THE PARIS PEACE CONFERENCE
HISTORY AND DOCUMENTS

PUBLISHED FOR
THE CARNEGIE ENDOWMENT FOR INTERNATIONAL PEACE
DIVISION OF ECONOMICS AND HISTORY

REPARATION AT THE
PARIS PEACE CONFERENCE

IN TWO VOLUMES

REPARATION AT THE PARIS PEACE CONFERENCE
From the Standpoint of the American Delegation

By PHILIP MASON BURNETT

★ VOLUME II ★

1965
OCTAGON BOOKS, INC.
New York

Reprinted 1965
by special arrangement with Columbia University Press

OCTAGON BOOKS, INC.
175 FIFTH AVENUE
NEW YORK, N. Y. 10010

LIBRARY OF CONGRESS CATALOG CARD NUMBER: 65-25889

Printed in U.S.A. by
NOBLE OFFSET PRINTERS, INC.
NEW YORK 3, N. Y.

THE GERMAN COUNTERPROPOSALS
(MAY 8–29, 1919)

DOCUMENT 347

Letter from the Secretariat General of the Peace Conference to the American Delegation Regarding the Greek Request for an Immediate Assignment of Enemy Merchant Marine, May 8, 1919

[From Peace Conference Bulletin No. 257 (May 10, 1919), in Miller, XVIII, 185-86. "Partition of Enemy Tonnage." See also Documents 95, 150, and 170.]

The Supreme Economic Council in its meeting of April 22nd, came to the conclusion that it would not be possible to approve a request of the Grecian Government to obtain an assignment of a part of the enemy fleet to Greece.

The Greek Delegation, in a note addressed to the General Secretariat of the Peace Conference, points out "that inasmuch as Greece is a maritime Power and comprises a very numerous seafaring population, who are thrown out of employ as a result of the losses of the Grecian merchant marine, due to enemy submarines, Greece feels entitled to claim a part of the management of enemy tonnage; without wishing to insist on this claim, Greece feels herself forced to bring up once again her point of view, considering the decision that the Supreme Economic Council arrived at."

The Secretariat General, following its communication of March 22nd on the same subject,[1] has the honor to inform the Secretary of the Delegation of the United States of America of these new remarks by the Grecian Delegation.

DOCUMENT 348

Note from Brockdorff-Rantzau to Clemenceau Regarding the Draft Treaty as a Whole, May 9, 1919

[Translated by the editor from the German text in *Materialien*, I, 19. French translation in PV, Notes, p. 3; also in Peace Conference Bulletin No. 260 (May 12, 1919), in Miller, XVIII, 193.]

MR. PRESIDENT:

The German Peace Delegation has completed its first examina-

---

[1] This document is missing, although a footnote in Miller at this point refers the reader to Bulletin No. 108. The documents in this Bulletin are those already reproduced as Documents 95, 150, and 170.

tion of the Conditions of Peace which were handed to it. It has had to recognize that the agreed basis of the peace of justice has been abandoned on important points; it was not prepared to see that the promise given expressly to the German people and to all mankind would be rendered illusory in this fashion.

The Draft Treaty contains demands which are not tolerable to any people. Much of it, moreover, in the opinion of our experts, is not possible of fulfillment. The German Peace Delegation will assemble in detail its information and will communicate to the Allied and Associated Governments in installments its remarks and material.

Accept, Mr. President, the expression of my highest consideration.

BROCKDORFF-RANTZAU.

DOCUMENT 349

Note from Clemenceau to Brockdorff-Rantzau Replying to Document 348, May 10, 1919

[Translated by the editor from the French text in PV, Notes, pp. 3-4; also in Peace Conference Bulletin No. 260 (May 12, 1919), in Miller, XVIII, 193-94. German translation in *Materialien*, I, 21.]

MR. PRESIDENT:

The representatives of the Allied and Associated Powers have taken cognizance of the note setting forth the observations of the German Delegates Plenipotentiary regarding the text of the Conditions of Peace.

In reply to this communication, they desire to remind the German Delegates that, in establishing the conditions of the Treaty, they have been constantly inspired by the principles according to which the Armistice and the Negotiations of Peace have been proposed.

The Representatives of the Allied and Associated Powers cannot admit any discussion of their right to maintain the fundamental conditions of the Peace such as they have been established.

They can consider only suggestions of a practical nature that the German Plenipotentiaries may submit to them.

Pray accept, Mr. President, the assurance of my high consideration.

CLEMENCEAU.

DOCUMENT 350

Communication from the Secretariat General Regarding the Establishment of Committees to Deal with Questions of Detail, etc., Submitted by the German Delegation, May 10, 1919

[Miller, IX, 316.]

The following communication has been received from the Secretariat General of the Peace Conference:

ARTICLE I.—In order to deal with questions of detail, requests for explanations, and the like referred by the German Delegates during the 15 days which intervene before they furnish their global reply to the Treaty of Peace to be handed to them, the Secretary General is empowered to refer to the following [thirteen] Committees, each of which will be composed of one representative each of the United States of America, the British Empire, France and Italy (in the event of the Italian Delegation returning): . . .

    8. Committee on Reparation and Restitution.[1]
    9. Committee on Financial Clauses.[2]
    10. Committee on Economic Clauses.[3] . . .

ARTICLE II.—The Secretary General will refer all questions of policy to the Supreme Council but will use his discretion to refer all questions of detail to the above committees, who should themselves in addition exercise their judgment if they consider questions of policy are involved to refer the questions to the Supreme Council.

DOCUMENT 351

Dulles' Draft of the Agreement with Belgium Regarding Priority, May 10, 1919

[TPG, III, 241-42. "(Translation) Belgium. First draft of Declaration." At the end of the present document, there are penciled initials, "J.F.D." Document 333 precedes generally. Document 352 follows.]

[a] WHEREAS, the Reparation Clauses of the draft text of the Treaty of Peace with Germany provide, among other things, that the several payments made by Germany by way of reparation

---

[1] McCormick was the American member, with Davis as an alternate. *Ibid.*, p. 317.
[2] Davis was the American member, with Lamont as an alternate. *Ibid.*, p. 317.
[3] Baruch was the American member, with Lamont as an alternate. *Ibid.*, p. 318.

will be divided by the Allied and Associated Governments on a basis determined upon by them in advance; and

[b] WHEREAS, it is deemed just and equitable that Belgium should receive a certain priority out of payments to be made by Germany;

[c] NOW, THEREFORE, the undersigned, for and on behalf of their respective Governments, agree that out of the first actual cash received from Germany in respect of reparation, Belgium shall receive, on account of her reparation claims, the equivalent of 2.500.000.000 gold francs [2 milliard marks].

[d] For the purpose of the foregoing, there shall be reckoned as cash:

1°—Currency received by the Reparation Commission

2°—Proceeds of sales by the Reparation Commission of assets received from Germany;

3°—The value of deliveries effected in kind and debited against any of the Allied or Associated Governments, which may be applied by the Reparation Commission towards reparation in accordance with the second paragraph of Article 237 of Treaty. This last item shall first be brought to account as of January 1, 1921: in case the settlement of account would necessitate some transfers in view of making up the amount of 2.500.000.000 above mentioned, these transfers will be at the charge of any of the Allied or Associated Governments as per ratio stated in paragraph 1 of Article 237 of Treaty, and may be effected by bills received by said Governments, according to terms of par. 12, C, 1° and 2° of Annex II of Clauses of the Reparation Treaty.

[e] Any sums, values or deliveries received by Belgium, through the execution of the Armistice of November 11, 1918, renewals of same, and Treaty, will be previously taken into account.

[f] Payments for occupation expenses and revictualling of Germany in food or raw materials, which may have been received by the Allied or Associated Governments in accordance with Article 235 of Treaty, will not be taken into account.

[g] The undersigned, on behalf of their respective Governments, further instruct the Reparation Commission to do all in its power to expedite the payment to Belgium of the 2.500.000.000 gold francs above referred to.

DOCUMENT 352

Draft of the Agreement with Belgium Regarding Priority, May, 1919

[TPG, III, 245. "Schedule B. Agreement with Belgium as to Priority of 2,500,-000,000 Gold Francs." This was enclosed as Schedule B in Lamont's Memorandum of June 14 (see Document 424). Document 351 precedes. Document 386 follows.]

[a] WHEREAS, Article 237 of the Conditions of Peace with Germany provides, among other things, that the payments to be made by Germany by way of reparation will be divided by the Allied and Associated Governments, in proportions which have been determined upon by them in advance, on a basis of general equity and of the rights of each; and

[b] WHEREAS, it is deemed equitable that Belgium should receive a certain priority out of such payments to be made by Germany;

[c] NOW, THEREFORE, the undersigned, for and on behalf of their respective Governments, agree that out of the first actual cash received from Germany, in respect of reparation, Belgium shall receive on account of her reparation claims the equivalent of 2,500,000,000 gold francs. For the purpose of the foregoing, there shall be reckoned as cash, currency and securities received by the Reparation Commission from Germany and the proceeds of sales by the said Commission of assets received from Germany. Reparation in kind made by Germany in execution of any of the provisions of the Armistice of November 11th, and the extensions and protocols thereof, or in pursuance of any of the provisions of the Treaty of Peace, shall not, for the purpose of the foregoing, be reckoned as cash.

[d] Sums received as reimbursement of the expenses of the Armies of Occupation, or in payment of food and raw materials as contemplated by Article 235 of the Conditions of Peace with Germany, shall not be taken into account as creating cash for the purposes of the priority in favor of Belgium.

[e] The undersigned, on behalf of their respective Governments, further instruct the Reparation Commission to do all in its power to expedite the payment to Belgium of the 2,500,000,000 gold francs or equivalent above referred to.

May   , 1919.

DOCUMENT 353

First Note from Brockdorff-Rantzau to Clemenceau Regarding Responsibility for the War, May 13, 1919

[Taken from the English translation in *German White Book*, p. 6. German text in *Materialien*, I, 28; VI, 5. French translation in PV, Notes, p. 13. English translation, with slight differences, also in Peace Conference Bulletin No. 275 Revised (May 21, 1919), in Miller, XVIII, 242-43.]

MR. PRESIDENT:

In the draft of a peace treaty submitted to the German delegates, Part VIII, concerning reparation, begins with Article 231, which reads as follows:

The Allied and Associated Governments affirm and Germany accepts the responsibility of Germany and her allies for causing all the loss and damage to which the Allied and Associated Governments and their nationals have been subjected as a consequence of the war imposed upon them by the aggression of Germany and her allies.

Now the obligation to make reparation has been accepted by Germany by virtue of the note from Secretary of State Lansing of November 5, 1918, independently of the question of responsibility for the war. The German delegation can not admit that there could arise, out of a responsibility incurred by the former German Government in regard to the origin of the World War, any right for the Allied and Associated Powers to claim indemnification by Germany for losses suffered during the war. The representatives of the Allied and Associated States have moreover declared repeatedly that the German people should not be held responsible for the wrongs committed by their Government.

The German people did not will the war and would never have undertaken a war of aggression. They have always remained convinced that this war was for them a defensive war.

Nor do the German delegates share the views of the Allied and Associated Governments in regard to the origin of the war. They are unable to consider the former German Government as the party solely or chiefly responsible for this war. The draft treaty of peace transmitted contains no facts in support of this view; no proof on the subject is furnished therein. The German delegates, therefore, request the communication to them of the report of the Commission set up by the Allied and Associated Governments for the purpose of establishing the responsibility of the authors of the war.

Pray accept, Mr. President, the assurances of my high consideration,   BROCKDORFF-RANTZAU.

DOCUMENT 354

Note from Brockdorff-Rantzau to Clemenceau Regarding the Effect of the Treaty on the German Population, May 13, 1919

[Translated by the editor from the German text in *Materialien*, I, 29-31. French translation in PV, Notes, pp. 15-16. There is also an English translation made from the French in Peace Conference Bulletin No. 277 Revised (May 22, 1919), in Miller, XVIII, 253-55.]

MR. PRESIDENT:

In accordance with the announcement in my note of May 9 of this year [see Document 348], I have the honor to present to Your Excellency the following declaration of the Economic Commission charged with studying the effect of the proposed Conditions of Peace on the situation of the German people:

"In the course of the last two generations, Germany had changed from an agricultural to an industrial state. As an agricultural state, Germany could support 40 million inhabitants. As an industrial state, she could assure the maintenance of a population of 67 million. In 1913, the importation of food amounted in round numbers to 12 million tons. Before the war, about 15 million persons in Germany owed their existence to foreign trade and to shipping—either directly or indirectly through the consumption of foreign raw materials.

"In accordance with the provisions of the Treaty of Peace, Germany is to surrender its serviceable merchant tonnage and that under construction, in so far as these are designed for commerce overseas. In the same way, the shipyards are to construct as their first work for a period of five years tonnage for the Allied and Associated Governments. Besides this, Germany gives up her colonies; all her overseas possessions, all her interests and titles in the Allied and Associated countries and in their colonies, dominions and protectorates will be, as a partial payment on the reparation account, subjected to liquidation and will be exposed to all other measures of economic war the Allied and Associated Powers may decide to maintain or to introduce during the years of peace.

"With the execution of the territorial clauses of the Treaty of Peace, the regions in the east most important for the production of grain and potatoes would be lost; that would be equivalent to a falling-off of 21 per cent of the total yield of these foodstuffs. Moreover, the intensity of our agricultural production will be considerably decreased. If, on the one hand, the importation of certain raw materials for the German fertilizer industry, such as phosphates, would be made more difficult, so, on the other, this industry would suffer, like every other, from the scarcity of coal, since the Treaty provides for the loss of almost one-third of our coal production; besides this decrease, Germany is burdened for the first ten years with enormous deliveries of coal to various Allied countries. What is more, in accordance with the Treaty, Germany is to cede to its neighbors nearly three-quarters of its production of iron ore and more than three-fifths of its production of zinc.

"After this deprivation of specific products, after the economic crippling caused by the loss of her colonies, of her merchant fleet and of her foreign possessions, Germany would not be any longer in a condition to import from abroad sufficient raw material. German industry would then have to die out on a large scale. At the same time, the need of importing food would increase considerably, while the possibility of satisfying that need would diminish extraordinarily.

"At the end of a very short time, Germany would then no longer be in a condition to give bread and work to the many millions of persons dependent for their living upon shipping and upon commerce. These people would then have to leave the country; but that is technically impossible, all the more since many of the most important countries of the world are opposed to a German immigration. Besides, hundreds of thousands of Germans expelled from the territories of the Powers at war with Germany as well as from the territories that Germany is to cede, will stream back again into the remaining German territory.

"If the Conditions of Peace are put into force, it simply means that many millions in Germany will perish. This process would develop quickly since the health of the population has been broken during the war by the blockade and during the armistice by its increased severity.

"No aid, important and of long duration as it might be, could bring a halt to this wholesale death. The peace would demand of Germany a greater human sacrifice than the war devoured in four years and a half ($1\frac{3}{4}$ million fallen in the field, almost 1 million as victims of the blockade).

"We do not know—and we doubt—whether the Delegates of the Allied and Associated Powers realize the consequences that would be inevitable if Germany, an industrial state with a dense population, tied to a world economy and dependent upon an enormous importation of raw materials and foodstuffs, finds itself all at once pushed back into a phase of its development that would correspond to her economic position and population of half a century ago. Those who sign the Treaty will pass a sentence of death upon many millions of German men, women and children."

I have believed it my duty, before the transmittal of further details, to bring to the attention of the Allied and Associated Delegation this general statement of the effect of the Peace Treaty upon the problem of the population of Germany. The statistical proofs are available on demand.

Accept, Mr. President, the expression of my high consideration.

BROCKDORFF-RANTZAU.

DOCUMENT 355

Letter from Pašić to Clemenceau Demanding a Portion of the Austro-Hungarian Merchant Fleet, May 14, 1919

[From Peace Conference Bulletin No. 300 (May 22, 1919), in Miller, XVIII, 359-60.]

MR. PRESIDENT:

I have the honor of calling your attention to Par. 5, of the Naval clauses of the Armistice with Austria-Hungary. That paragraph reads as follows:

"Maintenance of the blockade by the Allied and Associated Powers in the present conditions; the Austro-Hungarian ships found at sea shall be subject to capture, *with the exception of cases which shall be decided upon by a Commission to be designated by the Allies and the United States of America.*"

The clause contained in the last part of this paragraph: "with the exception . . . . ," has been adopted and unanimously approved upon the proposal of Mr. Vesnitch, Serbian Minister, for the purpose of freeing the ships belonging to the Austro-Hungarian subjects, which the Allied and Associated Powers consider, and which they treat as friends, namely the Jugo-Slav ship owners.

This fact made us believe that the Jugo-Slavs of Austria-Hungary could obtain the ships in order to furnish their country with manufactured products which she needs so badly.

Unfortunately, these stipulations of the Armistice have not been executed. Our countrymen ship owners, have not been able to obtain their ships.

The moment is drawing near when the fate of these boats shall be decided upon; the whole economical existence of our country depends on this decision.

It would be unjust that the Jugo-Slavs, who have fought for the common cause of the Allies since the beginning of the war, and who form now, by their union with Serbia, and Allied States, deprived of their ships, should find themselves after the war, in such conditions that their economic life should be stopped.

I ask you, Sir, to be kind enough to intervene, so that the part of the Austro-Hungary merchant fleet which belongs to Jugo-Slav nationals shall be returned by the Peace Treaty, to the Jugo-Slav ship owners.

Please accept, Sir, etc.,

NIK. P. PACHITCH.

DOCUMENT 356

Letter from the Drafting Committee to the Council of Four Regarding the Phrase "During the Period of the Belligerency of Each [Etc.]," May 14, 1919

[TPA, I, 67-69. RICMC, pp. 194-96. TPG, III, 185-86. This letter was part of the Appendix to the Minutes of the Council of Four of May 22, 4:15 P. M. (see Document 591).]

The following question with regard to the Reparation Clauses in the Draft Treaty of Peace with Germany has been brought to the notice of the Drafting Committee.

The following is the English text of the second paragraph of Article 232:—

"The Allied and Associated Governments, however, require, and Germany undertakes, that she will make compensation for all damage done to the civilian population of the Allied and Associated Powers and to their property *during the period of the belligerency of each as an Allied and Associated Power* against Germany by such aggression by land, by sea and from the air, and in general all damage as defined in Annex I hereto."

There are no words in the French text corresponding to those in the English text. There is, therefore, a divergence which must be put right, but the question arises as to whether the French text is to be brought into accord with the English or the English with the French.

The history of the matter is as follows: On May 3rd, Sir M. Hankey addressed a letter to the Secretary General of the Conference saying that in order to exclude any application of Reparation funds to new States such as Poland, the words "during the belligerency, etc. . . . " were to be introduced. The Drafting Committee accordingly introduced, the phrase which thenceforward figures in the French and English text. The order of the phrase however, in the two versions differed as it had not been easy to arrange the English draft precisely in the same way as the French.

On the morning of May 6th at a meeting of the Council of Prime Ministers, various modifications were made in the Reparation Articles on the suggestion of M. Loucheur who was present at the meeting. The instructions were communicated verbally to the Drafting Committee who were also present at the time. One of these alterations was to Article 232 and was to the effect that the wording was to be changed and a new phrase introduced after the word "air" which figures in the paragraph. The alterations were made accordingly but in the press of work on that day it was not noticed that the effect was to suppress the words "during the belligerency of each, etc. . . ." in the French text and not to suppress them in the English text.

Later on that same day a further letter from Sir M. Hankey was sent to M. Dutasta, containing the official record of this amendment but it was not received until after the Draft Treaty had gone to the printer in its final form. According to these later instructions the phrase "during the belligerency of each, etc. . . ." would be excluded, but there seems great doubt as to whether it was really intended to suppress the phrase which had been inserted expressly for the purpose of excluding any claims by the new States such as Poland.

On the other hand, this phrase affects other governments besides the new states and it may be that the full effect of the addition of the phrase had not been fully appreciated when instructions were given on May 3rd to insert it.

In view of the above, the Drafting Committe can only ask for further instructions from the Council of Prime Ministers.

On behalf of the Drafting Committee,

(signed)   HENRI FROMAGEOT.
14th May, 1919.

DOCUMENT 357

Letter from House to Whitlock Regarding Belgian Claims for Priority and Other Matters, May 14, 1919

[From the carbon copy in the Edward M. House Collection, Yale University Library, New Haven, Connecticut.]

My dear Friend:

There is nothing dearer to my heart than that Belgium should feel the warmth of the friendship which our people have for her. From the beginning of the Conference I have made Belgium and her desires my especial care. At the very inception of the suggestion that a closer economic union should be brought about between Belgium and Luxembourg I approached both the British and French Governments in order to secure their cooperation. This brought about many talks with Clemenceau, and enlisted Balfour's active help in the enterprise.

The same may be said of the Priority Claim for two and a half milliard of francs [2 milliard marks]. Hymans and I conferred upon this matter, concluded that this was the maximum sum that might be obtained, and I immediately approached the British and later had many conferences with the French Minister of Finance and others.

I have also kept in close contact with our economic and financial advisers as well as our experts upon boundaries and statistics and have urged liberal treatment for Belgium at every turn of the negotiations. I have been helped beyond measure by the advice you have given in letters and telegrams.

The suggestion you make regarding the President sailing from Antwerp is a good one were it not for the fact that the George Washington cannot go into that port. Her draft is 35 feet, 6 inches. However, I do not think there is any doubt that the President will visit Belgium before returning home.

With affectionate greetings, I am,

Your devoted friend,

DOCUMENT 358

Letter from Pašić to Clemenceau Regarding Apportionment, State Property, and German Currency, May 15, 1919

[From Peace Conference Bulletin No. 300 (May 22, 1919), in Miller, XVIII, 363-68.]

Sir:

The Delegation of the Kingdom of the Serbs, Croats and Slovenes, after having read the text of the disposition decided upon by the Allied and Associated Powers, which must be inserted in the Peace Treaty with Germany, and serve also as the basis for the drafting of the Peace Treaties with Austria-Hungary and the other Allies of Germany, considers that it will be just and necessary to precise more in the Peace Treaties with Austria-Hungary and the other Allied States of Germany, the dispositions contained in Art. 237, and Art. 256, as well as in Annex VIII of said Treaty.

We take the liberty of pointing out briefly, the reasons which justify our request and to formulate dispositions which in our opinion should be inserted in the above-mentioned articles.

I.

ARTICLE 237 OF THE PEACE TREATY WITH GERMANY.

The belligerent parties being composed of several Allied States, the questions of the responsibility of the enemy states, on account of the war damages on the one hand and of the distribution of the payments to be made by the enemy states between the Allied and Associated Powers on the other hand, must be decided upon by the Peace Treaties.

The question of responsibility could be resolved in two different ways: either the state which has done the damage pays the full value of it directly to the state which has to stand the damage, or, the amount of the indemnity shall be placed into a common fund from which shall be taken the funds for the indemnity of the Allied and Associated Countries, in application of a scale to be drawn up by a common agreement.

Any other solution would be contrary to the elementary juridical principles as well as to justice. Considering that the second solution is in conformity with the sentiments and the ideas of the Allied and Associated Powers, we have the honor of proposing that there should be inserted in the Peace Treaties with Germanic-Austria, Hungary and the other Allied States of Germany, the following clause, in place of Art. 237 of the Treaty with Germany:

"The successive payments, including those mentioned in the preceding articles made by Austria to satisfy the above claims, shall constitute a common fund, with the payments made by Germany or the other Allies; this common fund shall be divided by the Allied and Associated Governments according to proportions fixed by them in advance based on justice and on the rights of each one of them."

II.

ARTICLE 256 OF THE PEACE TREATY WITH GERMANY.

In this article, it is stipulated that all the Powers receiving German territory, shall be obliged to buy from Germany all property belonging to the Empire or to the other German States, situated on these territories.

This disposition is contrary to the rules established by international law, according to which the cessionary state comes into possession of the property of the ceding state, without any expense.

The cessionary states in question are in the act of discarding ties which existed between them and oppressory states; the latter have drawn them into a war of which the cessionary states were obliged to stand the greater part of the burden, although it took place in spite of them.

Worn out by the war, which has been imposed upon them in spite of them, the cessionary states can hardly stand the burden resulting from Art. 256, according to which they are obliged to assume part of the debt which was contracted for the greater part against their own interests.

In taking upon themselves, in accordance with Art. 256, the heavy burden of the enemy debt, the cessionary states pay very dearly for the property which comes into their possession.

The obligation of having to buy the property from the enemy, would be the equivalent for the cessionary states of signing the decree of their own economic ruin. The proposal which we make is in complete agreement with the decision by majority of 10 to 6 by the first sub-Commission of the Financial Commission.

We have therefore the honor of proposing in place of Art. 256, the insertion in the Peace Treaties to be concluded with Germany's Allies of the following resolution, of the first sub-Commission:

"The states which shall be granted territory from the former Austro-Hungarian Monarchy shall enter into possession of all property of this state situated within the liberated territories without having to pay, nor to credit on that score any of the states making the cession." (See Annex A, Art. VII, page 3, 5 April, 1919. Minutes of the Financial Commission.)

III.

ANNEX I, PART VIII.

The question of categories and damages which must be charged to the enemy has been the subject of deep study on the part of the Commission on Reparation. The result of these deliberations was submitted to the Supreme Economic Council of the Allies, and, among the damages giving right to reparation is:

The damage caused by the imposition of enemy fiduciary money to the population of invaded countries. This proposal was *unanimously* adopted.

The same question was discussed by the mixed sub-Commission on Monetary Questions, which ended by accepting *unanimously* the opinion of the Commission on Reparations.

Thus were we greatly surprised in noticing that this category of damages had been taken off from the list of damages in Annex I, Part VIII.

The enemy has put in circulation in Serbia about 1,000,000,000 francs of paper money, which is at present without any value. All the negotiable property of Serbia which was not destroyed, stolen, or plundered was bought by the enemy authorities and by their nationals for that paper money which had been given legal value. On the other hand, the Serbian population was obliged to exchange Serbian bank-notes still in their possession for that paper money; at the time of that forced exchange, the Serbian bank-notes were exchanged for half of their face value, causing bearers a loss of 50%.

It is one of the most important and one of the most disastrous damages suffered by Serbia among all those that she has suffered under the yoke of the enemy. The population is therefore now in possession of a large quantity of paper money which is worthless. When these banknotes were put on the market, their value was guaranteed only by a cash deposit in the proportion of one kreutzer for one crown; as these notes were used in payment for all transactions in occupied Serbia, one can say that they played the part of disguised "bons" of requisition. As it has been admitted, without opposition, that "bons of requisition" must be reimbursed, we ask that this paper money which had no and has real monetary value, and which represents really "bons of requisition" should be reimbursed; if this was not done and in view of the mass of those notes which the enemy has put in circulation on our territory, the economic re-awakening of the country will be impossible.

Consequently, we have the honor of proposing the insertion in the Peace Treaty with the Allies of Germany, at the end of Annex I, Part VIII, the following text:

(1) The enemy powers will be obliged to reimburse at a rate of gold or at a higher rate as they themselves have imposed, in pounds sterling, in francs, or in dollars, the choice of the Allied Powers concerned, the moneys, the "bons of requisition" and in general all enemy paper money still in the possession of the inhabitants (public or private people), of the territories which have been occupied by the enemy powers or still in existence in the hands of the prisoners of war, or interned civilians.

(2) All expenses and charges resulting from the redeeming by an Allied or Associated Power of the total amount of moneys imposed by the enemy, shall be reimbursed by the latter, together with interest of 6% starting from the day of the Armistice up to the date when the enemy moneys are reimbursed in the conditions above mentioned.

Such are, Mr. President, the dispositions which we should like to have inserted in the Treaty with Austria, Hungary, and the other States, Allies of Germany, and on which we beg you to call the kind attention of the Supreme Council.

Please accept, Sir, etc.,

NIK. P. PACHITCH.

DOCUMENT 359

Dillon's Memorandum to McCormick Suggesting an Organization for the Reparation Commission, May 20, 1919

[TPG, II, 92-98. "Organization for Reparation."]

1. In compliance with your instructions of this morning there is outlined below a plan for the general organization of the "Reparation Commission" and suggestions regarding the steps that should be taken by the American Delegation during the interim before the final organization has been completed.

2. Under the assumption that the Treaty will take effect practically as it stands the American Delegate and Assistant Delegate to the Reparation Commission should be designated at once subject to confirmation upon the organization of that Commission. It is highly to be desired that the continuity between the present organization and the new organization should not be lost and immediate steps should be taken to gather up the notes, records and reports from the various sub-sections, committee members, etc., of the American Peace Delegation. Otherwise a great part of these records will disappear with the disappearance of the personnel, as has already occurred, and in all probability the remainder will be filed away where it cannot be found. All of the

information which is here now will be of greater future value here than in Washington. The proper measures can be taken for obtaining the necessary records for the State Department without transporting everything to the United States.

3. If it is impracticable to designate the American Delegate at once, then someone can at least be immediately designated to carry over all Reparation matters until the American Delegate has been appointed and can get together his organization. This man should be given the necessary authority to at once organize a small office and to obtain from each of the various sub-sections, committee members, technical advisers, experts, etc., all the information, files, records, etc., pertaining to Reparation matters. He should also have the necessary authority to retain such clerical personnel from the various offices as necessary to get this information indexed and filed.

AMERICAN ORGANIZATION FOR REPARATION

4. The American Organization for Reparation will doubtless consist of—

    (a) *American Delegate and Assistant Delegate.*

    (b) *Secretary's Office,* with a limited personnel to handle
        Office matters
        Correspondence
        Records
        Translations, etc.

    (c) *Technical Advisers**
        Financial
        Economic
        Legal
        Valuation (Engineer)
        * Note: The technical advisers listed above could very properly be the American members of the Advisory Boards of the various sections of the Reparation Commission.

The General Secretary of the American Delegation to the Reparation Commission could well be appointed at once (temporary appointment only) to take over the work outlined in Paragraph 3 above.

ORGANIZATION OF THE REPARATION COMMISSION

5. It is unnecessary to invite your attention to the enormous task before the Reparation Commission and to the fact that very little time (two months in certain cases) is allowed for results. It seems

urgent therefore that the American Delegation should study the matter of its organization and endeavor to reach an immediate agreement concerning it with the foreign delegations concerned. Everything should be prepared to go into effect not later than the date of going into force of the Treaty itself. Otherwise the two months period allotted for obtaining certain results prescribed by the Treaty will be more than taken up in the throes of an attempted inter-allied organization. The organization of such a force as will be required by the Reparation Commission would be simple in plan but difficult of execution were it an ordinary business corporation matter. It becomes extremely complicated as an inter-allied matter. On account of the urgency of this matter I have presumed to suggest a general scheme of organization which at least may be useful for discussion with the foreign delegations. It would seem that the general working organization should consist of the following:—

    (a) Secretariat.
    (b) Damages Section.
    (c) Financial Section.
    (d) Economics Section.
    (e) Restitution Section.
    (f) Legal Section.
    (g) Special Sub-Committees.

    6. The composition, duties, jurisdiction, and general method of procedure of the Reparation Commission are outlined in the Treaty.

    7. All questions of policy, interpretation and general decisions concerning all matters arising under the Treaty provisions will naturally be under control of the Commission as a whole. The active control by a commission of such an enormous work, where plans must be promptly made and decisions quickly arrived at, has been many times proven impracticable. Such active control by an Inter-Allied Commission where each member is in turn more or less controlled by his government is believed to be impossible within the time allotted to obtain the necessary results. The active control of the organization, the employment of personnel, the actual planning and execution of the work should, therefore, be concentrated, as nearly as may be, in the hands of one man and this man should be the Chairman of the Reparation Commission as its Executive Officer. To him should report directly the Chiefs of the Secretariat, the Damages, Financial, Economics, Restitution, and Legal Sections outlined on the Organization Chart herewith, as well as the Chairman of the various Sub-Committees that may be appointed from time to time.

SECRETARIAT

8. The duties of the *Secretariat* would include Administration, Correspondence, Translations, Supplies, Disbursements, Employment of Personnel, Procedure, Diplomatic arrangements, etc. The *Secretary General* should report directly to the Chairman. His office should be at the Paris Headquarters. He should be permanently appointed subject to removal for cause by the Chairman. He should have as Assistant Secretaries General one for matters relating specifically to the German Treaty and one for matters relating to Austria, Hungary, Bulgaria and Turkey.

DAMAGES SECTION

9. The duties of the Damages Section would consist of the evaluating of damages in all countries concerned as included in Annex I. In accordance with Treaty provisions the sum total must be notified to the enemy countries by May 1, 1921. It would seem that each country should organize its own machinery for the determination of its own claims for damages, but should accord the Reparation Commission (Damages Section) the rights of supervision and inspection, and in general, comply with its instructions. In all probability the Reparation Commission (Damages Section) would accept the facts of loss so established, but would have the authority to reject the claim as not coming under a permissible category of damage, or to decrease or increase the amount claimed in order to place all valuations on a comparative basis. There should be a Chief of the Damages Section with headquarters at the Central Office in Paris. He should report directly to and receive his instructions from the Chairman. He should be permanently appointed, subject to removal for cause by the Chairman. He should have full authority over his organization and the planning and execution of his work subject to instruction from the Chairman. There should be a Board of Review consisting of one member appointed by each of the interested governments to finally pass upon all claims and to decide matters of general policy and interpretation with reference to categories of damage and methods of evaluation. The Chief of the Damages Section should be ex-officio the Chairman of this Board. The necessity for having such a Board and others specified herein is explained later.

It will probably be necessary to have a sub-section of the Damages Section at the capitals of each of the countries claiming damages. The chiefs of these sub-sections should be directly under the control of the Chief of the Damages Section at Paris in order to coordinate their work and have all damages assessed on a comparative basis in accordance with Treaty provisions and decisions of the Reparation Commission. The chiefs of these sub-sections should have all necessary authority to inspect the work of the various governmental agencies, attend the hearings of courts of claims, etc. set up in each country for adjudicating claims, and in general, should have ready access to all necessary information.

FINANCIAL SECTION

10. The duties of the Financial Section would include the carrying out of the financial clauses of the Treaty. They would also include the determination of the Belgian Loans (Art. 232), the schedule of payments (Art. 233), the distribution of the moneys received (Art. 237), and of the initial payments etc. They would also include the investigation and supervision of the financial arrangements of enemy countries and the obtaining of the necessary information concerning all such matters. There should be a Chief of the Financial Section with headquarters in Paris. He should be permanently appointed, subject to removal for cause, by the Chairman. He should report directly to and receive his instructions from the Chairman. He should have the necessary control over the selection and removal of his personnel.

There should be a Financial Advisory Board consisting of one member from each country concerned to determine questions of policy, interpretations, etc. The Chief of the Financial Section should be ex-officio the chairman of this Board.

It would be necessary to establish sub-sections of the Financial Section in each of the enemy countries. The chiefs of these sub-sections should be appointed by and report directly to and receive their instructions from the Chief of the Financial Section in Paris.

ECONOMICS SECTION

11. The duties of the Economics Section include in general the carrying out of the Economic clauses of the Treaty, with special reference to capacity of enemy countries to pay, trade relations, ability to make payments in kind, etc.

The organization would be similar to that of the Financial Section.

RESTITUTION SECTION

12. The duties of the Restitution Section would include the handling of all matters relating to return of cash, machinery, art treasures, and other objects removed for which no credit is given for Reparation (Art. 238) and the execution of Treaty clauses con-

cerning replacement of shipping and new tonnage to be constructed, the supervision of all arrangements for the supply of labor and materials for reconstruction and in general all payments made in kind, coal, iron, lumber, chemicals, dye stuffs, and questions covering such matters as the Saar Basin, submarine cables, etc.

Its organization would be similar to the Financial and Economics Sections.

LEGAL SECTION

13. A small Legal Section would probably be necessary to decide questions of law, interpretations of Treaty clauses and for assistance in reviewing the decisions of courts of claims, etc., in the various countries. Its organization would be somewhat similar to but much more limited than the other sections.

EXECUTIVE BOARD

14. There should be an Executive Board of which the ex-officio chairman should be the Vice Chairman of the Commission. The other members should be the Secretary-General, the Chiefs of the Damages, Financial, Economics, Restitution, and Legal Sections of the Commission. This Board should decide questions of distribution of duties among the various Sections, and general matters relating to rates of pay, employment and discharge of personnel, and to prepare and refer to the Commission such questions concerning matters of policy as may arise.

ADVISORY BOARDS

15. It will be observed that I have recommended an Advisory Board for each of the various Sections except the Secretariat. Such Boards would neither be necessary nor desirable were it the case of a well controlled organization but in the case of inter-allied organizations it is believed to be required. Each country can thus be represented directly on each important phase of the work where questions of policy are concerned and these representatives can be changed by local governments as often as their policy dictates. The Chiefs of Sections could therefore have that greatly to be desired permanency of office and practical freedom of control over their organizations and the planning and execution of their work.

SUB-COMMISSIONS

16. Various Sub-Commissions will probably be formed, but should be limited to absolute necessity.

T. H. DILLON,
Colonel, Corps of Engineers

Inc.

REPARATION COMMISSION

DELEGATES AND ASSISTANT DELEGATES

CHAIRMAN AND VICE CHAIRMAN

AMERICAN   BRITISH   FRENCH   ITALIAN   BELGIAN   SERBIAN   JAPANESE

EXECUTIVE BOARD { Consisting of the General Secretary and the Chiefs of the Damages, Financial, Economics, Restitution and Legal Sections.

SECRETARIAT Paris

SECRETARY
—Office
—Correspondence
—Records
—Interpreters
—Translations
—Etc.

DAMAGES—Chief—
- Board of Review—Paris—Representative of each country concerned.
- Executive Office—Paris—
- Sub-sections—at capital of each country concerned

FINANCIAL SECTION—Chief—
- Financial Board—Paris—Representative of each country concerned.
- Executive Office—Paris—
- Sub-sections in Germany, Austria, Hungary, Bulgaria, Turkey.
- Executive Office—Paris.

ECONOMICS SECTION—Chief—
- Economics Board—Paris—Representative of each country.
- Sub-sections in Germany, Austria, Hungary, Bulgaria and Turkey.

RESTITUTION SECTION—Chief {
- Executive Office—Paris.
- Restitution Board—Paris.
- Representative of each Country.
- Sub-sections in each of enemy countries.

LEGAL SECTION—Chief— {
- Executive Office—Paris.
- Advisory Board—Representative of each country.

SPECIAL SUB-COMMITTEES—(As Necessary).

TECHNICAL ADVISORS*
—Financial
—Economic
—Legal
—Valuation (Engineer)

*Note. These advisors should be the American members of the Advisory Boards of the Sections of the Reparation Commission.

DOCUMENT 360

Report of the Meeting of the Council of Four, May 20, 1919

[Slosson's Annotations, in Miller, XIX, 293.]

. . . It was provisionally agreed on May 19 to reinsert the words ["during the period of the belligerency of each as an Allied and Associated Power against Germany"] in the French text (C. F. 19).

This decision was confirmed on May 20 (C. F. 20). M. Orlando, however, asked for reconsideration on the ground that an expert committee which had examined the question had agreed on the American proposal to omit the words in question and substitute others.

President Wilson said "he had some vague recollection of the incident. The proposal had been made by Mr. Dulles, whose thought had been for the United States citizens on board the *Lusitania* who, unless some special provision was made, would get no reparation. Whatever had been the attitude of the experts, however, it was evident that nothing had got into the Treaty."

M. Orlando reserved his assent until he has seen the Italian experts on the question.

DOCUMENT 361

Decision of the Council of Four on the Phrase "During the Period of the Belligerency of Each [Etc.]," May 20, 1919

[RICMC, p. 193. TPG, III, 184. TPA, I, 66. "Appendix." This was part of the Appendix to the Minutes of the Council of Four of May 22, 4:15 P. M. (see Document 591). See Document 356.]

The Council of the Principal Allied and Associated Powers have considered the attached letter from M. Fromageot and have agreed that the following words "during the period of the belligerency of each as an Allied and Associated Power against Germany," which had been omitted from the French text but retained in the English text of Article 232 of the Treaty of Peace with Germany, should be re-instated in the French text.

(Initialled)   G.C.

W.W.

D.Ll.G.

V.O.[1]

20th May, 1919.

[1] Not initialed by Orlando until May 22.

DOCUMENT 362

Note from Clemenceau to Brockdorff-Rantzau Replying to Document 353, May 20, 1919

[Taken from the English translation in *German White Book*, p. 7. French text in PV, Notes, p. 14. German translation in *Materialien*, I, 41-42; VI, 7. English translation also in Peace Conference Bulletin No. 275 Revised (May 21, 1919), in Miller, XVIII, 244-45.]

MR. PRESIDENT:

In your note of May 13, you state that Germany, while "accepting" in November, 1918 "the obligation to make reparation" did not understand such an acceptance to mean that her responsibility was involved either for the war or for the acts of the former German Government.

It is only possible to conceive of such an obligation if its origin and cause is the responsibility of the author of the damage.

You add that the German people would never have undertaken a war of aggression. Yet, in the note from Secretary of State Lansing of November 5, 1918, of which you approve, and adduce in favor of your contention, it is stated that the obligation to make reparation arises out of "Germany's aggression by land, sea and air."

Since the German Government did not at the time make any protest against this allegation, it thereby recognized it as well founded.

Therefore Germany recognized in November, 1918, implicitly and clearly, both the aggression and her responsibility. It is too late to seek to deny them today.

It would be impossible, you state further, that the German people should be regarded as the accomplices to the wrongs committed by the "former German Government." However, Germany has never claimed, and such a declaration would have been contrary to all principles of international law that a modification of its political form of government or a change in its governing personnel would be sufficient to extinguish an obligation already undertaken by any nation. She did not act upon the principle she now contends for either in 1871, in regard to France, after the proclamation of the Republic, or in 1917, in regard to Russia after the revolution abolished the Czarist régime.

Finally, you ask that the report of the Commission on Responsibility may be communicated to you. In reply we beg to say that the Allied and Associated Powers consider the reports of the commissions set up by the Peace Conference as documents of an internal character which can not be transmitted to you.

Accept, Mr. President, the assurance of my highest consideration.

CLEMENCEAU.

DOCUMENT 363

Extract from Miller's Diary Regarding the Shipping Agreement, May 21, 1919

[Miller, I, 325-26.]

. . . Colonel House showed me [*time of day uncertain!*] the agreement[1] regarding shipping which had been signed by President Wilson and George. Under the President's signature was a reservation referring to the annexed paper, which said that the disposition of the money was subject to the decision of Congress. The agreement provided in substance that (1) Everybody that had captured ships of the enemy or taken them in harbors should keep them. (2) That the ceded ships should be distributed on the basis of tonnage lost, ton for ton and class for class in three classes, liners, fishing boats and one other. (3) That States like the United States, Brazil, Siam, and China, which captured more ships than their losses should pay the value of the surplus to the other people.

Colonel House asked me if I thought this should be presented to Orlando. I told him it ought to be signed by the French and Japanese as well as by the Italians and that it was a grossly unjust agreement to the Italians who would get practically no tonnage out of it. I pointed out that distribution was not to be made on the basis of per cent. of tonnage lost but actual tonnage lost, which of course favored the British enormously.

No decision was reached as General Pershing was announced when I was there. . . .

DOCUMENT 364

Report of the Meeting of the Council of Four, May 21, 1919

[Slosson's Annotations, in Miller, XIX, 276-277.]

On May 21 President Wilson advocated that the economic and financial experts of the Allied and Associated Powers discuss questions of detail with the German experts. "If our experts could show that no heavier burden had been laid on the German people than justice required, it might make it easier for the German Delegates to explain to their own people" (C. F. 22 A).

[1] See Document 337.

M. Clemenceau said that he thought the Germans would sign.

Mr. Lloyd George said that a few small concessions would give them excuse to sign. He thought before deciding what these concessions should be, it would be well to await the German counter-proposals on questions of reparation.

President Wilson said that German financial experts, like Herr Melchior, were anxious for peace to get German industries started again. "If it could be shown to Melchior that the Reparation Commission was allowed to consider the condition of Germany and to adjust the arrangements accordingly from time to time, it might enable him to persuade the German people."

M. Clemenceau said that he agreed with Mr. Lloyd George that it would be well to await the German counter-proposals.

DOCUMENT 365

Extract from Smuts' Criticism of the Treaty, May 22, 1919

[Baker, III, 459-61.]

3. *The Reparation Clauses.*

I am advised that while a very large amount of reparation could be obtained from Germany in the long run, the actual scheme adopted in our Reparation Clauses is unworkable, and must.kill the goose which is to lay the golden eggs. We could not get anything like one milliard sterling out of Germany within the first two years. Apart from ships, foreign securities and certain raw material, we could get nothing but worthless paper. So far from getting anything more out of Germany the first couple of years, the real practical problem is to find credit for Germany wherewith she could purchase food and the necessary raw materials to restart her industrial life. There is actually sitting a Commission, whose object it is to find out how to finance Germany and other European countries in the immediate future.

Besides the impossibility of paying this milliard in two years, I am also advised that the scheme of the five milliard bonds is unworkable and should be scrapped.

I think we should be prepared to listen to what the Germans have to say in criticism of our scheme of Reparation, and to modify it with a view to making it practicable and not crippling German industry irreparably in the next few years. Our policy should rather be to begin nursing German industry and finance in order to obtain heavy contributions from them when they have become productive.

In particular I think the coal demands we are making on Germany are too heavy, and must seriously cripple her industry. Three separate commissions have taken coal from Germany: one confiscated the Saar Basin, another cut off the Silesian coal fields, and the third laid heavy contributions on the Westphalian fields in favour of France, Belgium and Italy. The combined result of all this is a burden which it will probably be too heavy for German industry to bear. All this requires reconsideration, and would probably have received it but for the hurry in which the Treaty was finally put together from the various Commission Reports.

While sticking generally to our scheme of Reparation, I would eliminate the above objectionable or unworkable features, and in particular I would scrap the schedules dealing with the future delivery of coal and coal products, and the future construction of ships. I would give the Reparation Commission full power to settle not only the amount but also the form in which the payments are to be made (in money or kind). I would certainly take away the power from the French and Belgian manufacturers to rove about German factories in order to despoil them of machinery which they may allege to be necessary for their works (para. 4 of the Fourth Annex to Reparation Clauses). This industrial looting would be most mischievous, and could not in peace time be justified as a reprisal for crimes committed in war time. The proper reprisal is to make the Germans pay.

DOCUMENT 366

Note from Clemenceau to Brockdorff-Rantzau Replying to Document 354, May 22, 1919

[English translation, "Approved by the Council of the Principal Allied and Associated Powers on 21st May, 1919," from Peace Conference Bulletin No. 277 (May 22, 1919), in Miller, XVIII, 256-61. French text in PV, Notes, pp. 17-20. German translation in *Materialien*, II, 15-19.

The English translation, in addition to the date of approval, carries the date of the note as May 21. The French and German sources give May 22.]

1. The Allied and Associated Powers have received and have given careful attention to the report of the Commission appointed by the German Government to examine the economic conditions of the Treaty of Peace.

This report appears to them to contain a very inadequate presentation of the facts of the case, to be marked in parts by great exaggeration, and to ignore the fundamental considerations arising both out of the incidence and the results of the war, which explain and justify the terms that it is sought to impose.

2. The German Note opens with the statement that the industrial resources of Germany were inadequate before the war for the nourishment of a population of 67 millions, and it argues as though this were the total for which with diminished resources she will still be called upon to provide. This is not the case. The total population of Germany will be reduced by about six million persons in the non-German territories which it is proposed to transfer. It is the needs of this smaller aggregate that we are called upon to consider.

3. Complaint is made in the German Note that Germany is required to surrender her merchant tonnage, existing or in course of construction, and that a prior claim is made upon her shipbuilding capacity for a limited term of years. No mention, however, is made of the fact that a considerable portion of the smaller tonnage of Germany is left to her unimpaired; and it seems to have entirely escaped the notice of her spokesmen that the sacrifice of her larger shipping is the inevitable and necessary penalty imposed upon her for the ruthless campaign which, in defiance of all law and precedent, she waged during the last two years of the war upon the mercantile shipping of the world. As a partial offset against the $12\frac{3}{4}$ million tons of shipping sunk, it is proposed to transfer four million tons of German shipping. In other words, the shipping which it is proposed to take from Germany constitutes less than one-third of that which was thus wantonly destroyed. The universal shortage of merchant shipping is the result, not of the terms of Peace, but of the action of Germany, and no surprise can reasonably be felt if she is called upon to bear her share, and it is a very moderate share, of a loss for which her own criminal deeds have been responsible.

4. Great stress is laid upon the proposal that on the Eastern side Germany shall be deprived of the regions specially devoted to the production of wheat and potatoes. This is true. But the Note fails altogether to observe that there is nothing in the Peace Treaty to prevent either the continued production of these commodities in the areas in question, or their importation into Germany. On the contrary, the free admission of the products of the Eastern districts is provided for during a period of three years. Moreover, it is fortunate for Germany that these regions have lost none of their productivity owing to the ravages of war. They have escaped the shocking fate which was dealt out by the German armies to the corresponding territories in Belgium and France on the West,

and Poland, Russia, Roumania and Serbia on the East. There appears to be no reason why their produce should not continue to find a market on German soil.

5. Stress is laid upon the proposed restriction of the import of phosphates. It is, however, forgotten, that Germany has never produced but has always imported the phosphates of which she stands in need. Nor is there anything in the Terms of Peace which will prevent or hinder the importation of phosphates into Germany in the future. Other countries, which do not produce phosphates, are also compelled to import them in common with many other products from the outside; and the only difference in the two situations will arise from the relative degree of wealth or impoverishment in the countries concerned.

6. The German Note makes special complaint of the deprivation of coal, and asserts that nearly one-third of the production of the existing coal mines will be lost. But it omits to notice that one-fourth of the pre-war consumption of German coal was in the territories which it is now proposed to transfer. Further it fails to take into account the production of lignite, eighty million tons of which were produced annually in Germany before the war, and none of which is derived from the transferred territories. Neither is any reference made to the fact that the output of coal in the non-transferred districts was rapidly increasing before the war, and that there is no reason to doubt that under proper management there will be a continuing increase in the future.

7. But should not the coal situation be viewed from a different and wider standpoint? It cannot be forgotten that among the most wanton acts of devastation perpetrated by the German armies during the war was the almost complete destruction by her of the coal supplies of Northern France. An entire industry was obliterated with the calculation and a savagery which it will take many years to repair. The result has been a grave and prolonged shortage of coal in Western Europe. There can be no reason in equity why the effect of this shortage should be borne exclusively by the Allied nations who were its victims, or why Germany, who deliberately made herself responsible for the deficiency, should not, to the full limit of her capacity, make it good.

8. Stress is also laid upon the hardships alleged to be inflicted upon Germany by the necessity of importing in future iron ores and zinc. It is not understood why Germany should be supposed to suffer from conditions to which other countries contentedly submit. It would appear to be a fundamental fallacy that the political

control of a country is essential in order to procure a reasonable share of its products. Such a proposal finds no foundation in economic law or in history.

9. The Allied and Associated Powers cannot accept the speculative estimate presented to them in the German Note on the future conditions of German industry as a whole. This estimate appears to them to be characterized and vitiated by palpable exaggerations. No note is taken of the fact that the economic disaster produced by the war is wide-spread, and, indeed, universal. Every country is called upon to suffer. There is no reason why Germany, which was responsible for the war, should not suffer also.

10. Similarly, as regards the population of the future, no reliance can be placed on the data which are contained in the German Note. On the other hand, it is sought to prove that immigration from Germany will be necessary, but that few countries will receive the intending immigrants. On the other hand, it is sought to show that there will be a flood of Germans returning to their native land to live under the conditions which have already been described as intolerable. It would be unwise to attach too much weight to either speculation.

11. Finally, the German Note rashly asserts that the peace conditions will "logically bring about the destruction of several millions of persons in Germany," in addition to those who have perished in the war or who are alleged to have lost their lives in consequence of the blockade. Against the war losses of Germany might very fairly be placed the far greater losses which her initiative and conduct of the war have inflicted upon the Allied countries, and which have left an ineffaceable mark upon the manhood of Europe. On the other hand, the figures and the losses alleged to have been caused by the blockade are purely hypothetical. The German estimate of future losses could be accepted only if the premises upon which it is presumed to rest are accepted also. But they are entirely fallacious. There is not the slightest reason to believe that a population is destined to be permanently disabled because it will be called upon in future to trade across its frontiers instead of producing what it requires from within. A country can both become and can continue to be a great manufacturing country without producing the raw materials of its main industries. Such is the case, for instance, with Great Britain, which imports at least one-half of her food supplies and the great preponderance of her raw materials from abroad. There is no reason whatever why Germany under the new conditions should not build up for herself

a position both of stability and prosperity in the European world. Her territories have suffered less than those of any other continental belligerent State during the war. Indeed, so far as pillage or devastation is concerned, they have not suffered at all. Their remaining and untouched resources, supplemented by the volume of import trade, should be adequate for recovery and development.

12. The German reply also ignores the immense relief that will be caused to her people in the struggle for recovery by the enforced reduction of her military armaments in future. Hundreds of thousands of her inhabitants, who have hitherto been engaged either in training for armies or in producing instruments of destruction, will henceforward be available for peaceful avocations and for increasing the industrial productiveness of the nation; no result should be more satisfactory to the German people.

13. But the first condition of any such recuperation would appear to be that Germany should recognize the facts of the present state of the world, which she has been mainly instrumental in creating, and realize that she cannot escape unscathed. The share which she is being called upon to bear of the enormous calamity that has befallen the world has been apportioned by the victorious Powers, not to her deserts, but solely to her ability to bear it. All the nations of Europe are suffering from losses and are bearing and will long continue to bear burdens which are almost more than they can carry. These burdens and losses have been forced upon them by the aggression of Germany. It is right that Germany, which was responsible for the origin of these calamities, should make them good to the utmost of her capacity. Her hardships will arise not from the conditions of peace, but from the acts of those who provoked and prolonged the war. Those who were responsible for the war cannot escape its just consequences.

DOCUMENT 367

Second Note from Brockdorff-Rantzau to Clemenceau Regarding Responsibility for the War, May 24, 1919

[Taken from the English translation in *German White Book*, pp. 8-11. German text in *Materialien*, II, 28-31; VI, 8-11. French translation in PV, Notes, pp. 40-44. English translation, with differences, also in Peace Conference Bulletin No. 275 (May 26, 1919), in Miller, XVIII, 245-50.]

MR. PRESIDENT:

The contents of Your Excellency's note of the twentieth instant, concerning the question of Germany's responsibility for the consequences of the war, have shown the German peace delegation that the Allied and Associated Governments have completely mis-understood the sense in which the German Government and the German nation tacitly gave their assent to the note of Secretary of State Lansing of November 5, 1918. In order to clear up this misunderstanding the German delegation feel compelled to recall to the memory of the Allied and Associated Governments the events which preceded that note.

The President of the United States of America had several times solemnly declared that the World War should be terminated not by a peace of might, but by a peace of right, and that America had entered the war solely in behalf of this peace of right. For this war-aim the formula was established: "No annexations, no contribu-tions, no punitive damages." On the other hand, however, the President demanded the unconditional restitution of the violated right. The positive side of this demand found expression in the fourteen points which were laid down by President Wilson in his message of January 8, 1918. This message contains two principal claims against the German nation: First, the surrender of important parts of German territory in the west and in the east on the basis of national self-determination; secondly, the promise to restore the occupied territories of Belgium and the north of France. Both demands could be acceded to by the German Government and the German people, since the principle of self-determination was concordant with the new democratic constitution of Germany, and since the territories to be restored had been subjected by Germany to the terrors of war through an act contrary to the law of nations, namely, the violation of Belgium's neutrality.

The right of self-determination of the Polish nation had, as a matter of fact, already been acknowledged by the former German Government, just as had the wrong done to Belgium.

When, therefore, there was given in the note of the Entente trans-mitted by Secretary of State Lansing to the German Government, on November 5, 1918, a more detailed interpretation of what was meant by restoration of the occupied territories, it appeared from the German point of view to be a matter of course that the duty to make compensation, established in this interpretation, could relate to no other territories than those the damaging of which had already been admitted as contrary to right, and the restoration of which had been emphasized as war-aims by the leading enemy statesmen. Thus President Wilson in his message of January 8, 1918, expressly termed the reparation of the wrong done to Belgium as the healing act without which the whole structure and validity of international law would be forever impaired. In a like manner the English Prime Minister, Mr. Lloyd George, in his speech in the House of Commons on October 22, 1917, proclaimed:

The first requirement . . . always put forward by the British Government and their Allies, has been the complete restoration, political, territorial and economic, of the independence of Belgium, and such reparation as can be made for the devastation of its towns and provinces. This is no demand for war indemnity, such as that imposed on France by Germany in 1871. It is not an attempt to shift the cost of warlike operations from one belligerent to another.[1]

What is here said in behalf of Belgium, Germany had to acknowledge also with regard to the north of France, since the German Armies had only reached French territory by the violation of Belgium's neutrality.

It was for this aggression that the German Government admitted Germany to be responsible, it did not admit Germany's alleged responsibility for the origin of the war, nor the merely incidental circumstance that the formal declaration of war had emanated from Germany. The importance of Secretary of State Lansing's note for Germany lay rather in the fact that the duty to make reparation was not limited to the restoration of material values, but was extended to every kind of damage suffered by the civilian population in the occupied territory, in person or in property, during the continuance of warfare, be it by land, by sea or from the air.

The German nation was fully conscious of the one-sidedness lying in their being charged with the restoration of Belgium and northern France, while they were denied compensation for the territories in the east of Germany which had been invaded and devastated by the troops of Russian Czarism acting on a long-premeditated plan. They have, however, recognized that the Russian aggression must bear a different relation to the formal provisions of the law of nations than would the invasion of Belgium and have therefore abstained from demanding compensation on their part.

If the Allied and Associated Governments should now maintain the view that, for every violation of the law of nations which has been committed during the war, compensation is due, the German delegation will not dispute the correctness in principle of this standpoint; they beg, however, to point out that in such an event Germany also would have a considerable damage account to be settled, and that the duty to compensate, incumbent

[1] This speech was made really before The Trade Union Conference at London on January 5, 1918 See Document 7.

upon her adversaries—particularly in the case of the German civilian population, which has suffered immeasurable injury by the hunger blockade, a measure contrary to the law of nations—is not limited to the period when actual warfare was still being carried on from both sides, but applies particularly to the time when war was waged from one side only, by the Allied and Associated Powers against a Germany which had voluntarily laid down arms. This view of the Allied and Associated Governments, at any rate, differs from the agreement which Germany had entered into before the Armistice was concluded. It raises an endless series of controversial questions on the horizon of the peace negotiations and can only be brought to a practical solution through a system of impartial international arbitration, such arbitration as is provided for in Article 18, Part 2, of the draft of the conditions of peace.[2] This clause prescribes:

> Disputes as to the interpretation of a treaty, as to any question of international law, as to the existence of any fact which if established would constitute a breach of any international obligation, or as to the extent and nature of the reparation to be made for any such breach, are declared to be among those which are generally suitable for submission to arbitration.

Your Excellency has further pointed out in your note of the twentieth instant that, according to the principles of international law no nation could, through an alteration of its political form of government or through a change in the personnel of its leaders, cause to be extinguished an obligation once incurred by its government. The German peace delegation is far from contesting the correctness of this principle; nor do they protest against the execution of the agreement proposed by the former government on October 5, 1918, but they do make objection to the punishment, provided for by the draft of the peace treaty, for the alleged offenses of the former political and military leaders of Germany. The President of the United States of America, on December 4, 1917, declared that the war should not end in vindictive action of any kind; that no nation nor people should be robbed or punished because the irresponsible rulers of the country had themselves done deep and abominable wrong. The German delegation does not plead these or other promises to evade any obligation incumbent on Germany by the law of nations, but they feel justified in recalling them to memory if the German nation is to be held responsible for the origin of the war and made liable for its damages.

While the public negotiations immediately preceding the con-

---

[2] Error for "Article 13, paragraph 2."

clusion of the Armistice were still in progress, the German nation was promised that Germany's fate would be fundamentally altered if it were severed from that of its rulers. The German delegation would not like to take Your Excellency's words to mean that the promise made by the Allied and Associated Governments at that time was merely a ruse of war employed to paralyze the resistance of the German nation, and that this promise is now to be withdrawn.

Your Excellency has finally contended that the Allied and Associated Governments were justified in treating Germany after the same methods as had been adopted by her in the peace treaties of Frankfort and Brest-Litovsk. The German delegation for the present refrains from examining in what respects these two treaties of peace differ from the present draft, for it is now too late for the Allied and Associated Governments to found a legal claim on these precedents. The moment for so doing was when they had before them the alternative of accepting or rejecting the fourteen points of the President of the United States of America as [a] basis of peace. In these fourteen points the reparation of the wrong done in 1870-1871 was expressly demanded, and the peace of Brest-Litovsk was spoken of as a deterrent example. The Allied and Associated Governments at that time declined to take a peace of violence belonging to the past as a model.

The German nation never having assumed the responsibility for the origin of the war, has a right to demand that it be informed by its opponents for what reasons, and on what evidence are the conditions of peace based upon Germany's being to blame for all damages and all sufferings of this war. It can not, therefore, consent to be put off with the remark that the data relating to the question of responsibility, collected by the Allied and Associated Governments through a special commission, are documents of an internal nature of those Governments. This, a question of life or death for the German nation, must be discussed in all publicity; methods of secret diplomacy are out of place here. The German Government reserve for themselves the right to return to the subject.

Accept, Sir, the assurance of my high esteem.

BROCKDORFF-RANTZAU.

DOCUMENT 368

Mc Kinstry's Memorandum to McCormick, "Final Report of War Damage Board," May 26, 1919

[TPG, II, 1-10, 21-34. The irregular paging is due to a mistake in the binding. There are 24 pages in all. This is a signed original.]

1. Under date of 31 March 1919, I submitted a report covering the activities of the War Damage Board from the time of its inception to the suspension of work ordered by the American Commission to Negotiate Peace on February 12, 1919.[1] In that report (Par. 1) I mentioned that certain officers had been retained by the Commission as technical advisers to the American members of the Reparation Commission. The present is a report of the work done by these officers.

2. Among the officers retained were Colonel Brooks and two others, who had been engaged for some time in investigating the coal and steel situation in Belgium, northern France, the Saar Basin and Alsace-Lorraine. Colonel Brooks' report, dated April 8th, was forwarded by me to the American Commission (through Mr. McCormick) on April 9th,[2] and the three officers referred to had been relieved from duty by April 11th.

3. Early in February the Peace Conference appointed five commissions, (1) to work out the details of the Constitution of the League of Nations, and to examine and report (2) on Breaches of the Laws of War, (3) on International Legislation on Industrial Labor Questions, (4) on Reparation and (5) on Regulation of Waterways. The American appointees to the Reparation Commission were Messrs. Baruch, Davis, and McCormick. On the organization of the Reparation Commission, three sub-committees were formed to consider (1) the amount for reparation which the enemy countries ought to pay, (2) what they are capable of paying, (3) the method, form and time within which payment should be made. Mr. McCormick was appointed to the First Sub-Committee (Valuation of Damage).

4. The officers of the War Damage Board retained, other than Colonel Brooks and his two assistants, have been engaged in completing the report of March 31 (mentioned in Par. 1 above) and in advising Mr. McCormick on questions arising in connection with the work of the First Sub-Committee.

5. At the first meeting of the Reparation Commission, held

[1] This report is missing.   [2] This report is missing.

February 3, 1919, M. Klotz submitted on the part of France a "Memorandum on Principles of Reparation for Damage," in which, in effect, France claimed that reparation was due from the enemy states for all destruction, loss and expense which the Allied and Associated governments had suffered from the fact of war. Later this view was supported by the other delegations, except that of the United States. The U. S. delegation held that the field of reparation had been greatly narrowed by the President's Fourteen Points (as amended Nov. 4, 1918) and that these Points constituted the basis of the terms of peace. In the beginning the principal point of contention was whether the Allied and Associated governments (except Belgium) could exact reparation for "war costs." Principles of reparation substantially in accord with the French principles were submitted by the Italian, British, and Serbian delegations. These principles are printed in full as annexes to the Proceedings of the Reparation Commission and are analyzed and summarized in an annex to the proceedings of the Fifth Meeting (February 13, 1919.) Briefly, the majority of the powers claimed that Germany must be held bound to make good *all* damage caused by her. The position taken by the United States was that "no reparation can be exacted unless (1) it is clearly due in accordance with accepted principles of international law; or (2) it is stipulated for in the understanding embodied in President Wilson's points regarding reparation of invaded territories" (as amended). The American principles of reparation and extensive comments in explanation of them are printed as Annex 6 of the Proceedings of the Reparation Commission. The principles were as follows: . . . [3]

6. Principle I above includes war costs (all damages) for Belgium, but not for other countries. It was immediately obvious that this difference as to principles of reparation would have an important influence upon the work of the First Sub-Committee, since it would affect the categories of damage under which claims might be made against Germany and, therefore, the amount of the indemnity which could be demanded. The course of action which Mr. McCormick was obliged to take in the First Sub-Committee by reason of this difference is referred to below. When the issue had been fairly joined, the Reparation Commission decided (9th Meeting, 19 February 1919) to transmit to the President of the Peace Conference for submission to the Supreme War Council as constituted on the 4th November, 1918, the question

---

[3] The text of the American principles have been omitted here. They may be found in Annex VI of Document 454.

"Would an affirmation of M. Klotz's motion, i.e., that the rights of the Allied and Associated Powers are all inclusive, be contrary to the intentions of the members of the Supreme War Council (as then constituted) as expressed in the American note of 5 November 1918?"

7. At the 11th Meeting (March 3, 1919) of the Reparation Commission, the President "reported that the motion adopted by the Commission at its 10th Meeting, by which the President of the Peace Conference was requested to obtain a ruling from the Supreme War Council, as constituted in November, 1918, upon the extent of the right of reparation, had been brought to the attention of the Council of Ten at its last meeting. Colonel House had asked that the matter be deferred until President Wilson arrived in France. The Council had, therefore, decided that the Reparation Commission should be invited to prepare a two-fold report: first, on the assumption that war costs might be included, and second, on the assumption that they ought to be excluded from the claims presented against Germany." The question submitted has never been formally decided, but in the Peace Treaty as drawn by the Council of Four "the Allied and Associated Governments affirm and Germany accepts the responsibility of Germany and her allies for causing all the loss and damage to which the Allied and Associated Governments and their nationals have been subjected as a consequence of the war imposed upon them by the aggression of Germany and her allies," but "the Allied and Associated Governments recognize that the resources of Germany are not adequate * * * to make complete reparation for all such loss and damage. The Allied and Associated Governments, however, require, and Germany undertakes that she will make compensation for all damage done to the civilian population of the Allied and Associated Powers and to their property during the period of the belligerency of each as an Allied and Associated Power against Germany by such aggression by land, by sea, and from the air, and in general, all damages as defined in Annex hereto."

8. From the wording of the duties assigned to the First and Second Sub-Committees of the Reparation Commission, Mr. Mc-Cormick and his advisers assumed that the Peace Treaty would call upon Germany to pay by way of reparation-indemnity a definitely expressed capital sum. This apparently was Colonel House's idea in November. Under the principle of "no punitive indemnity" the sum demanded could not be in excess of the

amount of the damage done. It was obvious from the beginning that the sum which Germany could pay was less than the value of the damage done if, as claimed by all the powers except the United States, *all* categories of destruction and loss were included in the word "damage." As pointed out above, the views of the United States as to the proper scope of reparation were much less extensive. For example, the American interpretation of the Fourteen Points did not (except in the case of Belgium) cover remote indirect damage, "war costs," or even military pensions. It was therefore necessary for the American delegate to obtain, for comparison with the amount of the indemnity to be demanded, an evaluation of damage *in the categories covered by the American principles of reparation.* As a result Mr. McCormick at the 1st Meeting of the First Sub-Committee, February 15, 1919,

"* * * * * * * * presented a motion calling for lists of claims, supported by detailed figures, and providing for a sub-committee of experts to classify and verify the claims presented by each country. MM. Danielopol, Van den Heuvel, and Olchowski insisted on the impossibility of such detailed statements of total claims being furnished by their respective countries. Mr. McCormick urged the necessity of reaching at least approximate estimates, which could be laid before the Commission, and would thus aid in determining methods of valuation. MM. Van den Heuvel and Chiesa agreed that it was possible to furnish certain figures: in some cases precise, in others approximate. The President urged that the Delegates make every effort to accomplish this, in view of the importance of having figures as soon as possible. M. Baykitch (expert for Serbia) declared himself unable to appreciate the usefulness of partial figures. The President (Lord Sumner) pointed out that partial figures would serve at least to indicate the relative importance of different claims.

After observations by M. Danielopol, Mr. McCormick, M. Olchowski, Lord Sumner, and M. Baykitch,

M. Lebrun (France) urged again the adoption of the procedure he had proposed, in order to avoid a confusion which would be fatal to the progress of the work of the Sub-Committee.

The President, summarizing the discussion, then declared that the sense of the meeting was in favor of determining first the categories and the method of valuation. He thus asked each delegation to present as soon as possible a memorandum drawn up on this basis. * * *"[4]

9. Mr. McCormick's motion, worded finally by himself, was based upon a paper presented to him as the result of a conference between Messrs. Summers, Chase, Leith, Young, and the undersigned, at which the general subject of reparation, categories of damage admissible under the American principles of reparation, priorities, bases of distribution for the indemnity paid, etc., and drafts prepared by three of the advisers relating to the need for

[4] See Document 467.

the immediate presentation of figures for damage by the various nations had been discussed.[5] The rumor had already reached us that the French would oppose the production of figures. (See my memorandum of January 29, 1919, addressed to Mr. Baruch, copy herewith).[6]

10. It had likewise been assumed from the commencement of the work of the War Damage Board that information as to damage would be needed by the American members of the Peace Commission for reaching an agreement by the date of the signature of the preliminary treaty, on a basis for the distribution of the reparation-indemnity, or at least of the first payments thereof. Not that it was expected that the distribution would be based upon damage alone. Certainly not that a preliminary distribution could be based upon an accurate ascertainment of damage. An accurate ascertainment of the value of damage in any important category of damage could not possibly be made by the time the preliminary treaty was signed. Whatever system might be adopted for the final distribution, and whatever adjustments of the deferred payments might be necessary to accomplish the final distribution, it was realized that the preliminary distribution could be based:—

(1) On approximate figures for total damage, or

(2) On approximate figures for damage in *certain* categories, which would thus be given a priority, or

(3) On some arbitrary system, influenced probably by the value of damage, total or partial.

11. The advantage of an early adoption of a basis of distribution would lie in the fact that the powers could use their credits as a basis for borrowing and for beginning reconstruction, and such a plan having been adopted, the Allies as a whole would have no concern with the adjudication of claims in the different countries or with the distribution of the indemnity therein, and the danger of differences among the Allies would be avoided. Moreover, the difficulties which would beset an agreement on distribution were evident, and it was reasonable to believe that this subject would engage the attention of the President and the Prime Ministers while they were all together in Paris. This forecast proved to be correct. In fact, the turn which events have taken is such as completely prove the wisdom of Colonel House's original idea in inaugurating the work of the War Damage Board. The information which the technical advisers have been asked to furnish is about the same information as the War Damage Board was originally

---

[5] See Documents 117 and 118.   [6] See Document 92.

directed to obtain, but which it was unable to obtain in full on account of suspension ordered February 12, 1919. The suspension has, of course, made it impossible for us to furnish *accurate* figures as to damage suffered by any of the nations. Nevertheless as information as to claims was furnished from time to time by the various delegations, and as there came to be a consensus of opinion in the Sub-Committee as to categories and methods of evaluation the work done by the War Damage Board in Italy, Belgium, and especially in France, was useful in interpreting the claims, in deciding which items were or were not in consonance with the American principles of reparation, and in reducing to a comparable basis the claims of the various nations in the same categories. Thus the figures we have been able to furnish have proved of use in considering the amount which it would be just to demand of Germany under the American principles of reparation, in estimating the liability of enemy states under the various lists of categories of damage that have been considered from time to time, and in discussing plans for distributing the indemnity.

12. At its first meeting, the First Sub-Committee adopted as its order of business the drawing up of categories of damage and methods of evaluation. The memoranda on categories and methods submitted by the various powers are printed as annexes to the minutes of the meetings of the Sub-Committee. The American memorandum was submitted February 20, 1919, and is as follows:— ... [7]

13. This office submitted to Mr. McCormick, on March 3rd, a memorandum (copy herewith) on methods of evaluation. The memorandum actually submitted by Mr. McCormick was prepared by Mr. Dulles in consultation with Colonel Dillon and Lieutenant Colonel Jackson. It is quoted below:— ... [8]
Other delegations, notably the French and British, likewise submitted memoranda on Categories of Damage and Methods of Evaluation.

14. The Sub-Committee devoted parts of twenty-six meetings to the consideration of categories of damage and methods of evaluation. The final report on these subjects is printed as Annex 15, Proceedings of the Commission on Reparation. It was adopted (subject to reserves) by the Commission on Reparation on April 7th (Proceedings of 14th Meeting, April 7th). [9]

---

[7] The text of the American memorandum has been omitted here. It may be found as Annex XI of Document 470.

[8] The text of the American memorandum has been omitted here. It may be found as Annex IV of Document 475.　　[9] See Document 464.

15. The effort made by Mr. McCormick at the first meeting to secure the production of figures has been recounted above. Without following the proceedings from day to day it will suffice to say that subsequently Mr. McCormick made frequent efforts to have figures produced; that he caused the American figures for damage to be formally introduced and explained before the Sub-Committee; that Lord Sumner, aided by Mr. McCormick, endeavored to have at least minimum figures produced; that while the British, Italian, Belgian, Japanese, Polish, Jugo-Slavic, Portuguese, and Czecho-Slovak delegations presented memoranda of their figures to the President of the Sub-Committee, these figures were never formally presented to the Sub-Committee, and that at the 26th Meeting (March 31) the French delegation declared its inability to furnish figures. Following is an extract from the minutes of the 26th Meeting:— . . . [10]

The decision of the Chairman of the First Sub-Committee to take up this matter with his government and obtain further instructions resulted in effect that the Council of Four took up the work of the Reparation Commission, both as to categories of damage and the distribution.

16. The Council of Four on April 7th tentatively agreed to the clauses on Reparation, which with the various revisions and final text as submitted to the Germans on May 7th follows:— . . . [11]

Note:—In addition to the above categories of damage Article 232 of the Treaty provides that Germany shall "make reimbursement of all sums which Belgium has borrowed from the Allied and Associated Governments up to November 11, 1918, together with interest at the rate of 5% per annum on such sums."

Paragraph 16 of Annex II to the Reparation clauses of the Treaty states that the Commission in fixing "the total amount of the debt of Germany, may take account of interest due on sums arising out of the reparation of material damage as from November 11, 1918, up to May 1st, 1921."

The records of the meetings of the Council of Four should be consulted for the proper interpretation of these categories.

17. From the Treaty clauses it appears that the expectation that a basis of distribution would be decided on in advance of the signing of the Treaty was correct; that the expectation that the amount of the indemnity was to be definitely expressed in the Treaty was not fulfilled, but that nevertheless it is implied that

[10] The extract has been omitted here. It is taken from Document 492, beginning with the words—
"The Chairman proposed that the Sub-Committee should now discuss the Memoranda as to figures of actual claims, in so far as such Memoranda had been presented by different Delegations."
—and continuing to the end of the minutes.

[11] The quoted text, omitted here, is that of Annex I of the Treaty with Germany. See Document 440.

the payment will come to at least $25,000,000,000. Information as to the value of the damage done under the categories finally adopted, and information by which the claims under these categories could be tested and at least reduced to a comparable basis has therefore proved necessary. But as will appear below, the technical advisers were called upon for and furnished information which was used for other than these purposes alone.

18. With respect to the American claim for war damages: I informed the American members of the Reparation Commission, January 29th, that the War Damage Board had had nothing to do with drawing up an American claim and were not even informed that one would be submitted. Later it was learned that Colonel Ayres was concerning himself with this matter. We have assisted slightly by suggesting the wording of a cable requesting the State Department to furnish certain necessary information.

19.[12] From the cabled reply and information already in Colonel Ayres' possession, the first American claim was made up and submitted to the Sub-Committee, March 5th. It is printed as an annex to the minutes and was explained in detail to the Sub-Committee on March 11th (11th Meeting).[13] The American claim revised to accord with additional (but not entirely detailed) information, and with the categories of damage adopted by the Council of Four on April 7th, 1919, follows:—

"15 April 1919.

"Memorandum for: Mr. Dulles, American Section, Reparation Commission.

"1. In response to your telephone request, there is submitted herewith the items and totals going to make up the American claim in accordance with the list of categories approved by the 'Council of Four' at their meeting of April 7, 1919.

"2. The item for Pensions is based upon the French scale. The number of Americans killed and wounded was furnished through kindness of Colonel Ayres.

"3. The item for Separation Allowances is based upon the French scale. The number of American troops was furnished by the same source.

"4. These two items (Pensions and Separation Allowances) are approximate only, as many details needed for an accurate estimate are not available, and probably will not be available for several months.

"5. The items of other claims are based upon information contained in cables received by you from the United States. It will be noted that the item for property in enemy territory and in enemy occupied territory has been entered at its full estimated value.

"6. Government owned cargo losses are not included nor is the item for loss of business (Items P & S of U. S. Cable 907). The capital letters in parenthesis refer to U. S. Cable 907, and will serve to identify the corresponding items.

"C. H. McKINSTRY,
"Brigadier General, U.S.A."

[12] This section 19 is abstracted separately as Document 273.
[13] This memorandum was not printed in the Subcommittee's minutes.

Categories.	*Damage.*	*$ Amounts.*
I. (a)	Personal injuries and deaths of civilians	
	(A) 800 civilians killed	20,000,000
	(R) 43 civilians injured—not complete—say	1,000,000
(b)	Cruelty, exposure, etc.—relief of stranded seamen (U)	250,000
(c)	Injury to health, etc.—(no estimate)	—
(d)	Maltreatment of prisoners of war (no estimate)	—
(e)	Military Pensions	500,000,000
(f)	Assistance to prisoners of war (no estimate)	—
(g)	Separation allowances	400,000,000
II.	Forced labor, etc. (no estimate)	—
III.	Damage to Property—	
	By enemy agents in U. S. (estimated)	10,000,000
	Property in enemy countries including Turkey (See U. S. cable #1451 dated April 5, 1919)	475,000,000
(D)	Merchant vessels sunk before April 6, 1917.	25,638,850
	" " " after April 6, 1917.	127,665,750
(E)	Merchant vessels under navy control	10,792,670
(G)	" " " army "	2,206,625
(H)	One light ship	150,000
(I)	Two Dutch ships	1,980,180
(J)	One Swedish vessel	278,300
(K)	One cargo steamer (U. S.) under British flag	1,457,480
(L)	Six ships believed to have been sunk	2,500,000
(M)	Twenty vessels damaged	5,000,000
(N)	Charter losses (questionable)	10,000,000
(O)	Merchant cargo losses	58,407,490
(P)	Government cargo losses $48,272,800	—
(Q)	Personal effects sunk	773,742
(R)	Combined with I (a) and (b)	—
(S)	Loss of business $248,870 (See U. S. cable 1373 dated March 29, 1919)	—
(T)	War Risk premiums $227,500,000 (included under Pensions)	—
(U)	War risk paid to seamen $236,270 (covered by item Pensions)	—
	Maintenance and care of interned civilians and prisoners of war estimated at $10,000,000—(This item not included in total, since it apparently is not covered by the categories of April 7.	
IV.	Levies, fines, etc.—(no estimate)	—
	Total claims	$1,653,101,087
	Expenses of Army of Occupation estimated to Aug. 15, 1919.	150,000,000
	Total	$1,803,101,087

Summary—

Pensions	$500,000,000	[2.000 milliard marks]
Separation allowances .	400,000,000	[1.600 " "]
Other claims	752,000,000	[3.008 " "]
Army of Occupation . .	150,000,000	[0.600 " "]
Total	$1,803,101,087	[7.212, 404, 348 milld. mks.]

Damages before and after our entry into the war are shown as far as information was available.

ESTIMATES OF DAMAGE

20. The attempt on the part of the American Delegation to obtain figures concerning damages has been mentioned herein. While there has never been any doubt but that the total damages under all categories would exceed the capacity of Germany (enemy states) to pay, there has always been considerable doubt whether or not the damages under the American principles would exceed the capacity of Germany (enemy states) to pay. In order to be a party to the treaty it was necessary for the American Delegation to be assured that the bill for damages under their principles was equal to or greater than the sum to be demanded of Germany. To demand more would, in accordance with our ideas, have been to exact a punitive indemnity.

21. Immediately upon the appointment of the American members of the Reparation Commission, they therefore requested all available information as to the money value of the damages in the various countries. This was before the First Sub-Committee had begun its work on Categories and Methods of Evaluation, and at a time when no information had been furnished by any countries except France, and to a lesser degree, Belgium and Italy. The French figures in our possession were not entirely official, but our parties had been at work in France for one and one-half months and considerable independent information had been collected. We had also sent parties to Belgium and Italy, but these had been recalled before any credible results could be obtained.

22. It is apparent, therefore, that the figures which we have submitted upon request from time to time are incomplete and inaccurate, but they served a useful purpose in giving the American delegates an approximate idea of the conditions and extent of damage included in the categories under consideration from time to time. Our knowledge of the conditions and extent of damage to the invaded regions of France has enabled us to make rough approximate estimates for other countries which have been fairly

well substantiated by the British experts. The final rejection of the "Fixed Sum" idea in the Treaty has rendered this work more or less unnecessary and the inclusion herein of these estimates, made at different stages of agreements concerning permissible categories, are of no particular interest. The table last submitted (made up in cooperation with Mr. Cumberland) is appended as giving an approximate idea of the damages under the categories appearing in Annex I to the Reparation clauses of the Treaty. The table also contains some interesting data on per capita wealth, national debts, etc. All the figures given should be considered as approximate only. From this table it will be observed that the sum of the total damages (exclusive of Russia, Poland, and Czecho-Slovakia) is in the neighborhoood of $40,000,-000,000. In general, this figure is arrived at by accepting the claims of France (which have been fairly closely checked by our own estimates) and comparing damages in other countries by per capita of their invaded regions after taking into consideration their per capita national wealth, etc. Shipping losses, pensions and separation allowances which have no relation to the population in the invaded regions were estimated independently for each country concerned.

23. On March 7, 1919, I was designated as a member of a Special Committee together with Lieutenant Colonel Peel (British Empire) and M. Jouasset (France) "to secure and report to the Sub-Committee (Valuation of Damage) information relative to the amount and character of such reparation as may be claimed by or due to the Governments and peoples not represented on the Commission on Reparation of Damage." The report of this Special Committee, of which I was chairman, was submitted to Lord Sumner, the chairman of the First Sub-Committee, under date of April 14th, 1919. One copy of this report is submitted herewith.[14]

24. On April 22, 1919, I (together with Admiral Long, U. S. Navy) was designated a member of an Inter-Allied Commission on the Repatriation of Prisoners of War. This Commission held several meetings, prepared clauses for the Treaties and submitted reports to the Council of Four which will be found elsewhere in the Records of the Peace Conference.[15]

25. By letter from the Secretary General of the American Peace Delegation, dated May 13, 1919, I was designated the American member of the "Committee on Prisoners of War and Graves, established to deal with questions of detail, requests for explana-

---

[14] See Document 497.　　　[15] Not in TPG.

tions and the like, referréd by the German delegates during the fifteen days which intervene before they furnished their global reply to the Treaty of Peace as presented to them." Up to the present all questions relating to such matters have been referred to the Commission mentioned in the preceding paragraph.

26. Various letters, memoranda, reports, etc., have been submitted from time to time by my office, the more important of which are attached as appendices to this report.

[*signed*] C H McKINSTRY
C. H. McKINSTRY,
Brigadier General, U.S.A.

(Detailed list of inclosures attached).

_____

APPENDICES ACCOMPANYING FINAL REPORT OF WAR DAMAGE BOARD, DATED MAY 26, 1919, TO AMERICAN COMMISSION TO NEGOTIATE PEACE, HON. VANCE McCORMICK, REPARATION COMMISSION.

Date.		From.	To.	Purport.
January 29, 1919	Letter	Gen. McKinstry	B. Baruch	Sub-committee on claims.
January 29, 1919	Memo.	"	"	Progress of work of W.D.B.
January 29, 1919	Memo.	"	"	American Claims.
Feb. 10, 1919	Memo.	Col. Dillon	A.C.N.P.	Amer. Principles on Reparation.
Febry. 14, 1919	Memo.	Gen. McKinstry	Rep. Com.	Proposed policy for drafting & examining claims.
Febry. 14, 1919	Memo.	"	V.McCormick	Proposed procedure with respect to claims (Conference between Gen. McKinstry, Mr. Summers, Dr. Leith, Dr.Young, Mr. Dulles & Col. Dillon.
Febry. 16, 1919	Memo.	Gen. McKinstry	"	Duties of Inter-Allied Reparation Commission.
Febry. 17, 1919	Memo.	Col. Dillon	Gen. McK.	Categories of Damages.
Febry. 18, 1919	Memo.	Gen. McKinstry	V. McCormick	Categories of damage to be submitted by all nations.
Febry. 21, 1919	Memo.	"	Messrs. Dulles, Warren [*sic*], & Leith.	Duties of Reparation Com.
Febry. 21, 1919	Memo.	"	V. McCormick	Suggestion for daily conferences.

Febry.	28, 1919 Note	M. Jouasset	Rep. Com.	Work of 1st Sub-Committee.
Febry.	28, 1919 Memo.	Gen. McKinstry	V. McCormick	What Germany can pay. (Decision of 2nd Sub-Committee.
March	3, 1919 Memo.	"	V. McCormick	Methods of Evaluation.
March	7, 1919 Letter	"	V. McCormick	Methods of Allied Govts. of affording relief for war damages.
March	14, 1919 Memo.	"	V. McCormick	Distribution of amounts obtained for reparation.
March	31, 1919 Memo.	"	V. McCormick	Non-submission by French of minimum estimate of war damage.
March	31, 1919 Memo.	"	V. McCormick	Consideration of figures for dam.
April	18, 1919 Letter	Gen. McKinstry	V. McCormick	Table of Estimated Damages.
April	26, 1919 Memo.	Col. Dillon	V. McCormick	Distribution of amounts received for reparation among the Balkan States.
May	2, 1919 Letter	Gen. McKinstry	V. McCormick	War Damages.
May	3, 1919 Letter	"	"	Reparation
May	6, 1919 Table			Comparison of the Post-War Financial Situation of the Principal Allied Nations.
May	19, 1919 Memo.	Col. Dillon	Mr. Dulles	Estimates of proportion of pre-war debts and liability for damages in acquired territory for Poland, Czecho-Slovakia, Roumania, & Jugo-Slavia.
May	20, 1919 Letter	Col. Dillon	V. McCormick	Organization for Reparation.

DOCUMENT 369

Letter from Robinson to House Regarding the Shipping Agreement, May 27, 1919

[From the signed original in the Edward M. House Collection, Yale University Library, New Haven, Connecticut. The writer's address is given as "United States Shipping Board, Washington"; but it is clear that the letter was written in Paris.]

Dear Colonel House:

The negotiations between the British and Italians relating to ship tonnage in the Adriatic are very likely to be determined today at a meeting of the Council of Four. I have a feeling that they will not be concluded to the liking of either of them, especially to the liking of the Italians.

However, when it is concluded, I feel that we should press for the Italian signature to the agreement relating to seized ships. I am enclosing the original signed by President Wilson and Mr. Lloyd George, so that you may obtain Mr. Orlando's signature as suggested by the President.

Very respectfully yours,
[*signed*] HENRY M. ROBINSON

DOCUMENT 370

Memorandum from Robinson to House Regarding the Shipping Controversy and Agreement, May 28, 1919

[From the original in the Edward M. House Collection, Yale University Library, New Haven, Connecticut. "In Compliance with Ambassador Davis's request for Information With Relation to Seized Ships."]

The net war losses of the Allied and Associated Powers are 9,105,-000 gross tons; enemy tonnage over 1600 tons gross, approximately 5,300,000 gross tons. The percentage interests of each of the countries in the ships so to be distributed are as follows:

U. K.	77.65
France	6.75
Italy	6.70
U. S.	3.00
Greece	3.49
Japan	1.32
Belgium	.77
Portugal	.14
Brazil	.14
Roumania	.04

At first the British advanced the idea that enemy tonnage, which included all over 1600 gross tons (and a relatively small amount of tonnage under 1600 gross tons) should be taken over en masse and redistributed on the basis of ton-for-ton and class-for-class. It developed that the enemy ships in the possession of some of the

Allied and Associated Governments had been carried through prize court proceedings and that in other cases had been seized and made use of for war purposes and under other legal forms.

After full discussion by the British representatives, it was agreed by Great Britain that each Allied and Associated Power should keep the enemy tonnage in its possession at the signing of the Armistice, and that distribution of the balance of the enemy ships to be taken over should be on the basis of the balances due for ship losses, and the ships should be shared on the basis of remaining unsatisfied claims.

In certain cases, to wit: the United States, Brazil, Cuba, Siam and China, the seized tonnage exceeds the dividend that would be received by these States respectively had all tonnage been pooled and redistributed. It has been agreed, however, that the tonnage involved in such excess is relatively small and that there are many difficulties in the way of compelling the turning over of such excess into a pool.

It is understood, however, that in cases where one of the powers has an excess over what would be a dividend on the basis of a pooling of all of the ships and a redistribution, is to be paid for by such Power at a reasonable rate, payment to go into reparation.

France has agreed that the United States shall retain its ships on this basis, but has made a temporary reservation as to Brazil because of some inter-relations with that country. France agrees, however, that when it has resolved its difficulties with Brazil it proposes to make the same agreement that all Allied and Associated countries shall retain their seized ships.

The Italians state that they propose to sign the agreement that all Allied and Associated countries shall retain their seized ships, and would have done so before this but that certain questions as to Adriatic shipping should be solved before the execution of the general agreement.

Japan has agreed to the same basis of distribution if certain conditions are met, which can be met.

With the exception of Greece the interests of the other Powers are trifling, and the feeling is that their interests will not prove to be an obstacle.

It may not be amiss to state that Great Britain has substantially the same ship tonnage that she had at the outbreak of the war, that her relative position in the world's shipping is even stronger than at the outbreak of the War. Germany has been eliminated, the United States may be considered as a new competitor but at present is certainly not as strong as Germany was. And recognizing this, the British have shown proper liberality in connection with the ship-distribution.

DOCUMENT 371

Memorandum from Robinson to Gordon and to Palmer Regarding the Shipping Agreement, May 28, 1919

[From an original in the Edward M. House Collection, Yale University Library, New Haven, Connecticut. "Question of the Enemy Tonnage Seized by the United States."]

I wish to call your attention to the following:

Mr. Lloyd George, on behalf of England, has agreed with the President that the United States, Brazil, Cuba, Siam and China shall retain their seized ships. A copy of that agreement is attached.

The French have agreed that the United States shall retain the seized ships, but have made reservation as to the remaining States in the hope that they may in some way make an arrangement to get the Brazilian ships. My understanding is that when they have finished their negotiations with Brazil they are willing to waive on the other ships.

The Italians have stated that they expect to sign the agreement already signed by Mr. Lloyd George and the President, and are only waiting until the question of the ships in the Adriatic is settled in order that the signing of the agreement may not confuse the issue on the Adriatic ships. It is possible that this may be cleared up before I leave, but if not will you follow this up with Mr. Hipwood, the British representative, and with Attolico acting for the Italians, and obtain the Italian signature to the agreement as early as possible. The original which is to be signed by Mr. Orlando, is in Colonel House's possession, and if you will let Colonel House know when the Adriatic question has been settled, he will ask Mr. Orlando to sign.

The Japanese make a condition of their signature of the Lloyd George-President Wilson agreement that they be furnished with something over 5,000 tons of shipping. I am enclosing copy of the letter written to the President on this subject which outlines roughly how this might be handled, and which the President approves if feasible.[1] It is possible that it may not be necessary to go this far, but if it is, Mr. Bradley Palmer understands how to work the problem out.

[1] This letter is missing.

DOCUMENT 372

Letter from Brockdorff-Rantzau to Clemenceau Covering the Observations of the German Delegation on the Conditions of Peace, May 29, 1919

[English translation of French translation of German original, from Peace Conference Bulletin No. 322 (May 30, 1919), in Miller, XVIII, 466-72. German text in *Materialien*, III, 7-11. French translation in PV, Notes, pp. 107-11.]

Mr. President:

I have the honor to address to you, herewith, the observations of the German Delegation with regard to the proposed Peace Treaty. We came to Versailles, expecting to receive propositions of Peace on the proclaimed basis. We had the firm desire to do all we possibly could, to accomplish obligations accepted by us. We expected the Peace of Right which had been promised to us. We were grieved when we read this document to see what conditions victorious Might demanded of us. The more we entered the spirit of that Treaty, the more we were convinced of the impossibility of carrying it out. The demands of that Treaty are beyond the strength of the German people.

It is demanded that we renounce, with a view to the reconstitution of Poland, a territory which is indisputably German, that we renounce Eastern Prussia, entirely German, German parts of Pomerania, Dantzig, a city which is essentially German, a former Hanseatic city which we must allow to be constituted into a free State under the sovereignty of Poland. We must accept that Eastern Prussia be cut off the political body of which she is a part, that she be condemned to decay, and bereaved of her northern extremity, essentially German. We must renounce, in favor of Poland and Czecho-Slovakia, Upper Silesia, in spite of the narrow political bond which has kept it united to Germany for over 750 years, in spite of the German life which fills it and though it constitutes the very basis of industry in the whole of Eastern Germany. Districts where the German element is in majority must be given to Belgium, without sufficient guarantees in favor of the independence of a plebiscite which shall only be made after they are given away. The country of the Saar, essentially German, must be separated from our Empire, and its reunion to France must be prepared, though we do not owe France any populations but only coal.

During 15 years, the Rhine territory must be occupied and

the Allies will keep after 15 years, the facility of refusing to retrocede this country; during this period they will be free to do all that may cause the economic and moral ties to slacken between that country and the mother-land, and finally warp the mind of the population.

A Germany, thus partitioned and weakened, must, though the payment of war expenditures has expressly been given up, declare herself ready to bear the weight of all the expenditures of her adversaries, which amount to twice the national and individual wealth of Germany. The adversaries, even now, going beyond the basis agreed to, demand the reparation of the damage supported by the civil population, reparations for which Germany must also answer in the name of her Allies. The sum to be paid is to be settled and ulteriorly modified and increased in a unilateral manner by the adversaries. The limit will be indicated by the capacity of payment of the German people, the degrees contemplated do not depend on the conditions of its existence but solely on the possibility in which it will find itself to satisfy the demands of its enemies by its work. The German people would thus be condemned to a perpetual slavery.

In spite of these exorbitant demands, the reconstruction of our economic life is, at the same time, made impossible. We must give our merchant fleet, give up all foreign property. We must transfer to the adversaries our property rights over all German enterprises in foreign lands even in our Allies' countries. Even after the conclusion of Peace the enemy states will have the right to confiscate the totality of German wealth. No German business man, in the countries of these States, will be sheltered against such war measures. We must give up the whole of our colonies, German missionaries will not even have the right to exercise their profession. Therefore it is our very existence, from a political, economic and moral point of view, which we must renounce.

Even at home we must sacrifice our right of self-determination. The International Commission on Reparations has received a dictatorial power even over our whole national life, in the realm of economy and culture, its rights being much in excess of those ever possessed, over the territory of the Empire, by the Emperor, the Bundesrat and the Reichstag together.

This Commission has full power over the economy of the State, the communities and the individuals. Education and Public Health are absolutely under its control. It can maintain the whole German people in intellectual slavery; it can, with a view to raising the payments to which she is obliged, fetter the work of social provision in favor of the German workers.

.   .   .

Thus, a whole nation must sign her own proscription, more than that, her condemnation to death.

Germany knows that she must consent to sacrifices, in order to obtain peace. She knows that, in conformity with a convention, she has promised these sacrifices; she is ready to go to the extreme limit of what is possible.

1. . . .

2. . . . Germany is ready to insure the economic supply of France in coal, especially from the Saar coal field, until restoration of the French mines. . . .

3. Germany is ready to make the payments incumbent upon her according to the peace program agreed upon, up to the maximum sum of 100 billion marks gold, of which 20 billion marks gold are to be paid by May 1, 1926, the other 80 billion marks gold in annual sums without interest. These sums are in principle to represent a percentage fixed according to the revenue of the Empire and the German States. The quota will approach the former budget of peace times. For the first ten years, it shall not exceed a billion marks gold. The German taxpayer shall not be taxed less than the most highly taxed taxpayer among those represented on the Commission of Reparations.

Germany supposes from this that she will not have to make other territorial sacrifices than those heretofore cited, and that she will be permitted all liberty of movement at home and abroad.

4. Germany is ready to put all her economic force at the service of reconstruction. She desires to collaborate by her work in the reconstruction of the ravaged districts of Belgium and the North of France. For the deficit in the production of the mines destroyed in the North of France she will furnish as high as 20 million tons of coal for the first five years, 8 million tons a year for the next five years. Germany will facilitate other deliveries of coal to France, Belgium, Italy and Luxembourg.

Moreover, Germany is ready to furnish important quantities of benzol, coal tar, sulphuric ammonia and dye-stuffs and pharmaceutical products.

5. Finally, Germany offers to put her entire merchant tonnage at the disposal of the world's commerce, to put at the disposal of the enemy a part of the cargoes, which shall be put to her credit

toward the damages to be repaired, and for a term of years to construct for them in German yards a tonnage whose figure exceeds their demands.

6. To replace the river boats destroyed in Belgium and the North of France, Germany offers her own river fleet.

7. Germany thinks that she sees an appropriate means of rapidly fulfilling her obligations in the way of reparation, by according industrial participation, especially in the coal mines, to insure the delivery of coal.

8. In accord with the wish of organized laborers the world over, Germany desires to see the laborers of every country free and equal in their rights. She wishes to see them insured, by the Peace Treaty, in their right to participate, by their own decisions, in social politics and social insurance.

9. The German Delegation reiterates its demand for a neutral examination of the responsibility for the war and crimes committed during the war. An impartial commission should have the right to examine under its own responsibility the archives of all the belligerent countries and of all the principal participants.

Only the assurance that the question of guilt will be examined without prejudice can give to the hostile countries the state of mind necessary to the constitution of the League of Nations.

These are only the most important propositions that we have to make. As to the other great sacrifices and details, the Delegation refers to the inclosed memorandum and its supplement.

The time limit given us for the drawing up of this memorandum was so short that it was impossible to exhaust all the questions. A fruitful and useful discussion could take place only by means of oral conversations. This peace is to be the greatest treaty of history. It is without precedent to carry on such vast negotiations by means of written notes only. The sentiment of nations that have made such enormous sacrifices requires that their fate be decided by a public and unrestricted exchange of ideas, after the principle: "Public Peace Treaties," which have been drawn up publicly; and henceforth there must be no international conventions of any sort, but diplomacy must always operate publicly and under the eyes of the world.

Germany must sign the treaty that has been presented to her and must carry out its conditions. Even in her misfortune, right is too sacred to her for her to stoop to accept conditions that she can not promise to fulfil. It is true that in the course of the last centuries the peace treaties of the great powers have always proclaimed the right of might. But each one of these treaties is one of the causes that has started or prolonged the world war. Wherever in the course of this war the conqueror has spoken to the conquered, as at Brest-Litovsk or at Bucharest, the affirmations of power were only the germs of future discord. The lofty aims which our enemies have been the first to give to their way of conducting the war, require a treaty in a different spirit. Only the collaboration of all nations, the common labor of all arms and brains, can create a durable peace. We are under no illusions as to the depth of the hatred and bitterness which are the fruits of this war; and nevertheless the forces working for harmony in humanity are to-day stronger than ever. The historic task of the Peace Conference at Versailles is to bring about this harmony.

BROCKDORFF-RANTZAU.

DOCUMENT 373

Extracts from the Observations of the German Delegation on the Conditions of Peace, Undated

[English translation taken from *International Conciliation*, No. 143, October 1919, pp. 1203-05, 1212-13, 1220-21, 1258-77. German text in *Materialien*, III 12-14, 20-21, 27-28, 60-77. French translation in PV, Notes, pp. 112-14, 120-21, 128, 160-76.

These Observations were enclosed in the German Note of May 29 (see Document 372).]

[*pp. 1203-5*]   The German Delegation have entered upon the task of concluding peace in the legal conviction that the essential contents of the treaty of peace which is to be concluded, are in principle outlined by the events preceding it, and that thereby a definite platform is established for the negotiations at Versailles. This conviction is founded upon the following facts:

On the 5th of October, 1918, the German Government requested President Wilson to take into his hands the task of establishing peace on the basis of the fourteen points contained in his message to Congress of January 8, 1918, and on the basis of his subsequent proclamations, especially his speech of September 27, 1918, to invite all belligerent powers to send delegates for the purpose of entering into negotiations and to bring about the immediate conclusion of a general armistice.

On the 8th of October, 1918, President Wilson asked if the German Government accepted his fourteen points and if the sole object of their discussion would be to agree upon the practical application of their details. The German Government expressly confirmed this and at the same time said it expected that the Allied Governments also stood on the platform of President Wilson's proclamations. Moreover, it declared its readiness to evacuate the occupied territories, this being demanded by President Wilson as a prerequisite to concluding the armistice.

After further correspondence President Wilson, on the 23rd of October, 1918, declared that he was willing to take up with the Allied Governments the question of an armistice. He made it known at the same time that, in carrying out this intention, he had transmitted to the Allies his correspondence with the German Government and had suggested that, in case the Allies agreed to the terms and principles of peace accepted by Germany, they point out through their military advisers such terms for an armistice as would be fit to safeguard or to enforce the details of the peace to which the German Government had agreed. Germany, it was thus expressly said, could by the acceptance of such terms of armistice afford the best concrete evidence that she accepted the fundamental terms and principles of the whole treaty of peace.

The German Government having, in its reply of the 27th of October, given satisfactory information concerning further matters of internal politics which President Wilson had touched upon in his last mentioned note of October 23rd, President Wilson notified the German Government on the 3rd of November, that, in reply to the correspondence with the German Government which he had transmitted to the Allies, he had received from the Allied Governments the following memorandum:

"The Allied Governments have given careful consideration to the correspondence which has passed between the President of the United States and the German Government. Subject to the qualifications which follow, they declare their willingness to make peace with the Government of Germany on the terms of peace laid down in the President's address to Congress of January 8, 1918, and the principles of settlement enunciated in his subsequent addresses. They must point out, however, that what is usually described as the freedom of the seas, is open to various interpretations, some of which they could not accept. They must, therefore, reserve to themselves complete freedom on this subject when they enter the peace conference.

Further, in the conditions of peace laid down in his address to

Congress of January 8, 1918, the President declared that invaded territories must be restored as well as evacuated and freed. The Allied Governments feel that no doubt ought to be allowed to exist as to what this provision implies. By it they understand that compensation will be made by Germany for all damage done to the civilian population of the Allies and their property by the aggression of Germany by land, by sea and from the air."

On the 11th of November, 1918, the armistice was concluded. From the correspondence that led to this armistice, the following points became evident:

1. As a basis of peace, Germany has expressly accepted nothing but President Wilson's fourteen points and his subsequent proclamations. No other bases have been demanded either by President Wilson, or after him, by any of the Allied Governments.

2. The acceptance of the terms of armistice was, according to President Wilson's own assurance, to be the best evidence of the unequivocal acceptance of the above mentioned fundamental terms and principles of peace on the part of Germany. Germany has accepted the terms of armistice and thereby furnished the proof demanded by President Wilson. Beyond that she has with all her might endeavored to fulfill those terms in spite of their great severity.

3. The Allies also have accepted Wilson's fourteen points and his subsequent proclamations as a basis of peace.

4. A solemn agreement as to the basis of peace therefore exists between the two Contracting Parties. Germany has a right to this basis of peace. By abandoning it the Allies would break an international legal agreement.

The historical facts stated show that between the German Government on the one hand and the Governments of the Allied and Associated Powers on the other a *pactum de contrahendo* has been concluded which is, without a doubt, legally binding and whereby the basis for the peace is for both parties unalterably fixed.

The practical application of the principles agreed upon must, according to President Wilson's own words, be the subject of negotiation. Germany has a right to a discussion of the terms of peace. This discussion can only extend to the application of the fourteen points and of the subsequent proclamations of Mr. Wilson. If a peace of a different character were to be forced upon Germany, that would be a breach of a solemn pledge.

.   .   .

[*pp. 1212-13*]   Although President Wilson, in his speech of October 20th [*26th*], 1916, has acknowledged that "no single fact caused the war, but that in the last analysis the whole European system is in a deeper sense responsible for the war, with its combination of alliances and understandings, a complicated texture of intrigues and espionage that unfailingly caught the whole family of nations in its meshes," "that the present war is not so simply to be explained and that its roots reach deep into the dark soil of history," Germany is to acknowledge that Germany and her allies are responsible for all damages which the enemy Governments or their subjects have incurred by her and her allies' aggression. This appears all the less tolerable as it is an indisputable historical fact that several of the hostile Powers, such as Italy and Roumania, on their part entered the war for the purpose of territorial conquests. Apart from the consideration that there is no incontestable legal foundation for the obligation for reparation imposed upon Germany, the amount of such compensation is to be determined by a commission nominated solely by Germany's enemies, Germany taking no part in the findings of the commission. The commission is plainly to have power to administer Germany like the estate of a bankrupt.

As there are innate rights of man, so there are innate rights of nations. The inalienable fundamental right of every state is the right of self-preservation and self-determination. With this fundamental right the demand here made upon Germany is incompatible. Germany must promise to pay an indemnity, the amount of which at present is not even stated. The German rivers are to be placed under the control of an international body upon which Germany's delegates are always to be but the smallest minority. Canals and railroads are to be built on German territory at the discretion of foreign authorities.

.   .   .

[*pp. 1220-21*]   All this shows that the draft of a peace treaty as submitted to the German Government stands in full and irreconcilable conflict with the basis agreed upon for a just and durable peace. Scarcely a single stipulation of the draft corresponds with the conditions agreed upon, and with regard to the territorial questions, the draft demands the annexation of purely German territory and the suppression of the German nationality. It involves the utter destruction of German economic life. It leads the German people into a financial thraldom unknown in history up to the present day. Therefore, in the session of the National Assembly on the 12th of May, it was characterized as being impossible of realization, by the Government as well as by all the parties. The application of this draft of a treaty would be equivalent to a new disaster for the whole world. Did not ex-President Roosevelt on October 10, 1914, utter the warning that "A destruction or even mere crippling of Germany apt to lead to its political powerlessness, would be a catastrophe for mankind." This would make itself felt first in the sphere of economics. From an economically pauperized Germany, as would be the inevitable result of such a peace, her creditors cannot obtain those immense sums which Germany is to pay to them. The disadvantageous consequences of such a peace would range far beyond any diminution of the enemies' demands. The economic prosperity of the world is, taking everything into account, dependent on the total sum of the produced goods. The entire elimination of Germany from the world's trade may, to be sure, oust an obnoxious competitor; as a result of the economic breakdown of Germany, the world as a whole must become infinitely poorer. Such a lasting damage to the welfare of the world is doubly disastrous because the war has consumed a large portion of the national wealth of most of the belligerents. What the world is in need of is international cooperation in all fields.

. . .

[*pp. 1258-77*]   IV.   REPARATION

1. Legal basis of the German obligation for reparation

According to the interpretation of the German Delegation, the general legal basis for the treaty of peace, as explained in the introductory remarks, contains a detailed stipulated agreement regarding Germany's obligation for reparation of damages. The main features of this agreement were explained in the note of the German Delegation of May 24, 1919. According to this, President Wilson's message of January 8, 1918, and the note of the Secretary of State, Mr. Lansing, of November 5, 1918, are decisive in fixing the extent of the German obligation for reparation of damages. President Wilson's message demanded the "restoration of the occupied territories." Thereupon the term "restoration of the occupied territories," as regards Germany, has been defined in the note of the Secretary of State, Mr. Lansing, as meaning that Germany would have to make reparation for all damages which have been done to the civilian population of the

Allies and their property by her aggression by land, by sea and from the air.

According to the German interpretation it seemed, and still seems today, obvious that the obligation to make reparation, as thus defined could not apply to any other territories than those whose restoration has been demanded in President Wilson's message, and which has always been declared by the leading statesmen of our opponents to be their aim in the war. An obligation for the reparation of these territories—but for these territories only—was acceptable to Germany inasmuch as she had brought the terrors of war upon a foreign country by a breach of international law, *viz.*, the violation of Belgian neutrality. It is, therefore, solely the attack upon Belgium for which the German Government accepted responsibility when signing the armistice. The responsibility, consequently, applies only to Belgium. It will, however, be acknowledged likewise for the north of France, as the German armies reached the territory of Northern France by passing through Belgian territory, whose neutrality had been violated. An extension of the obligation of reparation to the occupied territories of Italy, Montenegro, Servia and Roumania must, however, be opposed, for the simple reason that in these countries there is no question of an attack by Germany contrary to international law. Italy and Roumania even took part in the fighting against us, notwithstanding their obligations to Germany as allies at the beginning of the war. Neither can any obligation for reparation as regards Poland be accepted since Poland was on peaceful terms with Germany on November 5, 1918, nor was the reparation of Poland mentioned in the message of January 8, 1918.

The obligation of Germany which was agreed upon amounts, therefore, to the following: that compensation should be made for all damages sustained by the civil population of the Allies in those territories in Belgium and France which were occupied by the German troops. Moreover, the obligation is not limited to the property destroyed; it includes, on the contrary, every damage which the said civilian population has suffered in person or in property.

The draft of the terms of peace presented by the Allied and Associated Powers exceeds the solemn declarations and agreements of 1918. Article 231 of the draft demands that Germany and her allies accept, in principle, full responsibility for all losses and damages which the Allied and Associated Governments and their respective subjects have suffered through the war. The

Allied and Associated Governments demand further, according to Article 232, paragraph 2, that Germany should, in the first place, hold herself responsible for making compensation for all damages which have been inflicted, by her attacks on land, on water and from the air, upon the civilian population of the Allied and Associated Powers and their property, and, in addition, in general for the reparation of the damages defined in Annex I to Article 232. This annex, however, deals only in the smallest degree with the damages inflicted upon the civilian population of the occupied territories.

Mention is made of:

1. Losses to civilian subjects of the Allied and Associated Powers, which were caused in other than the occupied territories;

2. Losses to the Allied and Associated States themselves;

3. Losses to military persons of these States;

4. Damages which Allied, not German, attack has inflicted upon the Allied and Associated Powers, their military persons and their civilian population.

The demands thus stipulated by the Allied and Associated Governments lead to the belief that they wish to establish, in excess of the arrangements agreed upon, an obligation for reparation for every action committed in violation of international law during the war. As already declared in the note of May 24, the principle of responsibility for violations of international law has been recognized by Germany. It goes without saying, however, that, if the point of view agreed upon in the arrangement should be abandoned, Germany could no longer abide by the renunciation of her demands for reparation contained in this arrangement, but that she, on her part, would have to make considerable claims for compensation for damages. The only practical solution of the great difficulties which would result from such claims of breaches of international law on both sides would be—as already mentioned in the note of May 24—the establishment of an impartial international court of arbitration.

The German Government, however, believes that it should limit its counter-proposals to the sphere of obligations established by the arrangements made in the fall of 1918. Nevertheless, Germany declares her readiness to assume responsibility for those loans which the Belgian State has placed with its Allies up to November 11, 1918, for war purposes. This is not to be regarded as a renunciation of the legal position as it has been explained, but as a voluntary concession.

2. Financial Obligations

As regards the damages to be made good in each particular case, the German Government considers it proper to follow the principle of the French Indemnification Draft of 1916, according to which these damages must be certain, material and direct ("certains, matériels et directs"). In this connection, the German Government wishes to point out the fact that some parts of the population of the occupied districts, especially Belgium, have had an opportunity to realize considerable profits during the period of occupation, a fact which is obviously proved by the extraordinarily large circulation of German bank-notes in the districts in question.

From this point of view, the German Government is willing to recognize, on principle, its liability for compensation as mentioned in Annex I to Article 232 under paragraphs 1, 2, 3, 8, 9, and 10. In all these cases, liability for compensation can only be recognized with respect to such damages as have been caused by Germany to civilians in the occupied districts of France and Belgium.

As regards paragraph 4, the German Government repeatedly asserts the principle of reciprocity, in consideration of the sufferings to which German nationals abroad, and in the Colonies—in the latter case partly in violation of the Congo Acts—have been exposed. For the claims mentioned under paragraphs 5-7, the German Government cannot recognize a legal title, as they apply to direct war costs, and not to damages done to the civilian population by an act of war.

As to the expenses of an army of occupation, the German Government is of the opinion that security by occupation is not necessary. In view of the demobilization by land and by water as agreed to, Germany is completely disarmed. An army of occupation will simply impair Germany's financial power and diminish the payments available each year.

Germany is agreed that the total amount of damages for which she must make compensation shall be definitely fixed according to these principles on or before May 1, 1921, for France in French francs and for Belgium in Belgian francs.

As, in accordance with general principles of justice, no one can at the same time be a party and a judge, and in view of the fact that the injured states are also represented on the Inter-Allied Commission, the German Government does not consider it proper that the "Reparation Commission" (Article 233) should have sole authorization to fix definitively the amount of the damages. The German Government, therefore, proposes that a German Commission be allowed to cooperate so that the two commissions may arrive at an understanding regarding the amount of damage, and that the items which cannot be settled between them be submitted for final decision to a mixed court of arbitration, under neutral presidency.

The same procedure should be applied in fixing the value of the liabilities in kind which Germany has already delivered or will deliver on the indemnity account, including an agreement on the amounts required to supply Germany with food and raw materials, in case such an agreement cannot be reached by the time the treaty is signed (Articles 235 and 236).

The German Government is anxious to cooperate in the restoration of France and Belgium in order to pay off the indemnity in part in German labor, and will, in due course, submit proposals as to the way in which this this task, which is common to all civilized nations, can be accomplished with the Allied and Associated Powers in the quickest possible manner.

Moreover, the German Government reserves to itself the right to submit details, either in writing or verbally, respecting those points of the peace draft which it is proposed in the foregoing to alter. It is the intention of the German Government to indicate here only such general principles as it considers fair.

Germany is resolved to do all in her power to fulfill her obligations to make reparation. In doing so, the German Government is fully aware that the German people will have to bear greater burdens for generations than any other nation.

Germany declares herself ready, in accordance with her ability, to pay as an annuity a certain percentage of the total revenue from the taxes and surplus production of the German Republic and of the individual states.

Germany also recognizes the principle, laid down in Article 234 and in 12b of Annex II, that the German tax system, as a whole, shall not burden the tax payer less than the tax system of the most burdened of the states represented on the "Reparation Commission." In doing so, Germany trusts that the tax system in these states will be worked out on the principle of social justice and upon the basis of economic endurance, in the same manner as in Germany. It is of vital importance to democratic Germany that its political organization should be inspired with a social spirit. For this reason, Germany can bear these heavy burdens only on condition that she will not be dismembered by the final treaty of peace, and that her industrial system as well as the basis of her food supply will not be destroyed, except in so far as this may result from the right of self-determination of the inhabitants of Alsace-Lorraine, Schleswig and parts of the province of Posen. Germany also expects that she will not be refused the right to resume her oversea connections and to regain her colonies, oversea trading settlements and the like; furthermore, that she may retain a mercantile fleet of large ships sufficient to her needs, and finally, that it will be possible, by way of international legal redress, to assess such property as has been removed from the territory of the German Republic.

Germany has assumed the obligations involved in the Lansing Note on the basis of the extent of her territory at that time. Otherwise it would have been an unintentional act of folly to take such heavy burdens on her shoulders, regardless of the diminution of her area, working capacity, raw materials, and food. Should a diminution of her territory take place, as a result of the application of the right of self-determination, the indemnity to be paid on the 1st of May, 1921, will have to be distributed proportionately and in accordance with the point of view set forth above. The National Assembly has granted credits for that damage which is considered as a resultant of the war. It may be pointed out that the delegates from all the territories, the transfers of which is claimed by our opponents in the draft of the peace treaty, joined in granting these credits. For this reason these districts should also be under an obligation to pay their proportionate share in the debts resulting from the war. The Allies should collect the share and credit it to the reparation account. Any other procedure would seem unjust. Reparation can only result from the industry and activity of the whole population, from which single parts cannot be exempted by putting them under some other government.

As regards the establishment of the annuity, the German Government cannot submit to its being fixed in a one-sided manner by the representatives of the creditors, the "Reparation Commission." The German Government is prepared to submit to this Commission without delay all the material necessary for examining Germany's ability to pay so that the percentage of the government revenues which is to form the annuity can be fixed in connection with a competent German Commission. Matters in dispute should be settled by a mixed commission under neutral presidency.

By these means, it will be possible to ascertain objectively and impartially what obligations Germany can meet without destroying her social and industrial life. Not even the harshest creditor can demand more from a debtor who is willing to fulfill his obligations, but whose capacity to pay is greatly impaired.

It is recognized that due provision should be made for keeping in reserve such sums as are to be paid at certain dates. But it is going too far to appoint a commission for Germany with such dictatorial powers as provided in Annex II to Article 233. It is impossible for any state, especially for a democratic one, to renounce its sovereign rights to the extent demanded. In particular, Germany cannot agree to the demand that she issue laws and regulations as required from time to time by the Commission. The whole constitution, which for Germany also should be based on the right of self-determination, would be endangered, nay, even made null and void. The power of the purse is, in all democratic states, a means by which the National Assembly exercises its control over the commonwealth. Moreover, the powers vested in the Commission would make it necessary for it to examine each household budget in the German Republic as well as in the individual states and communities. Such a task could never be performed by foreigners. Herein, furthermore, lies a great danger with regard to the payment of the indemnity. It needs merely to be mentioned that, not only the readiness of the whole population to work, but also its willingness to pay taxes will suffer as a consequence, inasmuch as no nation can be compelled to devote its services permanently to foreign powers and to renounce its right of self-government. It follows, as a matter of course, that the payment of the greater part of the German direct taxes would have to be exacted by force.

According to the German proposals the Inter-Allied Commission would be competent in the following matters:

1. In determining the amount of the damage.

2. In determining the value of the payments in kind.

3. In arriving at an agreement concerning the amount to be deducted from payments in kind, in order to supply Germany with food and raw materials.

4. In conducting the examination, which is to be undertaken forthwith, of Germany's capacity to pay, for the purpose of determining the percentage of taxes from Government revenues.

For the technical execution of the payment of the indemnity to be made on or before May 1, 1921, and to be stipulated in accordance with the above, and of the payments to be made on the basis of the fixed boundaries of the respective countries, Germany makes the following proposal:

Germany is ready, within four weeks after the ratification of peace, to issue government bonds for 20,000,000,000 gold marks, payable not later than May 1, 1926, in instalments to be stipulated by the Allied and Associated Powers, and for the remainder of the total indemnity to draw up the required deeds in the same manner and to pay them in yearly instalments without interest, beginning May 1, 1927, with the understanding that the total compensation shall on no account exceed the sum of 100,000,000,000 gold marks, including both the discharges to Belgium for the amounts advanced to her by the Allied and Associated Powers, and the above-mentioned 20,000,000,000 gold marks.

All those payments are to be placed to the credit of the first debentures of 20,000,000,000 gold marks, which Germany, on the basis of the armistice, has already fulfilled or will fulfill, such as railway material, agricultural machinery, war and peace material of all kinds, and the like; also the value of all payments which Germany will have to make after the treaty of peace, and which are to be credited to her on the indemnity account, as for instance the value of railways and public property, the final assumption of national debts, the claims to be ceded to the powers allied with Germany in the war, a certain portion of the freightage gained by the entrance of German commercial tonnage in the world pool; also those payments in kind, which in connection with Annexes III-VI to Part VIII are to be determined by negotiation; further-more, the value of the work done and the materials supplied by the Germans in the restoration of Belgium and France; and finally, the restitutions to be made to Belgium, in the shape of a contingent special loan, for the amounts advanced to her by the Allied and Associated Powers. For the instalments payable annually and bearing no interest up to the maximum amount of the 80,000,-000,000 marks still due, limits provided in view of Germany's solvency shall apply. The instalments shall not exceed the stipu-lated percentage of the receipts of the German Republic and of the States. Germany is prepared to assume, in favor of the indemnity to be paid to the Allied and Associated Powers, an annual burden equal to its hitherto net peace budget.

Accordingly, the annuity to be paid each year should be fixed as a certain percentage of Germany's revenues from direct and indirect taxes, and from the surplus production and customs, with the understanding that for the customs, payment in gold may be prescribed. This tax, however, in the first ten years shall not exceed the equivalent of 1,000,000,000 gold marks in each case. Two years before the expiration of the ten years there shall be further negotiation regarding the stipulation of a maximum amount.

The payment of the annuities may be secured by a guarantee fund. The German Republic could pledge itself to pay an annuity into this fund up to the year 1926 from the income of indirect taxes, monopolies and duties, and after that to keep this amount permanently at the same level. Only in case Germany should be in arrears with an annuity, could control of this fund by the Allied and Associated Governments be admitted, and then only until such annuity had been duly paid. It is impossible to admit measures of an arbitrary nature, such as are threatened in Section 18 of Annex II to Article 233 (page 107).

Germany reserves to herself the right to submit additional notes in writing; at the same time the Delegation propose to discuss details verbally.

3. Economic Liabilities

As a basis for the further discussions proposed, our position regarding the demands in Annexes III-VI to Part VIII are defined in the following:

Re Annex III: Ships

In the opinion of the German Delegation, the demands of Annex III are, in the main, in contradiction to the demands made in Article 236. If Germany is to cooperate with all her economic strength in the reconstruction of what has been destroyed by the war, she can, with good faith, accept only such an obligation as is within the limits of her already diminished productive power. Therefore, the German Delegation feel that it would be a mistake for the Allied and Associated Governments to reduce her productive power further by insisting upon the surrender not only of goods and securities, but also of such important means of production as merchant ships, the loss of which must unavoidably lead to a breakdown, and in consequence, to the absolute impotence of the German economic apparatus.

As to the demand for the surrender of fishing-vessels, we must add to the points mentioned above, the extraordinary importance of these fishing-vessels just at present for the food supply of the German people as a result of the insufficient supply of meat. Up to date, it has been possible to put to use in Germany only 157 fishing-steamers and 53 luggers. The rest of the fishing-steamers are required for mine-sweeping for several months to come. The draft of the peace treaty demands the surrender of 146 fishing-vessels, *i. e.*, almost the whole of the German fleet of fishing-vessels in use at present. The satisfaction of this demand is therefore impossible simply because of the necessity of securing food for the German people.

The demand for the surrender of the whole oversea mercantile fleet actually existing and under construction is quite inacceptable as planned in Annex III to Article 244. The German Delegation are willing, however, to comply with the provision in Annex III that the German fleet should replace the gaps caused by the eventualities of the war. This could be done by Germany's assuming her share in the universally necessary transport service by sailing her ships in an international pool, which provides a cooperation in the management for all nations concerned upon uniform and equal terms. The Delegation, refusing once more to accept the principle of restitution, "ton for ton," declare their willingness to accept engagements for the construction of merchant vessels, according to Section 5 of the Annex referred to, and even to extend such engagements to a larger number of tons and for a longer period, taking into consideration the productivity of the shipyards and further agreements. In this connection the reservation must, of course, be made that the tonnage demanded be reduced in the first year on account of the general situation.

The Delegation further suggest that the question of reciprocal cooperation of Allied and German shipping interests in shipping undertakings on either side be made the subject of negotiation.

So far as the cession of river tonnage for reparation purposes is concerned, the German Delegation point out that Germany can consider only a restitution of such losses as fall within the limits of the reparation obligations recognized by her. As far as the reparation, according to the first paragraph of Section 6, is not covered by the restoration of vessels the identity of which is established, Germany is willing to cede to the Reparation Commission a portion of her river tonnage up to the amount of this difference, but not exceeding ten per cent. of the whole tonnage existing November 11, 1918. This agreement is, however, subject to the following conditions:

1. That river vessels which have come into the hands of the Allied and Associated Governments in Belgium, France and Alsace, shall be taken into account.

2. That in the restoration of vessels purchased in the open market, Germany must be compensated for the value of the vessels, which is yet to be determined. Germany is willing to agree that these values be credited on the reparation account. In determining the value the estimates of both sides must be taken into account; in case there is no agreement, it must be determined by a neutral court of arbitration.

3. That in every case ships of the same class and tonnage shall be substituted for the ships destroyed. If, in this connection, a delivery from the existing supply is not possible without considerably endangering German inland shipping, Germany is willing to restore the rest of the ships by building new ones.

Mention will be made in another connection of the way in which Germany will meet the further question of the cession of river tonnage according to Articles 339 and 357 of the draft.

Re Annex IV: Machinery, etc.

The German Delegation are ready to acknowledge the principle that Germany should hold her economic resources directly liable for purposes of reparation. In this point they are willing to meet the demands made upon Germany as far as they possibly can. But they must take care that the economic sovereignty of the German Government is not threatened by the fulfillment of these obligations, or by the control of the Allied and Associated Governments. So far as infringements upon the economic liberty of the German population are necessary in order to perform the accepted obligations, the German Government will undertake them according to its own resolution. From this standpoint the German Delegation must refuse to cede to the Reparation Commission, which is to be constituted according to Article 233, any rights exceeding the above-mentioned principles.

The German Delegation have noted that, according to Section 11 of Annex II, the Commission shall be bound in its work by justice, equity and good faith. The German Delegation are also of the opinion that these principles are the necessary and foremost condition for a successful settlement of all questions connected with the matter of reparation. For this reason the German Government must claim rights for itself and decline the one-sidedness of the decisions and power of the Commission. In the interests of a practical solution they think it necessary to constitute, in their turn, a commission for the question of the rehabilitation of economic production. This commission shall be bound by the same principles that are laid down in paragraph 11 of Annex II for the Commission to be constituted by the Allied and Associated Governments. The Delegation propose to leave the execution of the obligations that are to be accepted by Germany in regard to economic liabilities to the cooperation of the two commissions. The rules for cooperation should be reserved for a special agreement.

In case the two commissions should come to no agreement regarding the execution of the accepted obligations, or with respect to the interpretation of certain prescriptions of the final peace treaty relating to reparation, the decision thereof shall be conferred upon a court of arbitration with a neutral chairman, each of the parties proposing one member for it who, in their turn, shall elect the neutral third member.

Under these conditions the German Delegation are willing to consent to the demands in Annex IV as a whole, but to the several single paragraphs only so far as they are not in contradiction to the above-mentioned reservations and proposals concerning the rights of the Commission. Considering the extraordinary importance of these stipulations, it seems necessary, however, that they shall be made the object of special and detailed discussion. In particular, it must be pointed out here that there are grave objections to these stipulations, especially those in Section 4 of Annex IV. According to Section 4, the disorganization of Germany's industrial life as a result of the requisition of materials, etc., shall be avoided only to the extent of not affecting adversely Germany's ability to perform the acts of reparation stipulated. That is impossible. The German people cannot accept any stipulations that aim at its disorganization. It does not live only to perform reparation; it wants, rather, to reestablish itself while freeing itself from the burden laid upon it.

The demand of Section 4, Annex IV, according to which Germany shall be bound, on request of the Commission, to deliver for reparation purposes machinery, equipment, tools, and the like articles which are in actual use, up to thirty per cent. of the quantity of such articles, should there be no free stock, cannot be accepted in this general form. The German Delegation declare that they are willing, on principle, to undertake expropriation within the limits of the counter-proposals already made or still to be made in further discussions. But, in doing so, it is supposed that these articles are the private property of undertakings not at all or little engaged, and that, therefore, taking all circumstances into consideration, the expropriation seems appropriate. Moreover, if there is no free stock of machinery, etc., available, it must be considered whether it would not be possible to avoid the removal or seizure of material from plants capable of production by constructing new similar machinery, etc., without serious loss of time.

In this connection the German Delegation declare that they are, on principle, willing to fulfill the demands of Article 238, already accepted in the armistice, and since then performed. As far as restitution of machinery, equipment, tools, and the like articles in actual use are concerned, they must demand that the principle of Section 4, Annex IV be applied, by which restitutions of this kind may be made, first of all, from free stocks of like articles as far as they exist. This principle must be extended so far as to provide that, in case there are no free stocks of like articles, the restitution of such articles shall not be demanded if, by the supply of newly constructed machinery, equipment, tools, and the like, reparation would be neither impaired nor essentially deferred.

The restitution of stallions, as demanded in Section 6, Annex IV, can be performed so far as their identification during the period fixed is possible. On the other hand, the capacity for agricultural production and the state of the food supply make it impossible to fulfill the rest of the demands within the time fixed for the delivery. This is in particular impossible in the case of the delivery of milch cows, which would result in a further increase in infant mortality, which has already grown considerably as a result of the hunger blockade. Already, as the Allied and Associated Governments are aware, the quantity of milk produced in Germany is insufficient to provide the necessary quantity of milk for the sick and the infants. Germany cannot think of delivering cattle, goats, etc., until, by a greater import of fodder, German livestocks have grown better in quantity and quality.

On the other hand, in order to fulfill the stipulated restitution of livestock, the German Delegation are willing to consent to purchases in neutral countries, or in the countries of the Allied and Associated Governments, which shall be charged to the account of the German Government. Representatives of the German Government should take part in these purchases. The German Delegation will submit special proposals for annual supplies of horses and other livestock, which they will undertake to deliver at fixed dates, and which are to be credited to the reparation account.

Re Annex V: Coal

Provided that the regulation of territorial and economic questions and of the question of reparation will permit her, Germany is willing to do everything in her power to produce for export to France the amount of coal needed by that country and corresponding to the difference between the annual pre-war production of the destroyed mines and their occasional production during the next ten years. Germany acknowledges that these quantities may amount, in the first period, to twenty million metric tons, and after five years, to eight million metric tons annually, and declares herself in accord with these maximum estimates.

Germany and France have a common interest in the prompt reconstruction of the French mines. Germany has at her disposal a great number of firms of wide experience in the sinking of pits in difficult mountainous districts and in the construction of surface equipment of all kinds. It is, therefore, to the interest of both countries that Germany should be given an opportunity to cooperate, in a wide measure, in the promptest reconstruction of the mines. She is also willing to undertake the total or partial reconstruction herself.

It is materially impossible to accord the options for coal demanded in Sections 2 to 5. Neither can they be demanded under the term of reparation. Even in 1913, when the German production of coal reached its maximum with 191.5 million metric tons, only 32.8 [*33.8?*] million metric tons—coke being computed in coal equivalent—were exported. But since 1913 the production of coal has considerably diminished. In 1918, it amounted to only 161.5 million metric tons, and in the first quarter of 1919, to about twenty-nine million metric tons, which would mean an annual production of 116 million metric tons. Even if it must be admitted that the production during the first quarter of 1919 was unfavorably influenced by strikes and revolts, the main causes of the decrease in production still continue to exist: the reduction, as a result of the war, of the number of skilled and experienced miners, the shortening of the shifts from eight and one-half to seven hours, the decline in working capacity caused by the hunger blockade, and the present bad condition of the equipment. These causes can be gradually abolished only if it shall be possible to remove the difficulties attending production by the import of the necessary raw materials, to improve slowly the condition of the German food supply, and, after the construction of the necessary houses, to balance the shortening of the shifts by increasing the amount of work. Nevertheless, the German Delegation feel that they must reckon with a decrease of production for the next few years of about thirty per cent. as against that of 1913, that is, a production of 131 million metric tons. Of course, it is true that Germany's own needs will not be as great as they were in 1913, but will amount to about eighty per cent. of the amount required in 1913, *i. e.*, about 116 million metric tons. These calculations do not include the production and the needs of Alsace-Lorraine, but the production and the needs of the Saar district and of Upper Silesia are included. Without the latter Germany could export no coal at all, but would have to import coal.

In Section 10, Annex V, the Allied and Associated Governments have acknowledged the necessity of taking into account the industrial requirements of Germany. It need hardly be mentioned how difficult it is to state in advance Germany's production and requirements. The numbers given above are the result of most careful calculations on the part of experts, and prove that the delivery of the amounts stated in Sections 2-5 is quite impossible. From these calculations it follows that there will be a surplus of fifteen million metric tons available for export. The German Government is willing, however, by continuing the present rationing, to make available another five million metric tons as long as the decrease in the production of the destroyed mines amounts to twenty million metric tons.

The German Delegation must add to the foregoing declaration the condition that, in exchange for these deliveries of coal and coke, the German smelting works will be supplied with their requirements of minette from Lorraine and France. The 1913 supplies should be accepted as a basis, unless the exchange of minette and coke is independently regulated by special agreements or connections between the works on either side.

In order to meet the requirements of France and Belgium, the German Delegation are also willing to agree to an option for the next ten years on the surplus of the whole German production of coal over the home needs of Germany's requirement. Should this surplus not suffice to cover the requirements of these three countries, the German Delegation propose to ration the consumption in Germany, France and Belgium equally. A commission of German, French and Belgian representatives should be constituted in order to supervise the execution of these measures. In these agreements the interests of Italy and Luxemburg should be considered.

As to the price and conditions of delivery, the German Delegation must demand that the general competitive prices be taken into account or paid. The German Delegation are willing to agree that the price, including cost of transport, must not exceed the general export price of British coal of the same quality, including cost of transport. On the other hand, the price must not be less than the price within Germany. Unless the full value brought by her export products abroad is paid or, within the limits of the financial proposals, credited to Germany, Germany could not arrange for the imports necessary for the maintenance of her economic life, and, in consequence, she would not be able to make the payments arising from her reparation obligations.

The details of the above proposals should be regulated by sub-commissions of experts, which should be constituted similarly to the above-mentioned commission.

The German Delegation think it their duty to point out that 13.6 million metric tons out of the above-mentioned export of 33.8 [*32.8?*] million metric tons in 1913 went to countries of the former Austro-Hungarian Monarchy, and other considerable amounts to countries which have favorable transport conditions to and from the German mining districts. Considering the difficulties of transport existing in Germany and in some countries of the Allied and Associated Governments, and the present lack of tonnage, it would not be in the general interest to deliver only to France the whole surplus available for export. The German Delegation do not make this objection in order to escape their obligations of delivery or to raise difficulties, but they think that they are in agreement with the Allied and Associated Governments in the conception that the economic life of Europe, which has been so severely shaken by the war, requires the most careful distribution of all raw materials and the most economical utilization of means of transport. They suggest, therefore, the constitution of an international commission, which should examine the question of coal distribution and which, by some manner of adjustment, could save many million of transport-kilometres. The German Delegation must draw attention to the fact that in the near future it will be impossible to deliver to France fifteen to twenty million metric tons of coal annually by German means of transport. A large portion of these amounts would, therefore, have to be conveyed by French means of transport. Even in this case it seems uncertain whether the existing ways of transports (railways, canals) would be sufficient to convey such quantities.

As to the derivatives of coal demanded in Section 8, Annex V, Germany is at present unable to deliver 35,000 tons of benzol annually. In 1913, the production amounted to 10,600 tons monthly, but it has now for several reasons, chiefly on account of the bad condition of the equipment, sunk to 4,000 tons monthly at best. Stocks do not exist. The present production does not even meet the most urgent domestic requirements. Hoping that it will be possible, by the import of benzine and by increasing the production, to improve this state of affairs in Germany, the German Delegation are willing to undertake, for the next three years, the delivery to France of thirty per cent. of that amount of the German production of benzol in excess of 4,000 tons monthly.

Germany is ready to deliver, for the next three years, 50,000 tons of coal tar annually (from coke works or gas works) if they are conveyed for the greater part in French tanks. In consequence of the cessions to the Allied and Associated Governments, and of other losses as well, *e. g.*, in Hungary, it is materially impossible for Germany to convey these quantities in her own tanks.

Germany is further willing to deliver to France, for the next three years, 30,000 tons of sulphate of ammonia annually.

The German Delegation are also willing to undertake to deliver, instead of 50,000 tons of coal tar, the corresponding amounts of the demanded products of distillation from raw tar.

In the fixing of prices, the principles laid down above for coal must be applied accordingly.

Re Annex VI: Chemical Industry

No connection can be found between the aims of reparation and the demands of Annex VI.

This notwithstanding, the German Government declares itself ready to concede the option demanded in Section 1 of Annex VI, in order to satisfy the immediate requirements of the Allied and Associated Governments. The demand respecting the fixing of the prices of these quantities cannot, however, be agreed to, as it implies that the right to control the cost prices of dyestuffs and chemical drugs would be conceded to the Commission. To ask for such a surrender of business secrets is, according to the views of the German Delegation, not compatible with the principles of justice, equity, and good faith, laid down in Section 11 of Annex II.

The demand contained in Section 2 of Annex VI cannot be

conceded. The grant of the option asked for would certainly in no way mean an increase in the financial capacity of Germany to fulfill her obligations; on the contrary, the provisions of Section 3 of Annex VI would be at variance with the principle of Section 4 of Annex IV regarding the stipulation of prices, and would in certain circumstances considerably impair the proceeds to be credited to Germany on her reparation account. The advantages which the holders of options would derive from the re-sale of the goods delivered would represent a sort of indirect reparation which cannot be granted, as it would not be credited to Germany on her reparation account.

Re Annex VII: Cable

These demands are not connected with the reparation, and are treated elsewhere.

———————

Considering the shortness of the time conceded for the examination of these extraordinarily complicated and momentous proposals, this rejoinder cannot give an exhaustive representation of the German point of view. However, the German Delegation believe that in further negotiations, which in order to be successful ought to be conducted by word of mouth, a settlement may be reached acceptable to both parties on the basis of the proposals submitted and in spite of the reservations made in particular cases. Doubtless, ways and means, which have so far not been considered in the proposals of the Allied and Associated Governments, could be found to attain the desired aim.

In this connection the German Delegation beg to refer to the proposals made in its note of May 16, concerning the safeguarding of coal deliveries through the acquisition of shares in German coal mines. The German Government is ready to extend the principle applied in this instance to other industries as well, *i. e.,* partially to compensate the owners of destroyed industrial enterprises in Northern France and Belgium by transferring to them a proportionate share in enterprises of the same or similar character in Germany. How to effect these partnerships in each particular case, and how to fix the value of the compensation thus made and to get it credited on the reparation account, could be arranged in the course of further negotiations. The German Government points out, furthermore, that these means afford considerable possibility of the financing of the reconstruction of Belgium and northern France. From this point of view, the German Government is ready, on principle, to effect the transfer of interest in enterprises in Germany to an even greater extent than that indicated above.

.   .   .

DOCUMENT 374

Note from Brockdorff-Rantzau to Clemenceau Communicating an Observation of the German Finance Commission, with Annex, May 29, 1919

[Translation of the Supplement from *International Conciliation*, No. 143, October, 1919, pp. 1299-1316. Translation of the covering note made by the editor. German text in *Materialien*, III, 115-31. French translation in PV, Notes, pp. 219-35.]

VERSAILLES, *May 29, 1919.*

MR. PRESIDENT:

I have the honor to communicate to Your Excellency an observation of the Finance Commission of the German Peace Delegation on Parts VIII and IX of the Draft of the Conditions of Peace. The German Peace Delegation concurs with the position of its Finance Commission and makes this position its own.

Accept, Mr. President, the expression of my high consideration.

BROCKDORFF-RANTZAU.

SUPPLEMENT

FINANCIAL QUESTIONS

The German finance commission has to treat mainly Part VIII, including Annexes 1 and 2, and Part IX of the draft of the peace conditions concerning the indemnity and other financial questions. It must preface its comments with the following observations upon the spirit and content of the draft as a whole.

There is doubtless only one way in which to heal the frightful unhappiness into which the war has plunged humanity and to solve the staggering financial and economic problems, which, differing only in degree, threaten in the same manner all the nations affected by the war, namely this: after the wretched years of mutual strife and devastation the nations of the earth must now *unite in peaceful work in common,* in order to be able to carry the burdens more easily and to hasten the reconstruction of the world through mutual helpfulness.

The draft of the peace treaty presented to us by the enemy governments has not adopted this way. On the contrary, they indulge in the hope that a Germany which has been drained and then kept down by every kind of political and economic handicap, would yield greater advantages to their nations and would be able to relieve them of more burdens than could that new Germany which we want to establish.

If the territorial, political, and economic clauses contained in the draft of the Allied and Associated Powers should be carried out, Germany would be condemned to economic and financial decay even without the imposition of an indemnity. Enormous agricultural districts, which we need for the nourishment of our population as well as for the colonization of at least a part of the people who can no longer be employed in industry, are to be detached from Germany. We must give up indispensable supplies of raw material, above all, almost one-third of our coal production; Germany's organization for world trade, insofar as it has not already been destroyed by the war, must now, after the conclusion of peace, suffer complete annihilation. We are to lose the sources of revenue and the productive force of important parts of the country. There would remain a Germany which in the future, even more than in the past, would have to turn to foreign countries for the satisfaction of her immediate needs in regard to food, clothing and industrial labor, because she would be deprived to a great extent of her own resources; moreover, *her only means of payment,* namely her labor, would not only have been requisitioned in advance to an enormous extent, but it would also meet on every hand almost insuperable obstacles. We cannot conceive how our people, so congested and encircled, could exist at all. There is frightful danger that the only means of relief would be emigration on a huge scale, or, if this should become impossible, death *en masse.* One thing, however, is certain: the idea of extracting the enormous indemnities stipulated in the draft of the peace treaty from what would be left of Germany according to the draft, is impossible. A Germany, in whose population any delight in work would be killed at the very outset by the despair of the present and the hopelessness of the future, cannot even be counted upon in the question of the payment of indemnities. That the draft of the Allied and Associated Powers fails to recognize this, that it seeks first to make Germany incapable of existing and then expects enormous payments from such a Germany, this is unjust and impossible of realization.

In regard to the size of the indemnities which the Allied and Associated Governments intend to impose on us, we observe that we do not intend to discuss here the legal bases of these demands, since these are treated elsewhere (by the legal commission of the Peace Delegation). *In any case it is of importance to examine the limits of Germany's financial capacity;* the following observations were made from this point of view.

From this purely financial standpoint it is, *in the first place, impossible for Germany to indemnify all the war damages of her opponents.* It is equally out of the question that Germany should be able to assume the *guarantee for her allies.* In the same way, for purely financial reasons the provisions of paragraphs 5-7 of Annex I, concerning military pensions, allowances to dependents of war victims, etc., cannot be taken into consideration.

As regards the amount of the obligations to be assumed by Germany in addition to the indemnities, the commission must call attention to the extraordinary significance of Article 249 which imposes upon Germany the full costs of the maintenance of any army of occupation even for the time following the conclusion of peace. These costs, which are to be paid in gold or in an amount based upon the gold parity of the mark, may be extraordinarily high and beyond the weakened financial power of Germany. *Today the costs of the foreign troops of occupation, as far as can be determined at present, exceed the former cost of maintenance of* the German army and navy on a peace footing. It would be unjust to impose upon *Germany the expense of a continued occupation, for among the troops of occupation would be parts of the regular peace time armies of the enemy States,* whose maintenance would be paid for by the enemy Powers likewise.

A military occupation would be all the more detrimental, since every occupation has exceedingly pernicious economic consequences, which could only too easily be seriously augmented by the interference of the troops of occupation in the field of administration and of political economy.

Germany's capacity for taxation and her ability to pay depend upon the uniformity of administration in the economic domains left to her; but the authority of the German Government in regard to the collection of imposts, of customs duties, etc., can only be restored when there is no longer an army of occupation in the country. Even the period of the armistice has produced chaotic conditions in the matter of import and financial transactions in the region on the left bank of the Rhine. An occupation lasting many years and accompanied, as is planned, by the introduction of a special customs tariff, would deprive Germany of the possibility of a determined economic and financial policy.

III

Moreover, we must object to Germany's being deprived, without any legal claim, of the important elements of her financial power. Article 254 of the draft provides for a settlement of the debts for the regions which Germany is forced to cede. The method of calculation prescribed, according to which the amount of the debt to be taken over is to be determined by the revenues of certain classes of taxation in the ceded territories as compared with the same revenues in the whole German population, is very difficult of execution on account of the dissimilarity of the systems of taxation in the various federal states of Germany. But the provision according to which the assumption of the debts is to extend only to those contracted before August 1, 1914, so that the full costs of the war would have to be paid by the remaining German population alone, seems quite unjustified. The nationals of the territories to be ceded were just as ready as the rest of the German people to defend their fatherland, when they believed it was attacked. Not a single deputy from the regions which are now to be separated from Germany voted against the war credits. They were all deputies who had been elected according to what was then the freest electoral system in the world (equal, universal, secret, direct), and if now single parts are to be detached, this can as a matter of course take place only in this form: that all the debts contracted up to the day of separation, debts of the Empire as well as of the federal States to which the ceded territories belong, be taken over by the former nationals of the Empire into their new country.

Not August 1, 1914, but the day of the signature of the peace treaty must, therefore, be fixed as the date for the calculation of the parts of the debts to be assumed, including the charge resulting from the peace treaty itself.

In Alsace-Lorraine should be taken over at least the *public debts of Alsace-Lorraine, the debts for the building of the Alsace-Lorraine railway and those loans for which new values have been created in Alsace-Lorraine since 1871.* In 1871 Germany rendered compensation to France for the railways constructed in Alsace-Lorraine by taking them into account in the war indemnity. It should be demanded, quite in general, that whenever railways are ceded, Germany should be credited with an amount corresponding to their present value.

The exclusion of any compensation for the cession of the property of the Empire and the State in Alsace-Lorraine (Article 256) seems to us unjustified by the reference to the regulation of

1871, especially as regards new constructions. For the corresponding demand of Belgium (Article 256, paragraph 4) no justification is given, and we recognize none. The special regulation in the case of Poland in Article 92, paragraph 3, can also not be granted.

The provision that *Poland* is not to participate in that part of the debt of the Empire and of the State which was expended for German colonization in Posen (Article 255, paragraph 2) can be carried out only in case *corresponding guarantees for the payment of interest incumbent upon the Prussian State due to that colonization* and further modifications be granted.

Without intending to anticipate in any way the question of the required cession of the colonies, we must emphasize the following from the financial point of view. They are to be taken away without taking over a part of the debts of the Empire or the federal States. *In case Germany should agree to the cession of her colonies, she would have to demand that the ceded territories continue to be charged with those debts which they have assumed partly with, partly without the guarantee of the Empire;* that the Empire should be released from the guarantee; and that the State acquiring the colonies should compensate the Empire for all the expenses incurred by the Empire for the benefit of the ceded territories. Moreover, the seizure of the colonies conflicts in any case with the fundamental principles of the armistice. Point 5 of President Wilson's fourteen points provides for "A free, open-minded, and absolutely impartial adjustment of all colonial claims, based upon a strict observance of the principle that in determining all such questions of sovereignty the interests of the population concerned must have equal weight with the equitable claims of the government whose title is to be determined." According to this, there is in President Wilson's program no question of a seizure of colonies in general, and especially without making deduction therefor. Moreover, the colonies have become for Germany to such an extent integral parts of her own social economy, they are such valuable parts of her national capital, that she cannot, if only for financial reasons, *renounce her colonial possessions.*

In conclusion, we must mention the provisions of Article 250, according to which the surrender of material which has already been delivered in accordance with the clauses of the armistice is to be confirmed, and the property right of the Allied and Associated Powers thereto recognized. For such a recognition, it would be necessary to conduct a detailed investigation, which was impossible in the short time given; but in any case we must demand that not only the surrendered material of non-military value, but also the Army and Navy material, which the draft excludes from the reckoning, be credited to Germany on her reparation account.

IV

Even the above observations show, in single instances, the profound difference in the conception of what may be charged against Germany's account and what she is to be compensated for. But these detailed considerations become almost insignificant when we attempt to get a general conception of what the financial sections of the draft of the peace treaty seek to impose upon us. The definitive sum which Germany is to pay is not yet named. It is not to be fixed before May 1, 1921; from that date the sum is to bear five per cent. interest, which amount is to be inscribed likewise among our permanent debts. Temporarily, provision is made for a payment in three instalments of 20,000,000,000 marks, 40,000,-000,000 marks, and, when the Reparation Commission considers Germany capable of paying it, another 40,000,000,000 marks in bonds. Further issues of bonds may be demanded later. *If the calculation is to be made in accordance with the principle described* above, it is evident that we should be confronted with a simply fantastic sum, an indebtedness which we could not hope to discharge even with generations of the hardest labor. The Allied and Associated Governments themselves are evidently aware of these facts, else they would not have made the above-mentioned reservation in the case of the issue of the last 40,000,000,000 of the 100,-000,000,000 marks in bonds demanded by them. What they do not seem to understand clearly, is this: If they impose upon Germany a debt which robs her of every possibility of a future; if as a consequence every improvement of Germany's economic condition, which the German people might achieve by tireless diligence and Spartan thrift, would lead simply to this, that even greater payments for the discharge of this debt would be imposed upon us, then any delight in creative work, any joy in work, any spirit of initiative would perish for all time in Germany. *The German people would feel themselves condemned to slavery, because everything that they accomplished would benefit neither themselves nor even their children, but merely strangers.* But the system of slave labor has never been successful. It is unbearable to a people like the German; any ability and inclination to pay taxes would disappear, and Germany would be for decades to come the scene of uninterrupted social class struggles of the bitterest kind. Instead of taking this danger into account, the object is, on the contrary, to subject Germany to pressure and surveillance financially, economically, and politically in a manner unexampled in the history of the civilized world. *The instrument for this purpose is the " Reparation Commission" and the extraordinary plenitude of power which the draft of the peace treaty provides for it.*

For the payment of the reparations and for all money requisitions arising from the peace treaty and the treaties supplementary thereto, as well as from the obligations of the armistice, a first charge is established, according to Article 248, upon all assets and revenues of the Empire and its constituent States. According to Section 12, Annex II, [Article 233], the Commission shall have the most extensive power to control and regulate the German system of taxation in order to make sure that, first, all Germany's assets, including the amounts set aside for the service or the redemption of any domestic loan, are applied preferentially to the sums to be paid by Germany to the account of reparation; and that, secondly, the German system of taxation, as regards charges upon individuals, shall be just as heavy as that of any one of the Powers represented upon the Commission. *These provisions would mean absolute financial control of Germany by the Allies and complete mastery on their part over the budget of the Empire.* They are impossible of execution even technically. For the granting of a priority of the first rank for the total capital of the debt upon all assets and revenues of the Empire and the constitutent States is impossible, because thereby the credit of the Empire and the States would be so undermined, that a further independent financial management of these States would no longer be conceivable. How could Germany float new loans at home or abroad (except through the Reparation Commission), when the service of such a loan would be jeopardized by the previous charge, of an actually unlimited sum, upon all possible means of payment? Even the service of loans contracted up to this time by the German Empire or its constituent States is made completely dependent upon the judgment of the Commission, and yet the preservation of the economic life of Germany depends entirely upon the maintenance of this service. People who save both on a large scale and on a small, the industrial enterprises, the banks, the savings banks, the insurance companies and all other enterprises for the management of the capital of others, have invested great parts of their holdings in imperial and state loans, especially in war loans. If these should become even partially worthless, it would cause a new and final collapse of the economic life of Germany, even more fatal in its results than all the economic effects of the war and the provisions of the armistice. From such a collapse Germany would not be able, for an incalculable period of time, to recover sufficiently to meet any of her financial obligations, not even the reparation.

It follows from our very situation that Germany will have to bear a burden of taxation no less than the States represented upon the Commission. This burden of taxation will probably be considerably greater than anywhere else.

The Reparation Commission, as is planned at present, would actually be the absolute master of Germany. It would order Germany's economic affairs at home and abroad. *According to Article 260, the Commission may demand that all German nationals cede their rights and interests in all enterprises of public interest (a very comprehensive and not clearly definable concept) and in all concessions in Russia, China, Austria, Hungary, Bulgaria and Turkey, as well as in the possessions and colonies of these countries or in territories which, according to the demands of the Allied and Associated Powers, are to be separated from Germany.* The German Government itself must aid in the execution of this clause; it must prepare and submit a list of all these concessions and rights; must undertake the expropriation; must compensate those dispossessed, and then deliver all the property thus expropriated to the Commission. Thus the Commission obtains an unheard-of power. *It can expropriate almost all German property in the countries mentioned, while the expropriation of German possessions in the enemy countries themselves can take place, according to the draft of the peace treaty, at any time until further notice by continued liquidations and sequestrations.* But how can Germany continue to work and discharge her financial obligations, especially payments to foreign creditors, for instance to the Allied and Associated Governments themselves, if every foreign possession is taken away from her beforehand and if she forfeits all sources of income of this kind? This expropriation would cause all the more serious injury to those affected by it, since the Empire could undertake to compensate those dispossessed in no other way than by titles to new domestic loans, the value of which would be prejudiced in the highest degree by the peace treaty. The expropriation would almost amount to a confiscation.

The peace proposal speaks very *frequently of the obligation of the Empire to make compensation for the private property* which is to be expropriated for the benefit of the Allied and Associated Powers, without considering that *this method can be applied only within certain limits for reasons having to do with the money market.* In the immediate future it will be impossible to place German state loans in large amounts either at home or abroad, so that compensation could be made only by means of large issues of notes. The inflation, already excessive, *would increase constantly if the peace conditions as proposed should be carried out. Moreover, great deliveries of natural products can take place only if the state reimburses the producers for their value; this means further issues of notes.* As long as these deliveries last, there could be no question of the stabilizing of German currency even upon the present level. *The depreciation of the mark would continue. The instability of the currency would affect not only Germany, however, but all the countries engaged in export, for Germany, with her currency constantly depreciating, would be a disturbing element and would be forced to flood the world market with goods at ridiculously low prices.* Therefore, quite apart from all the other reasons mentioned, we must reject the proposals for expropriations and excessive deliveries of natural products set forth in the peace conditions by reason of this consideration for the state of the money market.

In the draft of the peace conditions *all the countries at war with Germany have mechanically added their manifold wishes; there is no unified fundamental conception; contradictions multiply from chapter to chapter. A revision is necessary in order to prevent the breakdown, because of this mechanical addition, of the economic organization upon which these demands are made.* A fundamental solution could be found only in connection with all related questions and through the cooperation of all the parties interested.

According to Article 251, the Commission is also to have power to decide how much should be spent for the food supply and for the purchase of raw materials from abroad; that actually gives the Commission the power to decide whether and to what degree the German people is to be supplied with food, and to what extent industry may be carried on, so that there can no longer be any question of economic self-determination and initiative.

According to Article 241, Germany would be under obligation to promulgate all the laws necessary to assure the complete execution of the agreements. Is this to be taken to mean, in conjunction with Article 234 and section 12 of Annex II, that Germany would have to promulgate, by regulation of the Commission, all laws concerning taxation which the Commission should demand? This matters little, when the Commission is to decide, first, how the revenues of the German State are to be spent; when, moreover, at their behest, expenditures for the payment of interest on the war loans, for the allotments of the disabled German soldiers and for the pensions of the dependents of fallen soldiers, must cease or be cut down, as well as the expenditures for cultural purposes, schools, higher education, etc.; *then indeed is German democracy destroyed at the very moment when the German people, after mighty efforts, was on the point of establishing it; destroyed by the very ones who during the whole war never grew weary of insisting that they wanted to bring democracy to us!* When the right to dispose of the income of the state is taken away, parliamentary government disappears, and the right of the Reichstag to vote upon the budget becomes a hoax. Popular representation and governments in Germany would have only one task left, namely, to render to the Commission the services of a bailiff in the collection of the debts. Germany is no longer a nation and a state, but it becomes a commercial firm, forced into bankruptcy by its creditors, without being given the chance to prove whether it be willing to fulfill its obligations voluntarily. *The Commission, which is to have its permanent seat outside Germany, will possess incomparably greater rights in Germany than a German emperor has ever had; under its régime the German people would be for many decades without rights, deprived of all independence and of all initiative in commerce and industry and even in popular education, to a greater extent than ever a nation was in the time of absolutism.*

V

All these important questions, which are subject to the decision of the Reparation Commission, may be decided by this Commission entirely at its own good pleasure. Whether it is a question of the valuation of the Saar mines, or of the fixing of the amount of the indemnity to be imposed on Germany, or of the reduction and alteration of the schemes for the payments and the valuation of material to be returned by Germany, or of the fixing of the price of the goods and the foreign assets to be delivered by Germany, or of the calculation of the share of the imperial and state debts to be assumed by the territories ceded by Germany, or of the fixing of the value of the property in the ceded territories formerly belonging to the Empire or to the single States and now devolving upon foreign States—all this and much more, which cannot be enumerated in detail, the Commission is to have full power to decide. Even Annex II, according to whose provisions the problems here discussed are to be settled, may be modified, consonant with the provisions of the treaty, by a unanimous decision of the Governments represented upon the Commission, without even any right of consultation on the part of Germany. Germany has the right to a hearing in many questions, not in all, but she is to have no voice in the decisions made by the Commission in secret sessions. *We are to be denied the right granted as a matter of course in all civilized countries to every person, in the simplest kind of private dispute, namely, that both parties state each their own view of the case and defend their case before the other party, and that in case of failure to agree, a third person, who is not a party to the dispute, decides. The Commission is, at the same time, party to the dispute and judge.*

In other ways, too, Germany is deprived of her rights. *The Allied and Associated Governments reserve the right to retain and to liquidate German property of every kind, even after the armistice, or to subject it to other war measures, either already in force or to be introduced in the future* (Article 297, Annex, section 9), while they, on the contrary, demand the most extensive protection for the property of their nationals in Germany. In Article 252, they demand for themselves the right to dispose of all property of enemy subjects in their countries, while they immediately thereupon, in Article 253, take the position that the charges and mortgages effected in favor of the enemy Powers or their nationals before the war must not be affected by the provisions of the peace treaty. *Thus there are formulated different conceptions of private property for the conqueror and for the conquered;* what is demanded on behalf of the one is expressly denied to the other.

We must lodge an equally decisive protest against Article 258, according to which *Germany is to renounce all representation upon, or participation, etc., in the administration of commissions, state banks or other financial and economic organizations. There is no justification to be found for this exclusion, which would reduce Germans all over the world to the status of pariah. It is without doubt contrary to the principles accepted by us and by the other Powers in the exchange of notes concerning the armistice.*

Finally, Articles 259 and 261 are contrary to every conception of justice and wholly contradictory in themselves: *on the one hand Germany is to deliver large sums of money in gold to the Allied and Associated Governments on behalf of Turkey, Austria and Hungary, and to recognize her obligations in this respect; on the other hand, it is demanded that Germany transfer her claims against Austria, Hungary, Bulgaria and Turkey, especially claims dating from the period of the war, to the Allied and Associated Governments, but it is not stated what*

*value is to be attributed to these claims in the general reckoning. But
it follows from the nature of the case that the obligations of Germany
toward her former allies can not be separated from the claims of Germany against the same allies.* A balancing of accounts is here absolutely necessary. The relation with Turkey in particular is so
complicated that partial obligations could not be treated separately
without an agreement at the same time between the original
parties to the treaty.

VI

On account of the shortness of the time given for discussion we
must renounce, for the time being, a more detailed discussion of
all the single stipulations of the draft which were to be treated
here. While reserving other details for later discussions, for the
present we limit ourselves to a brief mention of the following:

In Article 248, paragraph 2, it is stipulated that no gold may be
exported before May 1, 1921, without authorization of the Reparation Commission. Even though the Reichsbank cannot be counted
on to redeem its notes in gold in the immediate future, nevertheless
the Reichsbank must be allowed to export gold in the case of guarantees which the bank itself has furnished, and which she is not in
a position to redeem by other means.

Article 262 provides that all payments which are to be made in
currency and which are expressed in terms of gold marks, shall be
payable, at the option of the creditors, in pounds sterling payable
in London; in dollars payable in New York; in francs payable in
Paris; in lire payable in Rome; the coins mentioned being of the
weight and fineness of gold according to the currency laws in force
January 1, 1914. In reply to this we must state emphatically that
Germany is in a position to organize her delivery of goods and her
other financial measures in an orderly manner only if she is authorized once for all *to effect her payments in the currency in which the
debt was contracted. For reparation in Belgium and France, sums
would of course have to be indicated which would be payable definitively
in Belgian and French francs respectively.*

In the paragraphs dealing with Germany's financial obligations
it is repeatedly stated that the payments are to be effected in gold.
But on account of the disastrous terms of payment for the provisions imported during the armistice, the gold reserve of the Reichsbank will, in the immediate future, be extraordinarily small, so
that it will be impossible to effect payments in actual gold. In order
to avoid mistakes, it ought to be understood that all payments in

gold marks or in gold may be effected by Germany in foreign currency at the rate of gold parity in force on January 1, 1914.

Above all, the Commission must call attention to the great dangers in Article 296, paragraph 4 d, according to which the German debtors of an enemy country are to be forced to discharge the *debts contracted by them in German marks, in the currency of the enemy country concerned, the value of the mark to be computed according to the rate of exchange prevailing before the outbreak of the war.* In this way grave injury will be done, in a quite arbitrary manner, to the German debtor, as well as to the German Empire in its capacity of guarantor, for we do not recognize any legal right upon which to base the demand for this conversion into foreign money of the debts contracted in marks. *Furthermore, the clearing will not accomplish its purpose if a period of six months is granted in which the different states can declare their adherence or non-adherence.* If the idea of "clearing" is intended to be carried out, the uniform and immediate adherence of all the states must be demanded.

VII

We are about to conclude. *The proposals of the Allied and Associated Governments are in their present form and extent positively impossible of execution.* Even if they could be imposed upon Germany, they would most severely disappoint the hopes of our present adversaries. This would become apparent even with the first instalment of 20,000,000,000 marks. For even if they should succeed in collecting a considerable part of these 20,000,000,000 marks, by confiscation of the German merchant marine, by forced construction of ships in German shipyards, by forced deliveries of coal, dyestuffs and chemical drugs, by placing to their account all German credits and the proceeds of the sale of all German property in the Allied and Associated countries as well as in the German territories to be ceded, they would still have gained very little for the satisfaction of the reparation demands. After deducting the costs of the military occupation, accumulated in the meantime, and the very considerable amounts necessary for furnishing Germany with even the scantiest supplies of food stuffs and raw materials, very little, if anything at all, would be left for the purposes of reparation. Any further payments whatsoever could not be counted on from a Germany deprived in such a manner of her most important means of subsistence. No German administration would be equal to the task of extracting further payments. But a foreign power which should attempt to practice still further extortion upon the devastated land, would soon have to recognize that the costs of an administration which could work only under the protection of a strong military force, occupying the whole country, would cause the Allied Governments financial losses so great that, within a short time, they would exceed all Germany's previous payments on account.

A different method must be sought, *the method of negotiation.* In all countries, just as in ours, there are people who preach revenge, hate, militarism and chauvinism. But in all countries there are also people who fight for right and equality, men of insight who know that the whole world would become poorer if the German people, with its capacity for work, its needs as a consumer, and its intellectual attainments, were excluded from the cooperation of the world. *It is not Germany alone that at present needs credit on a most extensive scale in order to replenish her exhausted stores, to procure the absolutely indispensable amounts of food stuffs and raw materials, and to consolidate the great floating debts, but almost all the belligerent countries of Europe must resume their normal economic life under the most difficult conditions. To concentrate all the forces of the world upon this problem and to give to all peoples the chance of continued existence is the first and most pressing task.* Only when that is accomplished will Germany be in a position to discharge the heavy obligations for reparation assumed by her, obligations which she is determined to discharge according to the best of her abilities. This is based upon the assumption, however, that Germany shall be allowed to preserve that territorial integrity which the armistice promises; that we keep our colonial possessions and merchant ships, even those of large tonnage; that we have the same freedom of action both in our own country and in the world at large as all other peoples; that all war laws shall be abrogated at once; and that all infringements of our economic rights in German private property, etc., which were suffered during the war, shall be settled according to the principle of reciprocity. Only if these assumptions are recognized can we make great financial sacrifices and present the following proposal:

The amount of the debt to be fixed shall be recognized and the loans which Belgium has contracted for purposes of war with her allies up to November 11, 1918, shall be paid by us. The manner of payment shall be regulated as follows:

The debt to France is to be fixed in French francs, the debt to Belgium in Belgian francs.

Germany is ready, within four weeks after the exchange of the ratifications of the peace treaty, to issue a certificate of indebtedness to the amount of 20,000,000,000 gold marks payable not later than May 1, 1926, in instalments to be determined by the Allied and Associated Powers; she is ready, furthermore, to issue in the same manner the necessary documents of indebtedness for the remainder of the sum of the fixed damages and to make yearly payments upon the same, beginning May 1, 1927, in instalments bearing no interest, with the reservation that the sum total of the damages shall in no case exceed the sum of 100,000,000,000 gold marks, including the payments to Belgium for the sums advanced to her by the Allied and Associated Powers, as well as the above-mentioned 20,000,-000,000 gold marks.

In the first certificate of indebtedness of 20,000,000,000 gold marks should be counted all those payments which Germany has already effected or shall effect by virtue of the armistice, such as railway materials, agricultural machinery, all kinds of war materials and non-military materials, and other things; as well as the value of all payments to be effected by Germany according to the peace treaty and to be credited to her reparation account, as for example, the value of railways and state property; the final assumption of state debts; the claims to be ceded to the Powers allied with Germany in the war; a part, to be fixed by agreement, of the freight revenues arising from placing the German merchant marine in the international pool; further, those payments in kind which are to be fixed by negotiation in conformity with Annexes III to VII of Part VII; further, the value of the labor performed and materials furnished on the part of Germany for the reconstruction of Belgium and France as well as the restitutions to be made to Belgium, possibly in the form of a special loan, for the amounts advanced to her by the Allied and Associated Powers. The limitations provided for in the preceding in regard to Germany's capacity to pay are applied to the annual non-interest-bearing instalments of amortization to be paid up to the amount of 80,000,000,000 marks. The instalments shall not exceed a fixed percentage of the German imperial and state revenues. Germany is prepared to assume, for the benefit of the indemnities to be paid to the Allied and Associated Powers, an annual charge approximating the total net budget, up to the present time, of the German Empire in times of peace.

Accordingly, the annuity to be paid every year is to be fixed as a certain percentage of the revenues of Germany from direct and indirect taxes, excess profits and customs dues; in the case of the latter, payment in gold may be exacted. These dues, however, shall not, in the first ten years of payment, exceed the equivalent at the time of 1,000,000,000 marks in gold. Two years before the expiration of the ten years the sum total is to be fixed by fresh negotiations. The payment of the annuities may be insured by a guarantee; Germany could undertake to deposit in this fund up to the year 1926 an annuity derived from the proceeds of the indirect taxes, monopolies and customs duties and, subsequently, to maintain this fund at the same level.

Only in case Germany should be in arrears with the payment of an annuity would she consent to permit the Allied Powers the control of the administration of this fund until the deficit had been wiped out, but not to accept measures of an arbitrary sort, such as are threatened in section 18, Annex II to Article 244 (page 107).

The amount of the damages shall be determined by the Reparation Commission in collaboration with a German commission, and in case no agreement should be reached, by a mixed court of arbitration with a neutral chairman; the same procedure should be followed in fixing the value of the payments in kind, and in negotiating concerning the necessary amounts of food stuffs and raw materials to be supplied to Germany insofar as it is a question merely of revenues from payments in kind, etc.

The burden assumed by the German system of taxation shall be at least as great as that of the most heavily taxed of the states represented on the Reparation Commission.

The territories to be ceded shall assume from the date of the conclusion of peace a pro rata share of the burden of debts, as well as their proportional part of the damages to be paid to the enemy.

It is quite clear to us what extraordinary financial burdens Germany has to assume. If, nevertheless, we dare to make such a proposal, it is done with the conviction that if our adversaries renounce the other demands made upon us, then the German people will have the resolution and the strength to bear these financial burdens.

But then it is necessary that Germany should be admitted on a basis of equality into the League of Nations from the very beginning, that is from the beginning of the new era of peace. In our opinion, it should also be one of the duties of the League of Nations, by uniting the forces of all its members, to make it easier and cheaper for each of them to procure the necessary capital to restore their economic life to a normal peace condition. The more valuable this aid becomes for Germany in particular, the more easily she will be able to discharge the heavy obligations assumed by her.

We are aware that we cannot, even then, build up again a world trade of approximately the same extent as before the war, and that our economic life will be considerably more restricted. What we demand is merely this, that we shall not be required to lead a life of inaction, without honor and without liberty. Although suffering from heavy misfortune, we want to be able to live as a self-respecting working people.

The world, and more especially Germany, longs for a speedy peace. We propose that the finance commission be given an opportunity to enter into negotiations at once with the financial delegates of the Allied and Associated Governments. So far there has been no opportunity for a free discussion of the peace conditions. Only by that means can there exist any hope of at last finding a way to allay the misery of all countries. Merely to allay, not to remove. We must not set to work under false illusions. In the countries of our opponents there are still many who believe that a country like Germany, can, by itself, repair to a great extent the damages of war in almost thirty countries; the experts in those countries know as well as we do that that is impossible. But the obligation which Germany now assumes in the way of reparation, she will strive to fulfill in long years of most arduous labor; only she must be allowed a chance to live and to live honorably.

Versailles, May 1919

The Finance Commission of the German Peace Delegation

THE ACCEPTANCE OF THE TREATY BY GERMANY (MAY 30, 1919, AND AFTER)

DOCUMENT 375

Extract from Riddell's Diary Regarding the German Reply, May 30, 1919

[Riddell, pp. 83-84.]

MAY 30TH.—Dined with L[loyd]. G[eorge]. After dinner we discussed the German reply. . . .

L. G.: . . . the question of reparations is bound up with this [*i.e.*, with the Silesian question]. If the Poles won't give the Germans the products of the mines on reasonable terms, the Germans say they cannot pay the indemnity. Therefore the Allies may be cutting off their noses to spite their faces if they hand the mines to the Poles without regard to the question of the indemnity. . . .

DOCUMENT 376

Lamont's Summary of the German Counter Proposals, Undated

[TPG, VIII, 1-3. "The German Counter-Proposals—Reparation." At the head of this document, there is written in Dulles' handwriting, "From T W L".]

[*Summarizes main points of counter proposals; and text of this summary is repeated in Document 377. Present memorandum has only summary, not Lamont's comment.*]

DOCUMENT 377

Lamont's Summary of and Comment on the German Counter Proposals, Undated

[TPG, VIII, 4-8. This document was probably drawn up about the same time as Dulles' Summary and Comment of June 1 (see below). The summary column of the present document appeared separately, without "TWL's Suggestions," in another and presumably earlier paper (see Document 376). For a similar summary and comment by Dulles, see the introductory paragraph to Document 393.]

*German Counter Proposals
Reparation*

1. An argument that Germany is actually liable for reparation and restitution only for Belgium and Northern France. In this connection she agrees to hold herself liable for Belgium's war debts, but declares that this amount shall be deducted from the total for which she makes herself liable.

2. Army of Occupation should be eliminated, as being unnecessary, on account of Germany's disarmament and as resulting as follows: "An Army of Occupation will only diminish the German resources and lessen the annual payments it (Germany) can make.

3. It is unfair that a partisan commission should assess the damage. There should be a German commission to work with the Allied Commission and arrangements made for arbitration under a neutral chairman.

4. "In order to fulfill its obligations in regard to reparation, Germany is determined to do

*TWL's Suggestions as to the
Manner of Meeting the
Points as stated*

This argument cannot be admitted for a moment. Furthermore, the reimbursement for Belgium's war debts is a special matter falling outside of reparation, and in effect merely a fulfillment of a promise Germany has already made to Belgium. Therefore, this reimbursement must be over and above general reparation.

It is admitted by all hands that the Army of Occupation should be maintained on as low a basis as possible. The proposed setting up of a civilian commission to handle the matter of the Rhine provinces so that their administration will not be under military domination ought to be a fairly satisfactory answer.

There is nothing in the Treaty that prevents Germany from establishing a special German Commission upon reparation; there is no reason why such a commission should not work in harmony with the Allied Commission. In fact, Germany seems to have overlooked certain of the Treaty clauses which especially provide that she shall have a just opportunity to be heard, &c., &c.

This is merely a declaration made by Germany, and is quoted as one possibility of

everything that lies in its power. The German Government entertains no doubt that the German people will for generations have to bear heavier burdens than any other in this respect."

5. "Germany declares itself willing to pay a proportion of the total income from taxation and surpluses on State undertakings of both the German Empire and the several German States, in proportion to its capacity to pay, as a regular annuity.

"It further recognizes the principle expressed in Article 234 and in paragraph 12-D of Annex II. that the German taxation system should impose in general on the taxpayer at least as great a burden as those prevailing in the most heavily burdened of the States represented on the Reparation Commission. Germany does this, confident in the belief that the development of the taxation system in those States will be determined on the basis of social justice and in conformity with the principle of economic solvency, as in Germany.

6. Germany states that her capacity to pay will be based upon the restoration of her overseas relations and upon having left with her a sufficient commercial fleet, &c., &c.

satisfactory evidence to the Allies that Germany realizes the situation.

These are further declarations to the same end, and are also satisfactory as indicating an acceptance by Germany of principles laid down by the Allies.

Political considerations must be taken into account in this paragraph. As a practical measure, Germany should have made available to her in some form or other a sufficient number of commercial vessels to enable her to carry on ocean traffic, either

7. She proposes, also, that her total liability should be based upon the territorial extent of the Empire as it existed at the time of the signing of the Armistice. Therefore, if any portions of the Empire are lopped off, those portions have been equally responsible for war aggression and should pay their proportionate share of the damage. "The Allied Powers should collect these proportionate shares and deduct them from the account for reparation; no other procedure would be just."

by way of purchase, charter or otherwise. America will have become such a considerable maritime power in the near future that some proposition along this line should be worked out by the American and British shipping experts.

This point is inadmissible. Germany must remember that the territories lopped off from her Empire and incorporated into other governments must bear their share of the very heavy war liabilities of such governments.

8. Germany cannot admit that Germany's capacity to pay shall be determined solely by "an assembly of creditors, namely, the Reparation Commission." The capacity should be settled with a Commission of German experts; points of disagreement should be settled by a mixed commission under a neutral chairman.

The comment in general is the same as on paragraph 3. Here Germany seems to be under the impression that the Reparation Commission plans to work arbitrarily and in the dark. Necessarily, it must work very closely in touch with the German authorities, preferably a commission of German experts, but the suggestion as to arbitration is inadmissible.

9. A democratic state like Germany cannot yield over its sovereignty, and therefore "most of all is Germany unable to yield to the demand that it

It is important that the misunderstanding which is evident, on this point, should be cleared up. It is not surprising that on a reading of the Treaty clauses

should issue decrees and regulations such as the (Reparation) Commission may from time to time require." To give the Reparation Commission the effective right to impose taxation would mean inquisitorial methods into "every individual household in the Empire."

"It need only to be observed that not only the joy of work, but also the willingness to pay taxes would suffer throughout the whole population, since no people can be permanently compelled to place the whole result of its efforts at the service of foreign powers or to give up its right to a voice in their disposal. The consequence would be that direct taxes in Germany would have to be collected for the most part by force."

Germany should gain the idea that the proposed Reparation Commission shall have inquisitorial and, in fact, supreme power. The Treaty clauses can readily be construed in this sense. Every effort, therefore, must be made to show Germany the spirit which underlies these clauses and the intent that the Reparation Commission shall not undertake to deal with the internal and domestic affairs of Germany. It will be remembered that when the clause giving the Reparation Commission power to impose upon Germany continuing decrees in order to carry out the provisions of reparation, we all had much discussion on this point. The final wording was not particularly fortunate, and some amplification and qualification should well be made on this point. To me it seems that the fear aroused by the clause in question is the one that dominates Germany's consideration of the whole Treaty.

10. Germany undertakes to pay 20 milliards in gold marks by May 1, 1926,

(N. B.—This date is to be contrasted with the date of May 1, 1921, set forth in the Allied text of the proposed Treaty)

but on this amount are to be credited military material and various other assets taken over

Germany is willing to pay the initial 20 milliard francs [*sic*], but wants 7 instead of 2 years to pay it in. I do not think that we should be sacrificing any principle if we give her 4 years to pay it in. As to the offsets against this initial sum, I am informed, although the figures have not been checked, that the [*these?*] will amount to some-

since the Armistice, the values of railways and state property taken over, &c.

11. Germany undertakes to execute necessary bonds covering additional amount of reparation payment on condition that the total payments shall not exceed 100 milliards of gold marks, including the initial 20 milliards, including also the payment of Belgium's war debts, and that none of the installments shall bear interest.

thing like 8 milliard marks, a a very considerable amount.

Under this paragraph Germany is in effect proposing that the total indemnity which she pays shall not exceed 100 milliard marks gold, without interest—that is to say, 25 billion dollars. It will be remembered that the original American estimate of the total amount principal sum that Germany could pay was given as 30 billion dollars. This estimate was, however, made before the extent of Germany's present bad financial plight was realized, and further, it was provided that fifty per cent of the payment might be made in German marks. The principle of naming a fixed sum was always advocated by the American Delegation, by the Italian Delegation, and by the conservative members of the British and French Delegations. It was only Mr. Lloyd George and Mr. Clemenceau who, on account of political considerations, upset this principle of a fixed sum. I think now that we should go back to it, and name as a total principal sum 100 milliard marks, bearing such interest as [the] Reparation Commission might determine and payable in such form as the Reparation Commission might determine.

By adopting this principle of

the fixed sum, the reparation clauses could be vastly simplified. Germany could address her economic life to the fixed end, and all the other Governments would know in the same way what they could count upon.

12. The payments during the first ten years shall not exceed one milliard of gold marks per annum.

No such limit as this should be fixed in the Treaty, and the limitation should be left to the Reparation Commission.

13. Germany undertakes the obligation to assume a liability for the payment of annual sums by way of reparation to the Allied and Associated Powers, which will approximate to the total net peace Budget of the German Empire as hitherto constituted.

This is a general declaration by Germany, which, in so far as it goes, is very satisfactory, inasmuch as it indicates that Germany will appropriate for reparation a sum equivalent to her total net budget prior to the war, such budget amounting to $

In general, I am inclined to believe that if we can devise something along the lines just indicated (which, as a matter of fact, would be easy for the Allies to bring about without any sacrifice of principle) we could arrive at a basis with Germany very quickly.

I have dictated the foregoing very hastily. N. H. D[avis]. is also preparing some suggestions which will be promptly available.

DOCUMENT 377-A

Davis' Comment on the German Counter Proposals, June 1, 1919

[Davis Papers, carbon copy. "*Duplicate*. Personal and Confidential Observations of Mr. Norman H. Davis to the President, on the Subject of the German Reply to the Allied Conditions of Peace, with Particular Reference to the Reparation Clauses, Paris, June 1st, 1919."]

(1) We shall not attempt to discuss the German arguments to the effect that the conditions submitted by the Allied and Associated Governments go far beyond the terms laid down and agreed upon—leading up to the Armistice. We shall only attempt to treat the question from a practical standpoint.

(2) After an examination of the reply and proposals of the German Financial Delegation, respecting reparation and the financial economic questions in relation thereto, we agree substantially with the arguments of the German Delegation which accord with the position which we have always taken, namely, that it was a mistake not to fix in the Peace Treaty a definite amount which Germany shall pay, and that the amount so fixed should be in relation to the amount of damage which she is obligated to repair and such as she may reasonably be expected to pay within one generation.

(3) We must say that in our opinion the reasons for naming a fixed amount now greatly outweigh those for leaving this question open for future determination. Under the present plan, if the Germans are unable to restore their economic life, they will pay practically nothing, while on the other hand, if they buckle down to work and increase their efficiency, the more they work and save, the more they will be called upon by the Reparation Commission to pay. This is a poor incentive. Under such conditions, it will, in our opinion, be impossible to get the German people to work, a chaotic condition will develop, and the German people will leave their country.

(4) As a matter of fact, only two arguments have ever been advanced against fixing a definite amount at present: *First*, that it is impossible to tell just now how much Germany might be able to pay within the next 25 or 30 years, and that as they owe so much as a result of the damage which they have caused and for which they should make good, it would be a mistake not to make them pay to the uttermost of their capacity; *Second*, that for political reasons, it is inadvisable to fix an amount because the people are expecting Germany to pay so much more than she will ever be able to pay, that it would be impossible to agree upon a reasonable amount to be fixed.

(5) In reply to this, our opinion is that it is much more dangerous and expensive to fix an amount which may be too large than to fix an amount which may be too small. If Germany thinks that she may be able to pay 100,000,000,000 marks over a period of thirty years, the business world is very apt to have confidence in her ability, and it is most probable that she will succeed, because she will have the incentive to buckle down to it to get through it and beyond it. On the other hand, if the German people think that they cannot possibly pay a certain amount and that they can only pay half that amount, it is most probable that they would not be able under any circumstances to pay the larger amount because they

would not have the spirit and hope as a necessary incentive for doing their best. And if, for political reasons, the amount is left open to be determined later on over a period of many years, such a procedure will, in our opinion, be very expensive, because, for the above reasons, it is most probable that a much smaller amount would be collected from Germany than the amount which Germany would now agree to undertake to pay, and the delay thus caused in the reestablishment of confidence and credit would cost more than any possible temporary benefit which might be derived from putting off the inevitable.

(6) The German situation and its treatment is the key to the whole financial situation of Europe. France and Italy and other countries of Europe will need immediately large quantities of raw materials and supplies and the credit with which to purchase them. Without this, they cannot restore their normal economic life and begin reconstruction. $5,000,000,000 to these countries within the next two or three years will be worth very much more to them than five times that amount in ten or fifteen years. Under the present reparation plan, it will, in our opinion, be impossible for them to collect any appreciable amount of money from Germany within the next ten years, and furthermore, it will be impossible for them to obtain any appreciable amount of money against the bonds to be delivered by Germany. The bankers and investors of the world will not have any confidence in the bonds delivered by Germany until they know definitely how many bonds are finally to be delivered, and what policy the Reparation Commission is going to follow, and they will not have any confidence in any unreasonable amount of obligations issued by Germany which Germany herself thinks and states publicly that she will be unable to pay. On the other hand, if a definite amount is fixed, which Germany and the rest of the world think she can meet, France and Italy and the other beneficiary governments should be able to use these bonds as collateral or to sell them in order to obtain funds as required to meet their necessities, and thus further the reestablishment of the economic and industrial life of Europe.

(7) Unless Germany is permitted to retain a requisite working capital and is given the necessary freedom of action for reestablishing her industrial life, it will be utterly impossible for her to pay anything at all, and she might soon get in the same position that Austria is in today; namely, that credits will have to be given to her for the purchase of food with which to keep her people alive, instead of collecting from her, as will be possible if a constructive

policy is pursued. If Germany is not at work and consequently is in a chaotic condition and unprosperous, it is impossible for the rest of Europe to get to work and to be prosperous. It is most essential for the future stability of Europe that confidence and credit be restored at the earliest possible moment, and these can never be restored as long as any large nation in Europe is struggling under a financial burden which the investors of the world think she cannot carry. There is nothing, in our opinion, which could be done which would go further toward re-establishing confidence, credit, and the normal economic and industrial life, than to make an agreement with Germany which the business people of the world think is just and can be carried out, so that the bonds so issued by Germany can act as a basis of credit. After all, the crux of the whole matter is really not so much what Germany will be able to pay, as what the business men, bankers, and investors of the world think she will be able to pay, and they are most likely to think she will be able to pay any reasonable amount which Germany herself admits she can pay. Six to twelve months delay in getting the masses of Europe at work will cost more, from an economic and financial standpoint, than the extra amount which might be gotten out of Germany by following the present indefinite, so-called elastic plan, even assuming that such plan could be eventually worked out. And if the conditions in Germany and the rest of Europe should become worse from a social, economic, and financial standpoint, which in our opinion is very probable if steps are not taken as above indicated, then the loss will simply be irreparable and far in excess of any amount that anyone has hoped could be gotten out of Germany. The solution of the problem of our friends in Europe is bound up with a practical treatment of the reparation problem in respect to Germany.

(8) Europe's need is immediate, and for political reasons the Reparation Commission would undoubtedly be as reluctant to fix an amount and announce a definite policy within the near future, as are some of the present Heads of State to do so at the present moment. This delay, in our opinion, will be fraught with most serious consequences, and will cost much more than it can ever be hoped Germany can repay. We therefore strongly recommend that a definite amount be fixed, that Germany be permitted to retain her present required working capital, that some arrangement be made whereby Germany may retain enough of her own mercantile marine for her own requirements, and that the Reparation Commission be given more constructive and fewer destructive powers.

DOCUMENT 378

Dulles' Summary of and Comment on Several Major German Counter Proposals, June 1, 1919

[TPG, VIII, 9-13. Penciled, "J. F. D." See Document 393.]

[*Feels that German fears chiefly directed at powers of Reparation Commission, and that Allies should seriously consider the specific objections presented. (1) Allies might endorse setting-up of German Commission, but proposal of equal power and arbitration is unacceptable. (2) Commission's power to modify schedule assumed to be in favor of Germany; German offer of 100 milliard only about half, because without interest; but perhaps offer would open door to new effort to get fixed sum; German offer of immediate 20 milliard assumes offsets of military supplies, etc. German offer of 1 milliard annuity for first 10 years seems low and inconsistent with offer of payments equal to prewar budget (which was 3 milliard). (3) German objection to requirement to promulgate legislation suggests their having secured copy of old print of clauses where German interpretation implied. (4) Commission's power to investigate taxes only so that may have intelligent basis of modifying payments in Germany's favor. (5) General power of Commission to require information is for same end, but wording might be redrafted. (6) Might consider giving Germany definite sum for food and raw materials to remove German fear of Commission's discretionary power. (7) German objection to Commission's powers to evaluate deliveries unfounded, since Commission must insure correspondence between damage and reparation. (8) Would revise Annex VI to remove German fear of betrayal of trade secrets. (9) Germany, not Commission, is understood to be chief power in selecting methods of reparation.*]

DOCUMENT 379

Dulles' Summary of and Comment on the Minor German Counter Proposals, June 2, 1919

[TPG, VIII, 14-15. Penciled, "J. F. D." See Document 393.]

[*World shipping pool not feasible, but might leave Germany some ships. Would limit size of Army of Occupation. Allocation of reparation to ceded territory not acceptable. Allied participation in German enterprises not practicable. Germany liable for her allies' damage, but should be pointed out that their payments constitute credit for Germany. Understands reparation by means of German labor acceptable in principle. Pensions and damage outside France and Belgium cannot be removed from Treaty. Poland excluded from reparation since claims only for belligerents. Objections to cattle deliveries inadmissible, but Germany can buy, if she wishes, from neutrals. Restitution by equivalents acceptable only if so to owners. Might make concession on fishing-boats. Understands French willing to exchange minette ore for German coal. Cannot accept demand that minimum coal price be internal German price because Germany cannot be given full competitive price on reparation. German objection to surrendering machinery in use cannot be admitted. Commission will judge Germany's capacity to deliver coal. Accepts German proposal to build less ships in first year but more later. German criticism of Annex VI is well-founded.*]

DOCUMENT 380

Report of the Meeting of the Council of Four, June 2, 1919

[Slosson's Annotations, in Miller, XIX, 277-78.]

On June 2, Mr. Lloyd George informed the Council that his colleagues, both in the Cabinet and in the Peace Delegation, considered it imperative that concessions should be made to Germany if this were the only means of preventing a renewal of the war (C. F. 43 A).

One of the principal objections to enforcing the Treaty as it stood related to the question of reparations. "The next point, and every one of his colleagues had made it, referred to compensation. All thought that more had been asked for than Germany could pay. They had pointed out that the scheme was indefinite and no figure had been fixed. He himself had two alternative suggestions on this subject which he would elaborate later, if desired, but he would rather have them examined by experts before they were discussed in detail by the Council."

President Wilson and M. Clemenceau said that they also would like to consult their own experts.

M. Clemenceau said that "In regard to compensation, France was convinced that Germany was not being asked to pay as much as she ought" and that even moderate men had criticised his own position in the matter.

Mr. Lloyd George said that "he would not cut out a single one of the categories of reparation, and so he had informed his colleagues." His first alternative suggestion "was to take a contract from Germany to make restoration within a certain time or else to pay. Outside restoration every item could, he believed, be fixed; for example, pensions, ships, etc. He would fix a definite sum for all these, and beyond it allow Germany to take a contract for restoration." The second alternative was to give Germany "three months within which she could make a definite offer of a figure. If at the end of three months Germany could not give a figure, then the Treaty would stand."

DOCUMENT 381

Dulles' Memorandum on the Desirability of a Fixed Sum,
June 3, 1919

[TPG, VIII, 34-36. Reprinted in Baruch, pp. 66-69. At the foot of this document, there are penciled initials, "J. F. D."]

(1) The German counter-proposal offering, subject to various credits, payments to aggregate 100 milliards of marks gold, raises the question of whether a determined effort should not again be made to fix Germany's reparation liability in terms of definite figures.

(2) The American Reparation Delegates have always been unanimous in the belief that the Treaty should fix a definite sum for Germany to pay. The considerations advanced by the German reply in favor of a fixed sum are not new in themselves, but are reinforced by a comprehension, daily becoming clearer, of the critical financial situation of Europe.

(3) There have been but two principal arguments against the the fixation of a definite sum, namely:

(a) It is impossible to tell today just how much Germany might be able to pay within the next generation. A miscalculation might release Germany, at heavy cost to the Allies, from a just liability which, it would subsequently develop, Germany was fully capable of discharging. Germany's liability should, therefore, be expressed elastically, so as to ensure the utilization of Germany's full future capacity of payment to make good the almost unlimited damage caused by her.

(b) The political situation among the Allies is so unsettled, and the popular expectation of relief by payments from Germany runs so high, that it might have serious political consequences to name definitely Germany's liability. Even the highest figure which has been considered would disappoint popular expectations.

(4) With respect to the latter argument, it may be observed that the financial and economic situation of Europe is so serious that no government would adopt, merely as a matter of domestic politics, a policy which is not defensible on its merits. The only political consequences to be taken into account are those relating to the stability of government in general. It is conceivable that a severe popular disillusionment at this time might lead to social unrest which would have really serious national and international consequences. It seems far more probable that to continue to per-

petuate uncertainty as to the amount of Germany's payments will merely postpone an awakening until a time when the situation may be even more critical. In the intervening period the people will not have exerted their fullest efforts to aid themselves, as would have been the case had they earlier realized their real situation.

(5) With regard to the argument that there is danger today of underestimating Germany's capacity to pay, it may be said that this risk is perfectly real and fully recognized. It is, however, a risk which must be balanced against the risk of attempting to secure from Germany more than she can pay, or adopting a procedure which destroys Germany's incentive to pay. Of the two risks the latter is infinitely the more serious. To seek too much jeopardizes the whole; to obtain too little involves only the loss of the difference between what is, and what might have been, paid.

(6) It is further to be observed that what the world requires, and requires immediately, is a new basis of credit. A dollar today is probably worth two dollars five years from now. A definite obligation assumed by Germany under conditions which warrant us in believing that Germany herself has the will and believes she has capacity to discharge such obligation, will serve as an immediate basis of credit. A far larger amount assumed under equally satisfactory conditions eighteen months from now would not begin to have the same practical value. Also a larger amount imposed today at the point of the bayonet and in the face of declarations by Germany (which will be accepted by conservative persons throughout the world) that the sum is far in excess of her capacity, would prove of little or no value as a basis of credit.

(7) The present reparation plan is, in our opinion, open to the serious objection that it may, in practice, operate to destroy economic incentive on the part of the present generation of Germany. Germany is set a task without end, and the more she labors the more will be taken from her. Furthermore, little is obtainable under the plan in the immediate future, aside from deliveries of bonds, which will not command the confidence of investors because, among other things, they may be followed by an indefinite amount of similar bonds. And it will be in the interests of Germany herself to destroy popular confidence in the initial instalments of bonds taken from her, as once these bonds acquire any marketable value, still further issues will be taken from Germany.

(8) Europe's need is immediate. Any substantial delay in securing from Germany an obligation having a substantial present

value may involve consequences which will approach a disaster. The risks involved in delay far outweigh the difference between such definite sum as might be fixed today and the most optimistic estimates which have been made as to Germany's capacity.

(9) We therefore strongly recommend that the opportunity offered by Germany's counter-proposal be taken advantage of to fix a definite obligation which Germany will assume in a manner at least semi-voluntary. The German people can then be left free from the continuing interference and control of the Reparation Commission to work out their own problem in their own way. Under such conditions there is every reason to believe that the German people will again become a stabilizing productive and consuming factor in the world's economy.

(10) To secure acceptance by Germany of a high figure it may be necessary to leave Germany a certain amount of working capital and sufficient shipping to meet her domestic requirements. This, in principle, we are prepared to recommend.

DOCUMENT 382

Extract from the Minutes of a Meeting of the American Delegation Regarding Changes in the Treaty with Germany, June 3, 1919, 11 A. M.

[Baker, III, 469-81. According to Baker, a mimeographed copy. "Book No. 4. Secret. Stenographic Report of Meeting between the President, the Commissioners, and the Technical Advisers of the American Commission to Negotiate Peace, Hotel Crillon, Paris, June 3, 1919, at 11:00 O'clock a. m."
Present: Wilson, Lansing, White, House, and Bliss. Also McKinstry, Baruch, McCormick, Davis, Lamont, Summers, Dulles, and Dillon. Also 26 others.]

THE PRESIDENT: Gentlemen, we have come together in order that we may hear from you on the question of the German counter-proposals. We all have moving recollections of the struggles through which we have gone in framing the treaty, and the efforts we made that were successful, and the efforts we made that were unsuccessful to make the terms different from what they are, and I have come here not to express an opinion but to hear opinions, and I think perhaps the best course to follow will be to get a general impression from each other as to which parts of the German counter-arguments have made the greatest impression upon us.

Just as a guide, I find that the parts that have made the greatest impression on our British colleagues are the arguments with regard to the eastern frontier with Poland, the parts with regard to reparations, the parts about the period of occupation, together with the point about the League of Nations, their impression being that the Germans might very well be given reasonably to expect that the period of their probation would not be long in the matter of admission into the League. Those are the four points, the four subjects upon which the German counter-proposals have made the deepest impressions upon them. That might be the start.

The reparation is the biggest point. That involves left-overs of the financial clauses. I would be glad to hear from anyone of our financial group who would like to express himself on that point.

MR. NORMAN H. DAVIS: We feel that the Germans have really given us a basis for getting together properly on reparation, by coming back with a fixed sum. It is a rather rigid fixed sum, which can be modified and made more workable. There is a considerable possibility of getting together there, if we can get the French to agree upon a fixed sum. As you know, we have always insisted on the necessity of having a fixed sum, because by leaving it indefinite we had to give considerable powers to the Reparations Commission, and that is what seems to worry the Germans more than anything else—the powers given to the Reparations Commission, which, as they claim, are rather destructive than constructive, and if we come back and make a fixed amount, it will be possible to do away with the functions of the Reparations Commission which most worry the Germans, and it will avoid the necessity of interfering with their internal affairs, and so on.

COLONEL HOUSE: Have not the Germans misconstrued what the treaty says on that point? That it really does not go as far as the Germans think it goes, and if the matter were explained to them personally, that they would understand it differently from what they now understand it?

MR. THOMAS W. LAMONT: I believe that they could be made to understand that, Colonel House. Certainly the intent of the Reparations Commission is nothing like as inquisitorial nor as arbitrary as the Germans have construed it to be, and I believe that we could explain that to a very large extent, provided, as Mr. Davis says, there was coupled with it the change from an indefinite, vague sum to be determined two years from now, to a definite sum to be determined to-day, because that very change would do away with a large part of the necessity of such a commission.

THE PRESIDENT: May I ask if you saw Messrs. Tardieu and Loucheur this morning?

MR. LAMONT: We saw Mr. Tardieu. Mr. Loucheur did not come.

THE PRESIDENT: What was his statement?

MR. LAMONT: Mr. Tardieu's first reply was that they could consider no change, because Mr. Lloyd George had brought up so many changes. He alluded to the conference at the President's house yesterday afternoon. But during the last part of the conference he finally came around and said that if it were a question of reparation alone and not a question of the Army of Occupation and these other things, he did not know but that they could devise with us the machinery that could work out the idea of a fixed sum, provided the sum were adequate enough. He alluded to the first answer, Mr. President, that you made to the first German note, in which you indicated that execution might be changed somewhat, or made to conform, and he said that if we could work reparation under the head of execution rather than change of principle, "I believe we could be with you."

THE PRESIDENT: May I ask that what I say by way of reference to our British colleagues be not repeated outside of this room, because I am at liberty to use it only for the purposes of this conference. But here are the alternative methods of reparation which were suggested: first, that the Germans should undertake as a contract the whole task of restoration, that is to say, the physical restoration of the ravaged parts of northern France, and that a sum should be fixed in the treaty of peace, under several items in the category of damages, the principle being that inasmuch as it was impossible now to estimate what the actual restoration would cost, that they should be put under contract to restore northern France within a definite period, and that, since the rest of the categories would perhaps hold them, a definite sum ought to be arrived at in regard to that.

The alternative plan was—and it is a rather vague one—that the Germans should sign the reparation clauses as they stand, but that three months should be given them to effect an arrangement for fixing a definite sum in cash as a compensation of all claims. That the reparation clauses were to stand, giving them three years for proposals as to the definite sum.

MR. BARUCH: We discussed those two alternatives that you speak of, Mr. President, yesterday, but we still feel that the best solution would be to come to a fixed sum now, to start with. We went over this yesterday.

THE PRESIDENT: And reject the idea of a contract for restoration?

MR. DAVIS: It would be difficult, as a matter of practice, to carry that out.

MR. SUMMERS: There is an economic unsoundness in it, because many of the districts and places that were devastated and destroyed were located many years ago, and have now no economic basis for being there. For instance, they could combine into one steel mill several destroyed mills. Many of the existing mills could be combined into one; one could be substituted for many. Unless there was a latitude given, it would be economically unsound.

MR. LAMONT: Mr. President, with all respect to Mr. Lloyd George, he is simply trying to postpone the evil day, as far as public opinion is concerned.

THE PRESIDENT: I think he has stated the way it is to be gone about.

MR. LAMONT: Still, whichever way one looks at it, from the Allied point of view or from the German point of view, it is better to make it definite. Germany cannot start her economic and industrial life, cannot gain any credit, as long as it remains open.

MR. DAVIS: He is trying to play both ways undoubtedly there, and as a matter of practice, it is very hard to work that out, because we can never get together as to the distribution of this fixed amount, because they would have to calculate all the time what would be France's share in the restoration of the Germans.

COLONEL HOUSE: It would be something like rewriting the treaty.

MR. DAVIS: We are convinced, Mr. President, that on account of Europe's financial situation to-day it is a most important thing to fix an amount, and an amount which Germany and the world itself have some hope of her being able to pay, and carrying out, which can be used as a basis for France and Italy and the other countries getting on their feet and meeting their requirements.

Under the present arrangements, as the Germans very properly state, if they are not prosperous and cannot get back to work they will pay nothing, but on the other hand, if they buckle down to work and work hard and save, the harder they work and the more they save, the more they will pay. And that is a rather poor incentive for the Germans to buckle down and work hard. But if there is a fixed amount which will let them see a chance of getting from under some day, I believe that would be a better incentive for them.

THE PRESIDENT: How about the other side of it: a fixed sum will form a basis of credit for the other nations, but what will form a basis for Germany's credit?

COLONEL HOUSE: It was practically a fixed sum.

THE PRESIDENT: Yes, there would be that definiteness in it, but where would her assets be?

MR. DAVIS: We must insist upon her being left with sufficient assets as a working capital.

THE PRESIDENT: As a matter of fact the Reparations Commission can do that.

MR. DAVIS: They are permitted to leave her with certain assets, except the ships. We feel that some arrangement certainly must be made whereby Germany can at least have a sufficient number of those ships, either retaining them or making some arrangement for getting them back, so that she will have enough for her own trade, and which I understand amounts to about one-third of the ships which she has turned over.

SECRETARY LANSING: Now Germany offers a fixed sum, does she?

MR. DAVIS: Yes.

SECRETARY LANSING: It is 100 milliards of marks?

MR. DAVIS: Yes. Of course they make quite a large amount of deductions. They say that they will pay the first sum of 20 milliards of marks in the first seven years, but that you must deduct from that the war materials they have turned over and everything else they have turned over and will turn over under the treaty, and also the proportionate share of the pre-war and the war debt of Alsace-Lorraine and of that part of the territory that Poland gets, which they estimate roughly would amount to about three million dollars.

MR. LAMONT: Still, Mr. Secretary, it is very striking that they have made two definite offers: the offer of 20 milliards, and the further offer to devote to reparations a sum annually amounting approximately to the total net peace budget of the German Empire, between $750,000,000 and one billion dollars [between 3 and 4 milliard marks].

SECRETARY LANSING: As I recall it, they offer to pay 20 milliards of marks on or before May 1st, 1926, and then they offer to pay one milliard a year after that. But they will increase it, on the basis that their people shall not be taxed more than the greatest amount paid by any injured country.

MR. DAVIS: They say that as a result they will be compelled, according to that, to tax that heavily; but at least 20 milliards they offer to pay within seven years, and without interest. That is not a capital sum. If you reduce that to a capital sum that will amount to $12\frac{1}{2}$ or 15 milliards. We feel, from a practical standpoint, that it is better to have it interest bearing. Of course you have to give them a few years before they can afford to pay interest, because otherwise it would run so fast against them that they could not catch up.

SECRETARY LANSING: It does not come so very far from the 15 billions of dollars talked about.

MR. LAMONT: It is a little bit less. After you take away deductions it would amount to the capital sum of 10 billion dollars.

THE PRESIDENT: Do you understand that the French this morning were not willing to consider an alteration or change of that sort?

MR. LAMONT: I think they are willing to consider a change of that sort if some one will tell them that that is the only change that would be discussed. At least that was Mr. Tardieu's attitude. Mr. McCormick could better tell us that.

MR. VANCE MCCORMICK: He said that every modification proposed by the British was against the French. The British never mentioned any concession regarding ships or the colonies, and Mr. Tardieu called Mr. Lloyd George's attention to that fact. Mr. Tardieu's position was that they should not agree to a change in the present treaty; that during these five months the experts have discussed these questions pro and con, and having finally come to a decision, it would be fatal to change any principle whatever. The question of machinery of execution, as you stated in your note, might be considered; that was the position the French took. And as he went out of the room he intimated to Mr. Lamont that he might consider such questions as the question of the reparation clauses, along the line we have just been discussing, provided it was not opening the door to concessions along the other lines. France could not afford to concede anything further.

THE PRESIDENT: Would he regard fixing a capital sum as a modification of principle, or a method?

MR. MCCORMICK: A method. Didn't you gather that? (Addressing Mr. Lamont.)

MR. LAMONT: Yes. Mr. Loucheur, of course, has more to say about that than Mr. Tardieu has. If it had not been for the British "Heavenly Twins" we could have gotten together with Loucheur months ago.

MR. DAVIS: Now he is a little bit worried about that political aspect of it, but if there are some changes made which would affect the British I think it would have a certain influence on the French, but, as Tardieu says, the only changes that are proposed are practically those that affect the French.

COLONEL HOUSE: Premier Clemenceau told me last night that he was willing to discuss Silesia. He was not willing to discuss the period of occupation, and he was not willing to discuss any of the other things that Lloyd George wanted.

THE PRESIDENT: Did he say that he would not discuss reparation?

COLONEL HOUSE: No, and I gathered that he would. I think we could get him to discuss reparation. And I also think—much to my surprise—that he would about the League of Nations. He said he would not consider for a moment letting the Germans in now, and I said: "Well, your attitude about that I think is the worst attitude for France, and I cannot understand it. It seems to me that you can see that the sooner the League of Nations gets its grip on Germany the better it would be for France." He said: "I concede that; that is all right; but not for the moment. Presently." So I don't think he is going to be very bad on that. I think the Germans could be told privately that Germany will come in very shortly. I think we could get him to consent to that.

THE PRESIDENT: Well, if you gentlemen of the reparation group had a free hand—if only we ourselves were concerned—what would you propose with regard to the reparation?

MR. DAVIS: Well, we have not definitely agreed among ourselves as to just what we would propose, but we certainly are in accord with this, that we would propose and insist upon a fixed sum, and that that fixed sum would be as high as we really could get Germany to agree to without having a bayonet at her throat, because, after all, the important thing, as stated before, is to get something which can be used as a basis for France and Italy to get more credit, and which will not be so burdensome as will prevent Germany from going ahead with restoring her industrial life, because, after all, what they need to do more than anything is to get people to work, and they have pretty nearly all exhausted their credit. Loucheur is worried about that now, and the important thing is not so much what Germany can pay now, really just now, as fixing a reasonable amount which the German people are willing to buckle down to attempting to pay, and which the investors of the world think she will pay,—and they are rather apt to believe that Germany will pay what she undertakes to pay.

THE PRESIDENT: The aspect of the subject which interests me is the world aspect of it. Unless these securities that Germany is going to give are known to be worth something they cannot be used as a basis for credit, and somebody else will have to supply the credit. Now they cannot be made worth anything unless Germany has the means of going to work and producing. Which is the result of saying that they cannot be made worth anything unless she has assets to begin with to establish her own credit. And therefore the thing has two sides to it; not only the aspect of Germany and France and Italy—but the world aspect; working out a method by which this sum would be made not only definite but worth something, by having means for Germany to get to work.

MR. DAVIS: Yes, we think so.

THE PRESIDENT: Now it seems to me that we could have made it evident to the Germans, by explaining to them, that the real functions of the Reparations Commission, are, as I understand them to be, to help them in carrying out their obligations. The only trouble is, that it is one thing to say that this is the way the Reparations Commission is going to work, and another thing to find it in the treaty. Because we, of the present group of persons, are putting a certain interpretation on the treaty, but there will be others following us who may not put the same interpretation upon it.

MR. DAVIS: We probably have not got in there as clear a picture of what our idea was as to the policy that would be followed by the Reparations Commission as we should have, and it would be well, and it would undoubtedly affect the Germans, if they could be told.

THE PRESIDENT: Why not write—I don't know what the language would be—an accompanying memorandum, agreed to by all the powers, as to the method of administration by the Reparations Commission?

MR. BARUCH: Of course if we fixed a sum the Reparations Commission would die. If we fixed a definite sum, and Germany agreed to it, and she delivered, the Reparations Commission, as we have got it set up, would die, and another would be set up to receive the funds and bonds.

MR. DAVIS: The Reparations Commission was set up principally because they were leaving this matter indefinite, and because we were imposing a burden upon Germany concerning which there was some doubt as to her capacity to meet. But as it was clearly understood that they must follow a constructive policy, and that Germany could not pay anything unless she was given facilities and working capital it was absolutely necessary to set up this commission, with the idea of getting all they could out of Germany, but doing this in a broad way. But that is not the picture that is really conveyed in there (i. e., in the Treaty). The powers of the Reparations Commission are, in a sense, destructive as far as Germany is concerned—they could be—but it ought to be explained to the Germans that no intelligent people could perform its destructive powers unless Germany wilfully failed to comply.

There is no limitation on what the Reparations Commission can do, and since the armistice the agreements with the Germans have been outrageously violated by the French, as for instance, the Luxembourg protocol, etc., and the Germans have had an experience of what the giving of this power has meant, and they complained of it, to which I responded and asked them if they did not think they were entitled to it. They have got evidence to show that the commissions have thus far been outrageously unfair.

THE PRESIDENT: You think that difficulty would be met then by a fixed sum?

MR. SUMMERS: Unquestionably. We have always rewarded, by pensions and in similar ways, deeds of heroism, and each nation has chosen to reward its heroes as it saw fit, and to place that on the Germans on the basis that the French have awarded theirs is unprecedented in the history of the world. And if we had stood for actual reparation we might get some place within a rational sum, which Germany could pay, and we would have a basis for understanding upon that amount.

MR. LAMONT: Mr. President, I believe our difficulties with Germany would fade away if you and Mr. Clemenceau and Mr. Lloyd George would instruct your technical committees to arrive at a definite sum within twenty-four hours instead of two years, and at the same time to reach an agreement as to how much working capital should be left in Germany's hands.

THE PRESIDENT: We instructed them once to find a definite sum. And then we got Klotz on the brain.

MR. LAMONT: Mr. Lloyd George kicked over the traces, but now he has come back to the fold.

MR. DAVIS: You remember they used to change commissions such as this, in times gone by, every time they decided against the wishes of the heads of the states.

COLONEL HOUSE: Do you remember how we always knew, when the individual members would come into a meeting just what the trend of the meeting was going to be that day?

THE PRESIDENT: Now the joke of it is that Lord Sumner was one of those who contributed to the unanimous counsel of the British the other day, and he takes a different position now.

MR. LAMONT: I believe we could get together on this point.

MR. DAVIS: Of course on those constructions you should make the necessary consequential changes in the Reparations Commission, and if possible do something to get away with it. I am afraid you will have to have a reparations commission for a while.

But it is necessary to have a commission, really, to receive the funds and the bonds, and open the trust for the proper distribution at the proper time.

[*This is the end of the discussion on reparation.*]

DOCUMENT 383

Report of the Meeting of the Council of Four, June 3, 1919

[Slosson's Annotations, in Miller, XIX, 278-79.]

On June 3 the discussion was continued [from Document 380] (C. F. 44). President Wilson said that there was nothing unjust in demanding complete reparation from Germany, but it was impracticable. "The idea in the Treaty had been to leave the total amount undecided for two years, and to set up the Reparations Commission, first to decide on the amount, and then, to supervise the process and means by which Germany would make good. Germany's objection was that this constituted an undefined obligation, and that the whole industrial life of Germany would be at the disposal of the Commission, which could prescribe this or that method of payment."

Mr. Lloyd George said that the Germans overstated the case.

President Wilson agreed and said that one of his experts had told him that if the exact intention of the reparations clauses could be made clear to the Germans they would not feel the same objections. But in a plan prolonged over thirty years "what guarantee was there that the members of the Reparation Commission would understand the scheme in the same way as those who had drawn it up?" He thought it would partly satisfy the Germans if a definite sum were fixed.

Mr. Lloyd George said that the question of instalments and of guarantees would still remain. The strongest point in the German case was that Germany's credit would be gone until the whole liability could be ascertained. To fix an exact sum at present "had not been found possible."

President Wilson said that the Germans had mentioned five thousand million pounds sterling [100 milliard marks]. "It was true that the Germans did not mean the same as the Allies by this. The Germans meant the five thousand millions as a total, whereas the Allies had contemplated the same sum with interest. If we were to say that we would accept five thousand millions sterling if treated as a capital sum with interest to be paid after the first year or two, during which, by common consent, Germany could not pay much, would it not form a good basis?"

M. Clemenceau said that M. Loucheur was opposed to this.

Mr. Lloyd George asked if the American and French experts had as yet studied the two alternative methods of dealing with reparations which he had suggested.

M. Clemenceau said that three months was a very short period, in the opinion of M. Loucheur, for estimating the extent of damage as proposed in Mr. Lloyd George's second plan.

Mr. Lloyd George said that it could be extended to four months.

It was agreed that the following Committee should examine the proposals of Mr. Lloyd George: Mr. Baruch for the United States; M. Loucheur for France; M. Crespi for Italy, and Mr. Lloyd George in person for Great Britain (C. F. 44).

DOCUMENT 384

Preliminary American Memorandum Regarding the Functions of the Reparation Commission, June 4, 1919

[TPG, VIII, 37-38. Probably by Dulles. The first five paragraphs of Document 390 follow. The first five paragraphs of a First American Proposed Reply of June 5 (see Document 389) intervene but are not printed, since they are almost exactly like the present draft.]

The Allied and Associated Governments, coincidentally with the signature of the Conditions of Peace with Germany,[1] make the following statement of their intentions relative to the operations of the Reparation Commission and their understanding of certain of the Treaty Clauses dealing with Reparation:

The vast extent and manifold character of the damage caused to the Allied and Associated Governments in consequence of the war has created a reparation problem of extraordinary magnitude and complexity, only to be solved by a continuing body, limited in personnel and invested with broad powers. All of the parties to the Treaty recognize this situation and unite in delegating power and

[1] The phrase "coincidentally . . . with Germany" was omitted from the intervening First American Proposed Reply of June 5. It reappeared in the following draft.

authority to the Reparation Commission. The Reparation Commission is, however, instructed to exercise its powers constructively to insure in the interest of all as early and as complete a discharge by Germany of her reparation obligations as is consistent with the due maintenance of the social, economic and financial structure of a Germany earnestly striving to exert her full power to repair the loss and damage she has caused.

Realizing that such efforts can best attain a maximum result with a minimum of interference from without, the Reparation Commission will not interfere vexatiously in the internal affairs of Germany. The provisions of Article 241 are not to be construed as giving the Commission power to dictate the domestic legislation of Germany. Nor does Paragraph 12 (b), of Annex II, give the Commission power to prescribe or enforce taxes or to dictate the character of the German budget. The Commission is required to inform itself as to the German system of taxation and of the character of the German budget, in order that it may intelligently and constructively exercise the discretion accorded it in Germany's interest particularly by Article 234. The provisions of Article 240 are similar in character and purpose and there should be no occasion for the exercise of these powers after May 1, 1921, if Germany is in a position to, and does conform to, the schedule of payments then to be notified to her and to the specific provisions of the several Annexes relative to reparation in kind. It is further to be observed that the power of modification accorded by the said Article 234 is designed to permit of a modification in Germany's interest of a schedule of payments which events may demonstrate to be beyond Germany's reasonable capacity.

The purposes for which the powers granted to the Commission are to be utilized are plainly indicated on the face of the Treaty, and the Commission, in exercising the power conferred by Article 240 and by Paragraphs 2, 3 and 4 of Annex VI, will scrupulously protect, and not require the divulgence of, trade secrets and similar confidential data.

It is understood that the action necessary to give effect to the provisions of Annex IV, relative to reparation in kind, will be taken by Germany on its own initiative, and the Commission has no direct power of action in Germany to give effect to Germany's obligations expressed in this Annex.

DOCUMENT 385

Preliminary American Memorandum Regarding Certain Concessions to Germany, Undated

[TPG, VIII, 39-40. This memorandum develops an American point of view and is shown, by its style of typewriting, to be an American document. It seems likely that it was drawn up at about the same time as the Preliminary American Memorandum Regarding the Functions of the Reparation Commission of June 4, 1919 (see Document 384); and it is also likely that Dulles himself was the author. In the original, there are several penciled amendments.

Paragraphs 7-10 of Document 390 follow. Paragraphs 6-9 of a First American Proposed Reply of June 5 (see Document 389) intervene but are not printed since they are so much like the present draft.]

The A. and A. Governments, after examining the considerable data which is available, have unanimously reached the conclusion that the total damage under Annex I, when estimated on a gold basis, will [not exceed] the principal sum of [120] milliards of marks gold. These Governments further recognize that the financial situation of Europe requires that Germany's liability be rendered as precise as circumstances will permit and that the benefits to follow from any reasonable and prompt decision in this respect will greatly outweigh any loss consequent upon an error in estimation. Accordingly the sum of [120] milliards of marks gold may be regarded as an accepted maximum of the damage for which Germany is liable in accordance with Article 232. Inasmuch as the damage specified in Annex I includes damage caused by the former allies of Germany, any sums received by the Allies from Germany's former allies will be credited against Germany's liability. Further, while not recognizing any right of contribution as between Germany and her former allies, the Reparation Commission will give to the Government of Germany an opportunity to present such facts as that Government deems relevant as to the capacity of payment of Germany's former allies.[1]

The Allied and Associated Governments recognize that the utilization of German labor falls within the principle enunciated by Article 236 and proposals for reparation in such form may be taken up either with the Reparation Commission or directly with the A. and A. Governments concerned. Furthermore, the Reparation Commission by virtue of paragraph 19 of Annex II, is authorized to accept payment in the form of shares, securities, etc. The Government of Germany accordingly may present to the

---

[1] This paragraph appears in the intervening First American Proposed Reply of June 5 only as a typewritten insert. It reappeared in the following draft in the body of the text.

Reparation Commission such proposals as it may have to make relative to effecting reparation through the grant of participating interests in German industrial concerns.

Recognizing the necessity of permitting the utilization by Germany of certain ships in order that Germany may proceed at once to performance of her reparation obligations, the A. and A. Governments authorize the Commission to defer the delivery by Germany of ships [required for her domestic needs, pending the date when Germany can herself provide ships for her own use.]

[In accordance with the provisions of paragraph 10 of Annex V, the Reparation Commission is required to take into account such facts as the German Government may desire to present relative to her capacity to supply the amounts of coal specified in this Annex. If such facts convince the Reparation Commission that there should be a suspension or cancellation of certain deliveries to prevent undue interference with the industrial requirements of Germany, the Commission will so do. Furthermore, the principle of an exchange with France of minette ore on reciprocal conditions is accepted.]

[It is understood that the options accorded by Annex VI for the purchase of dyestuffs and chemicals are for the benefit of the domestic requirements only of the Allied and Associated Powers.]

DOCUMENT 386

First Belgian Draft of the Agreement with Belgium Regarding Priority, June 5, 1919

[From the Edward M. House Collection, Yale University Library, New Haven, Connecticut. "Text Proposed by the Belgian Delegation." This was enclosed with Document 387. Document 352 precedes. Document 425 and 423 follow.]

[a] *Whereas*, article 237 of the conditions of Peace with Germany provides, among other things, that the payments to be made by Germany by way of reparation will be divided by the Allied and Associated Governments, in proportions which have been determined upon by them in advance, on a basis of general equity and of the rights of each; and

[b] *Whereas*, it is equitable that Belgium should receive a certain priority out of such payments to be made by Germany.

[c] *Now, therefore*, the undersigned, for and on behalf of their respective Governments, agree that out of the first actual cash received from Germany, in respect of reparation, Belgium shall receive on account of her reparation claims the equivalent of 2.500.000.000 gold francs.

[d] For the purpose of the foregoing, there shall be reckoned as cash

1°) the cash received by the Reparation Commission;

2°) the proceeds of sales, by the said Commission, of currency or securities received from Germany;

3°) the value of the reparations in kind, received from Germany in execution of the conditions of the armistice of the 11th of November 1918 and its renewals and the articles of the Peace Treaty and debited against the Allied and Associated Governments other than Belgium.

[e] It will be an instruction to the Reparation Commission to do its utmost to expedite all payments of the above sum of 2.500.-000.000 before the first of May 1921.

[f] Belgium shall retain in addition to the above sum of 2.500.-000.000 francs the full value of reparations in kind received by her from Germany and debited against her.

[g] From May 1st, 1921, the sum of two and a half billion francs and the eventual excess of the reparations in kind made to Belgium over her share as fixed by article 237 above mentioned will be redeemed to the amount of 1/30 of their whole on any one of the successive payments to be made by Germany for Belgian account.

Paris, June 5, 1919

DOCUMENT 387

Letter from Hymans to House Regarding Belgian Priority and Communicating a Text on Belgian Priority, June 5, 1919

[From the signed original in the Edward M. House Collection, Yale University Library, New Haven, Connecticut. House replied to this letter in Document 394.]

Dear Colonel House,

One month has passed, since the Allied and Associated Governments have made to Belgium a final proposal, concerning the priority on her reparation claims of two and a half billion francs, and the cancellation of Belgium war debt up to the Armistice.[1]

We accepted this proposal in the very general terms in which it was made to us, trusting that the Allies would draft without delay a document embodying the said proposal in terms satisfactory to us, to our Government and to our people, who are very anxious to see a question of such importance to them definitively

[1] Apparently Document No. 333.

settled. But we have not yet received such document and we would be very grateful to you if you would give your attention to this matter.

Our financial advisers have drafted a text of the document which we submit to your consideration.[2]

Faithfully yours,

[*signed*]   HYMANS.

DOCUMENT 388
Loucheur's Plan for Reparation, June 5, 1919

[TPG, VIII, 41. Three extra carbon copies, pp. 42-44. "M. Loucheur's Plan on Reparation." At the head of this document is written: "Jun 5".]

M. Loucheur proposes:

1. That a separate arrangement shall be made with the lesser nations, Roumania, Serbia, Czecho-Slovakia and Poland, to the end that their claims against Germany will be reduced to a minimum. He expects to accomplish this by means of various offsets in the way of debiting them with value of State properties, &c., giving them prior claims against Bulgaria and Turkey—the net result of all this being the total net claims against Germany on the part of these lesser States lumped together would not exceed 500 million to one billion dollars [2-4 milliard marks]. Handling Italy in the same way would reduce her claim against Germany not to exceed one to two billion dollars [4-8 milliard marks].

2. The foregoing plan, if successfully carried out, would leave the Reparation Commission only France, Great Britain and Belgium to deal with—would enormously simplify the work of the Commission, and would, in Loucheur's judgment, reduce the claims against Germany to about 30 billion dollars [120 milliard marks].

3. Assuming that the foregoing plan in general is arranged, Loucheur would not alter the text of the Treaty and Reparation clauses in the slightest degree, but would have the A & A powers execute a memorandum which would have the binding force of the Treaty, stating that Germany would have an opportunity in the next 90 days to survey the damage and to offer to commute the whole amount to a sum which he thinks the A & A powers would be able to accept. Mr. Clemenceau wants to get over the crisis of public opinion until the Peace Treaty has been actually signed and the summer has gone. Then he will let his people into any figures that may be necessary in the early autumn.

[2] See Document No. 386.

4. In the same memorandum there must be a more clear definition of the powers of the Reparation Commission, more satisfactory
to the Germans, &c. There should also be word of mouth explanations which will show favors but to which Clemenceau has not
yet given his consent.

DOCUMENT 389

First American Proposed Reply to the German Observations,
June 5, 1919

[TPG, VIII, 45-49.]

[Derived from Documents 384 and 385. Former incorporated practically without change. Latter incorporated with certain changes: first paragraph regarding setting of maximum damage figure omitted; and paragraph regarding ships has extra sentence which permits retention by Germany of limited but unspecified amounts of working capital.]

DOCUMENT 390

Second American Proposed Reply to the German Observations,
June 6, 1919

[TPG, VIII, 50-52. Documents 384 and 385 precede. A First American Proposed Reply of June 5 (see Document 389) intervenes but is not printed because it is much like the present draft. Document 396 follows. At the head of the present draft there is written in Dulles' handwriting: "Copy handed Loucheur VI/6/19/ 10.30 a. m." The heading on the following draft refers to the present one as having been drafted by "J. F. D."]

[1] [The Allied and Associated Governments coincidentally with the signature of the Conditions of Peace with Germany,[1] make the following statement of their intentions relative to the operations of the Reparation Commission and their understanding of certain of the Treaty Clauses dealing with Reparation:]

[2] The vast extent and manifold character of the damage caused to the Allied and Associated Governments in consequence of the war has created a reparation problem of extraordinary magnitude and complexity, only to be solved by a continuing body, limited in personnel and invested with broad powers. [All of the parties to the Treaty] recognize this situation and [unite in delegating] power and authority to [the] Reparation Commission. The Reparation Commission is, however, instructed to exercise its powers [constructively] to insure in the interest of all as early and as complete a discharge by Germany of her reparation obli-

---

[1] The phrase "coincidentally . . . with Germany" was omitted from the intervening First American Proposed Reply of June 5.

gations as is consistent with the due maintenance of the social, economic and financial structure of a Germany earnestly striving to exert her full power to repair the loss and damage she has caused.

[3] Realizing that such efforts can best attain a maximum [result] with a minimum of interference from without, the Reparation Commission will not interfere vexatiously in the internal affairs of Germany. The provisions of Article 241 [are not to] be construed as giving the Commission power to dictate the [domestic] legislation of Germany. Nor does Paragraph 12 (b), [of Annex II,] give the Commission power to prescribe [or enforce] taxes or to dictate the character of the German budget. The Commission is required to inform itself as to the German system of taxation and of the character of the German budget, only[2] in order that it may intelligently and constructively exercise the discretion accorded it [in Germany's interest] particularly by Article 234. The provisions of Article 240 are similar in character and purpose and there should be no occasion for the exercise of these powers after May 1, 1921, if Germany is in a position to, [and does,] conform to the schedule of payments which then will have been notified to her and to the specific provisions of the several Annexes relative to reparation in kind. [It is further to be observed] that the power of modification accorded by [the said] Article 234 is designed to permit of a modification in Germany's interest of a schedule of payments which [events] may demonstrate to be beyond Germany's reasonable capacity.

[4] The purposes for which the powers granted to the Commission are to be utilized are plainly indicated on the face of the Treaty, and the Commission, in exercising the power conferred by Article 240 and by Paragraphs 2, 3, and 4 of Annex VI, will scrupulously protect, and not require the divulgence of, trade secrets and similar confidential data.

[5] It is understood that the action necessary to give effect to the provisions of Annex IV, relative to reparation in kind, will be taken by Germany on its own initiative, [and the Commission has no direct power of action in Germany to give effect to Germany's obligations expressed in this Annex.]

[6] [The provisions of the Conditions of Peace point unmistakably to the mutual advantage of a close cooperation of Germany with the Reparation Commission. It is in recognition of this that

---

[2] The word "only" appeared for the first time in the intervening First American Proposed Reply of June 5.

full facilities are to be afforded] the German Government to present facts and arguments with respect to claims, [means of payment, etc. The Allied and Associated Governments would welcome the constitution by Germany of a Commission to promote such cooperation and invested with broad power to aid in the performance by Germany of her reparation obligations.] No reason is perceived why such a Commission could not work in harmony with the Reparation Commission [and greatly facilitate the practical application of the Reparation clauses of the Conditions of Peace.][3]

[7] [The Allied and Associated Governments, after examining the considerable data which is available, have unanimously reached the conclusion that the total damage under Annex I, when estimated on a gold basis, will approximate the principal sum of   milliards of marks gold.[4] These Governments further recognize that the financial situation of Europe requires that Germany's liability be rendered as precise as circumstances will permit and that the benefits to follow from any reasonable and prompt decision in this respect will greatly outweigh any loss consequent upon an error in estimation. Accordingly the sum of   milliards of marks of gold may be regarded as an accepted maximum of the damage for which Germany is liable in accordance with Article 232. Inasmuch as the damage specified in Annex I includes damage caused by the former allies of Germany, any sums received by the Allies from Germany's former allies will be credited against Germany's liability. Further, while not recognizing any right of contribution as between Germany and her former allies, the Reparation Commission will give to the Government of Germany an opportunity to present such facts as that Government deems relevant as to the capacity of payment of Germany's former allies.]

[8] [The Allied and Associated Governments recognize that the utilization of German labor falls within the principle enunciated by Article 236 and proposals for reparation in such form may be taken up either with the Reparation Commission or directly with the Allied and Associated Governments concerned. Furthermore, the Reparation Commission by virtue of Paragraph 19, of Annex

---

[3] This paragraph appeared for the first time in the present draft. A penciled text of it, however, may be found as an insert in the intervening First American Proposed Reply of June 5.

[4] This whole paragraph appeared in the intervening First American Proposed Reply of June 5 only as a typewritten insert. In that insert, the present sentence was amended with pencil to its wording here. Also in that insert the figures "120" in this and the third sentence were crossed out.

II, is authorized to accept payment in the form of shares, securities, etc. The Government of Germany accordingly may present to the Reparation Commission such proposals as it may have to make relative to effecting reparation through the grant of participating interests in German industrial concerns.]

[9] [Recognizing the necessity of permitting the utilization by Germany of certain ships in order that Germany may proceed at once to performance of her reparation obligations, the Allied and Associated Governments authorize the Commission to defer for _____ years the delivery by Germany of ships, designated by the Commission, representing _____ % in tonnage of the total amount of ships referred to in Paragraph 1 of Annex III. These ships, the delivery of which is deferred, will be available for use by Germany to meet her domestic needs.[5] In the same end, the provisions of Article 235 will be so applied as to permit the retention by Germany of such limited amounts of working capital as will facilitate a renewal of economic activity, and no gold will be required to be delivered for reparation purposes.[6]

[10] [(Here insert further observations relative to coal deliveries, exchange of minette ore, and chemical and dyestuff options.)[7]]

DOCUMENT 391

French Draft of a Reply to the German Observations, June 6, 1919

[TPG, VIII, 73-77. "Remarques de la Délégation Allemande. Réparations. 1ère Note." There is also an English translation of this document (dated June 7) made by the French Delegation (see Document 397). Certain differences between the original and the translation have been pointed out in footnotes. At the top of this document, there has been written in pencil, "French memo."]

–I–

Les deux considérations éventuelles auxquelles les puissances alliées et associées ont obéi en ne fixant pas immédiatement le

---

[5] In the intervening First American Proposed Reply of June 5, this paragraph read down to this point just as it did in the preceding draft.

[6] This sentence appeared for the first time in the intervening First American Proposed Reply of June 5; but the last clause ("and no gold [etc.]") appeared for the first time in the present draft.

[7] This sentence appears here for the first time as a substitute for the last two paragraphs of the preceding draft and of the intervening First American Proposed Reply of June 5.

montant définitif de la dette de l'Allemagne à leur égard sont les suivantes:[1]

Cette dette doit être la représentation aussi exacte que possible du montant des dommages à réparer. Les puissances alliées et associées entendent rompre désormais avec le principe d'une indemnité pécuniaire imposée au vaincu à titre de châtiment. Désormais le vaincu ne saursit être contraint de payer que les sommes nécessaires à la réparation des dommages qu'il a causés. Or si le montant des pensions et allocations peut être à bref délai établi avec une approximation suffisante, il n'en est pas de même des dommages matériels et des frais de reconstruction. Un temps assez long s'écoulera encore avant qu'il soit possible de parvenir à leur égard à des chiffres satisfaisants.

Le second élément à envisager est représenté par la capacité financière de l'Allemagne, par les moyens et facultés dont elle dispose pour faire face à ses obligations. A cet égard les experts les plus qualifiés ne sauraient encore hasarder que des hypothèses. Comme toutes les puissances belligérantes, l'Allemagne vit encore au point de vue économique sous un régime exceptionnel. Elle subit actuellement les conséquences du blocus, le contre coup de la défaite. Il est présentement impossible de prévoir avec quelle rapidité et avec quelle ampleur s'effectuera son relèvement économique. Au cours des deux années qui viennent l'économie nationale allemande va s'adapter à une situation nouvelle; l'Allemagne va réapparaître sur le marché mondial et reprendre rang dans la concurrence économique. C'est alors, mais alors seulement qu'il sera possible de déterminer si les craintes manifestées par la délégation allemande sont justifiées, si vraiment l'Allemagne est hors d'état de faire face aux charges qu'elle a acceptées.

Le délai de deux ans prévu dans le traité est dès lors conforme à son intérêt comme à celui des Puissances alliées. A quoi servirait en effet de fixer d'ores et déjà un chiffre forfaitaire, s'il apparaissait en 1921 que l'Allemagne ne saurait en acquitter le montant?[2]

Au double point de vue qui vient d'être précisé: évaluation des dommages et appréciation de la capacité financière de l'Allemagne, la fixation immédiate d'une indemnité maximum est inadmissible.

---

[1] In the English translation of June 7, this preamble reads:

"Germany demands that we settle immediately the total amount of its debt of reparation and part [*sic*] it down in the Treaty.

"Why did not the Allied and Associated Powers think they could do so?

"The two essential considerations they obeyed to are the following:"

[2] This paragraph is crossed out in the English translation of June 7.

–II–

La délégation allemande trace de la Commission des Réparations une image bien faite assurément pour apitoyer l'opinion publique, mais qui ne correspond nullement à la réalité.

Sur les problèmes essentiels, cette Commission ne prend aucune décision sans avoir mis l'Allemagne à même de présenter ses observations et ses arguments.

ANNEXE II—§9. "La Commission devra . . . . entendre tous "arguments et témoignages présentés par l'Allemagne sur toutes "questions se rattachant à sa capacité de payement."

§10. "La Commission étudiera les réclamations et donnera "au gouvernement allemand l'équitable faculté de se faire en-"tendre."

Par ailleurs quels sont les prétendus pouvoirs dictatoriaux de la Commission?

Aux termes de l'article 240 le gouvernement allemand doit fournir à la Commission "tous les renseignements dont elle "pourra avoir besoin . . . . ." ainsi que toutes informations rela-"tives aux opérations militaires."

L'Article 241 ajoute que "l'Allemagne s'engage à faire pro-"mulguer, à maintenir en vigueur et à publier toute législation, "tous règlements et décrets qui pourraient être nécessaires pour "assurer la complète exécution des stipulations ci-dessus."

Il s'agit exclusivement d'enlever à l'Allemagne la possibilité d'opposer à des décisions de la Commission soit certaines dispositions de sa législation intérieure, soit au contraire l'absence de textes législatifs,—et nullement de donner à la Commission le droit de dicter des lois à l'Allemagne.

En effet les paragraphes 16 et 17 de l'Annexe II prévoient le cas, le premier "de manquement par l'Allemagne à l'exécution "qui lui incombe de l'une quelconque des obligations visées à la "présente partie du présent traité," et le second le "cas de man-"quement volontaire par l'Allemagne" auxdites obligations.

Dans l'un et l'autre cas, la Commission n'est pas autorisée à agir par elle-même, elle ne peut qu'en référer aux Puissances intéressées. Sans doute le paragraphe 12 de la même annexe prévoit que "la "Commission examinera le système fiscal allemand afin que tous les "revenus de l'Allemagne y compris les revenus destinés au service et "à l'acquittement de tous emprunts intérieurs soient affectés par "privilège au paiement des sommes dues par elle au titre des "réparations." Il serait en effet inadmissible que l'Allemagne payât sa dette intérieure avant de s'être acquittée de l'intégralité de sa dette de réparation.

Mais ici encore la Commission ne peut qu'en référer aux Puissances intéressées.

La Commission est exclusivement munie de pouvoirs de décisions et de droits de contrôle; le traité ne prévoit en sa faveur aucun empiètement sur la souveraineté ou sur le sol allemands; aucune branche des revenus nationaux allemands ne lui est spécialement affectée.

La déformation que la Délégation allemande a fait subir sur ce point au projet de traité l'amène à formuler une contre-proposition dont le résumé suffit à démontrer à quel point elle est inacceptable.

Toutes les décisions de la Commission des Réparations interalliée seraient soumises à une Commission allemande pourvue d'un droit de veto. Les conflits entre ces deux organismes seraient déférés à des tribunaux ou à des Commissions mixtes d'arbitrage présidées par des neutres.

En d'autres termes, le vote du représentant d'une Puissance qui n'a pas pris part à la guerre pourrait décider de la nature et de l'étendue des droits à réparation des nations belligérantes, ce qui est évidemment inacceptable.[3]

–III–

L'Allemagne reconnaît avoir accepté et les 14 points du Président Wilson et la note du 5 novembre 1918 du secrétaire d'État Lansing.

Elle prétend toutefois que cette double acceptation a limité l'obligation allemande de réparer à la Belgique et aux contrées de la France envahie, et, dans ces deux régions, tous dommages subis par les biens de la population civile ainsi que par les personnes en tant qu'il s'agissait de civils non mobilisés:

Il suffira, pour répondre une dernière fois à cette argumentation de deux courtes citations.

Le 12 octobre 1918, le secrétaire d'État Solf écrivait: "Le gouver-"nement allemand a accepté comme base d'une paix de droit durable "les 14 points du Président Wilson":

Or, parmi ces 14 points figure, entre autres, au même titre que le 7ᵉ (Belgique) et le 8ᵉ (France envahie) le 11ᵉ relatif à la restauration de la Roumanie, de la Serbie et du Montenegro.

---

[3] In the English translation of June 7, this paragraph is expanded into two to read:

"Such a system would come to the organisation of a permanent conflict. It would continually be necessary to refer to the Commission of arbitration. And then the vote of the representative of a Power which took no part in the war could decide of the nature and extent of the rights toward reparation of the belligerent countries, which evidently cannot be admitted.

"Moreover nothing in the Treaty forbids Germany to present its observations through a permanent german Commission."

Dans la note du 5 novembre 1918, M. le Secrétaire d'État Lansing écrivait:

"Les territoires envahis"—et non *certains* d'entre eux—"doivent être restaurés."

Il ajoutait: "L'Allemagne devra réparer tous dommages subis "par les populations civiles des nations alliées et associées et par "leurs propriétés du fait de l'agression de l'Allemagne sur terre, sur "mer ou par les airs."

Enfin, on peut se demander à quoi sert d'engager des discussions théoriques sur l'étendue de la responsabilité de l'Allemagne, du moment que cette Puissance demande d'ores et déjà et quoi qu'il advienne, qu'on limite ses obligations à un chiffre forfaitaire.

DOCUMENT 392

Hughes' Draft of a Reply to the German Observations, June 6, 1919

[TPG, VIII, 83-85, 86. The last paragraph of this document is, in the original, on a separate sheet of paper not paged continuously with what precedes. At the head of the text is written "Hughes proposal June 6 1919".]

The demands of the Allied and Associated Powers as regards reparation are extraordinarily moderate. Whilst they affirm the undeniable principle that Germany and her Allies are responsible for all the loss and damage caused by the war, they recognize that the resources of Germany are not adequate to pay that amount, and they limit the categories of damage, for which they claim reparation, to such an extent that they only cover a fraction of the total obligation.

The German Delegation, in order to justify its contention that the Allies have pledged themselves to waive all claims except for the restoration of Belgium and Northern France, and for damage done to the civil population and its property in those areas, attempts to isolate the "Fourteen Points" enunciated by President Wilson on 8th January, 1918, from the "subsequent addresses" which, in all the Armistice negotiations, were associated with the address of 8th January, 1918.

The Allied and Associated Governments have, in drafting the Peace Terms, borne the principles referred to in negotiations constantly in mind. They are satisfied that the terms imposed are absolutely consistent with them. The principles of Justice which are affirmed in those addresses, and of which the "Fourteen Points" are particular illustrations, are nowhere exceeded; though the reparation demanded falls very far short of that full reparation for wrong done which the principles of justice require.

The German Delegation makes the vitally important admission that not only the invasion of Belgium but also the consequential invasion of France through Belgium was a violation of international law, which calls for reparation. But it is impossible to draw the line there. The whole war costs of all the Allies are a direct consequence of the same violation and stand on precisely the same footing.

The German Delegation attempts to limit the obligation of restoration to the occupied districts of Belgium and Northern France—to the exclusion of all damage done elsewhere, including Italy, Serbia, Rumania and Montenegro. It makes this contention, in defiance of the facts—

(1) that the Fourteen points themselves expressly mention the restoration of Serbia, Rumania and Montenegro;

(2) that the Allied and Associated Governments in the Note of 5th November, 1919, expressly insisted on compensation for *all damage* done to the civilian population of the Allies and their property by the aggression of Germany *by land, by sea, and from the air*—without any limitation to particular occupied districts, and in language which is quite incompatible with any such limitation.

The German counter-proposals as to the payment of compensation are quite inadequate. The sum of 20 milliards in gold marks, which the Allies demand during 1919, 1920 and the first four months of 1921, they offer to pay on or before 1st May, 1926; and they further name a maximum total amount of 100 milliards, and a maximum *annual* amount (till 1936) of one milliard. Neither of these proposals can be accepted.

If anything approaching to full reparation were demanded, the request for an exact figure would be reasonable; but such a figure would be many times greater than that named. As the categories of damage claimable have been strictly limited, the amount corresponding to those categories ought to be paid in full, and a limitation to a maximum total of 100 milliards cannot be agreed to.

The Treaty provides for the ascertainment of the total before 1st May, 1921, and for the German Government being fully heard by the Commission in the settlement of the total. These provisions go to the limit of concession. The further contention that the assessment by the Commission should only be operative if agreed to by a co-ordinate German Commission or by arbitration is quite out of the question.

The idea that the Commission is a dictatorial body, with power to make decrees and exercise rights of sovereignty in Germany, is unfounded, and seems to be due to a misreading of the terms of the Treaty—particularly Article 241 and Annex II to Article 244. The function of the Commission is to supervise and facilitate the fulfilment of the terms of the Treaty, and its "dictatorial" powers are mainly its discretion to grant or refuse extensions or reliefs of various kinds to Germany. Obviously, its existence and powers are beneficial to Germany.

DOCUMENT 393

Dulles' Summary of and Comment on the German Observations, June 6, 1919

[TPG, VIII, 53-57. "Reparations. Memorandum of Points of German Counter-Proposal together with Comment Thereon." At the head of this document is written: "Copies to Mr. Hughes (Gt Britain) Klotz (France) Mori (Japan) at meeting of Rep Committee—June 6/19 J. F. D." The two parts of this document combine two memoranda made by Dulles on June 1 and on June 2 (see Documents 378 and 379). The memorandum of June 1, which dealt with the German objections to the Reparation Commission set up by the Treaty, had an introductory statement that read:

"After examining the German's reply, I conclude that Germany's major objection to the Reparation clauses, and one of her principal objections to the Treaty as a whole, is the constitution of the Reparation Commission.

"Germany understands that she is compelled to grant this Commission a vast and continuing power which, while ostensibly limited to economic and financial spheres, will in fact enable the Commission to control all forms of national activity. The Commission does not merely operate from without Germany, defining in general terms the financial obligations of the German Government, but is to intervene directly in Germany's internal affairs, both public and private. This Germany states involves the renunciation, for an indefinite time and in favor of a body presumably hostile in character, of sovereign rights. The operation of such a scheme cannot fail to destroy all economic initiative and political aspiration on the part of the German people.

"We might answer Germany merely by stating that she must trust the Reparation Commission not to operate in a way to produce the results which Germany dreads and which the Allied and Associated Governments are also desirous of avoiding. I cannot but feel, however, that such a general reply would fail utterly to meet the not unnatural apprehensions of the Germans and that serious consideration should be given to the specific objections and practical suggestions which the German reply makes with respect to this phase of the Reparation clauses.

"The German points (stated in my own language) and my comment thereon follow:— . . ."]

German Points	*Comment*
1. The extent of Germany's liability is not fixed by the Treaty, but is to be fixed only at a future date and on the basis of uncertain factors, by Germany's adversaries acting through the Reparation Commission. A maximum limit of Germany's liability is suggested, namely, 100 milliards of marks gold, not bearing interest and subject to numerous credits.	1. The desirability from all points of view of rendering Germany's liability as definite as possible is clearly recognized. There are, however, a number of practical and political considerations.[1]
2. It is proposed that a German commission should cooperate with the Reparation Commission in the determination of the amount of damage and points of difference between the two commissions should be submitted to neutral arbitration.	2. The Treaty provides that the Reparation Commission shall give Germany a just opportunity to be heard on the allowance of claims. There appears to be no reason why Germany should not be heard through a special commission constituted by her, and the A. and A. Governments might indicate that they would welcome the establishment by

[1] In his memorandum of June 1, Dulles' comment on the German proposal to pay a definite sum of 100 milliard marks ran as follows (in separated paragraphs which have been combined here):

"Our rough estimates indicate total damage under the categories approximating 160 milliards of marks. A limit of 100 milliards could, therefore, only be considered in connection with the limits of Germany's capacity, as to which see below.

"100 milliards of marks gold corresponds closely with U. S. estimates as to the principal sum Germany is capable of paying. The German proposal, which eliminates interest and contemplates payments running through a period, presumably as long as 50 years, operates however to cut the actual value of 100 milliards as a principal sum to only about 50% thereof. German agreement, however, to a debt of 100 milliards when taken in conjunction with the Treaty revision [*provision*] requiring the delivery by Germany of bonds to precisely this amount seems to create a situation where a renewed effort might advantageously be made to secure the fixation of 100 milliards as Germany's obligation, such sum to be payable with interest, the burden of which interest might, however, be relieved by authorizing payment of part of the principal and interest to be made in domestic currency. Should it be possible to arrive at a fixed sum, it would be unnecessary to have a Reparation Commission with the broad powers of that contemplated by the Treaty.

"The suggestion of a payment of 20 milliards by 1926 is to be compared with the present proposal for the payment of this sum by 1921. Also the 20 milliards offered by Germany [is] subject to deductions in the form of credit for military supplies and for a share of reparation to be borne by detached portions of Germany. Both such credits appear inadmissible. On the other hand, it does not appear that out of the 20 milliards Germany offers are to be deducted payments for food, raw materials, or for the Army of Occupation.

"The suggestion of 1 milliard per annum for 10 years beginning 1926 seems too low and inconsistent with the suggestion relative to payments equivalent to the pre-war budget, which latter approximated 3 milliards of marks."

Germany of a commission endowed with broad powers to aid in the performance by Germany of her reparation obligations. The suggestion that this commission should be co-equal with the Allied Reparation Commission and that points of difference should be arbitrarily settled is, of course, unacceptable.

3. Even when Germany's debt is fixed the power to prescribe, modify, and increase the instalments by which it is payable constitutes a vexatious arrangement which would destroy financial stability and penalize economic effort.

3. The Treaty gives the Commission power from time to time to "modify" the schedule of payments after consideration of Germany's resources. It has always been assumed that this modification would be in Germany's interest, but the language is susceptible of the construction Germany gives it.

4. Germany is required to issue all such decrees and regulations as the Reparation Commission may from time to time require. This, in effect, means depriving Germany's own governmental agencies of their principal functions.

4. A print of the draft of the Reparation clauses (April 21)[2] required Germany in terms, allowing for variations in translation, almost identical to those quoted in the German's reply to pass legislation to give effect to the decisions and orders of the Commission from time to time. This phrase was stricken out by the Supreme Council on April 23, with the result that Germany is required only to pass legislation to give effect to the provisions of the Treaty.[3] The German note suggests that they may have secured a copy of an early print of the Reparation clauses. Possibly, however, Arti-

[2] See Article 10 of the British First Print of April 21 (Document 284).
[3] See Document 286, section 15. See also footnote 12 to Document 315.

cle 241 is still ambiguous and should be redrafted to exclude the possibility of the interpretation the Germans suggest.

5. The Reparation Commission has complete control over and right to enforce execution of the German system of taxation. Control of taxation is one of the fundamental rights of a democratic people and it is the chief means of controlling the executive branch of the Government. To deprive the German people of the right to prescribe their own taxation is to reduce them virtually to foreign enslavement.

5. This objection arises from a misapprehension of Annex II, Par. 12-B, requiring the Commission to "examine the German system of taxation" so as to insure that reparation is a charge upon all revenues prior to that for the service of any domestic loan, and so that the Commission will be satisfied that the German scheme of taxation is as heavy, proportionately, as that of any of the powers represented on the Commission.

The paragraph in question is awkwardly worded and might well be re-drafted to indicate clearly that no direct power over German taxation is created thereby, but only that the Commission before modifying in Germany's interest any part of her obligations shall be satisfied of the facts referred to. Incidentally, it may be noted that Germany accepts the principle of higher taxation than any power represented on the Commission.

6. Every individual householder in Germany may be subjected to an inquiry by the Commission.

6. This presumably refers to Article 240, requiring the German Government to supply the Commission all information which it may require, relative to the financial situation and operations and to the property, stocks, etc., of Germany and her nationals. The power is indeed

very broad, but it is to be noted that the information sought is primarily to be used in Germany's interest so as to enable the Commission intelligently to revise the initial obligations placed on Germany for payments in money and in kind. The clause might very well be eliminated, as Germany is practically certain to request the postponement of payments and relief from obligations to deliver materials, and the Commission can always condition the consideration of such requests upon receiving full information upon which to act intelligently.

7. The Reparation Commission is given full power to determine the extent to which the German people shall be fed and clothed and permitted to obtain the materials necessary to permit them to labor.

7. This refers to Article 235 authorizing the Commission to permit deductions out of the initial payment for the purchase of food and raw materials. Serious consideration has on several occasions been given to reducing the amount of the initial payment by setting aside a specific sum to be at the disposal of the German Government for the purposes indicated. It might be worth while to reconsider this.

8. The valuation of a substantial part of Germany's economic effort for many years is placed entirely in the hands of the Reparation Commission, which alone values reparation in kind.

8. While the Commission is authorized to place a value on Germany's reparation in kind, yet this is a bookkeeping rather than a substantial matter. The Commission is required to insure a correspondence on the one hand between damage debited to Germany and on the other hand

reparation of such damage in kind, so that provided the instructions are carried out no injustice to Germany can result. It is not unnatural that the provisions in this respect, which are quite complicated, are not fully understood by the Germans.

9. The Reparation Commission will be an agency for securing for the Allied Governments Germany's most valuable trade secrets, as Germany is obligated to furnish to the Commission information of this character.

9. This presumably refers to Article 240 above referred to and in particular to Paragraphs 2, 3 and 4 of Annex VI, dealing with dyestuffs and chemical products. Under this Annex Germany is in fact required to furnish the Reparation Commission full particulars as to the production of dyestuffs, etc., "in such form as may be considered necessary by the Commission," and "all necessary information" which the Commission may require. It is believed that the language of Annex VI may well be modified to meet the German objections.

10. Germany can only give effect to her obligations for reparation in kind through the exercise of her own initiative and without outside interference with the economic liberty of the German people.

10. We have always understood that Germany was to select her own methods for giving effect to her obligations for reparation in kind and that there was to be no direct interference by the Reparation Commission in this matter.

11. Merchant ships as means of production cannot be surrendered in toto unless there is a general world's shipping pool in which Germany will participate.

11. The idea of a world's pool does not seem feasible, but it will undoubtedly be necessary to leave Germany, as working capital, a substantial number of ships and her gold, and perhaps some other assets.

12. Germany's economic vitality will be destroyed by an Army of Occupation which must be supported by Germany. This will mean in fact that Germany is compelled to bear a substantial portion of the French peace budget.

12. There seems to be considerable force in the German objection on this score, and if military considerations permit an effort should be made to indicate a limit to the size of the Army of Occupation.

13. There should be an allocation of Germany's reparation liability to ceded territory.

13. This is inadmissible.

14. Germany should be allowed to make reparation in part by offering a participation interest to the Allies in Germany's shipping and industrial concerns.

14. The Reparation Commission is authorized to deal with such proposals (see Annex II, Par. 19).[4]

15. Germany should not be held liable for damage caused by her Allies.

15. This contention is inadmissible, but at the same time it might well be pointed out to Germany that payments made by Germany's Allies will be credited against the general debt and correspondingly reduce Germany's liability. There is no such provision in the Treaty.

16. Germany offers to work out reparation in part by undertaking reconstruction work, notably of the coal mines of France and in general for all reconstruction purposes

16. It is understood that this would be acceptable in principle, as the French have already indicated their desire to utilize German labor, and a requirement for Germany to supply labor was at one time introduced in the Treaty at the request of the French.

17. There should be no German liability for pensions and separation allowances, which are purely military expenses.

17. This is inadmissible.

[4] In his memorandum of June 2, Dulles' comment on this point was limited to: "It does not appear that such an arrangement would be practicable."

18. Germany's liability should be limited to damage resulting directly from the violation of Belgium, i.e., damage to Belgium and to northern France invaded via Belgium. In no case should Germany be liable for damage to Italy and Roumania who were not subjects of German aggression but who attacked Germany in their own interests.

18. Inadmissible.

19. There should be no reparation for Poland, with whom Germany was in friendly relations up to the date of the Armistice.

19. As the Treaty stands, damage is only recoverable during the period of belligerency. This would exclude reparation to Poland.

20. It is impossible for Germany on account of food conditions to make deliveries of cattle contemplated by Annex IV. Germany offers to buy cattle in neutral countries for delivery.

20. Germany's impossibility to deliver cattle cannot be recognized. At the same time, where no delay would be involved, there is no objection to her buying in and delivering from neutral countries.

21. The restitution of identifiable articles provided for by Article 238 should be allowed through the delivery of equivalent objects not necessarily the identic ones taken away and which may be in actual use.

21. This would be permissible if, and only if, the owners were satisfied with an equivalent object rather than their own specific property.

22. The delivery of fishing boats required by Annex III is impossible owing to the acute food shortage in Germany and the necessity of utilizing large numbers of trawlers for minesweeping purposes.

22. If the facts are as Germany alleges, it would seem that the time within which fishing vessels are to be delivered might be somewhat extended.

23. If German coal is to be delivered as required, there must

23. It is recognized as important that the Germans be

be an exchange of minette ore for German smelting works.

advised that an equitable arrangement for exchange of minette ore will be made.[5]

24. The price of German coal pursuant to the options should be the British export price, but not lower than the price to German consumers.

24. Presumably this more favorable price arrangement cannot be admitted on the theory that Germany cannot be allowed full competitive prices on deliveries made for reparation purposes.

25. Machinery, etc., which is in being and in use in Germany should not have to be surrendered up even to the extent of 30% of the amount in use in any one factory, unless the machinery in Germany is not fully employed.

25. The conditions surrounding such deliveries are already carefully safeguarded, and further German limitation seems inadmissible.

26. The amount of coal required to be delivered by Annex V is physically beyond Germany's capacity.

26. The German analysis of her capacity does not take into account reduction of German domestic needs or further possibilities of development. In any case the Commission is authorized to judge as to whether the foreign deliveries are beyond Germany's power; however, some changes in this schedule may be desirable.[6]

27. Germany accepts the shipbuilding requirements of Annex III with a modification that the amount during the first year should be somewhat less than suggested, but that the amount may be increased in subsequent years.

27. This suggestion would seem to be satisfactory.

---

[5] In his memorandum of June 2, Dulles' comment on this point read: "It is understood that the French are willing to make an arrangement of this sort."

[6] In Dulles' memorandum of June 2, the last clause of his comment on this point read: "therefore, any change in the schedule seems unnecessary."

28. Germany accepts Paragraph 1 of Annex VI relating to deliveries of dyestuffs and chemical drugs actually in stock, but rejects Paragraphs 2, 3 and 4, giving options until 1925. Also Paragraph 1 is accepted subject to stipulation that the chemicals delivered are for domestic use.

28. The German criticism of Annex VI seems well founded, and the Annex was never regarded by the United States as entirely equitable.

DOCUMENT 394

Letter from House to Hymans Regarding Belgian Priority, June 6, 1919

[From the carbon copy in the Edward M. House Collection, Yale University Library, New Haven, Connecticut.]

Dear M. Hymans:

I hasten to acknowledge the receipt of your letter of June 5, 1919, relating to the question of priority for Belgium on her claims for reparation.[1]

I need not assure you that it will give me great pleasure to continue to urge the settlement of this important question on the lines proposed by you.

Sincerely yours,
Signed: E. M. HOUSE.

DOCUMENT 395

McKinstry's (?) Revised Table of Damages, June 6, 1919

[TPG, II, 103a. This table stands by itself in McKinstry's papers and is an estimate that was presumably prepared by him or under his direction.]

[1] See Document 387.

ESTIMATES OF DAMAGE IN MILLIONS OF DOLLARS.

In accordance with Categories of Damages as contained in Treaties.
(Revised June 6, 1919, to replace all previous tables).

[Figures in brackets show milliards of marks, converted at ratio of 1:4]

Categories	France	Great Britain	Belgium	Italy	United States	Japan	Serbia & Montenegro	Roumania	Greece	All others, Portugal, China, Siam, Armenia, etc., but not including Russia, Poland, and Czecho-Slovakia.	Totals
10. Levies, fines, cash requisitions, etc. (Estimated from incomplete claims.)	400 [1.60]	—	500 [2.00]	50 [.20]	—	—	100 [.40]	100 [.40]	—		1,150 [4.60]
1, 2, 3, 4, 6, 8. Personal injuries, maltreatment of prisoners & assistance to prisoners of war & families. (Estimated from incomplete claims.)	600 [2.40]	250 [1.00]	200 [.80]	200 [.80]	25 [.10]	10 [.04]	150 [.60]	50 [.20]	5 [.02]		1,490 [5.96]
9. Damage to property. A. Shipping losses. (Estimated at $250 per gross registered ton for ships and cargoes.)	250 [1.00]	2,000 [8.00]	10 [.04]	200 [.80]	75 [.30]	30 [.12]	—	—	—		2,565 [10.26]
9. Damages to property. B. Other than shipping. (Estimated at pre-war prices plus 25%.)	4,000 [16.00]	125 [.50]	1,000 [4.00]	375 [1.50]	—	—	250 [1.00]	250 [1.00]	25 [.10]		6,025 [24.10]
5. Military Pensions.	7,500 [30.00]	4,500 [18.00]	200 [.80]	2,000 [8.00]	400 [1.60]	25 [.10]	300 [1.20]	250 [1.00]	30 [.12]		15,205 [60.82]
7. Separation Allowances.	3,000 [12.00]	2,000 [8.00]	75 [.30]	600 [2.40]	300 [1.20]	25 [.10]	150 [.60]	100 [.40]	15 [.06]		6,265 [25.06]
War Loans to Belgium.	—	—	1,200 [4.80]								1,200 [4.80]
										100* [.40]	100*[.40]
Totals (Mils. of Dollars)	15,750 [63.00]	8,875 [35.50]	3,185 [12.74]	3,425 [13.70]	800 [3.20]	90 [.36]	950 [3.80]	750 [3.00]	75 [.30]	100* [.40]	34,000 [136.00]
Suggested Reparation	15,000 [60.00]	8,000 [32.00]	3,000 [12.00]	3,000 [12.00]	75 [.40]	75 [.30]	750 [3.00]	—	75 [.30]	100 [.40]	30,100 [120.40]

DOCUMENT 396

*Loucheur's Revise of the Second American Proposed Reply,
June 6, 1919*

[TPG, VIII, 63-65. "Translation of Loucheur revise of J. F. D. draft." Document
390 precedes. Document 398 follows. This is a translation, presumably by Dulles.
The French original (*ibid.*, pp. 58-62) is not printed.]

[The A. & A. Governments are forced] to point out that the
interpretation given by Germany to certain [clauses of the treaty,
relative to reparations, are] entirely at variance with [the text and
with the intent which underlies it.] For the purpose of clarification
[they] make the following declaration, to render precise their
intentions as formed and as expressed in the Treaty:

The vast extent and manifold character of the damage caused to
the A. & A. Governments in consequence of the war [has] created
a reparation problem of extraordinary magnitude and complexity,
only to be solved by a continuing body, limited in personnel and
invested with broad powers. [The A. & A. Governments recognize
this situation and] themselves propose to delegate power and
authority to [a] Reparation Commission. The Reparation Commission is however instructed by the Treaty itself so to exercise and
interpret its powers as to insure in the interest of all as early and as
complete a discharge by Germany of her reparation obligations
as is consistent with the due maintenance of the social, economic
and financial structure of a Germany earnestly striving to [exert]
her full power to repair the loss and damage she has caused.

[Realizing that such efforts can best attain a maximum of
efficiency with a minimum of interference from without, the Reparation Commission will not interfere vexatiously in the internal affairs
of Germany.]

The provisions of Article 241 [cannot be construed] as giving
the Commission power to dictate the [internal] legislation of
Germany. Nor does Paragraph 12(b) give the Commission power
to prescribe taxes or to dictate the character of the German
Budget. The Commission is required to inform itself as to the
German system of taxation and of the character of the German
budget only in order that it may intelligently and constructively
exercise the discretion accorded it [*in the interest of Germany*] by
Article 234.

The provisions of Art. 240 are similar in character and purpose and there should be no occasion for the exercise of these powers after May 1, 1921, if Germany is in a position to [conform to] the schedule of payments which then will have been notified to her and to the specific provisions of the several Annexes relative to reparation in kind. [It is important to observe again] that the power of modification accorded by Art. 234 is designed [specifically] to permit of a modification *in Germany's interest* of a schedule of payments which [circumstances] may demonstrate to be beyond Germany's reasonable capacity.

The purpose for which the powers granted to the Commission are to be utilized are plainly indicated on the face of the Treaty, and the Commission in exercising the power conferred by Art. 240 and by Paragraphs 2, 3 and 4 of Annex VI, [will scrupulously protect, and not] require the divulgence of, trade secrets and similar confidential data.

It [is] understood that the action necessary to give effect to the provisions of Annex IV, relative to reparation in kind, will be taken by Germany on its own initiative. [The obligations assumed by Germany presumably will be carried out by her in accordance with the precise provisions of the Annex thereby obviating any occasion for intervention.]

The provisions of the Treaty are in no wise incompatible with the creation by Germany of a Commission, which will represent her in dealings with the Reparation Commission [and which will afford] such cooperation as may be necessary. The Treaty specifically [affords] opportunities for the German Government to present fact and arguments with respect to claims and modes of payment, within the limits of the principles and express provisions of the Treaty. This may be done through a Commission and [there is not, *a priori*, any reason] why such a Commission [should] not work in harmony with the Reparation Commission. Certainly this is greatly to be desired.

Germany proposes to assist in the restoration of the devastated areas by supplying labor. The A. & A. Governments had not desired to stipulate for [the supplying of] labor lest they be charged with demanding forced labor. [It is however to be noted that by Par. 19 of Annex II the Commission is already authorized to accept payment in numerous forms. There is no reason why Germany should not, immediately after the signature of the Treaty, take up with France and Belgium, the nations principally interested, a plan for the restoration by Germany of such parts of the devastated areas as these nations may be willing to have restored in this manner. Germany might, for example, 4 months after the signature of the Treaty, make a firm offer for such restoration, and at the same time offer a fixed sum for the balance of restoration and for the other categories of damage. A reply would be made within 2 months, either accepting or declining; and in the latter event the existing provisions of the treaty would continue to be applied. The Allied nations themselves look forward to an arrangement of this character, and it is only material difficulties which have prevented, and still prevent, them from adopting at once such a plan.]

[The A. & A. Governments have full regard for the economic needs of Germany, the more so as the ability of Germany to make reparation is directly related thereto. To this end instructions to the Reparation Commission which are in preparation contemplate according to Germany adequate economic facilities, notably in allowing Germany to retain for a certain time, a portion of the shipping referred to in Par. 1 of Annex III so that Germany may meet her domestic needs. Similar instructions are to be given relative to a retention of working capital essential to industry.]

[Similar observations may be made relative to the objections of Germany to the various deliveries of materials contemplated by Annexes V and VI.]

[Without entering into a detailed discussion relative to the deliveries of coal, it should however be noted that so far as relates to *quantities*, the production of the Sarre Basin, not utilized in this district itself, corresponds to the consumption of Alsace-Lorraine; that measures are taken to insure a distribution of Silesian coal as formerly, during a period equal to that of the options given by Germany; and finally that Par. 10 of Annex V was introduced expressly to insure within reasonable limits the satisfaction of the needs of all interested parties, including Germany.]

DOCUMENT 397

English Translation of French Draft of a Reply to the German Observations, June 7, 1919

[TPG, VIII, 78-82. "French Delegation. Memorandum or Answer to the Observations of the German Delegation. Reparations."]

[French original is Document 391. There are one or two small differences between the two versions, especially: Paragraph in French is omitted in English, which says that equally to Germany's advantage to postpone fixing her debt.]

DOCUMENT 398

Third American Proposed Reply to the German Observations, June 7, 1919

[TPG, VIII, 66-70. "Draft of Proposed Reply to German Counter Proposals Dealing with Reparation Clauses." Document 396 precedes. Document 407 follows. A Fourth American Proposed Reply of June 8 (see Document 406) intervenes but is not printed. *Except as shown by footnotes and except for unimportant differences, this intervening draft is identical with the following draft.*]

[On May 10th You were advised by the President of the Peace Conference that the Allied and Associated Governments would not engage in any discussions of the principles underlying the proposed conditions of Peace, but would only consider observations dealing with the practicable details of the operation of general principles. This communication you appear singularly to have ignored and in your counter proposals you attempt to open a discussion relative to fundamental questions of principle.] The Allied and Associated Governments, [consistently with] their policy already enunciated [will not] enter into a discussion [on questions of principle. They are, however, prepared to point out that the interpretation given by Germany to certain of the provisions of the Conditions of Peace dealing with reparations is entirely at variance with both the letter and spirit of these principles. For the purpose of clarification, the Allied and Associated Governments make the following declarations to render precise their intentions as formed and as expressed in the Treaty:][1]

[1] The first paragraph of the intervening Fourth American Proposed Reply of June 8 reads:

"On May 10th you were advised that the Allied and Associated Governments would not engage in any discussion of the principles underlying the Conditions of Peace, which had been prepared with scrupulous regard for the correspondence leading up to the Armistice of November 11, 1918. This com-

The vast extent and manifold character of the damage caused to the Allied and Associated Governments in consequence of the war, have created a reparation problem of extraordinary magnitude and complexity only to be solved by a continuing body limited in personnel and invested with broad powers to deal with the problem in relation to the general economic situation. The Allied and Associated Powers recognizing this situation, themselves propose to delegate power and authority to the Reparation Commission. The Reparation Commission is, however, instructed by the Treaty itself so to exercise and interpret its powers as to insure in the interest of all, as early and [as] complete [a] discharge by Germany of her reparation obligations as is consistent with the due maintenance of the social, economic and financial structure of a Germany earnestly striving to exercise her full power to repair the loss and damage she has caused.

The provisions of Article 241 are not to be misconstrued as giving the Commission power to dictate the domestic legislation of Germany. Nor does Paragraph 12 (b), of Annex II, give the Commission power to prescribe or enforce taxes or to dictate the character of the German budget. The Commission is required to inform itself as to the German system of taxation and of the character of the German budget, only in order that it may intelligently and constructively exercise the discretion accorded it in Germany's interest particularly by Article 234. The provisions of Article 240 are similar in character and purpose and there should be no occasion for the exercise of these powers after May 1, 1921, if Germany is in a position to, and does, comply with the schedule of payments which then will have been notified to her and [to] the specific provisions of the several annexes relative to reparation in kind. It is further to be observed that the power of modification accorded by the said Article 234 is expressly designed to permit of a modification *in Germany's interest* of a schedule of payments which events may demonstrate to be beyond Germany's reasonable capacity.

The purposes for which the power granted to the Commission

munication you appear singularly to have ignored and in your counter proposals you attempt again to open a discussion relative to fundamental questions of principle involving Germany's liability for reparation. The Allied and Associated Governments, consistent to their policy already enunciated, again decline to enter into a discussion with you on questions of principle.''

The second paragraph of this intervening draft is practically the same as that of the following draft.

are to be utilized are plainly indicated on the face of the Treaty, and the Allied and Associated [Governments must definitely reject any suggestions] that the Commission, in exercising the power conferred by Article 240 and by paragraphs 2, 3 and 4 of Annex VI, [would] require the divulgence of trade secrets and similar confidential data.

It [has always been] understood, [and it clearly appears from the text,] that the action necessary to give effect to the provisions of Annex IV, relative to Reparation in kind, will be taken by Germany on its own initiative, after receipt of notification from the Reparation Commission.

The provisions of the Treaty are in no wise incompatible with the creation by Germany of a commission which will represent Germany in dealing with the Reparation Commission and which will constitute an instrumentality for such cooperation as may be necessary. The Treaty specifically and repeatedly provides opportunities for the German Government to present facts and arguments with respect to claims and modes of payment, within the limits of the principles and express provisions of the Treaty. This may be done through a commission and no reason is perceived as to why such a commission could not work in harmony with the Reparation Commission. Certainly this is greatly to be desired.

The Allied and Associated Governments, after examining the considerable data which is available, have unanimously reached the conclusion that the total damage under Annex I, when estimated on a gold basis, will approximate the principal sum of one hundred and twenty milliards of marks gold. These Governments [further] recognize the desirability that Germany's liability be rendered as precise as circumstances will permit and that the benefits to follow from any reasonable and prompt decision in this request will greatly outweigh any loss consequent upon a possible error in estimation. Accordingly, the sum of 120 milliards of marks gold may be regarded as an accepted maximum of the damage for which Germany is liable in accordance with Article 232. Inasmuch as the damage specified in Annex I includes damage caused by the former allies of Germany, any sums received by the Allies from Germany's former allies will be credited against Germany's liability. Further, while not recognizing any right of contribution as between Germany and her former allies, the Reparation Commission will give the Government of Germany an opportunity to present such facts as that Government deems relevant as to the capacity of payment of Germany's former allies.[2]

Germany proposes to assist in the restoration of the devastated areas by supplying labor. The Allied and Associated Governments had not desired to stipulate for German labor lest they be charged with demanding forced labor. [In view, however, of the proposal of Germany, the Reparation Commission will be instructed to invite and to consider, within four months after the signature of the Treaty, a definite proposal by Germany to undertake herself the restoration of substantial portions of the devastated areas of Belgium and France, and concurrently therewith a proposal from Germany for a cash settlement of so much of the Categories of Damage as will not be repaired through physical reconstruction by Germany. Germany will be accorded all suitable facilities to permit of her making such a proposal in acceptable form. The offer to be made by Germany in accordance with the foregoing would be made within four months of the signature of the Treaty and would be open for acceptance or rejection for two months after its receipt by the Reparation Commission. In the event of rejection the regular procedure provided for by the Treaty would be followed. The Allied and Associated Governments anticipate that an arrangement of the character contemplated above can be made and it is only material difficulties which prevent them from at once putting forward a detailed plan of this character.]

The Allied and Associated Governments do not ignore the economic needs of Germany. The Commission is instructed in all of its activities to take into account the social and economic requirements of Germany. In furtherance of such general instructions, specific instructions are now in preparation directing the Commission to permit the retention by Germany for two years of ships, designated by the Commission, representing [35%[3]] in tonnage of the total

[2] This paragraph is derived from and very close in its wording to the seventh paragraph of the Second American Proposed Reply of June 6 (see Document 390).

[3] This number is almost illegible. It may be "33%."

amount of ships referred to in Paragraph I of Annex III. These ships, the delivery of which is deferred, will be available for use by Germany to meet her [domestic] needs and to assist in the fulfillment of Germany's external [obligations. The Commission will similarly receive detailed][4] instructions to apply the provisions of Article 235 so as to permit the retention by Germany, at home and abroad, of amounts of working capital [essential for industry.]

With reference to the provisions of Annexes V and VI, it is, of course, understood that the options therein referred to will be exercised exclusively to meet the domestic requirements of the country exercising the option. In further precision of the general principle above referred to [as guiding the Commission and the Allied and Associated Governments,] additional detailed instructions are in preparation, advising the Commission that to [prevent undue] interference with the economic and industrial life of Germany the option for delivery of coal to France will, for the first year, be exercised as to 50% only of the maximum amounts mentioned and that deliveries should commence with small monthly amounts, gradually increasing.

The Government of France has always contemplated that an arrangement would be made for the exchange of minette ore on mutually acceptable conditions.

With reference to the cost of maintaining the Army of Occupation, it is impossible for obvious reasons for the Allied and Associated Governments to [arrive at any fixed decision] which would operate to limit the size of such army. The Allied and Associated Governments perceive [no reason],[5] however, [why the German Government should not be advised] that it is their hope and expectation that it will be unnecessary for such army to be of a size such that the cost of maintenance would exceed 240 millions of marks per annum.

[4] Since these words are necessary to the sense of the text and since they are to be found in both the intervening and following drafts, it may be assumed that they were omitted from the present draft only by accident.

[5] See note 4 above.

DOCUMENT 399

Alternative Preamble to the Third American Proposed Reply, June 7, 1919

[TPG, VIII, 71-72. "Alternative Preamble to Proposed Reply on Reparation Clauses (NOTE: This Preamble is not suitable for adoption in the event that the American proposal for the immediate fixation of a sum is adopted.)" At the head of this draft, there is written in pencil, "June 7, 1919."]

The Allied and Associated Governments in the preparation of the Reparation Clauses of the Conditions of Peace, as well as the other provisions thereof, have had constantly in mind the events leading up to the conclusion of the armistice on November 11, 1918. The principles which were affirmed as constituting the basis of the peace to follow the conclusion of the armistice include among other things the "Fourteen Points" of President Wilson and his subsequent addresses, and the Allied declaration communicated to Germany on November 5, 1918, to the effect that compensation would be required for *all damage* done to the civilian population of the Allies and their property by the aggression of Germany by land, by sea and from the air. It is to be noted that in these several statements of principle nothing is contained to justify the conclusion that Germany's liability should be limited to damage occasioned to Belgium and northern France. The Fourteen Points expressly refer to the restoration of Serbia, Roumania and Montenegro, and the declaration of November 5 stipulates on compensation for "all damage" without limitation as to the theater where the damage arose.

That Germany should be held liable for damage resulting immediately from the action of Germany's former allies should not occasion surprise, in view of the repeated declarations of Allied statesmen made publicly prior to the armistice that Germany was deemed responsible for the actions of her allies, and in view of the repeated declarations made by the Governments of Germany and of her allies as to the unity of effort and of purpose which guided their activities.

The impossibility of fixing at the present moment the definite extent of Germany's liability results from the very extent and intensity of the damage Germany has caused, and it is clearly impossible for the Allied and Associated Governments at the present time to determine accurately either the amount of the damage or the times and modes of payment. The exceptional economic conditions in which Germany is at present placed, resulting from the practical cessation and from years[1] of any important export and import trade, and the physicological [*sic*] effect of the military reverses which Germany has suffered, also obviously render it impossible to fix immediately the precise amounts and payment. The counter-proposals of Germany which obviously are entirely speculative in character and wholly inadequate in amount, cannot, therefore, be considered. The proposals of the Conditions of Peace for a determination of these questions by a Reparation Commission are believed to insure a just and equitable treatment of the reparation problem. It is obvious however that Germany grossly misinterprets certain of the provisions of peace dealing with the purpose and functions of the Reparation Commission. For the purpose of clarification the Allied and Associated Governments are accordingly prepared to render precise their intentions as formed and as expressed in the Conditions of Peace.

(Here follow with other draft[2] beginning with second paragraph.)

DOCUMENT 400

Report of the Meeting of the Council of Four, June 7, 1919

[Slosson's Annotations, in Miller, XIX, 279-80.]

On June 7, Mr. Lloyd George said that the American experts were anxious to fix a definite figure for Germany to pay, but that he and M. Loucheur considered this difficult. The Germans would not accept as high a figure as would have to be fixed.

President Wilson said "the object of the figure was to get the Germans to agree."

Mr. Lloyd George said that he preferred the plan by which Germany would be given three or four months to name a figure and which she could pay a part in material and labor. He thought that this would be also more acceptable to the Germans.

M. Clemenceau agreed (C. F. 52).

---

[1] A penciled amendment makes this read: "practical cessation for several years of any".
[2] See Document 398.

DOCUMENT 401

Extract from Riddell's Diary Regarding Bonar Law's Views on the German Reply, June 8, 1919

[Riddell, p. 87.]

[JUNE] 8TH (SUNDAY).—... We drove to Pontoise, about thirty miles from Paris, where we had lunch at a small restaurant. ... Bonar Law spoke a good deal about the reply to the German Peace Note. He thinks that the amount of the indemnity should be fixed and that the Germans should issue bonds for it, payable so much per annum—say eight thousand millions [160 milliard marks] payable at three hundred millions [6 milliard marks] per annum. . . .

DOCUMENT 402

Draft of the Report of the Reparation Experts to the Supreme Council Regarding the Reply to the German Observations, June 8, 1919

[TPG, VIII, 87-90.]

Par lettre en date du 4 Juin.

Le Conseil Suprême a transmis pour avis et rapport les "re-"marques de la Délégation allemande sur les conditions de paix" à la Commission des Réparations.

Après plusieurs réunions l'accord n'a pu se faire entre les délégations américaine, anglaise, française, italienne et japonaise sur le projet de réponse commune.

J'ai l'honneur en conséquence de vous transmettre le rapport suivant qui précise les points sur lesquels l'accord s'est fait et ceux à l'occasion desquels un désaccord subsiste.

Il importe de faire ressortir immédiatement que le problème essentiel que, faute de parvenir à une entente, la Commission des Réparations soumet au Conseil Suprême, est celui de savoir s'il convient ou non de fixer immédiatement le chiffre global de la dette allemande.

En matière de Réparations, les Contre-propositions allemandes sont essentiellement au nombre de cinq.

I.—L'initiation de la responsabilité et de l'obligation de réparer de l'Allemagne à certaines d'entre les catégories de dommages figurant à l'Annexe I.

II.—L'initiation des pouvoirs de la Commission des Réparations interalliée subordonnée à une Commission allemande et à des tribunaux arbitraires présidés par des neutres.

III.—Fixation immédiate du chiffre global de la dette de Réparations de l'Allemagne.

IV.—Limitation des obligations de l'Allemagne en ce qui concerne la livraison de bateaux, de charbon et de certaines matières premières.

V.—Suppression de l'armée d'occupation ou tout au moins limitation de charger que son entretien imposerait à l'Allemagne.

I

Limitation de la responsabilité de l'Allemagne.
Accord unanime pour repousser l'argumentation allemande.
(Projet français)

II

Pouvoirs de la Commission.
Accord unanime pour écarter l'interprétation allemande et sa contre-proposition, préciser le rôle et le fonctionnement de la Commission, justifier sa raison d'être.
(Début du projet Lord SUMNER; suite: Projet M. DULLES—Rejet de la contre-proposition allemande
Projet Français).

III

Fixation immédiate du montant de la dette allemande:
1° Réponse affirmative— Délégation américaine
Texte A. Duller [*sic*].
2° Réponse négative— Délégation anglo-française.
Moyens invoqués:
1° Impossibilité matérielle d'établir le montant du dommage au risque de créer des injustices au détriment des pays envahis.
(Lord SUMNER)
2° Impossibilité d'évaluer actuellement la capacité de paiement de l'Allemagne.
(Projet Français)
3° Écroulement de tout le système établi par les Puissances Alliées et Associées et qui a trouvé son expression dans le Traité.
(Projet Français)

IV

Limitation des obligations de l'Allemagne en ce qui concerne les livraisons de bateaux, de charbon et de certaines matières premières.

1° Projet américain.—Admettre le principe des limitations fournies à cet égard des chiffres et des précisions dans la réponse aux propositions allemandes.

(Projet Duller [*sic*]).

2° Projet anglo-français.—Accepter pour l'avenir d'examiner dans un esprit pratique et conciliateur les propositions que pourrait formuler l'Allemagne.

(Projet LOUCHEUR et certains éléments,
Note Lord SUMNER).

V

Armée d'occupation.

1° Projet américain.—Fixer et communiquer à l'Allemagne un chiffre maximum du coût d'entretien des armées d'occupation.

(Traité Duller [*sic*]).

2° Projet franco-anglais.—Refus de discuter cette question dans la note transmise à l'Allemagne.

Par contre elle peut et doit faire l'objet de délibération interalliée.

DOCUMENT 403

Separate Recommendations of the American Delegates Regarding the Reply to the German Observations, June 8, 1919

[TPG, VIII, 95.]

[*Contents of present document largely embodied in Documents 404 and 405. Americans unable to concur in majority recommendations for following reasons: (1) Believe it unwise to discuss principles of matter as controversial as subject like reparation; would frame reply showing Allied intentions as to powers of Commission. (2) Feel formal defense of machinery now may make later simplification difficult. (3) Want fixed sum as basis of credit and as incentive for Germany to work. (4) Would give definite assurances on retention of working capital, operation of options, and cost of Army of Occupation.*]

DOCUMENT 404

Preliminary Copy of the Report of the Reparation Experts to the Supreme Council Regarding the Reply to the German Observations, June 8, 1919

[TPG. VIII, 91-94. "Report of the Reparation Commission to the Supreme Council."]

[*Erratically typed by a French stenographer. As directed by letter of June 4, Committee met on June 6 and 7 and examined three principal objections: (1) that powers of Reparation Commission were objectionable, (2) that no fixed sum in Treaty, (3) that*]

*certain deliveries and cost of Army of Occupation were objectionable. As to (1), unan-
imous in pointing out that Germans have misinterpreted. As to (2) and (3):*

*[(I) British and French agree that impossible now to estimate damage, that would
be willing to have Germany make offer, that Germany's capacity impossible to determine
now. Americans dissent; would frame reply showing Allied intentions. Americans
want fixed sum of 120 milliard marks as basis of credit and as incentive for Germany
to work.*

*[(II) Americans would give definite assurances on retention of working capital,
operation of options, and cost of Army of Occupation. British and French feel unwise
to volunteer offers at present.*

*[(III) Italians would leave questions of fixed sum, deliveries, and Army of Occupa-
tion to future. Japanese object to fixing sum that will not both be accepted and satisfy
claims in full; oppose any retention of ships.]*

DOCUMENT 405

Report of the Reparation Experts to the Supreme Council Regarding the Reply to the German Observations, June 8, 1919

[TPG, VIII, 108-11. "Report of the Reparation Commission to the Supreme
Council." This is apparently the final report as it was sent to the Council. It is a
carbon copy in American typewriting. An earlier text, June 8, not printed, but
practically identical with the present one, was typed very erratically by a French
stenographer (see Document 404). There is also a draft of separate American
recommendations, June 8, also not printed, which is the text from which several
of the paragraphs dealing with American objections in Document 404 and in
the present draft were derived (see Document 403).

This American draft is as follows (see Document 403):

"The American Delegates have submitted a separate recommendation as to the
reply which in their opinion should be made to the German counter reply on Reparations. They have felt unable to concur in the recommendations of the majority
report for the following principal reasons:

"1) It is believed to be unwise to enter into a discussion of principle with reference to a matter as controversial as reparations.

"[*inserted in pencil*] The proposed American reply does not contemplate any
changes in the text of the conditions of peace. . . . [*The rest of this penciled insertion
appears slightly altered in the present document as paragraph 2 of part I.*]

"2) It is felt that any formal defense of the machinery established by the present
clauses, leaving amounts, times and modes of payment in uncertitude, will prove
embarrassing in the event, in the near future, an effort is made to simplify the
machinery and fix a sum.

"3) It is believed that a fixed sum should be named now. . . . [*The rest of this
section appears in the present document as paragraph 3 of part I.*]

"4) It is believed that definite assurances should be given with reference to:
(a) the powers and duties of the Commission, as not involving any vexatious interference in Germany's internal affairs; (b) the retention by Germany. . . . [*The rest
of this section appears slightly altered in the present document as paragraph 1 of
part II.*]"]

Mr. President:

As directed in your letter dated 4th of June 1919 the Committee
met on June 6 and 7 to draft a reply to the German comments on

the reparation clauses contained in the letter of count Brockdorff-Rantzau dated 29th May 1919.

They examined particularly the three principal objections:

1—That the constitution and powers of the Reparation Commission were objectionable;
2—That the clauses named no fixed sum as the amount of liability of Germany;
3—That they took objections to the deliveries of certain articles and to the cost of the army of occupation.

As to (1) in pointing out that the comments on the Reparation Commission were founded on misconceptions of the meaning and effect of the clauses, the Delegations were unanimous.

As to (2) and (3)

I

The Delegations of France and Great Britain were prepared to concur in a reply to the following effect: (1) that it was impossible to fix the amount of the liability of Germany now, because the damage done was so vast, so various and so recent that it could not yet be calculated correctly; that in matters of such magnitude errors would either gravely prejudice the sufferers or result in serious overcharge against Germany; and they considered that they had no right to resort to mere conjectures in a matter of such vast importance; (2) that the Allied and Associated Powers, through the Commission, would in their own interest be willing to consider any bona fide proposals made by Germany, whereby the amount might be more readily fixed or agreed, or any other useful proposal purpose might be served and that it was competent to Germany to present arguments, evidence or proposals by nominating a commission or otherwise as she may think fit;[1] (3) further, as to the financial capacity of Germany, at present little more can be done than to hazard a hypothesis. Like all the other belligerent Powers, Germany is still living under an exceptional regime. The rate and extent of her recovery cannot at present be forecasted, but the period mentioned in the treaty was chosen in order to give time for the national economy to adapt itself to the new situation. The substitution of a sum fixed now by an arbitrary hypothesis for the system established by the treaty after very full and arduous discussion appears to be very undesirable, and to abandon without any sufficient advantage a plan which secured to Germany the opportunity and the right to be heard and to have decision taken in accordance with equity.

[1] Something seems to have been left out of this sentence, but the present wording is the same as that of the earlier, erratic text.

The Delegation of the United States declined to concur in such a reply. The proposed American reply does not contemplate any change in the text of the conditions of peace. It should take the form of a statement of intentions of the Allied and Associated Governments with reference to directing the activities of the Commission and indicate the spirit which animates these Governments.

The American Delegation believes that a fixed sum should be named now. The U. S. proposal contemplates a reply containing a finding that the total damage under the categories will approximate 120 milliards of marks gold, which, for practical reasons, is accepted as a maximum of Germany's liability. The American delegates have been convinced, not by German arguments, but by current developments of the soundness of their original view that, in the interest of the *Allies,* Germany's reparation liability should be limited *now* to a definite amount which there is reason to believe Germany can pay. Only in this way can there be secured what the world instantly requires, a new basis of credit. Only under such conditions is it reasonable to expect that Germany will put forward those efforts which are indispensable to create a value behind what are otherwise paper obligations.

II

The American Delegation believes that definite assurances should be given with reference to (a) the retention by Germany of certain amounts of working capital in the form of ships, gold, and investments abroad; (b) the operation of the coal and chemical options, and the possibility of Germany securing minette ore; (c) the intentions of the Allied and Associated Governments as to the cost of the army of occupation which Germany is to support. The American Delegation expresses its view that vagueness on these subjects will react to produce the contrary impression to what may be desired. Unless, therefore, these subjects are susceptible of specific treatment, they question whether they should be alluded to at all.

On the other hand the Delegations of Great Britain and France oppose themselves to these concessions, not only upon grounds connected with the terms of the proposals themselves, but also because they believe it to be unwise and inopportune for the Allied and Associated Powers to volunteer particular offers under present circumstances, especially as Germany has made no definite offer at all. They think that nothing is to be gained and much may be lost by such an attitude.

III

1—The Italian Delegation agrees with the English and French Delegations in thinking that it is impossible to fix in a document such as is now in preparation the total amount of Germany's liability. They believe, however, that it shall be wise at a future and early date to fix by negotiations with Germany a definite sum.

About Germany's requests concerning the delivery of ships and raw materials, the Italian Delegation thinks that it shall belong to the Reparation Commission to take such requests into account in so far as it shall think them equitable, and that the said Commission disposes to that effect of all necessary Powers.

Further they believe that the delimitation of the cost of the army of occupation should be the matter of later negotiations.

2—The Japanese Delegation desires it to be reported that they concur in objecting to any sum being fixed, if it will not both be accepted by Germany and satisfy the reparation claims in full. Further they oppose any proposal for the retention of any ships.

DOCUMENT 406

Fourth American Proposed Reply to the German Observations, June 8, 1919

[TPG, VIII, 96-101. "Reparation. U. S. Project for Reply to German Counter Proposals."]

[*Derived from Document 398, with minor and drafting amendments; and also: Statement that principles prepared with scrupulous regard for Pre-Armistice Agreement. Severer judgment on German misinterpretations. Footnote that 120 milliard sum could be increased by giving Germany credit for property and war debt attaching to ceded territory. Omission of provision by which Germany could make definite offer within 4 months; but still may offer proposals for reparation by means of German labor. Retained ship tonnage reduced from 33 to 30 percent. No gold required for reparation at present time. Last paragraph saying conditions are reasonable and just and that Germans have clearly misinterpreted them.*]

DOCUMENT 407

Fifth American Proposed Reply to the German Observations, June 9, 1919

[TPG, VIII, 103-7. "Reparation. U. S. Project for Reply to German Counter-Proposals." On an extra title-page at the beginning of this document (p. 102) is written: "Copy handed President on June 9, 1919—at conference with Baruch, Davis, Lamont, McC., & J. F. D." Document 398 precedes. A Fourth American Proposed Reply of June 8 (see Document 406) intervenes but is not printed. *Except as shown by footnotes and except for a few unimportant differences, this intervening draft is identical with the present draft*. Document 412 follows. A Sixth American Proposed Reply of June 10 (see Document 411) intervenes but is not printed. *Except as shown by footnotes, this intervening draft is identical with the present draft.*]

The Allied and Associated Governments, [consistent to] their policy already [enunciated,] decline to enter into a discussion of the principles underlying the Reparation Clauses of the Conditions of Peace, which [had] been prepared with scrupulous regard for the correspondence leading up to the Armistice of November 11, 1918.[1]

To the extent that your reply deals with practical phases of the execution of the principles enunciated in the Conditions of Peace, you appear to proceed on the basis of a complete misapprehension, which is more difficult to understand as the inferences you draw and the statements which you make are wholly at variance with both the letter and [with] the spirit of the Treaty clauses. In order, however, that there may be no possible excuse for misunderstanding, and for purposes of clarification, the Allied and Associated Governments submit the following observations:[2]

The vast extent and manifold character of the damage caused to the Allied and Associated Governments in consequence of the war, [have] created a reparation problem of extraordinary magnitude and complexity, only to be solved by a continuing body, limited in personnel and invested with broad powers to deal with the problem in relation to the general economic situation. The

---

[1] The first paragraph of the intervening Fourth American Proposed Reply of June 8 reads:

"On May 10th you were advised that the Allied and Associated Governments would not engage in any discussion of the principles underlying the Conditions of Peace, which had been prepared with scrupulous regard for the correspondence leading up to the Armistice of November 11, 1918. This communication you appear singularly to have ignored and in your counter proposals you attempt again to open a discussion relative to fundamental questions of principle involving Germany's liability for reparation. The Allied and Associated Governments, consistent to their policy already enunciated, again decline to enter into a discussion with you on questions of principle."

The second paragraph of this intervening draft is practically the same as that of the present draft.

[2] The first two paragraphs of the intervening Sixth American Proposed Reply of June 10 read:

"The Allied and Associated Governments decline to enter into a discussion of the principles underlying the Reparation Clauses of the Conditions of Peace, which have been prepared with scrupulous regard for the correspondence leading up to the Armistice of November 11, 1918.

"To the extent that your reply deals with practical phases of the execution of the principles enunciated in the Conditions of Peace, you appear to proceed on the basis of a complete misapprehension. The inferences which you draw and the statements which you make are, indeed, so fundamentally at variance with both the letter and with the spirit of the Treaty clauses that it is difficult to avoid the conclusion that this portion of your reply proceeds not from a sincere effort at real comprehension, but rather from a conscious desire to present for public effect a grotesque caricature of the Reparation Commission to be established pursuant to the Conditions of Peace. In order, however, that there may be no possible excuse for misunderstanding, and for purposes of clarification, the Allied and Associated Governments submit the following observations:"

Allied and Associated Powers recognizing this situation, them-selves propose to delegate power and authority to [the] Reparation Commission. The Reparation Commission is, however, instructed by the Treaty itself so to exercise and interpret its powers as to insure, in the interest of all, as early and complete discharge by Germany of her reparation obligations as is consistent with the [due] maintenance of the social, economic and financial structure of a Germany earnestly striving to exercise her full power to repair the loss and damage she has caused.

The provisions of Article 241 are not to be misconstrued as giving the Commission power to dictate the domestic legis-lation of Germany. Nor does Paragraph 12 (b), of Annex II, give the Commission power to prescribe or enforce taxes or to dictate the character of the German budget. [The Commission is required to inform itself as to the German system of taxation and of the character of the German budget, only] in order that it may intelligently and constructively exercise the discretion accorded it in Germany's interest particularly by Article 234. The provisions of Article 240 are similar in character and purpose and there should be [no] occasion for the exercise of these powers [after May 1, 1921,] if Germany is in a position to, and does, comply with the schedule of payments which then will have been notified to her and with the specifc provisions of the several Annexes relative to reparation in kind. It is further to be observed that the power of modification accorded by the said Article 236 [*234*][3] is expressly designed to permit of a modification *in Germany's interest* of a schedule of payments which events may demonstrate to be beyond Germany's reasonable capacity.

[The purposes for which the powers granted to the Commission are to be utilized are plainly indicated on the face of the Treaty, and] the Allied and Associated Powers vigorously reject the sug-gestion that the Commission, in exercising the power conferred by Article 240 and by Paragraphs 2, 3 and 4 of Annex IV [*VI*],[4] might require the divulgence of trade secrets and similar confidential data.

It is understood that the action necessary to give effect to the pro-visions of Annex IV, relative to reparation in kind, will be taken by Germany on its own initiative, after receipt of notification from the Reparation Commission.

The provisions of the Treaty are in no wise incompatible with the

[3] This error was introduced in the intervening Fourth American Proposed Reply of June 8 and was not corrected thereafter.

[4] See note 3 above.

creation by Germany of a commission which will represent Germany in dealings with the Reparation Commission and which will constitute an instrumentality for such cooperation as may be necessary. The Treaty specifically and repeatedly provides opportunities for the German Government to present facts and arguments with respect to claims and modes of payments, within the limits of the principles and express provisions of the Treaty. This may be done through a commission and no reason is perceived as to why such a commission could not work in harmony with the Reparation Commission. Certainly this is greatly to be desired.

[The Allied and Associated Governments, after examining the considerable data which is available, have unanimously reached the conclusion that the total damage under Annex I, when estimated on a gold basis, will approximate the principal sum of 120 milliards of marks gold. These Governments recognize the desirability from every aspect that Germany's liability be rendered as precise as circumstances will permit and that the benefits to follow from any reasonable and prompt decision in this respect will greatly outweigh any loss consequent upon a possible error in estimation. Accordingly, the sum of 120 milliards* of marks gold may be regarded as an accepted maximum of the damage for which Germany is liable in accordance with Article 232.[5] Inasmuch as the damage specified in Annex I includes damage caused by the former Allies of Germany, any sums received from Germany's former Allies will be credited against Germany's liability. Further, while not recognizing any right of contribution as between Germany and her former Allies, the Reparation Commission will give to the Government of Germany an opportunity to present such facts as that Government deems relevant as to the capacity of payment of Germany's former Allies.]

[Germany proposes to assist in the restoration of the devastated areas by supplying labor. The Allied and Associated Governments had not desired to stipulate for German labor lest they be charged with demanding forced labor. The principle, however, of the general application of Germany's entire economic resources to reparation, is consecrated by Article 236 and the provisions of Paragraph 19

---

* This sum might be still further increased were Germany given credit for various property to be taken from her without payment (e.g. in the Colonies) and were Germany further given credit for portions of war debt attaching to ceded territory. To give such credit appears just in principle.

---

[5] In the intervening Sixth American Proposed Reply of June 10, the first three sentences of this paragraph were omitted.

of Annex II authorize the Reparation Commission to accept payment in various forms. It is thus within the plain contemplation
of the Conditions of Peace that Germany may address direct proposals to the Reparation Commission for the supplying of German
labor for reparation purposes.][6]

[The Allied and Associated Governments do not ignore the economic needs of Germany. To do so would be contrary not only to
their own material interests but to the spirit which has animated
them in the preparation of the Conditions of Peace and of which
ample evidence is to be found. The Commission is instructed in all
of its activities to take into account the social and economic requirements of Germany. In furtherance of such general instructions
specific instructions are now in preparation[7] directing the Commission to permit the retention by Germany for two years of ships,
designated by the Commission, representing 30 per cent in tonnage
of the total amount of ships referred to in Paragraph 1 of Annex III.
These ships, the delivery of which is to be deferred, will be available
for use by Germany to meet her economic needs and to assist in
the fulfillment of Germany's external obligations. The Commission
will similarly receive detailed instructions to apply the provisions
of Article 235 so as to permit the retention by Germany at home
and abroad of certain amounts of working capital and so that for
the present no gold will be required to be delivered by Germany for
reparation purposes.]

[6] In the intervening Sixth American Proposed Reply of June 10, the last two sentences of this paragraph were omitted. In their place appeared additional material so that the whole paragraph then read
as follows:

"Germany proposes to assist in the restoration of the devastated areas by supplying labor. The Allied
and Associated Governments had not desired to stipulate for German labor lest they be charged with
demanding forced labor. In view, however, of the proposal of Germany, the Reparation Commission
will be instructed to invite and to consider, within four months after the signature of the Treaty, a
definite proposal by Germany to undertake herself the restoration of substantial portions of the devastated areas of Belgium and France, and concurrently therewith a proposal from Germany for a cash
settlement of so much of the Categories of Damage as the interested Allied and Associated Governments will not desire to have repaired through such physical reconstruction by Germany. Germany
will be accorded all suitable facilities to permit of her making such a proposal in acceptable form. The
offer to be made by Germany in accordance with the foregoing would be made within four months of the
signature of the Treaty and would be open for acceptance or rejection for two months after its receipt
by the Reparation Commission. In the event of rejection the regular procedure provided for by the
Treaty would be followed."

This text will be recognized as directly derived from the plan of Loucheur's Revise of June 6 (see
Document 396).

[7] In the intervening Sixth American Proposed Reply of June 10, this sentence began: "In furtherance
of such general instructions and in accordance with the advice of experts with respect to the retention
by Germany of certain instrumentalities which will facilitate Germany's discharge of her reparation
obligations, specific instructions are now in preparation [etc.]"

[With reference to the provisions of Annexes V and VI, it is, of course, understood that the options therein referred to will be exercised exclusively to meet the domestic requirements of the country exercising the option. In further precision of the general principle above referred to enunciated by the Allied and Associated Governments for the guidance of the Commission, additional detailed instructions are in preparation, advising the Commission that to avoid any possibility of interference with the economic and industrial life of Germany the option for delivery of coal to France will, for the first year, be exercised as to 50 per cent only of the maximum amounts mentioned and that deliveries should commence with small monthly amounts, gradually increasing.]

[The Government of France has always contemplated that an arrangement would be made for the exchange of minette ore on mutually acceptable conditions.]

[With reference to the cost of maintaining the Army of Occupation, it is impossible for obvious reasons for the Allied and Associated Governments to make any commitment which would operate to limit the size of such army. The Allied and Associated Governments, however, perceive no reason for not advising the German Government that it is their hope and expectation that it will be unnecessary for such army to be of a size such that the cost of maintenance would exceed 240 millions of marks per annum.]

The foregoing should suffice to demonstrate the reasonableness of the conditions under which Germany is to discharge her reparation obligations, and how utterly unfounded are the criticisms of the German reply. These are, indeed, explicable only on the theory that the German plenipotentiaries have read into the Conditions of Peace, in clear [defiance] of their express terms, an intent which it would be not unnatural to see evidenced by victorious nations which have been the victims of cruelty and devastation on a vast and premeditated scale. The burdens of Germany undeniably are heavy, but they are imposed under conditions of justice by peoples whose social well-being and economic prosperity have been gravely impaired by wrongs which it is beyond the utmost power of Germany to repair.

DOCUMENT 408

Report of the Meeting of the Council of Four, June 9, 1919

[Slosson's Annotations, in Miller, XIX, 280-81.]

This question [of fixing a definite figure (see the Report of June 8, Document 405)] was further debated on June 9 (C. F. 54). The United States Delegation proposed the following concessions to Germany (C. F. 54, Appendix I and Appendix II):

The fixing of 120 milliards of gold marks as the maximum of Germany's liability.

Assurances to Germany that she might retain a certain amount of working capital in the form of ships, gold and foreign investments.

Arrangements for assuring coal, chemicals and minette ore in sufficient quantity for Germany's needs.

Assurances to Germany as to the maximum cost of the army of occupation which Germany is to support.

The other Delegations refused to accept the American recommendations on these points. The Commission on Reparations reported this divergence of view to the Supreme Council.

Mr. Lloyd George said that he was confident that it was impossible at the present date to fix a figure which would satisfy public opinion either in Allied or enemy countries. For example, the French Government could not afford to accept a sum for the reconstruction of devastated regions which public opinion would consider inadequate, but when a detailed survey had been made it might be found that a small [*smaller?*] sum would suffice for the work than was now considered possible. For the Supreme Council to fix a definite figure in the limited time at its disposal and with so many other questions pressing for immediate decision "is like asking a man in the maelstrom of Niagara to fix the price of a horse."

President Wilson said that personally he was satisfied with the reparations arrangements of the Treaty, provided it was properly explained to the Germans, but the important thing was to induce the Germans to make peace quickly and if the concession of naming a definite sum, even arbitrarily, would reassure the Germans the concession was worth making. It was also important to leave the Germans sufficient assets to start their trade again and to bear the burden of reparations; "he could not ask the United States bankers to give credit if Germany had no assets." "The only argument in favor of fixing a sum was to provide a basis for credit. Supposing that the sum were fixed at twenty-five billion dollars, the financial world could then form a judgment. If it was thought that Germany could pay this sum, many would be willing to lend to her on the strength of the bonds to be issued under the reparation scheme in the Treaty."

Mr. Lloyd George said that he thought the American concessions were in excess of what was necessary.

DOCUMENT 409

Report from the Chairman of the Finance Commission to the President of the Peace Conference Regarding the Reply to the German Observations, June 9, 1919

[TPG, VIII, 128-29. Mimeographed. An extra copy, *ibid.*, pp. 130-31.]

The Secretariat General of the Peace Conference transmitted to the Finance Commission on June 5 a resolution of the Supreme Council, asking the commissions interested to submit to it on Monday morning [June 9] a memorandum treating in detail the special questions examined in the German remarks on the Peace conditions.

The Finance Committee was of the opinion that it should limit its examination solely to those observations of Annex II of the German remarks which refer to the clauses contained in Part IX of the Treaty with Germany (Financial Clauses).

The drafting of the Financial Clauses did not proceed by a single plan and a general method; it seems difficult even to group several articles under a single category. The Finance Commission has thought therefore that it was preferable not to try to present an expose of all the principles that had guided it in the working out of the various clauses, and that it was better to examine the articles one after the other.

Nevertheless, the Commission has thought it necessary to recall at the beginning of its reply that Germany will have to assume very heavy burdens, and that these burdens entail obligations and restrictions, which Germany can not escape, whatever effort may be made to take her interests into consideration.

The Finance Commission has tried to reply to the German observations, but it has tried especially to explain and to justify the stipulations inserted in the Treaty.

The examination of the articles, and the observations presented concerning them, has led the Finance Commission to submit to the Supreme Council the following remarks:

Articles 248 and 251, which establish a first charge on all the assets and revenues of the Empire and the German states for the settlement of reparation and other charges resulting from the Treaty, have called forth very vigorous remarks from the German Delegation, to which the Finance Commission proposes to give partial satisfaction by providing the Reparation Commission with the power to grant exceptions to the charge. This provision already appears in the draft of the Treaty with Austria.—The Finance Commission thinks that the maintenance of the privilege stipulated in Article 248 is indispensable to allow the Reparation Commission to exercise the prerogatives accorded to it in Part VIII. The suppression of this first charge could not be considered unless the methods at present provided for the payment of reparation were entirely changed.

Article 249 lays the cost of the Armies of Occupation on Germany.

The Finance Commission thinks that from the financial point of view solely, it would be advantageous to prevent the amount to be paid by Germany on this score from reaching too high a figure in proportion to the amount to be devoted to reparation. The Commission realizes that the financial point of view is not the only one to be considered, but it thinks that it would be advantageous to define the cost of the Armies of Occupation better, and to limit it if possible.

Signed: KENGO MORI.

DOCUMENT 410

Extract from P. W. Slosson, "Considerations on the Difficulty of Making a Peace Treaty," Undated

[From the typed original in the Edward M. House Collection, Yale University Library, New Haven, Connecticut. Professor Slosson writes:

"The memorandum you quote is undoubtedly part of a general article, a carbon (my only copy) of which I enclose herewith, prepared during the Peace Conference, probably in May or June 1919, tho I find no date to it. It was certainly not intended for the use of the American Peace Delegation itself, being quite general in character. I think it was intended as material for publicity, as indicating a line of defence which might be taken against that portion of the press which was criticizing the delay in completing peace negotiations. No doubt it was prepared at Professor Shotwell's request. Whether it was ever used or not I cannot tell." (Letter to the editor, January 17, 1937.)

Professor Shotwell has referred in his Diary to the preparation by himself of certain memoranda for Colonel House in the second week of June, 1919. One of these, concerning the difficulties of making a treaty, is very close in its subject matter to the present document. As Professor Slosson was at the time the assistant of Professor Shotwell, it is as good a guess as any to say that the present document was drawn up about the same time as Professor Shotwell's paper. That would put it about June 10 and later. See James T. Shotwell, *At the Paris Peace Conference* (New York: The Macmillan Company, 1937), pp. 366-67.]

The problem of exacting the necessary indemnity to rebuild the victim countries.

Then there is the question of indemnities. It is not be questioned by anyone who knows the facts that heavy indemnities—heavy beyond precedent—must be exacted from the enemy on behalf of those nations whose most fertile lands and most prosperous cities have been the battleground for more than four years of unremitting combat. If this is not done, even the victorious nations may be crushed by the financial burden of reconstruction coming on top of all the burdens of the war itself. Yet these essential indemnities must be exacted from nations themselves exhausted by stress of war and brought to the verge of bankruptcy by civil war and internal disorder of every kind consequent upon defeat.

How shall Germany pay? A payment in money must be inadequate. A payment in goods or in labor may create unemployment in Allied countries.

Some would say: "Take German gold." But there is not in all Germany, perhaps not in all the world, enough coined money to pay what should be expected from Germany to her victims. Wealth is a much broader and more complicated matter than "money," and we must mobilize Germany's productive power to exact an indemnity worth the collection. Shall Germany pay in goods? Certainly; but here, too, is a danger. We must not discourage the industries of the Allied and Associated nations by taking all that is needed from the German factories. How would Belgium profit if Essen rebuilt Louvain while Brussels workmen tramped the street under the banner of the unemployed? Shall Germany pay in labor? But here the same danger again confronts us, that the enemy shall compete in the labor market to the detriment of the workers of the nation which it is designed to benefit. All these factors must be weighed before the best method of levying the indemnity can be found.

DOCUMENT 411

Sixth American Proposed Reply to the German Observations, June 10, 1919

[TPG, VIII, 112–17. "Reparation. U. S. Project for Reply to German Counter-Proposals."]

[*Derived from Document 407, with differences: Preamble suggests deliberate German intention of presenting "grotesque caricature" of Commission. Omits provision for fixed sum, but retains provision that Germany will be credited with any sums received from her allies. Reinsertion of provision by which Germany may make offer for restoration and definite figure for balance within 4 months.*]

DOCUMENT 412

Proposed Reply of the Supreme Council to the German Observations, June 10, 1919

[TPG, VIII, 119–24. "Secret. Reparation. Project for Reply to German Counter Proposals."

Document 407 precedes. A Sixth American Proposed Reply of June 10 (see Document 411) intervenes but is not printed. *Except as shown by footnotes in the preceding draft, this intervening draft is identical with the preceding.* Document 429 follows. The present draft may be the "memorandum prepared by Lord Sumner," referred to in the opening sentence of Document 413.]

The Allied and Associated [Governments,] consistently with their policy already expressed, decline to enter into a discussion of the principles underlying the Reparation Clauses of the Conditions of Peace, which have been prepared with scrupulous regard for the correspondence leading up to the Armistice of November 11th, 1918, the final memorandum of which dated 5th November, 1918, contains the following words:—

"Further, in the conditions of Peace laid down in his address to Congress of the 8th January, 1918, the President declared that the invaded territories must be restored as well as evacuated and freed, and the Allied Governments feel that no doubt ought to be allowed to exist as to what this provision implies. By it they understand that compensation will be made by Germany for all damage done to the civilian population of the Allies and their property by the aggression of Germany by land, by sea and from the air."

To the extent that [your] reply deals with practical phases of the execution of the principles enunciated in the Conditions of Peace, you appear to proceed on the basis of a complete misapprehension, which is the more difficult to understand as the inferences [you draw] and the statements [which you make] are wholly at variance with both the letter and the spirit of the Treaty Clauses. For purposes of clarification, however, and in order that there may be no possible [excuse] for misunderstanding, the Allied and Associated [Governments] submit the following observations:—

The vast extent and manifold character of the damage caused to the Allied and Associated [Governments] in consequence of the war, [had] created a reparation problem of extraordinary magnitude and complexity, only to be solved by a continuing body, limited in personnel and invested with broad powers to deal with the problem in relation to the general economic situation. The Allied and Associated Powers, recognizing this situation, themselves propose to delegate power and authority to a Reparation Commission. This Reparation Commission is, however, instructed by the Treaty itself so to exercise and interpret its powers as to ensure in the interest of all, [as] early and complete [a] discharge by Germany of her reparation obligations [as is consistent with the] maintenance of the social, economic and financial structure of a Germany earnestly striving to exercise her full power to repair the loss and damage she has caused.

The provisions of Article 241, by which the German Government is to invest itself with such powers as may be needed to carry out its obligations, are not to be misconstrued as giving the Commission power to dictate the domestic legislation of Germany. Nor does paragraph 12 (b), of Annex II, give the Commission power to prescribe or enforce taxes or to dictate the character of the German Budget, [but] it is to examine the latter for two specified purposes. This is necessary in order that it may intelligently and constructively exercise the discretion accorded it in Germany's interest particularly by Article 234, with regard to extending the date and modifying the form of payments. The provisions of Article 240 with regard to the supply of information are similar in character and purpose and there should be little occasion for the exercise of these powers when once the amount of the liability of Germany is fixed, if Germany is in a position to, and does, comply with the schedule of payments which then will have been notified to her and with the specific provisions of the several Annexes relative to reparation in kind. It is further to be observed that the power of modification accorded by the said Article 236 [*234*] is expressly designed to permit of a modification *in Germany's interest* of a schedule of payments which events may demonstrate to be beyond Germany's reasonable capacity. The Allied and Associated Powers vigorously reject the suggestion that the Commission, in exercising the power conferred by Article 240 and by Paragraphs 2, 3 and 4 of Annex IV [*VI*], might require the divulgence of trade secrets and similar confidential data.

The observations of the German Delegation present a view of this Commission so [unjustified] and so inexact, that it is difficult to believe that the clauses of the Treaty have been calmly or carefully examined. It is not an engine of oppression or a device for interfering with German Sovereignty. It has no forces which it commands; it has no executive powers within the territory of Germany; it cannot, as is suggested, direct or control the educational or other systems of the country. Its business is to fix what is to be paid; to satisfy itself that Germany can pay; and to report to the Powers, whose Delegation it is, in case Germany makes default. If Germany raises the money required in her own way, the Commission cannot order that it shall be raised in some other way; if Germany offers a payment in kind, the Commission may accept such payment, but, except as specified in the Treaty itself, the Commission cannot require such a payment. The observations [of the German plenipotentiaries] appear to miss the point that the Commission is directed to study the German system of taxation equally for the protection of the German people [and] for the protection of their own. Such study is not inquisitorial, for the German system of taxation is not an object of curiosity to other powers, nor is a knowledge of it an end in itself. If any plea of inability which the German Government may advance is to be properly considered, such a study is necessary. The Commission must test whether a sincere application is being given to the principle, accepted in the observations, "that the German taxation system should impose in general on the taxpayer at least as great a burden as those prevailing in the most heavily burdened of the States represented on the Reparation Commission." If the German resources are to be properly weighed, the first subject of inquiry, [and perhaps the first ground for relief,] will be the German fiscal burden.

It is understood that the action necessary to give effect to the provisions of Annex IV, relative to reparation in kind, will be taken by Germany on its own initiative, after receipt of notification from the Reparation Commission.

The provisions of the Treaty are in no wise incompatible with the creation by Germany of a Commission which will represent Germany in dealings with the Reparation Commission and which will constitute an instrumentality for such cooperation as may be necessary. The Treaty specifically and repeatedly provides opportunities for the German Government to present facts and arguments with respect to claims and modes of payments, within the limits of the principles and express provisions of the Treaty. This may be done through a Commission and no reason is perceived [as to] why such a commission could not work in harmony with the Reparation Commission. Certainly this is greatly to be desired.

Immediately after the Treaty is signed, Germany may present [forthwith] and the Allied and Associated Powers will receive and examine such evidence, estimates and arguments [in writing,] as she may think fit to present. Such documents need not be final but may be presented subject to corrections and additions.

At any time within four months of the signature of the Treaty, Germany shall be at liberty to submit, and the Allied and Associated Powers will receive and consider such proposals as Germany may choose to make. In particular, proposals will be [acceptable] on the following subjects and for the following purposes. Germany may offer a lump sum in settlement of her whole liability, or in settlement of her liability under any of the particular categories which have been decided upon and laid down. Germany may offer [to undertake to repair and reconstruct part or the whole of any damaged district, or] certain classes of damage in [each country] or in all the [countries] which have suffered. Germany may offer labour, materials or technical [assistance] for use in such work even though she does not [undertake to do] the work herself. She may suggest any practicable plan, category by category, or for the reparation as a whole, which will tend to shorten the period of enquiry and to bring about a prompt and effectual conclusion. Without making further specifications, it may be said in a word that Germany is at liberty to make any suggestion or offer of a practical and reasonable character for the purposes of simplifying the assessment of the damage, eliminating any question or questions from the scope of the detailed enquiry, promoting the performance of the work and accelerating the definition of the ultimate amount to be paid. [Two] conditions [and two only] are imposed upon the tender of these proposals. [Firstly, they] must be unambiguous, [they] must be precise and clear, [and they must be practical.] [Secondly,] they must accept the categories and the reparation clauses as matters settled beyond discussion. The Allied and Associated Powers will not entertain arguments or appeals directed to any alteration. The Allied and Associated Powers have to remark that in the Observations submitted the German Delegation has made no definite offer at all but only vague expressions of willingness to do something undefined, [and that the one suggestion, namely, as to the payment of £5,000,000,000 [100 milliard marks], which appears to be expressed in concrete terms, is so hedged about with conditions and qualifications as to appear to be more apt to provoke controversy than to promote peace.][1]

Within two months thereafter the Allied and Associated Powers will, so far as may be possible, return their answer to [the above] proposals. It is impossible to declare in advance that they will be accepted, and if accepted, they [will be subject] to proper conditions, which can be discussed and arranged. The Allied and Associated Powers, however, declare that such proposals will be seriously and fairly considered; no one could be better pleased than they, [no one could profit more than they,] if, in the result, a fair, a speedy and a practical settlement were arrived at. The questions are bare questions of fact, namely, the amount of the liabilities, and they are susceptible of being treated in this way. Beyond this, the Powers cannot be asked to go. The Powers will, however, make a declaration on another point, as follows. The resumption of German industry involves access for German manufacturers to the necessary raw materials and provision for their transport to [German factories] from overseas. The resumption of German industry is an interest of the Allied and Associated Powers as well as an interest of Germany. They [recognize] this fact and therefore declare that they will not withhold from Germany the commercial [intercourse and assistance] without which this resumption cannot take place, but that, subject to conditions and within limits which cannot be laid down in advance, they are prepared to afford to Germany facilities in these directions for the common good.[2]

Even if no settlement were arrived at, it must be evident that the early production of the German evidence would greatly abbreviate

---

[1] In the following draft, this sentence is placed somewhat further along.

[2] The last four sentences of this paragraph are placed, in the following draft, somewhat further along.

the enquiry, and accelerate the decisions. [The information at present at hand comes from one side only. A great part of the damage done has been done by German hands in deliberate execution of German plans.] The German authorities have had long occupation of a large part of the damaged areas and have been over the ground, forwards and backwards, within the last twelve or fifteen months. [Their information must be extensive and exact.] The Allied and Associated Powers have as yet had no access to this mass of material. [The mere comparison of the evidence forthcoming on the one side and the other must greatly narrow the field of dispute and may eliminate dispute altogether.] It is obvious that, if the class of damage done in the devastated areas can be dealt with in this fashion, the liability under the other categories can be quickly established, for it depends on statistics and particulars of a far simpler character. By giving a satisfactory covenant to execute the work of rebuilding themselves, the Germans could at once dispose of the only difficult or long subject of inquiry.

Meanwhile, the draft Treaty must be accepted as definitive and must be signed. The Allied and Associated Powers cannot any longer delay to assure their security. Germany cannot afford to deny to her populations the peace which is offered to them. The Reparations Commission must be constituted and must commence its task. The only question open will be how best to execute the provisions of the Treaty.

The foregoing should suffice to demonstrate the reasonableness of the conditions under which Germany is to discharge her reparation obligations, and how utterly unfounded are the criticisms [of] the German reply. These are, indeed, explicable only on the theory that the German plenipotentiaries have read into the conditions of Peace in clear [contradiction] of their express terms, an [intent] which it would be not unnatural to see [evidenced] by victorious nations which have been the victims of cruelty and devastation on a vast and premeditated scale. The burdens of Germany undeniably are heavy, but they are imposed under conditions of justice by peoples whose social well-being and economic prosperity have been gravely impaired by wrongs which it is beyond the utmost power of Germany to repair.

Paris,   10th *May*, 1919.

?

DOCUMENT 413

Report of the Meeting of the Council of Four, June 10, 1919

[Slosson's Annotations, in Miller, XIX, 281–82.]

On June 10 Mr. Lloyd George presented a memorandum prepared by Lord Sumner,[1] which corresponds generally to the wording of the Reply of the Allied and Associated Powers to the Observations of the German Delegation on the Conditions of Peace, outlining a plan for permitting the German Government to make proposals for the method of reparations during the four months subsequent to the Treaty signature (C. F. 55).

M. Clemenceau said that he accepted it in principle.

In regard to the American proposal to permit Germany to retain 30% of her shipping tonnage, referred to in paragraph one of Annex III, for a period of two years, Mr. Lloyd George said that France had lost about a million tons of shipping during the war and would receive about 40,000 tons and Britain would receive from one to one and a half million tons to compensate for six and a half million tons lost during the war. If concessions were made every nation must contribute its share; the United States as well as Great Britain and France.

M. Clemenceau again spoke against fixing a definite sum of reparations. We could not be sure that a fixed sum would cover all the categories of damage for which it was agreed that Germany should be liable. To make excessive concessions would encourage the Germans to demand more.

President Wilson said that the American proposals were not made as surrender to Germany but in a spirit of co-operation with the Allies. If not acceptable, they could be withdrawn.

Mr. Lloyd George said that he agreed with President Wilson that a general proposal might be made that Germany should have access to raw materials, shipping facilities and other necessities for her industrial life, and he asked Lord Sumner to draft such a proposal. He admitted that his offer was more vague than the American proposals but he thought that a specific offer ran the risk of being incomplete.

The draft reply to the Germans on the subject of reparations was elaborated by the Council of Four and its expert advisers in a series of subsequent meetings (C. F. 57 [not earlier than June 10]; C. F. 58 [not earlier than June 10]; C. F. 61 [June 12]; C. F. 70 [June 16]; C. F. 76 [June 17-21]).

[1] This may be Document 412.

DOCUMENT 414

Letter from Lamont to McCormick, to Baruch, to Davis, and to Dulles, June 10, 1919

[TPG, VIII, 118.]

The President has sent in this proposed reply on Reparation, which has in general been adopted by the Big Four.[1] He is anxious to have us scan it tonight and make any suggestions that we may have by morning.

We will get together the first thing in the morning.

T.W.L.

DOCUMENT 415

Extract from Letter from Tardieu to House Regarding the Inadvisability of Changes in the Treaty with Germany, June 10, 1919

[From the signed original in the Edward M. House Collection, Yale University Library, New Haven, Connecticut. The typing of this letter is liberally corrected with pen and ink; and a small piece of letter paper is attached, on which is written by hand: "I apologize for a very bad copy   Cordially A. T."

A French version of this letter has appeared in Tardieu, pp. 134-36; English translation, pp. 121-22. The published English version (also in House, IV, 476-78), being undoubtedly a translation from the French, differs in wording but not in sense from what Tardieu sent to House.]

My dear Colonel House,

I believe, as I told you this morning, that, for the last eight days, great mistakes have been made and that we are still just in time to retrieve them.

For nearly five months, the heads of the Governments and their experts have studied the conditions of peace to be offered to Germany. They have agreed together, and they have communicated to the Germans a draft by which in any case and obviously they [sic] allies are bound, if Mr. Von BROCKDORFF is not.

Have they supposed that this draft of conditions should gratify Germany? Certainly not. All the same, they have adopted it. Germany is raising a protest, as expected. At once, there is an attempt to modify this draft.

.   .   .

Therefore on the general principle, this is my opinion: One ought, eight days ago, to have answered to the Germans: "We shall

[1] Probably Document 412.

not change anything." Should this have been the answer, by now the treaty would have been signed. This has not been done. To-day, what shall we do?

On the special points, about which modifications are being studied, what is the situation?

Reparation? The British, who brought forth the first proposal of a modification, are to-day with us against any modification, and your delegation is offering, (with other changes which France would not possibly accept), the figure of 120 billions,[1] which, as far as France is concerned, would not even amount to one half[2] of that kind of damages, the reparation of which is exacted from Germany by the draft of May 7th.

.   .   .

You know, dear friend, that I have always talked with you outspokenly. That is why I have wished to sum up in this letter our recent interviews.

Believe me, with high regard,

Very truly yours[3]

[*signed*] André Tardieu.

DOCUMENT 416

Memorandum Suggested by the American Reparation Experts as a Supplement to the Proposed Reply of the Supreme Council, Undated

[TPG, VIII, 127. "Reparation." The probable date of this memorandum is derived from the covering letter of June 11 (see Document 417).]

1. Germany is to be allowed to retain for two years tonnage (not to exceed 30% of total German tonnage) necessary for her import of food and raw materials. The Reparation Commission will be instructed accordingly.

2. The Reparation Commission will be instructed not to require the surrender by Germany before May 1, 1921, of any gold in payment of reparation and the Reparation Commission shall also permit Germany to retain the working capital requisite for compliance with her reparation obligations.

3. France will for the first year exercise the coal option given to her to the extent only of 50% of the maximum amount.

4. The options on chemicals and dye-stuffs[1] are to be availed

---

[1] The published versions read 125.   [2] The published versions read two-thirds.   [3] In handwriting.

[1] A written amendment makes this read: "The options on coal, chemicals and dye-stuffs [etc.]"

of only for the domestic use of the Allied and Associated Governments.

5. France will permit Germany to obtain minette ore under equitable conditions as to price, deliveries, etc.

6. The expenses of the Army of Occupation will be held to a minimum and, except in case of emergency, the charge to Germany on account thereof should not exceed 200,000,000 marks per annum.

DOCUMENT 417

Letter from the American Reparation Experts to Wilson Regarding a Supplementary Memorandum to the Proposed Reply of the Supreme Council, June 11, 1919

[TPG, VIII, 126. At the bottom of the page are written in Dulles' handwriting the names of the four signatories of this letter: "Norman Davis B M Baruch T W Lamont Vance C McCormick." There is also added: "(Drafted by J. F. D.)"]

My dear Mr. President:

In general reference to the proposed reply to Germany on Reparations,[1] we have, as you know, all along thought that specific reference could with advantage be made in this reply to the matter of allowing Germany to retain sufficient ships for her own actual requirements and also to retain certain other assets necessary as working capital. We also feel that assurances should be given that Germany will have a fair deal in such questions as coal, minette ore, dyestuffs, etc. Mr. Lloyd George accepted this in principle and Mr. Loucheur was, in fact, at one time agreeable to putting clauses of this sort in the reply itself. Later on he said that Mr. Clemenceau did not approve of this, but that the French would gladly execute with her Allies a separate memorandum embodying a precise understanding on these points, which are so important to the resumption by Germany of her industrial life.

We feel that if, as now appears to be the case, no specific assurances on the matters alluded to above will be included in the reply to Germany, at least Mr. Loucheur's suggestion as to an Inter-Allied memorandum should be adopted. You will, I am sure, appreciate how much it will simplify the task of the Reparation Commission if an agreement can be reached on this subject at the present time and before the heads of the principal Allied Governments have separated.

In case you should concur in this view you may wish to endeavor

[1] See Document 412.

to have a memorandum, along the lines of the enclosed,[2] initialed by Mr. Lloyd George, Mr. Clemenceau and Mr. Orlando, as well as yourself.

DOCUMENT 418

Letter from the American Reparation Experts to Wilson Regarding the Proposed Reply of the Supreme Council, June 11, 1919

[TPG, VIII, 125. At the bottom of the page are written in Dulles' handwriting the names of the four signatories of this letter: "Norman Davis B M Baruch T W Lamont Vance C McCormick."]

Dear Mr. President:

We return herewith your text of the proposed reply on Reparations, and you will note that on this text we have made only a few slight verbal suggestions, chiefly for the sake of clarity.[1]

On page 4 we think the phrase in writing should be omitted altogether, otherwise Germany will get the idea that even for the long future she must deal at arms length with us, as she has in the last few weeks and not ever be able to discuss any details.[2]

On page 5 the sum alluded to should be expressed in marks and not in sterling.[3] In the same paragraph the final phrase appeared to us as alluding not to the present peace, and, therefore, it is perhaps better if we were to say "more apt to provoke than to prevent controversy."[4]

In the next paragraph the allusion to the possible proposals from Germany should be linked up a little more closely because of the fact that so much text has come in between.[5]

On page 6 all allusion to food is omitted. We think that food, as well as raw materials, should be mentioned.[6] In the second paragraph we have suggested the addition of one phrase, which, however, is not essential, but which serves to bring out a little more clearly the systematic effort of the Germans in destruction.[7]

Respectfully yours,

[2] See Document 416.

---

[1] See Document 412.
[2] Quotation marks have evidently been left out here. The meaning apparently is: We think the phrase "in writing" should be omitted. Page 174, line 9.
[3] Page 175, line 7.
[4] Page 175, line 10.
[5] Page 175, line 13.
[6] Page 175, line 25.
[7] The reference is obscure here, although it is somewhere in the paragraph beginning at the bottom of p. 175. There is no penciled amendment in the TPG copy of the Proposed Reply.

DOCUMENT 419

Letter from House to Orlando Requesting the Italian Signature of the Shipping Agreement, June 12, 1919

[From the carbon copy in the Edward M. House Collection, Yale University Library, New Haven, Connecticut.]

My dear Prime Minister:

The President has asked me to find whether it would be agreeable to you now to sign the agreement which Mr. Lloyd George and M. Clemenceau have already signed regarding the German Merchant Ships, which were interned in the United States.

I am leaving for London to be gone for a few days, otherwise I would have called in person instead of asking Mr. Shepardson to represent me.

With all good wishes, I am

Faithfully yours,

DOCUMENT 420

Decision of the Council of Four Regarding the Resolutions of the Labor Commission, June 13, 1919

[Slosson's Annotations, in Miller, XIX, 282. Since these minutes are numbered "C. F. 65" (see last line), we know that the meeting fell on June 13. That is because other minutes with the same number have been identified. See Miller, XIX, 426, 436, 440.]

The Labor Commission, in view of the German offer to supply German labor for the rebuilding of the devastated area in France and Belgium (Observations of the German Delegation on the Conditions of Peace; Section IV, 2), passed resolutions declaring:

That the option of supplying labor at will should not rest with Germany;
That Germany should not be required to supply labor against her will;
That France and Germany reach a separate agreement for the employment of German labor in the work of restoration, subject to the conditions that Allied countries neighboring to France be offered opportunity to supply foreign labor and that all foreign labor, including German, be paid at the rates customary in the trade and district (C. F. 65, Appendix IV).

These resolutions, however, were not adopted by the Council of Four (C. F. 65).

DOCUMENT 421

Preliminary Text of the Agreement with Belgium Regarding Her Debt to the Allies, Undated

[TPG, III, 244. "A Schedule. Agreement with Belgium as to Handling of Her Debts to Allied and Associated Governments." Dated: "Paris, May , 1919." The latest date is derived from the fact that Lamont enclosed it in a memorandum of June 14 (see Document 424).]

[*Reparation clauses obligate Germany to reimburse sums which Belgium borrowed from Allies up to November 11, 1918; and, as evidence of obligation, Germany is to make special issue of bonds. Clemenceau, Lloyd George, and Wilson will each recommend to own government that these bonds be accepted in satisfaction of Belgium's obligation to that government.*]

DOCUMENT 422

Report of the Meeting of the Council of Four, June 14, 1919

[Slosson's Annotations, in Miller, XIX, 306-7.]

The principle of the liability of liberated territories, formerly enemy, for a share in the reparations debt was mainly discussed in connection with the Austrian rather than the German Treaty; but on another occasion it was raised in connection with the latter; when, on June 14, the question of revising the Articles relating to Poland was under consideration (C. F. 69).

Mr. Lloyd George objected to the freeing of certain liberated territories from the reparations obligations of the States to which they formerly belonged. "For example, were Danzig and Upper Silesia, both very wealthy States, to bear no part of the burden of the reparation?"

M. Clemenceau said that they ought to pay.

Mr. Hurst said that as regards Danzig nothing had been provided as a contribution for reparation.

President Wilson said that the Poles had been compelled to fight for Germany and that they had suffered greatly from the war. "The question which Mr. Lloyd George raised, he said, had been discussed again and again and had been given up because no decision could be reached. He recalled the discussions on the subject in connection with Austria and the proposals for a bookkeeping arrangement."

Mr. Lloyd George said that as regards the Austrian Treaty an arrangement had been reached which was to be discussed with the States formerly constituting Austria.

M. Sonnino said that as Danzig was separated from Germany against its will it was right to allow some consideration to the inhabitants.

M. Clemenceau said that the amount involved was small.

Mr. Lloyd George thought it was very considerable. "He would like to make some provision that if any part of Upper Silesia went to Poland, there should be a joint consideration between Germany, Poland and the Commission as to how much of the burden of reparation was to be borne." To exempt a district that voted for Poland from all share in reparations would "load the dice" in a plebiscite.

M. Clemenceau said that Mr. Lloyd George was right in principle but his proposal was not politic under existing circumstances.

DOCUMENT 423

Second Belgian Draft of the Agreement with Belgium Regarding Priority, June 14, 1919

[TPG, III, 252-55. "Formule proposée par la Délégation belge." At the head of the draft proper, and also of the Annex, there is written in ink, "14 juin 1919." Document 386 precedes. Cf. Document 425. Document 437 follows.]

[a] Attendu que l'article 237 du Traité de Paix avec l'Allemagne stipule entre autres choses que chaque paiement à faire par l'Allemagne au titre des réparations sera réparti entre les gouvernements alliés et associés suivant les proportions déterminées par eux à l'avance et fondées sur l'équité et les droits de chacun, et

[b] Attendu qu'après la priorité reconnue par l'article 235 du Traité aux dépenses des armées d'occupation et aux paiements du ravitaillement de l'Allemagne, il est équitable de donner à la Belgique une certaine priorité sur les versements effectués au compte des réparations.

[c] En conséquence, les soussignés, au nom de leurs gouvernements respectifs, se déclarent d'accord pour que la Belgique reçoive en acompte sur les indemnités de réparations auxquelles elle a droit, l'équivalent de 2½ milliards de francs or à prélever sur les premiers paiements effectivement reçus en espèces de l'Allemagne.

[d] A cet effet seront considérés comme espèces:

1) le numéraire reçu par la Commission des Réparations;

2) le produit de la vente par la dite Commission des devises ou valeurs reçues de l'Allemagne;

3) la valeur des prestations et réparations en nature reçues de l'Allemagne en exécution des clauses du Traité de Paix et portées

au débit des gouvernements alliés et associés autres que la Belgique. Ce dernier élément n'interviendra qu'au 1er mai 1921.

[e] Il est entendu que les restitutions visées par l'article 238 du Traité n'entreront pas en compte.

[f] La Commission des Réparations recevra comme instructions de faire tout ce qui est en son pouvoir pour effectuer tous les paiements de la comme susvisée de 2½ milliards avant le 1er mai 1921.

[g] La Belgique conservera, indépendamment des 2½ milliards susvisés, la pleine valeur des prestations et réparations en nature reçues de l'Allemagne avant le 1er mai 1921 et portées à son débit.

[h] A partir du 1er mai 1921 cette avance de 2½ milliards et l'excédent éventuel des livraisons en nature faites à la Belgique sur sa quote-part fixée en vertu de l'article 237 précité, seront amortis à concurrence de $1/30^e$ de leur montant total sur ce qui reviendra à la Belgique dans chacun des versements successifs de l'Allemagne. Si toutefois cette dernière réglait complètement sa dette en moins de 30 années, l'amortissement serait accéléré, de façon à être terminé en même temps que le règlement par l'Allemagne.

L'annexe ci-jointe fournit un exemple du mode d'application de la présente disposition.

FORMULE DE LA DÉLÉGATION BELGE. ANNEXE.

Supposons que l'Allemagne verse jusqu'au 1er mai 1921, en dehors des sommes qui seront consacrées à son ravitaillement, en vivres et en matières premières, et aux dépenses des armées d'occupation, une somme totale de 13 milliards de francs à affecter aux réparations.

Supposons que cette somme ait été obtenue comme suit:

En espèces ou valeurs converties en espèces 1½ milliard
En prestations diverses . . . . 11½ milliards

Supposons de plus que la part proportionnelle de la Belgique soit fixée par exemple à 7%.

Ceci posé, la Belgique aura droit:

1°) à recevoir les espèces, soit 1½ milliard;

2°) au 1er mai 1921 la Belgique a droit à la totalité des prestations en nature qu'elle a reçues, soit par exemple la valeur de 1 milliard 200 millions. Reste donc 10 milliards 300 millions. Le 1er mai 1921, chacun des pays intéressés, sauf la Belgique, est debité de la totalité des prestations en nature reçues par lui, et pour parfaire les 2½ milliards accordés en priorité à la Belgique, le fonds commun paie à ce pays la somme de 1 milliard. La Belgique reçoit ainsi 2½ milliards plus 1 milliard 200 millions.

En conséquence, la valeur des prestations en nature reçues par la Belgique, soit 1 milliard 200 millions, dépasse la part de 7% qui lui a été attribuée. Ce pourcentage lui aurait donné 735 millions calculés sur 10 milliards et demi restant à partager après déduction de la priorité de 2½ milliards. L'excédent de la valeur des prestations en nature sur la part normale de la Belgique est donc de 465 millions.

Après 1921, par exemple en 1922, si l'Allemagne a versé cette année-là 10 milliards et que la Belgique a reçu en nature 300 millions son compte de 1922 s'établira comme suit:

Reçu en nature. 300   millions
Part d'amortissement de la priorité de
2½ milliards et de 465 millions reçus
en excédent . . . .   98.88 millions
                                                                                                   ———————
                                                                                                   398.88

Somme due à la Belgique: 700 millions dont à déduire 398.88 millions, reste dû par le fonds commun à la Belgique 301.12 millions.

DOCUMENT 424

Lamont's Memorandum to Davis, to Baruch, to McCormick, to Dulles, and to Hankey Regarding the Special Agreements with Belgium, June 14, 1919

[TPG, III, 243. "Memorandum. Subject: Special Agreement with Belgium."]

The special agreement with Belgium has never been signed, although we have made constant efforts to get it out of the way. As to the form of the first agreement (as per Schedule A, attached hereto),[1] covering the undertaking by the Chiefs of State to make certain recommendations to their respective legislative bodies, there has been entire agreement among all four delegations, and the formula is acceptable to Belgium.

As to the agreement making effective Belgium's priority of $500,000,000 [2 milliard marks], the American Delegation drew up a formula (Schedule B attached hereto),[2] which was approved by the British and I think the Italian Delegation, but not by the French; Mr. Loucheur stating his opinion that it did not go far enough in favor of the Belgians.

---

[1] See Document 421.   [2] See Document 352.

Since this draft was first made, Belgium has submitted a counter draft,[3] which has not been acceptable to any of the delegations. Mr. Loucheur has charged himself with the task of submitting a final formula which should be in satisfactory form to all concerned. 2 enc.

DOCUMENT 425
Loucheur's Draft of the Agreement with Belgium Regarding Priority, June 14, 1919

[TPG, III, 246-48. "Formule proposée par M. Loucheur." At the head of the draft itself, and also of the Annex, there is written in ink, "14 juin 1919." For an English translation of the present text, see Document 426. Document 386 precedes. Cf. Document 423. Document 437 follows.]

[a] Attendu que l'article 237 du Traité de Paix avec l'Allemagne stipule entre autres choses que chaque paiement à faire par l'Allemagne au titre des réparations sera réparti entre les Gouvernements alliés et associés suivant les proportions déterminées par eux à l'avance et fondées sur l'équité et les droits de chacun, et

[b] Attendu qu'après la priorité reconnue par l'article 235 du Traité aux dépenses des armées d'occupation et aux paiements du ravitaillement de l'Allemagne, il est équitable de donner à la Belgique une certaine priorité sur les versements effectués au compte des réparations.

[c] En conséquence les soussignés, au nom de leurs gouvernements respectifs se déclarent d'accord pour que la Belgique reçoive en acompte sur les indemnités de réparations auxquelles elle a droit, l'équivalent de 2½ milliards de francs or à prélever sur les premiers paiements effectivement reçus en espèces de l'Allemagne.

[d] A cet effet seront considérés comme espèces:

1) le numéraire reçu par la Commission des Réparations;

2) le produit de la vente par la dite Commission des devises ou valeurs reçues de l'Allemagne;

3) la valeur des prestations et réparations en nature reçues de l'Allemagne en exécution des clauses du Traité de Paix et portées au débit des gouvernements alliés et associés. Ce dernier élément n'interviendra qu'au 1er mai 1921.

[e] Il est entendu que les restitutions visées par l'article 238 du Traité n'entreront pas en compte.[1]

---

[3] See Document 386 or Document 423.

[1] Following this sentence, another sentence has been crossed out. It is not in the English translation. It reads: "Les sommes reçues de l'Allemagne en remboursement des dépenses des armées d'occupation ou en paiement du ravitaillement de l'Allemagne en produits alimentaires et en matières premières resteront également hors de cette prise de compte." Note, however, that the idea behind this sentence is included in the second paragraph.

[f] La Commission des Réparations recevra comme instructions de faire tout ce qui est en son pouvoir pour effectuer tous les paiements de la somme susvisée de 2½ milliards avant le 1er mai 1921.[2]

[g] Indépendamment de cette avance de 2½ milliards, la Belgique participera, dans la proportion qui lui sera attribuée, à la répartition des premiers versements et aux répartitions ultérieures prévues par l'article 237 précité.

[h] A partir du 1er mai 1921 la somme susvisée de 2½ milliards sera amortie à concurrence de 1/30e par an sur ce qui reviendra à la Belgique, dans chacun des versements successifs de l'Allemagne. Si toutefois cette dernière réglait complètement sa dette en moins de 30 années, l'amortissement serait accéléré de façon à être terminé en même temps que le règlement par l'Allemagne.

L'annexe ci-jointe fournit un exemple du mode d'application de la présente disposition.

FORMULE DE MONSIEUR LOUCHEUR   ANNEXE

Supposons que l'Allemagne verse jusqu'au 1er mai 1921, en dehors des sommes qui seront consacrées à son ravitaillement, en vivres et en matières premières,[3] et aux dépenses des armées d'occupation, une somme totale de 13 milliards de francs à affecter aux réparations.

Supposons que cette somme ait été obtenue comme suit:

En espèces ou valeurs converties en espèces I ½ milliard
En prestations diverses . . . . 11 ½ milliards

Supposons de plus que la part proportionnelle de la Belgique soit fixée par exemple à 7%.

Ceci posé, la Belgique aura droit:

1°) à recevoir les espèces, soit 1½ milliard;

2°) au premier mai 1921 chacun des pays intéressés étant débité de la totalité des prestations en nature reçues par lui, le fonds commun paiera à la Belgique un milliard sur les 11½ milliards mentionnés ci-dessus.

Sur les 10½ milliards restant, la Belgique a droit à 7% soit 735 millions.

Si elle a reçu en nature 1 milliard 200 millions, elle devra verser au fonds commun la différence entre cette somme et la part de 735 millions à laquelle elle a droit, soit 465 millions.

---

[2] This sentence is omitted from the English translation.
[3] The phrase, "en vivres et en matières premières," is omitted from the English translation.

Après 1921, par exemple en 1922, si l'Allemagne a versé cette année-là 10 milliards et que la Belgique ait reçu en nature 300 millions, son compte pour 1922 s'établira comme suit:

Reçu en nature 300 millions		300.000.000
Part d'amortissement de la priorité de 2½ milliards		83.330.000 fr
	total	383.330.000

Somme due à la Belgique 700 millions dont à déduire 383.33 millions; reste dû par le fonds commun à la Belgique 316.67 millions.

DOCUMENT 426

English Translation of Loucheur's Draft of the Agreement with Belgium Regarding Priority, June 14, 1919

[TPG, III, 249-51. "Formula Proposed by Monsieur Loucheur."]

[*A translation of Document 425, with a few differences pointed out there in footnotes.*]

DOCUMENT 427

Letter from Hymans to Clemenceau Regarding the Proposed Reply to the German Observations, June 15, 1919

[Translation, in Peace Conference Bulletin No. 395 (June 24, 1919), in Miller, XVIII, 538-40.]

Mr. President:

The Belgian Delegation has the honor to submit to the Council of the Great Allied and Associated Powers the following considerations suggested to it by the draft of the answer to the German counter-proposals concerning Reparations, which was communicated to it yesterday.

The Powers declare themselves ready to take into serious consideration a certain number of new counter-proposals which might be made by Germany.

1. It is said in this document that special facilities shall be granted in view of allowing German Agents to inspect or to ascertain the damages done in the occupied regions.

We wish to call your attention to the fact that the populations will hardly admit that Germany, guilty and responsible of these damages, should come and make inquiries on the spot concerning the crimes, the reparation for which it is their duty to assure. On the other hand, it can hardly be admitted that an intervention of the German authorities could modify or suppress the authority of a thing judged by the national tribunals which were charged by a law to verify the damages.

2. The answer of the Allied and Associated Powers also says that within the limit of four months after the signing of the Treaty, Germany shall be admitted to make proposals concerning the mode of payment of the indemnities which the Treaty imposes upon her. Germany could notably offer to undertake the work of reparation and reconstruction of all or part of the devastated regions or the reparation of certain categories of damages. She could offer labor, materials, or technical assistance.

There exists, it is true, a special and restricted category of works for which the Belgian Government has taken the initiative, asking the Allied and Associated Powers that they should oblige Germany to furnish labor. In my letter of June 4th, addressed to the President of the Conference,[1] I have asked indeed that the German Government should be obliged to place at the disposal of the Belgian Government, 2,000 special workmen, who, under the direction of the Belgian Military authorities and at the expense of the German Government, should execute the work of transportation, of collecting, and of destruction of the munitions and explosives abandoned by the German authorities on the Belgian territory. I seize this opportunity to beg again the Great Powers to take this request into serious consideration and to try to give satisfaction to our desires.

But the Delegation feels obliged to make some reservations concerning the proposals of the Council of the Principal Allied and Associated Powers relative to the use of labor, materials and technical assistance from Germany in the undertaking of reparations and reconstruction in general.

The use of German labor in countries where national labor is abundant, as in Belgium, might be detrimental to the people who have been the victims of the German violence and depredations. The plundering of our factories, the destruction and the removal of the machinery have thrown hundreds of thousands of Belgian workmen out of employment. Many of them will find an occupation in the work of reparation. And they might not understand that foreign labor, especially that of the enemy of yesterday, could be substituted by authority for national labor.

In a general way, any German proposal concerning the undertaking by Germany of the reconstruction and reparation in Belgium should be submitted to the examination and to the agreement of the

---

[1] This letter is missing.

Belgian Government. The latter shall be sole judge in the matter and free to decide according to the economic, social, and political consideration which it will have to appreciate.

Please accept, etc.

HYMANS.

DOCUMENT 428

Extracts from the "Letter [from Clemenceau] to the President of the German Delegation [Brockdorff-Rantzau] Covering the Reply of the Allied and Associated Powers," June 16, 1919

[Bound with Document 429 (see citation there). From *Lettre d'envoi au président de la délégation allemande de la réponse des Puissances alliées et associées* (one copy of which is in TPG, VIII, 140 ff.). pp. 2, 3, 3-4, 5, 8-9. Only the English text is given here; the original is also in French. This is a covering letter to Document 429. This TPG copy seems to be an uncorrected proof; its several typographical errors have, however, been corrected here.

The English text is also in *International Conciliation*, No. 144, November, 1919, pp. 1341, 1342, 1343, 1344-45, 1349-50; and in Great Britain, Parliament, *Parliamentary Papers*, 1919, LIII, Cmd. 258, pp. 2, 3, 3-4, 5, 8-9. French text, in PV, Notes, pp. 239 ff. German translation, in *Materialien*, IV, 77 ff.]

[*p. 2*]   The Allied and Associated Powers have given the most earnest consideration to the observations of [the] German Delegation on the Conditions of Peace. The reply protests against the peace both on the ground that it conflicts with the terms upon which the Armistice of November 11th, 1918 was signed, and that it is a peace of violence and not of justice. The protest of the German Delegation shows that they utterly fail to understand the position in which Germany stands to-day. They seem to think that Germany has only to "make sacrifices in order to attain peace," as if this were but the end of some mere struggle for territory and power.

I

The Allied and Associated Powers therefore feel it necessary to begin their reply by a clear statement of the judgment passed upon the war by practically the whole of civilised mankind.

In the view of the Allied and Associated Powers the war which began on August 1st, 1914, was the greatest crime against humanity and the freedom of peoples that any nation, calling itself civilised, has ever consciously committed.

[*p. 3*]　　Germany's responsibility, however, is not confined to having planned and started the war. She is no less responsible for the savage and inhuman manner in which it was conducted.

.　　.　　.

[*pp. 3-4*]　　The conduct of Germany is almost unexampled in human history. The terrible responsibility which lies at her doors can be seen in the fact that not less than seven million dead lie buried in Europe, while more than twenty million others carry upon them the evidence of wounds and sufferings, because Germany saw fit to gratify her lust for tyranny by resort to war.

The Allied and Associated Powers believe that they will be false to those who have given their all to save the freedom of the world if they consent to treat this war on any other basis than as a crime against humanity and right.

This attitude of the Allied and Associated Powers was made perfectly clear to Germany during the war by their principal statesmen.

.　　.　　.

[*p. 5*]　　Justice, therefore, is the only possible basis for the settlement of the accounts of this terrible war. Justice is what the German Delegation asks for and says that Germany had been promised. Justice is what Germany shall have. But it must be justice for all. There must be justice for the dead and wounded and for those who have been orphaned and bereaved that Europe might be freed from Prussian despotism. There must be justice for the peoples who now stagger under war debts which exceed £30,000,000,000 that liberty might be saved. There must be justice for those millions whose homes and land, ships and property German savagery has spoliated and destroyed.

That is why the Allied and Associated Powers have insisted as a cardinal feature of the Treaty that Germany must undertake to make reparation to the very uttermost of her power; for reparation for wrongs inflicted is of the essence of justice. That is why they insist that those individuals who are most clearly responsible for German aggression and for those acts of barbarism and inhumanity which have disgraced the German conduct of the war, must be handed over to a justice which has not been meted out to them at home. That, too, is why Germany must submit for a few years to certain special disabilities and arrangements. Germany has ruined the industries, the mines and the machinery of neighbouring countries, not during battle, but with the deliberate and calculated purpose of enabling her industries to seize their markets before their industries could recover from the devastation thus wantonly inflicted upon them. Germany has despoiled her neighbours of every thing she could make use of or carry away. Germany has destroyed the shipping of all nations on the high seas, where there was no chance of rescue for their passengers and crews. It is only justice that restitution should be made and that these wronged peoples should be safeguarded for a time from the competition of a nation whose industries are intact and have even been fortified by machinery stolen from occupied territories. If these things are hardships for Germany, they are hardships which Germany has brought upon herself. Somebody must suffer for the consequences of the war. Is it to be Germany, or only the peoples she has wronged?

Not to do justice to all concerned would only leave the world open to fresh calamities. If the German people themselves, or any other nation, are to be deterred from following the footsteps of Prussia, if mankind is to be lifted out of the belief that war for selfish ends is legitimate to any State, if the old era is to be left behind and nations as well as individuals are to be brought beneath the reign of law, even if there is to be early reconciliation and appeasement, it will be because those responsible for concluding the war have had the courage to see that justice is not deflected of the sake of convenient peace.

.   .   .

[*pp. 8-9*]   V

The German Delegation have greatly misinterpreted the Reparation proposals of the Treaty.

These proposals confine the amount payable by Germany to what is clearly justifiable under the terms of armistice in respect of damage caused to the civilian population of the Allies by German aggression. They do not provide for that interference in the internal life of Germany by the Reparation Commission which is alleged.

They are designed to make the payment of that reparation which Germany must pay as easy and convenient to both parties as possible and they will be interpreted in that sense. The Allied and Associated Powers therefore are not prepared to modify them.

But they recognise with the German Delegation, the advantage of arriving as soon as possible at the fixed and definite sum which shall be payable by Germany and accepted by the Allies. It is not possible to fix this sum to-day, for the extent of damage and the cost of repair has not yet been ascertained. They are therefore willing to accord to Germany all necessary and reasonable facilities to enable her to survey the devastated and damaged regions, and to make proposals thereafter within four months of the signing of the Treaty for a settlement of the claims under each of the categories of damage for which she is liable. If within the following two months an agreement can be reached, the exact liability of Germany will have been ascertained. If agreement has not been reached by then, the arrangement as provided in the Treaty will be executed.

.   .   .

DOCUMENT 429

Extracts from the "Reply of the Allied and Associated Powers to the Observations of the German Delegation on the Conditions of Peace," Undated

[From Allied and Associated Powers (1914-   ), *Réponse des Puissances alliées et associées aux remarques de la délégation allemande sur les conditions de paix* (one copy of which is in TPG, VIII, 161 ff.), pp. 2-3, 32-36. Only the English text is given here; the original is also in French. Document 412 precedes the section entitled "Part VIII. Reparation." This TPG copy seems to be an uncorrected proof; its typographical errors have, however, been corrected.

The English text is also in *International Conciliation*, No. 144, November, 1919, pp. 1353-55, 1384-90; and in Great Britain, Parliament, *Parliamentary Papers*, 1919, LIII, Cmd. 258, pp. 2-3, 32-36. French text, in PV, Notes, pp. 250 ff. German translation, in *Materialien*, IV, 7 ff.

This was enclosed in the Letter of June 16 (see Document 428).]

[*pp. 2-3*]   INTRODUCTION
BASIS OF THE PEACE NEGOTIATIONS

The Allied and Associated Powers are in complete accord with the German Delegation in their insistence that the basis for the negotiation of the Treaty of Peace is to be found in the correspondence which immediately preceded the signing of the Armistice on November 11, 1918. It was there agreed that the Treaty of Peace should be based upon the Fourteen Points of President Wilson's address of January 8, 1918, as they were modified by the Allies' memorandum included in the President's note of November 5, 1918, and upon the principles of settlement enunciated by President Wilson in his later addresses, and particularly in his address of September 27, 1918. These are the principles upon which hostilities were abandoned in November 1918, these are the principles upon which the Allied and Associated Powers agreed that peace might be based, these are the principles which have guided them in the deliberations which have led to the formulation of the Conditions of Peace.

It is now contended by the German Delegation that the Conditions of Peace do not conform to these principles which had thus become binding upon the Allied and Associated Powers as well as upon the Germans themselves. In an attempt to prove a breach of this agreement the German Delegation have drawn quotations from a number of speeches, most of which were before the Address to Congress and many of which were uttered by Allied statesmen at a time when they were not at war with Germany, or had no responsibility for the conduct of public affairs. The Allied and Associated Powers consider it unnecessary, therefore, to oppose this list of detached quotations with others equally irrelevant to a discussion concerning the basis of the peace negotiations. In answer to the implication of these quotations, it is sufficient to refer to a note of the Allied Powers transmitted to the President of the United States on January 10, 1917, in response to an inquiry as to the conditions upon which they would be prepared to make peace:

"The Allies feel a desire as deep as that of the United States Government to see ended, at the earliest possible moment, the war for which the Central Empires are responsible, and which inflicts sufferings so cruel upon humanity. But they judge it impossible today to bring about a peace that shall assure to them the reparation, the restitution and the guarantees to which they are entitled by the aggression for which the responsibility lies upon the Central Empires—and of which the very principle tended to undermine the safety of Europe—a peace which shall also permit the establishment upon firm foundations of the future of the nations of Europe."

In the same note, in addition to a reference to Poland, they declared the War Aims of the Allies to include:

". . . first of all, the restoration of Belgium, Serbia, Montenegro, with the compensation due to them; the evacuation of the invaded territories in France, in Russia, in Roumania with just reparation; the reorganization of Europe, guaranteed by a stable regime and based at once on respect for nationalities and on the right to full security and liberty of economic development possessed by all peoples, small and great, and at the same time upon territorial conventions and international settlements such as to guarantee land and sea frontiers against unjustified attacks; the restitution of provinces formerly torn away from the Allies by force against the wish of their inhabitants; the liberation of the Italians, as also of the Slavs, Roumanians, and Czecho-Slovaks from foreign domination; the setting free of the populations subject to the bloody tyranny of the Turks; and the turning out of Europe of the Ottoman Empire as decidedly foreign to Western civilisation."

It cannot be disputed that responsible statesmen, those qualified to express the will of the peoples of the Allied and Associated

Powers, have never entertained or expressed a desire for any other peace than one which should undo the wrongs of 1914, vindicate justice and international right, and reconstruct the political foundations of Europe on lines which would give liberty to all its peoples, and therefore the prospect of a lasting peace.

But the German Delegation profess to find discrepancies between the agreed basis of peace and the draft of the Treaty. They discover a contradiction between the terms of the Treaty and a statement taken from an address delivered at Baltimore on April 6, 1918, by President Wilson:

"We are ready, whenever the final reckoning is made, to be just to the German people, as with all others. . . . To propose anything but justice to Germany at any time, whatever the outcome of the war, would be to renounce our own cause, for we ask nothing that we are not willing to accord."

This quotation does not stand alone. It should be read in conjunction with one of the cardinal principles of the Mount Vernon address of July 4, 1918, which demanded:

"The destruction of every arbitrary power everywhere that can separately, secretly, and of its single choice disturb the peace of the world or, if it cannot be presently destroyed, at the least its reduction to virtual impotence."

Neither of these two principles of the agreed basis of peace has been lost sight of in the formulation of these Conditions.

[*pp. 32-36*]   PART VIII

REPARATION

The Allied and Associated Powers, consistently with their policy already expressed, decline to enter into a discussion of the principles underlying the Reparation Clauses of the Conditions of Peace, which have been prepared with scrupulous regard for the correspondence leading up to the Armistice of November 11th, 1918, the final memorandum of which, dated 5th November, 1918, contains the following words:

"Further, in the conditions of Peace laid down in his address to Congress of the 8th January, 1918, the President declared that the invaded territories must be restored as well as evacuated and freed, and the Allied Governments feel that no doubt ought to be allowed to exist as to what this provision implies. By it they understand that compensation will be made by Germany for all damage done to the civilian population of the Allies and their property by the aggression of Germany by land, by sea, and from the air."

To the extent that the German reply deals with practical phases of the execution of the principles enunciated in the Conditions of

Peace, it appears to proceed on the basis of a complete misapprehension, which is the more difficult to understand as the inferences drawn and the statements made are wholly at variance with both the letter and the spirit of the Treaty Clauses. For purposes of clarification, however, and in order that there may be no possible ground for misunderstanding, the Allied and Associated Powers submit the following observations:

The vast extent and manifold character of the damage caused to the Allied and Associated Powers in consequence of the war has created a reparation problem of extraordinary magnitude and complexity, only to be solved by a continuing body, limited in personnel and invested with broad powers to deal with the problem in relation to the general economic situation.

The Allied and Associated Powers, recognising this situation, themselves delegate power and authority to a Reparation Commission. This Reparation Commission is, however, instructed by the Treaty itself so to exercise and interpret its powers as to ensure, in the interest of all, an early and complete discharge by Germany of her reparation obligations. It is also instructed to take into account the true maintenance of the social, economic and financial structure of a Germany earnestly striving to exercise her full power to repair the loss and damage she has caused.

The provisions of Article 241, by which the German Government is to invest itself with such powers as may be needed to carry out its obligations, are not to be misconstrued as giving the Commission powers to dictate the domestic legislation of Germany. Nor does paragraph 12 (b) of Annex II give the Commission powers to prescribe or enforce taxes or to dictate the character of the German budget.

It is only to examine the latter for two specified purposes.

This is necessary in order that it may intelligently and constructively exercise the discretion accorded to it in Germany's interest, particularly by Article 234, with regard to extending the date and modifying the form of payments. The provisions of Article 240 with regard to the supply of information are similar in character and purpose, and there should be little occasion for the exercise of these powers when once the amount of the liability of Germany is fixed, if Germany is in a position to, and does, comply with the schedule of payments which then will have been notified to her and with the specific provisions of the several Annexes relative to reparation in kind. It is further to be observed that the power of modification accorded by the said Article 236 [*234*] is expressly designed to permit of a modification in Germany's interest of a schedule of payments which events may demonstrate to be beyond Germany's reasonable capacity.

The Allied and Associated Powers vigorously reject the suggestion that the Commission, in exercising the power conferred by Article 240 and by paragraphs 2, 3 and 4 of Annex IV [*VI*], might require the divulgence of trade secrets and similar confidential data.

In short the observations of the German Delegation present a view of this Commission so distorted and so inexact that it is difficult to believe that the clauses of the Treaty have been calmly or carefully examined. It is not an engine of oppression or a device for interfering with German sovereignty. It has no forces, at its command; it has no executive powers within the territory of Germany; it cannot, as is suggested, direct or control the educational or other systems of the country. Its business is to fix what is to be paid; to satisfy itself that Germany can pay; and to report to the Powers, whose Delegation it is, in case Germany makes default. If Germany raises the money required in her own way, the Commission cannot order that it shall be raised in some other way; if Germany offers payment in kind, the Commission may accept such payment, but, except as specified in the Treaty itself, the Commission cannot require such a payment.

The German Observations appear to miss the point that the Commission is directed to study the German system of taxation for the protection of the German people no less than for the protection of their own. Such study is not inquisitorial, for the German system of taxation is not an object of curiosity to other Powers, nor is a knowledge of it an end in itself; but if any plea of inability which the German Government may advance is to be properly considered, such a study is necessary.

The Commission must test whether a sincere application is being given to the principle, accepted in the Observations,"that the German taxation system should impose in general on the taxpayer at least as great a burden as that prevailing in the most heavily burdened of the States represented on the Reparation Commission." If the German resources are to be properly weighed, the first subject of inquiry will be the German fiscal burden.

It is understood that the action necessary to give effect to the provisions of Annex IV, relative to reparation in kind, will be taken by Germany on its own initiative, after receipt of notification from the Reparation Commission.

The provisions of the Treaty are in no wise incompatible with the creation by Germany of a Commission which will represent Germany in dealings with the Reparation Commission and which will constitute an instrumentality for such co-operation as may be necessary. The Treaty specifically and repeatedly provides opportunities for the German Government to present facts and arguments with respect to claims and modes of payment, within the limits of the principles and express provisions of the Treaty. This may be done through a commission and no reason is perceived why such a commission could not work in harmony with the Reparation Commission. Certainly this is greatly to be desired. The Allied and Associated Powers are therefore ready to agree to such a procedure as the following:—

Immediately after the Treaty is signed, Germany may present, and the Allied and Associated Powers will receive and examine, such evidence, estimates and arguments as she may think fit to present. Such documents need not be final but may be presented to the Commission subject to corrections and additions.

At any time within four months of the signature of the Treaty, Germany shall be at liberty to submit, and the Allied and Associated Powers will receive and consider, such proposals as Germany may choose to make. In particular, proposals will be received on the following subjects and for the following purposes. Germany may offer a lump sum in settlement of her whole liability, as defined in Article 232, or in settlement of her liability under any of the particular categories which have been decided upon and laid down. Germany may offer, either to carry out by her own means the restoration, and reconstruction, whether in part or in its entirety, of one of the devastated areas, or to repair under the same conditions certain classes [of] damages in particular regions or in all the regions which have suffered from the war. Germany may offer labour, materials or technical service for use in such work, even though she does not execute the work herself. She may suggest any practicable plan, category by category or for the reparations as a whole, which will tend to shorten the period of enquiry and to bring about a prompt and effectual conclusion.

Without making further specifications, it may be said in a word that Germany is at liberty to make any suggestion or offer of a practical and reasonable character for the purposes of simplifying the assessment of the damage, eliminating any question or questions from the scope of the detailed enquiry, promoting the performance of the work and accelerating the definition of the ultimate amount to be paid.

The necessary facilities for making reliable estimates of the offers to be presented by her will be afforded to Germany at reasonable times. Three conditions only are imposed upon the tender of these proposals. Firstly, the German authorities will be expected before making such proposals to confer with the representatives of the Powers directly concerned. Secondly, such offers must be unambiguous, and must be precise and clear. Thirdly, they must accept the categories and the reparation clauses as matters settled beyond discussion. The Allied and Associated Powers will not entertain arguments or appeals directed to any alteration.

Within two months thereafter, the Allied and Associated Powers will, so far as may be possible, return their answer to any proposals that may be made. It is impossible to declare in advance that they will be accepted, and, if accepted, they may be subjected to conditions which can be discussed and arranged. The Allied and Associated Powers, however, declare that such proposals will be seriously and fairly considered; no one could be better pleased than they if, in the result, a fair, a speedy and a practical settlement were arrived at. The questions are bare questions of fact, namely, the amount of the liabilities, and they are susceptible of being treated in this way. Beyond this, the Allied and Associated Powers cannot be asked to go.

Even if no settlement were arrived at, it must be evident that the early production of the German evidence would greatly abbreviate the enquiry and accelerate the decisions. The German authorities have had long occupation of a large part of the damaged areas and have been over the ground, forwards and backwards, within the last twelve or fifteen months. The Allied and Associated Powers have as yet had no access to this mass of material.

It is obvious that, if the class of damages done in the devastated areas can be dealt with in this fashion, the liability under the other categories can be quickly established, for it depends on statistics and particulars of a far simpler character. By giving a satisfactory covenant themselves to execute the work of rebuilding, the Germans could at once dispose of the only difficult or long subject of inquiry.

The Allied and Associated Powers have to remark that in the Observations submitted the German Delegation has made no definite offer at all but only vague expressions of willingness to do something undefined. A sum of 100,000,000,000 marks (gold) is indeed mentioned, and this is calculated to give the impression of an extensive offer, which upon examination it proves not to be. No interest is to be paid at all. It is evident that till 1927 there is no substantial payment but only the surrender of military material and the devolution upon other Powers of large portions of Germany's own debt. Thereafter a series of undefined instalments is to be agreed, which are not to be completed for nearly half a century. The present value of this distant prospect is small, but it is all that Germany tenders to the victims of her aggression in satisfaction for their past sufferings and their permanent burdens.[1]

The Allied and Associated Powers will, however, make a declaration on another point, as follows: The resumption of German industry involves access by the German people to food supplies and by the German manufacturers to the necessary raw materials and provision for their transport to Germany from overseas. The resumption of German industry is an interest of the Allied and Associated Powers as well as an interest of Germany. They are fully alive to this fact and therefore declare that they will not withhold from Germany commercial facilities without which this resumption cannot take place, but that, subject to conditions and within limits, which cannot be laid down in advance, and subject also to the necessity for having due regard to the special economic situation created for Allied and Associated countries by German aggression and the war, they are prepared to afford to Germany facilities in these directions for the common good.[2]

Meanwhile, the draft Treaty must be accepted as definitive and must be signed. The Allied and Associated Powers cannot any longer delay to assure their security. Germany cannot afford to deny to her populations the peace which is offered to them. The Reparation Commission must be constituted and must commence

[1] In the preceding draft, this paragraph is placed somewhat further back as the conclusion of another paragraph.

[2] See note 1 above.

its task. The only question open will be how best to execute the provisions of the Treaty.

The foregoing should suffice to demonstrate the reasonableness of the conditions under which Germany is to discharge her reparation obligations, and how utterly unfounded are the criticisms in the German reply. These are, indeed, explicable only on the theory that the German plenipotentiaries have read into the Conditions of Peace, in clear defiance of their express terms, an intention which is not there, but which it would be not unnatural to see displayed by victorious nations which have been the victims of cruelty and devastation on a vast and premeditated scale. The burdens of Germany undeniably are heavy, but they are imposed under conditions of justice by peoples whose social well-being and economic prosperity have been gravely impaired by wrongs which it is beyond the utmost power of Germany to repair.

DOCUMENT 430

"*Declaration by the Governments of the United States of America, Great Britain and France in Regard to the Occupation of the Rhine Provinces,*" *June 16, 1919*

[From the facsimile of the signed original in Baker, II, 118. Same text, in Great Britain, Parliament, *Parliamentary Papers*, 1919, LIII, Cmd. 240. There is also printed here another text (TPG, VIII, 311), perhaps issued as a press release. A French translation of this latter is also reproduced (TPG, VIII, 312); and this has been printed, with unimportant differences, in France, Ministère des Affaires Étrangères, *Documents relatifs aux réparations*, I, 24 (dated: "17 juin, soir").]

The Allied and Associated Powers did not insist on making the period of occupation last until the Reparation Clauses were completely executed, because they assumed that Germany would be obliged to give every proof of her good will and every necessary guarantee before the end of the fifteen years time.

As the cost of occupation involves an equivalent reduction of the amount available for reparations, the Allied and Associated Powers stipulated, by Article 431 of the Treaty, that if, before the end of the fifteen years' period, Germany had fulfilled all her obligations under the Treaty, the troops of occupation should be immediately withdrawn.

If Germany, at an earlier date, has given proofs of her goodwill and satisfactory guarantees to assure the fulfilment of her obligations the Allied and Associated Powers concerned will be ready to come to an agreement between themselves for the earlier termination of the period of occupation.

Now and henceforward, in order to alleviate the burden on the reparations bill, they agree that as soon as the Allied and Associated Powers concerned are convinced that the conditions of disarmament by Germany are being satisfactorily fulfilled, the annual amount of the sums to be paid by Germany to cover the cost of occupation shall not exceed 240 million marks (gold). This provision can be modified if the Allied and Associated Powers agree as to the necessity of such modification.

[*signed*]   WOODROW WILSON.
G. CLEMENCEAU.
D. LLOYD GEORGE.

16th June, 1919.

GERMAN GOODWILL MAY SHORTEN RHINE OCCUPATION

Text of Declaration signed in June
by "Big Three" is published in London.

Relative to the Allies' occupation of the Rhine provinces, the British Government has distributed to members of Parliament the English text of the Declaration signed on June 16 by President Wilson, M. Clemenceau and Mr. Lloyd George, which is as follows:—

"The Allied and Associated Powers have not insisted that the period of occupation last until the complete execution of the reparation clauses because they considered that Germany would be obliged to furnish every proof of her goodwill and all necessary guarantees before the expiration of the period of 15 years.

"As the expenses of occupation imply an equivalent reduction of the sum available for reparation, the Allied and Associated Powers, have stipulated by Article 431 of the Treaty that if, before the expiration of the delay of 15 years Germany has fulfilled the obligations imposed upon her by the Treaty, the troops of occupation will be immediately withdrawn.

"If Germany at an earlier date has given proofs of her goodwill and sufficient guarantees of the execution of her obligations, the Allied and Associated Powers interested will be willing to conclude an arrangement between them for putting an earlier end to the occupation.

"With a view to lightening the weight of the reparation charges, the Allied and Associated Powers interested agree that, as soon as they are convinced that the conditions of Germany's disarmament have been fulfilled in a satisfactory manner, the annual amount payable by Germany to cover the cost of occupation shall not exceed 240,000,000 marks in gold. This prescription may be modified if the Allied and Associated Powers agree that such modification is necessary."

L'OCCUPATION MILITAIRE DES TERRITOIRES RHÉNANS

Le gouvernement britannique a fait distribuer aux membres du Parlement le texte anglais de la déclaration signée le 16 juin par MM. Wilson, Clemenceau et Lloyd George. En voici la traduction:

Les puissances alliées et associées n'ont pas insisté pour faire en sorte que la période d'occupation dure jusqu'à l'exécution complète des clauses relatives aux réparations, parce qu'elles estimaient que l'Allemagne serait obligée de fournir toutes les preuves de sa bonne volonté et toutes les garanties nécessaires avant l'expiration de la période de quinze années.

Comme les dépenses entraînées par l'occupation impliquent une réduction équivalente de la somme disponible pour les réparations, les puissances alliées et associées ont stipulé par l'article 431 du traité que si, avant l'expiration du délai de quinze années, l'Allemagne avait satisfait aux obligations que lui impose le traité, les troupes d'occupation seraient immédiatement retirées.

Si l'Allemagne, à une date plus rapprochée, a donné des preuves de sa bonne volonté et des garanties satisfaisantes, pour assurer l'exécution de ses obligations, les puissances alliées et associées, qui sont intéressées, seront prêtes à conclure un arrangement entre elles pour mettre fin plus tôt à la période d'occupation.

Actuellement et à l'avenir, en vue d'alléger le poids de la charge des réparations, elles conviennent que, aussitôt que les puissances alliées et associées qui sont intéressées seront convaincues que les conditions du désarmement de l'Allemagne sont remplies d'une manière satisfaisante, le montant annuel des sommes que l'Allemagne doit payer pour couvrir le coût de l'occupation ne devra pas dépasser 240 millions de marks en or. Cette prescription pourra être modifiée, si les puissances alliées et associées conviennent qu'une telle modification est nécessaire.

16 juin 1919.

DOCUMENT 431

Intermediate Treaty Text (English) (Including Annexes 1-7 and Section II), Undated

[Allied and Associated Powers (1914-   ), *Conditions de paix—Conditions of Peace*, Épreuve avant tirage définitif [Paris? 1919?], pp. 102-22. This seems to be the draft of the whole treaty as it was sent to the Germans on June 18.]

[*Derived from Document 344, with minor and drafting amendments; and also:* [*Annex 2.—(2) Reinsertion of sentence providing right of withdrawal.*]

DOCUMENT 432

Intermediate Treaty Text (French) (Including Annexes 1-7 and Section II), Undated

[Allied and Associated Powers (1914-   ), *Conditions de paix—Conditions of Peace*, Épreuve avant tirage définitif [Paris? 1919?], pp. 102-22. This seems to be the draft of the whole treaty as it was sent to the Germans on June 18.]

[*Derived from Document 345, with minor and drafting amendments; and also:* [*General provisions.—(232) Romanized phrase added—"que soient réparés tous les dommages causés* . . . pendant la période où cette Puissance a été en état de belligérence avec l'Allemagne".]

DOCUMENT 433

Memorandum from Shepardson to House Regarding Negotiations with the Italians on the Shipping Agreement, June 19, 1919

[From the initialed original in the Edward M. House Collection, Yale University Library, New Haven, Connecticut.]

Memorandum for Colonel House:

I saw Bradley Palmer on Saturday [June 14] and discussed with him the advisability of asking Orlando now for his signature to the memorandum concerning German merchant vessels seized by the United States.

Bradley Palmer talked with Gordon, who is now taking Mr. Robinson's place, and he thought it best to talk the matter over with Attolico. On Tuesday afternoon [June 17] they talked it over with him and Attolico reiterated what he had said before, that the Italian Delegation were ready in principle to sign such a statement but in practice they had rather delay signature until certain outstanding questions were settled.

On Wednesday morning [June 18] I talked with Mr. Palmer who related this conversation to me and told me that his discussion with Attolico had taken a rather delicate trend and that he thought it inadvisable to press it further at this time.

He asked me whether he should press it now and I told him that, on the contrary, it would be much more preferable to postpone further discussion until your return.

[initialed] WS [or "WHS"]

DOCUMENT 434

Letter from Brockdorff-Rantzau to Clemenceau Regarding Certain Differences between the Preliminary Text of May 7 and the Intermediate Changes in the Treaty, with Covering Letter from von Haniel, June 20, 1919

[English translation of French translation of German original, from Peace Conference Bulletin No. 387 (June 23, 1919), in Miller, XVIII, 519-23. German text, in *Materialien*, IX, 9-12. French translation, in PV, Notes, pp. 62-64.

All three sources give the date of the covering letter as June 20. The English and French sources give the date of the main note as June 19; the German gives it as June 20.]

Sir:

In the name of the German Delegation I have the honor to

submit to the Allied and Associated Governments the Note contained in the attached Annex.

I have the honor, etc.,

VON HANIEL.

GERMAN PEACE DELEGATION.

19th [*20th*] June, 1919.

Sir:

On examining the four documents forwarded on the 16th inst. to the Commissary General of the Delegation it appears that a certain number of concessions are announced in the covering letter and in the memorandum[1] which do not appear in the text as modified by hand.[2] Among the most important contradictions of this nature the German Delegation has collected the [twelve] following:

.   .   .

8. On page 33 [of the memorandum] it is stipulated that the Reparation Commission cannot require the divulgation of trade secrets and similar confidential data. It is furthermore stipulated that it will have no executive powers within the territory of Germany, and that it is not to interfere in the direction or control of German establishments.

9. On page 34 and the following pages of the memorandum special procedure is provided to establish and cover the reparations demanded of Germany.

10. On page 36 of the memorandum facilities are promised for Germany to import food supplies and raw material.

.   .   .

It is the duty of the German Delegation to render an exact account to its Government and to the National Assembly: it is therefore necessary that it should know absolutely to what degree its adversaries will give binding force to those concessions; it begs Your Excellency to confirm in writing that the contents of the covering letter and of the memorandum dealing with the points mentioned above constitute an integral part of the new peace proposals of the Allied and Associated Governments. In such case it would be sufficient to establish this fact in a final protocol on the text of which the contracting parties would have previously to come to an agreement. A doubt was also raised in regard to a

---

[1] See Part VIII of the Reply of June 16, Document 429.

[2] The Germans appear to have received a second copy of the Preliminary Text of May 7, with the amendments of the Intermediate Text of June 18 inserted in handwriting.

second point when the documents were examined. The printed copy of the Draft Peace Treaty handed to us differs not only in manuscript corrections and additions from the printed copy which the President of the German Delegation received on the 7th May from the Secretary-General of the Peace Conference.

Owing to the exceptional amount of labor imposed on the Delegation by the short time allowed for examination of the documents, it has not yet been able to compare word by word the printed copy of the 7th May with the one and only copy which a great number of persons have constantly to use. I am therefore obliged to reserve to the Delegation the right to make subsequent communications on this subject. For the moment I draw attention to the following differences:

1. On page 103 of the copy which was most recently transmitted[3] Paragraph 2 contains a third sentence beginning with these words: "Each Government" (Chacun des Gouvernements): this sentence is missing from the copies previously transmitted.[4]

2. On page 104, the English text of Paragraph 12, differs in different copies: the paragraph of the previous copies is only one sentence, whereas the copy transmitted in the last instance is divided into two sentences, of which the second begins by these words: "The Commission shall in general. . . . . ."[5]

Naturally, the German Delegation cannot consider as authoritative, modifications in the text which are not made by hand, or which are not evidently in the nature of additions, unless the Allied and Associated Governments confirm the fact that these differences are not due to the erroneous use of a false printed copy, but that they answer to a deliberate intention. In the latter case, the Delegation requests that all differences of such a character should be notified to it before the expiration of the time allowed to it to make a decision.

For these reasons, which it is easy to understand, the Delegation must consider it to be of the greatest importance that it should receive a reply by return messenger if possible.

I have the honor, etc.

BROCKDORFF-RANTZAU.

[3] This appears to refer to the Intermediate Text of June 18, either as printed separately or as hand-written amendments to the Preliminary Text of May 7.

[4] See paragraph 2 of Annex II of the Final Treaty Text, with appropriate footnotes.

[5] See paragraph 12 of Annex II of the Final Treaty Text, with appropriate footnotes.

DOCUMENT 435

Letter from Clemenceau to von Haniel Regarding the Concessions to Germany, with Protocol, June 21, 1919

[English translation "Approved by the Council of the Principal Allied and Associated Powers on June 21st, 1919" from Peace Conference Bulletin No. 387 (June 23, 1919), in Miller, XVIII, 523-28. French text, in PV, Notes, 65-68. German translation, in *Materialien*, IX, 19-24.]

By your note of the 20th instant[1] you brought to the attention of the Allied and Associated Governments certain points on which in the opinion of the German Delegation a divergence existed between the text of the Treaty and the Memorandum sent to you on June 16th, 1919, in answer to the German observations.

I have the honor to inform you that the views of the Allied and Associated Governments on these various [twelve] points are as follows:

· · ·

(8) The Allied and Associated Powers, as stated on page 33 of the memorandum, do not intend to give the Reparation Commission power to require trade secrets and other confidential information to be divulged. As regards the exercise of executive authority on German territory and interference in the direction or control of the educational establishments of Germany, the Treaty contains no provisions giving any power to the Reparation Commission.

(9) On page 34 and the following pages of the memorandum the Allied and Associated Powers have not laid down any special procedure for fixing the reparation demanded from Germany. The Allied and Associated Powers have provided for the possibility that Germany may present at any time after the signature of the Treaty and within the next four months documents and proposals for examination by the said Powers, in order to expedite the work relating to reparation, and thereby greatly shorten the investigation and accelerate the decisions.

(10) As to the facilities contemplated on page 36 of the memorandum for the importation of foodstuffs and raw materials into Germany, mention was only made of them "subject to conditions and within limits which could not be indicated in advance and subject also to the necessity for having due regard to the special economic situation created for Allied and Associated countries by

[1] See Document 434.

German aggression and the war." Such cannot be regarded as a binding engagement which departs from the terms of the Treaty, but as the expression of the intention of the Allied and Associated Powers to facilitate, as far as it may be possible to them, the resumption of the economic life of Germany.

. . .

Those of the explanations given above, which, in the opinion of the Allied and Associated Powers may be regarded as constituting a binding engagement, have been incorporated in the annexed Protocol, which the Allied and Associated Governments are prepared to annex to the Treaty.

PROTOCOL[2]

With a view to indicating precisely the conditions in which certain provisions of the Treaty of even date are to be carried out, it is agreed by the High Contracting Parties that:

. . .

(4) The Reparation Commission referred to in Article 240 and paragraphs 2, 3 and 4 of Annex IV cannot require trade secrets or other confidential information to be divulged.

(5) From the signature of the Treaty and within the ensuing four months, Germany will be entitled to submit for examination by the Allied and Associated Powers documents and proposals in order to expedite the work connected with reparation, and thus to shorten the investigation and to accelerate the decisions.

. . .

DOCUMENT 436

Letter from Clemenceau to von Haniel Regarding the Authenticity of the Intermediate Text of June 18, June 21, 1919

[English translation from Peace Conference Bulletin No. 387 (June 23, 1919), in Miller, XVIII, 523. French text, in PV, Notes, p. 65. German translation, in *Materialien*, IX, 13. According to the French and German sources, this note was dated June 21; according to the English, June 22.]

Sir:

I have the honor to acknowledge the receipt of your letter of the 20th June, 1919 [see Document 434]. In reply the Allied and Associated Powers hasten to inform you that the 200 copies of the Conditions of Peace forwarded to the German Delegation on the 19th June must be regarded as the authentic text containing the correc-

---

[2] Document 444 follows.

tions and alterations made, largely in consequence of the various German Notes, in the printed text delivered on the 7th May, 1919.

Accept, sir, the expression of my high consideration.

CLEMENCEAU.

DOCUMENT 436-A

Extract from Letter from Von Haniel to Clemenceau Regarding Article 231, June 22, 1919

[Editor's translation from German text in *Materialien*, IX, 27.]

Mr. President:

The Reichsminister of Foreign Affairs has ordered me to communicate the following to Your Excellency:

.   .   .

"Germany lays, moreover, the greatest emphasis on the declaration that she cannot accept and does not cover with her signature Article 231 of the Treaty of Peace, which demands from Germany that she confess herself the sole author of the war. From this it follows directly that Germany must also refuse to recognize the derivation of her imposed burden from the war-authorship unjustly attributed to her.

.   .   .

"The Government of the German Republic makes, consequently, in the following form, the declaration of its acceptance demanded in the Note of June 16:

" 'The Government of the German Republic is prepared to sign the Treaty of Peace without, however, thereby recognizing that the German people is the author of the war and without undertaking an engagement for surrender according to Articles 227-230 of the Treaty of Peace.'

"Weimar, June 21, 1919.   "BAUER,

"President of the Ministry of the Reich."

Accept [etc.] . . .   VON HANIEL.

DOCUMENT 436-B

Letter from Clemenceau to Von Haniel Replying to Document 436-A, June 22, 1919

[Editor's translation from French text in PV, Notes, p. 73.]

Mr. President:

The Allied and Associated Powers have examined the note of the

German Delegation under date of today, and, because of the little time that remains, they judge that their duty is to make to it an immediate reply. Of the period within which the German Government is to make its definitive decision on the signature of the Treaty there remain less than twenty-four hours. The Allied and Associated Governments have examined with the greatest attention all the observations presented by the German Government on the subject of the Treaty. They have replied to them with complete frankness and have made the concessions that it has appeared just to them to make. The last note of the German Delegation contains no argument, no remark, which has not already been the object of their examination. The Allied and Associated Powers consider themselves, then, obliged to declare that the time for discussion has passed. They cannot accept or recognize any modification or reservation and they see themselves forced to demand from the representatives of Germany an unequivocal declaration of their willingness to sign and accept as a whole, or to refuse to sign and accept, the Treaty in its final form.

After the signature, the Allied and Associated Powers will hold Germany responsible for the execution of the Treaty in all its stipulations.

Accept [etc.] . . .

Signed: CLEMENCEAU.

DOCUMENT 437
Final Text of the Agreement with Belgium Regarding Priority,
Undated

[TPG, III, 257-59. At the end of this document, there has been added in Dulles' handwriting: "Signed by Mr Clemenceau Mr Lloyd George Pres Wilson June 24, 1919." However, a French text of this agreement, *dated June 16* (by the French editor in the title; but no date in text), was published in France, Ministère des Affaires Étrangères, *Documents relatifs aux réparations*, I, 21-23. The editor feels that Dulles' statement and the fact that the Supreme Council approved this agreement on June 24 (see Document 439) justify the later date. Documents 425 and 423 precede.]

[a] WHEREAS, Article 237 of the Conditions of Peace with Germany provides, among other things, that the payments to be made by Germany, by way of reparation, will be divided by the Allied and Associated Governments in proportions which have been determined upon by them in advance and on a basis of general equity and of the rights of each; and

[b] WHEREAS, it is deemed equitable that after the priority

accorded by Article 235, in respect of the expenses of the Armies of Occupation and payments for the supply of Germany, a certain priority should be granted to Belgium in respect of the payments made by Germany by way of reparation;

[c] Now, THEREFORE, the undersigned, in the name of their respective Governments, agree that out of the first cash received from Germany, in respect of reparation, Belgium shall receive, on account of the reparation payments to which she is entitled the equivalent of 2,500,000,000 gold francs.

[d] For the purposes of the foregoing there shall be reckoned as cash:

(1) Currency received by the Reparation Commission;

(2) The proceeds of the sale by the said Commission of negotiable instruments or securities received from Germany;

(3) The value of deliveries and reparation in kind made by Germany pursuant to the provisions of the Conditions of Peace and debited to the Allied and Associated Governments. This last item shall not be taken into account before May 1, 1921.

[e] It is understood that the restitutions contemplated by Article 238 of the Treaty will not be taken into consideration.

[f] Irrespective of this priority of 2,500,000,000 francs, Belgium will participate in the proportion which will be accorded to her in the division of the first payments and the subsequent division contemplated by Article 237 above referred to.

[g] Beginning with May 1, 1921, the above mentioned sum of 2,500,000,000 francs will be amortized at the rate of one-thirtieth per year out of Belgium's share in each of the subsequent payments made by Germany. If, however, Germany should complete payment of its debt in less than thirty years, such amortization will be accelerated so that it will conclude coincidentally with the final settlement of Germany.

The Annex attached hereto will serve as an illustration of the method of applying the foregoing provisions.

ANNEX

Let us assume that Germany pays up to May 1, 1921, in addition to sums which will be applied to its supply of food and raw materials and to the expenses of the Armies of Occupation, the total sum of 13 milliards of francs applicable to reparation. Let us suppose that this sum has been paid as follows:

In cash or securities converted into cash, 1½ milliards.

In different deliveries, 11½ milliards.

Let us further assume that Belgium's share is fixed at 7%, for example. On the foregoing hypothesis Belgium will be entitled:

(1) To receive the cash, that is, 1½ milliards;

(2) On May 1, 1921, each of the interested Powers, having been debited with the total amount of deliveries in kind received by it, payment will be made to Belgium out of the common fund of 1 milliard of the 11½ milliards mentioned above.

Out of the balance of 10½ milliards, Belgium will be entitled to 7%, that is to say, 735 millions.

If Belgium has received in kind 1,200,000,000, she should pay into the common funds the difference between this sum and the share of the 735 millions to which she is entitled, that is to say, 465 millions.

After 1921, for instance in 1922, if Germany has paid in that year 10 milliards and Belgium has received in kind 300 millions, its account will stand as follows:

Received in kind, 300 millions,	300,000,000
Amortization payment on the priority of 2½ milliards,	83,330,000
Total	383,330,000

Amount due to Belgium 700 millions, from which are to be deducted the above 383,330,000; balance due from the common fund to Belgium, 316,670,000.

DOCUMENT 438

Final Text of the Agreement with Belgium Regarding Her Debt to the Allies, June 24, 1919

[TPG, III, 256. At the head of this document is written, "Drafted by J. F. D." The typed date of the agreement is June 16, but a "24" has been written over the "16." In the lower left-hand corner of the page, there is added in Dulles' handwriting: "Signed by Mr Clemenceau Mr Lloyd George Pres Wilson June 24, 1919"; and the minutes of the Supreme Council of June 24 (see Document 439) make it clear that the agreement was not definitely approved until that date. These facts have, therefore, been permitted to govern the date of the document in this edition.

When Wilson later transmitted this agreement to Congress, however, recommending appropriate legislation, the date was given at that time as June 16. See Wilson's message to Congress, February 22, 1921, in United States, Congress, *Congressional Record* (66th Cong., 3d sess.), LX (Part IV), 3598, 3692. Again, in an oral answer in the House of Commons, March 22, 1921, Austen Chamberlain, Chancellor of the Exchequer, referred to the agreement also as dated June 16. See Great Britain, Parliament, *The Parliamentary Debates: Official Report*, 5th series (House of Commons), Vol. CXXXIX, column 2367. Finally, in an official French text, the date was given as June 16. See France, Ministère des Affaires Étrangères, *Documents relatifs aux réparations*, I, 21.

An earlier draft of this agreement (see Document 421) has not been printed since it is almost like the present one. It was enclosed by Lamont in his Memorandum of June 14 (see Document 424).]

Paris, June 16, 1919.

M. Hymans,
Ministre des Affaires Étrangères,
Hotel Lotti, Paris.
Sir:

The Reparation Clauses of the draft Treaty of Peace with Germany obligate Germany to make reimbursement of all sums which Belgium has borrowed from the Allied and Associated Governments up to November 11, 1918, on account of the violation by Germany of the Treaty of 1859.[1] As evidence of such obligation Germany is to make a special issue of bonds to be delivered to the Reparation Commission.

Each of the undersigned will recommend[2] to the appropriate governmental agency of his Government that, upon the delivery to the Reparation Commission of such bonds, his Government accept an amount thereof corresponding to the sums which Belgium has borrowed from his Government since the war and up to November 11, 1918, together with interest at 5% unless already included in such sums, in satisfaction of Belgium's obligation on account of such loans, which obligation of Belgium's shall thereupon be cancelled.

We are, dear Mr. Minister,

Very truly yours,

DOCUMENT 439

Report of the Meeting of the Supreme Council, June 24, 1919

[Slosson's Annotations, in Miller, XIX, 299.]

On June 24, the Supreme Council approved proposals of the financial experts relating to Belgian claims for priority in payments (C. F. 89). It was agreed . . . (C. F. 89, Appendix I).[1]

An illustrative hypothetical distribution of the indemnity is appended in Appendix II to C. F. 89;[2] and a letter to M. Hymans, assuring him that the Allied and Associated Governments would

[1] Error for "1839."

[2] The earlier draft of this agreement (see Document 421) read, "Each of the undersigned agrees to recommend [etc.]." This is the only difference between them, aside from the fact that the earlier draft, not being in the form of a letter, had only the text.

---

[1] See Document 437 for the text of the agreement.

[2] Last part of Document 437.

accept the German bond issue provided in Article 232 "in satisfaction of Belgium's obligation on account of such loans" is appended in Appendix III to C. F. 89.[3]

DOCUMENT 440

Part VIII of Final Treaty (English) with Germany (Including Annexes 1-7 and Section II), June 28, 1919

[Allied and Associated Powers (1914-1919), Treaty with Germany, June 28, 1919, *Traité de paix entre les Puissances Alliées et Associées et l'Allemagne et protocole signés à Versailles, le 28 juin 1919—Treaty of Peace between the Allied and Associated Powers and Germany and Protocol Signed at Versailles, June 28, 1919* (Paris? 1919?), pp. 101-21. The print of the Treaty from which the present edition is taken has the following two errors (and no doubt many others): (*a*) at the beginning of the Treaty (on p. 3), Smuts' middle name is spelled "Christiaan" in the French text and "Christian" in the English; (*b*) in Article 235, in the last sentence but one, "reckoned" is misspelled "cerkoned" in the English text. These two mistakes are pointed out for purposes of identification.

Document 315 precedes. These intervene but are not printed: (*a*) The Amended Fourth Revise of *about* April 30 (see Document 317); (*b*) the Fifth Revise of May 1 (see Document 326); (*c*) the Preliminary Text (English), of May 7, as handed to the Germans (see Document 344); (*d*) the Intermediate Text (English) of June 18 (see Document 431). Important differences between these intervening drafts and the present one have been indicated by footnotes.]

PART VIII
REPARATION

SECTION I
GENERAL PROVISIONS

ARTICLE 231

The Allied and Associated Governments affirm and Germany accepts the responsibility of Germany and her allies for causing all the loss and damage to which the Allied and Associated Governments and their nationals have been subjected as a consequence of the war imposed upon them by the aggression of Germany and her allies.

ARTICLE 232

The Allied and Associated Governments recognize that the resources of Germany are not adequate, after taking into account permanent diminutions of such resources which will result from other provisions of the present Treaty, to make complete reparation for all such loss and damage.

[3] See Document 438.

The Allied and Associated Governments, however, require, and Germany undertakes, that she will make compensation for all damage done to the civilian population of the Allied and Associated Powers and to their property during the period of the belligerency of each as an Allied or Associated Power against Germany[1] by such aggression by land, by sea and from the air, and in general all damage as defined in Annex I hereto.[2]

In accordance with Germany's pledges, already given, as to complete restoration for Belgium, Germany undertakes, in addition to the compensation for damage elsewhere in this Part[3] provided for, as a consequence of the violation of the Treaty of 1839, to make reimbursement of all sums which Belgium has borrowed from the Allied and Associated Governments up to November 11, 1918, together with interest at the rate of five per cent. (5%) per annum on such sums. This amount shall be determined by the Reparation Commission, and the German Government undertakes thereupon forthwith to make a special issue of bearer bonds to an equivalent amount payable in marks gold, on May 1, 1926, or, at the option of the German Government, on the 1st of May in any year up to 1926. Subject to the foregoing, the form of such bonds shall be determined by the Reparation Commission. Such bonds shall be handed over to the Reparation Commission, which has authority to take and acknowledge receipt thereof on behalf of Belgium.[4]

ARTICLE 233

The amount of the above damage for which compensation is to be made by Germany shall be determined by an Inter-Allied Commission, to be called the *Reparation Commission* and constituted in the form and with the powers set forth hereunder and in Annexes II to VII[5] inclusive hereto.

[1] The words "during the period of the belligerency of each as an Allied or Associated Power against Germany" appeared first in the Preliminary Text of May 7.

[2] In the Amended Fourth Revise of April 30, this last phrase read, "in accordance with the definition contained in Annex 1." In the Fifth Revise of May 1, it was apparently unchanged. In the Preliminary Text of May 7, it has its present form.

[3] *Preliminary Text of May 7:* "in this Chapter".
Intermediate Text of June 18: "in this Chapter".

[4] This entire paragraph appeared for the first time in the Preliminary Text of May 7. It is derived from Dulles' Memorandum of May 5 (see Document 340), almost without change.

[5] *Preliminary Text of May 7:* "Annexes II to VI". *Intermediate Text of June 18:* "Annexes II to VII".

This Commission shall consider the claims and give to the German Government a just opportunity to be heard.

The findings of the Commission as to the amount of damage defined as above shall be concluded and notified to the German Government on or before May 1, 1921, as representing the extent of that Government's obligations.

The Commission shall concurrently draw up a schedule of payments prescribing the time and manner for securing and discharging the entire obligation within a period of thirty years from May 1, 1921. If, however, within the period mentioned, Germany fails to discharge her obligations, any balance remaining unpaid may, within the discretion of the Commission, be postponed for settlement in subsequent years, or may be handled otherwise in such manner as the Allied and Associated Governments, acting in accordance with the procedure laid down in this Part of the present Treaty, shall determine.

ARTICLE 234

The Reparation Commission shall after May 1, 1921, from time to time, consider the resources and capacity of Germany, and, after giving her representatives a just opportunity to be heard, shall have discretion to extend the date, and to modify the form of payments, such as are to be provided for in accordance with Article 233; but not to cancel any part, except with the specific authority of the several Governments represented upon the Commission.

ARTICLE 235

In order to enable the Allied and Associated Powers to proceed at once to the restoration of their industrial and economic life, pending the full determination of their claims, Germany shall pay in such instalments and in such manner (whether in gold, commodities, ships, securities or otherwise) as the Reparation Commission may fix, during 1919, 1920 and the first four months of 1921, the equivalent of 20,000,000,000 gold marks. Out of this sum the expenses of the armies of occupation subsequent to the Armistice of November 11, 1918, shall first be met, and such supplies of food and raw materials as may be judged by the Governments of the Principal Allied and Associated Powers[6] to be essential to enable

---

[6] *Amended Fourth Revise of April 30 and Fifth Revise of May 1:* "by the Five Allied and Associated Governments". In the Preliminary Text of May 7 and in the Intermediate Text of June 18, it appeared as in the present text.

Germany to meet her obligations for reparation may also, with the approval of the said Governments, be paid for out of the above sum. The balance shall be cerkoned [*sic*] towards liquidation of the amounts due for reparation. Germany shall further deposit bonds as prescribed in paragraph 12 (*c*) of Annex II hereto.

ARTICLE 236

Germany further agrees to the direct application of her economic resources to reparation as specified in Annexes III, IV, V, and VI, relating respectively to merchant shipping, to physical restoration, to coal[7] and derivatives of coal, and to dyestuffs and other chemical products; provided always that the value of the property transferred and any services rendered by her under these Annexes, assessed in the manner therein prescribed, shall be credited to her towards liquidation of her obligations under the above Articles.

ARTICLE 237

The successive instalments, including the above sum, paid over by Germany in satisfaction of the above claims will be divided by the Allied and Associated Governments in proportions which have been determined upon by them in advance on a basis of general equity and of the rights of each.

For the purposes of this division the value of property transferred and service rendered under Article 243, and under Annexes III, IV, V, VI, and VII,[8] shall be reckoned in the same manner as cash payments effected in that year.

ARTICLE 238

In addition to the payments mentioned above Germany shall effect, in accordance with the procedure laid down by the Reparation Commission, restitution in cash of cash taken away, seized or sequestrated, and also restitution of animals, objects of every nature and securities taken away, seized or sequestrated, in the cases in which it proves possible to identify them in territory belonging to Germany or her allies.

Until this procedure is laid down, restitution will continue in accordance with the provisions of the Armistice of November 11, 1918, and its renewals and the Protocols thereto.[9]

---

[7] *Preliminary Text of May 7:* "to physical restoration and to coal". In the Intermediate Text of June 18, it appeared as in the present text.

[8] *Preliminary Text of May 7:* "Annexes III, IV, V and VI". In the Intermediate Text of June 18, it appeared as in the present text.

[9] This sentence appeared for the first time in the Preliminary Text of May 7.

ARTICLE 239

The German Government[10] undertakes to make forthwith the restitution contemplated by Article 238 and to make the payments and deliveries contemplated by Articles 233, 234, 235 and 236.

ARTICLE 240

The German Government[11] recognizes the Commission provided for by Article 233 as the same may be constituted by the Allied and Associated Governments in accordance with Annex II, and agrees irrevocably to the possession and exercise by such Commission of the power and authority given to it under the present Treaty.

The German Government will supply to the Commission all the information which the Commission may require relative to the financial situation and operations and to the property, productive capacity, and stocks and current production of raw materials and manufactured articles of Germany and her nationals, and further any information relative to military operations which in the judgment of the Commission may be necessary for the assessment of Germany's liability for reparation as defined in Annex I.[12]

The German Government will accord to the members of the Commission and its authorised agents the same rights and immunities as are enjoyed in Germany by duly accredited diplomatic agents of friendly Powers.

Germany further agrees to provide for the salaries and expenses of the Commission and of such staff as it may employ.

ARTICLE 241

Germany undertakes to pass, issue and maintain in force any legislation, orders and decrees that may be necessary to give complete effect to these provisions.

ARTICLE 242

The provisions of this Part of the present Treaty do not apply to the property, rights and interests referred to in Sections III and IV of Part X (Economic Clauses) of the present Treaty, nor to the product of their liquidation, except so far as concerns any final balance in favour of Germany under Article 243 (*a*).

---

[10] *Preliminary Text of May 7 and Intermediate Text of June 18:* "Germany".
[11] See note 10 above.
[12] This underlined phrase appeared for the first time in the American Fifth Revise of May 1.

ARTICLE 243

The following shall be reckoned as credits to Germany in respect of her reparation obligations:

(*a*) Any final balance in favour of Germany under Section V (Alsace-Lorraine) of Part III (Political Clauses for Europe) and Sections III and IV of Part X (Economic Clauses) of the present Treaty;[13]

(*b*) Amounts due to Germany in respect of transfers under Section IV (Saar Basin) of Part III (Political Clauses for[14] Europe), Part IX (Financial Clauses), and Part XII (Ports, Waterways and Railways);[15]

(*c*) Amounts which in the judgment of the Reparation Commission should be credited to Germany on account of any other transfers under the present Treaty of property, rights, concessions or other interests.

In no case however shall credit be given for property restored in accordance with Article 238 of the present Part.[16]

ARTICLE 244

The transfer of the German submarine cables which do not form the subject of particular provisions of the present Treaty is regulated by Annex VII hereto.[17]

ANNEX I

Compensation may be claimed from Germany under Article 232 above in respect of the total damage under the following categories:[18]

(1) Damage to injured persons and to surviving dependents by

---

[13] In the Preliminary Text of May 7 and in the Intermediate Text of June 18, the word order of this clause (*a*) is different from that of the present text. The reference to Alsace-Lorraine appeared first in the Fifth Revise of May 1.

[14] *Preliminary Text of May 7:* "in Europe".

[15] In the Preliminary Text of May 7, the word order of this clause (*b*) is different from that of the present text.

[16] *Fifth Revise of May 1:* "In no case, however, shall credit be reckoned for property restored in accordance with Article 8."

This sentence appeared for the first time in its present form in the Preliminary Text of May 7.

[17] This article appeared for the first time in the Preliminary Text of May 7.

[18] *Amended Fourth Revise of April 30* (in italics as a clause not finally agreed): "Compensation may be claimed under Article 2 above in report of the following categories of damage."

Fifth Revise of May 1: "Compensation may be claimed from Germany under Clause 2 above in respect of the total damage, under the following categories, in each theatre of war, in the proportion borne in that theatre by the naval and military effort of Germany to such effort of Germany and her Allies as a whole. These proportions shall be determined by the Reparation Commission."

In the Preliminary Text of May 7 and in the Intermediate Text of June 18, this heading appeared as it does in the present text.

personal injury to or death of civilians caused by acts of war, including bombardments or other attacks on land, on sea, or from the air, and all the direct consequences thereof, and of all operations of war by the two groups of belligerents wherever arising.

(2) Damage caused by Germany or her allies to civilian victims of acts of cruelty, violence or maltreatment (including injuries to life or health as a consequence of imprisonment, deportation, internment or evacuation, of exposure at sea or of being forced to labour),[19] wherever arising, and to the surviving dependents of such victims.

(3) Damage caused by Germany or her allies in their own territory or in occupied or invaded territory to civilian victims of all acts injurious to health or capacity to work, or to honour, as well as to the surviving dependents of such victims.

(4) Damage caused by any kind of maltreatment of prisoners of war.

(5) As damage caused to the peoples of the Allied and Associated Powers, all pensions and compensation in the nature of pensions to naval and military victims of war (including members of the air force),[20] whether mutilated, wounded, sick or invalided, and to the dependents of such victims, the amount due to the Allied and Associated Governments being calculated for each of them as being the capitalised cost of such pensions and compensation at the date of the coming into force of the present Treaty on the basis of the scales in force in France at such date.

(6) The cost of assistance by the Governments of the Allied and Associated Powers to prisoners of war and to their families and dependents.

(7) Allowances by the Governments of the Allied and Associated Powers to the families and dependents of mobilised persons or persons serving with the forces, the amount due to them for each calendar year in which hostilities occurred being calculated for each Government on the basis of the average scale for such payments in force in France during that year.

(8) Damage caused to civilians by being forced by Germany or her allies to labour without just remuneration.

---

[19] *Preliminary Text of May 7 and Intermediate Text of June 18:* "forced to labour by Germany or her allies".

[20] The words "including members of the air force" were first inserted in the Amended Fourth Revise of April 30.

(9) Damage in respect of all property wherever situated belonging to any of the Allied or Associated States or their nationals, with the exception of naval and military works or materials, which has been carried off, seized, injured or destroyed by the acts of Germany or her allies on land, on sea or from the air, or damage directly in consequence of hostilities or of any operations of war.

(10) Damage in the form of levies, fines and other similar exactions imposed by Germany or her allies upon the civilian population.

ANNEX II

1

The Commission referred to in Article 233 shall be called "The Reparation Commission" and is hereinafter referred to as "the Commission."

2

Delegates to this Commission shall be nominated by the United States of America, Great Britain, France, Italy, Japan, Belgium and the Serb-Croat-Slovene State. Each of these Powers will appoint one Delegate and also one Assistant Delegate, who will take his place in case of illness or necessary absence, but at other times will only have the right to be present at proceedings without taking any part therein.

On no occasion shall the Delegates of more than five of the above Powers have the right to take part in the proceedings of the Commission and to record their votes. The Delegates of the United States, Great Britain, France and Italy shall have this right on all occasions. The Delegate of Belgium shall have this right on all occasions other than those referred to below. The Delegate of Japan shall have this right on occasions when questions relating to damage at sea, and questions arising under Article 260 of Part IX (Financial Clauses) in which Japanese interests are concerned, are under consideration. The Delegate of the Serb-Croat-Slovene State shall have this right when questions relating to Austria, Hungary or Bulgaria are under consideration.[21]

---

[21] *British Final Revise of April 29* (the preceding draft): "Each of these Powers will appoint one Delegate and also one coadjutor Delegate [etc.]".

Amended Fourth Revise of April 30: "and also one assistant Delegate".

Fifth Revise of May 1: "Delegates to this Commission shall be nominated by the United States of America, Great Britain, France, Italy, Japan, Belgium and Serbia. Each of these Powers will appoint

Each Government represented on the Commission shall have the right to withdraw therefrom upon twelve months notice filed with the Commission and confirmed in the course of the sixth month after the date of the original notice.[22]

3

Such of the other Allied and Associated Powers as may be interested shall have the right to appoint a Delegate to be present and act as Assessor only while their respective claims and interests are under examination or discussion, but without the right to vote.

4

In case of the death, resignation or recall of any Delegate, Assistant[23] Delegate or Assessor, a successor to him shall be nominated as soon as possible.

5

The Commission will have its principal permanent Bureau in Paris and will hold its first meeting in Paris as soon as practicable after the coming into force of the present Treaty, and thereafter will meet in such place or places and at such time as it may deem convenient and as may be necessary for the most expeditious discharge of its duties.

6

At its first meeting the Commission shall elect, from among the Delegates referred to above, a Chairman and a Vice-Chairman, who shall hold office for one year and shall be eligible for re-election. If a vacancy in the Chairmanship or Vice-Chairmanship should

---

one Delegate and also one assistant Delegate who will take his place in case of illness or necessary absence but at other times will only have the right to be present at proceedings without taking any part therein. On no occasion shall the Delegates of more than five of the above Powers have the right to take part in the proceedings of the Commission and to record their votes. The Delegates of the United States, Great Britain, France and Italy shall have this right on all occasions. The Delegate of Belgium shall have this right on all occasions other than those referred to below. The Delegate of Japan shall have this right on occasions when questions relating to damage at sea and questions arising under Article 13 of Section (Financial Clauses), in which Japanese interests are concerned, are under consideration. The Delegate of Serbia shall have this right when questions relating to Austria-Hungary and Bulgaria are under consideration."

Preliminary Text of May 7: same as above except "The Delegate of Japan shall have this right on occasions when questions relating to damage at sea, and questions arising under Article 260 of Part IX (Financial Clauses) in which Japanese interests are concerned, are under consideration. The Delegate of Serbia shall have this right when questions relating to Austria, Hungary or Bulgaria are under consideration."

Intermediate Text of June 18: same as the present draft.

[22] This sentence did not appear in the Preliminary Text of May 7, but it did appear in the Intermediate Text of June 18.

[23] The term "coadjutor Delegate" in the British Final Revise of April 29 was changed to "Assistant Delegate" in the Amended Fourth Revise of April 30 and in all subsequent drafts.

occur during the annual period, the Commission shall proceed to a new election for the remainder of the said period.

7

The Commission is authorised to appoint all necessary officers, agents and employees who may be required for the execution of its functions, and to fix their remuneration; to constitute committees, whose members need not necessarily be members of the Commission, and to take all executive steps necessary for the purpose of discharging its duties; and to delegate authority and discretion to officers, agents and committees.

8

All proceedings of the Commission shall be private, unless, on particular occasions, the Commission shall otherwise determine for special reasons.

9

The Commission shall be required, if the German Government so desire, to hear, within a period which it will fix from time to time, evidence and arguments on the part of Germany on any question connected with her capacity to pay.

10

The Commission shall consider the claims and give to the German Government a just opportunity to be heard, but not to take any part whatever in the decisions of the Commission. The Commission shall afford a similar opportunity to the allies of Germany, when it shall consider that their interests are in question.[24]

11

The Commission shall not be bound by any particular code or rules of law or by any particular rule of evidence or of procedure, but shall be guided by justice, equity and good faith. Its decisions must follow the same principles and rules in all cases where they are applicable. It will establish rules relating to methods of proof of claims. It may act on any trustworthy modes of computation.

12

The Commission shall have all the powers conferred upon it, and shall exercise all the functions assigned to it, by the present Treaty.

[24] This sentence appeared for the first time in the Fifth Revise of May 1.

The Commission[25] shall in general have wide latitude as to its control and handling of the whole reparation problem as dealt with in this Part of the present Treaty and shall have authority to interpret its provisions. Subject to the provisions of the present Treaty, the Commission is constituted by the several Allied and Associated Governments referred to in paragraphs 2 and 3 above[26] as the exclusive agency of the said Governments respectively for receiving, selling, holding, and distributing the reparation payments to be made by Germany under this Part of the present Treaty. The Commission must comply with the following conditions and provisions:

a) Whatever part of the full amount of the proved claims is not paid in gold, or in ships, securities and commodities or otherwise, Germany shall be required, under such conditions as the Commission may determine, to cover by way of guarantee by an equivalent issue of bonds, obligations or otherwise, in order to constitute an acknowledgment of the said part of the debt.

(*b*) In periodically estimating Germany's capacity to pay, the Commission shall examine the German system of taxation, first, to the end that the sums for reparation which Germany is required to pay shall become a charge upon all her revenues prior to that for the service or discharge of any domestic loan, and secondly, so as to satisfy itself that, in general, the German scheme of taxation is fully as heavy proportionately as that of any of the Powers represented on the Commission.

(*c*) In order to facilitate and continue the immediate restoration of the economic life of the Allied and Associated countries, the Commission will as provided in Article 235 take from Germany by way of security for and acknowledgment of her debt a first instalment of gold bearer bonds free of all taxes and charges of every description established or to be established by the Government of the German Empire or of the German States, or by any authority subject to them; these bonds will be delivered on account and in three portions, the marks gold being payable in conformity with Article 262[27] of Part IX (Financial Clauses) of the present Treaty as follows:

(1) To be issued forthwith, 20,000,000,000 Marks gold bearer

[25] The words "The Commission" appeared first in the Intermediate Text of June 18.

[26] This amendment appeared for the first time in the Fifth Revise of May 1.

[27] The Preliminary Text of May 7 has a misprint: "Article 202".

bonds, payable not later than May 1, 1921, without interest. There shall be specially applied towards the amortisation of these bonds the payments which Germany is pledged to make in conformity with Article 235, after deduction of the sums used for the reimbursement of expenses of the armies of occupation and for payment of foodstuffs and raw materials. Such bonds as have not been redeemed by May 1, 1921, shall then be exchanged for new bonds of the same type as those provided for below (paragraph 12, *c*, (2).

(2) To be issued forthwith, further 40,000,000,000 Marks gold bearer bonds, bearing interest at 2½ per cent. per annum between 1921 and 1926, and thereafter at 5 per cent. per annum with an additional 1 per cent. for amortisation beginning in 1926 on the whole amount of the issue.

(3) To be delivered forthwith a covering undertaking in writing to issue when, but not until, the Commission is satisfied that Germany can meet such interest and sinking fund obligations, a further instalment of 40,000,000,000 Marks gold 5 per cent. bearer bonds, the time and mode of payment of principal and interest to be determined by the Commission.

The dates for payment of interest, the manner of applying the amortisation fund, and all other questions relating to the issue, management and regulation of the bond issue shall be determined by the Commission from time to time.

Further issues by way of acknowledgment and security may be required as the Commission subsequently determines from time to time.

(*d*) In the event of bonds, obligations or other evidence of indebtedness issued by Germany by way of security for or acknowledgment of her reparation debt being disposed of outright, not by way of pledge, to persons other than the several Governments in whose favour Germany's original reparation indebtedness was created, an amount of such reparation indebtedness shall be deemed to be extinguished corresponding to the nominal value of the bonds, etc., so disposed of outright, and the obligation of Germany in respect of such bonds shall be confined to her liabilities to the holders of the bonds, as expressed upon their face.

(*e*) The damage for repairing, reconstructing and rebuilding property in the invaded and devastated districts, including reinstallation of furniture, machinery and other equipment, will be calculated according to the cost at the dates when the work is done.

(*f*) Decisions of the Commission relating to the total or partial cancellation of the capital or interest of any verified debt of Germany must be accompanied by a statement of its reasons.

13

As to voting, the Commission will observe the following rules:

When a decision of the Commission is taken, the votes of all the Delegates entitled to vote, or in the absence of any of them, of their Assistant Delegates, shall be recorded.[28] Abstention from voting is to be treated as a vote against the proposal under discussion. Assessors have no vote.

On the following questions unanimity is necessary:

(*a*) Questions involving the sovereignty of any of the Allied and Associated Powers, or the cancellation of the whole or any part of the debt or obligations of Germany;

(*b*) Questions of determining the amount and conditions of bonds or other obligations to be issued by the German Government and of fixing the time and manner for selling, negotiating or distributing such bonds;

(*c*) Any postponement, total or partial, beyond the end of 1930, of the payment of instalments falling due between May 1, 1921, and the end of 1926 inclusive;

(*d*) Any postponement, total or partial, of any instalment falling due after 1926 for a period exceeding three years;

(*e*) Questions of applying in any particular case a method of measuring damages different from that which has been previously applied in a similar case;

(*f*) Questions of the interpretation of the provisions of this Part of the present Treaty.

All other questions shall be decided by the vote of a majority.

In case of any difference of opinion among the Delegates, which cannot be solved by reference to their Governments, upon the question whether a given case is one which requires a unanimous vote for its decision or not, such difference shall be referred to the immediate arbitration of some impartial person to be agreed upon by their Governments, whose award the Allied and Associated Governments agree to accept.

14

Decisions of the Commission, in accordance with the powers

[28] *Amended Fourth Revise of April 30:* same as preceding draft except "assistant Delegates".

Fifth Revise of May 1: "When a decision of the Commission is taken, the votes of all the Delegates qualified to vote, or in the absence of any of them of their assistant Delegates, shall be recorded."

Preliminary Text of May 7 and Intermediate Text of June 18: "entitled to vote".

conferred upon it, shall forthwith become binding and may be put into immediate execution without further proceedings.

15

The Commission will issue to each of the interested Powers, in such form as the Commission shall fix:

(1) A certificate stating that it holds for the account of the said Power bonds of the issues mentioned above, the said certificate, on the demand of the Power concerned, being divisible in a number of parts not exceeding five;

(2) From time to time certificates stating the goods delivered by Germany on account of her reparation debt which it holds for the account of the said Power.

The said certificates shall be registered, and upon notice to the Commission, may be transferred by endorsement.

When bonds are issued for sale or negotiation, and when goods are delivered by the Commission, certificates to an equivalent value must be withdrawn.

16

Interest shall be debited to Germany as from May 1, 1921, in respect of her debt as determined by the Commission, after allowing for sums already covered by cash payments or their equivalent, or by bonds issued to the Commission, or under Article 243. The rate of interest shall be 5 per cent. unless the Commission shall determine at some future time that circumstances justify a variation of this rate.

The Commission, in fixing on May 1, 1921, the total amount of the debt of Germany, may take account of interest due on sums arising out of the reparation of material damage as from November 11, 1918, up to May 1, 1921.

17

In case of default by Germany in the performance of any obligation under this Part of the present Treaty, the Commission will forthwith give notice of such default to each of the interested Powers and may make such recommendations as to the action to be taken in consequence of such default as it may think necessary.

18

The measures which the Allied and Associated Powers shall have the right to take, in case of voluntary default by Germany, and which Germany agrees not to regard as acts of war, may include economic and financial prohibitions and reprisals and in general such other measures as the respective Governments may determine to be necessary in the circumstances.

19

Payments required to be made in gold or its equivalent on account of the proved claims of the Allied and Associated Powers may at any time be accepted by the Commission in the form of chattels, properties, commodities, businesses, rights, concessions, within or without German territory, ships, bonds, shares or securities of any kind, or currencies of Germany or other States, the value of such substitutes for gold being fixed at a fair and just amount by the Commission itself.

20

The Commission, in fixing or accepting payment in specified properties or rights, shall have due regard for any legal or equitable interests of the Allied and Associated Powers or of neutral Powers or of their nationals therein.

21

No member of the Commission shall be responsible, except to the Government appointing him, for any action or omission as such member. No one of the Allied or Associated Governments assumes any responsibility in respect of any other Government.

22

Subject to the provisions of the present Treaty this Annex may be amended by the unanimous decision of the Governments represented from time to time upon the Commission.

23

When all the amounts due from Germany and her allies under the present Treaty or the decisions of the Commission have been discharged and all sums received, or their equivalents, shall have been distributed to the Powers interested, the Commission shall be dissolved.

ANNEX III

1

Germany recognises the right of the Allied and Associated Powers to the replacement, ton for ton (gross tonnage) and class for class, of all merchant ships and fishing boats lost or damaged owing to the war.

Nevertheless, and in spite of the fact that the tonnage of German shipping at present in existence is much less than that lost by the Allied and Associated Powers in consequence of the German aggression,[29] the right thus recognised will be enforced on German ships and boats under the following conditions:

The German Government, on behalf of themselves and so as to bind all other persons interested, cede to the Allied and Associated Governments the property in all the German merchant ships which are of 1,600 tons gross and upwards; in one-half, reckoned in tonnage, of the ships which are between 1,000 tons and 1,600 tons gross; in one-quarter, reckoned in tonnage, of the steam trawlers; and in one-quarter, reckoned in tonnage, of the other fishing boats.

2

The German Government will, within two months of the coming into force of the present Treaty, deliver to the Reparation Commission all the ships and boats mentioned in paragraph 1.

3

The ships and boats mentioned in paragraph 1 include all ships and boats which (*a*) fly, or may be entitled to fly, the German merchant flag; or (*b*) are owned by any German national, company or corporation or by any company or corporation belonging to a country other than an Allied or Associated country and under the control or direction of German nationals; or (*c*) are now under construction (1) in Germany, (2) in other than Allied or Associated countries for the account of any German national, company or corporation.

4

For the purpose of providing documents of title for the ships and boats to be handed over as above mentioned, the German Government will:

(*a*) Deliver to the Reparation Commission in respect of each vessel a bill of sale or other document of title evidencing the transfer to the Commission of the entire property in the vessel, free from all encumbrances, charges and liens of all kinds, as the Commission may require;

(*b*) Take all measures that may be indicated by the Reparation

---

[29] *Fifth Revise of May 1:* "lost by the Allied and Associated Powers, in consequence of the naval operations of Germany, the right thus".
The Preliminary Text of May 7 and the Intermediate Text of June 18 are like the present draft.

Commission for ensuring that the ships themselves shall be placed at its disposal.

5

As an additional part of reparation, Germany agrees to cause merchant ships to be built in German yards for the account of the Allied and Associated Governments as follows:

(*a*) Within three months of the coming into force of the present Treaty, the Reparation Commission will notify to the German Government the amount of tonnage to be laid down in German shipyards in each of the two years next succeeding the three months mentioned above.

(*b*) Within two years[30] of the coming into force of the present Treaty, the Reparation Commission will notify to the German Government the amount of tonnage to be laid down in each of the three years following the two years mentioned above.

(*c*) The amount of tonnage to be laid down in each year shall not exceed 200,000 tons, gross tonnage.

(*d*) The specifications of the ships to be built, the conditions under which they are to be built and delivered, the price per ton at which they are to be accounted for by the Reparation Commission, and all other questions relating to the accounting, ordering, building and delivery of the ships, shall be determined by the Commission.

6

Germany undertakes to restore in kind and in normal condition of upkeep to the Allied and Associated Powers, within two months of the coming into force of the present Treaty, in accordance with procedure to be laid down by the Reparation Commission, any boats and other movable appliances belonging to inland navigation which since August 1, 1914, have by any means whatever come into her possession or into the possession of her nationals, and which can be identified.

With a view to make good the loss in inland navigation tonnage, from whatever cause arising, which has been incurred during the war by the Allied and Associated Powers, and which cannot be made good by means of the restitution prescribed above, Germany agrees to cede to the Reparation Commission a portion of the German river fleet up to the amount of the loss mentioned above, provided that such cession shall not exceed 20 per cent. of the river fleet as it existed on November 11, 1918.

[30] *Preliminary Text of May 7 and Intermediate Text of June 18:* "Within twenty-four months".

The conditions of this cession shall be settled by the arbitrators referred to in Article 339 of Part XII (Ports, Waterways and Railways) of the present Treaty, who are charged with the settlement of difficulties relating to the apportionment of river tonnage resulting from the new international régime applicable to certain river systems or from the territorial changes affecting those systems.

7

Germany agrees to take any measures that may be indicated to her by the Reparation Commission for obtaining the full title to the property in all ships which have during the war been transferred, or are in process of transfer, to neutral flags, without the consent of the Allied and Associated Governments.

8

Germany waives all claims of any description against the Allied and Associated Governments and their nationals in respect of the detention, employment, loss or damage of any German ships or boats, exception being made of payments due in respect of the employment of ships in conformity with the Armistice Agreement of January 13, 1919, and subsequent Agreements.

The handing over of the ships of the German mercantile marine must be continued without interruption in accordance with the said Agreement.[31]

9

Germany waives all claims to vessels or cargoes sunk by or in consequence of naval action and subsequently salved, in which any of the Allied or Associated Governments or their nationals may have any interest either as owners, charterers, insurers or otherwise, notwithstanding any decree of condemnation which may have been made by a Prize Court of Germany or of her allies.

ANNEX IV

1

The Allied and Associated Powers require, and Germany undertakes, that in part satisfaction of her obligations expressed in the present Part[32] she will, as hereinafter provided, devote her economic

---

[31] This sentence was first inserted in the Preliminary Text of May 7.

[32] *Preliminary Text of May 7 and Intermediate Text of June 18:* "expressed in this Part of the present Treaty".

resources directly to the physical restoration of the invaded areas of the Allied and Associated Powers, to the extent that these Powers may determine.

2

The Allied and Associated Governments may file with the Reparation Commission lists showing:

(*a*) Animals, machinery, equipment, tools and like articles of a commercial character, which have been seized, consumed or destroyed by Germany or destroyed in direct consequence of military operations, and which such Governments, for the purpose of meeting immediate and urgent needs, desire to have replaced by animals and articles of the same nature which are in being in German territory at the date of the coming into force of the present Treaty;

(*b*) Reconstruction materials (stones, bricks, refractory bricks,[33] tiles, wood, window-glass, steel, lime, cement, etc.), machinery, heating apparatus, furniture and like articles of a commercial character which the said Governments desire to have produced and manufactured in Germany and delivered to them to permit of the restoration of the invaded areas.

3

The lists relating to the articles mentioned in 2 (*a*) above shall be filed within sixty days after the date of the coming into force of the present Treaty.

The lists relating to the articles in 2 (*b*) above shall be filed on or before December 31, 1919.

The lists shall contain all such details as are customary in commercial contracts dealing with the subject matter, including specifications, dates of delivery (but not extending over more than four years), and places of delivery, but not price or value, which shall be fixed as hereinafter provided by the Commission.

4

Immediately upon the filing of such lists with the Commission, the Commission shall consider the amount and number of the materials and animals mentioned in the lists provided for above which are to be required of Germany. In reaching a decision on

---

[33] This phrase appeared for the first time in the Amended Fourth Revise of April 30 as "upactery bricks". It was corrected in the Fifth Revise of May 1.

this matter the Commission shall take into account such domestic requirements of Germany as it deems essential for the maintenance of Germany's social and economic life, the prices and dates at which similar articles can be obtained in the Allied and Associated countries as compared with those to be fixed for German articles, and the general interest of the Allied and Associated Governments that the industrial life of Germany be not so disorganised as to affect adversely the ability of Germany to perform the other acts of reparation stipulated for.

Machinery, equipment, tools and like articles of a commercial character in actual industrial use are not, however, to be demanded of Germany unless there is no free stock of such articles respectively which is not in use and is available, and then not in excess of thirty per cent. of the quantity of such articles in use in any one establishment or undertaking.

The Commission shall give representatives of the German Government an opportunity and a time to be heard as to their capacity to furnish the said materials, articles and animals.

The decision of the Commission shall thereupon and at the earliest possible moment be communicated to the German Government and to the several interested Allied and Associated Governments.

The German Government undertakes to deliver the materials, articles and animals as specified in the said communication, and the interested Allied and Associated Governments severally agree to accept the same, provided they conform to the specification given, or are not, in the judgment of the Commission, unfit to be utilized in the work of reparation.

5

The Commission shall determine the value to be attributed to the materials, articles and animals to be delivered in accordance with the foregoing, and the Allied or Associated Power receiving the same agrees to be charged with such value, and the amount thereof shall be treated as a payment by Germany to be divided in accordance with Article 237 of this Part of the present Treaty.

In cases where the right to require physical restoration as above provided is exercised, the Commission shall ensure that the amount to be credited against the reparation obligation of Germany shall be the fair value of work done or materials supplied by Germany, and that the claim made by the interested Power in respect o [*sic*] the damage so repaired by physical restoration shall be discharged to the extent of the proportion which the damage thus repaired bears to the whole of the damage thus claimed for.

6

As an immediate advance on account of the animals referred to in paragraph 2 (*a*) above, Germany undertakes to deliver in equal monthly instalments in the three months following the coming into force of the present Treaty the following quantities of live stock:

(1) *To the French Government*

500 stallions (3 to 7 years);
30,000 fillies and mares (18 months to 7 years), type: Ardennais, Boulonnais or Belgian;
2,000 bulls (18 months to 3 years);
90,000 milch cows (2 to 6 years);
1,000 rams;
100,000 sheep;
10,000 goats.

(2) *To the Belgian Government*

200 stallions (3 to 7 years), large Belgian type;
5,000 mares (3 to 7 years), large Belgian type;
5,000 fillies (18 months to 3 years), large Belgian type;
2,000 bulls (18 months to 3 years);
50,000 milch cows (2 to 6 years);
40,000 heifers;
200 rams;
20,000 sheep;
15,000 sows.

The animals delivered shall be of average health and condition.

To the extent that animals so delivered cannot be identified as animals taken away or seized, the value of such animals shall be credited against the reparation obligations of Germany in accordance with paragraph 5 of this Annex.[34]

7

Without waiting for the decisions of the Commission referred to in paragraph 4 of this Annex to be taken, Germany must continue the delivery to France of the agricultural material referred to in

---

[34] This whole clause 6 appeared for the first time in the Preliminary Text of May 7.

Article III of the renewal dated January 16, 1919, of the Armistice.[35]

ANNEX V

1

Germany accords the following options for the delivery of coal and derivatives of coal to the undermentioned signatories of the present Treaty.

2

Germany undertakes to deliver to France seven million tons of coal per year for ten years. In addition, Germany undertakes to deliver to France annually for a period not exceeding ten years an amount of coal equal to the difference between the annual production before the war of the coal mines of the Nord and Pas de Calais, destroyed as a result of the war, and the production of the mines of the same area during the years in question: such delivery not to exceed twenty million tons in any one year of the first five years, and eight million tons in any one year of the succeeding five years.

It is understood that due diligence will be exercised in the restoration of the destroyed mines in the Nord and the Pas de Calais.

3

Germany undertakes to deliver to Belgium eight million tons of coal annually for ten years.

4

Germany undertakes to deliver to Italy up to the following quantities of coal:

July 1919 to June 1920	4½ million tons,
— 1920 — 1921	6 —
— 1921 — 1922	7½ —
— 1922 — 1923	8 —
— 1923 — 1924	} 8½ —
and each of the following five years	

At least two-thirds of the actual deliveries to be land-borne.

5

Germany further undertakes to deliver annually to Luxemburg, if directed by the Reparation Commission, a quantity of coal equal to the pre-war annual consumption of German coal in Luxemburg.

<hr>

[35] Clause 7 appeared for the first time in the Preliminary Text of May 7.

6

The prices to be paid for coal delivered under these options shall be as follows:

(*a*) For overland delivery, including delivery by barge, the German pithead price to German nationals, plus the freight to French, Belgian, Italian or Luxemburg frontiers, provided that the pithead price does not exceed the pithead price of British coal for export. In the case of Belgian bunker coal, the price shall not exceed the Dutch bunker price.

Railroad and barge tariffs shall not be higher than the lowest similar rates paid in Germany.

(*b*) For sea delivery, the German export price f.o.b. German ports, or the British export price f.o.b. British ports, whichever may be lower.

7

The Allied and Associated Governments interested may demand the delivery, in place of coal, of metallurgical coke in the proportion of 3 tons of coke to 4 tons of coal.

8

Germany undertakes to deliver to France, and to transport to the French frontier by rail or by water, the following products, during each of the three years following the coming into force of this Treaty:

Benzol...............................	35,000 tons.
Coal tar..............................	50,000 tons.
Sulphate of ammonia...................	30,000 tons.

All or part of the coal tar may, at the option of the French Government, be replaced by corresponding quantities of products of distillation, such as light oils, heavy oils, anthracene, naphthalene or pitch.

9

The price paid for coke and for the articles referred to in the preceding paragraph shall be the same as the price paid by German nationals under the same conditions of shipment to the French frontier or to the German ports, and shall be subject to any advantages which may be accorded similar products furnished to German nationals.

10

The foregoing options shall be exercised through the intervention of the Reparation Commission, which, subject to the specific provisions hereof, shall have power to determine all questions relative to procedure and the qualities and quantities of products, the quantity of coke which may be substituted for coal, and the times and modes of delivery and payment. In giving notice to the German Government of the foregoing options the Commission shall give at least 120 days' notice of deliveries to be made after January 1, 1920, and at least 30 days' notice of deliveries to be made between the coming into force of this Treaty and January 1, 1920. Until Germany has received the demands referred to in this paragraph, the provisions of the Protocol of December 25, 1918, (Execution of Article VI of the Armistice of November 11, 1918) remain in force.[36] The notice to be given to the German Government of the exercise of the right of substitution accorded by paragraphs 7 and 8 shall be such as the Reparation Commission may consider sufficient.[37] If the Commission shall determine that the full exercise of the foregoing options would interfere unduly with the industrial requirements of Germany, the Commission is authorised to postpone or to cancel deliveries, and in so doing to settle all questions of priority; but the coal to replace coal from destroyed mines shall receive priority over other deliveries.

ANNEX VI

1

Germany accords to the Reparation Commission an option to require as part of reparation the delivery by Germany of such quantities and kinds of dyestuffs and chemical drugs as the Commission may designate, not exceeding 50 per cent. of the total stock of each and every kind of dyestuff and chemical drug in Germany or under German control at the date of the coming into force of the present Treaty.

This option shall be exercised within sixty days of the receipt by the Commission of such particulars as to stocks as may be considered necessary by the Commission.

2

Germany further accords to the Reparation Commission an option to require delivery during the period from the date of the

[36] This sentence was first inserted in the Preliminary Text of May 7.
[37] This sentence was first inserted in the Amended Fourth Revise of April 30.

coming into force of the present Treaty until January 1, 1920, and during each period of six months thereafter until January 1, 1925, of any specified kind of dyestuff and chemical drug up to an amount not exceeding 25 per cent. of the German production of such dye-stuffs and chemical drugs during the previous six months period. If in any case the production during such previous six months was, in the opinion of the Commission, less than normal, the amount required may be 25 per cent. of the normal production.

Such option shall be exercised within four weeks after the receipt of such particulars as to production and in such form as may be considered necessary by the Commission; these particulars shall be furnished by the German Government immediately after the expiration of each six months period.

3

For dyestuffs and chemical drugs delivered under paragraph 1, the price shall be fixed by the Commission having regard to pre-war net export prices and to subsequent increases of cost.

For dyestuffs and chemical drugs delivered under paragraph 2, the price shall be fixed by the Commission having regard to pre-war net export prices and subsequent variations of cost, or the lowest net selling price of similar dyestuffs and chemical drugs to any other purchaser.

4

All details, including mode and times of exercising the options, and making delivery, and all other questions arising under this arrangement shall be determined by the Reparation Commission; the German Government will furnish to the Commission all necessary information and other assistance which it may require.

5

The above expression "dyestuffs and chemical drugs" includes all synthetic dyes and drugs and intermediate or other products used in connection with dyeing, so far as they are manufactured for sale. The present arrangement shall also apply to cinchona bark and salts of quinine.[38]

ANNEX VII[39]

Germany renounces on her own behalf and on behalf of her

---

[38] This sentence was first inserted in the Preliminary Text of May 7.

[39] Annex VII appeared for the first time in the Preliminary Text of May 7.

nationals in favour of the Principal Allied and Associated Powers all rights, titles or privileges of whatever nature in the submarine cables set out below, or in any portions thereof:

Emden-Vigo: from the Straits of Dover to off Vigo;

Emden-Brest: from off Cherbourg to Brest;

Emden-Teneriffe: from off Dunkirk to off Teneriffe;

Emden-Azores (1): from the Straits of Dover to Fayal;

Emden-Azores (2): from the Straits of Dover to Fayal;

Azores-New-York (1): from Fayal to New York;

Azores-New-York (2): from Fayal to the longitude of Halifax;

Teneriffe-Monrovia: from off Teneriffe to off Monrovia;

Monrovia-Lome:

from about.............	$\begin{cases} \text{lat. } : 2° 30' \text{ N.;} \\ \text{long.: } 7° 40' \text{ W. of Greenwich;} \end{cases}$
to about...............	$\begin{cases} \text{lat. } : 2° 20' \text{ N.;} \\ \text{long.: } 5° 30' \text{ W. of Greenwich;} \end{cases}$
and from about.........	$\begin{cases} \text{lat. } : 3° 48' \text{ N.;} \\ \text{long.: } 0° 00', \end{cases}$

to Lome;

Lome-Duala: from Lome to Duala;

Monrovia-Pernambuco: from off Monrovia to off Pernambuco;

Constantinople-Constanza: from Constantinople to Constanza;

Yap-Shanghai, Yap-Guam, and Yap-Menado (Celebes): from Yap Island to Shanghai, from Yap Island to Guam Island, and from Yap Island to Menado.

The value of the above mentioned cables or portions thereof in so far as they are privately owned, calculated on the basis of the original cost less a suitable allowance for depreciation, shall be credited to Germany in the reparation account.

SECTION II[40]
SPECIAL PROVISIONS

ARTICLE 245

Within six months after the coming into force of the present Treaty the German Government must restore to the French Government the trophies, archives, historical souvenirs or works of art carried away from France by the German authorities in the course of the war of 1870-1871 and during this last war, in accordance with a list which will be communicated to it by the French

---

[40] Section II (Special Provisions) appeared first in the Preliminary Text of May 7.

Government; particularly the French flags taken in the course of the war of 1870-1871 and all the political papers taken by the German authorities on October 10, 1870, at the chateau of Cerçay, near Brunoy (Seine-et-Oise) belonging at the time to Mr. Rouher, formerly Minister of State.

ARTICLE 246

Within six months from the coming into force of the present Treaty, Germany will restore to His Majesty the King of the Hedjaz the original Koran of the Caliph Othman, which was removed from Medina by the Turkish authorities and is stated to have been presented to the ex-Emperor William II.

Within the same period Germany will hand over to His Britannic Majesty's Government the skull of the Sultan Mkwawa which was removed from the Protectorate of German East Africa and taken to Germany.

The delivery of the articles above referred to will be effected in such place and in such conditions as may be laid down by the Governments to which they are to be restored.

ARTICLE 247

Germany undertakes to furnish to the University of Louvain, within three months after a request made by it and transmitted through the intervention of the Reparation Commission, manuscripts, incunabula, printed books, maps[41] and objects of collection corresponding in number and value to those destroyed in the burning by Germany of the Library of Louvain. All details regarding such replacement will be determined by the Reparation Commission.

Germany undertakes to deliver to Belgium, through the Reparation Commission, within six months of the coming into force of the present Treaty, in order to enable Belgium to reconstitute two great artistic works:[42]

(1) The leaves of the triptych of the Mystic Lamb painted by the Van Eyck brothers, formerly in the Church of St. Bavon at Ghent, now in the Berlin Museum;

(2) The leaves of the triptych of the Last Supper, painted by Dierick Bouts, formerly in the Church of St. Peter at Louvain,

[41] *Preliminary Text of May 7:* "incunabula, prints, maps". The Intermediate Text of June 18 is like the present draft.

[42] *Preliminary Text of May 7:* "her two great artistic works". The Intermediate Text of June 18 is like the present draft.

two of which are now in the Berlin Museum and two in the Old[43] Pinakothek at Munich.[44]

DOCUMENT 441

Part VIII of Final Treaty (French) with Germany (Including Annexes 1-7 and Section II), June 28, 1919

[See Document 440 for the title of the print of the Treaty from which this text is taken. Document 312 precedes. These intervene but are not printed: (*a*) French Third "Title *N*" Draft of April 30 (see Document 323); (*b*) French "Title VIII" Draft of May 3 (see Document 338); (*c*) Preliminary Text (French) of May 7 as handed to the Germans (see Document 345); (*d*) Intermediate Text (French) of June 18 (see Document 432). Important differences between these intervening drafts and the present one have been indicated by footnotes.]

PARTIE VIII
RÉPARATIONS

SECTION I
DISPOSITIONS GÉNÉRALES

ARTICLE 231

Les Gouvernements alliés et associés déclarent et l'Allemagne reconnaît que l'Allemagne et .ses alliés sont responsables, pour les avoir causés, de toutes les pertes et de tous les dommages subis par les Gouvernements alliés et associés et leurs nationaux en conséquence de la guerre, qui leur a été imposée par l'agression de l'Allemagne et de ses alliés.

ARTICLE 232

Les Gouvernements alliés et associés reconnaissent que les ressources de l'Allemagne ne sont pas suffisantes—en tenant compte de la diminution permanente de ces ressources qui résulte des autres dispositions du présent Traité,—pour assurer complète réparation de toutes ces pertes et de tous ces dommages.

Les Gouvernements alliés et associés exigent toutefois, et l'Allemagne en prend l'engagement, que soient réparés tous les dommages causés à la population civile de chacune des Puissances alliées et associées et à ses biens, pendant la période où cette

---

[43] *Preliminary Text of May 7:* "former Pinakothek". The Intermediate Text of June 18 is like the present draft.

[44] Article 247 as a whole appeared for the first time in the Preliminary Text of May 7. The underlining refers to the preceding draft for this article—Dulles' Memorandum of May 5 (see Document 340).

Puissance a été en état de belligérance avec l'Allemagne,[1] par ladite agression par terre, par mer et par les airs, et, d'une façon générale, tous les dommages tels qu'ils sont définis à l'Annexe I ci-jointe.[2]

En exécution des engagements pris antérieurement par l'Allemagne relativement aux restaurations et restitutions intégrales dues à la Belgique, l'Allemagne s'oblige, en sus des compensations de dommages prévues d'autre part à la présente Partie, et en conséquence de la violation du Traité de 1839, à effectuer le remboursement de toutes les sommes que la Belgique a empruntées aux Gouvernements alliés et associés jusqu'au 11 novembre 1918, y compris l'intérêt à 5 o/o (cinq pour cent) par an desdites sommes. Le montant de ces sommes sera déterminé par la Commission des réparations, et le Gouvernement allemand s'engage à faire immédiatement une émission correspondante de bons spéciaux au porteur payables en marks or le 1er mai 1926 ou, au choix du Gouvernement allemand, le 1er mai de toute année antérieure à 1926. Sous réserve des dispositions ci-dessus, la forme de ces bons sera déterminée par la Commission des réparations. Lesdits bons seront remis à la Commission des réparations, qui aura pouvoir de les recevoir et d'en accuser réception au nom de la Belgique.[3]

ARTICLE 233

Le montant desdits dommages, pour lesquels réparation est due par l'Allemagne, sera fixé par une Commission interalliée, qui prendra le titre de *Commission des réparations* et sera constituée dans la forme et avec les pouvoirs indiqués ci-après et aux Annexes II à VII ci-jointes.

Cette Commission étudiera les réclamations et donnera au Gouvernement allemand l'équitable faculté de se faire entendre.

Les conclusions de cette Commission, en ce qui concerne le montant des dommages déterminés ci-dessus, seront rédigées et notifiées au Gouvernement allemand le 1er mai 1921 au plus tard, comme représentant le total de ses obligations.

La Commission établira concurremment un état de payements

---

[1] The words "pendant la période ou cette Puissance a été en état de belligérance avec l'Allemagne" appeared first in the Intermediate Text (French) of June 18.

[2] The words "et, d'une façon générale, tous les dommages" appeared first in the Preliminary Text (French) of May 7.

[3] This entire paragraph appeared for the first time in the Preliminary Text (French) of May 7.

en prévoyant les époques et les modalités de l'acquittement par l'Allemagne de l'intégralité de sa dette dans une période de trente ans, à dater du 1er mai 1921. Au cas cependant où, au cours de ladite période, l'Allemagne manquerait à l'acquittement de sa dette, le règlement de tout solde restant impayé pourra être reporté aux années suivantes, à la volonté de la Commission, ou pourra faire l'objet d'un traitement différent, dans telles conditions que détermineront les Gouvernements alliés et associés, agissant suivant la procédure prévue à la présente Partie du présent Traité.

ARTICLE 234

La Commission des réparations devra, après le 1er mai 1921, étudier, de temps à autre, les ressources et les capacités de l'Allemagne, et, après avoir donné aux représentants de ce pays l'équitable faculté de se faire entendre, elle aura tous pouvoirs pour étendre la période et modifier les modalités des payements à prévoir en conformité de l'article 233; mais elle ne pourra faire remise d'aucune somme sans l'autorisation spéciale des divers Gouvernements représentés à la Commission.

ARTICLE 235

Afin de permettre aux Puissances alliées et associées d'entreprendre dès maintenant la restauration de leur vie industrielle et économique, en attendant la fixation définitive du montant de leurs réclamations, l'Allemagne payera, pendant les années 1919 et 1920 et les quatre premiers mois de 1921, en autant de versements et suivant telles modalités (en or, en marchandises, en navires, en valeurs ou autrement) que la Commission des réparations pourra fixer, l'équivalent de 20,000,000,000 (vingt milliards) marks or à valoir sur les créances ci-dessus; sur cette somme les frais de l'armée d'occupation après l'Armistice du 11 novembre 1918 seront d'abord payés, et telles quantités de produits alimentaires et de matières premières, qui pourront être jugées, par les Gouvernements des Principales Puissances alliées et associées,[4] nécessaires pour permettre à l'Allemagne de faire face à son obligation de réparer, pourront aussi, avec l'approbation desdits Gouvernements, être payées par imputation sur ladite somme. Le solde

[4] *French Third "Title N" Draft of April 30:* "par les cinq Gouvernements alliés et associés".
Preliminary Text (French) of May 7: "par les huit Gouvernements des Principales Puissances alliées et associées".
Intermediate Text (French) of June 18: as in the present draft.

viendra en déduction des sommes dues par l'Allemagne à titre de réparations. L'Allemagne remettra en outre les bons prescrits au paragraphe 12 (*c*) de l'Annexe II ci-jointe.

ARTICLE 236

L'Allemagne accepte, en outre, que ses ressources économiques soient directement affectées aux réparations, comme il est spécifié aux Annexes III, IV, V et VI, relatives respectivement à la marine marchande, aux restaurations matérielles, au charbon et à ses dérivés, aux matières colorantes et autres produits chimiques: étant toujours entendu que la valeur des biens transférés et de l'utilisation qui en sera faite conformément auxdites Annexes sera, après avoir été fixée de la manière qui y est prescrite, portée au crédit de l'Allemagne et viendra en déduction des obligations prévues aux articles ci-dessus.

ARTICLE 237

Les versements successifs, y compris ceux visés aux articles précédents, effectués par l'Allemagne pour satisfaire aux réclamations ci-dessus, seront répartis par les Gouvernements alliés et associés suivant les proportions déterminées par eux à l'avance et fondées sur l'équité et les droits de chacun.

En vue de cette répartition, la valeur des biens transférés et des services rendus conformément à l'article 243 et aux Annexes III, IV, V, VI et VII sera calculée de la même façon que les payements effectués la même année.

ARTICLE 238

En sus des payements ci-dessus prévus, l'Allemagne effectuera, en se conformant à la procédure établie par la Commission des réparations, la restitution en espèces des espèces enlevées, saisies ou séquestrées ainsi que la restitution des animaux, des objets de toute sorte et des valeurs enlevés, saisis ou séquestrés, dans les cas où il sera possible de les identifier sur le territoire de l'Allemagne ou sur celui de ses alliés.

Jusqu'à l'établissement de cette procédure, les restitutions devront continuer conformément aux stipulations de l'Armistice du 11 novembre 1918, de ses renouvellements et des Protocoles intervenus.[5]

ARTICLE 239

Le Gouvernement allemand s'engage à opérer immédiatement

[5] This sentence appeared first in the Preliminary Text (French) of May 7.

les restitutions prévues par l'article 238 ci-dessus et à effectuer les payements et les livraisons prévus par les articles 233, 234, 235 et 236.

ARTICLE 240

Le Gouvernement allemand reconnaît la Commission prévue par l'article 233, telle qu'elle pourra être constituée par les Gouvernements alliés et associés conformément à l'Annexe II; il lui reconnaît irrévocablement la possession et l'exercice des droits et pouvoirs que lui confère le présent Traité.

Le Gouvernement allemand fournira à la Commission tous les renseignements, dont elle pourra avoir besoin sur la situation et les opérations financières et sur les biens, la capacité de production, les approvisionnements et la production courante des matières premières et objets manufacturés de l'Allemagne et de ses ressortissants; il donnera également toutes informations relatives aux opérations militaires, dont la connaissance serait jugée nécessaire par la Commission pour fixer les obligations de l'Allemagne telles qu'elles sont définies à l'Annexe 1.[6]

Le Gouvernement allemand accordera aux membres de la Commission et à ses agents autorisés tous les droits et immunités dont jouissent en Allemagne les agents diplomatiques dûment accrédités des Puissances amies.

L'Allemagne accepte, en outre, de supporter les émoluments et les frais de la Commission et de tel personnel qu'elle pourra employer.

ARTICLE 241

L'Allemagne s'engage à faire promulguer, à maintenir en vigueur et à publier toute législation, tous règlements et décrets qui pourraient être nécessaires pour assurer la complète exécution des présentes stipulations.

ARTICLE 242

Les dispositions de la présente Partie du présent Traité ne s'appliquent pas aux propriétés, droits et intérêts visés aux Sections III et IV de la Partie X (Clauses économiques) du présent Traité, non plus qu'au produit de leur liquidation, sauf en ce qui concerne le solde définitif en faveur de l'Allemagne, mentionné à l'article 243 *a*).

[6] This underlined phrase appeared first in the French "Title VIII" Draft of May 3.

ARTICLE 243

Seront portés au crédit de l'Allemagne, au titre de ses obligations de réparer, les éléments suivants:

a) Tout solde définitif en faveur de l'Allemagne visé à la Section V (Alsace-Lorraine) de la Partie III (Clauses politiques européennes)[7] et aux Sections III et IV de la Partie X (Clauses économiques) du présent Traité;

b) Toutes sommes dues à l'Allemagne du chef des cessions visées à la Section IV (Bassin de la Sarre) de la Partie III (Clauses politiques européennes), à la Partie IX (Clauses financières) et à la Partie XII (Ports, Voies d'eau et Voies ferrées);

c) Toutes sommes que la Commission jugerait devoir être portées au crédit de l'Allemagne à valoir sur tous autres transferts de propriétés, droits, concessions ou autres intérêts prévus par le présent Traité.

En aucun cas, toutefois, les restitutions effectuées en vertu de l'article 238 de la présente Partie ne pourront être portées au crédit de l'Allemagne.[8]

ARTICLE 244

La cession des câbles sous-marins allemands, qui ne sont pas l'objet d'une disposition particulière du présent Traité, est réglée par l'Annexe VII ci-jointe.[9]

ANNEXE I

Compensation peut être réclamée de l'Allemagne, conformément à l'article 232 ci-dessus, pour la totalité des dommages rentrant dans les catégories ci-après:[10]

1° Dommages causés aux civils atteints dans leur personne ou dans leur vie et aux survivants qui étaient à la charge de ces civils par tous actes de guerre, y compris les bombardements ou autres

---

[7] The reference to Alsace-Lorraine appeared for the first time in the Preliminary Text (French) of May 7.

[8] This sentence appeared for the first time in the French "Title VIII" Draft of May 3.

[9] This article appeared first in the Preliminary Text (French) of May 7.

[10] *French "Title VIII" Draft of May 3:* "Compensation peut être réclamée de l'Allemagne, conformément à l'article 2 du présent Titre, pour la totalité des dommages rentrant dans les catégories ci-après et correspondant à chaque théâtre des hostilités, dans la proportion qui a existé, sur ce théâtre d'opérations, entre l'effort naval et militaire de l'Allemagne et l'effort naval et militaire total de l'Allemagne et de ses alliés. Ces proportions seront déterminées par la Commission des réparations."

Preliminary Text (French) of May 7 and Intermediate Text (French) of June 18: same as the present draft.

attaques par terre, par mer ou par la voie des airs, et toutes leurs conséquences directes ou de toutes opérations de guerre des deux groupes de belligérants, en quelque endroit que ce soit.

2° Dommages causés par l'Allemagne ou ses alliés aux civils victimes d'actes de cruauté, de violence ou de mauvais traitements (y compris les atteintes à la vie ou à la santé par suite d'emprisonnement, de déportation, d'internement ou d'évacuation, d'abandon en mer ou de travail forcé), en quelque endroit que ce soit, et aux survivants qui étaient à la charge de ces victimes.

3° Dommages causés par l'Allemagne ou ses alliés, sur leur territoire ou en territoire occupé ou envahi, aux civils victimes de tous actes ayant porté atteinte à la santé, à la capacité de travail ou à l'honneur, et aux survivants, qui étaient à la charge de ces victimes.

4° Dommages causés par toute espèce de mauvais traitements aux prisonniers de guerre.

5° En tant que dommage causé aux peuples des Puissances alliées et associées, toutes pensions ou compensations de même nature aux victimes militaires de la guerre (armées de terre, de mer ou forces aériennes),[11] mutilés, blessés, malades ou invalides, et aux personnes dont ces victimes étaient le soutien; le montant des sommes dues aux Gouvernements alliés et associés sera calculé, pour chacun desdits Gouvernements, à la valeur capitalisée, à la date de la mise en vigueur du présent Traité, desdites pensions ou compensations, sur la base des tarifs en vigueur en France, à la date ci-dessus.

6° Frais de l'assistance fournie par les Gouvernements des Puissances alliées et associées aux prisonniers de guerre, à leurs familles ou aux personnes dont ils étaient le soutien.

7° Allocations données par les Gouvernements des Puissances alliées et asociées aux familles et aux autres personnes à la charge des mobilisés ou de tous ceux qui ont servi dans l'armée; le montant des sommes qui leur sont dues pour chacune des années au cours desquelles des hostilités se sont produites sera calculé, pour chacun desdits Gouvernements, sur la base du tarif moyen appliqué en France, pendant ladite année, aux payements de cette nature.

8° Dommages causés à des civils par suite de l'obligation qui leur a été imposée par l'Allemagne ou ses alliés de travailler sans une juste rémunération.

---

[11] The words "ou forces aériennes" appeared first in the French Third "Title *N*" Draft of April 30.

9° Dommages relatifs à toutes propriétés, en quelque lieu qu'elles soient situées, appartenant à l'une des Puissances alliées et associées ou à leurs ressortissants (exception faite des ouvrages et du matériel militaires ou navals)[12] qui ont été enlevées, saisies, endommagées ou détruites par les actes de l'Allemagne ou ses alliés sur terre, sur mer ou dans les airs, ou dommages causés en conséquence directe des hostilités ou de toutes opérations de guerre.

10° Dommages causés sous forme de prélèvements, amendes ou exactions similaires de l'Allemagne ou de ses alliés au détriment des populations civiles.

ANNEXE II

§ 1er

Le Commission prévue par l'article 233 prendra le titre de «Commission des réparations»; elle sera désignée dans les articles ci-après par les mots «la Commission».

§ 2

Des Délégués à la Commission seront nommés par les États-Unis d'Amérique, la Grande-Bretagne, la France, l'Italie, le Japon, la Belgique et l'État Serbe-Croate-Slovène. Chacune de ces Puissances nommera un Délégué, elle nommera également un Délégué adjoint qui le remplacera en cas de maladie ou d'absence forcée, mais qui, en toute autre circonstance, aura seulement le droit d'assister aux débats sans y prendre aucune part.[13]

En aucun cas, les Délégués de plus de cinq des Puissances ci-dessus n'auront le droit de prendre part aux débats de la Commission et d'émettre des votes. Les Délégués des États-Unis, de la Grande-Bretagne, de la France et de l'Italie auront toujours ce droit. Le Délégué de la Belgique aura ce droit dans tous les cas autres que ceux visés ci-après. Le Délégué du Japon aura ce droit dans les cas où seront examinées des questions relatives aux dommages sur mer, ainsi que des questions prévues par l'article 260 de la Partie IX (Clauses financières) dans lesquelles les intérêts du Japon sont en jeu. Le Délégué de l'État Serbe-Croate-Slovène aura

---

[12] The words "ou navals" appeared first in the Preliminary Text (French) of May 7.

[13] This paragraph appeared first in practically its present form in the French "Title VIII" Draft of May 3. It read there "la Serbie". The change to "l'État Serbe-Croate-Slovène" appeared first in the Intermediate Text (French) of June 18.

ce droit lorsque des questions relatives à l'Autriche, à la Hongrie ou à la Bulgarie seront examinées.[14]

Chacun des Gouvernements représentés à la Commission aura le droit de s'en retirer après un préavis de douze mois notifié à la Commission et confirmé au cours du sixième mois après la date de la notification primitive.[15]

§ 3

Telle d'entre les autres Puissances alliées et associées, qui pourra être intéressée, aura le droit de nommer un Délégué qui ne sera présent et n'agira, en qualité d'assesseur, que lorsque les créances et intérêts de ladite Puissance seront examinés ou discutés; ce Délégué n'aura pas le droit de vote.

§ 4

En cas de mort, démission ou rappel de tout Délégué, Délégué adjoint ou assesseur, un successeur devra lui être désigné aussitôt que possible.

§ 5

La Commission aura son principal bureau permanent à Paris et y tiendra sa première réunion dans le plus bref délai possible après la mise en vigueur du présent Traité; elle se réunira ensuite en tels lieux et à telles époques qu'elle estimera convenables et qui pourront être nécessaires en vue de l'accomplissement le plus rapide de ses obligations.

§ 6

Dès sa première réunion, la Commission élira, parmi lesdits Délégués visés ci-dessus, un Président et un Vice-Président, qui resteront en fonctions pendant une année et seront rééligibles; si le poste de Président ou de Vice-Président devient vacant au cours d'une période annuelle, la Commission procédera immédiatement à une nouvelle élection pour le reste de ladite période.

§ 7

La Commission est autorisée à nommer tous fonctionnaires, agents et employés, qui peuvent être nécessaires pour l'exécution de ses fonctions, et à fixer leur rémunération, à constituer des comités, dont les membres ne seront pas nécessairement ceux de la

---

[14] With minor differences in drafting, the present paragraph appeared first in the French "Title VIII" Draft of May 3.

[15] This sentence did not appear in the French "Title VIII" of May 3 or in the Preliminary Text of May 7, but it did appear in the Intermediate Text of June 18.

Commission, et à prendre toutes mesures d'exécution nécessaires pour l'accomplissement de sa tâche, à déléguer autorité et pleins pouvoirs à ses fonctionnaires, agents et comités.

§ 8

Toutes les délibérations de la Commission seront secrètes, à moins que, pour des raisons spéciales, la Commission, dans des cas particuliers, n'en décide autrement.

§ 9

La Commission devra, dans les délais qu'elle fixera de temps à autre, et si le Gouvernement allemand en fait la demande, entendre tous arguments et témoignages présentés par l'Allemagne sur toutes questions se rattachant à sa capacité de payement.

§ 10

La Commission étudiera les réclamations et donnera au Gouvernement allemand l'équitable faculté de se faire entendre, sans qu'il puisse prendre aucune part, quelle qu'elle soit, aux décisions de la Commission. La Commission donnera la même faculté aux alliés de l'Allemagne, lorsqu'elle jugera que leurs intérêts sont en jeu.[16]

§ 11

La Commission ne sera liée par aucune législation ni par aucun code particuliers, ni par aucune règle spéciale concernant l'instruction ou la procédure; elle sera guidée par la justice, l'équité et la bonne foi. Ses décisions devront se conformer à des principes et à des règles uniformes dans tous les cas où ces principes et ces règles seront applicables. Elle fixera les règles relatives aux modes de preuve des réclamations. Elle pourra employer toute méthode légitime de calcul.

§ 12

La Commission aura tous les pouvoirs et exercera toutes les attributions à elle conférés par le présent Traité.

La Commission aura, d'une façon générale, les pouvoirs de contrôle et d'exécution les plus étendus en ce qui concerne le problème des réparations tel qu'il est traité dans la présente Partie du présent Traité et aura pouvoir d'en interpréter les dispositions. Sous réserve des dispositions du présent Traité, la Commission est constituée par l'ensemble des Gouvernements alliés et associés visés aux paragraphes 2 et 3[17] comme leur représentant exclusif, pour leur part

---

[16] This sentence appeared for the first time in the French "Title VIII" Draft of May 3.

[17] This amendment appeared for the first time in the French "Title VIII" Draft of May 3.

respective, en vue de recevoir, vendre, conserver et répartir le payement des réparations à effectuer par l'Allemagne aux termes de la présente Partie du présent Traité. Elle devra se conformer aux conditions et dispositions suivantes:

a) Toute fraction du montant total des créances vérifiées qui ne sera pas payée en or, ou en navires, valeurs et marchandises ou de toute autre façon, devra être couverte par l'Allemagne dans des conditions que la Commission déterminera par la remise, à titre de garantie, d'un montant équivalent de bons, de titres d'obligations ou autres, en vue de constituer une reconnaissance de la fraction de dette dont il s'agit.

b) En estimant périodiquement la capacité de payement de l'Allemagne, la Commission examinera le système fiscal allemand: 1° afin que tous les revenus de l'Allemagne, y compris les revenus destinés au service ou à l'acquittement de tout emprunt intérieur, soient affectés par privilège au payement des sommes dues par elle à titre de réparations, et—2° de façon à acquérir la certitude qu'en général le système fiscal allemand est tout à fait aussi lourd, proportionnellement, que celui d'une quelconque des Puissances représentées à la Commission.

c) Afin de faciliter et de poursuivre la restauration immédiate de la vie économique des Pays alliés et associés, la Commission, ainsi qu'il est prévu à l'article 235, recevra de l'Allemagne, comme garantie et reconnaissance de sa dette, un premier versement de bons au porteur en or, libres de taxe ou impôts de toute nature, établis ou susceptibles de l'être par les Gouvernements de l'Empire ou des États allemands ou par toute autorité en dépendant; ces bons seront remis en acompte et en trois fractions, comme il est dit ci-après (le mark or étant payable conformément à l'article 262 de la Partie IX [Clauses financières][18] du présent Traité):

1° Pour être émis immédiatement, 20 milliards (vingt milliards) de marks or en bons au porteur, payables jusqu'au 1ᵉʳ mai 1921 au plus tard, sans intérêts; on appliquera notamment à l'amortissement de ces bons les versements que l'Allemagne s'est engagée à effectuer conformément à l'article 235, déduction faite des sommes affectées au remboursement des dépenses d'entretien des troupes d'occupation et au payement des dépenses du ravitaillement en vivres et matières premières; ceux de ces bons qui n'auraient pas été amortis

---

[18] These brackets are in the original.

à la date du 1er mai 1921 seront alors échangés contre de nouveaux bons du même type que ceux prévus ci-après (12, *c*), 2°).

2° Pour être émis immédiatement, 40 milliards (quarante milliards) de marks or en bons au porteur, portant intérêts à 2½ o/o (deux et demi pour cent) entre 1921 et 1926 et ensuite à 5 o/o (cinq pour cent) avec 1 o/o (un pour cent) en supplément pour l'amortissement, à partir de 1926 sur le montant total de l'émission.

3° Pour être délivré immédiatement, en couverture, un engagement écrit d'émettre à titre de nouveau versement, et seulement lorsque la Commission sera convaincue que l'Allemagne peut assurer le service des intérêts et du fonds d'amortissement desdits bons, 40 milliards (quarante milliards) de marks or en bons au porteur, portant intérêts à 5 p. o/o (cinq pour cent), les époques et le mode de payement du principal et des intérêts devant être déterminés par la Commission.

Les dates auxquelles les intérêts sont dûs, le mode d'emploi du fonds d'amortissement et toutes questions analogues relatives à l'émission, à la gestion et à la réglementation de l'émission des bons seront déterminés de temps à autre par la Commission.

De nouvelles émissions, à titre de reconnaissance et de garantie, peuvent être exigées dans les conditions que la Commission déterminera ultérieurement, de temps à autre.

d) Au cas où des bons, obligations ou autres reconnaissances de dettes émis par l'Allemagne, comme garantie ou reconnaissance de sa dette de réparation, seraient attribués, à titre définitif et non à titre de garantie, à des personnes autres que les divers Gouvernements au profit desquels a été fixé à l'origine le montant de la dette de réparation de l'Allemagne, ladite dette sera à l'égard des ces derniers considérée comme éteinte, pour un montant correspondant à la valeur nominale des bons qui ont été ainsi attribués définitivement et l'obligation de l'Allemagne afférente auxdits bons sera limitée à l'obligation qui y est exprimée.

e) Les frais nécessités par les réparations et reconstructions des propriétés situées dans les régions envahies et dévastées, y compris la réinstallation des mobiliers, des machines et de tout matériel, seront évalués au coût de réparation et de reconstruction à l'époque où les travaux seront exécutés.

f) Les décisions de la Commission relatives à une remise totale ou partielle, en capital ou en intérêts, de toute dette vérifiée de l'Allemagne devront être motivées.

§ 13

En ce qui concerne les votes, la Commission se conformera aux règles suivantes:

Quand la Commission prend une décision, les votes de tous les Délégués ayant le droit de voter, ou, en l'absence de certains d'entre eux, de leurs Délégués adjoints, <u>seront</u> enregistrés. L'abstention est considérée comme un vote émis coutre la proposition en discussion. Les assesseurs n'ont pas le droit de vote.

Sur les questions suivantes l'unanimité est nécessaire:

a) Questions intéressant la souveraineté des Puissances alliées et associées ou concernant la remise de tout ou partie de la dette ou des obligations de l'Allemagne;

b) Questions relatives au montant et aux conditions des bons et autres titres d'obligations à remettre par <u>le Gouvernement allemand</u> et à la fixation de l'époque et du mode de leur vente, négociation ou répartition;

c) Tout report total ou partiel, au delà de l'année 1930, des payements venant à échéance entre le 1er mai 1921 et la fin de 1926 incluse;

d) Tout report total ou partiel, pour une durée supérieure à trois années, des payements venant à échéance après 1926;

e) Questions relatives à l'application, dans un cas particulier, d'une méthode d'évaluation des dommages différente de celle qui a été précédemment adoptée dans un cas semblable;

f) Questions d'interprétation des dispositions <u>de la présente Partie du présent Traité.</u>

Toutes autres questions seront résolues par un vote à la majorité.

Au cas où surgirait entre les Délégués un conflit d'opinion sur la question de savoir si une espèce déterminée est une de celles dont la décision exige ou non un vote unanime et au cas où ce conflit ne pourrait être résolu par un appel à leurs Gouvernements, les Gouvernements alliés et associés s'engagent à déférer immédiatement ce conflit à l'arbitrage d'une personne impartiale sur la désignation de laquelle ils se mettront d'accord et dont ils s'engagent à accepter la sentence.

§ 14

Les décisions prises par la Commission en conformité des pouvoirs qui lui sont conférés seront aussitôt exécutoires et pourront recevoir application immédiate sans autre formalité.

§ 15

La Commission remettra à chaque Puissance intéressée, en telle forme qu'elle fixera:

1° Un certificat mentionnant qu'elle détient pour le compte de ladite Puissance des bons des émissions susmentionnées, ledit certificat pouvant, sur la demande de la Puissance dont il s'agit, être divisé en un nombre de coupures n'excédant pas cinq;

2° De temps à autre, des certificats mentionnant qu'elle détient pour le compte de ladite Puissance tous autres biens livrés par l'Allemagne en acompte sur sa dette pour réparations.

Les certificats susvisés seront nominatifs et pourront, après notification à la Commission, être transmis par voie d'endossement.

Lorsque des bons sont émis pour être vendus ou négociés et lorsque des biens sont livrés par la Commission, un montant correspondant de certificats doit être retiré.

§ 16

Le Gouvernement allemand sera débité, à partir du 1er mai 1921, de l'intérêt sur sa dette telle qu'elle aura été fixée par la Commission, déduction faite de tous versements effectués sous forme de payements en espèces ou leurs équivalents ou en bons émis au profit de la Commission et de tous payements visés à l'article 243. Le taux de cet intérêt sera fixé à 5 p. o/o, à moins que la Commission n'estime, à quelque date ultérieure, que les circonstances justifient une modification de ce taux.

La Commission, en fixant au 1er mai 1921 le montant global de la dette de l'Allemagne, pourra tenir compte des intérêts dus sur les sommes afférentes à la réparation des dommages matériels à partir du 11 novembre 1918 ·jusqu'au 1er mai 1921.

§ 17

En cas de manquement par l'Allemagne à l'exécution qui lui incombe de l'une quelconque des obligations visées à la présente Partie du présent Traité, la Commission signalera immédiatement cette inexécution à chacune des Puissances intéressées en y joignant toutes propositions qui lui paraîtront opportunes au sujet des mesures à prendre en raison de cette inexécution.

§ 18

Les mesures que les Puissances alliées et associées auront le droit de prendre en cas de manquement volontaire par l'Allemagne, et que l'Allemagne s'engage à ne pas considérer comme des actes d'hostilité, peuvent comprendre des actes de prohibitions et de représailles économiques et financières et, en général, telles autres mesures que les Gouvernements respectifs pourront estimer nécessitées par les circonstances.

§ 19

Les payements, qui doivent être effectués en or ou ses équivalents en acompte sur les réclamations vérifiées des Puissances alliées et associées peuvent à tout moment être acceptés par la Commission sous forme de biens mobiliers et immobiliers, de marchandises, entreprises, droits et concessions en territoires allemands ou en dehors de ces territoires, de navires, obligations, actions ou valeurs de toute nature ou monnaies de l'Allemagne ou d'autres États; leur valeur de remplacement par rapport à l'or étant fixée à un taux juste et loyal par la Commission elle-même.

§ 20

La Commission, en fixant ou acceptant les payements qui s'effectueront par remise de biens ou droits déterminés, tiendra compte de tous droits et intérêts légitimes des Puissances alliées et associées ou neutres et de leurs ressortissants dans lesdits.

§ 21

Aucun membre de la Commission ne sera responsable, si ce n'est vis-à-vis du Gouvernement qui l'a désigné, de tout acte ou omission dérivant de ses fonctions. Aucun des Gouvernements alliés et associés n'assume de responsabilité pour le compte d'aucun autre Gouvernement.

§ 22

Sous réserve des stipulations du présent Traité, la présente Annexe pourra être amendée par la décision unanime des Gouvernements représentés à la Commission.

§ 23

Quand l'Allemagne et ses Alliés se seront acquittés de toutes sommes dues par eux en exécution du présent Traité ou des décisions de la Commission et quand toutes les sommes reçues ou leurs équivalents auront été répartis entre les Puissances intéressées, la Commission sera dissoute.

ANNEXE III

§ 1ᵉʳ

L'Allemagne reconnaît le droit des Puissances alliées et associées au remplacement tonneau pour tonneau (jauge brute) et catégorie pour catégorie de tous les navires et bateaux de commerce et de pêche perdus ou endommagés par faits de guerre.

Toutefois, et bien que les navires et bateaux allemands existant à ce jour représentent un tonnage très inférieur à celui des pertes subies par les Puissances alliées et associées, en conséquence de l'agression allemande,[19] le droit reconnu ci-dessus sera exercé sur ces navires et bateaux allemands dans les conditions suivantes:

Le Gouvernement allemand, en son nom et de façon à lier tous autres intéressés, cède aux Gouvernements alliés et associés la propriété de tous navires marchands de 1,600 tonnes brutes et au-dessus appartenant à ses ressortissants, ainsi que la moitié en tonnage des navires dont le tonnage brut est compris entre 1,000 et 1,600 tonnes et le quart en tonnage des chalutiers à vapeur, ainsi que le quart en tonnage des autres bateaux de pêche.

§ 2

Le Gouvernement allemand, dans un délai de deux mois après la mise en vigueur du présent Traité, remettra à la Commission des réparations tous les navires et bateaux visés par le paragraphe 1ᵉʳ.

§ 3

Les navires et bateaux visés par le paragraphe 1ᵉʳ comprennent tous les navires et bateaux: *a*) battant ou ayant le droit de battre le pavillon marchand allemand; ou *b*) appartenant à un ressortissant allemand, à une société ou à une compagnie allemande ou à une société ou compagnie d'un pays autre que les Pays alliés ou associés et sous le contrôle ou la direction de ressortissants allemands; ou *c*) actuellement en construction: 1° en Allemagne; 2° dans des pays autres que les Pays alliés ou associés pour le compte d'un ressortissant allemand, d'une société ou d'une compagnie allemande.

§ 4

Afin de fournir des titres de propriété pour chacun des navires remis comme ci-dessus, le Gouvernement allemand:

---

[19] This phrase appeared for the first time in the French "Title VIII" Draft of May 3.

a) Remettra pour chaque navire à la Commission des réparations, suivant sa demande, un acte de vente ou tout autre titre de propriété établissant le transfert à ladite Commission de la pleine propriété du navire libre de tous privilèges, hypothèques et charges quelconques;

b) Prendra toutes mesures qui pourront être indiquées par la Commission des réparations pour assurer la mise de ces navires à la disposition de ladite Commission.

§ 5

Comme mode supplémentaire de réparation partielle, l'Allemagne s'engage à faire construire des navires de commerce, sur les chantiers allemands, pour le compte des Gouvernements alliés et associés, de la façon suivante:

a) Dans un délai de trois mois à dater de la mise en vigueur du présent Traité, la Commission des réparations notifiera au Gouvernement allemand le montant du tonnage à mettre en chantier dans chacune des deux années qui suivront les trois mois ci-dessus mentionnés.

b) Dans le délai de deux ans à dater de la mise en vigueur du présent Traité, la Commission des réparations notifiera au Gouvernement allemand le montant du tonnage à mettre en chantier dans chacune des trois années qui suivront les deux années ci-dessus mentionnées.

c) Le montant du tonnage à mettre en chantier pour chaque année ne dépassera pas 200,000 tonneaux de jauge brute.

d) Les spécifications des navires à construire, les conditions dans lesquelles ils devront être construits ou livrés, le prix par tonneau pour lequel ils devront être portés en compte par la Commission des réparations, et toutes autres questions relatives à la commande, à la construction et à la livraison des navires ainsi qu'à leur entrée en compte, seront déterminés par ladite Commission.

§ 6

L'Allemagne s'engage à restituer en nature et en état normal d'entretien aux Puissances alliées et associées, dans un délai de deux mois à dater de la mise en vigueur du présent Traité, conformément à une procédure qui sera établie par la Commission des réparations, tous les bateaux et autres engins mobiles de navigation fluviale qui, depuis le 1er août 1914, ont passé, à un titre quelconque, en sa possession ou en possession de l'un de ses ressortissants, et qui pourront être identifiés.

En vue de compenser les pertes du tonnage fluvial, dues à n'importe quelle cause, subies pendant la guerre par les Puissances alliées et associées et qui ne pourront pas être réparées par les restitutions prescrites ci-dessus, l'Allemagne s'engage à céder à la Commission des réparations une partie de sa batellerie fluviale jusqu'à concurrence du montant de ces pertes, ladite cession ne pouvant dépasser 20 p. 100 du total de cette batellerie telle qu'elle existait à la date du 11 novembre 1918.

Les modalités de cette cession seront réglées par les arbitres prévus à l'article 339 de la Partie XII (Ports, Voies d'eau et Voies ferrées) du présent Traité, qui sont chargés de résoudre les difficultés relatives à la répartition du tonnage fluvial et résultant du nouveau régime international de certains réseaux fluviaux ou des modifications territoriales affectant ces réseaux.

§ 7

L'Allemagne s'engage à prendre toutes les mesures que la Commission des réparations peut lui indiquer en vue d'obtenir le plein droit de propriété sur tous les navires qui peuvent avoir été transférés pendant la guerre ou être en voie de transfert sous pavillons neutres, sans le consentement des Gouvernements alliés et associés.

§ 8

L'Allemagne renonce à toute revendication de quelque nature que ce soit contre les Gouvernements alliés et associés et leurs ressortissants, en ce qui concerne la détention ou l'utilisation de tous navires ou bateaux allemands et toute perte ou dommage subis par lesdits navires ou bateaux, exception faite des payements dus par suite de l'emploi de ces bateaux en conformité du Protocole d'Armistice du 13 janvier 1919 et des Protocoles subséquents.[20]

La livraison de la flotte commerciale allemande devra continuer à être effectuée sans interruption, conformément auxdits Protocoles.[21]

§ 9

L'Allemagne renonce à toutes revendications sur des navires ou cargaisons coulés du fait ou par la suite d'une action navale ennemie et sauvés ensuite, et dans lesquels un des Gouvernements alliés ou associés ou leurs ressortissants ont des intérêts, comme

[20] This last phrase appeared for the first time in the French Third "Title *N*" Draft of April 30.

[21] This sentence appeared first in the Preliminary Text (French) of May 7

propriétaires, affréteurs, assureurs ou à tout autre titre, nonobstant tout jugement de condamnation qui peut avoir été prononcé par un Tribunal des prises de l'Allemagne ou de ses alliés.

ANNEXE IV

§ 1er

Les Puissances alliées et associées exigent, et l'Allemagne accepte que l'Allemagne, en satisfaction partielle de ses obligations définies par la présente Partie, et suivant les modalités ci-après définies, applique ses ressources économiques directement à la restauration matérielle des régions envahies des Puissances alliées et associées, dans la mesure où ces Puissances le détermineront.

§ 2

Les Gouvernements des Puissances alliées et associées saisiront la Commission des réparations de listes donnant:

a) Les animaux, machines, équipements, tours, et tous articles similaires d'un caractère commercial qui ont été saisis, usés ou détruits par l'Allemagne, ou détruits en conséquence directe des opérations militaires, et que ces Gouvernements désirent, pour la satisfaction de besoins immédiats et urgents, voir être remplacés par des animaux ou articles de même nature, existant sur le territoire allemand à la date de la mise en vigueur du présent Traité;[22]

b) Les matériaux de reconstruction (pierre, briques, briques réfractaires,[23] tuiles, bois de charpente, verres à vitres, acier, chaux, ciment, etc.), machines, appareils de chauffage, meubles et tous articles d'un caractère commercial que lesdits Gouvernements désirent voir être produits et fabriqués en Allemagne et livrés à eux pour la restauration des régions envahies.

§ 3

Les listes relatives aux articles mentionnés dans le paragraphe 2 *a)* ci-dessus seront fournies dans les soixante jours qui suivront la mise en vigueur du présent Traité.

Les listes relatives aux articles mentionnés dans le paragraphe 2*b)* ci-dessus seront fournies le 31 décembre 1919, dernier délai.

Les listes contiendront tous les détails d'usage dans les contrats commerciaux relatifs aux articles visés, y compris spécification, délai de livraison (ce délai ne devant pas dépasser quatre ans) et

---

[22] This phrase appeared first in the French Third "Title *N*" Draft of April 30.
[23] The words "briques réfractaires" appeared first in the French Third "Title *N*" Draft of April 30.

lieu de livraison; mais elles ne contiendront ni prix, ni estimation, ces prix ou estimation devant être fixés par la Commission, comme il est dit ci-après.

§ 4

Dès réception des listes, la Commission examinera dans quelle mesure les matériaux et animaux mentionnés dans ces listes peuvent être exigés de l'Allemagne. Pour fixer sa décision, la Commission tiendra compte des nécessités intérieures de l'Allemagne, autant que cela sera nécessaire au maintien de sa vie sociale et économique; elle fera état également des prix et des dates auxquels les articles semblables peuvent être obtenus dans les Pays alliés et associés et les comparera à ceux applicables aux articles allemands; elle fera état, enfin, de l'intérêt général qu'ont les Gouvernements alliés et associés à ce que la vie industrielle de l'Allemagne ne soit pas désorganisée au point de compromettre sa capacité d'accomplir les autres actes de réparation exigés d'elle.

Toutefois, il ne sera demandé à l'Allemagne des machines, des équipements, des tours et tous articles similaires d'un caractère commercial actuellement en service dans l'industrie, que si aucun stock de ces articles n'est disponible et à vendre; d'autre part, les demandes de cette nature n'excéderont pas 30 p. 100 des quantités de chaque article en service dans un établissement allemand ou une entreprise allemande quelconque.[24]

La Commission donnera aux représentants du Gouvernement allemand la faculté de se faire entendre, dans un délai déterminé, sur sa capacité de fournir lesdits matériaux, animaux et objets.

La décision de la Commission sera ensuite, et le plus rapidement possible, notifiée au Gouvernement allemand et aux différents Gouvernements alliés et associés intéressés.

Le Gouvernement allemand s'engage à livrer les matériaux, objets et animaux, précisés dans cette notification, et les Gouvernements alliés et associés intéressés s'engagent, chacun pour ce qui le concerne, à accepter ces mêmes fournitures, sous réserve qu'elles seront conformes aux spécifications données ou ne seront pas, de l'avis de la Commission, impropres à l'emploi requis pour le travail de réparation.

§ 5

La Commission déterminera la valeur à attribuer aux matériaux, objets et animaux, livrés comme il est dit ci-dessus, et les Gouverne-

---

[24] In the preceding draft, this sentence stands at the end of Article 2 (*a*). The change of position was made first in the French Third "Title *N*" Draft of April 30. At the same time, the words "des tours" were introduced.

ments alliés et associés qui recevront ces fournitures acceptent d'être débités de leur valeur et reconnaissent que la somme correspondante devra être traitée comme un payement fait par l'Allemagne, à répartir conformément à l'article 237 de la présente Partie du présent Traité.

Dans le cas où le droit de requérir la restauration matérielle aux conditions ci-dessus définies sera exercé la Commission s'assurera, que la somme portée au crédit de l'Allemagne représente la valeur normale du travail fait ou des matériaux fournis par elle et que le montant de la réclamation faite par la Puissance intéressée pour le dommage ainsi partiellement réparé est diminué dans la proportion de la contribution à la réparation ainsi fournie.

§ 6[25]

A titre d'avance immédiate, en acompte sur les animaux visés au paragraphe 2 (*a*) ci-dessus, l'Allemagne s'engage à livrer dans les trois mois qui suivront la mise en vigueur du présent Traité, à raison d'un tiers par mois et par espèce, les quantités ci-dessous de bétail vivant:

1° Au Gouvernement français.

500 étalons de 3 à 7 ans;
30,000 pouliches et juments de 18 mois à 7 ans, des races ardennaise, boulonnaise ou belge;
2,000 taureaux de 18 mois à 3 ans;
90,000 vaches laitières de 2 à 6 ans;
1,000 béliers;
100,000 brebis;
10,000 chèvres.

2° Au Gouvernement belge.

200 étalons de 3 à 7 ans, de la race de gros trait belge;
5,000 juments de 3 à 7 ans, de la race de gros trait belge;
5,000 pouliches de 18 mois à 3 ans, de la race de gros trait belge;
2,000 taureaux de 18 mois à 3 ans;
50,000 vaches laitières de 2 à 6 ans;
40,000 génisses;
200 béliers;
20,000 brebis;
15,000 truies.

Les animaux livrés seront de santé et de condition normale.

[25] This entire article appeared for the first time in the French "Title VIII" Draft of May 3.

Si les animaux ainsi livrés ne peuvent pas être identifiés comme ayant été enlevés ou saisis, leur valeur sera portée au crédit des obligations de réparations de l'Allemagne, conformément aux stipulations du paragraphe 5 de la présente Annexe.

§ 7[26]

Sans attendre que les décisions de la Commission prévue au paragraphe 4 de la présente Annexe puissent être prises, l'Allemagne devra continuer à effectuer à la France les livraisons de matériel agricole, prévues à l'article III du renouvellement d'Armistice en date du 16 janvier 1919.

ANNEXE V

§ 1er

L'Allemagne s'engage à livrer, sur leur demande respective, aux Puissances signataires du présent Traité ci-dessous mentionnées,[27] les quantités de charbons et de dérivés du charbon ci-après définies.

§ 2

L'Allemagne livrera à la France sept millions de tonnes de charbon par an, pendant dix ans. En outre, l'Allemagne livrera chaque année à la France une quantité de charbon égale à la différence entre la production annuelle avant la guerre des mines du Nord et du Pas-de-Calais détruites du fait de la guerre et la production du bassin couvert par ces mines pendant l'année envisagée. Cette dernière fourniture sera effectuée pendant dix ans et ne dépassera pas vingt millions de tonnes par an pendant les cinq premières années et huit millions de tonnes par an pendant les cinq années suivantes.

Il est entendu que toute diligence sera faite pour la remise en état des mines du Nord et du Pas-de-Calais.

§ 3

L'Allemagne livrera à la Belgique huit millions de tonnes de charbon par an pendant dix ans.

§ 4

L'Allemagne livrera à l'Italie les quantités maxima de charbon ci-après:

---

[26] This article appeared for the first time in the Preliminary Text (French) of May 7.

[27] The words "aux Puissances signataires du présent Traité ci-dessous mentionnées" appeared for the first time in the Preliminary Text of May 7, as a substitute for the words "à la France, à la Belgique et à l'Italie".

Juillet 1919 à juin 1920 : 4 millions ½ de tonnes,
— 1920 — 1921 : 6 millions de tonnes,
— 1921 — 1922 : 7 millions ½ de tonnes,
— 1922 — 1923 : 8 millions de tonnes,
— 1923 — 1924 : 8 millions ½ de tonnes.

et, pendant chacune des cinq années suivantes: 8 millions ½ de tonnes.

Les deux tiers au moins des livraisons seront faites par voie de terre.

§ 5

L'Allemagne livrera au Luxembourg, si elle en est requise par la Commission des réparations, une quantité annuelle de charbon égale à la quantité annuelle de charbon allemand consommée par le Luxembourg avant la guerre.

§ 6

Les prix à payer pour les livraisons de charbon effectuées en vertu desdites options seront les suivants:

a) Fourniture par voie de fer ou par eau.—Le prix sera le prix allemand sur carreau de la mine payé par les ressortissants allemands, plus le fret jusqu'aux frontières française, belge, italienne ou luxembourgeoise,[28] étant entendu que le prix sur le carreau de la mine n'excédera pas le prix, sur le carreau de la mine, du charbon anglais pour l'exportation. Dans le cas du charbon de soute belge, le prix ne dépassera pas celui du charbon de soute hollandaise.

Les tarifs de transport par voie de fer ou par eau ne dépasseront par les tarifs les plus bas appliqués aux transports de même nature en Allemagne.[29]

b) Fourniture par voie de mer.—Le prix sera soit le prix d'exportation allemand f.o.b. dans les ports allemands, soit le prix d'exportation anglais f.o.b. dans les ports anglais et dans tous les cas le plus bas des deux.

§ 7

Les Gouvernements alliés et associés intéressés pourront demander la livraison de coke métallurgique en remplacement de charbon, à raison de 3 tonnes de coke par 4 tonnes de charbon.

§ 8

L'Allemagne s'engage à fournir à la France, et à transporter à la

---

[28] The words "ou luxembourgeoise" appeared for the first time in the French Third "Title *N*" Draft of April 30.

[29] The words "en Allemagne" appeared for the first time in the French Third "Title *N*" Draft of April 30.

frontière française, par voie de fer ou par eau, les produits suivants, pendant chacune des trois années qui suivront la mise en vigueur du présent Traité:

Benzol..35,000 tonnes.
Goudron de houille..............................50,000 —
Sulfate d'ammoniaque...........................30,000 —

Tout ou partie du goudron de houille pourra être remplacé, au choix du Gouvernement français, par des quantités équivalentes des produits de distillation, tels que huiles légères, huiles lourdes, anthracène, naphtaline ou brai.[30]

§ 9

Le prix payé pour le coke et les autres produits visés au paragraphe 8 sera le prix payé par les ressortissants, toutes conditions d'emballage et de port jusqu'à la frontière française ou jusqu'aux ports allemands étant les plus avantageuses consenties pour les mêmes produits aux ressortissants allemands.

§ 10

Les options de la présente Annexe seront exercées par l'intermédiaire de la Commission des réparations. Celle-ci aura pouvoir, pour l'exécution des dispositions ci-dessus, de statuer sur toutes questions relatives à la procédure, aux qualités et quantités des fournitures, à la quantité de coke à fournir en remplacement de charbon, aux délais et modes de livraison et de payement. Les demandes accompagnées des spécifications utiles[31] devront être notifiées à l'Allemagne cent vingt jours avant la date fixée pour le commencement de l'exécution, en ce qui concerne les livraisons à faire à partir du 1er janvier 1920, et trente jours avant cette date pour les livraisons à faire entre la date de mise en vigueur du présent Traité et le 1er janvier 1920. En attendant que l'Allemagne ait reçu les demandes prévues au présent paragraphe, les stipulations du Protocole du 25 décembre 1918 (Exécution de l'article VI de l'Armistice du 11 novembre 1918) restent en vigueur.[32] Les demandes relatives aux substitutions prévues par les paragraphes 7 et 8 seront notifiées au Gouvernement allemand avec un délai préa-

---

[30] The words of the preceding draft, "conformément aux spécifications qui seront remises en temps utile au Gouvernement allemand et jugées suffisantes par la Commission des réparations," did not appear in the French Third "Title N" Draft of April 30 or in any later drafts.

[31] These words appeared for the first time in the Preliminary Text (French) of May 7.

[32] This sentence appeared for the first time in the Preliminary Text (French) of May 7.

lable jugé suffisant par la Commission.[33] Si la Commission juge que la satisfaction complète des demandes est de nature à peser d'une façon excessive sur les besoins industriels allemands, elle pourra les différer ou les annuler, et ainsi fixer tous ordres de priorité; mais le charbon à fournir en remplacement du charbon des mines détruites sera fourni par priorité sur toutes livraisons.

ANNEXE VI

§ 1er

L'Allemagne donne à la Commission des réparations une option de livraison, à titre de réparation partielle, des quantités et des espèces de matières colorantes et produits chimiques pharmaceutiques qui seront désignés par elle, à concurrence de 50 p. 100 du stock total de chaque espèce de matières colorantes et produits chimiques pharmaceutiques existant en Allemagne ou se trouvant sous le contrôle allemand à la date de la mise en vigueur du présent Traité.

Cette option sera exercée dans les soixante jours de la réception, par la Commission, de l'état détaillé des stocks, fourni dans la forme demandée par elle.

§ 2

L'Allemagne donne en outre à la Commission des réparations une option pour la livraison, pendant la période qui s'écoulera entre la mise en vigueur du présent Traité et le 1er juin 1920, puis, pendant chaque période ultérieure de six mois, jusqu'au 1er janvier 1925, de toutes matières colorantes et tous produits chimiques pharmaceutiques, à concurrence de 25 p. 100 de la production allemande pendant la période des six mois précédents, ou, si la production, pendant cette période de six mois, était, de l'avis de la Commission, inférieure à la production normale, à concurrence de 25 p. 100 de cette production normale.

Cette option sera exercée dans les quatre semaines qui suivront la réception des états de production pendant la période de six mois précédente; ces états seront produits par le Gouvernement allemand à l'expiration de chaque période de six mois et dans la forme jugée nécessaire par la Commission.[34]

§ 3

Pour les matières colorantes et produits chimiques pharmaceutiques fournis en exécution du paragraphe 1er, le prix sera fixé

---

[33] This sentence appeared for the first time in the French Third "Title *N*" Draft of April 30.
[34] These words appeared for the first time in the French Third "Title *N*" Draft of April 30.

par la Commission en fonction du prix net d'exportation d'avant-guerre et des variations du prix de revient survenues.

Pour les matières colorantes et produits chimiques pharmaceutiques livrés en exécution du paragraphe 2, le prix sera fixé par la Commission en fonction du prix net d'exportation d'avant-guerre et des variations du prix de revient survenues, ou en fonction du prix de vente le plus bas des mêmes matières à un autre acheteur quelconque.

§ 4

Tous les détails, en particulier touchant le mode et les délais d'exercice de l'option et de la livraison, ainsi que toutes les questions soulevées pour l'exécution des prescriptions ci-dessus, seront réglés par la Commission des réparations à qui le Gouvernement allemand fournira toutes les informations nécessaires et toutes autres facilités qui seront requises par elle.

§ 5

Les matières colorantes et produits chimiques pharmaceutiques visés à la présente Annexe comprennent toutes les matières colorantes et tous les produits chimiques pharmaceutiques synthétiques, ainsi que tous les produits intermédiaires et autres employés dans les industries correspondantes et fabriqués pour la vente. Les dispositions qui précèdent s'appliquent également à l'écorce de quinquina et aux sels de quinine.[35]

ANNEXE VII[36]

L'Allemagne renonce en son nom et au nom de ses nationaux, en faveur des Principales Puissances alliées et associées, à tous droits, titres ou privilèges de toute nature qu'elle possède sur les câbles ou portions de câbles, énumérés ci-après:

Emden-Vigo : du pas de Calais au large de Vigo;
Emden-Brest : du large de Cherbourg à Brest;
Emden-Ténériffe : du large de Dunkerque au large de Ténériffe;
Emden-Açores (1) : du pas de Calais à Fayal;
Emden-Açores (2) : du pas de Calais à Fayal;
Açores-New-York (1) : de Fayal à New-York;
Açores-New-York (2) : de Fayal à la longitude d'Halifax;

[35] This section 5 became a separate article for the first time in the French Third "Title *N*" Draft of April 30. Its last sentence appeared first, in a slightly different form, in the French "Title VIII" Draft of May 3.

[36] Annex VII was joined to Part VIII (Reparation) for the first time in the Preliminary Text (French) of May 7.

Ténériffe-Monrovia : du large de Ténériffe au large de Monrovia;

Monrovia-Lome:

du point défini par........ $\begin{cases} \text{lat. : } 2° 30' \text{ N.;} \\ \text{long. : } 7° 40' \text{ O. de Greenwich;} \end{cases}$

du [au] point défini par .... $\begin{cases} \text{lat. : } 2° 20' \text{ N.;} \\ \text{long. : } 5° 30' \text{ O. de Greenwich;} \end{cases}$

et du point défini par....... $\begin{cases} \text{lat. : } 3° 48' \text{ N.;} \\ \text{long. : } 0° 00';} \end{cases}$

jusqu'à Lome;

Lome-Duala : de Lome à Duala;

Monrovia-Pernambouc : du large de Monrovia au large de Pernambouc;

Constantinople-Constantza : de Constantinople à Constantza;

Yap-Shanghaï, Yap-Guam et Yap-Menado (îles Célèbes): de l'île Yap à Shanghaï, de l'île Yap à l'île Guam et de l'île Yap à Menado.

La valeur des câbles ou des portions de câbles ci-dessus mentionnés, en tant que ceux-ci constituent des propriétés privées, ladite valeur calculée sur la base du prix d'établissement et diminuée d'un pourcentage convenable pour dépréciation, sera portée au crédit de l'Allemagne, au chapitre des réparations.

SECTION II[37]
DISPOSITIONS PARTICULIÈRES

ARTICLE 245

Dans les six mois qui suivront la mise en vigueur du présent Traité, le Gouvernement allemand devra restituer au Gouvernement français les trophées, archives, souvenirs historiques ou œuvres d'art enlevés de France par les autorités allemandes au cours de la guerre de 1870-1871 et de la dernière guerre, suivant la liste qui lui en sera adressée par le Gouvernement français, et notamment les drapeaux français pris au cours de la guerre de 1870-1871, ainsi que l'ensemble des papiers politiques pris par les autorités allemandes le 10 octobre 1870 au château de Cerçay, près Brunoy (Seine-et-Oise), appartenant alors à M. Rouher, ancien Ministre d'État.

ARTICLE 246

Dans les six mois qui suivront la mise en vigueur du présent Traité, l'Allemagne devra restituer à Sa Majesté le Roi du Hedjaz le Koran original ayant appartenu au Calife Osman et enlevé de

[37] Section II (Dispositions Particulières) appeared first in the Preliminary Text (French) of May 7.

Médine par les autorités turques pour être offert à l'ex-Empereur Guillaume II.

Le crâne du Sultan Makaoua ayant été enlevé du protectorat allemand de l'Afrique orientale et transporté en Allemagne sera, dans le même délai, remis par l'Allemagne au Gouvernement de Sa Majesté Britannique.

La remise de ces objets sera effectuée dans tels lieu et conditions que fixeront les Gouvernements, auxquels ils doivent être restitués.

ARTICLE 247

L'Allemagne s'engage à fournir à l'Université de Louvain dans les trois mois qui suivront la demande qui lui en sera faite par l'intermédiaire de la Commission des réparations, les manuscrits, incunables, livres imprimés, cartes et objets de collection correspondant en nombre et en valeur aux objets semblables détruits dans l'incendie mis par l'Allemagne à la Bibliothèque de Louvain. Tous les détails concernant ce remplacement seront déterminés par la Commission des réparations.

L'Allemagne s'engage à remettre à la Belgique, par l'intermédiaire de la Commission des réparations, dans les six mois qui suivront la mise en vigueur du présent Traité, et afin de lui permettre de reconstituer deux grandes œuvres d'art:

1° Les volets du triptyque de l'*Agneau mystique* peint par les frères Van Eyck, autrefois dans l'église de Saint-Bavon à Gand et actuellement au Musée de Berlin;

2° Les volets du triptyque de la *Cène*, peint par Dierick Bouts, autrefois dans l'église de Saint-Pierre à Louvain, et dont deux sont maintenant au Musée de Berlin et deux à l'ancienne Pinacothèque de Munich.

DOCUMENT 442

Articles 248 and 251 of Part IX (Financial Clauses) of Final Treaty (English) with Germany, June 28, 1919

[See Document 440 for the title of the print of the Treaty from which these extracts are taken.]

ARTICLE 248

Subject to such exceptions as the Reparation Commission may approve, a first charge upon all the assets and revenues of the German Empire and its constituent States shall be the cost of reparation and all other costs arising under the present Treaty or any treaties or agreements supplementary thereto or under arrangements concluded between Germany and the Allied and Associated Powers during the Armistice or its extensions.

Up to May 1, 1921, the German Government shall not export or dispose of, and shall forbid the export or disposal of, gold without the previous approval of the Allied and Associated Powers acting through the Reparation Commission.[1]

ARTICLE 251

The priority of the charges established by Article 248 shall, subject to the qualifications made below, be as follows:

(*a*) The cost of the armies of occupation as defined under Article 249 during the Armistice and its extensions;

(*b*) The cost of any armies of occupation as defined under Article 249 after the coming into force of the present Treaty;

(*c*) The cost of reparation arising out of the present Treaty or any treaties or conventions supplementary thereto;

(*d*) The cost of all other obligations incumbent on Germany under the Armistice Conventions or under this Treaty or any treaties or conventions supplementary thereto.

The payment for such supplies of food and raw material for Germany and such other payments as may be judged by the Allied and Associated Powers to be essential to enable Germany to meet her obligations in respect of reparation will have priority to the extent and upon the conditions which have been or may be determined by the Governments of the said Powers.

DOCUMENT 443

Articles 248 and 251 of Part IX (Financial Clauses) of Final Treaty (French) with Germany, June 28, 1919

[See Document 440 for the title of the print of the Treaty from which these extracts are taken.]

ARTICLE 248

Sous réserve des dérogations qui pourraient être accordées par la Commission des réparations, un privilège de premier rang est établi sur tous les biens et ressources de l'Empire et des États

---

[1] Article 248 of the Preliminary Treaty Text (English) of May 7 precedes. It begins:

"[The] first charge upon all the assets and revenues [etc.]"—and is otherwise practically identical with the present text.

See Document 344 for the title of the print of the Preliminary Treaty Text from which the above phrase is taken (p. 118).

This amendment was made at a meeting on May 27 of the Council of Four, according to the statement in the English Minutes of the Austrian Experts' Seventeenth Meeting, May 28, 1919, 11 A. M. (see Document 613).

allemands, pour le règlement des réparations et autres charges résultant du présent Traité, ou de tous autres traités et conventions complémentaires, ou des arrangements conclus entre l'Allemagne et les Puissances alliées et associées pendant l'Armistice et ses prolongations.

Jusqu'au 1er mai 1921, le Gouvernement allemand ne pourra ni exporter de l'or ou en disposer, ni autoriser que de l'or soit exporté ou qu'il en soit disposé sans autorisation préalable des Puissances alliées et associées représentées par la Commission des réparations.[1]

ARTICLE 251

Le privilège établi par l'article 248 s'exercera dans l'ordre suivant, sous la réserve mentionnée au dernier paragraphe du présent article:

a) Le coût des armées d'occupation, tel qu'il est défini à l'article 249, pendant l'Armistice et ses prolongations;

b) Le coût de toutes armées d'occupation, tel qu'il est défini à l'article 249, après la mise en vigueur du présent Traité;

c) Le montant des réparations résultant du présent Traité ou des traités et conventions complémentaires;

d) Toutes autres charges incombant à l'Allemagne en vertu des Conventions d'armistice, du présent Traité ou des traités et conventions complémentaires.

Le payement du ravitaillement de l'Allemagne en denrées alimentaires et en matières premières et tous autres payements à effectuer par l'Allemagne, dans la mesure où les Gouvernements alliés et associés les auront jugés nécessaires pour permettre à l'Allemagne de faire face à son obligation de réparer, auront priorité dans la mesure et dans les conditions qui ont été ou pourront être établies par les Gouvernements alliés et associés.

DOCUMENT 444

"Protocol" Supplementary to the Treaty with Germany Regarding Certain Concessions to Germany, June 28, 1919

[French and English, bound in at end of Document 440. English only, in Great Britain, Parliament, *Parliamentary Papers*, 1919, LIII, Cmd. 220. British Treaty Series, No. 5 (1919). Document 435 precedes.]

[1] Article 248 of the Preliminary Treaty Text (French) of May 7 precedes. It begins:
"Un privilège de premier rang est établi [etc.]"—and is otherwise identical with the present text.
See Document 345 for the title of the print of the Preliminary Treaty Text from which the above phrase is taken.
This amendment was made at a meeting on May 27 of the Council of Four, according to the statement in the English Minutes of the Austrian Experts' Seventeenth Meeting, May 28, 1919, 11 A. M. (see Document 613).

With a view to indicating precisely the conditions in which certain provisions of the Treaty of even date are to be carried out, it is agreed by the HIGH CONTRACTING PARTIES that:

. . .

(4) The Reparation Commission referred to in Article 240 and paragraphs 2, 3 and 4 of Annex IV cannot require trade secrets or other confidential information to be divulged;

(5) From the signature of the Treaty and within the ensuing four months Germany will be entitled to submit for examination by the Allied and Associated Powers documents and proposals in order to expedite the work connected with reparation, and thus to shorten the investigation and to accelerate the decisions;

. . .

Done at Versailles, the twenty-eighth day of June, one thousand nine hundred and nineteen.

> [The signatories of this proto-
> col were the same as those of the
> Treaty with Germany.]

DOCUMENT 445

Extract from E. M. House, "Memorandum for the President: Questions Remaining to Be Settled after German and Austrian Peace Treaties Are Disposed of," Undated

[Signed original from the Edward M. House Collection, Yale University Library, New Haven, Connecticut. This document is not dated. The heading also read, "There may be agreements with regard to some of these questions by the Council of Four that have not been announced."]

C^1

Commissions, etc., to be appointed under Peace Treaty with Germany.

. . .

9. Reparation Commission (Article 233, page 98)

One Delegate and an Assistant Delegate will be appointed by the United States of America, Great Britain, France, Italy, Japan, Belgium and Serbia. Other interested Powers may appoint a Delegate without vote.

. . .

G^2

SHIPPING MATTERS

The situation to this date is [*in*] relation to the enemy ships seized by the United States is about as follows:

[1] Original endorsed in Wilson's (?) writing: "none of these for the Conference."
[2] Original endorsed in Wilson's (?) writing: "not for the Conference."

We have taken the position that our title is good.

In interpreting one of the provisions proposed for the Treaty of Peace and which afterwards went into the Treaty of Peace, Great Britain questions our international title to the ships. Because of this, and since the Treaty was passed, and under the provisions of the Treaty that as between the Allies distribution of the materials, money, etc., for reparation is to be settled by agreement, Great Britain agrees to waive any question of title in the United States to the seized ships, and in the same way agrees that Brazil, Cuba, China and Siam shall retain the ships seized by them respectively provided payment is made for the same.

France has agreed with the United States that it does not question the United States' title, but has not to this date agreed with relation to the ships seized by the other states.

We are now negotiating with Italy and Japan.

If the seized ships were all to be pooled and divided on the ton-for-ton basis, the interests of the various countries would be according to the percentages shown below:

U. K.	77.65
France	6.75
Italy	6.70
U. S.	3.00
Greece	3.49
Japan	1.32
Belgium	.77
Brazil	.14
Portugal	.14
Roumania	.04

Great Britain and France have waived any question as to our title, and we hope for similar agreements on the part of Italy, Greece, Japan and Belgium. With such agreements we need fear no further difficulty in maintaining our title. However, that as a matter of courtesy we should present the matter to Greece and Belgium and possibly the other countries, and will do so as soon as we have arrived at an understanding with Japan.

We know of no other questions involved in the seized ships which might give difficulty from the standpoint of the United States. There are some rather complicated claims put forward by Italy, particularly with relation to Adriatic shipping, but in this question we should not be affected so far as ship tonnage is concerned.

DOCUMENT 446

Resolution of the Supreme Council Regarding the Distribution of Rolling Stock in Enemy Countries, July 29, 1919

[Council of Heads of Delegations, Resolution No. 11-F. "Appointment of Commission of Experts for the distribution of Rolling Stock in Enemy Countries. Resolution."]

It is decided that the immediate distribution of rolling stock will be made on the authority of the Commission of Experts, but this division will only be final when the financial side of the operation has been examined and approved by the Commission on Reparations.

(Submitted before final acceptance to the Commission on Reparations and on Ports, Waterways and Railways.)

DOCUMENT 447

Resolution of the Supreme Council Regarding the Coal Situation in Europe, August 5, 1919

[Council of Heads of Delegations, Resolution No. 17-D (H. D. 24). "The coal situation in Europe. Resolution."]

It is decided that the Supreme Council shall invite the British, French, Italian, Belgian, Polish and Czecho-Slovak Governments each to name a member to serve on a European Commission on Coal, which shall be immediately constituted in Paris, to undertake the coordination of production, distribution and transportation of coal for all Europe.

The Commissions on Reparations, on Teschen, on the Plebiscite for Silesia and the various Commissions charged with transportation by sea, by rail and by canal shall receive instructions to cooperate with this Commission on Coal and to aid it to the greatest possible extent.

It is moreover decided that conversations shall take place between Mr. Polk, Mr. Hoover and M. Loucheur on the subject of American representation on this commission.

The above-named delegations are requested immediately to announce the name of their representative to M. Loucheur; it would facilitate matters if these names could be communicated on the morning of August 6, 1919.

DOCUMENT 448

Letter from Jouasset to Dulles Regarding the Accounting Procedure to Be Followed by the Reparation Commission, August 27, 1919

[Copy in TPG, III, 276-78.]

Cher Monsieur Dulles,

Vous vous souvenez que nous avons eu ensemble un entretien au sujet des règlements de comptes à intervenir entre les Gouvernements Alliés et Associés à l'occasion de la répartition des paiements ou versements que l'Allemagne, en vertu du Traité de Versailles, devra effectuer au titre des réparations. Cette question avait d'ailleurs fait l'objet de conversations antérieures et notamment d'une proposition de Mr. KEYNES en date du 1er Mai 1919, qui avait été acceptée en principe, mais non rédigée.[1]

Au cours de notre entretien, nous étions tombés d'accord sur les points suivants:

1° Une seule règle existe pour la répartition susvisée: c'est celle que le Conseil Suprême des Principales Puissances Alliées et Associées a adoptée le 30 Avril dernier et qui consiste à répartir au prorata du montant des dommages respectivement subis par chaque Puissance intéressée et reconnus par la Commission des Réparations.[2] C'est à l'application stricte de cette règle que doivent tendre les règlements de compte dont il s'agit;

2° On pourrait envisager qu'il fut procédé à ces règlements de compte tous les ans par la Commission des Réparations, chaque Gouvernement devant reverser à la Commission, dans un délai déterminé, les sommes, valeurs ou livraisons reçues par lui en excédent de la part à laquelle lui donne droit l'application de la règle du 30 Avril; toutefois, le premier arrêté de compte ne pourrait avoir lieu que le 1er Mai 1921; d'une part, en effet, c'est seulement à cette date qu'aux termes même du Traité le montant des dommages vérifiés par la Commission sera normalement connu, et, par suite, que pourra s'appliquer la règle de répartition; d'autre part, l'accord approuvé le 24 Juin par le Conseil Suprême au sujet de la priorité de 2 milliards ½ de francs accordée à la Belgique suppose cette décision;[3]

3° Enfin, il est hors de doute que dans tous les cas il y aura lieu à reversement de la part de l'une quelconque des Puissances intéres-

---

[1] There are no other references to Keynes' proposal.
[2] See Documents 320 and 324.
[3] See Documents 437 and 439.

sées, c'est seulement au profit de la masse commune, c'est à dire de la Commission des Réparations, mais en aucun cas au profit de l'Allemagne ou de ses Alliés, que ces versements devront être effectués, puisqu'ils auront pour objet unique de respecter la règle du 30 Avril et de ne pas permettre une méconnaissance des proportions qu'elle assigne pour chaque Puissance Alliée ou Associée; cette observation a une importance toute particulière pour le premier arrêté de compte, au cas où, au 1er Mai 1921, on constaterait que le chiffre de 20 milliards de marks or indiqué par l'article 235 du Traité a été dépassé; en ce qui concerne l'Allemagne, ce dépassement ne pourrait que donner lieu à une déduction sur sa dette totale, telle qu'elle aura dû être fixée en conformité de l'article 233.

Je pense, Cher Monsieur Dulles, que vous voudrez bien me confirmer notre accord sur ces différents points. Vous estimerez sans doute, dans ce cas, qu'on pourrait accepter un texte conçu, par exemple, comme celui qui est annexé à la présente lettre.

Croyez-moi, je vous prie, bien sincèrement vôtre.

GEORGES JOUASSET.

ANNEXE

A la fin de chaque année, la Commission des Réparations établira le compte de chacune des Puissances Alliées et Associées, en tenant compte de tous les paiements ou versements effectués par l'Allemagne ou ses Alliés, des livraisons faites ou des réparations en nature réalisées, et de la part revenant à ladite Puissance conformément à la règle de répartition adoptée le 30 Avril 1919 par le Conseil Suprême des Principales Puissances Alliées et Associées.

Le solde débiteur de chaque Puissance, provenant de toute somme, valeur, livraison ou réparation en nature reçue par elle en excédent de sa part, devra être reversé par elle à la Commission des Réparations dans un délai de trois (3) mois après que l'arrêté de compte lui aura été notifié par ladite Commission. Sur les encaissements ainsi effectués, celle-ci fera alors aux Puissances intéressées dont le compte sera créditeur les versements auxquels elles auront droit.

Par exception, le premier arrêté de compte sera fait le 1er Mai 1921.

DOCUMENT 449

Reply from Dulles to Jouasset Regarding the Accounting Procedure to Be Followed by the Reparation Commission, August 28, 1919

[Copy in TPG, III, 279.]

My dear Mr. Jouasset:

I am in receipt of your letter of August 27 with respect to the procedure for accounting to be adopted by the Reparation Commission.[1]

Your understanding of this matter corresponds with my own and I should be prepared to accept a text [such] as that drafted by you with the understanding that among the values which are to be taken into account in determining the debit or credit of each nation at the annual accounting period are included the items specified by Article 243 of the Treaty.

I am, my dear Mr. Jouasset,

Very sincerely yours,

DOCUMENT 450

Cable from Polk Regarding the Interpretation of Article 235 of the Treaty with Germany, September 27, 1919

[Miller, XX, 432-35.]

At meeting Interim Reparations Commission, twenty-fifth, British Delegates raised question of interpretation Article 235 German Peace Treaty which question also involves interpretation of similar article in Austrian and other Peace Treaties. They claim article distinguishes between action of "Governments of the Principal Allied and Associated Powers" and the Reparations Commission proper.

British claim this distinction deliberately made by those drafting Peace Treaty and in their opinion should be recognized and maintained: that therefore, Reparations Commission is only a liquidatory engaged in releasing Germany's assets and "not preoccupied with any consideration but the extracting from the estate in its hands the last penny of the bill formulated under Annex 1." They claim that the Reparations Commission should have no responsibilities in determining what supplies of food and raw ma-

---

[1] See Document 448.

terials essential to enable enemy countries to meet their obligations for reparations which are to be paid for out of the sums provided under Article 235 or otherwise. They claim "Reparations Commission is *functus officio* when it has released whole of valuable assets" and "however great the ultimate interest in nursing this estate with a view to securing greater yielding, the future Reparations Commission could not safely accept this responsibility in view of magnitude of political and financial questions involved." British claim this latter operation would be function of the "Governments of the Principal Allied and Associated Powers" or somebody independent of the Reparations Commission authorized and empowered by these Governments to make such determinations. For this purpose they propose continuing either the Supreme Economic Council with its various agencies or giving a similar function to "the economic section of the League of Nations." They, therefore, propose that the Supreme Economic Council, with its existing agencies, either under its present name or under the name of "the economic Section of the League of Nations" be charged with determining requirements and sources of supplies and informing the Reparations Commission of the amount of finances necessary in meeting these requirements.

The British point out the Austrian case where assets at the disposal of the Reparations Commission will be too limited to meet minimum needs during next year, and in which case some other method of finance must be evolved to cover the difference.

British also point out that proposed agencies of the Supreme Economic Council or economic section of the League of Nations could also handle and arrange questions of procurement of supplies, oversea and inland transport and final distribution of food and raw materials with resulting benefit to all concerned.

American Delegates made reservations on all points raised by British Delegates pointing out that whole question one of broad and far reaching policy which at this time required instructions from American Government before definite action could be taken.

They pointed out that Supreme Economic Council with sub-agencies, was organized solely for purpose of operating during period of Armistice and until such time as Reparations Commission started to function and quoted Hoover's statement at London meeting that measures already taken had been hampered by Government's instruction which did not include future activities of Supreme Economic Council; that they had no knowledge of an "economic section of the League of Nations" and that they considered that the question as to whether or not such section should be established, as well as the delimitation of its functions, was wholly a matter for the determination of the League of Nations.

The acceptance of the British interpretation of Article 235 might, it is thought, have considerable effect on the provisions of economic and financial situation. The first endeavor of the Supreme Economic Council or the economic section of the League of Nations would possibly be directed to affect [sic], in one form or another, a control of purchase and distribution of world's commodities, which might be undesirable. This same Council or section might also attempt to pass on question of credits and amounts of same with some embarrassment to us.

The result of the British proposal, as we see it, would be to create two independent bodies each with independent sub-agencies throughout Europe, one responsible for reports on requirements in addition to endeavoring to exercise the controls already mentioned, while the other would be simply engaged in exploiting enemy States. The Reparations Committee in this latter capacity, it is believed, would very shortly assume the rôle of directing the bulk of enemy assets into the reparations accounts of the countries interested in reparation, leaving to the Supreme Economic Council or economic section the rôle of attempting to cover the deficit by procuring corresponding credits to meet the necessities of life of enemy countries. In view of our financial and raw material holdings, it may be readily seen how vitally this affects our interests.

Our opinion is that the Reparations Commission is not solely a liquidatory agency, but was created with the distinct understanding on the part of all our Allies that it should have much the same duties and functions as a receivership in commercial life and that on this account it is a definite function of the Reparations Commission to so "administer the estate as to insure securing not only its best and continued health, but also in this manner to assure greater yield from it in the future for the payment of its reparation account." It is, therefore, our opinion that there exists no good reason for the continuance of the Supreme Economic Council or for clothing the existing council under the name of the economic section of the League of Nations for the purpose indicated.

We have no one to consult here who participated in drawing up reparations clauses of treaty. In view importance of this matter, suggest that views of Hoover and Dulles be ascertained as to position our Delegates should take in this matter. Request reply earliest possible date.

THE MINUTES OF THE PLENARY COMMISSION
DOCUMENT 451
Plenary Commission: Minutes of the First Meeting (Including Annex), February 3, 1919, 3 P. M.

[EOM, CRD, pp. 5-7. French stenographic minutes, PV, CRD, pp. 13-16. The minutes of the first 10 meetings of the Plenary Commission are bound into one book. In addition to the minutes, this book also contains the following:

Cover. "PRELIMINARY PEACE CONFERENCE, COMMISSION ON THE REPARATION OF DAMAGE. MINUTES. MEETINGS: 1st—3 FEBRUARY . . . 10th—24 FEBRUARY. PARIS, 1919"]

Title Page. Same as Cover.

Page 3. "COMMISSION ON REPARATION OF DAMAGE
"TERMS OF REFERENCE

"At the Plenary Session of the Preliminary Peace Conference held 25 January, 1919, the following resolution was adopted:

" 'That a Commission be appointed with not more than three representatives apiece from each of the Five Great Powers and not more than two representatives apiece from Belgium, Greece, Poland, Roumania and Serbia, to examine and report:—

" '1. On the amount which the enemy countries ought to pay by way of reparation.

" '2. On what they are capable of paying; and

" '3. By what method, in what form and within what time payment should be made.'

"In accordance with action taken on 3 February, 1919, and on 22 February, 1919, respectively, the Czecho-Slovak Republic and Portugal were permitted each to have two representatives on the Commission."

Page 4. "COMMISSION ON REPARATION

"LIST OF MEMBERS

" *United States of America:*
  Mr. Bernard M. Baruch
  Mr. Norman H. Davis
  Mr. Vance C. McCormick

" *British Empire:*
  The Rt. Hon. W. M. Hughes
  The Rt. Hon. The Lord
    Sumner of Ibstone
  The Rt. Hon. The Lord
    Cunliffe

" *France:*
  Mr. L.-L. Klotz
  Mr. Loucheur
  Mr. Albert Lebrun

Belgium:
  Mr. Van den Heuvel
  Mr. Despret

Greece:
  Mr. Romanos
  Mr. Michalacopoulos

Poland:
  Mr. Olchowski
  Mr. Chamiec

Portugal:
  Mr. Moniz*
  Mr. Freire d'Andrade

"*Italy:*
Mr. Salandra
Mr. Chiesa
Mr. d'Amelio

"*Japan:*
Mr. Mori
Mr. H. Nagaoka
Mr. Tatsumi

Roumania:
Mr. Danielopol
Mr. Zahariade

Serbia:
Mr. Stoyanowitch
Mr. Miloch Savtchitch

Czecho-Slovak Republic:
Mr. Benes
Mr. Osuski

"SECRETARIAT

"Mr. Jerome D. Greene
"Colonel the Hon. S. Peel
"Mr. Ch. de Lasteyrie
"Mr. F. Foberti

"*Replaced by Mr. Alfonso Costa, after the meeting of 11th March, 1919. [*Footnote in original.*]"

Page 52. "TABLE OF CONTENTS (THROUGH THE TENTH MEETING) . . ."]

The Commission on Reparation of Damage met on Monday, 3 February, 1919, at 3 P. M., at the Ministry of Finance.

Present: Messrs. BARUCH, DAVIS and McCORMICK(*U. S. A.*); Mr. HUGHES, LORD SUMNER and LORD CUNLIFFE (*British Empire*); Messrs. KLOTZ, LOUCHEUR and LEBRUN (*France*); Messrs. CHIESA and D'AMELIO (*Italy*); Messrs. MORI and FUKAI (*Japan*); Messrs. VAN DEN HEUVEL and DESPRET (*Belgium*); Messrs. ROMANOS and MICHALACOPOULOS (*Greece*); Messrs. OLCHOWSKI and CHAMIEC (*Poland*); Messrs. STOYANOWITCH and SAVTCHITCH (*Serbia*); Messrs. DANIELOPOL and ZAHARIADE (*Roumania*).

Mr. KLOTZ, Minister of Finance and Delegate to the Peace Conference, opened the proceedings by welcoming the representatives of the Powers.

Election of Officers

He then presided at the election of the CHAIRMAN and VICE-CHAIRMEN.

On the proposal of Mr. HUGHES (*British Empire*), supported by Mr. VAN DEN HEUVEL (*Belgium*), Mr. CHIESA (*Italy*) and Mr. BARUCH (*U. S. A.*), Mr. KLOTZ was nominated CHAIRMAN of the Commission, and Mr. HUGHES and Mr. VAN DEN HEUVEL VICE-CHAIRMEN.

The composition of the Secretariat and the nomination of its members, as well as the details of the internal organization of the Commission, were deferred to a meeting to be held the next day, 4th February.

The CHAIRMAN returned thanks for himself and the VICE-CHAIRMEN, and described the task which was before the Commission in the following words:

"Merci! Au travail! Pour la Justice! Ce programme suffit!"

The CHAIRMAN proposed, and it was agreed, that the meetings of the Commission should take place three times a week, on Mondays, Wednesdays and Fridays at 10.30 A. M.

Discussion of Principles

In reply to an observation made by Mr. LOUCHEUR (*France*), the CHAIRMAN proposed that before dividing the work among the Sub-Committees the Commission should proceed to an exchange of views. Just as, before the conclusion of the armistice, the Allied and Associated Governments came to an understanding with respect to the principles laid down by President WILSON, so the Commission could not come to any practical conclusions unless its members were first agreed on the principles of reparation for damage. A summary of the principles had been prepared by the CHAIRMAN, which might serve as a basis for study and discussion by the Commission.

A draft of this summary, in French and English, was distributed to the members of the Commission. (See Annex.)

Terms of Reference

The CHAIRMAN called the attention of the Delegates to the programme fixed by the Peace Conference for the work of the Commission on Reparation. The Commission had to study:—

(a) The amount of reparation to be paid by the enemy Powers.
(b) Their capacity for payment.
(c) The method, form and period in which this payment had to be made, and the guarantees necessary to ensure its completion.

The business of the immediately succeeding meetings would then be as follows:—

At the meeting on Tuesday, 4th February, the Commission would decide on its internal organization; on Wednesday morning it would begin the examination of principles. There would then be an opportunity for the Commission to decide what is meant by "damage" and by "reparation."

These proposals of the CHAIRMAN were adopted.

The next meeting was fixed for the following day, Tuesday, 4th February, at 3 P. M.

The meeting adjourned at 3.45 P. M.   L.-L. KLOTZ,
                                                          Chairman.

MEMORANDUM ON PRINCIPLES OF REPARATION FOR DAMAGE

Presented by the French Delegation

1. All jurisprudence and all modern legislation (German, American, English, French, etc.) profess or apply identical principles with regard to reparation and damage.

All lay down, almost in the same terms, that he who through his own fault has done injury to "the life, body, health, liberty, property or any other right of another" (Art. 823 of the German Civil Code) should be condemned, on that ground, to "re-establish the conditions which would have existed if the circumstances giving rise to that obligation had not occurred." (Art. 249 of the same Code.)

Through Germany's action:—

Men, both combatant and non-combatant, women, children and old people have been killed, mutilated, wounded, attacked in the very sources of their life by diseases produced by the war—"injuries to life, body and health;"

Men, women and children have been reduced to slavery, driven into forced labor under the yoke of the invader—"injury to liberty;"

Whole populations, active and hard-working, have seen with their own eyes the product of the accumulated labor of generations destroyed in a few weeks, sometimes in a few hours—"injury to property."

Germany should make good in full the damage caused by her. This is the only means of re-establishing, as her own law decrees, "the conditions which would have existed" if the war "had not occurred" through her own act and her fault. Both as a penalty for the past and as an example for the future, she must pay the whole of her debt.

2. But if all her creditors—that is to say, the Allied and Associated Powers,—are equally worthy of consideration and should be placed on the same footing, this is not the case for all categories of claims. Some of these have a right to a privileged position.

The priority of a claim consists in the right which it derives from its very nature to be repaid before all others, irrespective of the identity of the creditor.

---

[1] French text, PV, CRD, pp. 17-18, and Miller, IV, 363-64. There are minor differences between the three versions.

3. Irrespective of and before these privileged claims, of which it will be the duty of the Commission to draw up a list and to establish an order of priority, there must be reserved the right of an owner to recover property wrongfully removed (l'action en revendication.)

If a debtor has taken possession of the goods of another, he is under an obligation to restore them before his creditors can claim from him any reimbursement. The owner of such goods has the right to take them back before any distribution of the goods of the debtor by his creditors. The goods of a debtor only constitute the common security of his creditors in so far as they are his lawful property.

The owner preserves his prior right to restitution, even when the goods seized have been destroyed or rendered useless by the debtor, and are, therefore, no longer to be found in kind among his possessions.

If this were not so, it would be possible for the debtor by malicious destruction or by the consumption for his own purpose of the goods taken, to prevent the victim of the depredation from exercising his proprietary rights. It would reduce the owner of the property to the rank of ordinary creditors, who have equal rights in the distribution of the property of the debtor.

1 February, 1919.

DOCUMENT 452

Plenary Commission: Minutes of the Second Meeting (Including Annex), February 4, 1919, 3 P. M.

[EOM, CRD, pp. 8-11. French stenographic minutes, PV, CRD, pp. 19-27.]

The Commission on Reparation of Damage met on Tuesday, 4 February, 1919, at 3 P. M., at the Ministry of Finance, MR. KLOTZ in the Chair.

Present: Messrs. BARUCH, DAVIS and MCCORMICK (*U. S. A.*); Mr. HUGHES, LORD SUMNER and LORD CUNLIFFE (*British Empire*); Messrs. KLOTZ, LOUCHEUR and LEBRUN (*France*); Messrs. SALANDRA, CHIESA and D'AMELIO (*Italy*); Messrs. MORI and TATSUMI (*Japan*); Messrs. VAN DEN HEUVEL and DESPRET (*Belgium*); Messrs. ROMANOS and MICHALACOPOULOS (*Greece*); Messrs. OLCHOWSKI and CHAMIEC (*Poland*); Messrs. DANIELOPOL and ZAHARIADE (*Roumania*); Messrs. STOYANOWITCH and SAVTCHITCH (*Serbia*).[1]

---

[1] According to the French minutes, Fukai, not Tatsumi, was present for Japan.

Czecho-Slovak Representatives

The CHAIRMAN informed the Commission of the wish expressed by certain Powers not yet represented on the Commission to be admitted to share its work. This wish on the part of the Czecho-Slovak Republic had been granted by the Peace Conference, and that State would be represented on the Commission by two delegates whose names were not yet known.

The Commission proceeded to the business of the day. A proposal for regulating the organization of the Commission, drawn up in French and English, was accepted as the basis of discussion. (See Annex).[2]

The CHAIRMAN read Article A:—

Organization of Secretaries

A Secretariat is established for the Commission on Reparation. The Secretariat is composed of four members, two English-speaking and two French-speaking. The Secretariat will summon the members to the meetings of the Commission. Its duty is to draw up minutes, which are to be drafted in French and English. If a comparison of the two texts (English and French) shows any discrepancy, the point will be referred to the Commission for decision. The same course will be followed if two texts of the same language show any discrepancy. It will also be the duty of the Secretariat to draft the Agenda, in accordance with the decisions taken by the Commission at its previous meeting. If, in addition to the prescribed Agenda, some urgent question should arise in the interval between two meetings, the Chairman may cause it to be added to the Agenda. He will inform the General Secretariat of the addition. Special mention of such question will be made in the notice of meeting sent out to the members by the Secretariat.

On an observation by MR. LOUCHEUR (*France*), and after discussion, it was decided that the following addition should be made to the Article:—

Language of Official Texts

The official text shall be drafted in the language or languages to be agreed upon by the Peace Conference.

On the suggestion of MR. VAN DEN HEUVEL (*Belgium*), the two sentences relating to possible discrepancies between the texts drafted by the Secretaries, in the same language or in different languages, were reduced to a single sentence, which read as follows:—

If a comparison of the texts shows any discrepancy, the point will be referred to the Commission for decision.

The CHAIRMAN then invited discussion on Article B:—

[2] Annex is text as finally adopted.

Sub-Committees

The Commission decides on the establishment of Sub-Committees, to the number of three.

The work will be divided as follows:—

Sub-Committee 1.—Valuation of damage.

Sub-Committee 2.—Study of the financial capacity of the enemy States and of their means of payment.

Sub-Committee 3.—Measures of control and guarantees.

On the request of MR. CHAMIEC (*Poland*), it was agreed that, although the number of Sub-Committees was provisionally fixed at three, the Commission did not intend to preclude the appointment of further Sub-Committees at a later date.

MR. HUGHES (*British Empire*), and MR. LOUCHEUR (*France*), agreed in thinking that general principles should be discussed by the Commission in full session.

Article B was adopted.

Article C was then read:—

National Representation

The Delegations of the United States of America, Great Britain, France, Italy and Japan shall each have one representative on each of the Sub-Committees.

The delegations of the other Powers shall agree among themselves to nominate from among their members their representatives on each of the three Sub-Committees, to the number of three members for each Sub-Committee.

This number is increased to four in the case of the Sub-Committee for the valuation of damages.

MR. ROMANOS (*Greece*) requested that each Power interested, especially those on whose territory military operations had taken place, should be entitled to a representative on each of the Sub-Committees.

After discussion, Article C was adopted with the suppression of the last paragraph and with the following addition:

The delegations of each Power shall have a representative on the First Sub-Committee.

Article D was adopted without discussion.

Technical Experts

As regards Article E, on the suggestion of MR. SALANDRA (*Italy*), the CHAIRMAN stated that the list of experts and technical advisers provided for therein was not intended to be final, but could be added to later if necessary.

MR. STOYANOWITCH (*Serbia*), requested that a special Sub-Committee be appointed to consider reparation the immediate execution of which is urgently required.

The CHAIRMAN asked that this proposal might be submitted in written form.

Article F was adopted without discussion, and the regulations as a whole were approved in the form shown in the Annex.

MR. LOUCHEUR (*France*) suggested that the Sub-Committees should begin their work without waiting for a decision on the general principles of reparation for damage.

After observations by MR. HUGHES (*British Empire*), and MR. VAN DEN HEUVEL (*Belgium*), and on the suggestion of the CHAIRMAN, it was agreed that the Sub-Committees should be appointed as soon as possible and that each delegation should forward to the Secretariat a list of its representatives.

The following were nominated members of the General Secretariat:—

Members of Secretariat

United States: MR. JEROME D. GREENE.
Great Britain: COLONEL THE HON. S. PEEL.
France: MR. DE LASTEYRIE.
Italy: MR. FOBERTI.

The CHAIRMAN further stated that he had appointed as his Private Secretary, Mr. Cheysson. MR. HUGHES and MR. VAN DEN HEUVEL had respectively appointed SIR ROBERT GARRAN and MR. BOURQUIN.

MR. STOYANOWITCH (*Serbia*) made the following proposal:—

Urgent Needs of Invaded Countries

A special Sub-Committee shall be appointed to study the means by which the most urgent necessities caused by acts of war in invaded and devastated territories should be met. Each of the great Powers as well as each of the invaded countries shall have its representative on such Sub-Committee.

After discussion, the Commission decided that that part of M. STOYANOWITCH'S motion which related to financial assistance asked for by the smaller Powers was not within its competence and that it would seem more appropriate to refer it for examination to the Financial Commission. The questions raised by MR. STOYANOWITCH and MR. DANIELOPOL during the course of the discussion in so far as they related to means of payment and reparation should be submitted for study to the Second Sub-Committee of the Commission on Reparation, the terms of reference for which should be amplified by the addition of the words "and reparation." The Second Sub-Committee would thus be charged with "the study of the financial capacity of the enemy States and of their means of payment and reparation."

The next meeting was fixed for Wednesday, 5 February, at 11 A. M.

The meeting adjourned at 4.45 P. M.

L.-L. KLOTZ,
Chairman.

JEROME D. GREENE,
S. PEEL,
CH. DE LASTEYRIE,
F. FOBERTI,
    Secretaries.

ANNEX[3]

ORGANIZATION

A

A Secretariat is established for the Allied Commission on Reparation. The Secretariat is composed of four members, two English-speaking and two French-speaking.

The Secretariat will summon the members to the meetings of the Commission. Its duty is to draw up minutes, which are to be drafted in French and English. If a comparison of the texts shows any discrepancy, the point will be referred to the Commission for decision. The official text will be drafted in the language or languages to be agreed upon by the Conference. It will also be the duty of the Secretariat to draft the Agenda, in accordance with the decisions taken by the Commission at its previous meeting. If, in addition to the prescribed Agenda, any urgent question should arise in the interval between two meetings, the President may add it to the Agenda. He will inform the Secretariat of the addition. Special mention of such question will be made in the notice of meeting sent out to the members by the Secretariat.

B

The Commission decides on the establishment of Sub-Committees, the number of which is provisionally fixed at three.

The work will be divided as follows:—

Sub-Committee No. 1.—Valuation of damage.

Sub-Committee No. 2.—Study of the financial capacity of the enemy States and of their means of payment and reparation.

Sub-Committee No. 3.—Measures of control and guarantees.

[3] French Text, PV, CRD, pp. 28-29.

C

The Delegations of each Power shall have a representative on the First Sub-Committee.

The Delegations of the United States of America, Great Britain, France, Italy and Japan shall each have one representative on each of the other Sub-Committees.

The Delegations of the other Powers shall agree among themselves to nominate from among their members their representatives on each of these Sub-Committees, to the number of three representatives for each Sub-Committee.

D

All the members of the Commission have the right to attend the meetings of the Sub-Committees.

The minutes of the Sub-Committees will be held at the disposal of the members of the Commission.

E

Technical advisers and experts may be appointed by the Powers to take part in the work of the Sub-Committees.

They will have a consultative voice.

A general list should be furnished to the Secretariat by each Delegation, indicating which Sub-Committees these advisers and experts have a right to attend.

F

The Secretariat will provide a Secretary for each of the Sub-Committees.

4 February, 1919.

DOCUMENT 453

Plenary Commission: Minutes of the Third Meeting, February 5, 1919, 11 A. M.

[EOM, CRD, pp. 12-14. French stenographic minutes, PV, CRD, pp. 30-38.]

The Commission on Reparation of Damage met on Wednesday, 5 February, 1919, at 11 A. M., at the Ministry of Finance, MR. KLOTZ in the Chair.

Present: Messrs. BARUCH, DAVIS and McCORMICK (*U. S. A.*); MR. HUGHES, Lord SUMNER and Lord CUNLIFFE (*British Empire*); Messrs. KLOTZ, LOUCHEUR, and LEBRUN (*France*); Messrs. SALANDRA, CHIESA and D'AMELIO (*Italy*); Messrs. MORI and TATSUMI (*Japan*); Messrs. VAN DEN HEUVEL and DESPRET

(*Belgium*); Messrs. Romanos and Michalacopoulos (*Greece*); Messrs. Olchowski and Chamiec (*Poland*); Messrs. Danielopol and Zahariade (*Roumania*); Messrs. Stoyanowitch and Savtchitch (*Serbia*); Messrs. Benes and Osuski (*Czecho-Slovak Republic*).[1]

The Chairman stated that the draft minutes of the first and second meetings were not yet ready and that they would be laid before the Commission at the next meeting.

The Chairman informed the Commission of a motion of Mr. Lloyd George, which had been adopted by the Peace Conference:

Substitution of Delegates

That the principle of rotation should be adopted for all Commissions, and that it should be understood that, if a Delegate is unable to be present at a meeting, he can always be represented by a substitute.

The Chairman opened the discussion on the principles in accordance with which the work of the Commission was to be governed.

Mr. Salandra (*Italy*) asked that in Article I of the French text the word "Germany" should be replaced by "the enemy States." (See Annex to 1st Meeting).

The Chairman agreed fully with Mr. Salandra. If 'Germany had been specially mentioned, it was because the suggested text laid particular emphasis on the German Civil Code. But the general tenor of its principles was not altered by that.

On a request made by Mr. Savtchitch (*Serbia*) that the Commission should define the different categories of damages, the Chairman stated that, before defining these categories, it was essential first of all to establish principles of law, from which the definitions asked for by Mr. Savtchitch would logically proceed. The Chairman had enunciated some of these principles in the text which had been submitted to the members of the Commission.

Documents Submitted to be Placed on Agenda

Mr. Davis (*U. S. A.*) asked whether the Chairman's text was of an official character or not, and Mr. McCormick (*U. S. A.*) observed that, when any documents were to serve as a basis for discussion, they ought to be notified as such to the members of

---

[1] According to the French minutes, Baruch, Beneš, and Osuský were absent; and Fukai was present instead of Tatsumi.

Slosson's Annotations read (Miller, XIX, 266): "At the plenary session [of January 25] the Portuguese and Czecho-Slovak Delegations requested special representation on the Commission. Two Czecho-Slovak Delegates were added on February 3 (B. C. 21) and two Portuguese Delegates on February 22 (B. C. 37). Seven small Powers therefore enjoyed representation on the Commission."

the Commission, and special mention should be made of them in the Agenda of the meeting.

MR. HUGHES (*British Empire*) stated, and the CHAIRMAN assented, that the text submitted to the Commission was a summary of the personal views of MR. KLOTZ, that it had been prepared before that gentleman's nomination to the Chairmanship, and that in consequence it had no official character, but was simply a contribution to the discussion and, as such, might serve as a basis for the deliberations of the Commission.

MR. CHIESA (*Italy*) proposed an amendment to the text:

> The valuation of war damage which it would be in accordance with justice to include must be founded on common principles, according to which there will be fixed several categories of damages, which will compose the respective totals due to each nation.

Suggested Programme for Discussion

The CHAIRMAN suggested a programme which he considered it would be expedient to adopt:

(1) Establishment of principles of law.

(2) Definition of damage.

(3) Definition of reparation.

MR. DAVIS (*U. S. A.*) while approving the procedure proposed by the CHAIRMAN stated that the American delegates were not in a position to enter on a legal discussion without consulting expert opinion, and that he reserved the rights of his Delegation.

MR. HUGHES (*British Empire*) considered that, in these circumstances, the discussion would be sterile, and proposed to postpone the deliberations of the Commission to a later meeting.

Mr. Van den Heuvel's Analysis of French Proposal

MR. VAN DEN HEUVEL (*Belgium*) analysed the CHAIRMAN'S text. This text, in his opinion, dealt successively with:

(1) The rights from which claims arise.

(2) The nature of the claims.

(3) The order of payment of the claims.

In his opinion, the claims on enemy states for reparation did not arise—as the text would seem to indicate—only from atrocities committed by them, but from the much more general fact that the enemy initiated and carried on an unjust war.

In the paragraph relating to the nature of the claims, the principle laid down as to the integral reparation of damages must be more precisely expressed. It would be necessary to indicate if indirect damages were regarded as on the same level as direct damages, and the principal categories of damages should be clearly defined. The order of payment and the preferred status to be accorded to certain of these claims ought, it seemed to him, to receive the fullest attention of the Commission.

He also proposed that the members of the different delegations should forward to the Secretariat any suggestions they might have to make on this subject.

Question of War Costs

MR. MICHALACOPOULOS (*Greece*) asked for an explanation of the CHAIRMAN's text. Was it intended to make the enemy pay all the expenses of the war, i.e., cost of the war and war damage? And did not the terms of the Armistice Convention limit further claims under this head?

The CHAIRMAN was of opinion that Article XIX of the Armistice Convention which read as follows: "With reservation that any future claims and demands of the Allies and the United States of America remain unaffected . . . " was a sufficient answer to the Greek Delegate's question.

MR. HUGHES (*British Empire*) expressed the view that it was useless to limit the discussion to the proposed text. There were principles of a more general nature which must be examined first of all.

The CHAIRMAN proposed that the discussion should be deferred until the next meeting.[2]

MR. DESPRET (*Belgium*) read the following:

The enemy Powers, having, through the fact of the war caused by their own fault, done injury to the life, bodies, health, liberty, property and all rights of of others—individuals and corporations, public and private bodies—must be condemned, on that ground, to re-establish the conditions which would have existed if the circumstances giving rise to that obligation had not occurred.

The principle herein enunciated was very general and might form a basis for discussion at Friday's meeting.

MR. HUGHES (*British Empire*) objected to being bound down by any text, whether it were the German Civil Code or any other Code. If the Commission did not find any code wide enough, it would create one. The only code it could recognize was the code of Justice.

MR. LOUCHEUR (*France*) objected that it was impossible to start any discussion without a precise programme. He asked MR. HUGHES to draft a memorandum which could be examined by the

---

[2] According to the French minutes, this was Hughes' proposal.

members of the Commission before the next meeting and discussed at that meeting.

Each Delegation to Submit Memorandum

MR. DAVIS (*U. S. A.*) considered that each of the delegations should present its point of view in a separate memorandum.

MR. HUGHES (*British Empire*) shared the opinion of MR. DAVIS. On Friday, even before receiving the memoranda, the Commission might commence its attempt to lay down general principles. Limits would thus be placed upon discussion, and certain propositions could be eliminated at once.

MR. LOUCHEUR (*France*) thought that such a discussion would yield no useful result.

The Commission accordingly decided to postpone the next meeting to Monday, 10 February, at 10.30 A. M. In the meantime, the Delegations would forward to the Secretariat memoranda setting out the principles which they intended to submit to the Commission for examination. The Secretariat would undertake to forward copies of these proposals to each member of the Commission.

Sub-Committees

The Commission then decided to nominate at its next meeting the members of the Sub-Committees.

Each of the Powers represented on the Commission would inform the Secretariat of the name of its Delegate on the First Sub-Committee. The five great Powers would also name their representatives on the two other Sub-Committees.

The Delegates of the Powers having special interests would meet under the presidency of MR. VAN DEN HEUVEL (*Belgium*) to choose their three representatives on each of the Second and Third Sub-Committees.

The meeting adjourned at 12.45 P. M.

L.-L. KLOTZ,
Chairman.

JEROME D. GREENE,
S. PEEL,
CH. DE LASTEYRIE,
F. FOBERTI,
 Secretaries.

DOCUMENT 454

Plenary Commission: Minutes of the Fourth Meeting (Including Annexes I-VI), February 10, 1919, 10:30 A. M.

[EOM, CRD, pp. 15-24. French stenographic minutes, PV, CRD, pp. 39-47.]

The Commission on Reparation of Damage met on Monday, 10 February, 1919, at 10.30 A. M., at the Ministry of Finance, MR. KLOTZ in the Chair.

Present: Messrs. BARUCH, DULLES and McCORMICK (*U. S. A.*); MR. HUGHES, LORD SUMNER and LORD CUNLIFFE (*British Empire*); Messrs. KLOTZ, LOUCHEUR and LEBRUN (*France*); Messrs. SALANDRA, CHIESA and D'AMELIO (*Italy*); Messrs. MORI, NAGAOKA and TATSUMI (*Japan*); Messrs. VAN DEN HEUVEL and DESPRET (*Belgium*); Messrs. ROMANOS and MICHALACOPOULOUS (*Greece*); Messrs. OLCHOWSKI and CHAMIEC (*Poland*); Messrs. DANIELOPOL and ZAHARIADE (*Roumania*); Messrs. STOYANOWITCH and SAVTCHITCH (*Serbia*); Messrs. BENES and OSUSKI (*Czecho-Slovak Republic*).[1]

The CHAIRMAN informed the Commission that the names of the Czecho-Slovak delegates were:

MR. BENES.

MR. OSUSKI.

The minutes of the first three meetings were presented and approved.

The CHAIRMAN requested that all papers which the delegations wished to submit to the Commission should reach the Secretariat by 12 noon of the day preceding the date of meeting.

The CHAIRMAN asked that those delegations which had not yet sent in the names of their representatives on the various Sub-Committees should do so as quickly as possible. This was done, and the Sub-Committees were constituted as shown in Annex 1.

It was agreed that MR. VAN DEN HEUVEL should take the initiative in convoking for the first time the First Sub-Committee, MR. LOUCHEUR in convoking the Second Sub-Committee, and that the CHAIRMAN, MR. HUGHES and MR. BARUCH should consult together as to convoking the Third Sub-Committee.

Representation on Sub-Committees

The question having been raised by MR. VAN DEN HEUVEL

---

[1] According to the French minutes, Markowski (instead of Chamiec) and Protić (instead of Savčić) were present; and Osuský was absent.

(*Belgium*) and MR. BENES (*Czecho-Slovak Republic*) as to the sufficiency of the representation of the Powers having particular interests upon the Second and Third Sub-Committees, the Commission decided, on the suggestion of MR. MICHALACOPOULOS (*Greece*) that the rule be modified, so that the representation on these Sub-Committees should be interchangeable, in order to allow the delegates of the States not otherwise represented to present their views on points which might particularly concern them.

The CHAIRMAN announced that the Secretariat had received memoranda from the Italian, British, Polish, Serbian, and American Governments.' (See Annexes 2-6.)

After ascertaining that no other delegation had the intention of presenting memoranda, the CHAIRMAN asked for observations on those already before the Commission.

MR. MCCORMICK (*U. S. A.*) proposed that the memoranda already submitted should be tabulated by a Committee of three, in order that points of agreement and of difference should be more clearly brought out.[2]

The CHAIRMAN agreed with MR. MCCORMICK, but suggested that a special Sub-Committee, consisting of two English-speaking and two French-speaking members, should be appointed for this purpose, and this course having met with the approval of the Commission, the Sub-Committee was constituted as follows:—MR. DULLES (*U. S. A.*), LORD SUMNER (*British Empire*), MR. LYON (*France*), MR. DESPRET (*Belgium*).

The Committee was to meet at once and present its statement in order to facilitate discussion at the next meeting.

In order to assist discussion, the CHAIRMAN proposed that one particular memorandum should be considered in the first instance .

British Memorandum of Principles

MR. LOUCHEUR (*France*) suggested that the British text, as it covered the widest field, should be taken as a basis, and this view was supported by the CHAIRMAN and MR. VAN DEN HEUVEL (*Belgium*).

MR. HUGHES (*British Empire*) was not prepared to enter on a detailed discussion of the text of the British memorandum or to criticise those presented by the other delegations. He was, however, willing, in deference to the CHAIRMAN, to make a general statement of the British position. It was accordingly agreed that the discussion of principles should be introduced by MR. HUGHES

---

[2] According to the French minutes, this proposal was made by Van den Heuvel and Loucheur.

on the basis of the British text, it being understood that, as suggested by MR. CHIESA (*Italy*) and MR. SALANDRA (*Italy*), any additions, eliminations or modifications might be freely suggested.

MR. HUGHES introduced his statement[3] by an apology to his American colleagues. As he had only received the American memorandum a few minutes before the meeting he had been unable to read it. Consequently, he could not make any allusion to it. He could not even refer to PRESIDENT WILSON'S Fourteen Points, but must confine himself to the discussion of fundamental principles.

It was, he said, a principle based on justice and not on revenge, that when a wrong had been done, the wrongdoer should right the wrong to the full extent of his capacity. This was recognized by every system of jurisprudence, not only by municipal but also by international law.

The principle of reparation demanded that the whole expenditure involved should be charged upon the enemy nations to the full extent of their capacity to pay. There was no distinction in logic or justice between a claim for restoration of ravaged territories and a claim for general compensation. Those whose fields and houses had not been destroyed had had their trade disorganized and had been involved in a crushing burden of debt. Millions of tons of merchant shipping had been destroyed. The losses suffered by the Allies of France, Belgium, and Serbia, through the military effort which saved those countries from complete destruction, were a direct consequence of the enemy's aggression and as truly a subject for compensation as the devastation in France, Belgium and Serbia. Ravaged territories must be restored and repaired, but justice would not have been achieved if the Allies were left to bear the burdens of the war. In that case, the rescuers would be worse off, not only than the intended victims, but also than the aggressors themselves. The application of the principle of reparation must be complete. This, and no less than this, justice required.

If we did not deal out justice to all men, the peace we made would not endure. To let the arch-criminals go free would make the coming League of Nations a subject for mockery and derision for those who plotted wars hereafter.

The CHAIRMAN expressed the thanks of the Commission to MR. HUGHES and proposed that consideration of the many questions raised in his speech should be postponed until the next meeting.

---

[3] Hughes' speech is reported in the French minutes only in the condensed form. See Document 110 for the full text in English, and the *Mémoire britannique* (PV, CRD, pp. 63-67) for a French translation of this.

At the suggestion of the CHAIRMAN, it was agreed that, in the meetings of the Sub-Committees, audience should be given only to technical advisers and experts. It was also agreed that the memoranda submitted by the various Delegations should be kept secret and not given to the Press.

Purchase of Food Stuffs for Germany

In reply to a statement by MR. HUGHES (*British Empire*) with reference to the use by Germany of gold for the purchase of foodstuffs through the Associated Governments, to which he took exception, the CHAIRMAN explained that the question would doubtless be dealt with by the Supreme Economic Council instituted on Saturday last at the proposal of PRESIDENT WILSON.

The next meeting was fixed for Wednesday, 12 February, 1919, at 10.30 A. M.

The meeting adjourned at 1 P. M.

L.-L. KLOTZ,
Chairman.

JEROME D. GREENE,
S. PEEL,
CH. DE LASTEYRIE,
F. FOBERTI,
  Secretaries.

ANNEX I[4]

CONSTITUTION OF SUB-COMMITTEES

*First Sub-Committee—Valuation of Damage.**

Great Powers	*Powers with Particular Interests*
United States of America, Mr. McCORMICK.	Belgium, Mr. Van den HEUVEL.
Great Britain, Lord SUMNER.	Greece, Mr. MICHALACOPOULOS.
France, Mr. LEBRUN.	Poland, Mr. OLCHOWSKI.
Italy, Mr. CHIESA.	Roumania, Mr. DANIELOPÒL.
Japan, Mr. MORI.	Serbia, Mr. SAVTCHITCH.
	Czecho-Slovak Republic, M. BENES.

Second Sub-Committee—Financial Capacity of Enemy States; Means of Payment and Reparation.

United States of America, Mr. DAVIS.	Roumania, M. DANIELOPOL.
Great Britain, Lord CUNLIFFE.	Serbia, M. STOYANOWITCH.
France, Mr. LOUCHEUR.	Poland, M. CHAMIEC.
Italy, Mr. SALANDRA.	
Japan, Mr. TATSUMI.	

---

* Upon the admission of Portugal to representation on the Commission (Minutes of Tenth Meeting, p. 50), Mr. Santos Viegas was appointed as Portuguese Delegate on the First Sub-Committee.

---

[4] French text, *ibid.*, pp. 39-41.

Third Sub-Committee—Measures of Control and Guarantees.

United States of America, Mr. BARUCH. Belgium, M. DESPRET.
Great Britain, Mr. HUGHES. Greece, Mr. MICHALACOPOULOS.[5]
France, Mr. KLOTZ. Czecho-Slovak Republic, Mr. OSUSKI.
Italy, Mr. D'AMELIO.
Japan, Mr. NAGAOKA.

ANNEX II[6]

PRINCIPLES OF REPARATION

(Presented by the Italian Delegation as an addition to the French Memorandum on Principles)

1. The legislation and jurisprudence of all civilized countries show that all those who have taken part in causing damage of the kind mentioned in the French draft (First Meeting, Annex: Paragraph 1), ought to be jointly responsible towards those who have suffered the damage. Germany, Austria-Hungary, Bulgaria and Turkey have jointly conducted the unjust war as on a single front, by mutual co-operation of forces and with identical methods and aims; they are therefore jointly liable for reparation toward those countries who have suffered on account of the war.

2. It is a recognized principle of justice, laid down in various legislations, that when several creditors have claims upon the property of a common debtor, or when several debtors are jointly liable, the assets are distributed in proportion to the respective claims, except when privilege or priority exists. The same principle should apply to reparation of war damages.

3. Interest on the amounts of reparation should be due from the same date for all countries. In fact, it may be anticipated that the ascertaining of damages in the various countries may extend over a longer or shorter period owing to circumstances over which the creditor country has no control. It will be for the Commission to fix this date.

6 February, 1919.

ANNEX III[7]

PRINCIPLES OF REPARATION

(Presented by the British Delegation)

1. Reparation is not a technical word. It is common to both languages and is well understood. It is the making good of the losses

---

[5] According to the French text, Romanos.
[6] French text, *ibid.*, p. 55.
[7] French text, *ibid.*, pp. 55-57.

which a party injured has sustained by wrongful acts and their natural consequences, so as to replace him in as good a position as that which he occupied before the wrong was done. It is effectuated by material means and affords full compensation for the real effects of the wrong.

2. Where objects, which have been taken from their owners against their will, continue to exist and can be identified, reparation involves that they should be re-delivered to their owners, who may also have a claim for compensation for having been deprived of them.

3. In other cases, reparation takes the form of material compensation. Justice requires that this compensation should be on the one hand complete and on the other hand not in excess of realities.

4. Claims are both public and private, direct and indirect. The claim is presented by the State and not by the individual, and the State claims (a) on behalf of the whole body of its citizens or (b) on behalf of smaller aggregates of citizens or (c) on behalf of single persons. The State claims for its own losses, that is to say the losses, sacrifices and outlays which fall as a burthen on the whole people now and in the future; it also claims on behalf of particular persons who have suffered wrong.

"Persons" include both natural and artificial persons, that is to say human beings, either singly or in partnerships or other personal associations, and artificial persons created by legal incorporation, such as companies, institutions, communes and municipalities.

5. The subject may be classed generally under two heads:— (a) what are the acts and what are the consequences of those acts direct and indirect, for which the Enemy Powers are responsible? (b) by what means are claims to be established and how are they to be measured for the purpose of fixing the compensation and damage from the Enemy Powers?

(a) It is a general principle of law that a wrong-doer is held to have contemplated and intended all the natural and necessary consequences of his acts. Accordingly he is bound to pay damages not merely for the act itself and its immediate result but also for its natural and necessary consequences. In the present case this is just not only in law, but in fact for, as we know, "all was foreseen" and the enemy calculated upon the injurious consequences of his outrages as an effectual means of breaking the will of the Associated Powers and their nationals. The war itself was an act of aggression and a wrong; it was therefore a wrong for which reparation is due. We have "an absolute right to demand the whole cost of the War."

(b) In measuring the damages so as to fix the compensation the following rules apply:—

(i) In all cases claims should be carefully framed with as much precision and detail as is practicable and should be supported by some form of credible proof or verification.

(ii) Claims are not to be excluded merely because of unavoidable uncertainty as to their exact nature or amount, arising out of the confusion and loss of documents or witnesses which are themselves the result of the aggressions of the Enemy Powers.

(iii) It is not desirable that claims should be presented which are too vague to be capable of reasonable estimation or which are not of a material kind but of a moral order only, or which would in effect involve payment twice over for the same thing.

(iv) In case of need any claim may be presented and reported upon provisionally or under reserves.

6. The Sub-Committees will avail themselves in their discretion of any or all codes of civilized law from which they think that they will derive assistance but without confining themselves to any particular code. Naturally they will be guided by the principles prescribed by the Plenary Commission. In reporting they should indicate what principle they have applied.

7. The Sub-Committees will receive orally or in writing the evidence of the experts and the official documents presented on behalf of the Associated Powers. They will be at liberty, if they think fit, to present alternative conclusions or to refer to the Plenary Commission questions upon which they are unable to agree upon a solution.

8. The Sub-Commitees will consider whether categories of cases can be formulated or typical instances can be selected. As it is impossible to foresee all the particular cases, to which the Sub-Committees will find it necessary to call attention, the Plenary Commission should reserve its right to reconsider the principles above laid down, if on further examination of cases and details it is found that they cannot be justly applied without adaptation or revision.

9. It is desirable that the Sub-Committees should report as soon as possible on the questions of the amount of the claims, the amount of the resources of the Enemy Powers and the appropriate forms of reparation and guarantees and afterwards take up the further

questions which do not concern the Enemy Powers but will arise between the Associated Powers alone.

ANNEX IV[8]

PRINCIPLES OF REPARATION

(Presented by the Polish Delegation)

1. Germany, Austria-Hungary, Turkey and Bulgaria as States responsible for the unjust war are liable for damages resulting from the war.
2. Reparation is due for damage caused:
   (a) to individuals, by any injury through the act of the enemy to their life, their capacity to work or their liberty.
   (b) to goods, movable or immovable, or to the interests of individuals, of corporations or of the State.
   (c) by the levying of war contributions, taxes or fines.
   (d) to States, by all expenditure involved through the declaration of war.
3. Every Allied or Associated State shall obtain integral reparation for all the damages specified in the preceding article.
4. Sums due for war damage will bear interest commencing from the date from which the claims arise.
5. Objects of all kinds appropriated by the enemy shall be immediately restored to their owners; in cases where this restitution shall be impossible the cost of such objects shall be paid in priority to all other payments.
6. Bank notes issued by the enemy on occupied territory shall be reimbursed by him in gold and in priority to all other claims. Allied and Associated States may each reimburse the holders of enemy paper for the sums which it represents in the money of their country. They shall then be reimbursed in gold for the exact amount of the advances which they have thus made.
7. The basis for the valuation of damage shall be common to all countries.
8. The Peace Conference shall fix the measure in which each of the responsible States must contribute reparation for damages.
9. The Allied and Associated Powers shall create a common organization charged on the basis laid down in Article 8 with receiving, recovering and distributing the amount of these damages.
10. Territories torn by violence from the mother country and which

---

[8] French text, *ibid.*, pp. 57-58.

now are returning to it shall not be liable for any reparation which shall be imposed on those countries from which they are separated by the re-establishment of their rights. On the contrary, they shall have a right to reparation as laid down above.

8 February, 1919.

ANNEX V[9]

DRAFT RESOLUTION

(Presented by the Serbian Delegation as a Conclusion to the Discussion of the Principles on which is Based the Right to Reparation)

The Commission on Reparation of Damage of the Peace Conference, in view of the fact that it has been irrefutably proved and demonstrated that the present war was willed, premeditated and provoked by the enemy Powers with the object of conquest, domination and profit, and that it is consequently an unjust war;

that a higher rule of morality and of justice, incumbent upon States as well as individuals, demands imperatively that everyone shall bear the consequences of his illicit actions;

that Points 7, 8 and 11 of the Peace Programme formulated by President Wilson in his Message of 8th January, 1918, and generally accepted as a basis for negotiations, provides for the complete restoration of countries and districts invaded by the enemy;

Proclaims the principle of the joint and several responsibility of the enemy countries for all damages resulting from the war, and the absolute right of the injured States to recover full and integral reparation for such damages, and charges its First Sub-Committee with the determination of the categories of these damages and with the method of their valuation.

8 February, 1919.

ANNEX VI[10]

PRINCIPLES OF REPARATION

(Presented by the Delegation of the United States of America)

I

Reparation to be made for all damage directly caused by acts of the enemy clearly in violation of international law as recognized at the time of the commission of the acts.

[9] French text, *ibid.*, p. 58.

[10] French translation, *ibid.*, pp. 59-63. At the head of the English text in TPG, there is written in Dulles' handwriting: "Approved by W. W." The first four paragraphs of the text are also in Miller, V, 154. Document 105 precedes.

II*

Belgium and the occupied areas of France, Roumania, Serbia and Montenegro to be physically restored to a condition as near as possible to that which would have existed had war not occurred; such restoration to be accomplished when practicable by a return of actual property abstracted, otherwise compensation to be made in money or goods.

III

Compensation to be made for all physical damage to property of a civilian (i. e., non-military) character, wherever located, provided such damage has been caused directly by German military operations.

IV

Compensation to be made for all damage directly caused by injuries to civilians directly due to German military operations; this to include death, personal injury, enforced labor, and loss of opportunity to labor or to secure a just reward for labor.

(NOTE:—These four principles do not purport to be mutually exclusive in their application).

APPENDIX I

The text of that portion of President Wilson's address of Jan. 8, 1918 which relates to restoration, and the text of the Allied qualification thereof.

(It is the view of the American Delegates of the Commission on Reparation that no reparation can be exacted unless (1) it is clearly due in accordance with accepted principles of international law, or (2) it is stipulated in the understanding embodied in the texts given below).

PRESIDENT WILSON'S POINTS REGARDING RESTORATION OF INVADED TERRITORIES

VII. Belgium, the whole world will agree, must be evacuated and restored, without any attempt to limit the sovereignty which she enjoys in common with all other free nations. No other single act will serve as this will serve to restore confidence among the nations in the laws which they have themselves set and determined for the government of their relations with one another. Without this healing act the whole structure and validity of international law is forever impaired.

VIII. All French territory should be freed and the invaded portions restored, and the wrong done to France by Prussia in

* Amended at meeting of 14 February.

1871 in the matter of Alsace-Lorraine, which has unsettled the peace of the world for nearly fifty years, should be righted, in order that peace may once more be made secure in the interest of all.

XI. Roumania, Serbia, and Montenegro should be evacuated; occupied territories restored; Serbia accorded free and secure access to the sea; and the relations of the several Balkan states to one another determined by friendly counsel along historically established lines of allegiance and nationality; and international guarantees of the political and economic independence and territorial integrity of the several Balkan states should be entered into.

QUALIFICATION OF THESE CLAUSES BY THE ALLIED GOVERNMENTS, CONVEYED TO GERMANY IN THE NOTE OF THE SECRETARY OF STATE OF THE UNITED STATES OF NOVEMBER 5, 1918

Further, in the conditions of peace laid down in his address to Congress of January 8, 1918, the President declared that invaded territories must be restored as well as evacuated and freed; the Allied Governments feel that no doubt ought to be allowed to exist as to what this provision implies. By it they understand that compensation will be made by Germany for all damage done to the civilian population of the Allies and their property by the aggression of Germany by land, by sea and from the air.

APPENDIX II
COMMENT ON THE PRINCIPLES OF REPARATION AS PROPOSED BY THE AMERICAN DELEGATES

I

Reparation to be made for all damage directly caused by acts of the enemy clearly in violation of international law as recognized at the time of the commission of the acts.

The reparation specified for in the Fourteen Points is not designed to be comprehensive and in derogation of reparation due in accordance with accepted principles of international law. Rather the Fourteen Points proceed from the basis of existing international law and specify the further and special acts of justice necessary for a proper settlement of the war.

We accordingly accept as a first principle that reparation is due for all damage directly consequent upon acts of the enemy clearly in violation of international law as recognized at the time of the commission of the acts in question.

In determining the practical application of this principle we have, to guide us, a large body of international precedent and considerable contractual law, such as the Hague Conventions. The details of the reparation which will be required in pursuance of this principle need not be gone into comprehensively at this time, but such reparation will include the following:

(1) The citizens of the associated countries to be restored to the enjoyment of their property which was in enemy countries at the outbreak of the war. Where restoration in kind cannot be made, pecuniary restitution to be made.

(2) Reparation to be made to Belgium for all losses of whatever character directly attributable to the war. This consequence flows from the fact that the war of Germany against Belgium, unlike that against the other Allies, was violative of international law, Germany having undertaken by treaty not to make war against Belgium.

(3) Reparation for damage caused by miscellaneous illegal acts, such as:

Deportation of civilians;

Sinking merchant vessels without warning;

Attacks on undefended towns;

Mistreatment of prisoners of war;

Destruction of property without military justification;

Etc., etc., etc.

II

Belgium and the occupied areas of France, Roumania, Serbia and Montenegro to be physically restored to a condition as near as possible to that which would have existed had war not occurred; such restoration to be accomplished when practicable by a return of actual property abstracted, otherwise compensation to be made in money or goods.

Unless reparation is due in accordance with clearly recognized principles of international law, it cannot be exacted except as specifically agreed to by the enemy. Principles II, III and IV are accordingly based on the Fourteen Points, as qualified by the Allies, which were accepted by Germany as an agreed basis of peace.

Principle II, set out above, flows directly from the original statement in the Fourteen Points relative to restoration. It is to be noted that restoration in Points VII, VIII and XI is coupled with evacuation and appears clearly to contemplate a physical, territorial restoration. The thought is that certain areas must be freed from enemy presence and restored to the condition which they would have been in had enemy invasion never occurred.

It might be argued that the complete restoration of Belgium and the occupied territories contemplated by the President's original statement is limited in scope or at least changed in point of view by the "Interpretation" placed thereon by the Allies; to-wit: "that compensation will be made by Germany for all damage done to the *civilian* population of the Allies and *their* property by the *aggression* of Germany by land, by sea, and from the air." (Italics ours).

The inherent improbability of the Allied statement being intended to operate as a limitation or as anything but an addition is so great that we take the view that the words of the Allies: "by it they understood that compensation will be made" should be construed as though they were "they understand that compensation also will be made."

Accordingly, we regard, in the first instance, President Wilson's language and derive therefrom, our Principle II which implies a complete physical restoration of the territory of Belgium, and the occupied areas of France, Roumania, Serbia and Montenegro. While such reparation would, in a large part, flow also from Principle III, it is not now clear that this latter principle would cover every case for reparation coming under Principle II and for this reason, as well as for the fact that Principle II embodies a somewhat special point of view, it is stated separately.

III

Compensation to be made for all physical damage to property of a civilian (i.e., non-military) character, wherever located, provided such damage has been directly by German military operations.

We have seen that the qualification by the Allies of President Wilson's Points VII, VIII and XI is to be regarded not as an interpretation of, but as an addition to, the reparation provided for by these points. We have also seen that Points VII, VIII and XI provide for adequate reparation for damage to property located in Belgium and the invaded areas of France, Roumania, Serbia and Montenegro. The addition of the Allies, however, extends the right of reparation to property located *outside* the areas covered by Points VII, VIII and XI. The only apparent qualifications are (1) that the property at the time of the damage be that of "the civilian population" and (2) that the damage be the result of "aggression of Germany" by land, sea or air. While the language of the Allied qualification thus refers clearly to damage to the civilian population and "to *their* property," we attribute "civilian" to the character of the property, rather than the character of the owner. The test of the character of the owner is a purely arbitrary and unreasonable one. The test of the character of the property and the use to which it is devoted is sound and in accord with international practice.

It is also necessary to give some definite and limited construction to the words "damage" and "aggression." Otherwise all war costs might be included in clear defiance of the spirit pervading the bases of settlement. We accordingly construe "damage by aggression" to mean physical damage to property resulting directly from military operations of the enemy, including defensive, or counter-offensive, operations of the Allies. Under this construction would be covered damage to civil property resulting directly from air raids, long-range bombardments, attack by sea, etc.

IV

Compensation to be made for all damage directly caused by injuries to civilians directly due to German military operations; this to include death, personal injury, enforced labor, and loss of opportunity to labor or to secure a just reward for labor.

The qualification of the Allies to Points VII, VIII and XI introduces the further element of reparation for injury to civilians. By this is to be understood violations of personal rights as distinct from damage to property. Adopting the same construction of the words "damage by aggression," as is outlined above, this Allied addition means that reparation must also be made for damage caused by injuries to civilians resulting directly from the military operations of Germany (this to include defensive and counter-offensive operations of the Allies). It is not, however, as easy to determine what is injury to a person as it is to determine what is damage to property. It is possible, of course, to limit damage to person to a physical injury occasioned directly, as a rifle wound. Damage to person should be given a more liberal construction than this. In view of the rather adequate provision made for damage to property, particularly in the invaded areas, it is both wise and just to construe damage to person in a liberal sense which will not invite the charge of according a special sanctity to property as distinguished from life and labor. We construe, therefore, damage to the civilian population to include damage resulting through injury to civilians in the way of death, personal injury, enforced labor and loss of opportunity to labor or to secure a just reward for labor.

February 8, 1919.[11]

[11] The French translation is dated February 9.

DOCUMENT 455

Plenary Commission: Minutes of the Fifth Meeting (Including Annex), February 13, 1919, 10:30 A. M.

[EOM, CRD, pp. 25-31. French stenographic minutes (except some paragraphs in short form) in PV, CRD, pp. 71-83.]

The Commission on Reparation of Damage met on Thursday, 13th February, 1919, at 10.30 A. M., at the Ministry of Finance, MR. KLOTZ in the Chair.

Present: Messrs. BARUCH, DAVIS and MCCORMICK (*U. S. A.*); MR. HUGHES, LORD SUMNER and LORD CUNLIFFE (*British Empire*); Messrs. KLOTZ, LOUCHEUR and LEBRUN (*France*); Messrs. SALANDRA, CHIESA and D'AMELIO (*Italy*); Messrs. MORI, NAGAOKA and TATSUMI (*Japan*); Messrs. VAN DEN HEUVEL and DESPRET (*Belgium*); Messrs. ROMANOS and MICHALACOPOULOS (*Greece*); Messrs. OLCHOWSKI and MARKOWSKI (*Poland*); Messrs. DANIELOPOL and ZAHARIADE (*Roumania*); Messrs. STOYANOWITCH and PROTITCH (*Serbia*); Messrs. BENES and OSUSKI (*Czecho-Slovak Republic*).

Unauthorized Reports in the Press

Before presenting for the Commission's approval the minutes of the last meeting, the CHAIRMAN expressed his regret that a French newspaper had published a report of the meeting of 10th February differing from that given officially to the press. In his opinion it was contrary to French usage to publish a denial such as Messrs. Hughes, Baruch and McCormick called for. On the other hand, the censorship could not keep watch over all news items relating to the Commissions of the Peace Conference, since American and English newspapers were free to publish whatever they saw fit. The CHAIRMAN proposed that the Commission should announce that "only such press notices as were communicated by the Secretariat at the close of each meeting should be regarded as authentic." After further representations had been made by MR. HUGHES, the CHAIRMAN gave the Commission his assurance that he would see to it in future that no such incident should occur again and that he would give the necessary protection to members of the Commission in the event of their being subjected to prejudicial or calumniating assertions in the press.

The minutes of the meeting of 10th February were adopted without comment.

The Tabulation by the Committee appointed at the last meeting was reported to have been circulated to the different Delegations. (See Annex).

Method of Procedure

At the suggestion of the CHAIRMAN, the Commission agreed that any text accepted on first reading should have a second reading. The discussion of articles or paragraphs, on first reading, would thus be followed by a discussion of the text as a whole.

Observations on the American Memorandum

Before the consideration of general principles from the American point of view was taken up, MESSRS. OLCHOWSKI (*Poland*), CHIESA (*Italy*) and ROMANOS (*Greece*) made a reservation of their position in regard to the text of the Tabulation (See Annex: *General Principles of Reparation*) and of the American Memorandum (Annex VI, 4th meeting), which seemed to them to exclude their respective countries from the right of reparation. They desired that these texts be modified accordingly. MR. DULLES (*U. S. A.*) explained that in the American Memorandum only four Powers had been cited because they alone were mentioned in Points VII, VIII and XI of PRESIDENT WILSON'S speech of 8th January, 1918. This specification of the four Powers by no means implied that the United States left out of account the rights of Italy, Poland and Greece.

Due note was taken of certain reservations made by M. ROMANOS (*Greece*) in regard to the claims of Greece against Turkey and Bulgaria, in view of the fact that PRESIDENT WILSON'S Fourteen Points did not enter into the Armistice concluded with those Powers.

Remarks of Mr. Dulles (U. S. A.)

MR. DULLES (*U. S. A.*) stated[1] that if the American memorandum made less drastic demands than the others, the American Delegates felt a real chagrin at the thought that the moderation of their statement might be attributed to a lack of severity in judgment. As a matter of fact, the views of the United States as to the enormity of the enemy's crime were in full accord with those of the Allies.

If, therefore, the American memorandum limited the rights of the victors, it was only because the United States did not consider itself free. The Associated Governments were confronted not by a blank page, but by one covered with writing, to which were ap-

---

[1] Dulles' speech is reprinted in Baruch, pp. 289-97. See Document No. 113.

pended the signatures of PRESIDENT WILSON, MR. ORLANDO, MR. LLOYD GEORGE and MR. CLEMENCEAU. There was in existence a basis of peace accepted by Germany, namely, the Fourteen Points of PRESIDENT WILSON and their acceptance, with certain qualifications, by the Allies.

Was it open to question that such a contract constituted a limitation? The object sought by Germany in November had been to have the Allies set the maximum demand to be made upon her; and the qualification desired by the Allies showed clearly that they recognized the limitations imposed on their demands by the acceptance of the Fourteen Points.

The fundamental proposition presented by the American Delegates was, therefore, reparation—the full reparation required by the agreement with Germany. This was a point on which, frankly, there could not be disagreement; and if the American Delegates had emphasized it, it was only because they had observed that none of the other Delegations, except that of Serbia, had mentioned the agreement in their memoranda.

If this proposition was sound, the task of the Commission was one of construction rather than of original thought. Each member of the Commission might have definite ideas on the subject of reparation. But, today, the question was prejudged. However convinced we might be that the reparation stipulated in November fell short of what was due, we could make no change today. Those who made the decision in November had to balance Germany's problematic capacity for payment against further loss of life and money.

As to the application of the agreed terms of peace, this had been set forth in the memorandum filed by the American Delegates. This memorandum held, moreover, that the conditions of reparation therein formulated should not be regarded as limiting those principles of jurisprudence upon which the French memorandum and MR. HUGHES' address purported to base themselves.

An act must be illegal, and not only unjust or cruel, in order to establish the right to reparation. But in every case where the enemy had committed an act in violation of international law, reparation was due. It was on this principle that the American Memorandum demanded complete repayment to Belgium for the damage resulting from the violation of her territory, attacks on undefended towns, etc.

In addition to the reparation due in accordance with international law, there was the reparation due by virtue of the agreement with the enemy. This reparation included that for damage done to the invaded regions of Northern France, Serbia, and Montenegro.

MR. DULLES proposed, in conclusion, that the Commission should accept as a fundamental principle that the reparation to be exacted is that which is due in accordance with a fair construction of the written agreement accepted by Germany.

Secondly, he proposed that the Commission next consider the most expeditious method of reaching an understanding as to the construction and application of the language of the agreement relative to reparation.

Remarks of Lord Sumner (British Empire)

The RT. HON. LORD SUMNER (*British Empire*) declared[2] that in replying to the speech of MR. DULLES, he too intended to speak from a legal and judicial point of view. Beyond any doubt, no Delegation had any desire to depart from the terms of a contract which bound the Power it represented. The divergences of views between the Memorandum of the United States and those of other Allied Powers were certainly based on the conviction of the latter that a different interpretation could be made of PRESIDENT WILSON's Fourteen Points.

The principle laid down by MR. DULLES (*U. S. A.*) was that the rights of the victor over the vanquished were derived from the Law of Nations in so far as it had not been modified or limited by special contracts.

But, in the Law of Nations there existed no text which maintained that the victor had not the right to impose upon the vanquished the costs of the war. If the contrary were the case, the consequence would be that an ambitious nation could attack its neighbors with impunity, as it could rest assured that if defeated it would suffer but slight losses, and in case of success could count upon large gains from its victory.

Moreover, Article 1 of the American proposal leaves out of account the chief historical examples. In 1815, the Allies imposed upon France the payment of seven hundred million francs in order to cover the costs of the war; in 1849, Sardinia had to pay Austria seventy-five million francs in order to cover the costs of the war; in 1866, after a very short war, Prussia imposed upon Austria an indemnity of forty million thalers and considerable sums upon several German states, in order to cover her war expenses. Finally,

---

[2] For the full text of Sumner's speech, see Document 114.

in 1871, Prussia imposed upon France an infamous indemnity which exceeded considerably the cost of the war. If custom was a source of the Law of Nations, the custom was, thus, that the victor might impose upon the vanquished the payment of the costs of war.

Article 1 of the American Memorandum should thus have been conceived in a wider sense, and should have enunciated the principle of the victor's right to recover the costs of the war.

A contract—so it was asserted—had been made, and this contract was stated in certain points to limit and in others to extend the Law of Nations. If it was subject to interpretation, might this interpretation not be different from that set forth by MR. DULLES?

In fact, how could PRESIDENT WILSON, at the beginning of 1918, have intended to exclude from the right to reparation Italy, Greece and Poland? How could it have been his idea that Belgium should only be restored and maintained in her sovereignty, and not reimbursed for the costs caused her by Germany's unjust attack? PRESIDENT WILSON's Fourteen Points aimed at the immediately necessary and practical reparation of certain damages; they could not be considered a limitation of the reparations which were due, without an explicit declaration to that effect.

The rights of nations could not be abandoned by implication, or without a specific renunciation.

Finally, it was an accepted principle that a contract bound the parties only when it had been really concluded. But in this case, negotiations were still going on. It was only when these negotiations were finished and were set forth in a document that the parties would be bound. The November agreement was only a basis of discussion. From this agreement, moreover, several parties were absent; Turkey, Bulgaria and Austria. Were they to be dealt with differently? Today all the Allied Powers were agreed in demanding the payment of the whole costs of the war. Could it be supposed that they intended to abandon that right by the agreement of November?

LORD SUMNER, in conclusion, laid down the two following principles:

1. According to the Law of Nations the victor has the right to impose upon the vanquished the payment of the costs of the war.

2. PRESIDENT WILSON's Fourteen Points should be given an extensive rather than a restrictive interpretation. This would certainly be in conformity with the ideas of PRESIDENT WILSON, whose only aim had been to further the well-being of humanity.

Rights of Italy, Greece and Poland

Messrs. SALANDRA (*Italy*); ROMANOS (*Greece*) and OLCHOWSKI (*Poland*) again maintained the point that the Nations they represented should be included amongst the invaded countries to which, according to the American Memorandum, reparation is due.

MR. DULLES (*U. S. A.*) declared that the rights of Italy, Greece and Poland were recognized and sanctioned by Points 3 and 4 of the American Memorandum. These Powers would have a right to the same reparation as the others. It was for historical reasons that certain nations only were mentioned in the American Memorandum.

M. BENES (*Czecho-Slovak Republic*) stated that he would present a memorandum setting before the Conference the situation of the interests he represented.

The CHAIRMAN took cognizance of the points raised by these various Delegations. The rights of all were reserved.

Meetings of Sub-Committees

Upon the proposal of the CHAIRMAN and after observations by Messrs. VAN DEN HEUVEL (*Belgium*), DAVIS (*U. S. A.*) and STOYANOWITCH (*Serbia*), it was decided that the Sub-Committees should meet as soon as possible and that, in particular, the First Sub-Committee should seek to establish the bases of a just sum to be demanded from the enemy at the Peace Preliminaries.

The next meeting was fixed for Friday, 14 February at 10.30 A. M.

The meeting adjourned at 1 P. M.

JEROME D. GREENE,	L.-L. KLOTZ,
S. PEEL,	*Chairman.*
CH. DE LASTEYRIE,	
F. FOBERTI,	
Secretaries.	

ANNEX[3]

TABULATION

Of the Memoranda Submitted by the Delegates of the United States of America, the British Empire, France, Italy, Poland and Serbia

General Observation:

Some Delegations have submitted no Memorandum. Their opinions on the various questions set forth below are therefore reserved.

[3] French text in PV, CRD, pp. 51-54.

I. GENERAL PRINCIPLES OF REPARATION

A.

France:

"Germany must make good in full the damage caused by her."
"She must pay the whole of her debt."

British Empire:

"Reparation is . . . the making good of the losses which a party injured has sustained by wrongful acts and their natural consequences, so as to replace him in as good a position as that which he occupied before the wrong was done.

"The war itself was an act of aggression and a wrong; it was therefore a wrong for which reparation is due."[4]

Italy:

Adheres implicitly to the French Note.[5]

Serbia:

"Asserts . . . the absolute right for the States having suffered a wrong to sue for the reparation in full of the whole of the damage caused by the war."

Poland:

The enemy Powers "considered as responsible for an unjust war . . . are bound to compensate all damage arising out of the war."

B.

United States of America:

"Reparation to be made for all damage directly caused by acts of the enemy clearly in violation of international law as recognized at the time of the commission of the acts.

"It is the view of the American Delegates of the Commission on Reparation that no reparation can be exacted unless: (1) it is clearly due in accordance with accepted principles of international law; or (2) it is stipulated for in the understanding embodied in President Wilson's points regarding restoration of invaded territories, and in the qualification of these clauses by the Allied Governments conveyed to Germany in the note of the Secretary of State of the United States of November 5, 1918."

[4] This sentence is omitted in the French text.
[5] There is an omission here. Cf. French text.

II. CLAIMS

1. PHYSICAL DAMAGE (DIRECT OR INDIRECT)

British Empire:

"Claims are both public and private, direct and indirect.

"The claims are presented by the State and not by the individual, and the State claims:

"(*a*) On behalf of the whole body of its citizens;

"(*b*) On behalf of smaller aggregates of citizens; or

"(*c*) On behalf of single persons.

"The State claims for its own losses, that is to say the losses, sacrifices and outlays which fall as a burden on the whole people now and in the future; it also claims on behalf of particular persons who have suffered wrong.

"It is a general principle of law that a wrong-doer is held to have contemplated and intended all the natural and necessary consequences of his acts. Accordingly he is bound to pay damages not merely for the act itself and its immediate result but also for its natural and necessary consequences."

To these proposals all the Memoranda expressly or impliedly agree except that of the United States of America whose views are expressed in the following paragraphs:

United States of America:

II. "Belgium and the occupied areas of France, Roumania, Serbia and Montenegro to be physically restored to a condition as near as possible to that which would have existed had war not occurred.

III. "Compensation to be made for all physical damage to property of a civilian (*i.e.*, non-military) character, wherever located, provided such damage has been caused directly by German military operations.

IV. "Compensation to be made for all damage directly caused by injuries to civilians directly due to German military operations; this to include death, personal injury, enforced labor, and loss of opportunity to labor or to secure a just reward for labor."

2. DAMAGE OF MORAL ORDER

No Memorandum claims damage of a purely moral order.

3. COSTS OF THE WAR

British Empire:

"We have an absolute right to demand the whole cost of the war.

"The State claims for its own losses, sacrifices and outlays which fall as a burden on the whole people now and in the future."

Poland:

The Polish Memorandum agrees expressly:
"Damage caused to the various States by all forms of expenditure imposed by the declaration of the war."

United States of America:

The other Memoranda do not suggest any contrary opinion, except the Memorandum of the United States of America which however admits the repayment of the war costs of Belgium.

III. JOINT AND SEVERAL LIABILITY

Italy:

"The legislation and jurisprudence of all civilized countries show that all those who have taken part in causing damage of such kind as mentioned in the French draft (par. No. 1) are to be jointly responsible towards those who have suffered the damage."

Serbia:

The Serbian Memorandum "asserts the principle of the joint and several liability to enemy countries for all damage arising out of the war."

Poland:

The Polish Memorandum appears in par. 8 not to be in accordance with the former principle:
"The Peace Conference shall state in what measure each of the responsible States shall have to contribute to the reparation of the damage."
Nothing is said in any of the other Memoranda.

IV. MODES AND MEANS OF MAKING REPARATION

Objects taken away against the will of their owners, if they can be identified, may be reclaimed by their owners. The enemy Powers may be required to make the reparation due from them either in goods or in money or in both.

All the Memoranda appear to recognize those principles.

V. INTERESTS

The Polish Memorandum proposes that the interest on the amounts of reparation should be due from the day of the opening of the claim. The Italian Memorandum proposes that interest should be due from the same date for all countries.

VI. PRIORITIES

France:

"If all the creditors of the enemy States—that is to say, the Allied and Associated Powers,—are equally worthy of consideration and should be placed on the same footing, this is not the case for all categories of claims. Some of these have a right to a privileged position.

"The priority of a claim consists in the right which it derives from its very nature to be repaid before all others, irrespective of the identity of the creditor.

"Irrespective of and before these privileged claims, of which it will be the duty of the Commission to draw up a list and to establish an order of priority, there must be reserved the right of the owner to recover wrongfully removed (l'action en revendication)."

The Italian Memorandum alludes to the priorities.

The other Memoranda do not mention them.

However the 9th paragraph of the British Memorandum refers to that question in the following words:

British Empire:

"It is desirable that the Sub-Committees should report as soon as possible on the questions of the amount of the claims, the amount of the resources of the enemy Powers and the appropriate forms of reparation and guarantees and afterwards take up the further questions which do not concern the enemy Powers but will arise between the Associated Powers alone."[6]

DOCUMENT 456

Plenary Commission: Minutes of the Sixth Meeting (Including Annex), February 14, 1919, 10:30 A. M.

[EOM, CRD, pp. 32-36. French stenographic minutes in PV, CRD, pp. 84-95.]

The Commission on Reparation of Damage met on Friday, 14th February, 1919, at 10.30 A. M., at the Ministry of Finance, MR. HUGHES in the Chair.

Present: Messrs. BARUCH, DAVIS and McCORMICK (*U. S. A.*); MR. HUGHES, LORD SUMNER and LORD CUNLIFFE (*British Empire*); Messrs. KLOTZ and LEBRUN (*France*); Messrs. CHIESA and D'AMELIO (*Italy*); Messrs. MORI, NAGAOKA and TATSUMI (*Japan*); Messrs. VAN DEN HEUVEL and DESPRET (*Belgium*); Messrs.

---

[6] The supplementary Italian proposition (Annex to meeting of February 14) is appended here in the French text.

ROMANOS and MICHALACOPOULOS (*Greece*); Messrs. OLCHOWSKI and MARKOWSKI (*Poland*); MR. ZAHARIADE (*Roumania*); Messrs. STOYANOWITCH and PROTITCH (*Serbia*); Messrs. BENES and OSUSKI (*Czecho-Slovak Republic*).

Amendment of American Memorandum

MR. BARUCH (*U. S. A.*) on behalf of the American Delegates, submitted an amendment of Article 2 of the principles of reparation contained in the American memorandum and this amendment was adopted so that the article should read as follows:

"Belgium and the occupied areas of France, Italy, Roumania, Serbia, Greece and Montenegro to be physically restored to a condition as near as possible to that which would have existed had war not occurred: such restoration to be accomplished when practicable by a return of actual property abstracted, otherwise compensation to be made in money or goods. Reservation made provisionally in respect of Poland and Czecho-Slovakia because of the special international situation of these countries."

The minutes of the meeting of 13th February were adopted.

Remarks of Mr. Dulles (U. S. A.)

MR. DULLES (*U. S. A.*) resuming the discussion of the principles of reparation, said[1] that the position of the British and the American Delegates was evidently in accord on two propositions: First, if there is a contract limiting the demands that can now be made upon Germany, it is to be scrupulously observed; second, if there are rights for reparation arising outside by the operation of international law, they are to be exercised unless expressly waived. Proceeding to the consideration of the second proposition, it might be pointed out that rights arise in two ways: (1) by operation of law and (2) by contract. In which of these two categories did war costs fall? Was there any principle of law which made the vanquished the debtor of the victor? LORD SUMNER had cited no such text. His examples did not arise from any right of the victor, but were contracts between belligerents—contracts in which the victor said: "I will give you peace in exchange for money." The sums thus demanded have never corresponded to the costs of the war, but have been such as the victor estimated it could secure.

(At this point MR. KLOTZ entered and took the Chair.)

As there was no law which made Germany our debtor for war costs, the discussion was brought back irresistibly to the question of contract—as to whether or not we were now free to make a

---

[1] For the full text of Dulles' speech, see Document 115.

contract with Germany requiring her to pay war costs. LORD SUMNER maintained that we were; that the negotiation in November was only a basis for discussion, guiding the negotiation but not binding it, and leaving us free to introduce war costs even if they had not figured in the basis which had been accepted.

If the British Delegation were right in this thesis, they might be right in their conclusion. He agreed that International Law gave the victor the right to claim war costs; we had that right now unless we had given it up.

This was not the first time that it had been suggested that the previous negotiations were only a basis for discussion. In October, 1918, the German Government announced that it was prepared to accept PRESIDENT WILSON'S programme as a basis of discussion. The President replied that the issue was too momentous to consider an armistice on terms which were merely a basis for discussion. The German Government thereupon agreed to accept the terms and to limit the discussion to the practical application of these terms—substituting, it will be noted, the expression *terms* for *basis*. This correspondence was then laid before the Allies, who, after consideration, declared their willingness to make peace on the terms already formulated.

Thus the November negotiation constituted not merely a basis for discussion, but terms of peace. Thus we had no longer the freedom of contract which LORD SUMNER claimed, and our task was confined to the practical application of accepted terms of peace.

We were thus brought back to the original proposition; our rights, arising from the operation of law, having not been waived, remained; our rights by contract were already fixed, it remaining only to determine the construction of its terms.

MR. DULLES further observed that the United States, not having expected to claim war costs, had not drawn up its bill, but a still incomplete, unofficial estimate had already reached the figure of 250 milliards of francs. The United States had not intended to present this bill, and it still did not intend to; but if, the bill were presented, what would be the consequence? What would be the status of the many other claims for reparation which had been presented?

Thus, the principle laid down by the United States was both logical and just.

Remarks of Mr. Hughes (British Empire)

MR. HUGHES (*British Empire*) pointed out[2] that the memorandum filed by the American Delegation admitted the existence of rights to reparation which had not by any implication been bargained away. The contention of the British Delegation was that these rights could not be limited as in that memorandum, but justified a claim by the Allies for reimbursement of all the damages and costs naturally resulting from the German aggression. If, however, the American view were correct, the recognition that Belgium was entitled to recover the costs of the war must still lead inevitably to the conclusion that the other Allies were also entitled to recover their costs.

The neutralization of Belgium was not a principle of international law, but the result of a treaty, a public international pledge, designed to secure the peace of the world. Certain Powers, as parties to that treaty, had the duty as well as the right of intervening, in case of its violation. They were surely entitled to be reimbursed by the aggressor for the costs involved in the discharge of this duty. But the whole world also was deeply interested in the maintenance of this treaty and had a corresponding right to enforce it. If so, all the Powers who had come to the rescue of violated Belgium had the same title as Belgium herself to recover their war costs.

The narrow basis adopted in the American Memorandum was, however, to be rejected. Examination of the relevant documents showed that both the Allies and Germany explicitly accepted the principle that the costs of a wrong must be borne by the wrongdoer —of an unjust war, by the aggressor. PRESIDENT WILSON's Fourteen Points must not be considered in isolation, but as expanded by the subsequent utterances mentioned in his Note of 5th November, 1918.

MR. HUGHES quoted from PRESIDENT WILSON's Fourteen Points speech of 8th January, 1918, his speech in Congress on 11th February, 1918, his Mt. Vernon speech of 4th July, 1918, and his New York speech of 27th September, 1918; and referred to the terms of the German Note of 4th October, 1918, PRESIDENT WILSON's reply of 8th October, 1918, the German reply of 19th October, 1918, and PRESIDENT WILSON's Notes of 23rd October,

---

[2] An English text of Hughes' speech is in TPG, I, 32-52; reprinted in Baruch, pp. 298-315. See Document 116. The French text, however, is evidently the way in which it was actually delivered, as the English is briefer and more formal. There is also annexed to Hughes' speech in TPG, I, 48-52, a memorandum entitled "Extracts from the German and American Notes and from the Addresses of President Wilson." This is merely the portion of his speech which begins at the heading *German and American Notes* (Baruch, p. 304) and ends with the words, ". . . equal rights of the several peoples concerned" (Baruch, bottom of p. 309).

and 5th November, 1918, upon which followed the armistice on 11th November, 1918. Referring to MR. DULLES'S speech, MR. HUGHES observed that presentation of the full bill for all war costs by the United States and other Powers need not mean any deferment of the more urgent claims for reparation. Certain claims could always be preferred.

Summary of British Argument

MR. HUGHES summarized the argument and conclusions of his speech in the following eight points:—

(1) The Fourteen Points are not exhaustive as to reparation.
(2) It is admitted by the American Memorandum that Belgium's full war costs must be paid, as Germany's attack on Belgium, whose neutrality she had guaranteed, was a violation of international law.
(3) Whatever rights Belgium has under international law by reason of her neutralization, are clearly shared by those Powers who guaranteed her neutrality and incurred fearful losses in enforcing it.
(4) The other Associated Powers (e.g. United States and Italy), who helped to defend Belgian neutrality, can also claim their war costs.
(5) Therefore, even on the narrow basis of the American Memorandum, reparation can be claimed for the whole war cost of the Associated Powers.
(6) But independently altogether of any question of violations of international law, full reparation is demanded by the principle of justice.
(7) The principle of justice, and the reign of law between States as between individuals, have been affirmed by PRESIDENT WILSON and incorporated in the terms and principles of peace accepted by the Associated Powers and by Germany in terms which clearly cover the demand for full reparation.
(8) Therefore, whether we apply the principles of the American Memorandum, or whether we independently apply the principles formulated by PRESIDENT WILSON and accepted, of "the reign of law" and a just peace, in either case we reach the same conclusion, that we are entitled to reparation for the full costs of the war.

It was decided that a further meeting of the Commission, to continue the discussion, should be convoked at 10.30 A. M., on Saturday, 15th February, and that meetings of the two Sub-

Committees on Valuation of Damages and on Financial Capacity of the Enemy States should be convoked at 3 P. M., on the same day.

The meeting adjourned at 12.45 P. M.

JEROME D. GREENE,   L.-L. KLOTZ,
S. PEEL,   *Chairman.*
CH. DE LASTEYRIE,
F. FOBERTI,
    Secretaries.

ANNEX[3]

PRINCIPLES OF REPARATION

(*Supplementary Proposition Presented by the Italian Delegation*)

The Italian Delegation considers that reparation is due both for damage directly occasioned by the enemy, and for indirect damage.

The fundamental justice of this principle was recognized in the following statement which was made to Germany in the Note of the 5th of November, 1918, in the name of the Allies by the Secretary of State of the United States of America:

"Further, in the conditions of peace laid down in his address to Congress on the 8th of January, 1918, the President declared that invaded territories must be restored as well as evacuated and made free. The Allied Governments feel that no doubt ought to be allowed to exist as to what this provision implies. By it they understand that compensation will be made by Germany for all damage done to the civilian populations of the Allies and to their property by the aggression of Germany by land, by sea and from the air."

This declaration is the latest in date.

It explains and completes the ideas expressed by President Wilson in his Fourteen Points. It was the basis of the negotiations for the armistice and must therefore, be regarded as accepted by the enemy. As a necessary consequence it must be observed as the rule governing the subject of reparations.

Now the declaration of the Allies, both in its terms and in its spirit, covers indirect damages, for it refers to all damages caused to the non-military population by the aggressions of the enemy.

The declaration is in conformity with the general principles of law. Reparation is, in fact, not secured unless the injured person is replaced in the exact position which he would have cocupied if the injury had not been inflicted.

This cannot be effected if reparation is restricted to the direct consequences of the aggression. The legal position would not be

---

[3] French text in PV, CRD, p. 54, paragraph 2 ff.

re-established, because the injured person would still remain in an economically inferior position and the consequences of the criminal act would still in part rest upon him. It is furthermore obvious that the direct consequences of the unlawful act might well constitute the lesser part of the damage suffered while the more serious part of the damage consisted in the reaction of these direct consequences upon the various activities of the injured person.

Both categories of damage spring from a single cause and raise a single responsibility. This is the more evident where the guilty person in performing his unlawful act willed its indirect effects or actually counted upon them as essential. This is exactly what happened in the war in which the Central Empires and their Allies deliberately planned and sought to destroy the economic existence of their adversaries.[4]

DOCUMENT 457

Plenary Commission: Minutes of the Seventh Meeting (Including Annex), February 15, 1919, 10:30 A. M.

[EOM, CRD, pp. 37-42. French stenographic minutes, PV, CRD, pp. 96-107.]

The Commission on Reparation of Damage met on Saturday, 15th February, 1919, at 10.30 A. M., at the Ministry of Finance, MR. HUGHES in the Chair.

Present: Messrs. BARUCH, MCCORMICK and DULLES (*U. S. A.*); MR. HUGHES, LORD SUMNER and LORD CUNLIFFE (*British Empire*); Messrs. KLOTZ, LOUCHEUR and LEBRUN (*France*); Messrs. CHIESA and D'AMELIO (*Italy*); Messrs. MORI, NAGAOKA and TATSUMI (*Japan*); Messrs. VAN DEN HEUVEL and DESPRET (*Belgium*); Messrs. ROMANOS and MICHALACOPOULOS (*Greece*); Messrs. OLCHOWSKI and MARKOWSKI (*Poland*); Messrs. DANIELOPOL and ZAHARIADE (*Roumania*); Messrs. STOYANOWITCH and PROTITCH (*Serbia*); Messrs. BENES and OSUSKI (*Czecho-Slovak Republic*).

M. BENES (*Czecho-Slovak Republic*) called attention to the omission of the word "international" from the last phrase of the French text of the amendment proposed by MR. BARUCH, at the sixth meeting, and this word was accordingly added. With this correction the minutes of the meeting of 14th February were approved.

The order of the day calling for the continuation of the discussion of the general principles of reparation:

---

[4] This last paragraph is not in the French text.

Remarks of Mr. Van den Heuvel (Belgium)

MR. VAN DEN HEUVEL (*Belgium*) remarked that the Commission had before it two propositions: first, the American proposition, which rested on international law and on the words of President Wilson, and included in the charge against Germany only the reparation of damage; second, the British proposition which rested on considerations of a more general character and included the costs of the war so far as these had not been expressly renounced.

Up to the present time the general form of the discussion had not permitted the participants to see clearly the application of their ideas to the actual situation in which the several countries found themselves. MR. VAN DEN HEUVEL wished to speak today from the Belgian point of view.

The American proposition, after stating in general that the costs of the war would not have to be paid by the enemy, made an exception in the case of Belgium. This was no more than just. Germany had committed a double violation of international law against Belgium: in the first place she had broken the Treaty of 1839 by which she had promised to guarantee the neutrality of Belgium; in the second place she had not kept the new engagement into which she had entered at the Hague Conference of 1907 to respect the neutrality of certain states among which Belgium was included.

In MR. VAN DEN HEUVEL'S opinion there were three phases in the negotiations preliminary to peace: the first was already accomplished,—for the Associated Powers, in agreeing to the Armistice with Germany had accepted certain preliminaries of peace, namely the Fourteen Points of PRESIDENT WILSON; the second phase was in progress today,—its object was to determine the details of execution and, in the opinion of some, to add new conditions; the third phase, which was about to ensue, was that of discussion with the enemy States. The latter were not going to accept with eyes closed the bill which was to be presented to them. They would seek to reduce the total; they would examine the reasons for which each of the Allied Powers entered the war and the date of their entry, and would do what they could to make discriminations among their creditors.

It was also greatly to the interest of the Allies to define the bases of their respective claims.

Belgium found herself in a position that had been prejudged; for on four different occasions Germany had committed herself in regard to the reparation due to Belgium: (1) just before the war,

when Germany sought to prevent the intervention of Great Britain;
(2) on 2nd August, in the ultimatum she sent to Great Britain; (3)
on 4th August, when the Chancellor publicly admitted that
injustice had been done and declared that Germany was ready to
make reparation; (4) on 9th August, when Germany proposed to
Belgium a separate peace with certain clauses providing for
reparation.

The exception recognized by the American Government was
enforceable in law, for it had been admitted by the German
Government itself.

Passing to the British proposition, MR. VAN DEN HEUVEL
remarked that it attributed to all the nations the right to recover
the costs of war, unless this right had been waived by contract—a
waiver which Great Britain did not admit.

Belgium, therefore, had the right to claim the costs of war. She
had, moreover, a privileged position; for the Powers had special
obligations towards Belgium arising from the obligations which the
treaty of 1839 imposed upon her. She had fulfilled these obligations
by defending her territory from all attacks.

This peculiar situation had already been recognized by the Great
Powers during the war, on 14th February, 1916. They then declared
that "Belgium would be liberally indemnified when peace should
arrive and that the Powers would help her substantially in her
economic and financial rehabilitation."

It seemed, therefore, that both from the American point of view
and from that of Great Britain, the rights of Belgium were equally
safeguarded.

It was something to be able to present a bill to a debtor, but it
amounted to little if the circumstances were such that there was a
probability of not being paid. For, along with the claims of Belgium
and the other Powers specially concerned, there were the claims of
the Great Powers. Facing an insolvent Germany with an enormous
total it would become necessary to reduce all claims proportionately.
The result would be that the Great Powers which had made
important territorial gains would be in an exceptionally advantageous position, to the detriment of the smaller Powers.

MR. VAN DEN HEUVEL was sure the Great Powers would not
desire such an outcome. But peace was still remote, and for
Belgium time was slipping·by. If it was to be understood that the
Great Powers might weigh down Germany's debt with huge war
costs and that they might fail to aid the smaller countries by

measures for immediate relief, there would be a bitter disillusionment for the whole world.

(At this point MR. KLOTZ entered and took the Chair.)

The British proposal was too general. It ought to be accompanied by special provisions. It was necessary to find some arrangement that would remove the danger that menaced Belgium and the smaller Powers.

Remarks of Mr. Stoyanowitch (Serbia)

M. STOYANOWITCH (*Serbia*) considered that there could be no reparation without indemnities. This war in no way resembled previous wars. The costs had been greater. It was inconceivable that the victors should be placed in a less favorable position than the vanquished, but this was just what would happen if the latter should fail to pay the entire costs of the war which they had started. There had been discussion of the principles and of the Fourteen Points of PRESIDENT WILSON. PRESIDENT WILSON himself, in a recent letter to the Press, said plainly that principles were valuable only for the results which were drawn from them.[1]

If the American view did not allow of the restoration of the devastated countries, it would certainly be MR. WILSON'S opinion, in accordance with his letter, that recourse must be had to payment of the costs of the war. What was the position of the belligerents at the moment of the Armistice? The enemy was in occupation of foreign territory. The Central Empires had not been invaded. They had been able to carry on the war so as to exploit the invaded districts and thus reimburse themselves for their war costs.

In Germany everything was intact—communications, houses, industries. Was this the case with Belgium, with Serbia? Germany's debt, thanks to her requisitions, had been paid in kind by the occupied countries. In the meantime the Allies' debts were growing from day to day with all the disorganization brought in his train by the invader.

Germany's future had not been so gravely prejudiced as was supposed. Her live stock was intact. Was this the case with France, Belgium or Serbia? The smaller Powers had been obliged to borrow enormous sums from their Allies. The service of these loans in itself would absorb all the sums obtainable by way of restoration, if payment of a war indemnity was rejected.

The interest upon the Serbian debt amounted to 250 millions. The budget before the war was 230 millions. The country had lost

---

[1] In the original, these last two sentences are repeated.

300,000 men, or one-third of its able-bodied male population. The service of pensions was estimated at 100 million francs. The war had thus involved an increase of 350 millions in the annual expenditure. Could one consider that Serbia had been restored if the country was left to bear an additional annual charge of 350 millions while her earning capacity had been diminished? Unless Serbia was granted 350 millions of war indemnity, the sum total of her debt, she could not live. Certain losses, such as moral damage, could not be repaired; this has a further reason for exacting to the utmost limit possible such reparation as could be made. Serbia must otherwise be in danger of falling a prey to strikes and social revolution.

The League of Nations would prevent the recurrence of wars; but if it did not compel the enemy to pay the debts which he had contracted, there would be no change in his mental attitude. Recent events in Germany were significant in this connection. While we must not be animated by ideas of vengeance, it was necessary that every country should be replaced in the position in which it stood before the war. There have been cases, such as that of Turkey, in which states have been unable to pay their debts. The enemy states could pay interest through the mediation of the League of Nations. Their indebtedness would prevent them from renewing the war. Germany was not the only state in question; there was Bulgaria, too, and Bulgarian atrocities. There must be a sanction to prevent for the future the repetition of such crimes.

It was also important to obtain as soon as possible for the purpose of reparation the return of property stolen by the enemy. A commission to conduct a search on a proper legal basis could be sent to Germany to examine, for example, the railways and take the material which was indispensable for our needs. The matter was a pressing one. Practical meaures must be taken.

All the costs of the war should be paid, and, if necessary, Germany should be declared debtor in perpetuity to the League of Nations.

Remarks of Mr. Klotz (France)

The CHAIRMAN did not wish for the time being to take sides between the British thesis and the American: at the proper time the French Government would state its position.[2] He now wished to change the ground of the debate. MR. KLOTZ contested the American thesis which refused to examine whether the principle

---

[2] A French text of Klotz's speech is in TPG, I, 53-59. An English translation is in Baruch, pp. 316-22. See Document 119.

set forth of the right to reparation was just or not, on the theory that the Associated Governments were bound by a contract. There was no relation of cause and effect between the exchange of Notes (in which the American Delegation sought to find the elements of a contract), and the German military capitulation. Germany had capitulated because she was vanquished by arms, not because she considered acceptable PRESIDENT WILSON'S Fourteen Points.

There existed only one document between Germany and the Associated Governments: the Armistice Convention of November 11, 1918. In that document neither Germany nor the Allies alluded to conditions which would limit subsequently the future treaty of Peace. Just as Germany consented in the Armistice Convention to guarantees which we had later been led to extend, so we were justified in formulating demands which were perhaps not explicitly comprised in PRESIDENT WILSON'S Fourteen Points but which were founded on justice and law. International Law was only too often no more than the sanction of the right of the strong; whereas we based our position on accepted principles of law.

It could not be admitted that France, which was robbed in 1871 —assailed, invaded, plundered—could have renounced by implication the application of these general principles of law.

Thus, the only written document which might have the form and produce the consequences of a contract—that is to say the Armistice Convention of November 11, 1918—from the point of view which now concerned us contained no specific statement limiting our right to put forward claims. On the contrary, under the section entitled "Financial Clauses" we found the words: (Article 19) "With reservation that any future claims and demands of the Allies and the United States of America remain unaffected, the following financial conditions are required: Reparation for damage done, etc., etc."

This was an express clause which reserved all our rights and which clearly had in view the future Treaty of Peace.

In conclusion the CHAIRMAN asked the Commission to declare the right to full reparation. The Commission would later judge as to whether or not the Associated Governments ought to push their rights to their extreme limit, and would determine the priority of certain debts, a priority which, it appeared, was recognized by all the States represented.

Foodstuffs Supplied to Germany

MR. HUGHES (*British Empire*) stated that a resolution was to be proposed to the Peace Conference to the effect that foodstuffs supplied to Germany should be paid for out of German assets and not by Allied credits. This was a matter which affected the Commission, as the suggested procedure, by depleting Germany's existing assets might in effect give a preference to her new over her old creditors. He suggested that the Commission authorize the CHAIRMAN to inform the President of the Peace Conference that, in the opinion of the Commission, the question of the mode of payment for foodstuffs supplied to Germany is one that should be referred to this Commission for report.

After a discussion in which MR. HUGHES (*British Empire*), MR. BARUCH (*U. S. A.*) and MR. DESPRET (*Belgium*) took part, it was decided to take up the question again at the next meeting, which was fixed for 10.30 A. M. on Monday, 17th February.

The meeting adjourned at 1 P. M.

JEROME D. GREENE,
S. PEEL,
CH. DE LASTEYRIE,
F. FOBERTI,
  Secretaries.

L.-L. KLOTZ,
  Chairman.

ANNEX[3]

PROPOSALS IN REGARD TO WAR COSTS

(*Presented by the Italian Delegation*)

The Italian Delegation to the Reparation Commission affirms that by the general principles of International Law and by the principles of natural justice, an enemy who is responsible for an unjust act of aggression owes to all those who have been victims of his aggression or who have aided in repelling it, full reparation for the costs of their defense. These costs must be considered as the direct and immediate consequence of the aggression, and their liquidation becomes an absolute necessity to the States which have incurred them.

It is to be noted that President Wilson's propositions are not in contradiction with this right to full reparation, and that this right has not been relinquished by the Allies in the clauses of the armistice signed with Germany, and still less in the armistice with Austro-Hungary, Turkey and Bulgaria—which powers are held jointly responsible for the reparation of all damage inflicted.

At the same time account must be taken of the economic capacity of the enemy; he should be placed in such a position as to be able to

[3] There is no French text of this annex in PV.

inflict no further injury; but his capacity to make reimbursement must be determined in the light of his resources, which must first of all be exactly established.

Accordingly, the Commission resolves that while admitting in principle the right of the Entente to require full reparation for war costs all deliberations on this point shall be reserved until the time when the First Sub-Committee shall have made a valuation of the different categories of damages (including the costs of war), and until the Second Sub-Committee shall have estimated the capacity of payment of the enemy states and shall have decided upon the method of payment.

DOCUMENT 458

Plenary Commission: Minutes of the Eighth Meeting, February 17, 1919, 10:35 A. M.

[EOM, CRD, pp. 43-45. French stenographic minutes in PV, CRD, pp. 108-14.]

The Commission on Reparation of Damage met on Monday, 17th February, 1919, at 10.35 A. M., at the Ministry of Finance, MR. KLOTZ in the chair.

Present: Messrs. BARUCH, DAVIS and McCORMICK (*U. S. A.*); MR. HUGHES, LORD SUMNER and LORD CUNLIFFE (*British Empire*); Messrs. KLOTZ, LOUCHEUR and LEBRUN (*France*); MR. CHIESA (*Italy*); Messrs. MORI, NAGAOKA and TATSUMI (*Japan*); Messrs. VAN DEN HEUVEL and DESPRET (*Belgium*); Messrs. ROMANOS and MICHALACOPOULOS (*Greece*); Messrs. OLCHOWSKI and CHAMIEC (*Poland*); MR. ZAHARIADE (*Roumania*); Messrs. STOYANOWITCH and PROTITCH (*Serbia*); Messrs. BENES and OSUSKI (*Czecho-Slovak Republic*).[1]

The CHAIRMAN announced that the minutes of the last meeting would be presented at the next meeting.

At the suggestion of MR. HUGHES (*British Empire*) the Commission decided to hold over until after the discussion of general principles his motion in regard to the method of paying for food supplies furnished to Germany.

The discussion of the general principles of reparation was then resumed.

MR. CHIESA (*Italy*) recognized that there was a certain correspondence between the French and the Italian propositions. The principle of the right to complete reparation was now clearly propounded. But this principle must be embodied in a definite measure.

---

[1] According to the French minutes, Danielopol was also present.

Along with the question of law there were also a political question and an economic question. The handling of all these questions was first of all a problem of accountability; it was a matter of establishing the total charges resulting from the war and then of proceeding to reparation. We should thereafter proceed to apportion these charges, having in view a method of collective payment which would provide for the contingency of our not being able to place the entire load of war costs—which it might prove futile to attempt—upon the shoulders of the enemy.

This problem of accountability could not be solved until the first and second Sub-Committees had presented their conclusions. MR. CHIESA proposed that until then all final decisions of the Commission be held in abeyance, except the affirmation of its principles as to our right to include the costs of war and the reparation of damages growing out of the war.

MR. PROTITCH (*Serbia*) stated that the Serbian Delegates agreed with the position taken by the British Delegates.

He thought it necessary to make it clear that the question he was considering was not one of an oppressive indemnity but rather of a rightful indemnity, such as that to which PRESIDENT WILSON had alluded in his address to the Senate of 4th December, 1917, and this indemnity was the repayment of the costs of the war.

MR. KLOTZ (*France*) had done justice to the proposition that we were bound by a contract with Germany. But we must not forget that peace is not to be made with Germany alone. Could it be asserted that a note of 5th September bound the Powers which signed the Convention of 29th September, 1918, with Bulgaria, the Convention of 30th October, 1918, with Turkey, and the Armistice protocol of 3rd November with Austria? If not, it would have to be admitted that the Allied and Associated Governments are free as regards the Powers just mentioned and that they are not free as regards Germany.

PRESIDENT WILSON'S Seventh, Eighth and Eleventh Points asserted the right to restoration. Real reparation involved the payment of the costs of war.

Mr. Loucheur's Summary of Arguments

MR. LOUCHEUR (*France*) said that he had been much impressed by MR. DULLES' argument, but that the three arguments subsequently presented had impressed him equally. These were:

1. The argument of MR. HUGHES: International law obliged the Powers which had guaranteed the neutrality of Belgium to stand

by her and it therefore gave them the same right of reparation as Belgium enjoys.

2. The argument of MR. KLOTZ: Article XIX of the Armistice reserved all future rights to enter claims.

3. The argument of MR. PROTITCH: The treaty of peace should apply generally to the enemy Powers and not to Germany alone. We must pay equal regard to the conventions entered into with the enemy States other than Germany.

These three arguments had modified M. LOUCHEUR's point of view and he wondered if they had not affected that of the American Delegates.

M. VAN DEN HEUVEL (*Belgium*) regretted that the statement he had made at the 7th meeting had not been understood. He insisted upon the special situation in which Belgium found herself and upon her indispensable right to reparation—a right which had been recognized by all the belligerents, without exception. This right would be compromised if the costs of war were included in the general liability of the enemy. The discharge of this liability would become, at best, highly problematical. It would afford no basis for any credits or advances.

The principle of priority was not enough to protect the indisputable rights of Belgium. All Belgium had been ravaged, and her economic activity had been ruined. She must be assured of complete reparation. For this reason MR. VAN DEN HEUVEL felt obliged to object to the inclusion of the costs of war in the debt owed by Germany.

The CHAIRMAN said that he would try to sum up the discussion and to widen its scope.

Before addressing himself to the special interests of any country and before examining the methods of applying the principles under consideration he wished to propose to the Commission that it enunciate the right of complete reparation. The Commission would then determine how this right should be applied.

Resolution Proposed by Mr. Klotz

The CHAIRMAN therefore asked the Commission to consider the following propositions:

"The right of the Allied and Associated Powers is all-inclusive.

"The enemy must make good all damage, an order of priority being preserved for certain claims."

At this point a recess was taken in order that the CHAIRMAN's propositions might be translated into English.

On calling the meeting to order the CHAIRMAN announced that MR. DULLES wished to reply to the comments made upon the American propositions. He suggested, however, that MR. DULLES' remarks be deferred until the next meeting, on Wednesday, the 19th February.

MR. HUGHES (*British Empire*) objected to this postponement and wished to be relieved of all personal responsibility for it. The Commission should, in his opinion, bring its work to completion as soon as possible. For this there was a public demand. The results obtained up to the present time amounted to practically nothing.

The CHAIRMAN took exception to the last assertion. An extended debate was indispensable before the Commission could make up its mind in regard to the principles underlying the right to reparation. He thought he could answer for the Commission's doing its utmost to expedite the discussion from Wednesday on.

The next meeting was fixed for Wednesday, 19th February, at 10.30 A. M.

The Commission adjourned at 12.35 P. M.

JEROME D. GREENE,   L.-L. KLOTZ,
S. PEEL,   *Chairman.*
CH. DE LASTEYRIE,
F. FOBERTI,
   Secretaries.

DOCUMENT 459

Plenary Commission: Minutes of the Ninth Meeting,
February 19, 1919, 10:30 A. M.

[EOM, CRD, pp. 46-49. French stenographic minutes in PV, CRD, pp. 115-30.]

The Commission on Reparation of Damage met on Wednesday, 19th February 1919, at 10.30 A. M., at the Ministry of Finance, MR. KLOTZ in the Chair.

Present: Messrs. BARUCH, DAVIS and McCORMICK (*U. S. A*); MR. HUGHES, LORD SUMNER and LORD CUNLIFFE (*British Empire*); MR. KLOTZ, LOUCHEUR and LEBRUN (*France*); Messrs. CHIESA and D'AMELIO (*Italy*); Messrs. MORI, NAGAOKA and TATSUMI (*Japan*); Messrs. VAN DEN HEUVEL and DESPRET (*Belgium*); MR. MICHALA-COPOULOS (*Greece*); Messrs. OLCHOWSKI and CHAMIEC (*Poland*); Messrs. DANIELOPOL and ZAHARIADE (*Roumania*); Messrs. STO-YANOWITCH and PROTITCH (*Serbia*); Messrs. BENES and OSUSKI (*Czecho-Slovak Republic*).[1]

---

[1] According to the French minutes, Dulles was present instead of Davis.

Sympathy Expressed for Mr. Clemenceau

MR. HUGHES (*British Empire*) rose to express, on behalf of the Commission, the sympathy excited by the attack which had been made upon the French President du Conseil, Mr. Clemenceau.

The CHAIRMAN thanked the Commission and stated that the first reports of MR. CLEMENCEAU'S condition were comparatively favorable.

The minutes of the 7th and 8th Meetings were adopted.

The business before the meeting was the continuation of the discussion of the principles on which the rights to reparation rests.

Remarks of Mr. Mori (Japan)

MR. MORI (*Japan*) observed that the legal and juridical aspects of the question had already been fully set forth, as well as the special point of view of each nation. The Japanese Delegates, however, felt it their duty to state their position.[2]

It was a question of principles and not of policy that the Commission was now discussing. It was a simple and innate principle that everyone is responsible for the wrong he has done and for its consequences. The question at issue was whether or not the costs of the war should be included in the reparation to be demanded from the enemy. Conflicts between nations were comparable to suits at law, in which the successful litigant was allowed to recover costs, otherwise a crafty defendant could count upon the gradual exhaustion of his opponent.

War costs were a consequence of the enemy's aggression. Germany should thus pay the costs of the war to Japan, who was drawn into the war by the menace of Germany in the Far East, and by fidelity to the Anglo-Japanese alliance. The reimbursement of war costs would furnish the only guarantee of a just and lasting peace.

The remarks of MR. HUGHES, LORD SUMNER and MR. KLOTZ had elucidated the question whether the note of November 5th, 1918, had placed a limit on our claims.

Germany's acceptance of that Note had simply resulted in our consenting to give her peace; she was in the position of a criminal bound over for good behavior.

Could it be supposed that, in making Germany accept the Note of November 5th 1918, we had contemplated curtailing the scope of our claims resting on right and justice? What was the use of International Law if it did not recognize the principle of right and

[2] For the full text of Mori's speech, see Document 126.

justice? If there were no precedent for such a claim, the sooner it was established the better.

Consequently, the Japanese Delegates had arrived at the conclusion that reparation should be made to its full extent and scope. They therefore subscribed to the principles enunciated in the British Memorandum.

Remarks of Mr. Dulles (U. S. A.)

MR. DULLES (*U. S. A.*) acknowledged[3] that the recent discussion had brought forward arguments which, unless answered, would affect the validity of the principles proposed by the American Delegates. MR. LOUCHEUR had very clearly summed up these arguments. MR. DULLES first wished briefly to restate the American position, which, he said, rested on the fundamental proposition that we were here not to create new rights but "to consider the details of the application" of existing rights. It was the conclusion of the American Delegates that *by agreement* Germany is liable to make compensation for all damage done to the civilian populations of the Allies and their property; that *by operation of law* those who had been the victims of admittedly illegal acts are entitled to reparation.

Dealing first with the argument of MR. PROTITCH that, not having reached any agreement with the three enemy Powers other than Germany, we were free to impose upon them any terms we thought just. MR. DULLES admitted that this position was technically correct. He insisted, however, that it had been understood that the settlement with these countries was to be in the spirit of the terms specifically agreed to in the case of Germany. He doubted whether Serbia was prepared to renounce the right to appeal to those terms.

If MR. KLOTZ's contention was correct, we had no agreement with Germany as to the terms of peace. The only document having the form and spirit of an agreement was the Armistice Convention. If that were so, where we thought we had a chart we had none.

Referring to an abstract[4] of the principal communications that

---

[3] The full text of Dulles' speech is in TPG, I, 63-74; reprinted in Baruch, 323-37. See Document 127.

[4] This abstract, entitled "Texts upon Which the American Argument Is Based," is in TPG, I, 75-77. It consists of five quotations from the American exchange of notes with Germany in October and November, 1918. Under the heading, "I. Correspondence between Germany and the United States," it quotes in part: (a) "Germany to United States, October 6, 1918" (see Document 16); (b) "United States to Germany, October 8, 1918" (see Document 17); (c) "Germany to United States, October 14, 1918" (see Document 19); (d) "United States to Germany, October 23, 1918" (see Document 20). Under the heading, "II. Note expressing agreement of Associated Governments as to terms of peace and consequent willingness to conclude armistice;" it quotes: "United States to Germany, November 5, 1918," the complete note except the introductory sentence, "I have the honor . . . to the German Government" (see Document 38).

had passed between Germany and the Associated Powers, MR. DULLES reminded his hearers that PRESIDENT WILSON had refused to treat the program therein set forth as the "basis for peace discussion," but had insisted that it could be taken only as the "terms of peace," discussion of which must be limited to the details of application. There were two series of negotiations, the one as to the terms of peace and the other as to the terms of Armistice. When the Allies declared to Germany their willingness to make peace with Germany "on the terms of peace laid down by the PRESIDENT'S address to Congress of January, 1918, and the principles of settlement enunciated in his subsequent addresses," that declaration had the form and substance of an agreement. It was inconceivable that France regarded herself as free to propose terms other than those of 5th November. It must be, then, that MR. KLOTZ meant only to say that the Armistice agreement had in some way modified the binding engagement already made. But the duty of this Commission was to construe and apply, not the terms of Armistice, but the terms of peace. The Armistice was an instrument to secure the realization of terms of peace which it had been insisted should be fixed before Armistice negotiations were so much as opened. It was a mere military convention and its clauses could not affect the terms of peace or govern the decisions of the Commission. Had the military authorities in framing the Armistice sought to modify those terms, they would have exceeded their authority.

Turning to the argument of MR. HUGHES, MR. DULLES held that there must, in law, be a causal relationship between the illegal act and the alleged damage. This had been made out in the case of Belgium and was arguable in the case of Great Britain, which had entered the war expressly on account of the violation of the neutrality of Belgium. But the war came to France as the result of the declaration of war by Germany. The invasion of Belgium was only incidental so far as France was concerned, and the same was true of the other Allied and Associated Powers. Moreover, the treaty of 1839 was a beneficiary contract, for the benefit of another, namely, Belgium. Any special position resulting from the violation of the treaty by Germany therefore redounded to the benefit of Belgium and not to that of the other contracting Powers. MR. HUGHES had repudiated the conclusion to which his own argument, as above interpreted, inevitably led, namely, that England enjoyed an exclusive benefit, along with Belgium, to complete reimbursement for war costs. But could he escape the logical absurdity of that conclusion, merely by extending the benefit, with however admirable generosity, to the other Powers?

It was clear that under no principle of international law had Germany become our debtor for war costs. Any such debt could only arise from an agreement, and thus we were brought back to the proceedings of 4th November and the terms of compensation there laid down which did not provide for the expense of maintaining extraordinary military establishments.

It was not agreeable to maintain an argument that seemed, even in principle, in the interest of Germany. But MR. DULLES believed that the propositions of the American Delegates were those which, practically, would secure the maximum reparation and its most equitable distribution.

In conclusion, MR. DULLES proposed that the gentlemen who had drafted the agreement in question be asked to express their understanding of its meaning and legal effect.

A Question of Competence

The CHAIRMAN pointed out that MR. DULLES' motion raised a question of competence. This point was discussed by Messrs. LOUCHEUR (*France*), HUGHES (*British Empire*) and VAN DEN HEUVEL (*Belgium*).

MR. CHIESA (*Italy*) in the name of the Italian Delegation supported the new American proposal, which prejudiced in no way the various proposals already put forward and offered an effective means of securing information on the point under discussion. Once the agreements formulated at the time of the Armistice had been elucidated, it would be easy for the Commission to arrive at unanimity in their decisions, which was an essential condition for making them respected by the enemy powers. This advantage was of so great importance that it would warrant the delay involved in referring the matter back (to the Supreme War Council); and in the meantime the Commission could continue its examination of other principles involved in the question of reparation.

Armistice Convention

The CHAIRMAN, while reserving his reply to MR. DULLES' argument, desired to make clear the point that the Armistice Convention was not a purely military act. Its text was discussed on the 2nd and 4th of November, 1918, by the Supreme War Council in session at Versailles, and was drawn up and agreed to by both the civilian and military representatives of all the Associated Governments, among whom was COLONEL HOUSE, as would appear from the minutes of the meetings.

MR. LOUCHEUR (*France*) insisted on the fact demonstrated by MR. KLOTZ that the Armistice Convention was not only a military act. The clauses relating to reparation had been inserted in the Armistice Convention on the demand of MR. HYMANS. It was MR. KLOTZ who had proposed and insisted on including in the Financial Clauses the stipulation reserving our rights to all further claims. Furthermore, MR. LOUCHEUR pointed out that the document of November 5th does not either grant or deny War Costs. Was it not to be understood that the expression "compensation . . . . for all damages . . . ." included the payment of War Costs, which otherwise would weigh down heavily upon the civil population in the form of taxes?

Question Submitted to Supreme War Council

After a further discussion in which MR. HUGHES (*British Empire*), MR. McCORMICK (*U. S. A.*), MR. MORI (*Japan*), the CHAIRMAN and MR. LOUCHEUR (*France*) took part. The Commission decided to submit to the Supreme War Council the following question:*

Would an affirmation of MR. KLOTZ' motion, viz, "that the rights of the Allied and Associated Powers are all-inclusive" be contrary to the intentions of the members of the Supreme War Council (as then constituted) as expressed in the American Note of November 5th, 1918?

The Commission decided that the minutes of the Commission and the Annexes thereto should also be laid before the gentlemen above-mentioned, and that MR. HUGHES should be authorized to include a written reply to the arguments put forward by MR. DULLES during the session of the 19th February, 1919.[5]

The next meeting was fixed for Monday, the 24th February, 1919, at 10.30 A. M.

The meeting adjourned at 1.20 P. M.

JEROME D. GREENE,	L.-L. KLOTZ,
S. PEEL,	*Chairman.*
CH. DE LASTEYRIE,	
F. FOBERTI,	
Secretaries.	

*Amended at meeting of 24 February.

---

[5] For the text of Hughes' reply, see Document 128.

DOCUMENT 460

Plenary Commission: Minutes of the Tenth Meeting,
February 24, 1919, 10:30 A. M.

[EOM, CRD, pp. 50-51. French stenographic minutes in PV, CRD, pp. 131-37.]

The Commission on Reparation of Damage met on Monday, 24th February, 1919, at 10.30 A. M., at the Ministry of Finance, MR. KLOTZ in the Chair.

Present: Messrs. BARUCH, DAVIS and McCORMICK (*U. S. A.*); MR. HUGHES, LORD SUMNER and LORD CUNLIFFE (*British Empire*); Messrs. KLOTZ, LOUCHEUR and LEBRUN (*France*); Messrs. CHIESA and D'AMELIO (*Italy*); Messrs. MORI, NAGAOKA and TATSUMI (*Japan*); MR. VAN DEN HEUVEL (*Belgium*); MR. MICHALACO-POULOS (*Greece*); Messrs. OLCHOWSKI and MARKOWSKI (*Poland*); Messrs. MONIZ and D'ANDRADE (*Portugal*); Messrs. DANIELOPOL and ZAHARIADE (*Roumania*); Messrs. STOYANOWITCH and PRO-TITCH (*Serbia*); MR. BENES (*Czecho-Slovak Republic*).[1]

The minutes of the meeting of the 19th February, 1919, were adopted.

Representatives of Portugal

The CHAIRMAN reported that the Supreme War Council had decided to accede to the request of the Portuguese Government for representation on the Commission on Reparation.[2] Messrs. MONIZ and FREIRE D'ANDRADE had been appointed. The CHAIRMAN welcomed them on behalf of the Commission.

The President, on behalf of the French Delegation, expressed the hope that the First Sub-Committee would not neglect to make an estimate of the damage done by Germany in Russia.

In reply to an observation by MR. HUGHES (*British Empire*), who expressed himself in general sympathy with the President's sentiments, the latter made it clear that his suggestion did not contemplate proceeding to the allocation of sums due to Russia but merely to register her claims and to reserve her rights.

Communication to Supreme War Council

The CHAIRMAN informed the Commission that he had transmit-

---

[1] According to the French minutes, Osuský and Chamiec (instead of Markowski) were also present; and Mori was absent.

[2] Slosson's Annotations read (Miller, XIX, 266): "At the plenary session [of January 25] the Portuguese and Czecho-Slovak Delegations requested special representation on the Commission. Two Czecho-Slovak Delegates were added on February 3 (B. C. 21) and two Portuguese Delegates on February 22 (B. C. 37). Seven small Powers therefore enjoyed representation on the Commission."

ted to the President of the Peace Conference the motion adopted by the Commission at its meeting of 19th February, 1919.

Mr. LOUCHEUR (*France*) pointed out that the Commission, being derived from the Peace Conference, could only correspond with the President of the Peace Conference and not directly with the Supreme War Council. He proposed in consequence to amend the text of the motion as set out in the minutes of the previous meeting so that it should read as follows:

"The Commission decided to transmit to the President of the Peace Conference for submission to the Supreme War Council as constituted on the 4th November, 1918. . . ."

The amendment was adopted.

The CHAIRMAN asked for the views of the Commission as to its further labors.

He proposed an adjournment until the reply of the Supreme War Council should have been received. In the interval the Sub-Committees could push on more rapidly with their work, so as in the near future to submit their reports to the Commission.

Mr. VAN DEN HEUVEL (*Belgium*) thought that public opinion was concerned at the failure of the Peace Conference and its Commissions to bring their work to a conclusion. He asked the Commission to proceed with its work.

Acceleration of Work of Commission

Mr. LOUCHEUR (*France*) thought that the Commission could hardly work to good purpose so long as most of the questions before it, like that of direct and indirect damages, for example, were dependent on the reply of the Supreme War Council. Moreover, the work of the Commission was partly dependent on that of the Sub-Committees; the latter must endeavor to reach as soon as possible conclusions which could be submitted to the Commission. He proposed to fix a period of eight days within which the Sub-Committees should present their reports, or at least interim reports. It would give satisfaction to public opinion and to the various Governments to see a rapid conclusion of the work of the Sub-Committees. This was agreed to.

The CHAIRMAN proposed that the Third Sub-Committee should meet immediately to elect its officers.

The meeting adjourned at 11.30 A. M.

JEROME D. GREENE,		L.-L. KLOTZ,
S. PEEL,	*Secretaries.*	*Chairman.*
CH. DE LASTEYRIE,		
F. FOBERTI,		

DOCUMENT 461

Plenary Commission: Minutes of the Eleventh Meeting (Including Annex), March 3, 1919, 11 A. M.

[EOM, CRD, pp. 53-57. French stenographic minutes in PV, CRD, pp. 138-49. The minutes of meetings 11-16 of the Plenary Commission are bound into one book. In addition to the minutes, this book also contains the following:

Cover. "PRELIMINARY PEACE CONFERENCE, COMMISSION ON THE REPARATION OF DAMAGE, MINUTES. MEETINGS: 11th—3 MARCH . . . 16th—19 APRIL. PARIS, 1919."

Title Page. Same as Cover, except that "MINUTES" is omitted.

Last Page. "TABLE OF CONTENTS (FROM THE ELEVENTH THROUGH THE SIXTEENTH MEETING) . . ."]

The Commission on Reparation of Damage met on Monday, 3rd March, 1919, at 11 A. M. at the Ministry of Finance, MR. KLOTZ in the Chair.

Present: Messrs. BARUCH, DULLES and LAMONT (*U. S. A.*); MR. HUGHES, LORD SUMNER and LORD CUNLIFFE (*British Empire*); Messrs. KLOTZ, LOUCHEUR and LEBRUN (*France*); Messrs. CHIESA and D'AMELIO (*Italy*); Messrs. MORI and TATSUMI (*Japan*); MR. DESPRET (*Belgium*); MR. MICHALACOPOULOS (*Greece*); Messrs. OLCHOWSKI and CHAMIEC (*Poland*); Messrs. MONIZ and D'ANDRADE (*Portugal*); Messrs. DANIELOPOL and ZAHARIADE (*Roumania*); Messrs. STOYANOWITCH and PROTITCH (*Serbia*); Messrs. BENES and OSUSKI (*Czecho-Slovak Republic*).[1]

The minutes of the last meeting were adopted.

Communication from Council of Ten

The CHAIRMAN reported that the motion adopted by the Commission at its tenth meeting, by which the President of the Peace Conference was requested to obtain a ruling from the Supreme War Council, as constituted in November, 1918, upon the extent of the right to reparation, had been brought to the attention of the Council of Ten at its last meeting. COLONEL HOUSE had asked that the matter be deferred until PRESIDENT WILSON arrived in Europe. The Council had therefore decided that the Commission should be invited to prepare a two-fold report: first, on the assumption that war costs might be included, and secondly on the assumption that they ought to be excluded from the claims presented against Germany.

MR. DULLES (*U. S. A.*) said that two principles had been

---

[1] According to the French minutes, Nagaoka and Romanos were also present; and Lamont and Beneš were absent.

proposed to the Commission.[2] One contemplated limited reparation based on specific principles as enunciated by the American Delegation; the other, unlimited reparation as enunciated by the French. The American proposition was accepted by all, at least as a minimum. The American Delegation therefore hoped for a unanimous report on its practical application but suggested that those who advocated unlimited reparation should work out its practical application and significance without active participation by the American Delegation in an effort which it considered mistaken in principle and involving claims so vague as to be impracticable in application.

MR. HUGHES (*British Empire*) stated that the Commission's enquiry had not been submitted to the proper authority. The suggestion of the Council of Ten was impracticable; one of the two views must be right, and the Commission could not follow both simultaneously. If no ruling from the competent authority could be obtained, the Commission must answer the question for itself. The British Delegation could not agree to continue the work of the Commission on a basis which excluded consideration of war costs.

The CHAIRMAN thought that in the circumstances the Council of Ten had authority to give a reply to the Commission.

In correction of MR. DULLES' statement the CHAIRMAN declared that the French Delegation had never maintained the principle of unlimited reparation, but only the unlimited right to reparation of damage, reserving always the possibility of not proceeding in the application of this principle to the utmost extent of the right.

MR. HUGHES (*British Empire*) said that the British Delegation also did not demand unlimited reparation but only the actual costs and damage occasioned by the war.

MR. CHIESA (*Italy*) thought that the instruction of the Council of Ten might be accepted. When the tabulation on the two bases had been completed, it might itself furnish the answer to the question.

The CHAIRMAN reminded the Commission that it was still faced by two conflicting proposals: that of MR. HUGHES to ignore the reply of the Council of Ten and that of MR. CHIESA to accept it.

MR. LOUCHEUR (*France*) urged that the Council of Ten was the Bureau of the Peace Conference, from which the Committee derived its origin. Its decision was binding upon the Commission

[2] For the full text of Dulles' statement, see Document 158.

and left it no longer at liberty to discuss the question of principle at issue.

MR. HUGHES (*British Empire*) denied that the Council of Ten had intended to give a binding instruction; the original terms of reference to the Commission still held good. If we admit that an amount less that [*sic*] what we claim to be entitled to is to be estimated, we arm Germany with a powerful weapon against us. The people of England, the only people who had had an opportunity of expressing an opinion, declared at the last election that Germany must pay to the utmost of her capacity.

MR. BARUCH (*U. S. A.*) noted that the delay in obtaining a specific answer to the Commission's question had been due to the absence, not only of PRESIDENT WILSON, but also of MR. LLOYD GEORGE and MR. ORLANDO. He agreed with MR. LOUCHEUR as to the necessity of following the instruction of the Council of Ten.

The CHAIRMAN took note of MR. BARUCH'S correction. He defined the precise question now before the meeting: should the Committee continue to discuss the principle of war costs in spite of the answer of the Council of Ten?

MR. HUGHES (*British Empire*) quoted the Terms of Reference received by the Commission from the Peace Conference, upon which it had hitherto proceeded. These original directions had not been limited by any competent authority. His instructions from the British Government did not allow him, without reference to it, to agree to the preparation of alternative statements of claim against Germany one of which would exclude war costs.

MR. STOYANOWITCH (*Serbia*) urged that the practical work of preparing estimates should not be delayed in order to await the final decision of questions of principle.

MR. CHIESA (*Italy*) noted that both the conflicting views called for valuation of war costs. The Sub-Committees should continue their work including war costs in their lists but without discussing the principle.

The CHAIRMAN thought the two proposals could be reconciled and suggested that claims should be entered in two columns, one for damage and one for war costs.

LORD SUMNER (*British Empire*) said that the entering of claims in two columns would necessitate their expression in figures. The experience of the First Sub-Committee showed that precise figures could hardly be obtained. The Sub-Committee had not even, as yet, been able to obtain computations of the minimum total claims of the various countries. He suggested that the Sub-Committees should be allowed to continue their work without being limited by too precise instructions.

The CHAIRMAN reminded the Commission that precise figures for war costs could easily be obtained, and that certain categories of damage could also be expressed in figures, as, for example, sums extorted from local authorities.

MR. HUGHES (*British Empire*) said that the objection raised by him was to the preparation of two estimates. A single complete statement should be made out from which the competent authority could eliminate any items it might desire on its own authority.

MR. DULLES (*U. S. A.*) asked if he was right in understanding that the Sub-Committees were to distinguish between costs of war and damage.

LORD SUMNER (*British Empire*) said the First Sub-Committee's task was not to define terms but to list and describe and, as far as possible, to value claims. Any person would be competent to decide on each item whether it fell within the description of war costs or of damage. The question was largely one of language and and not substance. War costs was a vague term including much which could equally well be considered as reparation; for example, compensation for personal injuries to soldiers. He did not think that two distinct columns should be drawn up. What was needed was a list as detailed as possible, such as would allow any person to distinguish for himself between war costs and damage.

On the proposal of the CHAIRMAN, the Commission decided that without there being imposed upon them any particular method, the Sub-Committees should actively press forward their work, having regard, as far as possible, to the opinion expressed by the Council of Ten.

The Commission decided also that the Chairmen of the Sub-Committees should inform the Secretariat as soon as their reports were ready for presentation.

MR. LOUCHEUR (*France*) explained that apart from the question of war costs, which was reserved by the Council of Ten, there were a certain number of questions of principle of which the Sub-Committees required solutions in order to proceed with their work.

The Commission decided that it should be the duty of the Sub-Committees to present to the Secretariat the lists of questions to be submitted to the Commission.

MR. MONIZ (*Portugal*) expressed his acknowledgments for the welcome given by the CHAIRMAN to the Portuguese Delegates at the last Meeting of the Commission. He presented the memorandum of the Portuguese Delegation, setting out the point of view of this Delegation in regard to reparation of damage. (See Annex.)

The next Meeting was fixed for Thursday, 6 March, 1919 at 10.30 A. M.

The meeting adjourned at 12.45 P. M.

JEROME D. GREENE,   L.-L. KLOTZ,
S. PEEL,   *Chairman.*
CH. DE LASTEYRIE,
F. FOBERTI,
   Secreiaries.

ANNEX[3]

PRINCIPLES OF REPARATION

Presented by the Poriuguese Delegation

The Portuguese Delegation maintains that the Allies have the right to demand complete reimbursement from the enemy countries for all damage including the expenditures which result from the aggression which they have suffered. The memoranda which have already been presented to the Commission on Reparation have made this point clear.

Ever since the month of August 1914, Germany has attacked the Portuguese Colonies, both of Mozambique and of Angola, and has instigated by her acts the uprising of the natives. The Southern part of Angola has been ravaged and many Portuguese subjects have been murdered. Finally, on 10 [*9*] March 1916, war was declared against Portugal because of her fidelity to the Anglo-Portuguese alliance and the services she had rendered to the cause of the Allies and of humanity.

The Portuguese Delegates are not of the opinion that the note of 5 November 1918 and its acceptance by Germany can operate as a limitation of claims of the Allies for war costs. By that note, President Wilson in effect said to Germany that the Allied Governments were disposed to conclude peace upon the conditions set forth in the President's address to Congress of 8 January 1918, and in accordance with the principles announced in his later declarations. They made reservations as to what is commonly called "freedom of the seas"; and they said that no doubt could be allowed to remain as to what was meant by the special stipulation included in the declaration of President Wilson when he said that the

---

[3] French text in PV, CRD, pp. 150-51. Portuguese text in Moniz, pp. 313-15, with unimportant differences.

invaded territories ought to be not only evacuated and freed, but also restored; and it is to make plain what the Allies mean by these words that the following passage appears in the note of 5 November:

"...... *compensation will be made by Germany for all damage done to the civilian population of the Allies and their property by the aggression of Germany by land, by sea and from the air.*"[4]

This passage refers to the stipulation above mentioned, the meaning of which it makes clear; and it cannot act as a limitation upon the claims of the Allies in regard to war costs, which latter, moreover, were contemplated in the financial clauses of Article XIX of the Armistice Convention.

In his speech to Congress of 8 January 1918, making known the objects of the United States in entering the war, President Wilson set forth the Fourteen Points of the programme of world peace, the only possible programme, according to him, and he said:

"An evident principle runs through the whole programme I have outlined. It is the principle of justice to all peoples and nationalities, and their right to live on equal terms of liberty and safety with one another, whether they be strong or weak."

Thus the principle underlying the Fourteen Points of the speech of 8 January is that of justice for all peoples. For if Germany does not pay the cost of the war which she has caused this would mean that upon the peoples who were the victims of her aggression there would fall the entire weight of the indebtedness which they have contracted in self defense; and this, most of all in the case of the small powers, would make their future development almost wholly impossible so that they would be left in a situation much more difficult and much more precarious than that of Germany, the vanquished power. That would be contrary to President Wilson's principle as expressed in the words "justice for all peoples," which are the sum and substance of his programme.

Holding, therefore, that there exists no document which limits the right of the Allies to demand complete payment for damage, including war costs, the Portuguese Delegates associate themselves entirely with the principles laid down in the British memorandum. Paris, 3 March 1919.

---

[4] French text reads: "du fait des forces armées de l'Allemagne". Portuguese text reads: "derivadas da acção das forças armadas da Alemanha".

DOCUMENT 462

*Plenary Commission: Minutes of the Twelfth Meeting,
March 6, 1919, 10:30 A. M.*

[EOM, CRD, pp. 58-61. French stenographic minutes, PV, CRD, pp. 152-66.]

The Commission on Reparation of Damage met on Thursday, 6 March, 1919, at 10.30 A. M. at the Ministry of Finance, MR. KLOTZ in the chair.

Present: Messrs. BARUCH, DAVIS and McCORMICK (*U. S. A.*); MR. HUGHES, LORD SUMNER and LORD CUNLIFFE (*British Empire*); Messrs. KLOTZ, LOUCHEUR and LEBRUN (*France*); MR. D'AMELIO (*Italy*); Messrs. MORI, NAGAOKA and TATSUMI (*Japan*); MR. DESPRET (*Belgium*); MR. MICHALACOPOULOS (*Greece*); Messrs. OLCHOWSKI and CHAMIEC (*Poland*); MR. D'ANDRADE (*Portugal*); Messrs. DANIELOPOL and ZAHARIADE (*Roumania*); Messrs. STOYA-NOWITCH and PROTITCH (*Serbia*); MR. BENES (*Czecho-Slovak Republic*).[1]

The CHAIRMAN announced that a certain number of questions had been submitted to the Commission by the First and Second Sub-Committees.

At the request of MR. BENES (*Czecho-Slovak Republic*), the first question from the First Sub-Committee, relative to the Czecho-Slovak Republic, was withdrawn from the Agenda.

Russian Claims

The CHAIRMAN then read the second question: "What is the nature and extent of the account which the Sub-Commission is desired to take of the case of Russia?"

LORD SUMNER (*British Empire*) said that, as Russia had no Delegate at the Peace Conference, it was impossible for the First Sub-Committee to study the question of damage suffered by Russia without receiving special instructions from the Commission. The Polish Delegation could give certain indications as to the case of the Polish Provinces of the former Russian Empire, but these indications could not suffice.

MR. OLCHOWSKI (*Poland*) added that he could also give figures for the Lithuanian Provinces and White Russia, which according to all probability, would in the future form a common State with Poland.

MR. HUGHES (*British Empire*) declared that the case of the

---

[1] According to the French minutes, Moniz and Osuský were also present.

Czecho-Slovak Republic must not be confused with that of Russia. He considered that the First Sub-Committee should not take up the case of Russia or of any portion of the former Russian State, exception being made, however, for Russian Poland, Esthonia, and Lithuania, which might have claims to present.

The CHAIRMAN pointed out that in its meeting of 24 February the Commission had, however, agreed to a proposal to the contrary.

MR. HUGHES (*British Empire*) objected that the Commission on Reparation of Damage had received no instructions from the Peace Conference to examine the case of Russia. Thus it was before the Council of Ten that the Russian question should be brought up.

The CHAIRMAN considered that the case of Russia could not be examined in detail by the full Commission. He proposed that the First Sub-Committee, after having been declared competent, should study the question of damage suffered by Russia and bring before the Commission such conclusions as it saw fit to adopt.

German Currency in Alsace-Lorraine

The CHAIRMAN then read the third question of the First Sub-Committee, relative to the buying up by the French Government of German money in Alsace-Lorraine. He considered that this was not a question of principle. The First Sub-Committee should thus study the subject in detail and present its report.

LORD SUMNER (*British Empire*) explained that the question had been brought before the full Commission because the First Sub-Committee had not come to an agreement upon it, and had therefore thought it natural and proper to refer it to the full Commission.

MR. HUGHES (*British Empire*) was of the opinion that the question of losses due to the depreciation of the mark should be referred to the Financial Commission, which alone was competent to deal with it.

Competence of Sub-Committees

MR. McCORMICK (*U. S. A.*) thought that the problem which had been raised was more general. In his opinion the question as it stood at present was as follows: "When there is a difference of opinion within a Sub-Committee, should the latter refer the question to the full Commission, or, on the contrary, draw up a majority and a minority report upon the question?"

The CHAIRMAN replied to MR. McCORMICK that the full Commission should not from day to day have to decide upon the questions of detail which continually arose. This was a bad method of work. The Sub-Committees were organs of information for the Commission. In case of disagreement they should join to their majority report a note setting forth the opinion of the minority. As to the particular question of the mark in Alsace-Lorraine, there could be no doubt that the First Sub-Committee was competent to deal with it.

The CHAIRMAN then proceeded to the discussion of the questions put by the Second Sub-Committee, taking up first the fifth question: "Should the Sub-Committee now consider the imposition of taxes on the enemy powers for the payment of reparation?"

MR. MCCORMICK (*U. S. A.*) thought that if the point of view stated by the CHAIRMAN was the correct one, the full Commission ought not to take up the questions put by the Second Sub-Committee, any more than those put by the First.

MR. LOUCHEUR (*France*) feared that a misunderstanding had arisen. He thought that a distinction must be made between questions of opinion, which should not be brought before the full Commission, and questions of principle, upon which the decision taken by the Commission would change completely the purpose of the work of the Sub-Committee. The question as to whether the imposition of taxes on the enemy Powers could be considered as a means of payment of reparation, appeared to belong to the latter category. It was thus proper to bring it before the full Commission.

Questions Submitted by Second Sub-Committee

MR. HUGHES (*British Empire*) returned to the subject of the questions put by the Second Sub-Committee, which he then read:

1. Shall not the recovery of objects that can be identified as having been carried off be sanctioned for the benefit of all the Allied States as against the enemy States?

2. In all cases where an immediate need exists, may not the Allied States take objects from the enemy countries, whether now actually in use or not, such as machines, rolling stock, equipment, tools, timber and animals—equivalent to the same kind of objects in the occupied territories that have been carried off, worn out, consumed, or destroyed by the enemy or by acts of war?

3. May the supply of a certain amount of labor be considered as one method of reparation to the Allies by the enemy States?

4. Should the replacement of destroyed or stolen works of art by other works of art equivalent and of the same kind taken from the enemy be considered as one means of reparation?

5. Should the Sub-Committee now consider the imposition of taxes on the enemy powers for the payment of reparation?

To all these questions MR. HUGHES replied in the affirmative. "Yes, we have the right to demand everything stated in these questions. Who would contest our right?"

The CHAIRMAN made note of MR. HUGHES'S statement.

MR. DAVIS (*U. S. A.*) could not see, from the point of view of the procedure to be followed, the difference between the questions put by the First Sub-Committee and those put by the Second. The Commission should send back both sets of questions to the Sub-Committees or discuss them both, and in the latter case he would have certain reservations to make in regard to the opinions expressed by MR. HUGHES.

MR. LOUCHEUR (*France*) pointed out that the questions put by each Sub-Committee had not been treated differently, as MR. DAVIS seemed to understand. The First Sub-Committee had put three questions. The first had been withdrawn at the request of MR. BENES (*Czecho-Slovak Republic*). As to the second and third questions, they had been answered by the decision that the Sub-Committee was competent to deal with them.

MR. DAVIS (*U. S. A.*) however, understood the CHAIRMAN to have decided that the questions put by the First Sub-Committee should not have been brought up before the full Commission, and that on these points the First Sub-Committee should present two reports, a majority and a minority report.

The CHAIRMAN replied that this answer was given to the question raised by MR. McCORMICK (*U. S. A.*), not to the questions put by the First Sub-Committee.

MR. LEBRUN (*France*) observed that, contrary to what had been first decided, the full Commission had laid down no general principle to serve as a guide for the work of the Sub-Committees. Today, the First Sub-Committee brought up questions of competence, and had received a reply in the affirmative. It now remained to reply to the questions of principle put by the Second Sub-Committee. The ability of the Second Sub-Committee to accomplish a useful result in its work depended upon whether the answer was yes or no.

MR. HUGHES (*British Empire*) here took the chair.

MR. DAVIS (*U. S. A.*) observed that the value of a principle and, thus, its acceptance, depended often on the way it was to be applied. He therefore made the following proposal: "The acceptance of these principles will depend upon the means adopted for their application. A definite position cannot be taken on this point until after a discussion which shall have made completely clear the method of application, in order that there be no conflict with other principles."

LORD CUNLIFFE (*British Empire*) examined the question of the supply of labor to be demanded from Germany, the taking of machinery from enemy countries, and the replacement of works of art. A careful study would be necessary to determine the application of these principles. It was desirable that the Second Sub-Committee be given clear directions by the Commission before undertaking such a task.

The CHAIRMAN proposed that the Second Sub-Committee be declared competent to study the five questions which it had submitted to the full Commission, that it should work out the details of application of the principles involved, and that the following reply be made to the questions put by the Second Sub-Committee:

"The Second Sub-Committee shall continue the study of these different problems, without prejudging the final decision to be taken by the full Commission after the report of the Second Sub-Committee."

This was agreed to.

MR. LOUCHEUR (*France*) asked that the question of joint responsibility of enemy countries be examined by the full Commission at its next meeting.

The next meeting was fixed for Tuesday, March 12,[2] at 3.30 P. M. The meeting adjourned at 12.45 P. M.

L.-L. KLOTZ,
Chairman.

JEROME D. GREENE,
S. PEEL,
CH. DE LASTEYRIE,
F. FOBERTI,
   Secretaries.

DOCUMENT 463

Plenary Commission: Minutes of the Thirteenth Meeting (Including Annex), March 11, 1919, 3:30 P. M.

[EOM, CRD, pp. 62-67. French stenographic minutes, PV, CRD, pp. 167-75.]

The Commission on Reparation of Damage met on Tuesday, 11 March, 1919, at 3.30 P.M., at the Ministry of Finance, MR. HUGHES in the Chair.

[2] Error for "March 11."

Present: Messrs. BARUCH, DAVIS and MCCORMICK (*U. S. A.*);
MR. HUGHES, LORD SUMNER and LORD CUNLIFFE (*British Empire*);
Messrs. LOUCHEUR and LEBRUN (*France*); Messrs. CHIESA and
D'AMELIO (*Italy*); Messrs. MORI, NAGAOKA and TATSUMI (*Japan*);
Messrs. VAN DEN HEUVEL and DESPRET (*Belgium*); MR. MICHALA-
COPOULOS (*Greece*); Messrs. OLCHOWSKI and CHAMIEC (*Poland*);
Messrs. MONIZ and D'ANDRADE (*Portugal*); Messrs. DANIELOPOL
and ZAHARIADE (*Roumania*); Messrs. STOYANOWITCH and PRO-
TITCH (*Serbia*); Messrs. BENES and OSUSKI (*Czecho-Slovak
Republic*).

The adoption of the minutes of the meeting of Thursday, 6
March, was reserved until the next meeting.

Joint Responsibility of Enemy Powers

The CHAIRMAN pointed out that the agenda called for the
examination of the question of the joint responsibility of the
enemy debtor States.

MR. D'AMELIO (*Italy*) maintained that this principle was
universally set forth in civil law and applied by jurisprudence in
cases similar to those with which the Commission was concerned.

The Penal Code also provided for the joint responsibility of the
participants in a crime. And it was indeed a crime which was the
sole source of the obligations of the enemy States, namely, the
unjust war which they sought and carried on with the utmost
co-operation and with complete concurrence of aim, means and
methods.

On the other hand, the Allied States had all suffered about the
same kind of damage. The extent of the damage alone varied. The
material damage caused by each of the enemy States was willed by
all the others. Their action was therefore in common and they were
responsible, as co-authors, for damage caused. It was therefore just
that the Allied States receive indemnity from the whole sum
represented by the assets of all the enemy States, in proportion
to the damage suffered.

Also, troops of several enemy States were often engaged on the
same front. Under these conditions it was impossible to differentiate
the damage caused by each body of troops.

MR. D'AMELIO presented a document to support his argument,
an agreement signed by Germany and Austria-Hungary to settle
the division of booty taken from Italy. He added that it was also
impossible to find out upon what enemy States fell the responsibility
for torpedoing vessels because, at least in the Adriatic, submarines
displayed the German or Austrian flag indiscriminately.

In conclusion, therefore, if the Commission were to seek to place the responsibility for each case of damage the task would be one of minute analysis. The Commission should, on the contrary, maintain the principle of joint responsibility corresponding to the larger joint responsibility which should inspire all the acts of the Peace Conference.

MR. PROTITCH (*Serbia*) showed that International Law did not cover the point with which the Commission was now concerned, but that penal law, at any rate, decreed that when a crime had been committed by several persons, complete joint responsibility existed where reparation for damage was concerned.

Besides, on many fronts, hostilities were carried on simultaneously or successively by forces belonging to several enemy States and it was often impossible to distinguish the true authors of the damage. Consequently, the Serbian Delegation maintained the validity of the principles of joint responsibility of the enemy debtor States.

MR. DANIELOPOL (*Roumania*) stated that the Treaty of Bucharest which sought to enslave Roumania was signed by the four enemy Powers. This agreement established beyond doubt the joint responsibility of the enemy States. But the question of joint responsibility was closely allied to another problem. Should the peoples who made part of Austria-Hungary against their will be counted among the responsible debtors? If the Reparation Commission maintained the principle of joint responsibility of all the enemy States it would seem that a reservation should be made upon this point. Austria proper and Hungary should, alone, be considered as joint debtors.

MR. OLCHOWSKI (*Poland*) remarked that the term "joint responsibility" could not be here employed in its usual sense in civil law. There could be no question, in fact, of each creditor State making claim against whatever debtor it saw fit. On the contrary it was the principle cf the joint responsibility of the creditors which must be established. All the States interested in the reparation of damage should, in his opinion, form a united group and create an international body for receiving the sums owed by the enemy.

The Peace Conference should also fix the amount which each of the responsible States had to contribute to the reparation of damage. These were the essential measures.

As for the countries which had been freed, by the war, from foreign domination, it must be taken as a principle that territories taken from their mother country by violence, and now being restored thereto, should in no way be held responsible for the reparation which would be imposed on the Powers from whom they had just been separated. They would on the contrary have right to reparation.

MR. OLCHOWSKI added:

"The justice of this principle is an axiom which needs no proof. Poland which has been the victim of German and Austrian policies for more than a century cannot be chastised for the crime of her executioners."

MR. PROTITCH (*Serbia*) supported the reservations set forth by MR. DANIELOPOL and by MR. OLCHOWSKI in the case of former Austrian provinces and of Bosnia-Herzegovina.

MR. LOUCHEUR (*France*) stated that the French Delegation was not, at present, ready to give its opinion on the question of joint responsibility. Because the question whether the new States should take part in the payment of the debt of the States of which they formerly were part, was a very serious one. He wondered, even, whether this question was in the province of this Commission. At any rate the French Delegation would have to consult its Government. It would only be able to give a reply early next week.

MR. STOYANOVITCH (*Serbia*) asked if the memoranda relative to damage to territories which were part of Austria-Hungary and Germany should be presented.

MR. LOUCHEUR (*France*) was of the opinion that these memoranda could be presented to the First Sub-Committee if they were presented separately.

MR. CHIESA (*Italy*) thought that the question of the new States participating in the debt was not in the province of the Commission but in that of the Council of Ten.

MR. VAN DEN HEUVEL (*Belgium*) supported the argument presented by MR. LOUCHEUR in favor of deferring the discussion as this question was one of the most serious before the Commission. Not only did the problem of the participation of new States in the debts of the States of which they formerly were part mingle with that of joint responsibility, but various other problems were also intimately connected therewith. Thus, the various Allied and Associated Governments entered the war at different times. And even those who entered the struggle at different times were not immediately at war with all the enemy States. For example, would the destruction caused by Austria-Hungary on the Italian front in 1915 be placed to the account of Germany upon whom Italy did not declare war until 1916?

MR. CHIESA (*Italy*) replied that if Italy did enter the war later than the other Nations, this could affect only the amount of her claims. But from the moment that damage had been caused the right to reparation became real, no matter what the time of the war in which this damage occurred. Besides, the damage in Italy did occur at the time when Italy was at war with Germany. Finally, the document submitted by MR. D'AMELIO proved the complete joint responsibility of Germany and Austria-Hungary because it showed that there had been division of spoils between the two countries.

The CHAIRMAN proposed that the Commission adjourn until such time as the Sub-Committee could present their reports. The Commission would be convened by the CHAIRMAN when necessary. This proposal was accepted.

LORD SUMNER (*British Empire*) felt obliged to say once more that the work of the First Sub-Committee could not proceed until the memoranda expressing in figures the damage suffered by each country had been submitted. He therefore asked the interested Delegations to submit their figures as soon as possible.

The meeting adjourned at 5 P. M.

L.-L. KLOTZ,
Chairman.

JEROME D. GREENE,
S. PEEL,
CH. DE LASTEYRIE,
F. FOBERTI,
  Secretaries.

ANNEX[1]

GERMAN-AUSTRIAN AGREEMENT IN REGARD TO THE DIVISION
OF MATERIAL SEIZED IN ITALY DURING THE INVASION

(*Presented by the Italian Delegation*)

By document dated 5 May, 1918, and signed at Vienna by the Consul-General Jovanovich for Austria-Hungary and further by Major Schaeffer (General Staff) for Germany, the preliminary agreement, signed by Gratz, for Austria-Hungary, and Handorff, for Germany, with the number Z.u.Z. 118,446, was ratified as follows, the preliminary document being entitled: "Apportionment of Property Taken from the Occupied Parts of Italy," under date of 16 December, 1917.

[1] French text in PV, CRD, pp. 176-78.

		Austria-Hungary	Germany
1.	War material found in fields and store-houses....	1	1
2.	Human material, taken prisoner...............	1	1
3.	Spun and twisted cotton......................	3	1
4.	Silk..	2	3
5.	Silk Floss.....................................	1	1
6.	Wool, carded, for mattresses..................	1	1
7.	Hemp, jute, silk shreds, sacking..............	1	1
8.	Animal hair (horse, goat and other animals, with the exception of sheep's and lamb's wool)......	1	1
9.	Textile manufactures..........................	2	3
10.	Dyeing materials.............................	1	1
11.	Special materials idem.......................	3	2
12.	Skins of large animals / Skins of rabbits / Skins of sheep / Skins of lambs / Skins of goats, etc. } (exclusive of skins capable of being made into gas masks)...........	3	2
13.	Shreds of skins, and skins dressed for boots......	3	2
14.	Paper, paste-board, and material for its manufacture..	1	1
15.	Candles and paraffin..........................	1	2
16.	Machine and mineral oils.....................	2	1
17.	Vulcanized oil................................	1	1
18.	Vulcanized oil, high grade....................	2	3
19.	Lubricating grease............................	1	1
20.	Wood—for building purposes, firewood, scraps, logs, etc....................................	All	None
21.	Fine woods, (except chestnut, walnut and pine)..	1	1
22.	Charcoal.....................................	2	1
23.	Excelsior.....................................	1	1
24.	Flowers of sulphur...........................	All	None
25.	Crude sulphur................................	3	1
26.	Sulphur in blocks............................	None	All
27.	Copper ore...................................	All	None
28.	Lead ore.....................................	None	All
29.	Coal...	All	None
30.	Pharmaceutical preparations..................	4	1
31.	Pharmaceutical herbs and their products........	1	1
32.	Old rubber, new rubber, and gutta-percha.......	1	1
33.	Receptacles—iron, wood for petroleum and oil...	4	1
34.	Crude copper, manufactured alloy of copper, bells, copper kitchen utensils.....................	200 cars (this proportion being continued if there is any more).	200 cars
35.	Crude and manufactured tin, old tin cans, organ pipes, household utensils of the same metal....	1	1
36.	New tin cans.................................	1	1
37.	Blades of white metal........................	All	None

38.	Aluminum	All	None
39.	Crude and manufactured lead	None	All
40.	Zinc	All	None[2]

(because Germany thereby paid off a debt in this metal due Austria-Hungary to the amount of 1250.)

41.	Nickel	1	1
42.	Iron alloy		
	chrome	1	1
	tungsten	1	1
	vanadium	4	1
	silicate	None	All
	manganese	All	None
43.	Metal alloys	1	1
44.	All other metals except iron, platinum and precious metals	4	1
45.	Platinum	(to be apportioned when the results of collection have been determined).	

46.	Graphite	None	All
47.	Magnesite	None	All
48.	Iron ore, chips, and burned stones	(to be apportioned).	
49.	Crude old iron, fragments, half-manufactured iron, iron piping and wire	1	1
50.	Organic acids, tartrates, and citrates	1	1
51.	Chemical products	4	1
52.	Carbide of calcium	2	1
53.	Electrodes	All	None
54.	Coal retorts	All	None
55.	Asbestos, long-strand	1	1
56.	Asbestos, short-strand	1	2
57.	Borax	1	1
58.	Crude tar	4	1
59.	Liquid gas	All	None
60.	Wine bottles	(to be considered as booty of war).	
61.	Vitriol (sulphuric acid)	All	None
62.	Sulphur pyrites	None	All
63.	Electric motors, electric lathes, workshop machinery, boilers, cordage machinery, steam engines for building roads, cylinders, rock-breakers, textile machines, cranes, farm machinery, etc.	Such as are of use to the Army are taken over by it. The remainder, to be destroyed; and material serviceable for military purposes, to be apportioned.	

[2] In the French text, "All   None" is omitted.

64. Lithograph stones...........................	1	1
65. Mill-stones...................................	2	1
66. Cement......................................	4	1

N. B. It is to be noted that when German troops were occupying the territory noted on the map exclusively, they made it very hard to carry out so much of the foregoing apportionment agreed upon as was in favor of Austria-Hungary.

DOCUMENT 464

Plenary Commission: Minutes of the Fourteenth Meeting (Including Annex), April 7, 1919, 10:30 A. M.

[EOM, CRD, pp. 68-76. French stenographic minutes, PV, CRD, pp. 925-33. The French text of the Annex may be found as the Annex to the minutes of the First Subcommittee, Twenty-seventh (and last) meeting, April 1, 1919, in PV, CRD, pp. 694-702. Annex I of Document 486 (second column) precedes the section entitled "Categories of Damage for which Reparation May Be Demanded." Annex II of Document 486 (second column) precedes the section entitled "Methods of Valuation of Damage." Articles I and II of Document 225 follow in a general way as indicated in footnotes 2 and 5 of the present text.]

The Commission on Reparation of Damage met on Monday, 7 April, 1919, at 10.30 A. M., at the Ministry of Finance, MR. HUGHES in the chair.

Present: GENERAL MCKINSTRY and MR. DULLES (*U. S. A.*); MR. HUGHES, LORD SUMNER and LORD CUNLIFFE (*British Empire*); Messrs. LOUCHEUR, LEBRUN and SERGENT (*France*); MR. D'AMELIO (*Italy*); Messrs. MORI, FUKAI and KIKUCHI (*Japan*); Messrs. VAN DEN HEUVEL and DESPRET (*Belgium*); Messrs. ROMANOS and MICHALACOPOULOS (*Greece*); Messrs. OLCHOWSKI and CHAMIEC (*Poland*); Messrs. AFFONSO COSTA and FREIRE D'ANDRADE (*Portugal*); Messrs. DANIELOPOL and ZAHARIADE (*Roumania*); Messrs. STOYANOWITCH and PROTITCH (*Serbia*); MR. BENES (*Czecho-Slovak Republic*).[1]

The minutes of the 11th, 12th and 13th meetings were adopted without discussion.

Consideration of Interim Report. First Sub-Committee

The business upon the Agenda was the consideration and discussion of the reports presented by'the Sub-Committees.

The CHAIRMAN presented to the Commission the report of the first Sub-Committee (Valuation of Damage). (See Annex.)

MR. SERGENT (*France*) stated that, although the report was

---

[1] According to the French minutes, Santos Viegas and Slavík were present; and McKinstry, Kikuchi, and Zahariade were absent.

merely provisional, he desired to point out that it made no mention of the following subjects:—

1. Those categories of damage which arose from repurchase of enemy money by the Allies.*

2. The method of valuing damage to persons. The French Delegation had made on this subject proposals which had not been adopted; and no other proposal had been presented.

Finally, certain proposals of the French Delegation had been reserved. MR. SERGENT reserved the right to bring forward these proposals.

The CHAIRMAN, in the name of the British Delegation and of LORD SUMNER, Chairman of the First Sub-Committee, called attention to the reservations made at the meetings of the Sub-Committee by the British Delegation.

MR. VAN DEN HEUVEL (*Belgium*) stated that, when the list of Categories of Damage had been completed, he had asked whether the two following classes of damage were included therein:

(1) The loss suffered in consequence of failure to inscribe in the budget various revenues received:

(2) The loss suffered in consequence of the appropriation of part of the receipts to expenditure contrary to international law.

In the Sub-Committee there had been hesitation, not as to the admissibility of such damage, but, in the absence of express mention thereof, as to the category in which it should be placed. In order to avoid all misunderstanding, the Belgian Delegation expressly made reserves on the subject of these classes of damage.

MR. AFFONSO COSTA (*Portugal*) requested, in the name of the Portuguese Delegation, that mention should be made of the reservations formulated by it.

The CHAIRMAN considered that three methods of procedure were possible:

(1) To adopt *en bloc* the report with the reservations which had been formulated.

(2) To reserve further discussion.

(3) To await the reports of the two other Sub-Committees in order to examine the three reports together.

He asked the Commission to express its views.

MR. LEBRUN (*France*), in the momentary absence of LORD SUMNER, the Chairman of the First Sub-Committee, stated that

---

* This question had been reserved, agreement not having been reached upon it. The method of valuation for this class of damage had also not been decided.

the report presented, although merely a provisional report, was the result of very detailed labor. As the text had been for several days in the hands of the Delegates, he proposed that the Commission should adopt the first course suggested by the CHAIRMAN.

Messrs. OLCHOWSKI (*Poland*), BENES (*Czecho-Slovak Republic*), VAN DEN HEUVEL (*Belgium*), DANIELOPOL (*Roumania*), AFFONSO COSTA (*Portugal*), STOYANOWITCH (*Serbia*) and MICHALACOPOULOS (*Greece*), supported this proposal while reserving all rights.

MR. VAN DEN HEUVEL (*Belgium*) pointed out that the provisional report in a special note *in fine* expressly reserved the rights of the various Delegations.

MR. AFFONSO COSTA (*Portugal*) proposed that the Commission should itself adopt this note contained in the report of the First Sub-Committee; and expressed the hope that the Peace Conference would adopt it in the same manner.

MR. DULLES (*U. S. A.*) stated that the American Delegation desired to record a general reservation as to what items of damage included in the report of the First Sub-Committee should be made the subject of a claim against the enemy States.

Adoption of Report

The CHAIRMAN declared the report of the First Sub-Committee to be adopted, subject to the reservations which had been made.

Second Sub-Committee

The CHAIRMAN then asked if the Second Sub-Committee was in a position to present its report.

LORD CUNLIFFE (*British Empire*) explained that, in consequence of the numerous difficulties which it had encountered, the Sub-Committee had not yet been able to draw up a report. He announced that he had prepared a draft which would be discussed in the course of the afternoon, and that this draft could without doubt be submitted to the Commission on the following day.

MR. SERGENT (*France*) stated that he had introduced two articles before the Financial Commission, which the latter had held to be outside its competence and had considered ought to be submitted to the Second Sub-Committee of the Commission on Reparation of Damage. He therefore submitted these two articles to the Commission on Reparation, in order to make certain that the question raised by them would be discussed.

Third Sub-Committee

The CHAIRMAN stated that the Third Sub-Committee was not

at the moment in a position to present its report, as its action depended upon the stage reached by the work of the other Sub-Committees.

Belgian Priority

MR. VAN DEN HEUVEL (*Belgium*) read a declaration upon the special situation of Belgium as regarded its right to indemnity. This exceptional situation necessitated a preferential treatment. MR. VAN DEN HEUVEL recalled PRESIDENT WILSON'S Seventh Point and the promises made on 14 February, 1916, by the Powers guaranteeing the neutrality of Belgium. He laid stress upon the dangers which must result for Belgium from inadequate reparation, and insisted that complete reparation must be accorded to her.

MR. STOYANOWITCH (*Serbia*) announced that, following the example of the Belgian Delegation, the Serbian Delegation would present a Memorandum upon the question of priority of claims.

MR. DANIELOPOL (*Roumania*) reminded the Commission that the motion presented by the French Delegation,[†] upon which no decision had yet been taken, had raised this question of priority. He considered that the question was one of the utmost importance to those countries which had directly suffered from invasion. The immediate problem was to decide whether the question lay within the competence of the Commission on Reparation.

The CHAIRMAN replied that there was nothing to prevent the Commission from examining the question; but he pointed out that the Council of Four was studying the question for itself, and that in such conditions it would be illusory for the Commission on Reparation to attempt to arrive at any result.

The next meeting was fixed for Tuesday, 8 April, at 3 P. M.

The meeting adjourned at 12 noon.

L.-L. KLOTZ,
Chairman.

JEROME D. GREENE,
S. PEEL,
CH. DE LASTEYRIE,
F. FOBERTI,
  Secretaries.

---

† "The right of the Allied and Associated Powers is all-inclusive. The enemy must make good all damage, an order of priority being reserved for certain claims."—Minutes of Eighth Meeting.

ANNEX

INTERIM REPORT

(Presented by the First Sub-Committee (Valuation of Damage).)

CATEGORIES OF DAMAGE FOR WHICH REPARATION
MAY BE DEMANDED

The following texts have been adopted, subject to reservations by certain Delegations which are stated in the footnotes.

FIRST PART

PRIVATE DAMAGE

CATEGORY A

Immovables

Chapter I.—DAMAGE CAUSED BY THE TWO GROUPS OF BELLIGER-ENTS IN EVERY THEATRE OF OPERATIONS.

Destruction, deterioration or depreciation of immovable property, on land or sea, belonging to private persons (natural or artificial) and to public persons other than the State.

1. Means employed:

The destruction, deterioration or depreciation may be the result either of an act of war or of the fact of invasion, *as:*

(*a*) Bombardment by gun or aircraft on land or sea;

(*b*) Voluntary or involuntary action of troops (including lodging, billeting, etc.);

(*c*) Defensive or offensive measures and measures pertaining thereto (including inundations, etc.);

(*d*) Torpedoes and submarine mines;

(*e*) Deterioration resulting from use by the enemy, felling and digging up;

(*f*) Requisitions, expropriations, etc.

2. Objects of destruction or deterioration:

(*a*) Land, forests, orchards and plantations, deposits, mines, quarries, roads, canals, railways in general, electric lines and conduits (telephone, telegraph or power), water supply (pipe lines, drains, works of all kinds, etc.);

(*b*) Private structures of all kinds, and all public structures, other than those belonging to the State, buildings or monuments, etc.—artistic property included.

Chapter II.—DAMAGE OTHER THAN THAT PROVIDED FOR IN CHAPTER I ABOVE WHICH MAY HAVE BEEN CAUSED IN ALLIED OR ENEMY COUNTRIES.

Damage caused to immovable property:

(*a*) In enemy territory by any act ordered or committed by enemy authority or population;

(*b*) In enemy territory or in invaded or occupied territory by the application of laws, or by any act whatsoever under enemy authority, relating to seizures, requisitions, sequestrations and liquidation of sequestrated property.

CATEGORY B

Movables

Chapter I.—DAMAGE CAUSED BY THE TWO GROUPS OF BELLIGERENTS IN EVERY THEATRE OF OPERATIONS.

1. Causes of damage.

All the causes referred to in clause 1 of Chapter I above, as well as all removals, with or without color of right, all thefts, forced sales, confiscations, or similar measures.

2. Objects of damage.

(*a*) Equipment and furnishings of private structures and public structures other than those belonging to the State, machinery and tools, articles of furniture, clothes, linen and personal effects of all sorts, art objects, raw and other materials, merchandise, live stock and animals of all kinds, crops, manufactured and non-manufactured products, provisions, drawings, models, patents, trademarks, records, instruments and documents of all kinds, etc.

(*b*) Merchant vessels, fishing-boats, etc., navigating upon the sea or inland water-ways as well as their equipment, freights and cargo.

Chapter II.—DAMAGE OTHER THAN THAT PROVIDED FOR IN CHAPTER I ABOVE WHICH MAY HAVE BEEN CAUSED IN ALLIED OR ENEMY COUNTRIES.

Damage caused anywhere to movables:

(*a*) In enemy territory by any act ordered or committed by enemy authority or population;

(*b*) In enemy territory or in invaded or occupied territory by the application of laws, or by any act whatsoever under enemy authority, relating to seizures, requisitions, sequestrations and liquidation of sequestrated property.

CATEGORY C

Miscellaneous Interests

Chapter I.—DAMAGE CAUSED BY THE TWO GROUPS OF BELLIGERENTS IN EVERY THEATRE OF OPERATIONS.

1. Causes of damage.

All causes referred to in clause 1 of Chapter I, Categories A and B above, as well as illegal or *ex parte* sentences of all kinds and every abolition or suspension by the enemy of laws or codes in force in invaded or occupied territories.

2. Objects of damage.

(*a*) Shares and securities of all sorts, coupons;

(*b*) Requisition or hiring of labor or service;

(*c*) Expenditure incurred under any form whatsoever by any public authority fulfilling an obligation (other than the State) for the food supply, transport or relief of the populations of invaded or occupied territories;

(*d*) Injury caused to industrial property by the discovery or use of special processes of manufacture, patents or special methods;*

(*e*) Losses to trade caused by the disclosure of business books or ledgers and of public or private correspondence or records—and in general all documents or information not of a public nature—as well as by the use made of such documents and information. Losses caused by the new competition set up through the knowledge of such documents and information;*

(*f*) Loss caused to any person who has been deprived, wholly or partially, as a direct consequence of the operations of war or of the measures taken by the enemy, and without compensation from new sources of revenue, of the exercise of his proprietary rights, his occupation, or generally of opportunity to work or to obtain fair remuneration for his work, during the whole period of such deprivation.

Chapter II.—THE SAME CLASS OF DAMAGE AS UNDER CHAPTER II OF CATEGORY B ABOVE.

CATEGORY D

Exactions of a Financial Character

Chapter I.—DAMAGE CAUSED BY THE TWO GROUPS OF BELLIGERENTS IN EVERY THEATRE OF OPERATIONS.

Destruction or disappearance of currency as a direct consequence of the causes referred to in Section 2 above.

Taxes, imposts, contributions of war, fines, levies in cash of all kinds, imposed by the enemy, thefts of currency by the enemy,— including balances of accounts transferred and assets converted into "bons," loans or other stock,—forced subscriptions and

* This category was accepted only under the reservation that its application should be limited to the practical possibilities of the case.

expenses imposed by the enemy upon individuals or corporations; issue, falsification, alteration or depreciation by the act of the enemy of bank-notes, "bons" or monetary instruments of any kind.

Chapter II.—THE SAME CLASS OF DAMAGE AS UNDER CHAPTER II, CATEGORIES B AND C ABOVE.

CATEGORY E

Damage to Persons

Chapter I.—DAMAGE CAUSED BY THE TWO GROUPS OF BELLIGERENTS IN EVERY THEATRE OF OPERATIONS.[2]

1. Damage caused to civilian victims of acts of war (bombardment on land, on sea or from aircraft and all the consequences of operations of war) or to persons claiming under them:

(*a*) To the surviving wife or husband, orphans, descendants or parents, or persons claiming under them;

(*b*) To mutilated, wounded or sick.

2. Damage caused to civilian victims of acts, cruelties, violence or maltreatment committed or ordered by the enemy or to persons claiming under them:

(*a*) To persons shot, put to death or dead from the consequences of maltreatment;

(*b*) To persons exposed by the enemy to the fire of the Allied troops;

(*c*) To persons injured in life or health as a consequence of imprisonment, deportation, internment or evacuation;

(*d*) To persons who have suffered accidental death or injury, or have become infirm or sick, in consequence of forced labor.

3. Damage resulting from all acts injurious to health or capacity for work or to honor.

4. Damage caused to every person forced to engage in any occupation contrary to the interests of his country, without injury to life, health or capacity for work.[3]

Chapter II.—DAMAGE WHICH MAY HAVE BEEN CAUSED IN ALLIED OR ENEMY COUNTRIES OUTSIDE OF EVERY THEATRE OF OPERATIONS OF THE TWO GROUPS OF BELLIGERENTS.

Damage resulting from any injury to life, health or the capacity to work of interned civilians.

Damage caused:

[2] Article I of Document 225 follows this chapter in a general way.
[3] Section 18 of the preceding draft.

(*a*) To victims of explosions in war factories;

(*b*) To victims of accidents while working in such factories.[4]

SECOND PART

DAMAGE TO THE STATE

Chapter I.—ALL DAMAGES ENUMERATED IN PART I ABOVE WHICH HAVE BEEN SUFFERED BY THE STATE IN ITS NON-MILITARY PROPERTY AND ITS OWN RESOURCES.

Avoiding any duplication of claims for damage to individuals or corporations other than the State.

Including:

1. The extraordinary expenditure which the State has been obliged to bear in consequence of invasion or occupation, in so far as such expenses have not been included in other claims.†

2. Loss resulting from the theft of stamps and articles which are the subject of State monopolies, from their removal or their sale at prices lower than those established by law; and loss resulting from the failure to collect taxes, imposts and other revenues due to the State in occupied territory or in the zone of operations, in so far as such non-collection has not been balanced by a reduction in charges, and in so far as no material for taxation from which the State could recover such losses has been created anew by the admission of individual claims.‡

3. Allowances to refugees, to persons evacuated and to all persons who have been deprived, wholly or partially, as a direct consequence of the operations of war or of the measures taken by the enemy, of the exercise of their proprietary rights or occupation, or generally of opportunity to work or to obtain fair remuneration for their work.

4. Expenses incurred, under whatsoever form, by the State or by any corporation or individual, intervening for the account and with the authority of the State, for the food supply, transport or relief of the populations of invaded or occupied territories.

---

† The British Delegation did not accept this category.

‡ The following Delegations did not accept this category: viz., British Empire, Japan and Portugal. The Delegation of the United States reserved its opinion on the question of principle.

---

[4] Section 19 of the preceding draft.

Chapter II.—EXPENDITURE OF THE STATE OR OF ITS POSSESSIONS OR COLONIES.[5]

A. Pensions, allowances and bonuses of every kind to military victims of the war or persons claiming under them:

1. To victims of acts of war or persons claiming under them:

(*a*) Widows, orphans, descendants or parents or persons claiming under them.

(*b*) Mutilated, wounded, sick and invalided.

2. To prisoners of war injured in life or health as a consequence of acts, cruelties, violence or maltreatment committed or ordered by the enemy.

B. Cost of assistance by the State to prisoners of war. Allowances to families of mobilized persons.

C. Other war costs.

All expenditures or charges resulting from the state of war imposed upon the Allied and Associated Powers.

Expenses of maintenance by the Allied States of enemy prisoners of war, officers and men, and of interned persons.

METHODS OF VALUATION OF DAMAGE

The following texts have been adopted, subject to reservations by certain Delegations, which are stated in the footnotes.

FIRST PART

GENERAL PRINCIPLES

It is understood throughout that claims cannot be admitted, under whatever categories, so as to involve payment twice over for the same damage, or payment to two persons of whatever sort for one injury.

Where injury is caused by acts for which the enemy Powers are responsible, the damage to be claimed will include all the natural and necessary consequences of those acts.

Claims are not admissible which are incapable of being estimated with reasonable certainty by some means or other of proof, whether direct and specific or statistical and general.

Claims shall have regard only to net losses, after deducting any values which may stand to the credit of the parties interested.

Statistical methods of computation and evaluation may be resorted to, in default of direct evidence of value or for other

[5] Article II of Document 225 follows this chapter in a general way.

sufficient reasons, subject to the application of proper methods for verification and corroboration.

The cost of restoration of things injured, whether movables or immovables, does not extend to the cost of substituting for the things injured other things of a more expensive or valuable character, or to rebuilding with better materials or on an enlarged scale.

Claims ought to be supported by credible testimony with reasonable certainty, but it rests with the Powers concerned to determine in the first instance the particular form in which such testimony is to be admitted.

SECOND PART

METHODS OF VALUATION

It will be the concern of the Allied and Associated Powers which have suffered damage, to set forth and evaluate the damage which the enemy will be required to make good, each nation having regard to its own case.

The valuations thus established, in support of claims to be filed, shall conform to general and uniform rules as set forth in the following paragraphs.

The general rules set forth in the following paragraphs apply exclusively to claims which are to be made on the enemy, and do not necessarily govern the relations of the Allied and Associated States as between themselves, nor the relations of each State to its subjects.

The registration and valuation of claims referred to in the preceding paragraph shall not be definitive until they have been verified by the Allied and Associated Powers.

Valuations of damage shall be made with careful regard to placing every person having the right to reparation in a situation as nearly as possible identical with that in which he would have found himself if he had not sustained the damage resulting from the state of war imposed by the enemy Powers upon the Allied and Associated Powers.

The valuations made shall cover all the natural and necessary consequences of the acts giving rise to the claims for damages.§

Whatever the procedure adopted for the classification of categories of damage, or for the registration and valuation of claims,

§ Paragraph adopted as reaffirming the principle, without in any way modifying the application, of the paragraphs relating to general principles.

it shall never be possible to obtain payment twice for the same damage, either wholly or in part, whether to the same person or to different persons.§

Claims should be supported, either by direct proof as to the reality and the amount of the damage suffered, or by any other acceptable evidence or credible testimony, the Allied and Associated Powers having the exclusive right to determine the form of evidence and the conditions under which it shall be admitted.§

Valuations shall be expressed in the currency each interested Power may consider it proper to adopt, without in any way prejudging the question of the currency in which payment shall be made by the enemy; and each Power shall state the rate of exchange upon which its calculation is based, so as to permit full verification.

The amount of a claim shall not be more than enough for the replacement of property or objects destroyed, whether movables or immovables, by other property of corresponding quality or importance, it being understood, however, that this provision does not refer to increases in value resulting from a rise in prices, or to the replacement of property or objects destroyed or damaged by similar property or objects in [the] new state.§

Destruction, deterioration and all damage caused to real or personal property, on land or at sea, which property is of such a nature that it can be reconstructed, replaced or repaired, shall be valued at the amount of the estimated cost of such reconstruction, replacement or repair on the date of the conclusion of peace; but in cases where the application of this rule would expose the persons injured to the risks of fluctuation of market prices, damage caused to the property above mentioned shall be evaluated at its value within a reasonable time after the time of the loss or damage, except in the case, provided for in the paragraph below, where there has been an actual replacement by purchase.

The cost of such reconstruction, replacement or repair is arrived at, wherever possible, by applying to the corresponding pre-war cost an appropriate co-efficient, calculated for each category of property in accordance with the market price at the date prescribed by the preceding paragraph in respect to materials, labor and all other factors to be considered.[6]

---

§ Paragraph adopted as reaffirming the principle, without in any way modifying the application, of the paragraphs relating to general principles.

---

[6] Section 21 of Document 486 (*first column*) precedes this paragraph.

In the case of labor hired or purchases made for reconstruction, replacement or repair, before the date of the conclusion of peace, the valuation may be based upon actual cost.

In case the same property or object has undergone repeated and successive damage, all labor and purchases which have actually gone to reconstruction, replacement or repair, are to be taken into account in the valuation.

Destruction, deterioration and all damage caused to real or personal property not susceptible of reconstruction, replacement or repair, are to be valued by reference to the amount which the property would have been worth at the date of the conclusion of peace, deduction to be made proportionately for salvage, if any.

Damage resulting from levies or seizures of sums of money, under whatever guise, including forced subscriptions, or of assets of any kind expressed in cash, and damage resulting from expenses incurred, for example for the relief of the population of invaded territories or of interned civilians, are taken at the capital value of the sum involved, with interest at 6 per cent from the date of the damage to the date of the conclusion of peace, the right being fully reserved to regulate in any manner determined all questions as to reciprocal claims or debts arising from pre-war contracts between subjects of the enemy Powers and subjects of the Allied and Associated Powers.

Damage resulting from the seizure, loss or destruction of securities is valued on the basis of their average price on the Bourse during the first six months of 1914, or, in the case of securities issued after 1 July, 1914, on the basis of their issue price, provided that such price be not lower than the average for the first quarter of 1919; there shall be added the value of coupons, interest or income in arrears, which the owners would have been able to realize up to the date of the conclusion of peace, if they had remained in possession of their securities.‖

Damage resulting from the deprivation, wholly or in part, of the exercise of any proprietary right is valued on the basis of the average net receipts or income from such property at the time of damage, for the whole period during which such deprivation shall have continued, both down to the date of the conclusion of peace and until such reasonable time after the said date as may be deemed necessary to secure the cessation of such deprivation. The valuation will be made by the application of a coefficient, appropriate to the cases and periods in question, to the average net receipts or income

‖ The Delegations of the British Empire and Japan did not accept this paragraph.

of the three calendar years, the three fiscal years or the three seasons last preceding the war. In such valuation account shall be taken of any new resources, or any subsidies, whose addition to the existing income of the parties interested may have furnished compensation, wholly or in part, for the loss suffered by them.

Damage resulting from the deprivation, wholly or in part, of the exercise of an occupation, or generally of opportunity to work or to obtain fair remuneration for work, is valued on the basis of the average wages or salaries of the parties interested at the time of the damage, for the whole period during which such deprivation shall have continued, both down to the date of the conclusion of peace and until such reasonable time after the said date as may be deemed necessary to secure the cessation of such deprivation. The valuation will be made by the application of a coefficient, appropriate to the cases and periods in question, to the average net wages or salaries for the three calendar years last preceding the war. In such valuation account shall be taken of any new resources, or any subsidies, whose addition to the existing income of the parties interested may have furnished compensation, wholly or in part, for the loss suffered by them.

Damage which consists in the disorganization of business houses, enterprises or professions, is valued on the basis of the cost of reorganization.

Damage caused to industrial property through the enemy's knowledge of special processes of manufacture, and the commercial damage resulting from the enemy's knowledge of books, correspondence and documents or information of a private nature, of all sorts, is to be valued in accordance with special rules agreed upon between the Allied and Associated Powers.

NOTE

Having concluded the first consideration of the Categories of Damage and Methods of Valuation, the Sub-Committee adopted the following resolution:

"It is understood that in adopting the principles and resolutions which have already been adopted, the Sub-Committee does not exclude the adoption of additional resolutions subsequently, or regard those already adopted as being exhaustive of all cases."

SUMNER,
Chairman of the First Sub-Committee.
31 March, 1919.

DOCUMENT 465

Plenary Commission: Minutes of the Fifteenth Meeting (Including Annex), April 8, 1919, 3 P. M.

[EOM, CRD, pp. 77-84. French stenographic minutes, PV, CRD, 934-43. The Annex to this meeting (pp. 80-84) is the First Interim Report of the Second Sub-committee, April 7, 1919, which was adopted at this meeting by the Plenary Commission. *It is not reprinted here.* For the text, see Annex I to Document 543.]

The Commission on Reparation of Damage met on Tuesday, 8 April, 1919, at 3 P. M., at the Ministry of Finance, MR. KLOTZ in the Chair.

Present: Messrs. McCORMICK and DULLES and GENERAL MC-KINSTRY (*U. S. A.*); MR. HUGHES, LORD SUMNER and LORD CUNLIFFE (*British Empire*); Messrs. KLOTZ, LOUCHEUR and LEBRUN (*France*); MR. D'AMELIO (*Italy*); Messrs. MORI, FUKAI and KIKUCHI (*Japan*); Messrs. VAN DEN HEUVEL and DESPRET (*Belgium*); Messrs. ROMANOS and MICHALACOPOULOS (*Greece*); Messrs. OLCHOWSKI and CHAMIEC (*Poland*); MR. FREIRE D'ANDRADE (*Portugal*); Messrs. DANIELOPOL and ZAHARIADE (*Roumania*); Messrs. STOYANOWITCH and PROTITCH (*Serbia*); MR. BENES (*Czecho-Slovak Republic*).[1]

The minutes of the 14th meeting were adopted without discussion.

The business on the Agenda was the presentation of the report of the Second Sub-Committee, which was distributed to the Delegates. (See Annex.)

MR. HUGHES (*British Empire*) considered that, having regard to the important character of this document, it would be wise to allow the Delegates to examine it carefully, particularly with a view to the alterations of detail which had been made in the course of yesterday's session of the Second Sub-Committee, at which the report had been adopted by the latter. After observations by LORD CUNLIFFE (*British Empire*), who pointed out the importance of adopting the report without undue delay, in order to be able to submit to the Peace Conference a report on this question of essential importance, MR. HUGHES' suggestion was agreed to, and the Commission adjourned for a short interval.

On the resumption of the sitting, the Chair was taken by the Vice-Chairman, MR. HUGHES (*British Empire*).

[1] According to the French minutes, Dulles, McKinstry, and Loucheur were absent; and Costa was present.

Figure for Total Reparation not Determined

The CHAIRMAN, referring to the section of the Report entitled "Method of Reasoning Employed," pointed out that no figure for the amount which should be paid by Germany in the period following upon the first eighteen months after the conclusion of peace was in fact specified in the Report, although the section in question appeared to contemplate such a statement of amount. Germany's ultimate liability was left to be determined by a Commission. In view of the danger that this projected Commission might be composed of persons inclined to be too lenient towards Germany, he expressed strongly his personal opinion that an amount should be specified which it would be impossible to reduce without the consent of the nations concerned.

LORD CUNLIFFE (*British Empire*), as Chairman of the Second Sub-Committee, explained that after careful consideration it had been impossible to agree as to a figure for the total amount which Germany would be able to pay; and that, therefore, it would serve no useful purpose to refer the Report back for insertion of such a figure. In conclusion, he urged strongly that the Report be adopted.

The CHAIRMAN considered that it might be wise to insert a figure, even although complete agreement was not attainable; if no figure was stated, he suggested that the passage to which he had referred should be redrafted.

LORD CUNLIFFE (*British Empire*) pointed out that the Report indirectly established a figure by its recommendation that the proposed Commission "shall be instructed and bound not to decide that the capacity of the Enemy Powers to pay will fall short of the full amount of the proved claims, unless and until the enemy Powers shall have imposed on their subjects taxation per head for the service of this debt at least as heavy as the highest taxation imposed on its subjects for the service of its debt by any Allied Power."

Payment in Kind

MR. BENES (*Czecho-Slovak Republic*) drew attention to the paragraph "Payment in Kind," which recommended that the Enemy Powers pay part of their reparation by deliveries of manufactured products. He urged that this provision might prove a double-edged weapon. If Germany was allowed to export manufactured articles on this basis to Allied States, she would exclude from their markets the exports of the other Allied States, whose workmen would thus in effect bear the burden of the indemnity. He urged that reparation by export of manufactures be limited to immediate deliveries; and considered that the paragraph should either be struck out or be redrafted in such a way as to limit it in the sense which he had indicated.

MR. DANIELOPOL (*Roumania*) supported the paragraph as it stood. The problem was whether Germany should pay or not. If the Allies expected to be paid, all possible means of payment must be allowed. To say to Germany, "You must pay us, but you shall not produce," involved a false conception. To propose that Germany should pay a certain number of billions *per annum* and at the same time to keep her frontiers closed was an economic absurdity. He agreed that Germany must not be allowed to compete with the exports of Allied States under the guise of reparation, but pointed out that any danger on this head was met by the recommendation of the Sub-Committee as to the establishment of a Committee of Control.

MR. BENES (*Czecho-Slovak Republic*), in reply to MR. DANIELOPOL, reaffirmed his fear that it would be dangerous to allow German products free entry into Allied countries.

Adoption of Report

LORD CUNLIFFE (*British Empire*) then formally proposed and MR. DANIELOPOL (*Roumania*) seconded the adoption of the Report.

The CHAIRMAN, in putting the motion to the vote, regretted that personally he must record his vote against it, as the Report contained no definite recommendation either as to the total sum obtainable from Germany or as to the period within which payment should be made.

MR. OLCHOWSKI (*Poland*) expressed regret that the First Sub-Committee had failed to fix a figure for the amount of the Allied claims, and the Second Sub-Committee to determine the amount obtainable from Germany.

A vote was then taken by Delegations.

The Delegations of the United States, France, Japan, Belgium, Greece, Portugal, Roumania and Serbia voted for the adoption of the Report.

The Delegations of Poland and the Czecho-Slovak Republic abstained from voting.[2]

The CHAIRMAN said that the British Delegation did not vote

---

[2] According to the French minutes, the Polish Delegation voted against the report.

either for the motion or against it. Two of the British Delegates were in favor of it, he himself opposed it.[3]

Reports to go to Council of Four

After a discussion in which LORD CUNLIFFE, the CHAIRMAN and MR. McCORMICK took part, it was agreed that the Secretariat be instructed to send immediately the Report of the Second Sub-Committee to the General Secretariat of the Peace Conference for submission to the Council of Four; that the Minutes of the present meeting be also sent at the earliest possible date for the information of the Council of Four; and that the Secretariat advise the General Secretariat of the intended submission of the Minutes.

On the proposal of MR. LEBRUN (*France*), seconded by LORD CUNLIFFE (*British Empire*), it was agreed that the Report of the First Sub-Committee, adopted at the previous meeting, together with the minutes of that meeting, be sent with the Report of the Second Sub-Commission to the General Secretariat for submission to the Council of Four.

Roumanian Bullion Deposited in Russia

MR. DANIELOPOL (*Roumania*) desired to lay before the Commission a question of great and immediate importance for Roumania. In 1916 Roumania had been forced for security to send her bullion reserves to Moscow. The Imperial Russian Government had given a receipt for this bullion and guaranteed its return; later the Allied Powers had given a corresponding guarantee. Subsequently there had likewise been sent to Russia the greater part of the securities owned by Roumania. The present state of Russia made it impossible to obtain the return, or even the promise of the return, of these deposits, although they were believed to be still intact. The Roumanian Delegation urged that, in the interest of their country and that of the guaranteeing Powers, some action should be taken to secure the restitution of this property, the total value of which exceeded 7,500 million francs.[4] It would perhaps be inadvisable at the moment to claim it as a category of damage against Germany, but he suggested that to make Germany guarantee its restitution might possibly have the effect of safeguarding it and securing its ultimate return.

MR. DANIELOPOL asked that by the Preliminaries of Peace the enemy should be bound to remit to Roumania an amount of gold

---

[3] According to the French minutes, the British Delegation was apparently two to one against the report, assuming that Hughes was considered opposed to it.

[4] According to the French minutes, 6,000 million francs.

equivalent to the deposits of gold and jewels which were guaranteed by the Allied Powers, and at the same time be bound to guarantee the restitution by Russia of the other deposits upon demanded [*demand*] by Roumania.

The CHAIRMAN considered that the Commission could not now discuss the important question raised by MR. DANIELOPOL, which in any case was perhaps rather a matter for the Financial Commission. He suggested that the Roumanian Delegation should submit the question to the latter Commission; and that, if it so desired, it should also send a Memorandum on the subject to the Secretariat of the Commission on Reparation,[5] which would be instructed to cause it to be submitted to the Council of Four.

The commission agreed to this procedure, it being understood that the position of the Roumanian Government would be fully stated in the Memorandum to be submitted.

The meeting adjourned at 6 P. M.

L.-L. KLOTZ,
Chairman.

JEROME D. GREENE,
S. PEEL,
CH. DE LASTEYRIE,
F. FOBERTI,
   Secretaries.

ANNEX

[*Not reprinted. See introductory note.*]

DOCUMENT 466

Plenary Commission: Minutes of the Sixteenth (and Final) Meeting (Including Annex), April 19, 1919, 5:30 P. M.

[EOM, CRD, pp. 85-95. This meeting is not included in the French minutes. The Annex to this meeting (pp. 86-95) is the Supplementary (or Second) Interim Report of the Second Subcommittee, April 18, 1919, which was adopted at this meeting by the Plenary Commission. *It is not reprinted here.* For the text (and citation to the French text), see Annex II to Document 543.]

[The] Commission on Reparation of Damage met on Saturday, 19 April, 1919, at 5.30 P. M., at the Ministry of Finance, MR. VAN DEN HEUVEL in the chair.

Present: Messrs. MCCORMICK and ROBINSON (*U. S. A.*); LORD SUMNER and LORD CUNLIFFE (*British Empire*); MR. SERGENT (*France*); MR. D'AMELIO (*Italy*); Messrs. FUKAI, KIKUCHI and

---

[5] According to the French minutes, to the Financial Commission.

TATSUMI (*Japan*); MR. VAN DEN HEUVEL (*Belgium*); Messrs. ROMANOS and MYLONAS (*Greece*); MR. MARKOWSKI (*Poland*); MR. MONIZ (*Portugal*); Messrs. DANIELOPOL and ZAHARIADE (*Roumania*); Messrs. STOYANOWITCH and SAVTCHITCH (*Serbia*); MR. SLAVIK (*Czecho-Slovak Republic*).

The minutes of the 15th meeting were approved.

Supplementary Interim Report of Second Sub-Committee

The CHAIRMAN presented the Supplementary Interim Report of the Second Sub-Committee (Financial Capacity of the Enemy States: their Means of Payment and Reparation), together with two additional documents, viz:—

(1) An article proposed for inclusion in the Peace Treaty by the Economic Commission and referred by it to the Second Sub-Committee.

(2) An "additional note" to the Report proposed by the American Delegation.

LORD CUNLIFFE (*British Empire*) explained the general purport of the Report, which was not based merely on the work of the last three meetings, but represented conclusions reached by thorough discussion during a long period. As regarded the two additional documents, he saw no reason why they should not be accepted and added to the Report. He formally proposed that the Report be adopted in order that the articles recommended for insertion in the Peace Treaty might at once be considered by the Drafting Commission of the Peace Conference.

The CHAIRMAN put the question as to the two additional documents, and the Commission accepted them.

The CHAIRMAN then put the question as to the Report as thus amended.

The Commission adopted the amended Report. The first additional document is incorporated therein as Clause E and the second as an "additional note" at the end of the Report.

The meeting adjourned at 6.15 P. M.

L.-L. KLOTZ,
Chairman.

JEROME D. GREENE,
S. PEEL,
CH. DE LASTEYRIE,
F. FOBERTI,
   Secretaries.

ANNEX

[*Not reprinted. See introductory note.*]

THE MINUTES OF THE FIRST SUBCOMMITTEE
(VALUATION OF DAMAGE)

DOCUMENT 467

First Subcommittee: Minutes of the First Meeting (Including Annex) February 15, 1919, 3:15 P. M.

[EOM, First Subcommittee, pp. 5–7. French stenographic minutes, PV, CRD, pp. 239-50. The minutes of the twenty-seven meetings of the First Subcommittee are bound into one book. In addition to the minutes, this book also contains the following:

Cover. "PRELIMINARY PEACE CONFERENCE, COMMISSION ON THE REPARATION OF DAMAGE, FIRST SUB-COMMITTEE, VALUATION OF DAMAGE, MINUTES. MEETINGS: 1st—15 FEBRUARY . . . 27th— 1 APRIL. PARIS, 1919."

Title Page. Same as Cover, except that "MINUTES" is omitted.

Page 3.   "COMMISSION ON REPARATION

"FIRST SUB-COMMITTEE
"VALUATION OF DAMAGE
"The Commission on Reparation of Damage resolved on 4 February, 1919 (see minutes of its second meeting) to appoint Sub-Committees, including 'Sub-Committee I, Valuation of Damage.' It was decided (see Annex to the minutes) that each Power should have a representative on the First Sub-Committee.

"The following were appointed to the Sub-Committee thus created:—
"United States of America.....................Mr. McCormick.
"British Empire................................Lord Sumner.
"France.......................................Mr. Lebrun.
"Italy...Mr. Chiesa.
"Japan..Mr. Mori.
"Belgium.............................Mr. Van den Heuvel.
"Greece.............................Mr. Michalacopoulos.
"Poland...........................Mr. Olchowski.
"Portugal*......................Mr. Dos Santos Viegas.
"Roumania.............................Mr. Danielopol.
"Serbia...Mr. Savtchitch.
"Czecho-Slovak Republic..........................Mr. Benes.
"The Rules as to substitution of Delegates and admission of experts with consultative voice adopted by the Commission on the Reparation of Damage (see minutes, pages 11 and 12) apply also to the Sub-Committee.

"*Portugal represented after 24 February. See minutes of Plenary Commission, Tenth Meeting. [*Footnote in original.*]"

Last Two Pages. "TABLE OF CONTENTS . . ."]

The First Sub-Committee of the Commission on Reparation of Damage (Valuation of Damage) met on Saturday, 15 February,

1919, at 3.15 P. M., at the Ministry of Finance, LORD SUMNER in the Chair.[1]

Present: MR. MCCORMICK (*U. S. A.*); LORD SUMNER (*British Empire*); MR. LEBRUN (*France*); MR. CHIESA (*Italy*); MR. MORI (*Japan*); MR. VAN DEN HEUVEL (*Belgium*); MR. MICHALACOPOULOS (*Greece*); MR. OLCHOWSKI (*Poland*); MR. DANIELOPOL (*Roumania*); MR. SAVTCHITCH (*Serbia*); MR. OSUSKI (*Czecho-Slovak Republic*).

Election of Officers

Upon the motion of MR. VAN DEN HEUVEL (*Belgium*) the meeting proceeded to the election of officers, and upon the motion of LORD SUMNER (*British Empire*), seconded by MR. LEBRUN (*France*), MR. VAN DEN HEUVEL (*Belgium*) was unanimously elected Chairman. After expressing his thanks MR. VAN DEN HEUVEL regretted that the pressure of work would not permit him to accept the office. He then nominated LORD SUMNER, who was chosen unanimously. LORD SUMNER took the Chair, and expressed his thanks to the Committee. He then proposed that a Vice-Chairman be elected. MR. VAN DEN HEUVEL proposed MR. CHIESA (*Italy*), who was elected by a unanimous vote. MR. CHIESA accepted the election with thanks.

Organization

The CHAIRMAN submitted to the meeting a proposal for its organization presented by MR. VAN DEN HEUVEL (*Belgium*). (See Annex.) In the subsequent discussion the various articles of this document were accepted.

Secretaries

MR. E. MINOST was designated Secretary by the Secretariat of the Commission.

MR. MCKINNON WOOD and MR. BOURQUIN were chosen assistant secretaries of the Sub-Committee.

Suggested Programme of Work. Categories and Methods of Valuation

MR. CHIESA (*Italy*) proposed that all Delegates should present a statement of their claims, classified by categories.

MR. OLCHOWSKI (*Poland*) asked that there be established a basis of valuation common to all countries.

MR. LEBRUN (*France*) urged that the expression "valuation of damage" be clearly defined. He considered that it meant, not the determination of figures, but the drawing up of a list of (1) damages by categories, and (2) the principles of valuation according to which

---

[1] According to the French minutes, Van den Heuvel was in the chair.

their sum total should be estimated. He pointed out, furthermore, in reply to an observation by MR. OLCHOWSKI (*Poland*) that no argument could be drawn from the French law for maintaining that France should limit her claims to direct damages.

After observations by Messrs. MICHALACOPOULOS (*Greece*), LEBRUN (*France*) and OLCHOWSKI (*Poland*), the CHAIRMAN moved that each Delegation present a Memorandum containing a list of damages, classified by categories, stating the method followed in valuation, and whenever possible giving approximate figures, in order to bring out the relative importance of the various claims.

After MR. LEBRUN (*France*) and the CHAIRMAN had developed their different points of view,

Figures of Claims for Damage

MR. McCORMICK (*U. S. A.*) presented a motion calling for lists of claims, supported by detailed figures, and providing for a sub-committee of experts to classify and verify the claims presented by each country.[2] Messrs. DANIELOPOL (*Roumania*), VAN DEN HEUVEL (*Belgium*) and OLCHOWSKI (*Poland*) insisted on the impossiblity of such detailed statements of total claims being furnished by their respective countries. MR. McCORMICK urged the necessity of reaching at least approximate estimates, which could be laid before the Commission and would thus aid in determining methods of valuation. Messrs. VAN DEN HEUVEL (*Belgium*) and CHIESA (*Italy*) agreed that it was possible to finish certain figures— in some cases precise, in others approximate. The CHAIRMAN urged that the Delegates make every effort to accomplish this, in view of the importance of having figures as soon as possible. MR. BAYKITCH (*Expert for Serbia*) declared himself unable to appreciate the usefulness of partial figures. The CHAIRMAN pointed out that partial figures would serve at least to indicate the relative importance of different claims.

After various observations by Messrs. DANIELOPOL (*Roumania*), McCORMICK (*U. S. A.*), OLCHOWSKI (*Poland*) and BAYKITCH (*Serbia*) and the CHAIRMAN, MR. LEBRUN (*France*) urged again the adoption of the procedure he had proposed, in order to avoid a confusion which would be fatal to the progress of the work of the Committee.

Memoranda to be Presented

The CHAIRMAN, summarizing the discussion, then declared that

---

[2] For McCormick's motion, see PV, CRD, pp. 244-45. This is very close to the wording of Document 118.

the sense of the meeting was in favor of first determining the categories and the method of valuation for each. He therefore asked each Delegation to present as soon as possible a Memorandum drawn up on this basis.

The next meeting was fixed for Monday, 19 February, at 3 P. M. The meeting adjourned at 5.30 P. M.

SUMNER,
Chairman.

E. MINOST,
Secretary.

ANNEX

ORGANIZATION OF THE FIRST SUB-COMMITTEE

1. The First Sub-Committee shall be organized as follows:
   (a) A Chairman and a Vice-Chairman, one English-speaking, the other French-speaking.
   (b) A Secretary appointed by the Secretariat, and two Assistant Secretaries, one English-speaking, the other French-speaking.

2. The official texts shall be written in the language or languages agreed upon by the Conference.

3. The technical advisers and experts appointed by the Powers to take part in the work of the Sub-Committee shall have a consultative voice.

4. The minutes of the meetings shall be written both in English and in French.

DOCUMENT 468

First Subcommittee: Minutes of the Second Meeting, February 17, 1919, 3:15 P. M.

[EOM, First Subcommittee, pp. 8-9. French stenographic minutes, PV, CRD, pp. 251-60.]

The First Sub-Committee of the Commission on Reparation of Damage (Valuation of Damage) met on Monday, 17 February, 1919, at 3.15 P. M., at the Ministry of Finance, LORD SUMNER in the Chair.

Present: GENERAL MCKINSTRY (*U. S. A.*); LORD SUMNER (*British Empire*); MR. LEBRUN (*France*); MR. MORI (*Japan*); MR. VAN DEN HEUVEL (*Belgium*); MR. MICHALACOPOULOS (*Greece*); MR. OLCHOWSKI (*Poland*); MR. DANIELOPOL (*Roumania*); MR. SAVTCHITCH (*Serbia*); MR. OSUSKI (*Czecho-Slovak Republic*).[1]

---

[1] According to the French minutes, McCormick (instead of McKinstry), Jouasset, Bajkić, and Beneš were also present; and Savčić was absent.

The minutes of the first meeting were adopted.

Discussion of Methods of Valuation

The CHAIRMAN pointed out that the Agenda for the meeting called for the discussion of methods of valuation of damage.

MR. OLCHOWSKI (*Poland*)[2] drew a distinction between two categories of damage: (1) damage to property; (2) damage to persons. For determining the nature of the claims arising from each of these categories, it would be necessary to fix at once a basis of valuation common to all countries, for the purpose of obtaining ultimately an equitable distribution of the available assets.

MR. LEBRUN (*France*) presented to the Sub-Committee MR. JOUASSET, Technical Adviser for France.

Projected French Legislation

MR. JOUASSET explained to the meeting the procedure adopted by French legislation for determining categories of damage and the methods of valuation. The French Bill dealt only with claims for certain, material and direct damage. This did not limit the claims which France might put forward, nor did it prejudge in any way the international problem now before the Commission. The Bill contemplated five categories of damage:

1. Requisitions of every kind under enemy authority.

2. Removal of personal property (biens meubles).

3. Deterioration and destruction of real property (biens immeubles).

4. Damage resulting from organizing certain areas for defense.

5. Damage to fishing vessels.

Two factors were recognized for purposes of valuation of real property: (1) pre-war selling value; (2) addition for increased cost of replacement (the amount to be added to the pre-war value in order to make the property substantially what it was before).

By "pre-war selling value" was to be understood the cost of construction at the outbreak of the war, less depreciation. The element of depreciation was not applied to personal property (biens meubles); on the other hand, the factor of the increased cost of replacement was particularly important for one category, namely, raw materials.

As to the procedure followed in valuation, the Bill had created a two-fold organization: (1) an Adjustment Committee (Commissions Cantonales); (2) a Judicial body (War-Damage Tribunals). Both of these proceeded according to certain categories of damage;

---

[2] According to the French minutes, Danielopol.

the bases of valuation were determined in each region according to prices fixed by local expert committees. Any questions of law were referred to the ordinary Courts.

This task of valuation was long and difficult, and it would not be until a considerable part of the work of these organizations had been accomplished that figures of any value could be provided.

Before the enemy could furnish reparation, the French State would have to make a great financial effort. First, in order to recompense the injured parties without delay, it would have to advance the reparation due to them. Next, it would have to assume the charges which would normally rest upon the community at large. Besides payment in money, the French Bill provided for payment in kind, which should be on as an extensive a scale as possible.

MR. JOUASSET, finally, pointed out that a whole series of damages remained outside of the provisions of the French Bill; notably, a certain number of injuries to property (cost of repairing the surface of land, repairing ways of communication, razed towns (re-establishing landed rights): so-called indirect damages (loss of opportunity for profit or for production); and injuries to persons.

Figures of Claims for Damage

After observations by Messrs. BAYKITCH (*Expert for Serbia*), LEBRUN (*France*) and DANIELOPOL (*Roumania*), the CHAIRMAN put certain questions in regard to MR. JOUASSET'S statement:

1. Would the French Government be able to insert precise figures in the Treaty of Peace?

MR. LEBRUN (*France*) replied that he thought it preferable to state in the Peace Treaty only the categories of damage to be made good and the system of valuation. Furthermore, the amount of payments in kind would be so uncertain that the total payments to be made in money could not be exactly calculated.

2. What were the claims with which the French Bill did not deal?

MR. JOUASSET replied that they included, for example, all classes of damage not susceptible of treatment by payments to individuals, all indirect damage and all damage to persons.

Memoranda of Categories of Damage

Upon the proposal of the CHAIRMAN, supported by Messrs. LEBRUN (*France*) and BENES (*Czecho-Slovak Republic*), it was decided that the Delegations should submit to the Secretariat before Thursday next, 20 February, memoranda giving the categories of damage to be claimed by their respective countries. MR. DANIELOPOL (*Roumania*) suggested that these various Memoranda include also general observations on the subject, which was agreed to. The Memoranda were directed to be co-ordinated by the Secretariat under the direction of the CHAIRMAN.

The next meeting was fixed for Monday, 24 February, at 3 P. M. The meeting adjourned at 5.15 P. M.

SUMNER,
Chairman.

E. MINOST,
Secretary.

DOCUMENT 469

First Subcommittee: Minutes of the Third Meeting, February 24, 1919, 3:45 P. M.

[EOM, First Subcommittee, pp. 10-12. French stenographic minutes, PV, CRD, pp. 261-73.]

The First Sub-Committee of the Commission on Reparation of Damage (Valuation of Damage) met on Monday, 24 February, 1919, at 3.45 P. M., at the Ministry of Finance, LORD SUMNER in the Chair.

Present: MR. McCORMICK (*U. S. A.*); LORD SUMNER (*British Empire*); MR. LEBRUN (*France*); MR. CHIESA (*Italy*); MR. NAGAOKA (*Japan*); MR. VAN DEN HEUVEL (*Belgium*); MR. MICHALACOPOULOS (*Greece*); MR. OLCHOWSKI (*Poland*); MR. SPIRITU SANCTU LIMA (*Portugal*); MR. DANIELOPOL (*Roumania*); MR. SAVTCHITCH (*Serbia*).[1]

The minutes of the second meeting were adopted.

Distinction between Direct Damage, Indirect Damage and War Costs

The CHAIRMAN explained that owing to the detailed character of the Memoranda on Categories of Damage presented by the various Delegations, it had been impossible for the Secretariat to complete the proposed tabulation in time for the meeting. On most points a complete agreement would be possible, but two main points of difficulty could be foreseen: (1) the distinction between direct and indirect damage; (2) war costs. Under the head of indirect damage there were often items which were questions of detail rather than of principle (such as loss of profits from the destruction of a building); other items raised wide questions of principle (for example, losses through a rise in the cost of living). Similarly, the expression "costs of the war" covered claims which

---

[1] According to the French minutes, Beneš was also present.

from another point of view might be regarded as damage to individuals; for example, bodily injuries to soldiers or requisitions of property. The question of war costs was thus to a large extent a question of language and less a question of substance than would at first appear.

MR. CHIESA (*Italy*) urged that the Committee avoid attempting to establish an absolute distinction between direct and indirect damage. In some cases, in fact, the indirect damage was more important than the direct. MR. CHIESA then explained that while claims arising from an increase in the cost of living were difficult to deal with as a general question, there were certain definite categories of specific expenses on that ground which could be presented. These claims were not vague; and furthermore they were the consequence of illegal acts in the conduct of the war. Such, for example, was the claim for extra freight costs presented by Italy.

MR. BENES (*Czecho-Slovak Republic*) noted that, in the case of his Government, it would be easy to distinguish between reparations and war costs,—the latter having for the most part been incurred outside of the country.

MR. OLCHOWSKI (*Poland*) urged that it would be possible to make a satisfactory distinction between direct and indirect damage by following the definition commonly laid down in law: claims for indirect damage should be limited to losses which were the immediate consequence of the wrongful act.

Messrs. BAYKITCH (*Expert for Serbia*) and VAN DEN HEUVEL (*Belgium*) insisted on the impossibility of establishing a distinction in principle between direct and indirect damage.

The Chairman thought that, while a philosophical distinction between direct and indirect damage was doubtless difficult to make, there was in fact general agreement that certain categories of indirect damage must be excluded. Existing systems of law applied tests, expressed in such phrases as "natural and necessary" consequences or "certain and immediate" consequences, to determine the limits of compensation for injuries. Corresponding tests could probably be usefully applied to the categories of damage claimed in the various Memoranda. The CHAIRMAN suggested, as a further test, that claims of too vague a character to be even approximately evaluated, or claims whose causal connection with the war could not be clearly demonstrated, might be excluded.

Provisional Figures of Claims for Damage

The CHAIRMAN then reminded the Committee that it had been

directed by the Main Commission to present at least an Interim Report within eight days. In view of this he desired to submit to the various Delegations certain questions to be answered by the day of the next meeting. Any Delegation was, of course, at liberty not to answer all or any of the questions, but he hoped that all Delegations would be prepared to answer at least the question No. 3 in the affirmative, so that the Committee might be able to present a minimum gross figure for the total claim against Germany.

The questions were:

1. Are you in a position within the next few days to ascertain and to state exactly the amount which you claim, and, if so, can you do so for all categories or only for some categories, indicating them?

2. Are you in a position within the next few days to state approximately and by estimates according to the various methods of statistical computation the amount which you claim? If so, kindly indicate the particular method of estimate or computation adopted.

3. If you are not in a position to present definite amounts by which you would be willing to be bound under either of the two heads, (1) and (2) above mentioned, are you in a position to state within the next few days, for report to the Plenary Commission and for the assistance of the Peace Conference:

    (a) A minimum which you feel assured your claims, when precisely ascertained hereafter, are certain to reach and even exceed; and

    (b) A maximum which you do not contemplate that your claims will exceed hereafter in any event?

Under question No. 3 it is understood that the Delegates are not asked to divide their minima and maxima into categories or subjects, or to consider any question except total figures, which could be added together and presented for the guidance of the authorities concerned.

MR. LEBRUN (*France*) recalled the previous decision of the Committee as to its mode of procedure and proposed: (1) that the Committee should not meet until the tabulation of the various Memoranda was ready for discussion; (2) that each Delegation prepare a Memorandum on Methods of Valuation.

The CHAIRMAN pointed out that there was no contradiction between his questions and MR. LEBRUN'S proposals.

After observations by MR. CHIESA (*Italy*) and MR. LEBRUN (*France*), MR. LEBRUN'S proposals were agreed to, and it was decided that the Delegations should reply to the CHAIRMAN'S questions if they found it possible to do so.

It was then agreed that the next meeting should be called for Thursday, 27 February, at 5 P. M., provided that the Tabulation of Memoranda could then be ready for discussion.

The meeting adjourned at 5.15 P. M.[2]

E. MINOST,
Secretary.

SUMNER,
Chairman.

DOCUMENT 470

First Subcommittee: Minutes of the Fourth Meeting (Including Annexes I- XIII), February 27, 1919, 5 P. M.

[EOM, First Subcommittee, pp. 13-43. French stenographic minutes, PV, CRD, pp. 274-84; French condensed minutes, *ibid.*, pp. 285-87. French text of Annexes I-XI and XIII, *ibid.*, pp. 185-214; of Annex XII, *ibid.*, pp. 215-20.]

The First Sub-Committee of the Commission on Reparation of Damage (Valuation of Damage) met on Thursday, 27 February, 1919, at 5 P. M., at the Ministry of Finance, LORD SUMNER in the Chair.

Present: MR. McCORMICK (*U. S. A.*); LORD SUMNER (*British Empire*); MR. LEBRUN (*France*); MR. CHIESA (*Italy*); MR. NAGAOKA (*Japan*); MR. VAN DEN HEUVEL (*Belgium*); MR. MICHALACOPOULOS (*Greece*); MR. OLCHOWSKI (*Poland*); MR. SPIRITU SANCTU LIMA (*Portugal*); MR. DANIELOPOL (*Roumania*); MR. SAVTCHITCH (*Serbia*); MR. BENES (*Czecho-Slovak Republic*).

The minutes of the last meeting were adopted.

Discussion of Tabulation of Categories of Damage

The CHAIRMAN pointed out that the business before the meeting was the examination of the Tabulation of the various Memoranda on the Categories of Damage which had been prepared by the Secretariat. (See Annex XII.) He suggested that the Committee should read the tabulation with a view to correcting any mistakes of detail and obtaining any necessary explanations. The American Delegation had handed him a summary of the first four pages of the Tabulation, embodying the points upon which there appeared to be general agreement. This the CHAIRMAN read.

In reply to MR. CHIESA (*Italy*), the CHAIRMAN said that the Committee was not now adopting a definite text, and that acceptance of the Tabulation as a satisfactory summary of the Memo-

[2] According to the French minutes, at 5:45.

randa would not bind any Delegation as to the form in which it presented its claims.

"Theatre of Operations"

MR. YANKOVITCH (*Expert for Serbia*) asked if the term "theatre of operations" meant exclusively invaded territories? It was agreed that the term was to be understood in the most general sense. MR. BENES (*Czecho-Slovak Republic*) took cognizance of this decision on behalf of his country.

Sec. 2 (b)

The CHAIRMAN asked whether the provision in regard to the lodging and billeting of troops (Sec. 2, b) referred to friendly as well as enemy troops, pointing out the danger of a possible duplication of claims. MR. LEBRUN (*France*), in reply, referred to the general provision against duplication of claims in the Second Part of the Tabulation (Sec. 20).

The CHAIRMAN then asked which country should present the claim in the case of damage done by quartering of British troops in France for which the British Government had already paid compensation. MR. LEBRUN (*France*) thought that in this case the claim should be made by the British Government. MR. VAN DEN HEUVEL (*Belgium*) asked whether the two general headings of the Tabulation, *Dommages Particuliers* and *Dommages Généraux*, meant respectively damage to private persons and damage to the State.

MR. MCCORMICK (*U. S. A.*) proposed that the Committee accept the American résumé of the points on which all Delegations were agreed, instead of discussing the whole Tabulation in detail. It was decided that the Delegates would require further time to consider this résumé.

MR. LEBRUN (*France*) replied to MR. VAN DEN HEUVEL that his interpretation of the phrases cited was correct.

Sec. 4

The CHAIRMAN asked for an explanation of Sec. 4.

MR. JOUASSET (*Expert for France*) recognized that the drafting of this section required amendment. It was too comprehensive; it should be amended so as to cover only damage caused (a) in enemy territory by any act ordered or committed by enemy authority or population and (b) either in enemy territory or in invaded or occupied territory by the application of laws dealing with seizures, requisitions, sequestrations and liquidations of sequestrated goods.

Sec. 6 (b)

On the proposal of the CHAIRMAN the words "and freights" were added after "cargoes" in Sec. 6 (b).

Sec. 8

The CHAIRMAN asked for an explanation of the following words: "illegal or *ex parte* sentences of all kinds, and every abolition or suspension of existing laws or codes." MR. JOUASSET replied that the draughtsman had in mind cases in which enemy courts or courts under enemy pressure had given judgments in violation of the laws in force in the occupied territory, or without hearing the party condemned, and such possible cases as the suspension of the Russian law by the Germans.

MR. OLCHOWSKI (*Poland*) proposed the words "and also the promulgation of new law." The CHAIRMAN thought MR. OLCHOWSKI'S proposal was too comprehensive.

Sec. 9

The CHAIRMAN then asked for an interpretation of this section, particularly the reference to assurances. After explanations by MR. JOUASSET, the CHAIRMAN said that this clause raised great difficulties, upon which he would reserve his comments until the Committee came to consider the corresponding clause in the division dealing with "Categories not mentioned by all or most of the Delegations."

Sec. 9 (d)

The CHAIRMAN asked whether the next clause (Sec. 9 d) as it stood, would include private charities such as the Red Cross, the Belgian Relief Fund, etc. After observations by Messrs. OLCHOWSKI (*Poland*), DULLES (*U. S. A.*) *and* BENES (*Czecho-Slovak Republic*), it was agreed to accept the distinction made by MR. VAN DEN HEUVEL (*Belgium*), which allowed claims for reimbursement only where assistance was given by an authority or persons under a duty so to do. MR. VAN DEN HEUVEL reserved the right to make such claims in the marginal cases where, for example, a manufacturer was compelled to give relief to his workmen who became unemployed through removal of his machinery by the Germans at a time when the proper authority was unable to give any assistance. The Committee agreed to the CHAIRMAN'S proposal to substitute for the words "any party" (qui que ce soit) the words "public authorities (other than the State) fulfilling an obligation or by private persons or societies upon whom has fallen the obligation of taking the place of the public authorities."

Sec. 9 (e) (f)

The CHAIRMAN suggested that the following clauses (Sec. 9 (e) and (f) allowed claims for damage which it would be excessively difficult to establish or estimate, and that it was perhaps unwise to maintain these categories.

MR. JOUASSET (*Expert for France*) urged that difficulties of application should not prejudice the principle. The CHAIRMAN accepted the principle of these sections on the understanding that its application should be governed by the practical possibilities of the case. MR. LEBRUN (*France*) quoted the pamphlet issued by the German General Staff under the title "French Industries in the Invaded Districts" as sufficient proof that the damage contemplated by these sections was not imaginary.

Sec. 9 (g).

After comments on the next clause (Sec. 9 g) by the CHAIRMAN and Messrs. DULLES (*U. S. A.*) and JOUASSET (*France*), its consideration was adjourned until the Committee came to consider the corresponding section in the part of the Tabulation dealing with "Categories not mentioned by all or the majority of the Delegations."

MR. BENES (*Czecho-Slovak Republic*) asked that regard should be had to the fact of occupation as well as to the fact of invasion as a basis of claims for reparation.

The CHAIRMAN suggested that the Committee might now desire to adopt the first part of the résumé presented by the American Delegation, but accepted MR. LEBRUN's objection that this course would be premature, as the Committee had not yet covered the ground.

The next meeting was fixed for Friday, 28 February, at 2.30 P. M.
The meeting adjourned at 6.45 P. M.

SUMNER,
Chairman.

E. MINOST,
Secretary.

ANNEX I
CATEGORIES OF REPARATION TO BE DEMANDED APART FROM WAR COSTS
(*Presented by the Italian Delegation.*)

1. Reparation for damages inflicted in invaded territories, including injuries to persons, damage to personal and real property of individuals, corporations and of the State, including the Artistic Patrimony of the State, and factories.

2. Reparation due under the same heads to the inhabitants of regions once in the possession of the enemy and at present reunited to the mother country.

3. Reparation for the loss of production (on account of the enemy invasion) of fouled lands (for example, by the destruction of improvements), which for several years after the war will yield no harvest.

4. Reparation due for loss of taxes in the regions invaded or indirectly affected by the war or in regions evacuated under military necessity—this loss being caused by non-production and the consequent lack of taxable revenue.

5. Reparation for damage inflicted by the issuing of spurious money in the regions occupied by the enemy.

6. Reparation due on account of depreciation of enemy currency caused by the wrongful issue of paper money, such reparation to be based on the amount put in the hands of the inhabitants of the invaded regions.

7. Reparation for supplies and merchandise requisitioned or subject to requisition, and then not secured because of enemy invasion.

8. Reparation for allowances to fugitives from invaded regions and the nationals returned from enemy countries, in consideration of the fact that their flight or repatriation was necessary in order to escape the ill-treatment of the enemy.

9. Reparation for damage suffered by inhabitants of Allied countries who fell into the hands of the enemy, such damage having resulted from internment on account of their nationality.

10. Reparation for damage suffered by subjects of the Allied Powers resident abroad through their internment in concentration camps, or through the sequestration, irregular liquidation or requisition of their property.

11. Reparation for maintenance of prisoners of war.

12. Reparation to Allied officers, prisoners of war, for pay not received.

13. Reparation on account of the death of prisoners or on account of infirmities contracted during captivity in consequence of maltreatment or excessive labor or insufficient and bad food—so that the rate of death and illness (tuberculosis, for instance) is far in excess of that amongst enemy prisoners in Allied countries.

14. Reparation for the arbitrary suspension by enemy Powers of payment of workmen's pensions to nationals.

15. Reparation for the allowances granted on account of unemployment to workmen repatriated from enemy countries.

16. Reparation for aid granted by the State to destitute families of soldiers called to the colors, such aid having been made necessary by the high cost of food.

17. Reparation for privileged war pensions (for death, mutilation and illness due to illicit methods of warfare, such as noxious gases, bombardment of undefended towns, etc.).

18. Reparation to the State and to individuals for the increased pay of military forces and civilian employees occasioned by the enemy (due to high cost of food, etc., etc.).

19. Reparation to individuals and to corporations for damage to persons and property in consequence of aerial and naval bombardments of undefended towns.

20. Reparation to individuals (passengers and crews) who have suffered injury or damage by the sinking of ships, etc., whether of allied or foreign register.

21. Reparation to the State and to individuals for merchant ships sunk by mines, etc., or stranded or rendered useless by enemy action.

22. Reparation for goods lost on sunken ships, including sequestrated enemy ships and foreign chartered ships.

23. Reparation for the difference between the cost price of industrial raw materials imported during hostilities, and remaining on hand at the time of the Armistice, and the price they could command at present.

24. Reparation for diminished agricultural and industrial output during the period of the war through lack of raw materials or of coal, on account of submarine warfare.

25. Reparation for pecuniary loss in the administration of food supplies (wheat and other food-stuffs of prime necessity).

26. Reparation for pecuniary loss in the administration of national fuel supply.

27. Reparation for damage due to deforestation, necessitated by the lack of fuel, in consequence of diminished importation of coal due to submarine warfare.

28. Reparation for abnormal freight-costs paid during the war.

29. Reparation for loss in exchange incurred in paying for materials imported during the four years of war in so far as it exceeds the average rate of preceding years.

NOTE. These categories may be added to or modified.

[no date]

ANNEX II

CATEGORIES OF DAMAGE

(*Presented by the Serbian Delegation.*)

A.   DIRECT DAMAGES

I. *Agriculture:*

(1) Devastated and damaged land; vineyards, fruit-trees, woods, parks, pasturages, waste lands and forests which have been annihilated, dried out and uprooted.

(2) Cattle and fowls: beasts of burden and of draught and cattle kept for breeding purposes (horned cattle, pigs, horses, donkeys, mules, sheep, goats); fowls of all sorts, silk-worms, bees, game and fishes.

(3) Inventory of the agriculture: all sorts of instruments and tools of agriculture, carriages, riding and driving implements.

(4) Food for men and animals which was in the country at the time of the invasion, i.e., all sorts of cereals, hay, straw, etc.; animal products: cheese, milk, cream (kaimak), skins, wool, etc.

II. *Industrial concerns:*

Handicraft, mines, quarries; installations, goods, raw and other used materials.

III. *Hydrotechnical objects:*

Aqueducts, canalizations, quays, barrages, etc.

IV. *Means of communication:*

All the railways of the country, with all their buildings, objects and installations, with their own and borrowed rolling-stock, installations for impregnation, plans of all sorts, material and complete inventory destined to the keep of the railway lines and the workshops; all the roads of the country; all the Post, Telegraph and Telephone Offices, and other means of communication, as carts, cabs, automobiles.

V. *Buildings:*

All buildings destined for habitation or for public services (schools, churches, hospitals, barracks, etc.).

VI. *Furniture and household goods, etc.:*

Furniture taken away from the whole population, household goods and plates, especially copper; furniture and other objects taken away from all public buildings (from all sorts of schools, churches, offices, monasteries, all the administrative offices, hospitals, pharmacies, barracks, stables, penitentiaries, etc.).

VII. *Scientific and Artistic Institutions:*

Libraries, museums, theatres, physical and chemical cabinets, collections, etc.

VIII. *Commerce and Institutions of credit:*

All sorts of goods, imported from abroad as well as produced in the country, manufactures and half-manufactured raw materials; cash, bonds and other valuable articles.

IX. *Other Direct Damages:*

(1) Repurchase of Austrian kronen imposed upon the country.
(2) Depreciation of the country's currency at the time of the invasion.
(3) Requisitions of all sorts.
(4) Compulsory purchase of products and goods at derisory prices.
(5) Compulsory sales and confiscations.
(6) Lost claims.
(7) Life insurance by insurance companies.
(8) Compulsory taxes and fines.
(9) Compulsory war loans.
(10) Invalid pensions and war pensions.
(11) Debts of the State, in kind and in cash, contracted during the war with the Allies:
　　(a) for military purposes;
　　(b) for the other branches of the State Administration;
　　(c) for the support of disabled soldiers, of a part of the population and of interned persons.

(12) Unpaid salaries and pensions to functionaries of the State of all categories, and help granted to the population during the occupation.

X. *Accoutrements and equipment of the Army* (up to the beginning of the war in 1914): all sorts of clothing, tools, material, equipment of the army service corps, ammunition, weapons, etc.

B.   INDIRECT DAMAGES

(1) Lost or reduced revenues: of agriculture, buildings, industry, handicraft and mines, commerce, banks, insurance societies, and capital in general; of the liberal professions: lawyers, engineers, physicians, journalists, etc.

(2) Increased expenditure, i.e., private debts contracted in consequence of the war.

N. B. In all these categories, enumerated above, the damages sustained by private people and by the State or other autonomous institutions will have to be dealt with separately.

[no date]

ANNEX III

CATEGORIES OF DAMAGE

(*Presented by the Japanese Delegation.*)

(1) The cost of war.

(2) The cost of maintenance of the prisoners of war.

(3) Damage inflicted on shipping by illegal acts of the enemy.

    (a) Damage in respect of ships.

    (b) Damage in respect of cargoes, and

    (c) Personal and material damages in respect of passengers and crews.

(4) Damage inflicted on individuals by illegal acts of the enemy.

    (a) Personal damage (including the loss of life, wounds, etc.).

    (b) Damage in respect of properties and other rights.

(With reserve for addition and correction.)

20 February, 1919

ANNEX IV

CATEGORIES OF DAMAGE FOR WHICH REPARATION MAY BE DEMANDED

(*Presented by the French Delegation.*)

I. DAMAGE TO THE PERSON

1. Allowances and pensions to civilian and military victims of acts of war or to persons claiming under them.

Allowances, bonuses or pensions:

    (a) to widows, orphans, parents and grandparents;

    (b) to soldiers maimed or invalided out of the army;

    (c) to civilian victims of bombardments;

    (d) to victims of explosions in factories;

    (e) to victims of accidents during employment in war factories.

2. Allowances and pensions to civilian and military victims, including prisoners of war, or to persons claiming under them, for acts of maltreatment or violence committed or ordered by the enemy.

3. Allowances or pensions to civilians or military persons, or persons claiming under them, who have

(a) been shot;

(b) suffered injury to the person in consequence of imprisonment, deportation, internment or evacuation;

(c) have suffered any accident, fatal or not fatal, through compulsory labor;

—damage in respect of maltreatment injurious to health or honor.

II.   DAMAGE TO PROPERTY

A. Damage caused by the armed forces of both groups of belligerents on all theatres of operations of the said forces:

(1) Destruction, deterioration or depreciation by land or sea to public or private property, whether movable or immovable.

Means employed:—

The destruction or deterioration may be the result either of an act of war or of the fact of invasion:

(a) bombardment by artillery or from the air, by land or sea;

(b) voluntary or involuntary destruction by troops;

(c) defensive or offensive arrangements;

(d) torpedoes, submarine mines;

(e) deterioration resulting from use by the enemy.

Objects of destruction or deterioration:—

(a) the soil, forests, mines, diggings and quarries, roads, canals, railways in general, electrical lines and canalizations (telephones, telegraphs, transmission of power), water supply, canalizations, drainage, etc.

(b) all kinds of structures, public or private, buildings or monuments, etc.

(c) installations and fittings in public or private edifices, machines, furniture, objects of art, raw materials, merchandise, live stock, crops, products and commodities, personal securities, documents of title and coupons, drawings, models, patents, trade-marks, archives, instruments and documents of every description, etc.

(d) merchant vessels and fishing-boats and their cargoes.

(2) Requisitions, removals or theft of all goods, public or private. Requisition of every kind whether or not made against requisition acknowledgments, including billeting of troops and hire of services. Removals by regularly constituted authorities or by any other person and thefts of the objects enumerated in item (c) of clause (1) above.

(3) Imposts, taxes, war levies, fines, levies in cash of all sorts, including balances of accounts transferred and assets transformed

into credit acknowledgments, loan and other vouchers, and expenses imposed by enemy authorities on individuals or corporations. Issue of bank-notes, credit acknowledgments and monetary instruments of all sorts.

(4) Expenses incurred by any person whatever in any form whatever for feeding the populations of territories invaded or occupied, for transporting or assisting such populations.

(5) Complete or partial deprivation of the free exercise of any proprietary right or occupation.

Loss caused to any public or private person by the fact that the normal development of his resources has been impeded by the invasion—

    (a) up to the date of the armistice.

    (b) from the date of the armistice up to the moment at which normal exercise of the proprietary right or occupation shall have become possible.

(6) Losses caused to industrial property by the discovery or use of special processes of manufacture, patents or methods of handicraft.

(7) Commercial losses occasioned by the investigation of business books or ledgers, correspondence or archives public or private, and, in general, all unpublished documents and information, as well as by the use made of such documents and information. Loss caused by the organization of new competition by the assistance of the investigation of such information and documents.

B. Damage other than that considered under A above which may have been caused in Allied or enemy countries:—

(1) Allowances to the families of men called to the colors, refugees and unemployed persons.

(2) Cost of assistance by the State or corporate bodies to prisoners of war and interned civilians.

(3) Damage caused in any place to property movable or immovable either by the application of enemy war legislation or by any act ordered or committed by enemy authority or an enemy population.

The reference is to sequestration or liquidation of Allied property.

(4) Loss resulting to the Allied nations from the necessity of buying up holdings of enemy money in the hands of the inhabitants (public or private persons) of the territories which have been in the power, *de jure* or *de facto*, of enemy Powers, or in the hands of prisoners of war and interned civilians.

(5) Damage of every sort suffered by the nation in its productivity.

III. EXPENSES OF WAR

All expenses or charges arising from the imposition of the state of war upon the Allied nations.

Cost of the maintenance by the Allied States of enemy prisoners of war, officers and men.

IV.

Damage suffered by the State and by Public Persons in consequence of the War of 1870-71:

(1) War indemnity.

(2) War captures.

(3) Imposts, taxes, contributions, fines and prestations imposed by enemy authority.

The right to make subsequent modifications or additions is reserved.

20 February, 1919

ANNEX V

CATEGORIES OF DAMAGE

(*Presented by the Greek Delegation.*)

I[1]

Greece owing to her geographical configuration, and the Hellenic Nation owing to its residence in enemy countries, have largely contributed to the great war for the liberty of the nations.

Submarine warfare, on the one hand, and the policy of extermination followed by the Turks and Bulgarians, on the other, have caused damage which necessitates reparation. This damage results from a series of acts contrary to the Law of Nations, namely

The action of submarines,

The devastation of territories occupied by an enemy,

The deportation and destruction systematically organized by the Bulgarians and Turks against the Hellenic populations.

Demands for indemnity will be formulated by the Hellenic Government as much in its own name as in that of the individuals concerned, actual or future subjects of the Kingdom of Greece, to whom it will undertake to distribute such indemnities as are eventually allowed.

It will further undertake to provide for the settlement of all indemnities due to Ottoman Greeks in consequence of persecutions

---

[1] In the French text, this figure "I" stands immediately above the "A" below, which seems more logical than its present position.

organized in Turkey, which should not be considered on the same basis or treated in the same manner as the reparation claimed by the Armenians.

The heads of indemnity claimed by Greece are as follows:

A

1. Indemnities due to the families of those who have perished or been disabled or invalided as the result of enemy operations at sea.

B

1. Indemnities for damage caused or loss suffered in ships flying the Greek flag by reason of enemy action and as the result of maritime warfare.

2. Indemnities for damage caused or loss suffered in ships or loss of ships flying Allied or neutral flags but belonging to Hellenic subjects, it being understood that there shall be no claim under this head in respect of ships for which the allied Power interested has already demanded compensation.

3. Indemnities for cargoes, goods or effects belonging to Greek subjects lost or damaged by enemy action and as the result of maritime warfare. This category shall include the effects of Greek nationals who were members of the crews of vessels sunk by enemy action, as also the luggage and effects of Greek nationals who were passengers on board ships of Greek, Allied or neutral nationality, and effects and luggage damaged as the result of enemy operations at sea.

4. Indemnities still outstanding and due to Greece according to the Treaty of Athens (1913) by reason of the embargo laid by Turkey on Greek ships in Turkish ports before the outbreak of the Balkan War, in respect whereof an expert valuation was made in concert by the two interested parties, but payment of which could not take place owing to the outbreak of the European War.

5. Insurance premiums for war risks paid by the Greek State and Greek nationals on sea transport connected with the national food supply and on vessels carrying on Greek import and export trade.

6. Reparation for damage resulting from the immobilization of ships flying the Greek flag which, by reason of the closing of the Straits and the Turkish ports, were laid under embargo without being granted the necessary period of grace to leave.

7. Expenditure incurred for the protection of the coast and ports of the Kingdom against the submarine blockade and the expenses

of convoying the merchant ships flying the Greek, Allied or neutral flags, which ensured the provisioning of the Kingdom and carried on its import and export trade; also the cost of arming merchant vessels.

II

A

1. Restitution to the Greek State of war indemnities, and compensation for the pensions to be paid to the families of the killed and missing and to those disabled and invalided by the war.

2. Indemnities for the expenditure incurred by the Greek State for assistance of refugees expelled from Turkey and Bulgaria into Greece.

3. Reparation for damage caused to Greeks expelled (by the enemy), whether Hellenic or Turkish nationals, by reason of having relinquished their business, profession or trade, in so far as they shall have been unable in their new place of residence to make good the losses caused by such expulsion. Under the denomination of "Greeks who are Turkish nationals" shall be understood Greeks who, being Turkish nationals and refugees in Greece, shall have served under the Greek flag or in the Allied Armies, and their families, as well as those inhabiting or residing in the provinces claimed by Greece.

4. Compensation payable to deportees and to persons interned for political reasons for damage specified under Paragraph 3 hereof and caused during their deportation or internment and to facilitate their return home, as also compensation for the assistance given by the Greek State under this head.

B

1. Reparation of damage done to property situate within the provinces of the Kingdom occupied by the enemy or situate on enemy territory and belonging to Hellenic or Turkish nationals residing in or inhabiting such localities, namely: Restitution and restoration of immovable estate situate within the provinces of the Kingdom occupied by the enemy or on enemy territory and belonging to Greeks who are Hellenic or Turkish nationals. Restitution and restoration of works, factories and agricultural, industrial and other undertakings situate within such localities and belonging to Greeks who are Hellenic or Turkish subjects. Compensation for merchandise and movable property belonging to Greeks expelled from such localities and which they were not permitted to remove.

In the latter category are included the securities (State securities and others) left behind in enemy territory, as well as those deposited by Hellenic subjects generally in enemy countries.

2. Indemnities for damage caused by aerial bombardment of the City of Salonica and all other damage caused by aerial bombardment or any other form of bombardment to unfortified towns or places in Macedonia and the islands of the Archipelago.

This class of indemnity shall include damage caused both to public buildings and private property, to movable and immovable estate, to persons or to inanimate objects.

3. Indemnification of the State for war material, railway rolling stock, etc. taken by the Bulgarians in Eastern Macedonia, and reparation for damage caused to public property, such as public buildings, railway lines, etc.

4. Compensation for the destruction of forests, live stock and other resources of the Kingdom to supply the needs of the Allied Armies.

5. Compensation for loss and damage resulting from defensive measures taken and works carried out by the Allied armies, such as flooding, destruction of railway bridges, etc.

6. Compensation for non-cultivation of land in Macedonia by reason of military operations.

7. Indemnities unpaid or fixed below their actual value by the enemy, for requisitions of buildings, means of transport and supplies in general made by the enemy on Greeks, whether Hellenic or Turkish nationals, in the occupied provinces or in enemy territory.

8. Reparation by Turkey for damage occasioned to Greek nationals by the abolition of the Capitulations which constituted the anti-war treaty relationship between Greece and Turkey, namely: Loss resulting from arbitrary requisitions, from the execution of illegal sentences, from taxes and other dues levied on Greek nationals, etc.

Lastly, the Greek Delegation leaves the question as to expenses of the war to the decision of the Great Powers.

Further, the Greek Delegation reserves to itself the right to obtain sanction for settlement of the claims against Turkey and Bulgaria prior to the European war, such as:—

1. Payment by Turkey and Bulgaria of the sums expended by the Greek Government for maintenance and repatriation of Turkish prisoners of war during the Balkan War.

2. Indemnities for illegal confiscations of property owned by

Greek private individuals or communities in Bulgaria or Turkey before 1914.

3. Indemnities to landowners in Thessaly for requisitions by and supplies furnished to the Turkish Army of Occupation in 1897, etc., etc.

[no date]

ANNEX VI

CATEGORIES OF DAMAGE

(*Presented by the Polish Delegation.*)

War damage is divided into the following categories, viz.:—

(1) Damage to persons;

(2) Damage to property;

(3) Damage to States in consequence of the total expenditure occasioned by the war.

1. Loss caused, within or without its territories, to all nationals of a State by any injury to life, working capacity, or liberty through acts of the enemy, such as:—

(a) physical injury caused by an act of war resulting in a wound, infirmity or sickness;

(b) physical injury unaccompanied by any wound, infirmity or sickness, but caused by imprisonment, deportation or any violence on the part of the enemy;

(c) if the victim has died in consequence of the violence done him by the enemy, reparation shall be made to the husband or wife (whichever shall be the survivor), descendants or parents;

(d) damage caused by the impossibility of working or obtaining fair remuneration for work.

N. B. To escape death or hunger owing to the destruction of industry, workpeople were forced, in some of the occupied territory, to take up work in Germany, after having signed contracts with the Government or with contractors. On arrival in Germany these unhappy persons found themselves in slavery, being deprived of personal liberty and all civil rights. This case should clearly come under the category of forced labor.

2. Damage caused by acts of war within the territory of a State to movable and immovable property belonging to private individuals and juridical persons without distinction of nationality, as well as to the State, such as:—

(a) all requisitions made by the enemy authorities or troops from private individuals or juridical persons, and including supplies in kind, imposts, taxes, fines and war contributions;

(b) all so-called "expropriations," "friendly purchases," "compulsory administrations," "sequestrations," "compulsory liquidations," etc., etc., with respect to movable and immovable property;

(c) the removal of all property, furniture, or other articles, and the depreciation and total or partial destruction thereof, comprising (*inter alia*) the removal of locomotives, wagons, rails, etc., whoever may have been the authors of such removal, depreciation or destruction;

(d) damage to immovable property, whether built upon or not, including forests; the total or partial destruction of buildings; the removal, depreciation or total or partial destruction of implements, accessories and cattle, belonging to any commercial, industrial or agricultural undertaking, which rank as immovable property by reason of the use for which they are intended; and destruction of the soil —whoever may have been the authors of such damage or destruction;

(e) the expenditure incurred by towns, communes, and other administrative bodies and by social organizations through the necessity of feeding, clothing, nursing and generally maintaining the populations which had been deprived of the means of gaining a livelihood;

(f) State loans to which the population was forced to subscribe;

(g) losses occasioned by the special issue of bank-notes and other securities for the invaded districts;

(h) losses occasioned by the fall in value of the money used by the enemy Powers to meet their liabilities in invaded districts;

(i) all damage caused by the enemy to movable or immovable property belonging to nationals of the State or the State itself within the boundaries of the four enemy Powers.

N. B. This list is incomplete and we reserve to ourselves the right to complete it.

By "war damage" we mean generally:—

(1) loss proved by the injured party;

(2) the profits of which he has been and will be deprived until restitution is made;

Either being a direct and immediate consequence of enemy action.

The war damage must be duly vouched for.

Moral damage is not a subject for compensation.

The bases of evaluation of damage and injury shall be the same in all countries.

20 February, 1919

ANNEX VII

CATEGORIES OF DAMAGE

(*Presented by the Czecho-Slovak Delegation.*)

I. Damage caused by military operations, including occupation.

A. Damage on territory of operations.

    (a) Legal Conduct of War.

        (1) *To National Properties.*

            Destruction and wear of war material.

            Destruction and wear of transport material.

            Destruction and wear of ways of communication (railways, bridges, tunnels, roads and destruction of canals).

            Destruction and wear of national and public buildings.

        (2) *Indirect damage caused to the State.*

            Destruction or decreasing of personal taxes, expenses of operations of immediate relief (deportation of population to the interior of the country and the keeping of fugitives as well as their transportation in the country).

            Restoration of the territory affected by the war, which renders impossible agricultural exploitation (digging of trenches, grenades, strewn fields, corpses, ruins, barbed-wire entanglements, excess of sterile material, flooding of mines, flooding of whole regions).

        (3) *Damage caused to persons.*

            Killing and wounding of combatants and the consequences (families deprived of their support or weakened in efficiency for labor).

            Killing and wounding of non-combatants who have failed to conform to the rules of international law, and the consequences (guerrillas).

            Damage caused to national property (fiscal) and private property, though not contrary to international law.

(b) Illegal Conduct of War.

All damage caused to the State, protected by neutrality.

All damage mentioned in (a) (if they have not been made necessary for war purposes), for instance: flooding of mines in the Briey region, cutting down of fruit trees in the North of France, destruction of all the swine in Serbia—for the reason that those acts were not dictated by war necessities but by the desire to cause the economic ruin of the enemy.

Forced enrolling of the population of an opponent State in the armies, and employment in camp with all its consequences.

Deportation of the population of the invaded territory for other purposes than to save it, bombarding cities and undefended places, torpedoing ships, contrary to the principles of international law.

B. Damage in occupied territory.

(a) Through legal occupation.

(1) Damage to the State.

Decreasing the proceeds of taxes and other revenues of the State (monopolies, customs, transportation, enterprises and institutions of the State), sequestration and seizures of the occupied territory, requisitions and contributions in accord with international law.

(2) To persons.

Killing and wounding non-combatants and the consequences as far as these non-combatants have observed the rules of international law.

Damage caused to State properties (fiscal) or to those belonging to private persons through acts in accord with international law.

(b) Illegal acts of the occupying Powers.

(1) To the detriment of the State.

Destruction or decrease of the resources of the State through abandonment of economic life (abandonment of measures for improvement of the soil, for development of industry, for means of transportation and for mines; the replacement of national funds with foreign funds, weakening the capacity for work and the morale of the population: floating of fiduciary money without value, converting funds into war-loan bonds, non-payment of supplies to the State, etc.

(2) Against persons.

Using the population contrary to the terms of Art. 52 of The Hague Conventions for war operations against their own country; illegal requisitions, unlawful exploitation of mines and forests, unlawful imposition of contributions on private persons or corporations (Art. 48 of The Hague Conventions), dispossession of the means of transport, stealing by bands or military detachments, illegal imposition of fines upon private individuals or corporations (Art. 50 of The Hague Conventions).

Execution of the population contrary to the regulations of Art. 50 of The Hague Conventions; illegal mutilation of the inhabitants and their deportation to other regions for the economic weakening of the occupied territory and the increase of the economic life of the invading State; and all acts affecting the physical strength, health, freedom and honor (women).

(3) Against Property.

Removal of furniture, especially of works of art; removal of cattle, removal of forage, requisition of clothing belonging to private individuals, seizure of raw material for industrial purposes; damage done to buildings and furniture, compulsion of the population to subscribe to war loans and in that way help the enemy contrary to Art. 49 of The Hague Conventions.

(c) Other damage caused by acts of the enemy.

(1) Damage caused to prisoners of war and interned persons, by acts contrary to International Law (ill treatment of prisoners and interned persons). These acts have as a consequence, on the one hand, damage to the State, whose vitality is weakened; on the other hand, both material and moral damage to the victims.

(2) All damage caused by other acts of the enemy, as, for example, damage resulting from the ban placed by the enemy on all commerce with the Allied countries and in prohibition of all maritime transportation to the Allied countries; all prejudice to the individual

rights of citizens of the Allied countries, including especially rights on intangible property (such as copyrights, patents, trade-marks); the sequestration and liquidation of property belonging to citizens of the Entente, as far as it does not include regular measures made necessary by the absence of the owner; confiscation of property belonging to Entente subjects; the fact that owners did not receive the part which ought to have come to them of the liquidations and auction sales; the fact that the owners were not heard by the tribunals; internment or confinement not in execution of a legal measure or of persons without military obligations; deportation of individuals without giving them time to settle their affairs; damage inflicted on citizens of the Entente by the arbitrary suppression of the foreign civil code (in Russia, for example); the deterioration of property belonging to Entente citizens during disturbances or disorders; the loss suffered on obligations on account of the depreciation of the paper money which was to be used as payment; the cancellation of contracts in the Entente countries; the loss, on account of the war, of possible profits by labor or capital in foreign countries.

CLASSIFICATION

Of War Claims of Czecho-Slovak Republic

I. Damage caused by military operations, including occupation.

A. Damage caused in the zones of operations.

As a rule the Czecho-Slovak territory has been spared by military operations; nevertheless, some parts of Slovakia, that is to say, the region situated East of the Poprad and North of Prosova Humanne and Uzhorod, as well as the territory situated South and West of this line, suffered as the zone of communication.

(a) Legal Conduct of the War.

1. *On national property.*

The Czecho-Slovak State did not possess in these territories either war material or means of transportation. It was therefore affected only indirectly; the assets of the Austro-Hungarian Empire have been reduced by the destruction and deterioration of material of war, and of the transport of that State, and have thus become insufficient to cover other obligations.

But, on the other hand, the Czecho-Slovak State is affected by the destruction and deterioration of railways, roads, bridges and public buildings in these regions, the wanton burning of churches and schools in 17 communes of the Sarys district and the destruction of buildings in the Zemplin, Uzhorod and Marmaros districts. It would be necessary by an inquiry on the spot to make an exact estimate of these damages.

2. *Indirect damage caused to the State.*

These are naturally more important. The regions which have suffered by the war, and which are now part of the Czecho-Slovak State are in such a lamentable condition that the revenue from taxes will be greatly reduced. The fields are, for the most part, covered with barbed wire and it was forbidden to remove it; so for four years these fields have not been tilled. Forests were cut down and the wood used for the construction of trenches, public buildings and roads; this cutting down of forests was necessitated also by artillery fire.

The resulting decrease of revenue from taxation must also be taken into account in the direct damage caused to the State by the legal conduct of the war. It will be easy to evaluate these damages by a comparison of fiscal revenues before and after the war.

3. Damage caused to individuals.

The Czecho-Slovak Republic has sustained a loss by death and injuries received on the battle-field of people living on the territories composing it. The Republic suffers not only as a whole by the lessening of production of its population but also by the duty imposed upon it to pay pensions to the maimed, widows and orphans, together with the care of sick soldiers. The balance of public funds and hospital statistics will furnish the basis to calculate this damage.

If during the war civilians have been murdered, especially in the territory of the above-mentioned operations, it will be necessary to make an inquiry on the spot whether a legal judgment has been made according to international law or not. In the former case, it will be necessary to include in this group of damages the detriment caused to the family of the victim. The full extent of damage caused by military operations in the region of the Republic already mentioned, to national and private property, can be calculated only on the basis of reports made out by the sufferers themselves. Thus many villages and hamlets were bombarded and burned, the fields damaged by the digging of trenches, the erection of barbed-wire entanglements, the cutting down of forests, the theft of furniture which, in their flight, the inhabitants had been unable to take with them. It will be necessary as far as this kind of damage also is concerned, to determine whether it was caused by legal warfare or not.

(b) Illegal Conduct of the War.

We may expect the proof by the most detailed evidence of the fact that many acts of damage mentioned above as examples were committed in infraction of the articles and principles relative to the legal conduct of warfare. It is certain that numerous Russian and Slovak farmers were executed without a legal trial by the Austro-Hungarian army at the time of its retreat across the territories mentioned above.

Moreover, we know that the evacuation of seventeen villages of the county (comitat) of Sarys was ordered so tardily that the populace were forced to leave their homes, abandoning the greater part of their possessions to the enemy.

It is necessary to emphasize the fact that the Austro-Hungarian soldiery, during the course of the winter, destroyed previously intact houses and agricultural buildings in order to procure firewood.

(c) Damage in the invaded territory.

It has been demonstrated in a special memorandum relative to the international relations between the Czecho-Slovak Republic and the Central Empires, and emphasizing the right of the Czecho-Slovak Republic to demand indemnification, that the territory of the Czecho-Slovak Republic, from the point of view of international law, must be regarded as having been occupied by a foreign Power. This memorandum describes in detail how the Austro-Hungarian authorities caused damages which were necessitated only in part by the circumstances of occupation, and often with other objects contrary to international law.

By ruining the economic life of the country, without the excuse of military necessity, the Austro-Hungarian authorities manifested their intention of rendering impossible in the future the revival of the economic power of the Czecho-Slovak Republic or at least of preventing the competition which its economic prosperity might offer for Germany, German Austria, and Hungary.

It is also necessary, therefore, to distinguish the damage caused by the agents on the territory of the Czecho-Slovak Republic of the administration, by two categories, the damage caused by legal occupation, and that resulting from illegal acts committed by an occupying Power.

(d) Legal occupation.

1. Damage to the State.

The economic life of the Czecho-Slovak Republic as a whole has so greatly suffered from the complete interruption of its relations with the outside world, that even after years fiscal receipts will be considerably less than before the war. We must add to this the regular requisitions made for the army installed in the country, which have already reduced the food supply and the economic capacity of the population. It would be difficult to determine precisely the extent of these damages, for, in the lowering of the fiscal capacity of the territory resulting therefrom, we must distinguish the effects of the legal occupation and those ensuing from the illegal acts of the occupying Power.

2. Damage to individuals.

With respect to the persons who during the war and in the territory of the Czecho-Slovak Republic have been condemned to death or to a punishment not encroaching upon personal liberty, it will be necessary to examine whether or not the acts took place legally or illegally. It was particularly in the territories proclaimed a war zone in which martial law was established that a great number of sentences have given rise to grave doubts. In the other parts of the territory, also since the very beginning of the war, civilians in an absolutely illegal manner were subjected to military justice for political offences. The sentences pronounced gave rise to doubts of the very gravest nature. As a consequence of these sentences the possessions of the condemned were confiscated. These sentences must be reviewed in order to establish whether or not they were pronounced legally.

In the same way, in the case of requisitions and labor imposed upon the civilian population according to the law of military operations, we shall have to distinguish whether the enemy acted legally or whether he abused the forms of law so as to accomplish the economic annihilation of the Republic.

(e) Illegal acts of the invading State.

1. To the detriment of the State.

The efforts toward the object mentioned above, and in contradiction to the fundamental principles of international law which state that war is not waged against the civil population but only against the armed forces of the enemy, have led during the entire duration of the war in Czech countries to a multitude of acts and infractions on the part of the occupying Power. Thus, the principle already mentioned in Art. 43 of The Hague Conventions, stating that it is the duty of the occupying Power to aid the public life and the maintenance of order as far as is possible, by respecting the laws of the country, has especially failed of observance. On the contrary, the force of the State has been employed to the end that, by supporting the separatist tendencies of the German part of the population, the political life not only during the war, but above all after the war, should be infected by the element which is threatening the public life of the country.

In the same way Art. 48 of The Hague Conventions, according to which the occupying Power must bear the expenses of administration in the same measure as the lawful government, has not been observed.

Above all, State institutions, public buildings and structures designed for transport service, have not only not been repaired, but have even been abused, damaged and destroyed. Thus, the schools have been used, without absolute necessity, for the military services; means of transportation have in general been in large part rendered unserviceable, from lack of timely repairs.

The principles of Arts. 49 H. k. and 52 H. k. especially have been neglected.[2] Not only has the population been forced to contribute to the payment of debts resulting from the conduct of the war and maintenance of the army, in the interior of the country, by subscriptions or war loans; but again public funds have been converted into war loans from the moment when they were placed at the disposal of the State. Economic prosperity also has been impaired by a deluge of unrealizable securities. Moreover, damages inflicted especially on private individuals by illegal proceedings have had ulterior consequences which have affected the economic capacity of the State. Thus, the damage of which mention will be made in the following articles must be considered as damage inflicted on the State, although they have been so only indirectly, at the time of the occupation by the Central Powers, by illegal acts.

2. To individuals.

From the time of the mobilization, not only the men of the standing army but also those of the reserve of the standing army and those of the territorials (Landwehr) have been obliged—and that illegally—to place themselves at the disposal of the military authorities and to leave their families. By this fact, damage has been suffered not only by these private individuals and their families (and this especially in frequent cases of illegal sending of

---

[2] The French text reads, "Les principes des articles 49 H. IV ont surtout été négligés."

these persons to the front), but also by the State, which lost, temporarily or permanently, the experienced and skilled manual labor furnished by these men who for the most part occupied positions of responsibility.

Requisitions were made in the Czecho-Slovak country more intensively than in the other countries, not only for the needs of the army of the interior, but also for the needs of the Austro-Hungarian army at the front or for the needs of the civil population of German Austria and of Germany.

In addition to live stock and products of the soil, harness, wagons, and machines or parts of machines were requisitioned.

This requisitioning had grave consequences, not only through the removal of these objects, but also by rendering impossible or diminishing all future exploitation. Not only did the owners of these objects suffer losses from this requisitioning, but also the whole civil population and the entire State; especially because of the difficulty of getting food, particularly for infants, since it was almost impossible to get milk.

Mines and forests were seized in the same way. By a rapacious exploitation the soil was prematurely exhausted, and it will be sterile for some years; and repeatedly the forests and mines were damaged in such a way that they will be unproductive during a long period, and it will be necessary to make large expenditures in order to be able to resume their exploitation.

Industry has suffered the same damage. Laborers, engineers, and skilled employees were sent into other countries, where they were employed in occupations unsuitable for them; while the industries which had been deprived of this skilled labor had to get along as best they could with labor less capable and often harmful. Raw materials were requisitioned in the same manner as were parts of machinery; their production was made impossible or diminished and industries were often obliged to keep their workmen, for whom they did not have enough work. Discharged workmen thus swelled the ranks of the unemployed who were helped by money from the public funds. Entire branches of industry, which formerly prospered, disappeared almost entirely, such as breweries, butcher-shops, glove-making shops.

The capital of industries was immobilized by a compulsory conversion into war loans. The insufficiency of coal in 1918 hindered the sugar industry; the larger part of the sugar beets were spoiled by frost. Glass factories produced nothing for three years because of the lack of coal. Blast furnaces were forced to limit their production, first from lack of coal, then because of the monopoly of ferro-manganese ores by the Magyars.

Unexpected requisitions also hindered the business of numerous industries. In addition to the fact that the public administration sought to support Viennese industries, it forbade the commerce of numerous enterprises, replacing them by central commercial enterprises which, to the detriment of commerce and of the legitimate consumers, achieved fabulous profits. Commerce suffered especially, and will continue to suffer, from the State policy concerning transportation and communications. Thus, on railroads the interior furnishings were intentionally destroyed by foreign armies; the seats of the cars were burned, windows broken. Metal objects were requisitioned. While in the German and Magyar districts the tracks and railway buildings continued to be normally maintained, and while they employed prisoners for this work, the upkeep in the Czecho-Slovak districts was totally neglected. For example, on the railway from Cmunt to Vienna, several thousand prisoners worked on the Alpine section and effected various improvements, while in Czecho-Slovak territory the track remained out of repair; even precautions of safety were not taken (rotten ties, worn-out rails, etc.).

The track was considerably damaged by the transportation, on a large scale, of material which the German armies occupying Serbia, Roumania, Russia and Venetia had illegally seized, and by express trains proceeding at an exceptional speed by right of priority. The best engines, cars and hand-cars were taken from the Czecho-Slovak countries in greater number than would have been required by a normal conduct of the war, and in the same way reserve rails, signal outfits, apparatus, instruments, accessory machinery, materials intended for construction and upkeep, etc. Transportation was decreased in the Czecho-Slovak countries, while in Germanic Austria the traffic was the same as before the war. Consequently, the larger part of the rolling-stock suffers for this reason an unwonted wear. Railway material and lubricants were requisitioned on such a scale that the material left, namely, the unrepaired portions and the worn parts, were damaged or destroyed. The experienced personnel were sent for political reasons to far-off lines; not only did they suffer injury on their own part from this fact, but traffic suffered likewise.

Postal service and road transport suffered similarly. With regard to private individuals and landed property other than farms, the same treatment was meted out as in the case of agricultural, industrial, and commercial enterprises. Buildings could not be repaired and even lightning-rods and metal parts were confiscated. In dwellings utensils were requisitioned—metal instruments and metallic furnishings.

Clothing, linen and worn shoes are either irreplaceable or to be acquired at an exaggerated price as a result of unfair requisitions and the creation of a central commission. The insufficiency of food and its poor quality have occasioned illness, especially among children, and among adults have caused a relative incapacity for labor. Bells and objects of art were requisitioned not for military purposes, as alleged, but rather with the result that the "Metallgesellschaft" in Vienna sold in November, 1918, great stores of metal to individuals or to factories in Upper and Lower Austria. Other requisitioned objects were likewise sold from Vienna—automobiles, bicycles, uniforms, harness, saddles, etc.

The occupation of the territory by foreign troops has caused unjustified expense, to individuals as well as to communes.

Credit and insurance firms have suffered great losses due to the depreciation of money and the forced conversion of their capital into war loans. A large part of this capital, deposited at postal savings-banks has been illegally seized by the State and used for war purposes.

II. Other damage caused by hostile acts.

1. There are many persons of Czecho-Slovak nationality who, as a result of political suspicion, have been illegally imprisoned or interned. They have thus suffered bad treatment, injurious to their health and safety. Moreover, it is impossible to estimate in material terms the intellectual and moral damage caused in Bohemia by the war, notably as a result of interruption of schools and the consequent injury to the education of youth.

2. The damage caused by other hostile acts of the first category have all been exemplified in Bohemia. It is impossible to establish at this moment a detailed list; for that it would be necessary to have the persons concerned fill out an agreed formula conforming to the category given in Paragraph II. 2.

For the present, it is certain that a large number of enterprises have suffered great damage as a result of the suspension of the protection offered by trade-marks registered in other States, and the prohibition of time deliveries in contracts for phosphates, nickel and iron ore.

21 February, 1919.

CATEGORIES OF DAMAGE AND INJURY RECOVERABLE
(*Presented by the British Delegation.*)

A. GENERAL. On behalf of the State.

The net expenditure, which the British Empire (including all possessions overseas) has been compelled to lay out from whatever source, including loans to British Dominions and to Allied Powers and the liabilities which the British Empire has been compelled to incur, though not yet satisfied, including compensation of all kinds and pensions of all kinds to members of the forces of Great Britain and the Overseas Dominions and to their dependents, support of persons interned and prisoners, support and relief of fugitives and persons evacuated, from the commencement of the war to the signature and ratification of the final peace.

B. PARTICULAR. On behalf of private persons (natural or juridical), public bodies, companies, etc.

(Where the State has already compensated such persons, it will be subrogated to their rights proportionately. These claims are made where the property of British subjects has been injuriously affected in territory belonging to or occupied by the enemy Powers as well as where it has been so affected in any part of His Majesty's dominions or on the high seas.)

The natural and necessary consequences of enemy action, and of all defensive or counter-offensive measures of war undertaken in order to resist or defeat enemy action, will constitute a claim for compensation where damage has been caused thereby in respect of:

1. *Immovables.*

Buildings and structures of all kinds (other than buildings and structures paid for out of the general war expenditure named above).

Land, whether urban or rural, unless wholly waste and unoccupied.

If the damage is reparable, the claim will be for repairs to restore the condition existing before the damage was done.

If the damage is not reparable or if there has been total destruction, the claim will be for rebuilding or otherwise reconstructing so as to restore the said condition.

Where reconstructing takes the form of replanting, as in the case of orchards destroyed, or of restoring cultivable surfaces impaired or destroyed by shell-fire or otherwise, reasonable account must be also taken of the length of time necessary to restore the former productivity.

Where damage to immovables has taken the form of severing and removing things, which would in ordinary course be severed and removed for the benefit of the parties interested, such as timber, coal, ores, stone, sand or clay, only the value of the things removed shall be claimed.

It is intended to include in buildings, structures and land above mentioned, railways, roads, canals and works of river canalization, with their bridges, embankments and locks, waterworks, railway stations, warehouses, etc., etc., also telegraphs and telephones, and drainage, sewerage and water supply works.

2. *Movables.*

Goods and merchandise of all kinds, live stock, farm implements, crops, household furniture, works of art, shopkeepers' stocks, merchants' stocks, manufacturers' stocks, machinery, tools and implements.

If movables taken away can be recovered and identified, they should be restored to their former owners, who may also claim in respect of damage to them. If they have not been taken away and can be repaired, the claim will be for the cost of repairing them; if they are irreparable, destroyed or carried off, without being capable of identification and restoration, the claim will be for their value.

Further, all kinds of ships (other than ships of war) and other vessels, whether used for marine or internal navigation, with their equipments and cargoes, and all freights contracted for, whether by charter or by bill of lading and actually in course of being carried. Claims are made whether these ships have been detained and held by the enemy or damaged or destroyed.

Where forced sales to the enemy have taken place but payments have been received by the sellers, the claim is for the value of the thing sold only to the extent to which it is in excess of the sum received.

3. *Other kinds of property.*

Stolen money, bank-notes, currency notes, and securities and instruments of all kinds destroyed or carried off and irrecoverable, unless, in the latter case, they are such that their destruction does not involve the loss of the sums which they represent.

4. *All enemy fines and requisitions in money.*

5. *Persons.*

All persons (other than those whose compensation is already

included in paragraph A), who have been physically damaged in their persons in consequence of the aforesaid acts of war, whether permanently or temporarily, or have been assaulted, unjustly imprisoned, deported, held as hostages or otherwise maltreated; and in cases where death has been thus caused the persons dependent on them, who thereby become deprived of their support or livelihood, to the extent of such deprivation.

Questions of price and value and of the times at which such prices or values should be taken, stand over.

Reservation is made in case of any omissions and for proper amendments or additions.

20 February, 1919.[3]

ANNEX IX

TABULATION OF CATEGORIES OF DAMAGE SUFFERED BY BELGIUM

(*Presented by the Belgium Delegation.*)

FIRST CATEGORY OF DAMAGE

I. Damage to Public Domains:

State Railways, electric plants, Navy, Postal and Telegraph Service, property damaged or removed.

Railways operated under concessions: property damaged or removed.

Public Works: roads, navigable waterways, public buildings, police barracks, military buildings in undefended towns.

Navigable waterways operated under concessions.

War: fortified positions of Antwerp, Liége, Namur, Camp of Beverloo, Artillery establishments.

Arts and Sciences: Universities, observatories, etc.

Churches, monuments, works of art belonging to the State, to Provinces, or to Communes.

Senate and Chamber of Representatives.

II. Damage to State Finances:

Advances from Great Britain and France; credits from the United States of America:

(a) war expenses;

(b) subsidies to Commission for Relief in Belgium.

Advances from the Banque Nationale: war expenses.

Advances from private banks and individuals:

(a) subsidies in aid of the Comité National de Secours et d'Alimentation.

[3] The French text omits the date.

(b) payments to the Administration of State Railways and to other public departments for relief and salaries during the period of occupation.

Arrears of salaries due to employees of the State during the period of occupation.

Increase of taxes and new taxes imposed by the invader (excluding war contributions and fines).

Capital to be set aside for the service of civil and military pensions.

Indemnity to be paid to persons deported.

Interest due on advances to the State from the Allies, from banks or from individuals.

Cost of the issue of Treasury Notes for the restoration of the currency.

III. Damage to Provinces:
War contributions (principal and interest).
Damage to Provincial public buildings.

IV. Damage to Communes:
Fines, war contributions, etc.
Subsidies to relief committees, etc.
Damage to Communal public buildings.
Damage to Communal roads and non-navigable waterways.
Requisitions from Communes.

V. Damage to Industry:
Destructions and requisitions.
Expenditures for relief and for the maintenance of factories during the period of occupation.

VI. Damage to Commerce:
Goods seized in the warehouses of the ports of Antwerp, Ghent and Brussels.

VII. Damage to Agriculture:
Depreciation of the land in the battle zone.
Loss of a part of the supply of live stock and decrease in the intrinsic value of the rest.
Deforestation of forests belonging to the State, to Communes, to public organizations and to individuals.

VIII. Damage to Individuals:
Houses destroyed.
Furniture and goods contained in these houses.
Houses pillaged.
Requisitions and thefts committed by the German Army.

Indemnity due to proprietors and tenants of houses occupied by German troops.

Fines inflicted by German war tribunals, interest due on money sequestrated, etc.

IX. Losses at Sea.

SECOND CATEGORY OF DAMAGE

I. Finances of the State and of the Public Administrations:
Arrears in service of public debt.
Losses in sources of taxation after the war.
Public Works: increased expenditure resulting from the stopping of work under way or contracted for before the declaration of war.
Railways operated under concession and local railways: arrears of financial service, loss of receipts, free transport of passengers, soldiers and freight.

II. Industry:
Losses due to interruption of business and profits during period of occupation.
Loss of production during period of restoration.

III. Commerce:
Loss of foreign markets.
Cancelling or non-execution of contracts.

IV. Agriculture:
Increased cost of transport and of living resulting from the diminution of the national supply of live stock.
Decreased production of the soil through lack of fertilizers.
Forests: extraordinary expenses of reforestation; loss of interest during period of restoration, etc.
Restocking of forests and water-courses (game and fish).[4]

V. Particular Damages.

[no date]

ANNEX X

CATEGORIES OF DAMAGE

(*Presented by the Roumanian Delegation.*)

I

DAMAGE INCURRED BY THE STATE, THE DEPARTMENTS AND THE COMMUNES

Division by Ministries:

1. Foreign affairs.

---

[4] The French text omits this item.

2. Finance.
3. Justice.
4. Industry and Commerce.
5. Education and Religion.
6. Public Works.
7. War.
8. Agriculture and Public Domain.
9. Interior.

II

DAMAGE INCURRED BY THE POPULATION OF THE KINGDOM

To be classed in four main categories:

A. Damage to Agriculture.
B. Damage to Industry.
C. Damage to Commerce.
D. Damage to Immovables, as well as damage resulting from the seizure, theft and requisition of installations, utensils, household effects, objects of art, valuables, documents, etc., belonging to private individuals.

A. *Damage to Agriculture.*

To be classified under seven sub-headings according to their nature:

1. Destruction and dilapidation of buildings (buildings and installations).
2. Destruction, seizure and deterioration of machinery and farm implements.
3. Seizure of cereals, seed, dried vegetables, oil seed, forage, etc
4. Seizure of cattle, poultry, as well as production of live stock during the whole period of occupation.
5. Seizure of the entire production of wine, alcohol and liquor produced from fruits and vegetables.
6. Destruction and seizure of the total stock of kegs, casks and barrels and similar receptacles indispensable to the wine industry, etc.
7. Damage to forests belonging to private individuals.

B. *Damage to Industry.*

a. Large industries.
b. Small industries.
c. Oil and mines:
  1. Coal mines.
  2. Quarries and mineral springs.
  3. Oil wells.

C. Damage to the Commerce of the Country.

D. Damage to immovables, as well as damage resulting from the seizure, theft and requisition of installations, utensils, household effects, objects of art, valuables, documents, etc., belonging to private individuals.

III

DAMAGE CAUSED BY THE LOSS OF USE OF PUBLIC AND PRIVATE CAPITAL AND RESTRICTIONS ON THE PRACTICE OF PROFESSIONS.

IV

DAMAGE CAUSED BY THE ILLEGAL ISSUE OF BANK-NOTES BY THE ENEMY IN ROUMANIA.

V

DAMAGE CAUSED BY THE NECESSITY OF RETIRING THE FIDUCIARY CURRENCY OF THE ENEMY FROM CIRCULATION.

VI

DAMAGE TO THE NATIONAL ECONOMIC LIFE AND FINANCES BY THE DESTRUCTION OR REDUCTION OF THE PRODUCTIVE FORCES AND RESOURCES OF THE COUNTRY, AS WELL AS BY THE INFLATION RESULTING FROM THE EXCESSIVE ISSUE OF BANK-NOTES BY THE ENEMY.

VII

WAR COSTS.

VIII

DAMAGE TO PRIVATE INDIVIDUALS AND SOLDIERS AS A CONSEQUENCE OF THE WAR (affecting their life, liberty, capacity for work, health, etc.)

a. Pensions, relief and all other indemnities paid to maimed, wounded and diseased soldiers and their wives and orphans, etc.

b. Idem, applied to civilians.

c. Damage caused by infringing the liberty of individuals (arrest, deportation, invasion of private dwellings, etc.)

(d) Damage caused by maltreatment of prisoners of war.

IX

DAMAGE CAUSED TO THE NATIONAL BANK OF ROUMANIA, TO ROUMANIAN CREDIT INSTITUTIONS AND TO INDIVIDUALS.

For example:

1. Restitution of the gold which the National Bank of Roumania possesses in the hands of the enemy or of enemy subjects.

2. Restitution of the gold, silver, nickel, etc., which the enemy has confiscated or seized in Roumania.
3. Restitution of disposable funds which the National Bank of Roumania or other banks, institutions or individuals possess in enemy countries.
4. Damage caused by the sequestration of such assets or by their having been disposed of.

X

DAMAGE CAUSED TO PROPERTY BELONGING TO THE STATE, TO PUBLIC AUTHORITIES OR OF INDIVIDUALS, SUBJECTS OF ROUMANIA LIVING IN ENEMY COUNTRIES.
DAMAGE CAUSED TO ROUMANIAN SUBJECTS LIVING OR SOJOURNING IN ENEMY COUNTRIES.

XI

DAMAGE CAUSED TO THE STATE, TO THE ECONOMIC CONDITION OF THE COUNTRY IN GENERAL AND TO INDIVIDUALS BY OCCUPATION AS A RESULT OF MEASURES OF A MILITARY, ECONOMIC, FINANCIAL NATURE, ETC. RESTORED TO BY THE ENEMY IN ROUMANIA FOR THE EXPLOITATION OF THE NATIONAL RESOURCES FOR THEIR OWN BENEFIT.

XII

DAMAGE CAUSED TO THE STATE, TO PUBLIC OR PRIVATE INSTITUTIONS AND TO INDIVIDUALS AS A RESULT OF MEASURES WHICH THE ALLIED STATES WERE COMPELLED TO TAKE IN ORDER TO CARRY ON THE WAR.

[no date]

ANNEX XI[5]

CATEGORIES OF DAMAGE

(*Presented by the American Delegation.*)

(Explanatory Note. The following categories of damage with supporting exhibits are submitted in accordance with the procedure decided upon by the First Sub-Committee of the Reparation Commission. Complete reservation is made of the right to withdraw or modify any or all of the categories of damage hereinbelow stipulated for, or to add thereto. The categories are submitted as a practical method of facilitating the work of the First Sub-Committee, and are not to be construed as affecting the principles proposed by the American Delegation, or as indicating any intention as to the filing of a claim, or the amount or character of such claim, if any, as might be filed.)

(1) Compensation for damage resulting from injuries to civilian subjects of the United States (including death, personal injury,

[5] Annex XI is also in Document 368,

enforced labor and/or loss of opportunity to labor or to secure a just reward for labor) done by the aggression of the enemy by land, by sea and from the air.

(2) Compensation for damage (other than that covered by (1), resulting from injuries to subjects of the United States (including death, personal injury, enforced labor and/or loss of opportunity to labor or to secure a just reward for labor) resulting from illegal acts of the enemy governments or of their agents.

(3) Compensation for interests of the American Government and its subjects in property in enemy countries of which they have been deprived by the action of the enemy governments.

(4) Compensation for damage to civilian (non-military) property wherever located in which the American Government or its subjects had an interest, done by the aggression of the enemy by land, by sea and from the air.

(5) Compensation for damage (other than that covered by (4), to property wherever located in which the American Government or its subjects had an interest, resulting from illegal acts of enemy governments or of their agents.

(6) Compensation for the cost of restraining and/or maintaining enemy aliens, whose restraint and/or maintenance devolved upon the Government of the United States in accordance with international law.

———

The American Delegation suggests, but reserves, the question of what if any treatment should be given claims of private subjects of the United States against private subjects of enemy governments, arising through pre-war transactions.

———

The American Delegation suggests, but reserves, the question of what if any waiver should be made by enemy governments of any and all claims against the Government of the United States and its subjects on account of events prior to or during the war.

———

NOTE. It is understood that compensation would be made in accordance with the foregoing categories, irrespective of whether the events specified as giving rise to the right or reparation occurred before or after the entry of the United States into the war.

Attached hereto are Exhibit A, "Property Losses," and Exhibit B, "Injuries to Civilians."[6]

[no date]

[6] The French text omits these exhibits.

A.—Property Loss

Schedules proposed by the representatives of the United States of America

	Damage in place, or sinkings	Removals	Money requisitions	Reorganization of business	Maintenance of idle plants or ships	Loss of revenue during dispossession	Permanent loss of part or all of business	Maintenance of civilians during dispossession	Care of refugees during dispossession	Cost of repatriation	Restraint and maintenance of enemy aliens	Losses to property in enemy and neutral countries (classified)	Total private	Total communal	Total national
Farms															
Dwellings															
Mercantile establishments															
Banks and financial institutions															
Public buildings															
Public service properties															
Transportation lines															
Ships															
Cargoes of ships															
Forests															
Mines:															
Coal															
Metal (classified)															
Industries:															
Textiles															
Metallurgical and chemical															
Sub-classes by commodities															
Miscellaneous manufacturing															
Sub-classes by commodities															
Other state and communal expenses															
TOTAL . . .															

Schedules Proposed by the representatives of the United States of America

CATEGORIES OF DAMAGE

B.—Injuries to Civilians

	Air Operations	Naval Operations	Military Land Operations, Including Executions	Deportation	Internment or Detention	TOTAL		
						Private	Communal	National
Compensation for Personal Injury								
Compensation for Death								
Compensation for Enforced Labor								
Compensation for Loss of Opportunity to Labor								
TOTAL								

NOTE—Compensation to be stated as a capital sum, whether paid as such, or by pension, by annuity, or by state care.

ANNEX XII[7]

CATEGORIES OF DAMAGE FOR WHICH REPARATION MAY BE DEMANDED

Tabulation for the Sub-Committee compiled from the various Memoranda submitted *

FIRST PART.   PRIVATE DAMAGE

Division I. *Categories mentioned by all or the majority of the Delegations.*

CATEGORY A.   IMMOVABLES

Chapter I. DAMAGE CAUSED BY THE TWO GROUPS OF BELLIGERENTS IN EVERY THEATRE OF OPERATIONS.

Sec. 1.

Destruction, deterioration or depreciation of immovable property on land or sea belonging to private persons (natural or artificial) and to public persons other than the State.

Sec. 2.

1. Means employed:

The destruction, deterioration or depreciation may be the result either of an act of war or of the fact of invasion, *as:*

    (a) Bombardment by gun or aircraft on land or sea.

    (b) Voluntary or involuntary action of troops (including lodgings or billeting, etc.).

    (c) Defensive or offensive measures and measures pertaining thereto (including inundations, etc.).

    (d) Torpedoes and submarine mines.

    (e) Deterioration resulting from use by the enemy, felling and digging up.

    (f) Requisition, expropriations, etc.

Sec. 3.

2. Objects of destruction or deterioration:

    (a) Land, forests, plantations and orchards, mines, quarries, roads, canals, railways in general, electric lines and conduits (telephone, telegraph or power), water supply, pipe lines, drains, works of all kinds, etc.).

    (b) Private structures of all kinds and all public structures other than those belonging to the State, buildings or monuments, etc., artistic property included.

* See Annexes II to XI inclusive.

---

[7] The text of this annex is identical with the text of the first column of Annex I of Document 486. See there for what follows.

Chapter II. DAMAGE OTHER THAN THAT PROVIDED FOR IN CHAPTER I ABOVE WHICH MAY HAVE BEEN CAUSED IN ALLIED OR ENEMY COUNTRIES.

Sec. 4.

Damage caused anywhere to immovables or to interests therein either by the application of enemy war legislation or by any act ordered or committed by enemy authority or enemy population (Allied property sequestrated or liquidated by the enemy).

CATEGORY B.   MOVABLES

Chapter I. DAMAGE CAUSED BY THE TWO GROUPS OF BELLIGERENTS IN EVERY THEATRE OF OPERATIONS.

Sec. 5.

1. Causes of Damage.
   All causes referred to in Paragraph 1, Chapter I, above, as well as all removals with or without color of right and all thefts, all forced sales, confiscations or similar measures.

Sec. 6.

2. Objects of Damage.
   (a) Equipment and furnishings of private structures and public structures other than those belonging to the State, machinery, tools, articles of furniture, clothes, linen and personal effects of all sorts, art objects, raw and other materials, merchandise, live-stock, animals of all kinds, harvests, manufactured and non-manufactured products, provisions, drawings, models, patents and trade-marks, records, instruments and documents of all kinds, etc.
   (b) Merchant vessels, fishing-boats, etc., navigating upon the sea or inland waterways, as well as their equipment and cargoes.

Chapter II. DAMAGE OTHER THAN THAT PROVIDED FOR IN CHAPTER I ABOVE WHICH MAY HAVE BEEN CAUSED IN ALLIED OR ENEMY COUNTRIES.

Sec. 7.

Damage caused anywhere to movables, either by the application of enemy war legislation or by any act ordered or committed by enemy authority or enemy population (property sequestrated or disposed of by the enemy, etc.).

CATEGORY C.   MISCELLANEOUS INTERESTS

Chapter I. DAMAGE CAUSED BY THE TWO GROUPS OF BELLIGER-
ENTS IN EVERY THEATRE OF OPERATIONS.

Sec. 8.

1. Causes of damage.

All causes set forth in Paragraph 1, Chapter I, Categories A
and B, above, as well as illegal or *ex parte* sentences of all kinds
and every abolition or suspension by the enemy of laws or codes
in force in invaded or occupied territories.

Sec. 9.

2. Objects of damage.
  (a) Shares and securities of all sorts, coupons.
  (b) Requisition or hiring of labor or service.
  (c) Claims of whatsoever description which can no longer be
       enforced (insurance included) and debts contracted.
  (d) Expenditures incurred by any party (other than the State)
       and in any form whatsoever for the food supply, trans-
       port or relief of the population of invaded or occupied
       territories.
  (e) Injury caused to industrial property by the discovery or
       use of special processes of manufacture, patents or special
       methods.
  (f) Losses to trade caused by the disclosure of business books
       or ledgers and of public or private correspondence or
       records—and in general all documents or information not
       of a public nature—as well as by the use made of such
       documents and information. Losses caused by the new
       competition set up through the knowledge of such docu-
       ments and information.
  (g) Partial or total deprivation of free exercise of proprietary
       rights of any kind, of the free exercise of any occupation
       or generally of opportunity to work or obtain fair remu-
       neration for work.

Loss caused by the total or partial unproductiveness, inactivity
or immobilization of property belonging to private or public persons, other than the State, the normal development of whose
resources has been impeded by the fact of invasion—(1) up to the
date of the Armistice; (2) from the date of the Armistice to the date
at which normal exercise of the proprietary right or occupation
shall again have become possible.

Sec. 10.

Chapter II. THE SAME CLASS OF DAMAGE AS UNDER CHAPTER II, CATEGORY B, ABOVE.

CATEGORY D.   EXACTIONS OF A FINANCIAL CHARACTER

Chapter I. DAMAGE CAUSED BY THE TWO GROUPS OF BELLIGER-ENTS IN EVERY THEATRE OF OPERATIONS.

Sec. 11.

(a) Taxes, imposts, contributions of war, fines, levies in cash of all kinds, thefts of currency—including balances of accounts transferred and assets converted into 'bons,' loan and other stock —forced subscriptions and expenses imposed by the enemy upon individuals or corporations.

(b) Issue of bank-notes, 'bons' and monetary instruments of any kind, falsification, alteration or depreciation of the same.

Sec. 12.

Chapter II. THE SAME CLASS OF DAMAGE AS UNDER CHAPTER II, CATEGORIES B AND C, ABOVE.

CATEGORY E.   DAMAGE TO PERSONS

Chapter I. DAMAGE CAUSED BY THE TWO GROUPS OF BELLIGER-ENTS IN EVERY THEATRE OF OPERATIONS.

Sec. 13.

1. Pensions and allowances of every kind to civilian victims of acts of war (bombardment on land, on sea or from aircraft, and all operations of war) or to persons claiming under them:
>   (a) to the surviving wife or husband, orphans, descendants, or parents;
>   (b) to mutilated, wounded or sick.

Sec. 14.

2. Pensions and allowances of every sort to civilian victims of acts, cruelties, violence or maltreatment committed or ordered by the enemy, or to persons claiming under them:
>   (a) to persons shot, put to death or dead from the conse-quences of maltreatment;[8]
>   (b) to persons exposed by the enemy to the fire of the Allied troops;
>   (c) to persons injured in life or health as a consequence of imprisonment, deportation, internment or evacuation;
>   (d) to persons who have suffered accidental death or injury

---

[8] The French text omits (a).

or have become infirm or sick in consequence of forced work, and especially of every kind of occupation contrary to the interests of their country.

Sec. 15.

3. Damages for every act injurious to health or capacity for work or to honor.

Chapter II. DAMAGE OTHER THAN THAT PROVIDED FOR IN CHAPTER I ABOVE WHICH MAY HAVE BEEN CAUSED IN ALLIED OR ENEMY COUNTRIES.

Sec. 16.

Pensions, allowances and compensation for injury to life, health or the capacity to work of interned civilians, including cost of relief of the said interned persons.

Division II. *Categories not mentioned by all or the majority of the Delegations.*

CATEGORY C.   MISCELLANEOUS INTERESTS

Chapter II. DAMAGE WHICH MAY HAVE BEEN CAUSED IN ALLIED OR ENEMY COUNTRIES OUTSIDE OF EVERY THEATRE OF OPERATIONS OF THE TWO GROUPS OF BELLIGERENTS.

Sec. 17.

(a) Claims no longer enforcible and debts contracted as a consequence of the war.

(b) Total or partial deprivation of the free exercise of any proprietary right, occupation or, generally, of opportunity to work or to obtain fair remuneration for work.

Loss caused by unproductiveness, inactivity or immobilization, total or partial, to any private or public person other than the State, the normal development of whose resources has been impeded by the fact of invasion—(1) up to the date of the Armistice; (2) from the date of the Armistice to the date at which normal exercise of the proprietary right or occupation shall again have become possible.

(c) All expenses imposed upon corporations other than the State and upon associations existing for the public benefit through the necessity of coming to the assistance of the population.

(d) All damage to individuals or corporations other than the State resulting from the annulment or suspension of contracts entered upon before the war with subjects of enemy Powers.

(e) All damage suffered by individuals or corporations other than the State, in consequence of the increase in prices, freights, salaries and remuneration, etc.

CATEGORY E.   DAMAGE TO PERSONS

Chapter I. DAMAGE CAUSED BY THE TWO GROUPS OF BELLIGERENTS IN EVERY THEATRE OF OPERATIONS.

Sec. 18.

Damage for every person employed in any occupation contrary to the interests of his country, without injury to life, health or capacity for work.

Chapter II. DAMAGE OTHER THAN THAT PROVIDED FOR UNDER CHAPTER I ABOVE WHICH MAY HAVE BEEN CAUSED IN ALLIED OR ENEMY COUNTRIES.

Sec. 19.

Pensions and allowances of every kind:
   (a) to victims of explosions in war factories;
   (b) to victims of accidents while working in such factories.

SECOND PART—PUBLIC DAMAGE

Division I. *Categories mentioned by all or the majority of the Delegations.*

Chapter I. ALL DAMAGE ENUMERATED IN DIVISIONS I AND II OF PART I ABOVE WHICH HAVE BEEN SUFFERED BY THE STATE IN ITS NON-MILITARY PROPERTY AND IN ITS OWN RESOURCES

Sec. 20.

(avoiding any duplication of claims for damage to individuals or corporations other than the State):

Sec. 21.

Including allowances to refugees, and to persons evacuated or out of work, and furthermore:

Sec. 22.

Injury resulting to Allied nations from the necessity to which they have been put of redeeming monetary instruments and in general all obligations expressed in terms of enemy money held by the inhabitants (public or private persons) of territories which have been in the power *de jure* or *de facto* of the enemy Powers, or held by prisoners of war and interned civilians.

Chapter II. MILITARY EXPENDITURE OF THE STATE OR OF ITS POSSESSIONS OR COLONIES.

Sec. 23.

A. Pensions, allowances and bonuses of every kind to military victims of the war or persons claiming under them.

Sec. 24.

1. To victims of acts of war or persons claiming under them:
   (a) to widows, orphans, descendants or parents;
   (b) to mutilated, wounded, sick and invalided.

Sec. 25.

2. To prisoners of war injured in life or health as a consequence of acts, cruelties, violence or maltreatment committed or ordered by the enemy.

Sec. 26.

B. Expenditure for aid by the State or corporations rendered to prisoners of war. Allowances to families of mobilized persons.

Sec. 27.

C. Other war costs.

All expenditures or charges resulting from the state of war imposed upon the Allied nations.

Sec. 28.

Expenses of maintenance by the Allied States of enemy prisoners of war, officers and men and of interned persons.

Division II. *Categories not mentioned by all or the majority of the Delegations.*

Chapter I. DAMAGE OF EVERY KIND SUFFERED BY THE NATION IN ITS PRODUCTIVENESS.

Sec. 29.

Especially: damage resulting from deaths or any injury to the health or physical capacity of subjects—from the diminution of agricultural and industrial production—from excessive exploitation of forests—from loss on exchange caused by excess importation, etc.

Chapter II. DAMAGE RESULTING FROM FORMER WARS.

Sec. 30.

A. Greek Delegation: settlement of claims against Turkey and Bulgaria of earlier date than the European War.

[Sec. 31.]

B. French Delegation: War of 1870-1871 (war indemnity, war seizures, taxes, imposts, contributions, fines and payments imposed by the enemy).

Subject to modifications and additions.

26 February, 1919.

ANNEX XIII
CATEGORIES OF DAMAGE
(*Presented by the Portuguese Delegation.*)
CLASS I
DIRECT DAMAGE

A. DAMAGE INFLICTED ON THE WEALTH OF THE PORTUGUESE PEOPLE AS A NATION.

Expenses incurred by the State through participation in military and naval operations in Europe and Africa to honor international treaties and defend national rights:

—Pensions, subsidies and compensations of different classes granted by the State to soldiers, sailors, civilians and corporations.

—Expenses incurred on account of Portuguese prisoners and interned subjects in enemy countries, and enemy subjects in Portugal.

—Relief and transport for individuals repatriated from invaded territories or enemy countries, and crews and passengers of boats lost by enemy action.

—National property which the State was debarred from making use of owing to requirements of the Allies for reasons of war.

B. DAMAGE INFLICTED ON THE PRIVATE WEALTH OF PERSONS (BOTH NATURAL AND ARTIFICIAL).

—Destruction and deterioration of property of every description on land or sea wrought by enemy action or by measures of defense.

—Loss and depreciation of the value of property in enemy countries, pertaining to Portuguese subjects, or of valuables and credits for which enemy States, corporations and persons are responsible.

—Compensations and subsidies awarded, as determined by law, by private persons (either natural or artificial) to mobilized men or their families.

—Compensation for damage, not chargeable to the State, awarded to different persons for various reasons (crews, passengers of ships sunk, individuals and corporations, for deaths, injuries and other causes).

CLASS II
INDIRECT DAMAGE
A and B (NATIONAL AND PRIVATE WEALTH).

—Industries paralyzed, raw materials and colonial produce lost, owing to the lack of tonnage due to the submarine campaign.

—Profits, derived from shipping, industry and agriculture (colonial), which ceased on account of destruction and depreciation.

—Economic loss involved in the devastation of forests owing to the imperative requirements of wood for use as fuel on railways and in factories.

—Economic loss suffered by the colonies owing to the scarcity of labor, the population having been reduced by the loss of some 130,000 natives in consequence of the war.

—Disturbance of the economic equilibrium arising from the greater increase of the price of imported goods as compared with that of exported goods.

Should a damage suffered be considered as sufficiently compensated to the person directly affected, the risk having been transferred in the usual way, the State shall, for purposes of reparation, stand in the place of such person, as the damage still rests with the nation.

Subject to alterations.

Paris, 27 February, 1919.

DOCUMENT 471

First Subcommittee: Minutes of the Fifth Meeting, February 28, 1919, 2:30 P. M.

[EOM, First Subcommittee, pp. 44-49. French stenographic minutes, PV, CRD, pp. 288-308; French condensed minutes, *ibid.*, pp. 309-14.]

The First Sub-Committee of the Commission on Reparation of Damage (Valuation of Damage) met on Friday, 28 February, 1919, at 2.30 P. M., at the Ministry of Finance, LORD SUMNER in the Chair.

Present: MR. McCORMICK (*U. S. A.*); LORD SUMNER (*British Empire*); MR. LEBRUN (*France*); MR. NAGAOKA (*Japan*); MR. VAN DEN HEUVEL (*Belgium*); MR. MICHALACOPOULOS (*Greece*); MR. OLCHOWSKI (*Poland*); MR. A. DOS SANTOS VIEGAS (*Portugal*); MR. DANIELOPOL (*Roumania*); MR. SAVTCHITCH (*Serbia*); MR. OSUSKI (*Czecho-Slovak Republic*).

The CHAIRMAN stated that the minutes of the preceding meeting would be submitted for approval later.

Discussion of Tabulation of Categories

The agenda called for the examination of the Tabulation of the various Memoranda relating to Categories of Damage (Annex XII, 4th meeting).

Sec. 3 (a)

MR. DANIELOPOL (*Roumania*) offered two observations under this section.

1. The tabulation classified mines and quarries under immovable property, but, according to the Roumanian law, oil wells and bituminous deposits were regarded as movables. This fact ought not to prejudice Roumania's claim for reparation on account of injury to her mines.

2. In Roumania, wells from which oil was drawn were considered as oil mines and the whole stretch of ground from which oil could be extracted was called the oil-bed. Injury to the wells had involved damage to the oil-beds and MR. DANIELOPOL proposed the addition to Section 3, a, of the word "deposits" (*gisements*).

The CHAIRMAN replied to the first point by stating that the heading "immovables" on the first page of the comparative statement did not imply any limitation. It was used only for convenience in classification and in every respect the right to reparation was the same whether the mines were considered as movable or as immovable property.

The CHAIRMAN expressed the opinion that the second point was rightly taken and accordingly the Committee approved the addition of the word "deposits" (*gisements*) to Section 3, a.

Sec. 11

A discussion followed on Category D, "Exactions of a Financial Character."

Financial Exactions

Messrs. YANKOWICH (*Expert for Serbia*), OLCHOWSKI (*Poland*) and DANIELOPOL (*Roumania*) explained the situation which the war had created in their countries. MR. DANIELOPOL in particular complained of Germany's action in continuing to print bank-notes in Berlin which were identical with the Roumanian bank-notes and in circulating them in neutral countries.

In order to meet the wishes of the preceding speakers, MR. LEBRUN (*France*) moved and the Committee accepted an amendment to sub-section (b) (Sec. 11) in the following form:

"Issue, falsification, alteration or depreciation of bank notes, 'bons' and monetary instruments of every sort."

The CHAIRMAN remarked that the section under discussion was borrowed from the French Memorandum (Annex IV, Tenth

Meeting) which contemplated taxes, levies and war contributions, the issue of bank paper and monetary instruments of all sorts. It seemed to him a pity that this paragraph of the French Memorandum had been split in two parts in the comparative statement, for its division might appear to imply a distinction between two sorts of damage, whereas in truth no distinction was intended. To MR. DANIELOPOL he replied that the notes put out by Germany were not genuine and imposed no obligation on the Roumanian banks, so that there could hardly be a question of listing them among the claims for reparation by Germany. To Messrs. BAY-KITCH and OLCHOWSKI, who had raised a question about the depreciation of the "ost-rubel" and of the "dinar," he said that the facts alluded to by them appeared to belong to the class of damage resulting from excessive levies and sales forced at a low price.

MR. DULLES (*U. S. A.*) expressed his accord with the views of the CHAIRMAN and stated his opinion that it would be better to consider the person who had suffered injury rather than to look at general categories which could but involve a risk of duplication.

Allied Gold in Enemy Countries

MR. DANIELOPOL (*Roumania*) having raised the question whether the Delegations would be allowed to claim rights to gold, silver or credits belonging to the Allies but situated in enemy countries, MR. LEBRUN (*France*) replied that the question had a double aspect:

1. Should the question raised by MR. DANIELOPOL be considered in the report of the Sub-Committee?

In MR. LEBRUN'S opinion, Chapter II of Category B of the comparative Tabulation which covered property sequestrated or disposed of should satisfy MR. DANIELOPOL'S requirements.

2. How were the Allied belligerents to realize their holdings situated in enemy countries?

To this second question MR. LEBRUN would answer that it was a question of priority, which, not being within the province of the Sub-Committee, should be reserved.

The CHAIRMAN, summing up the discussion, asked the Committee if it was clearly understood that sub-section (b) contemplated only forced loans and exactions in the guise of loans and consequently belonged with sub-section (a). The Committee assented to this interpretation.

MR. JOUASSET (*Expert for France*) explained, at the CHAIRMAN'S request, the meaning of the phrase "thefts of currency—

including balances of accounts transferred and assets converted into "bons".

The intention had been to consider along with general cases the conversion of credit balances belonging to French nationals found in the banks in the regions referred to in the paragraph, into German loans, or subscriptions to German obligations. Moreover, the words "including balances of accounts" did not refer only to thefts of currency but to the whole of what went before.

Secs. 13-16 and 18-19.

The CHAIRMAN proposed that Category E, "Damage to Persons," should next be considered simultaneously with the category which had the same title and was inserted in Division II (Categories not mentioned by all or the majority of the Delegations).

At the request of MR. OLCHOWSKI (*Poland*) and with the assent of MR. JOUASSET (*Expert for France*) the end of Section 14 (d) was deleted: "and especially of every kind of occupation contrary to the interests of their country."

Sec. 18

After a remark by MR. VAN DEN HEUVEL (*Belgium*) and an exchange of views in which Messrs. LEBRUN (*France*), OLCHOWSKI (*Poland*) and JOUASSET (*France*) spoke, the CHAIRMAN proposed the following amendment to Category E of Division II ("Categories not mentioned by all or the majority of the Delegations."): "All persons put at any kind of forced labor or compelled to be engaged in work contrary to the interests of their country." This amendment was accepted.

Sec. 15

In answer to a question of MR. VAN DEN HEUVEL (*Belgium*) MR. JOUASSET (*Expert for France*) explained that the term "against honor" in Chapter 1, Category E, 3 (Sec. 15) contemplated only material injuries such as every one must have in mind.

After an exchange of opinions by MR. DULLES (*U. S. A.*) and MR. JOUASSET (*Expert for France*) on the significance of the words "pensions or allowances," the CHAIRMAN expressed the view that the difference between these speakers was only a matter of terminology and that the text might stand if it was understood that the words contained no implication about "method of payment." Subject to the reservations implied in the preceding comments, the two categories marked E, which had been under discussion, were accepted.

MR. OLCHOWSKI (*Poland*) referred to the expression "claims no longer enforcible and debts contracted as a consequence of the war." Following a number of observations, MR. LEBRUN (*France*) pointed out that the Commission was engaged in a discussion about propositions included in a small number of Memoranda; it would be well if the Delegations which were raising these points would explain their own proposals.

Upon the CHAIRMAN'S approving this suggestion, MR. BAY-KITCH (*Expert for Serbia*) cited a number of definite examples of claims no longer recoverable and debts contracted as a result of the war: e.g., insolvent enemy debtors and enemy debtors who died leaving no representatives, cases in which the evidences of title had been destroyed, debts contracted in foreign countries by Serbian refugees, debts contracted by Serbians at home as a direct result of the impossibility of earning their own livelihood.

MR. LEBRUN (*France*) thought that these different sorts of damage were covered by the Category "Damage caused by the two Groups of Belligerents in every theatre of operations." How otherwise would one deal with the case of a manufacturer of Toulouse who, without having ever seen the enemy, had suffered war damage in the form of a list of unenforceable claims and liabilities incurred?

MR. DANIELOPOL (*Roumania*) explained that the invaders had prevented Roumanian capital from being invested in developments in order to secure the opportunities for German capital. The consequent loss should, according to him, be regarded as a direct damage giving right to a claim for reparation. The same would apply to the agricultural damage resulting from the invader's seizures of seed, agricultural machinery and cattle.

MR. CHIESA (*Italy*) reminded the Committee of the loss which Italy had suffered by reason of the increased freight rates which were a direct consequence of submarine warfare; the rise in prices, in wages and in salaries; allowances and allotments to the families of men who were mobilized.

The CHAIRMAN called the attention of the Committee to the gravity of the situation and to its responsibility before the bar of history. He considered it important to approach the discussion in a spirit of most serious deliberation. Certain claims, such particularly as claims on account of the increased cost of living, were too vague and appeared excessive. Could the British Empire present a claim for loss on administration of the wheat supply? The Members of the Committee must adopt the point of view of statesmen rather than of jurists, and, bearing this in mind, they must certainly find themselves influenced toward moderation. Furthermore, if prices had risen on the one hand, very considerable profits had been realized on the other hand. A truly exact estimate of the consequences of the war was impracticable. In conclusion, the CHAIRMAN asked the Delegations to make an effort to eliminate formulas which were so vague that he for one could hardly subscribe to them.

MR. CHIESA (*Italy*) thought it should be remembered that certain countries had suffered special injury, and that even if important gains had accrued which would tend to reduce certain losses, the enemy must still be held accountable for the difference. Furthermore, the injuries specified in the Italian Memorandum were in no respect vague and were susceptible of being figured accurately.

Sec. 17 (b)

MR. VAN DEN HEUVEL (*Belgium*) criticized the idea expressed in Section 17 (b), according to which it would be necessary to take account of the normal possible development of business during the war. To his mind one should take account only of the situation as it existed at the moment when injury was sustained.

Secs. 9 (g) and 17 (b)

MR. LEBRUN (*France*) elucidated the distinction between general damage and special damage resulting from the invasion. All countries, for instance, neutral as well as others, had been involved in expense due to the wheat shortage, but only certain countries have seen their territory invaded and their houses demolished. Besides, the destruction of property sustained by these countries might be said to have saved other Allied countries from similar destruction. For this reason special damage consequent upon invasion should have priority in reparation. Passing, then, to the application of this distinction, MR. LEBRUN (*France*) called attention to the classes of damage resulting from "partial or total deprivation of free exercises of proprietary rights of any kind, etc.," which figures both in Section 9 (g) and in Section 17 (b); the first case being when the damage was sustained within the theatre of operations; and the second case when the injury was sustained outside the theatre of operations. In his opinion, Section 9 (g) should be adopted. But he said that, for his part, subject to further examination of details, he would be tempted to omit entirely the damage contemplated by Section 17 (b).

The CHAIRMAN then proposed to postpone the discussion of Category C until particulars had been supplied by each of the interested Delegations. The proposal was accepted by the Sub-Committee.

After a recess of fifteen minutes, the discussion of the Second Part (Public Damage) was renewed.

Secs. 20, 21, 22

MR. DANIELOPOL (*Roumania*) called attention to the fact that Chapter I, referring as it did to Divisions 1 and 2 of Part I, would seem to cover only taxes and levies and war contributions imposed by the enemy. The fact was, however, that Roumania had suffered a direct injury by reason of the invaders having not imposed taxes, but prevented the collection of taxes (custom duties, e.g.). There ought to be a formula broad enough to include damage of this negative sort.

MR. LEBRUN (*France*) pointed out that the matter was covered by Section 9 (g) of Category C, which had already been made the subject of a reservation.

Upon the proposal of the CHAIRMAN, MR. DANIELOPOL'S question was accordingly reserved for future discussion.

Sec. 22

Upon the request of the CHAIRMAN, MR. JOUASSET (*Expert for France*) explained by means of examples what was the significance of the last paragraph, Chapter I ("Injury resulting to Allied Nations, from the necessity to which they had been put of redeeming acknowledgments," etc.). Repatriated citizens of the invaded regions, interned civilians and prisoners of war returning from Germany had marks in their possession which they had been forced to accept at par. In order not to inflict a loss upon them that would have been unfair from their point of view, the French Government had had to reimburse them in a manner which similarly reckoned the mark at par regardless of its actual depreciation. The same had been true with respect to the marks which remained in the hands of people who were liberated when the invaded territories were retaken. Similar measures had been taken on behalf of the population of Alsace-Lorraine.

The State had thereby suffered a loss the measure of which was the difference between the actual exchange value of the mark and its nominal value.

The CHAIRMAN was of the opinion that though the French Government was in a position to claim reimbursement for its loss resulting from assuming marks at par in the first two cases cited by MR. JOUASSET, its claim might be disputable in the case of Alsace-Lorraine.

MR. CHIESA (*Italy*) called attention to the fact that a similar question had been raised in Italy in respect to Venetia and the provinces that had been occupied under the terms of the Armistice.

MR. JOUASSET (*Expert for France*) insisted on the legitimacy of the claim on account of taking up the marks at par in Alsace-Lorraine. This claim could not be said to differ from the claim arising out of the reimbursement to the liberated population.

Sec. 11 (b)

MR. MICHALACOPOULOS (*Greece*) informed the Committee that the enemy had circulated its own paper money in Greece. He proposed accordingly that Section 11 (b) of Category D (First Part), "Extractions of a Financial Character," should be taken to cover the circulation of bank-notes.

MR. BAYKITCH (*Expert for Serbia*) drew attention to the injury suffered by his country through the issue of paper which had merely the value of receipts.

German Money in Alsace-Lorraine

In view of the lack of agreement upon the question of reimbursing the people of Alsace-Lorraine for German marks, the CHAIRMAN proposed to forward this question to the main Commission—the difference of views expressed in the Sub-Committee being noted in the report.

Finally the CHAIRMAN expressed the hope that the Delegations would soon make satisfactory replies to the questions which he had put to them relative to the total of the damage claimed by each, this to the end that figures might be presented to the main Commission by the end of next week.

The next meeting was fixed for Saturday, 1 March, 1919, at 5 P.M.

The meeting adjourned at 6.45 P.M.

SUMNER,
Chairman.

E. MINOST,
Secretary.

DOCUMENT 472

First Subcommittee: Minutes of the Sixth Meeting, March 1, 1919, 5:15 P. M.

[EOM, First Subcommittee, pp. 50-51. French stenographic minutes, PV, CRD, pp. 315-25; French condensed minutes, *ibid.*, 326-28.]

The First Sub-Committee (on Valuation of Damage) met at the Ministry of Finance on Saturday, 1 March, 1919, at 5.15 P. M., LORD SUMNER in the Chair.

Present: MR. DULLES (*U. S. A*); LORD SUMNER (*British Empire*); MR. LEBRUN (*France*); MR. CHIESA (*Italy*); MR. NAGAOKA (*Japan*); MR. VAN DEN HEUVEL (*Belgium*); MR. MICHALACOPOULOS (*Greece*); MR. OLCHOWSKI (*Poland*); MR. DOS SANTOS VIEGAS (*Portugal*); MR. DANIELOPOL (*Roumania*); MR. PROTITCH (*Serbia*); MR. BENES (*Czecho-Slovak Republic*).[1]

The presentation of the minutes of the last meeting was postponed.

Discussion of Tabulation of Categories

The Committee continued its examination of the Tabulation of the Memoranda on Categories of Damage.

MR. BAYKITCH (*Expert for Serbia*), referring to the CHAIRMAN'S observation during the last meeting that certain kinds of war costs were economically not an expense to the nation but merely a transfer of wealth within the nation, pointed out that the expenditures of Serbia had been a total loss.

The CHAIRMAN observed that MR. BAYKITCH'S remarks concerned methods of valuation rather than categories of damage, which the Committee was now considering.

MR. VAN DEN HEUVEL (*Belgium*) asked whether the Tabulation included any article which would cover the claim of the Belgian Government for necessary extra expenditure for civil administration due to its expulsion from Belgium. The CHAIRMAN explained that the claim was not excluded from the Tabulation.

Secs. 13 (a) and 24 (a)

MR. LEBRUN (*France*) proposed to add the words "or persons claiming under them" (*et leurs ayant droit*) after the word "parent" (*ascendants*) in Section 13 (a) and Section 24 (a). This was agreed to.

[1] According to the French stenographic minutes, Savčić was present instead of Protić.

Sec. 29

The CHAIRMAN then called for the discussion of the first clause of the last section of the Tabulation: "Damage of every kind suffered by the nation in its productiveness."

MR. CHIESA (*Italy*) pointed out that the losses due to extra freight costs and abnormal exchange had been suffered by Italy to a peculiar degree. These losses, as well as the destruction of forests to provide fuel, had been due to the special conditions created by illegal submarine warfare.

MR. BENES (*Czecho-Slovak Republic*) stated that the agricultural production of his country had been diminished by one third, largely on account of the lack of imported fertilizers, caused by the war. There had been large losses through the wasteful exploitation of coal mines and also through their destruction. Certain industries had been entirely annihilated, as, for example, the breweries of Pilsen.

The CHAIRMAN considered that the claims dealt with in this paragraph belonged to the class of claims under Section C (Miscellaneous Interests) in Part First, the consideration of which had been postponed. There were two obvious objections: First, that general diminution of productivity could not be valued; next, that the cases referred to were due, not to the war, but to the peculiar commercial position of the countries in question, which existed before the war and did not arise from it. As to the particular case of the Czecho-Slovak Republic, he pointed out that MR. BENES was claiming for damage which resulted from the blockade at a time when his country was unfortunately still a part of the Austro-Hungarian Monarchy.

The CHAIRMAN invited the Delegations interested to bring forward these claims again in a modified form which could be generally accepted.

Status of Poland and the Czecho-Slovak Republic

MR. BENES (*Czecho-Slovak Republic*) pointed out that his country claimed reparation as a country occupied by the enemy. His country had been recognized as an independent power during the war.

MR. OLCHOWSKI (*Poland*) added that the Kingdom of Poland had been invaded and occupied since 1915 and that Galicia had been a theatre of operations during the whole period of the war.

The CHAIRMAN said that the status of Poland and that of the

Czecho-Slovak Republic were special questions which must be decided by a higher authority and which he in no way prejudged.

Sec. 29

MR. CHIESA (*Italy*), replying to the CHAIRMAN'S observations, said that although Italy's fleet before the war was small, the damage she had subsequently suffered had been none the less due to submarine warfare. Her claims for excess freight costs and for losses on account of abnormal exchange were for a real damage, accurately and precisely known and due to an illegal form of warfare. This was a direct damage and was covered by Secretary Lansing's note.

Sec. 30

The CHAIRMAN, proceeding to the last paragraph of the Tabulation, pointed out that it was hardly within the competence of the Commission to deal with claims arising out of previous wars. He suggested that France and Greece reserve their rights and present their claims to the Peace Conference.

MR. MICHALACOPOULOS (*Greece*) said that the Greek Memorandum merely reserved the rights of his country in respect of such claims.

MR. LEBRUN (*France*) accepted the CHAIRMAN'S ruling so far as it concerned the Sub-Committee, but hoped that the Commission on Reparation itself would discuss the French claims arising from the War of 1870-71.

Memoranda on Methods of Valuation

The CHAIRMAN observed that the next task of the Committee would be to consider methods of valuation; he suggested, subject to the Committee's approval, that each Delegation should prepare a Memorandum on this subject.

After a brief discussion in regard to the reserved clauses of the Tabulation, it was agreed that the Delegations interested should bring forward revised drafts at their convenience.

The next meeting was fixed for Tuesday, 4 March, at 2.30 P. M.

The meeting adjourned at 7 P. M.

SUMNER,
Chairman.

H. McKINNON WOOD,
　Secretary.

DOCUMENT 473

First Subcommittee: Minutes of the Seventh Meeting, March 4, 1919, 2:30 P. M.

[EOM, First Subcommittee, pp. 52-55. French stenographic minutes, PV, CRD, pp. 329-47; French condensed minutes, *ibid.*, pp. 348-51.]

The First Sub-Committee of the Commission on Reparation of Damage (Valuation of Damage) met on Tuesday, 4 March, 1919, at 2.30 P. M., at the Ministry of Finance, LORD SUMNER in the Chair.

Present: MR. MCCORMICK (*U. S. A.*); LORD SUMNER (*British Empire*); MR. LEBRUN (*France*); MR. CHIESA (*Italy*); MR. MORI (*Japan*); MR. VAN DEN HEUVEL (*Belgium*); MR. MICHALACO-POULOS (*Greece*); MR. OLCHOWSKI (*Poland*); MR. DOS SANTOS VIEGAS (*Portugal*); MR. DANIELOPOL (*Roumania*); MR. PROTITCH (*Serbia*); MR. OSUSKI (*Czecho-Slovak Republic*).

The minutes of the fourth, fifth and sixth meetings were adopted.

In reply to MR. OLCHOWSKI (*Poland*) who asked that Poland and the other countries of the East of Europe might be admitted to the benefit of the clause in the Armistice Convention providing for Belgium and France immediate recovery of articles removed by the enemy, the CHAIRMAN, accepting the view which was expressed by MR. VAN DEN HEUVEL (*Belgium*), stated that this question was not within the competence of the Committee, as it had no executive powers.

Discussion of Tabulation of Categories

The CHAIRMAN then called for discussion of various amendments of the Tabulation of Categories which had been proposed.

MR. PROTITCH (*Serbia*) thanked MR. LEBRUN for a speech which had assisted him to understand the meaning of the main categories of damage. He laid stress upon the importance of direct damage to countries which had been invaded. Granted the impossibility in practice of assessing all the effects of the war upon economic life, he asked that Section 17 might be simply omitted.

Sec. 17

The CHAIRMAN took note of MR. PROTITCH'S statement and submitted for discussion the first amendment proposed by the French Delegation in substitution for Sections 4 and 7, viz.:

Secs. 4 and 7

"Damage caused to property, movable or immovable:

(a) In enemy territory by any act ordered or committed by enemy authority or population.

(b) In enemy territory or in occupied or invaded territory by the application of laws relating to seizure, requisitions, sequestrations and liquidations of sequestrated property."

MR. DANIELOPOL (*Roumania*) asked that the words "and by any administrative, legal or other act" be added at the end of sub-section (b) of the amendment.

The CHAIRMAN and MR. LEBRUN (*France*) replied that the cases thus provided for were already covered by sub-section (a); and MR. DANIELOPOL accepted this explanation.

After a request for an explanation by MR. PROTITCH (*Serbia*) and after an exchange of views between various Delegates, it was decided to add certain words to sub-section (b), which thus assumed the following form:

(b) In enemy territory or in occupied or invaded territory by the application of laws *or by any act whatever under enemy authority* relating to seizures, requisitions, sequestrations and liquidations of sequestrated property.

The amendment thus modified was unanimously accepted.

Sec. 9 (g)

The Sub-Committee proceeded to discuss the second amendment of the French Delegation, which proposed to substitute for Section 9 (g) the following:

Partial or total deprivation of the free exercise of any proprietary right, any occupation or generally of opportunity to work or to obtain fair remuneration for work.

Loss from any partial or total unproductiveness, inactivity or immobilization caused to any private person or public person (other than the State) whose resources have been injured by invasion; (1) up to the date of the Armistice; (2) from the date of the Armistice up to the moment at which normal exercise of such proprietary rights of occupation shall again have become possible.

MR. VAN DEN HEUVEL (*Belgium*) proposed for the same clause the following text:—

"Loss arising from unproductiveness of lands and buildings directly caused by operations of war or by the measures which the enemy has taken.

"Reparation for the obligatory charges which as a direct consequence of operations of war or of measures taken by the enemy have become a burden upon commercial and industrial undertakings."

He considered that the French text was too indefinite and would be difficult to apply in practice.

Mr. OLCHOWSKI (*Poland*) thought it would be fairer to claim for commercial and industrial undertakings, not merely reparation for obligatory charges, but also normal interest upon capital.

Mr. LEBRUN (*France*) could not accept the Belgian text, which provided no indemnification for the workman; and pointed out that the American Delegation admitted the category of "forced labor" and "loss of opportunity to labor or to secure a just reward for labor."

Mr. DULLES (*U. S. A.*) agreed that the rights of the workers must receive the same protection as those of property. He thought that the two views could be reconciled, if it was insisted that there must be a direct and necessary connection between the acts of the enemy and the loss suffered through forced labor or prevention of labor.

The CHAIRMAN felt that the French text was too wide, and that its categories of claim were covered by other parts of the Tabulation. He thought that an intermediate text could be agreed upon.

Mr. VAN DEN HEUVEL (*Belgium*), who was in no way opposed to the claims of labor, Messrs. CHIESA (*Italy*) and MCCORMICK (*U. S. A.*) supported this proposal.

Mr. DANIELOPOL (*Roumania*) asked that in the new draft account should be taken of the damage caused to his country during the occupation by the loss of the export taxes upon grain.

The CHAIRMAN preferred that this claim should form a special paragraph.

Mr. MCCORMICK (*U. S. A.*), in view of the urgency of the position, asked (1) that all these proposals should be put in writing, and (2) that the Sub-Committee should proceed forthwith to the discussion of figures.

The CHAIRMAN took formal note of Mr. MCCORMICK's declaration and asked Messrs. VAN DEN HEUVEL and JOUASSET to agree with him upon a fresh draft or clause (g).

The Committee proceeded to discuss the amendments proposed by the Italian Delegation, viz.:

Section 29 is withdrawn.

At Section 6 (b) it is proposed to add the following words:

"including the increase in freight costs in consequence of

the diminution in the number of ships; that in costs of exchange due to the diminution of exports, and the loss of the produce of fisheries."

In place of Section 17 (b) the following concrete formula is proposed:

> (b) Losses caused by the excessive exploitation of forests in consequence of the shortage of coal and by all unproductiveness of agriculture or industry due to the war, up to the time when production shall again have become possible.

MR. CHIESA (*Italy*) emphasized the fact that certain countries had suffered more from indirect damage than from direct damage. He made a moving appeal in favor of his country, where destruction of forests, economic stagnation, losses on foreign exchange, and from the increase in freight costs, had been due in a special degree to the submarine warfare, which was contrary to international law.

In order not to open the door to unlimited claims, the CHAIRMAN asked MR. CHIESA to submit a more precise and restricted formula.

MR. MCCORMICK (*U. S. A.*) returned to the question of figures, which was the more pressing in view of the fact that the Second Sub-Committee would soon have finished its work. He urgently requested each Delegation immediately to give a provisional figure. In reply to an observation with MR. JOUASSET (*Expert for France*), he remarked that figures would facilitate the study of the methods of valuation.

The CHAIRMAN and Messrs. CHIESA (*Italy*) and ANTONESCO (*Roumania*) supported this proposition. Messrs. JOUASSET (*Expert for France*) and MICHALACOPOULOS (*Greece*) made reservations on behalf of their respective countries.

MR. MCCORMICK (*U. S. A.*) presented the following declaration: "The American Delegation understands that the Second Sub-Committee is about to report a sum which the enemy can pay. The American Delegation, in frankness, desires to inform the other members of the Sub-Committee that for itself it will not be a party to demanding a fixed sum from the enemy, unless there is evidence sufficient to convince the American Delegation that there are just minima claims sufficient to absorb that sum."

MR. OSUSKI (*Czecho-Slovak Republic*) asked what were the points of principle upon which the Plenary Commission would be consulted.

It was agreed that the following points should be raised:—

(1) The question of the purchase of marks in Alsace-Lorraine and of kronen at Trieste.

(2) To what extent the Committee should take account of the case of Russia.

(3) The status of the Czecho-Slovak Republic.

France and Greece reserved their rights in regard to claims arising out of former wars.

The next meeting was fixed for Wednesday, 5 March, at 2.30 P. M.

The meeting adjourned at 6.15 P. M.

H. McKINNON WOOD,   SUMNER,
Secretary.   *Chairman.*

DOCUMENT 474

First Subcommittee: Minutes of the Eighth Meeting, March 5, 1919, 2:30 P. M.

[EOM, First Subcommittee, pp. 56-58. French stenographic minutes, PV, CRD, pp. 352-66; French condensed minutes, *ibid.*, pp. 367-69.]

The First Sub-Committee of the Commission on Reparation of Damage (Valuation of Damage) met on Wednesday, 5 March, 1919, at 2.30 P. M., at the Ministry of Finance, LORD SUMNER in the Chair.

Present: MR. DULLES (*U. S. A.*); LORD SUMNER (*British Empire*); MR. LEBRUN (*France*); MR. CHIESA (*Italy*); MR. MORI (*Japan*); MR. VAN DEN HEUVEL (*Belgium*); MR. MICHALA-COPOULOS (*Greece*); MR. OLCHOWSKI (*Poland*); MR. DOS SANTOS VIEGAS (*Portugal*); MR. DANIELOPOL (*Roumania*); MR. PROTITCH (*Serbia*); MR. BENES (*Czecho-Slovak Republic*).[1]

The presentation of the minutes of the seventh meeting was postponed.

The CHAIRMAN reported that Memoranda on methods of valuation had been presented by the Czecho-Slovak, Greek, Roumanian, American and Polish Delegations (Annexes I, II, III, IV and V).[2]

The CHAIRMAN and MR. LEBRUN (*France*) said that their Delegations also would each present a Memorandum on this subject.

Principles of Evaluation

The CHAIRMAN proposed a preliminary discussion on certain

---

[1] According to the French stenographic minutes, Savčić was present instead of Protić, and Osuský instead of Beneš.

[2] These memoranda are printed as annexes to the minutes of the Ninth Meeting (see Document 475).

fundamental principles of the question, even if they might appear self-evident. He had drawn up a number of propositions which might serve as a basis for this discussion. The formal acceptance of such principles would serve to show the world at large that the Sub-Committee had been guided by the idea of justice. He then submitted the following propositions:[3]

1. It is understood throughout that claims cannot be admitted under whatever categories so as to involve payment twice over for the same damages or payment to two persons of whatever sort for one injury.

2. Where injury is caused by acts for which the enemy Powers are responsible, the damage to be claimed will include all the natural and necessary consequences of those acts.

3. [Claims are not admissible which are not substantially due to the acts of war, including the making of the war itself, for which the enemy Powers are responsible, but which are only incidentally connected with them.]

4. Claims are not admissible which are incapable of being estimated with reasonable certainty by some means or other of proof, whether direct and specific or statistical and general.

5. [Claims should be net—that is to say, where the claimant has received already anything in reduction of or compensation for that which is the subject-matter of the claim, credit should be given for it and the claim should be made only for the residue.]

6. Statistical methods of computation and evaluation may be resorted to in default of direct evidence of value, subject to the application of proper methods for verification and corroboration.

7. The cost of restoration of things injured, whether movables or immovables, does not extend to the cost of substituting for the things injured other things of a more expensive or valuable character, or to rebuilding with better materials or on an enlarged scale.

8. [Where the thing injured is not intended to be physically replaced or reconstructed the amount of the claim is limited to its value without adding any expenses connected with replacement or reconstruction.]

9. Claims ought to be supported by credible testimony with reasonable certainty, but it rests with the powers concerned to determine in the first instance the particular form in which such testimony is to be admitted.

After Messrs. DULLES (*U. S. A.*), OLCHOWSKI (*Poland*) and

---

[3] This text is identical with the text of the First Part of the first column of Annex II of Document 486. The text of Annex VII of Document 475 follows.

VAN DEN HEUVEL (*Belgium*) had expressed general approval of the CHAIRMAN'S propositions, subject to certain reservations, in particular as to No. 8, MR. LEBRUN (*France*) suggested that they should be discussed one at a time on a first reading.

No. 1

Proposition No. 1 was accepted subject to possible verbal alterations.

No. 2

On proposition No. 2 the CHAIRMAN agreed with MR. DULLES (*U. S. A.*) that "responsible" meant "responsible in accordance with the approved categories of damage," and with Messrs. LEBRUN (*France*) and VAN DEN HEUVEL (*Belgium*) that the enemy, by wrongfully embarking upon an aggressive war, had made himself responsible for all the necessary and natural consequences, including the defensive, counter-offensive and other operations and measures of the Allies. The proposition was then accepted.

No. 3

After comments upon proposition No. 3 by Messrs. DANIELOPOL (*Roumania*), CHIESA (*Italy*) and OLCHOWSKI (*Poland*), the CHAIRMAN observed that there was so much legitimate doubt as to its meaning and application that he withdrew it.

No. 4

Discussing proposition No. 4, MR. LEBRUN (*France*) agreed that in all cases it must be proved that damage existed, but pointed out that there could be damage of the most serious character which might be difficult to value by any definite method, instancing the cases of outrage and abduction in occupied parts of France. After explanations by the CHAIRMAN the proposition was postponed for further consideration.

No. 5

After criticism by Messrs. OLCHOWSKI (*Poland*), DULLES (*U.S. A.*), LEBRUN (*France*) and VAN DEN HEUVEL (*Belgium*), proposition No. 5 was withdrawn by the CHAIRMAN.

No. 6

On proposition No. 6 being read, MR. DANIELOPOL (*Roumania*) pointed out that in the case of Roumania to value losses of material which must be replaced by foreign purchases, without allowing for the unfavorable exchange, might halve the compensation received.

A further problem would arise from the possible fluctuations of exchange during the probably lengthy period in which Germany was paying her debt.

The CHAIRMAN agreed that this question was of the utmost importance, but thought it should be deferred, as the proposition merely reserved complete liberty as to modes of proof of damage.

MR. DULLES (*U. S. A.*) favored making proposition No. 6 even more liberal and proposed to add the words "or for other sufficient reasons" after the words "direct evidence of value."

Proposition No. 6 was accepted with this amendment.

No. 7

MR. LEBRUN (*France*) approved proposition No. 7, but urged that, where an old building had been destroyed, the cost of erecting a new building of the same description might fairly be claimed.

The CHAIRMAN agreed with MR. LEBRUN and the proposition was accepted.

No. 8

Proposition No. 8 was withdrawn by the CHAIRMAN.

No. 9

Discussing proposition No. 9, MR. CHIESA (*Italy*) suggested that each country, in stating its claims, might well indicate the sources from which the figures were obtained, whether from inquiry by a Commission, Treasury information, etc.

The CHAIRMAN thought this was a good suggestion, which it was clearly in the interests of each country to adopt.

Proposition No. 9 was accepted.

It was agreed that the propositions, not withdrawn, should be submitted for second reading in a French translation.

MR. DULLES (*U. S. A.*) stated that the American Delegation had presented to the CHAIRMAN a provisional statement of the figures of the American claim. Copies had been handed to the Delegations and he asked that they might be treated as strictly confidential.[4]

The next meeting was fixed for Friday, 7 March, 1919, at 5 P. M.

The meeting adjourned at 5.45 P. M.

H. McKINNON WOOD,   SUMNER,
   Secretary.   *Chairman.*

[4] These figures are missing. See section 19 of Document 368.

DOCUMENT 475

First Subcommittee: Minutes of the Ninth Meeting (Including Annexes I-VII), March 7, 1919, 5:15 P. M.

[EOM, First Subcommittee, pp. 59-70. French condensed minutes, PV, CRD, pp. 370-73. French text of Annexes I–VI, *ibid.*, pp. 221-30 There is no French text of Annex VII.]

The First Sub-Committee of the Commission on Reparation of Damage (Valuation of Damage) met on Friday, 7 March, 1919, at 5.15 P. M., at the Ministry of Finance, LORD SUMNER in the Chair.

Present: MR. MCCORMICK (*U. S. A.*); LORD SUMNER (*British Empire*); MR. LEBRUN (*France*); MR. CHIESA (*Italy*); MR. MORI (*Japan*); MR. DESPRET (*Belgium*); MR. MICHALACOPOULOS (*Greece*); MR. OLCHOWSKI (*Poland*); MR. DOS SANTOS VIEGAS (*Portugal*); MR. ANTONESCO (*Roumania*); MR. PROTITCH (*Serbia*).

The minutes of the seventh and eighth meetings were adopted.

The CHAIRMAN presented the revised version of his proposals on methods of valuation as adopted at the last meeting. The French and English texts of this version were adopted (Annex VII).

Method of Valuing Movables

The CHAIRMAN considered that it would be useful to discuss rules for the method of valuing movables. In this it was necessary first of all to avoid anything that was purely arbitrary, and to base ourselves on reason and practice. A movable having been destroyed, its loser must have its value. This should be the value at the time it was destroyed. But the loser should not suffer by delay, and, if there was delay in payment, he should be accorded additional compensation for being deprived of the use or profit of his property in the interval between loss and replacement. The final reparation thus comprised three elements:

1. Value of the movable at the time it was destroyed.
2. Compensation for loss of gain.
3. Compensation for other advantages of which the owner had been deprived.

MR. LEBRUN (*France*) considered that there was no clear distinction between the latter two factors and pointed out that no account had been taken of extra cost of replacement. He maintained that in the case of property destroyed, for instance, at the outbreak of the war, the three factors of reparation were as follows:

1. Value of the movable in 1914.

2. Supplementary value due to extra cost of replacement at present.

3. Compensation for loss of gain.

The CHAIRMAN maintained that there was a real distinction between the second and third factors of his analysis. The value of what was being earned (e.g., by contract) was certain, while the value of expectation of earning was doubtful. There was a great difference between taking the value at the time of destruction and that at the time of peace. In the latter case the claimant would be exposed to the risk of a falling value. The claimant should receive the value of the movable at the time of loss, and be free to employ this value as he saw fit and not be forced to replace it.

MR. LEBRUN (*France*) agreed to the soundness of the distinction thus made by the CHAIRMAN between actual and expected earnings, but maintained his point of view in regard to the basis of valuation. The man who had had his house plundered wanted not money but furniture such as he had lost, in order to be able to live in his house. He must receive not the value at the time of loss, but the value which would make it possible to replace what he had lost. At present, the value at the time of destruction would be only one half or one third enough to repurchase. In the case of movables, as of immovables, it was the value of replacement which should be recovered.

The CHAIRMAN suggested that the case of furniture as cited by MR. LEBRUN might be a special case. Under existing circumstances furniture might be assimilated to the house, as to the rule to be applied to it. He had had in mind articles used for purposes of trade, in regard to which MR. LEBRUN'S rule might work very hardly against the loser, in case of a falling market.

MR. OLCHOWSKI (*Poland*) could not agree that there was a difference of principle between movables and immovables, as regards methods of valuation. He agreed with MR. LEBRUN that it was essential to provide the value of replacement, and suggested that the loser had the right to choose between the value at the time of destruction and that of replacement at present, according to his interest.

MR. DULLES (*U. S. A.*) warned against the danger of a rule which would make the enemy pay too much for goods which had artificially appreciated and too little for goods which had been depreciated at the date of destruction, a rule which would perpetuate the fortunate gains and also the unfortunate losses. The obligation of the enemy was to replace or to pay what was requisite for replacement, with a proper compensation for loss of enjoyment or use.

MR. MICHALACOPOULOS (*Greece*) thought that the cost of replacement should be paid, but suggested that this would be covered by the second and third factors of reparation as stated by the CHAIRMAN.

The CHAIRMAN confessed that he was not yet converted by the arguments he had heard. His proposition was: at the time a wrong was sustained the measure of that wrong was established. Injustice might be done by concentrating our attention on the idea that prices were higher in 1919 than during the war.

Valuation of Immovables

The CHAIRMAN then suggested that the subject of immovables be taken up. If a house were destroyed, its owner could not rebuild until after peace. He would have to pay the prices of labor and material then current—and he would have lost the use and occupation of his house and possible rents paid by tenants. All of these factors must be allowed in his claim.

MR. LEBRUN (*France*) agreed with the CHAIRMAN, but thought that his argument applied equally to movables and immovables. He proposed that both should have a common basis of valuation.

MR. CHIESA (*Italy*) pointed out that the methods of valuation already followed by the State, in meeting the claims of its nationals for reparation, offered a very practical basis. In estimating claims toward which the State itself was making advances, it was obviously in the interest of the State not to allow excessive valuations. In Italy, moreover, the State provided reparation only for the bare necessities, leaving other losses (such as luxuries) to be made up by the industry of the individual. Full compensation could never be expected; some reparation was essential, and he urged the importance of keeping within the limits of what was practicable in order to arrive at a tangible result. The salvation of the injured country depended not upon hoped-for reparation but upon the industry of its citizens. Finally, in order to hasten the work of the Committee, MR. CHIESA proposed, instead of a discussion of principles, that the methods of valuation presented by the various Delegations be tabulated.

MR. LEBRUN (*France*) supported this proposal, and mentioned that the French Memorandum (See Annex VI) was, to a certain extent, a tabulation of those previously presented.

MR. ANTONESCO (*Roumania*) considered that there was a common basis for the valuation of movables and immovables, i.e., their value, plus compensation for loss of gain. Both therefore could be treated as a single category from the point of view of the discussion.

As to movables, it was preferable that reparation be made in kind. Where this was not possible, MR. ANTONESCO made a distinction between consumable and non-consumable goods. The first should be valued as at the time of loss; the second according to their cost at the time of replacement. Compensation should be claimed, not only for the loss of gain, but also for damage due for non-fulfillment of contracts caused by loss of property.

As to immovables, there were two factors to be considered: first, the cost of reconstruction or repairs, according to the price of labor and material at the time of reconstruction, which, as far as the enemy was concerned, would be taken as the time of the signing of peace; second, the loss of gain, based on the earning at the time of destruction or upon the average for the preceding years.

MR. DESPRET (*Belgium*) agreed with the CHAIRMAN that, from a purely juridical point of view, damage should be based on the value at the time of the destruction. We were faced, however, by a practical case, and by claimants whose point of view would not be that of jurists. MR. DESPRET pointed out the danger of adopting any rule which would involve marked inequality in the results of its application, and urged, finally, that reparation must be made on the same basis for all.

Figures

The CHAIRMAN then suggested that the discussion of figures be taken up at the next meeting. This proposal was supported by MR. McCORMICK (*U. S. A.*) and, after discussion, it was agreed to begin the discussion of figures at the next meeting, although certain Delegations would not be able to provide their figures by that date.

MR. McCORMICK (*U. S. A.*) proposed that those Delegations which had figures ready submit them to other Delegations in confidence, through the Secretariat, so as to permit direct explanations and discussions between the different Delegations. This proposal was supported by the CHAIRMAN.

Special Committee on Countries not represented

MR. McCORMICK (*U. S. A.*) then made the following motion:
"It being noted that certain governments and people which may be entitled to reparation for damage suffered, are not repre-

sented on the Reparation Commission, it is moved that a Committee of three be appointed by the Chairman, which Committee shall be charged to secure and report to this Sub-Committee information relative to the amount and character of such reparation as may be claimed by or due to the Governments and people not represented on the Committee on Reparation of Damage."

This motion being carried, the CHAIRMAN accordingly appointed as members of the said Committee GENERAL MCKINSTRY (*U.S.A.*), COLONEL THE HON. S. PEEL (*British Empire*) and MR. JOUASSET (*Expert for France*).[1]

The next meeting was fixed for Monday, 10 March, at 2.30 P. M. The meeting adjourned at 7.20 P. M.

E. MINOST, SUMNER,
Secretary. *Chairman.*

ANNEX I

METHOD OF VALUATION OF WAR DAMAGE

(*Presented by the Czecho-Slovak Delegation.*)

The most dificult questions to decide are those dealing with the estimation of war indemnities and compensation. The damage caused by the war is so enormous, that all *a priori* valuation runs the risk of underestimating it. On the other hand, calculation of the separate items of damage and presentation of the total claim thus established involves a danger no less great, though of a different kind. Such an individual assessment of damage would take several years, whereas we must decide as quickly as possible how much we can demand of our defeated enemy; it would also involve an enormous expenditure, with the result that, as the available funds are limited, a large number of claims would remain unpaid. Finally, it is far from certain that long and expensive investigation would lead to equitable results. Experience proves that under normal conditions the result of a valuation depends on various details, such as the individuality of those concerned, the standard of valuation, etc. Imagination can hardly conceive the variety of the results which would be obtained by hundreds and thousands of commissions estimating separately each case of damage; one need only think of the different surroundings amid which the valuations would take place, the various points of view of the valuers, of their various moral and intellectual qualities. These divergencies could not be brought within tolerable limits by rules

[1] See Document 497.

which, without being uniform or even rigid, left little scope to those entrusted with the valuations. At the very least it may be anticipated that such individual valuations would alter the proportion of the claims made by each State. Methods should therefore be sought by which the dangers of hasty valuation would be avoided and such individual valuation rendered unnecessary.

The following plan does not pretend to be, and is not, complete, yet it seems possible to classify damage under three heads, viz.:

(1) Damage the existence and extent of which are obvious. Such damage would merely need to be recorded and described;

(2) Damage which is not obvious, but which can be determined by statistics, such as a given number of acres devastated (or at least a number which can be calculated approximately), a given number of acres of forest land laid waste, a given number of houses demolished, etc. It is not necessary to deal with objects *en bloc;* for instance, a uniform figure could be taken for each inhabited room in a house, for each story, for every acre cultivated for 10 or 20 years, etc. The results thus obtained might not be exact, but the mistakes made would hardly produce such serious consequences as those resulting from individual valuation.

(3) Finally, the amount of indemnity to be paid for certain kinds of damage, whether palpable or not, cannot be estimated in figures by any form of individual valuation, for the simple reason that the damage in question is not calculable. It would no doubt be possible to reckon the cost of reconstruction of the Hôtel de Ville at Louvain, or the rebuilding of Reims Cathedral, but the new Hôtel de Ville at Louvain and the reconstructed cathedral at Reims would not replace the former buildings. No compensation can make good such damage; it can only atone for it; and there must always be a certain element of arbitrariness. In such cases, an inventory of the damage and an estimate of the indemnity would be a suitable method, in conformity with the requirements of justice.

(4) In order that claims for compensation, treated as a whole in accordance with the present scheme, may not be too disproportionate to the actual damage, or those claims to indemnification which are not controlled remain unsatisfied, it would be advisable to add a round sum (not too small) to the total indemnity arrived at by the methods explained in paragraphs 1, 2 and 3.

(5) On the question of persons claiming indemnification from the enemy and that of the individual distribution of compensation to interested parties, the following proposition may be laid down:

"The only possible course is to consider that it will be for the State to assert against the enemy the claims for indemnification arising from injuries suffered either by its individual citizens or by legal persons. It will rest with each State to make a proper partition of such indemnities."

(E. and O. E.)

On behalf of the Czecho-Slovak Delegation,

Paris, 2 March, 1919.

(Signed) EDWARD BENES.

ANNEX II

METHOD OF ESTIMATING WAR DAMAGE

(*Presented by the Greek Delegation.*)

With respect to the method of estimating damage, the Greek Delegation is of opinion that it would be impossible to estimate the damage occasioned by the enemy's acts with even approximate accuracy. Greece, in particular, would encounter an insurmountable difficulty in collecting and verifying the necessary reports on outrages committed in Turkey upon the persons of Greek nationals or upon their property.

It has been established that the number of Greek victims of Turkish atrocities amounts to nearly one million. The recording of outrages, which include massacres, expulsions, deportations en masse, destruction and pillage of movable and immovable property, presents great difficulties by reason of the reign of terror which still prevails in Turkey and which is maintained by the Turkish officials, who prevent the victims and their families from making the depositions that are requisite.

For this reason the Greek Delegation considers that the method proposed by the French Delegation is the best. Accordingly, a special procedure would be put in force by legislation and internal regulations. It would be based on the principles embodied in the recently enacted French law. Such procedure would provide all practicable guarantees of an impartial estimate and record of each case of damage, and the total thus established would be presented to the enemy.

As the enemy's ability to pay these indemnities is limited and as it appears nearly certain that each State will unfortunately have to bear a large part of the damage, it is evident that the officials, who are charged with the estimation of damage and who will have to consider the interest of the Treasury at the same time, will by virtue of that fact offer additional assurance of their moderation in estimating the claims of their co-nationals.

In respect to damage inflicted upon Greeks in Turkey the Greek Delegation reserves its right to propose a method of estimation in accordance with the solution of the Turkish question which is to be decided upon by the Peace Conference.

The right to offer modifications later is reserved.

[no date]

ANNEX III

METHOD OF VALUATION OF WAR DAMAGE

(*Presented by the Roumanian Delegation.*)

The principle that the enemy is liable for the entire reparation of damage caused by war, in itself indicates the method of valuation.

The enemy must in fact restore all the countries that have suffered damage to the position in which they would have been if the act causing the damage had not been perpetrated.

This principle involves the necessity of estimating the value of the said damage as at the time when reparation is effected, and of calculating the total amount due by reference to current values at the date of reparation.

Let us first examine the various possible methods of valuation.

There are two principal methods which might be adopted:

A. Valuation as at the date when the damage was caused.

B. Valuation as at the date when reparation is effected.

A third method might also be possible, viz.:—valuation as at the date when the damage was caused, with the addition of a bonus in respect of rise in cost of living to be paid to the sufferers. This third method is immediately connected with the second method of valuation.

We consider that the first method should be eliminated as unjust.

For, though in cases of financial or other litigation between nationals of a State and the State itself, it may be admissible to discuss the question of the date in reference to which valuation should be made, and even to admit that compensation for damage should only be made to the extent of the actual value at the date of damage, no such discussion can be permitted when it is a case of reparation by the enemy.

In the latter case, it is certain that the liability of the enemy to make reparation has arisen from a criminal act, and that, in consequence, his responsibility being absolute, his liability to make reparation is so also.

He must, therefore, restore the injured party to the position in which the latter would have stood if the damage had not been caused.

How would it be possible to satisfy this principle of justice, if the injured party were only to receive compensation for the actual value at the date when the damage was caused, if such value amounted to less than the value at the time when reparation was to be effected? All principles of law forbid that the difference between the value of property at the date when damage is caused and the value at the date when reparation is effected, shall be a charge upon the injured party.

The method of valuation which we recommend appears to be in no way contradicted by any theory so far put before the Plenary Commission. We consider in fact that the principle of "restoration" so clearly and fairly laid down by President Wilson in his Fourteen Points implies valuation of damage as at the date when the "restoration" is to be effected.

It seems evident that the enemy will not have entirely fulfilled his obligation to "restore" damage caused, if the victim is compelled to bear part of the expense involved by the said "restoration."

[no date]

ANNEX IV

METHOD OF EVALUATING REPARATION TO BE MADE

(Submitted by the American Delegation as a supplement to its Memorandum of 20 February, entitled, "Categories of Damage," and subject to all the reserves in that Memorandum expressed. (See Annex XI., 4th Meeting.)

This Memorandum has exclusive reference to the preparation of claims by Associated Governments against enemy Governments and does not purport to have reference to the settlement of claims between the Associated Governments or between one of the Associated Governments and its subjects).

GENERAL PRINCIPLES

Reparation for damage within approved categories should be adequate to place the claimant in as nearly as may be the same position as he would have occupied had the damage in question not occurred. Items of alleged damage to be considered must be of a character susceptible of definite proof and of precise evaluation. Speculative damage is inadmissible.

In view of the magnitude of interests and multiplicity of cases involved, it will be impracticable to accord special consideration to each claimant. General rules for measurement of damages should be adopted.

In estimating damage we should, as far as possible, confine our attention to the specific individual who is the primary sufferer; otherwise it will be difficult to avoid duplications. When damage to an individual has in whole or in part been assumed by the State or some charitable organization, the relief thus accorded may be useful as a measure of the damage to the individual, but should not be treated as an additional item of damage. The State in its proprietary capacity should, of course, be treated as an individual proprietor.

Damage should be evaluated in terms of the same currency as that in which reparation by the enemy will be made payable (e.g., gold marks).

SUGGESTIONS APPLICABLE TO SPECIAL CASES

(1) Damage by destruction or injury of property which is capable of restoration or replacement should be measured in terms of the cost of replacement or restoration as of the date of the conclusion of peace. All factors entering into replacement, such as materials, labor, etc., should be estimated as of this date.

(2) Damage by destruction or injury of property not capable of replacement (e.g., forests, orchards, works of art, etc.) should be measured in terms of the value of the property, less salvage if any, as of the date of the conclusion of peace.

(3) Damage in the form of deprivation of use of non-income-producing private property should be estimated for the period of dispossession on the basis of an arbitrary percentage per annum on the pre-war value of the property.

(4) Damage in the form of deprivation of use of income-producing property should be estimated for the period of dispossession on the basis of net income for normal (e.g., pre-war) years.

(5) Damage in the form of requisitions of currency should be estimated on the basis of its value plus interest at an arbitrary rate for loss of use.

(6) Damage in the form of a disorganization of business establishments should be estimated on an arbitrary basis, designed to meet the cost of reorganization.

(7) Damage to civilians in the form of personal injury or death should be estimated on the basis of the Workmen's Compensation or similar national legislation, if any; otherwise in accordance with the similar law of some other country as may be agreed upon (e.g., Germany).

(8) Damage in the form of enforced labor or loss of opportunity

to labor should be based on total-disability figures, in accordance with (7), reduced to terms of the time involved, from which should be deducted the value of such support, maintenance and wages, if any, as were supplied by the enemy.

(9) Damage to civilians in the form of actual expenses in excess of normal, resulting directly from enemy military operations (e.g., expenses of flight from invaded areas, etc.), should be measured in terms of such actual expense with interest to the date of the conclusion of peace.

(10) It is believed that damage should be measured in terms of the actual damage to the person injured, and whether or not the State or any public or charitable organization has borne a part of such loss. In some cases the expenses of the benefactor may be useful as a measure of the damage.

[no date]

ANNEX V

METHOD OF VALUATION OF WAR LOSSES

(*Presented by the Polish Delegation.*)

Damage to Property.

(1) Reparation for war losses must be whole and complete. The guiding principle must therefore be that the value of every object which has suffered destruction, deterioration or seizure by the enemy owing to the war must be estimated as follows:

The object must be valued on the basis of its market price on 20 June, 1914. This date has been fixed because a few days later the murder of the Austrian Archduke and his wife took place at Sarajevo, shaking Europe politically and economically to its foundations and causing a serious fall in prices.

In the case of buildings the basis must be the net cost of construction at that date, with a suitable deduction for depreciation due to age.

A sum to cover the cost of restoration at the actual rates must be added to the above valuation. For this purpose, each Government will classify the objects which have suffered through the war into categories and will determine the percentage to be added to each category to cover the cost of reconstruction.

(2) Expenses incurred by communes, towns and other public institutions for feeding, clothing and supporting the population thrown out of employment as a result of the war will be settled according to the books kept by those organizations, such books having first been duly audited.

(3) The losses suffered by the population by forced subscriptions to State loans will be estimated by calculating the difference between the sums invested by subscribers and the market price of the said securities six months after the signature of peace.

(4) Taxes, imposts, fines and war levies of every kind raised by the enemy will be estimated according to the total amount paid, a mark being held to equal Fr. 1.25, a krone Fr. 1.05 and a rouble Fr. 2.68.

(5) Losses caused by compulsory administration will be estimated on the basis of the revenue of similar property at the same period. These losses will be refunded in francs at the rates of exchange mentioned in the preceding paragraph. No debts contracted by such administration will be binding on the rightful owner unless admitted by the legal authorities to have been incurred for the benefit of the property.

(6) The value of objects subjected to compulsory liquidation and which cannot by reason of their nature be restored, will be estimated according to the principle set forth in paragraph (1). Objects which by reason of their nature can be restored must be returned to the owner free of all charges and burdens.

The contract of sale drawn up between the liquidator and the purchaser will be considered *ipso facto* null and void, the purchaser merely being entitled to claim compensation from the enemy Government.

(7) Deterioration caused by the liquidator or administrator will be estimated according to general rules.

(8) Bank-notes issued by the enemy in invaded countries, and also all bank-notes left by the enemy in such countries, must be redeemed in gold at the rates above mentioned.

(9) Beside reparation for actual damage, the enemy will be liable to pay compensation for the resulting stoppage of work and production, such compensation being estimated on the basis of the normal revenue.

Personal Loss or Damage.

Indemnities for physical injury, such as wounds, illness, total or partial disablement, shall include the cost of treatment, the wages lost through illness, and a life annuity fixed in proportion to the capacity for work and degree of disablement.

Losses caused through being deprived of the possibility of working or of earning a fair wage will be estimated according to the rates of pay in operation in Germany at the same period.

2 March, 1919.

(Signed) OLCHOWSKI.

ANNEX VI

METHODS OF STATING AND EVALUATING DAMAGE FOR WHICH REPARATION WILL BE DEMANDED

(*Presented by the French Delegation.*)

CHAPTER I

A. It will be the concern of the Allied and Associated Nations which have suffered damage, to set forth and evaluate the damage which the enemy will be required to make good, each nation having regard to its own case.

B. The valuations thus established, in support of claims to be filed, shall conform to general and uniform rules, as set forth in Chapter II below.

C. The general rules set forth in Chapter II below apply exclusively to claims which are to be made on the enemy and do not necessarily govern the relations of the Allied and Associated States as between themselves, nor the relations of each State with its own nationals.

D. The registration and evaluation of claims referred to in the preceding paragraphs shall not be definitive until they have been passed upon, with a special view to uniformity, by Inter-Allied bodies composed of representatives of the Allied and Associated nations.

CHAPTER II

1. Valuations of damage should be made with careful regard to placing every person having the right to reparation in a situation as nearly identical as possible with that in which he would have found himself if a state of war had not been imposed by the enemy Powers upon the Allied and Associated Powers.

2. The valuations made should cover all the natural and necessary consequences of acts giving rise to a claim for damage.

3. Whatever the procedure adopted for the classification of categories of damage, or for the registration and valuation of claims, it should never be possible to obtain payment twice for the same damage, either wholly or in part, whether to the same person or to different persons.

4. Claims should be supported either by direct proof as to the reality and the amount of the damage suffered, or by any other aceptable evidence or credible testimony, the Allied and Associated Powers having the exclusive right to determine the form of evidence and the conditions under which it shall be admitted.

5. Valuations shall be expressed in the currency of each nation

concerned, without prejudice as to the currency in which the enemy will be obliged to make payment.

6. The amount of a claim should be not more than enough to replace property or objects destroyed by other property [of] corresponding quality or importance, it being understood, however, that this provision does not refer to increases in value resulting from a rise in prices, or to the replacement of property or objects destroyed or damaged by similar property or objects in a new state.

7. (a) Destruction, deterioration and all damage caused to real or personal property, which property is of such a nature that it can be reconstructed, replaced or repaired, should be valued at the amount of the estimated cost of such reconstruction, replacement or repair on the date of the conclusion of peace.

(b) The cost of such reconstruction, replacement or repair is arrived at by applying to the corresponding pre-war cost an appropriate co-efficient, calculated for each category of property in accordance with market prices at the date of the conclusion of peace, in respect to materials, labor and all other factors to be considered.

(c) In the case of labor hired or purchases made for reconstruction, replacement or repair, before the date of the conclusion of peace, the valuation may be based upon actual cost.

(d) In case the same property or object has undergone repeated and successive damage, all labor and purchases that have actually gone to reconstruction, replacement or repair are to be taken into account in the valuation.

8. Destruction, deterioration and all damage caused to real or personal property not susceptible of reconstruction, replacement or repair, are to be valued at the amount the property would have been worth at the date of the conclusion of peace, deduction to be made proportionately for salvage, if any.

9. Damage resulting from levies or seizures of sums of money, under whatever guise, or of assets of any kind expressed in cash, and damage resulting from expenses incurred, especially for the relief of the population of invaded territories or of interned civilians, are valued on the basis of the sum owed, as principal, expressed in the currency of the State making the claim, with interest at 6 per cent from the day of the damage to the date of the conclusion of peace.

10. Damage resulting from the seizure, loss or destruction of securities is valued on the basis of their average market price during the first six months of 1914 or, in the case of securities issued after

1 July, 1914, on the basis of their issue price—provided that such price be not lower than the average for the fourth quarter of 1918; to that should be added the value of coupons, interest, or arrears of income, which the owners would have been able to realize up to the date of the conclusion of peace if they had remained in possession of their securities.

11. Damage resulting from deprivation, wholly or in part, of the free exercise and enjoyment of any property right, is valued, for the period of such deprivation, on the basis of the average receipts or income of the property during the last three calendar years, the last three fiscal years or the last three seasons before the war, including, in the case of agricultural property, the income of the landlord and that of the tenant; it being specified that the compensation shall not be less than the amount necessary to pay interest charges at 6 per cent and also to amortize the principal invested in the enterprise or representing the value of the property of which the nationals of the Allied and Associated States shall have been deprived.

12. Damage resulting from the deprivation of opportunity to work or to obtain a just remuneration for one's work or profession is valued on the basis of the average wages or salary of the claimant during the three years preceding such deprivation.

13. Damage which consists in the disorganization of business houses, enterprises or professions is valued on the basis of the cost of reorganization.

14. Damage caused to industrial property through the enemy's knowledge of special processes of manufacture and the commercial damage resulting from the enemy's knowledge of books, correspondence and documents or information of a private nature, of every kind, are to be valued in accordance with special rules agreed upon between the Allied and Associated Powers.

15. Damage relating to currency (marks, monetary instruments issued or falsified by the enemy, etc.) is valued on the basis of the face value of such currency, with interest at 6 per cent from 11 November, 1918, to the date of the conclusion of peace.

16. (a) Damage resulting from every kind of personal injury, from every act, cruel treatment or violence, leading to the death or total incapacity for labor of the injured person, will be valued, for each person thus deceased or incapacitated, on the basis of a uniform scale of charges applicable to all individuals and to all countries, which shall be agreed upon between the Allied and Associated Powers.

(b) Damage resulting from every kind of personal injury, from every act, cruel treatment or violence leading to wounds, illness or partial incapacity for labor, shall be valued for each person thus affected by applying to the scale of charges above mentioned a formula which shall be uniform for all individuals and all countries and which shall be agreed upon between the Allied and Associated Powers.

(c) Compensation which is due on account of all injuries to honor or health shall be determined in accordance with rules which shall be uniform for all individuals and for all countries and which shall be agreed upon between the Allied and Associated Powers.

The right of future changes or additions is reserved.

7 March, 1919.

ANNEX VII

LORD SUMNER'S SUGGESTIONS FOR A BASIS OF DISCUSSIONS ON METHODS OF EVALUATION

(*Revised Version of Accepted Articles.*)[2]

(1) It is understood throughout that claims cannot be admitted under whatever categories so as to involve payment twice over for the same damage or payment to two persons of whatever sort for one injury.

(2) Where injury is caused by acts for which the enemy Powers are responsible, the damage to be claimed will include all the natural and necessary consequences of these acts.

(3) Claims are not admissible which are incapable of being estimated with reasonable certainty by some means or other of proof whether direct and specific or statistical and general.

(4) Statistical methods of computation and evaluation may be resorted to in default of direct evidence of value or for other sufficient reasons subject to the application of proper methods for verification and corroboration.

(5) The cost of restoration of things injured whether movables or immovables does not extend to the cost of substituting, for the things injured, other things of a more expensive or valuable character or to rebuilding with better materials or on an enlarged scale.

(6) Claims ought to be supported by credible testimony with reasonable certainty, but it rests with the Powers concerned to determine in the first instance the particular form in which such testimony is to be admitted.

[2] The text in Document 474 precedes. The text of the First Part of the *second* column of Annex II of Document 486 follows.

DOCUMENT 476

First Subcommittee: Minutes of the Tenth Meeting (Including Annexes I and II), March 10, 1919, 2:30 P. M.

[EOM, First Subcommittee, pp. 71-82. French stenographic minutes, PV, CRD, pp. 374-92. There is no French text of Annex I. French text of Annex II, *ibid.*, pp. 231-38.]

The First Sub-Committee of the Commission on Reparation of Damage (Valuation of Damage) met on Monday, 10 March, 1919, at 2.30 P. M., at the Ministry of Finance, LORD SUMNER in the Chair.

Present: MR. DULLES (*U. S. A.*); LORD SUMNER (*British Empire*); MR. LEBRUN (*France*); MR. D'AMELIO (*Italy*); MR. MORI (*Japan*); MR. DESPRET (*Belgium*); MR. MICHALACOPOULOS (*Greece*); MR. OLCHOWSKI (*Poland*); MR. DOS SANTOS VIEGAS (*Portugal*); MR. DANIELOPOL (*Roumania*); MR. PROTITCH (*Serbia*); MR. BENES (*Czecho-Slovak Republic*).[1]

The adoption of the minutes of the previous meeting was postponed until a later meeting.

The CHAIRMAN proposed to begin by examining the comparative list of the various Memoranda relating to the method of calculating damage (Annex II, Tenth Meeting).

Sec. 2

Sec. 2. MR. OLCHOWSKI (*Poland*) proposed to substitute the words "Allied and Associated Powers" for "Allied and Associated Nations."

This section was adopted with the above modification.

Sec. 3

Sec. 3. This section was set aside until the headings to which it refers could be examined.

Sec. 4

Sec. 4. At the suggestion of MR. LEBRUN (*France*) it was agreed that all the rules which might be later fixed upon by the Sub-Committee for the presentation of claims against the enemy should be included in this section.

Section 4 was adopted, subject to this suggestion.

Sec. 5

Sec. 5. After a discussion in which MR. OLCHOWSKI (*Poland*),

[1] According to the French minutes, Savčić was also present.

the CHAIRMAN, and Messrs. LEBRUN (*France*) and DULLES (*U. S. A.*) took part, Section 5 was reserved.

Sec. 8

Sec. 8. At the suggestion of MR. DULLES (*U. S. A.*) this section was adopted with the following addition: "in a situation identical with that in which he would have been if he had not suffered damage resulting from the state of war imposed by the enemy Powers."

MR. JOUASSET (*Expert for France*) drew attention to the fact that this new phraseology in no way prejudiced the question of determining whether the value considered at the time of reparation should be based on a state of affairs existing at one time more than another.

Sec. 11, 13, 15

Sec. 11, 13 and 15. These sections were adopted without remark.

Sec. 17

Sec. 17. MR. BENES (*Czecho-Slovak Republic*) proposed to leave it to each nation to establish the valuation in the monetary unit which it might choose. He was inclined to believe that it would be more practical to adopt the French franc as the common monetary unit.

MR. OLCHOWSKI (*Poland*) agreed with this last opinion, drawing attention to the fact that Poland had as yet no monetary unit of its own.

MR. JOUASSET (*Expert for France*) drew attention to the fact that the value of the franc might change between the time of the valuation and that of the final settlement. In fact, the object of the section in question was precisely to reserve the final establishment of the exchange rate against the time when the general settlement should be reached. At any rate, having regard to actual situations it might be considered that valuations would be made as a rule in the monetary unit of the nation interested or at least in so far as possible.

MR. DANIELOPOL (*Roumania*) thought that each country should be permitted to calculate the amount of its damage in its own national currency, taken at gold par, and that each country be allowed to take the rate of exchange into account in addition to the amount of such damage.

MR. YANKOWITCH (*Expert for Serbia*) proposed that the gold franc be taken as a basis.

The CHAIRMAN, after reviewing the discussion, proposed that each interested nation be allowed the right to make its valuation in the monetary unit it might feel constrained to choose, furnishing, however, such information as would permit of the verification of figures submitted.

Sec. 17 was adopted under the following form: "Valuation will be made in the monetary unit which each interested Power may see fit to adopt, without in any way prejudging the unit in which the enemy must pay and each Power shall indicate the rate of exchange upon which its calculations were based, so as to permit all necessary verification."

Sec. 21

Sec. 21. After a discussion in which the CHAIRMAN and Messrs. JOUASSET (*Expert for France*) and LEBRUN (*France*) took part, it was decided to add the words "movables and immovables" after the phrase "to the replacement of goods or objects destroyed or damaged."

Sec. 24

Sec. 24. In answer to a question by the CHAIRMAN, MR. LEBRUN (*France*) explained that the word "reparation," as used in this section, was only applicable to the same objects as were the words "reconstruction and replacement."

The CHAIRMAN observed also that it might perhaps be well to fix a date, instead of using the "date of the conclusion of peace," and proposed the date of the cessation of hostilities.

MR. MORI (*Japan*) supported this idea, but after a general discussion, in which Messrs. JOUASSET (*Expert for France*), DULLES (*U. S. A.*), OLCHOWSKI (*Poland*) and LEBRUN and the CHAIRMAN took part, it was evident that there would be difficulty in fixing upon a date for the present, and the section was finally adopted without change.

Sec. 25

Sec. 25. The CHAIRMAN asked for some explanations of Section 25. MR. JOUASSET (*Expert for France*) explained that the system of applying a coefficient corresponding to pre-war value was intended to permit the immediate beginning of the work of valuation.

The adjustment of these valuations at the time of the final settlement would be effected simply by the application of this coefficient.

After a discussion in which the CHAIRMAN, and Messrs. JOUASSET,

OLCHOWSKI (*Poland*) and ANTONESCO (*Roumania*) took part, Section 25 was reserved.

Secs. 26 and 27

Sec. 26 and 27. These two sections were adopted without remark.

Sec. 34

Sec. 34. The CHAIRMAN feared that this section did not provide for enough compensation to owners of destroyed merchandise which might suffer a decline in value at the conclusion of peace.

MR. MORI (*Japan*) announced that the Japanese Delegation was disposed to accept the principles presented by the French Delegation and the three kinds of compensation proposed by the CHAIRMAN, on condition that the following addition be made to the first of these points: "On condition that the damaged person may choose the highest value which may have been reached by a similar object during the period elapsed between the time of destruction and the time of compensation therefor."

MR. MICHALACOPOULOS (*Greece*) thought that this proposal was entirely in accord with the principles of Roman law and with equity.

MR. JOUASSET (*Expert for France*) proposed the following phraseology: "In any case the valuation can never be less than the value of the goods at the time of damage."

The CHAIRMAN proposed to consider before the next meeting a new draft upon which every one could agree.

The next meeting was fixed for Tuesday, 11 March, 1919, after the meeting of the Plenary Commission.

The meeting adjourned at 6.30 P. M.

SUMNER,
Chairman.

E. MINOST,
  Secretary.

ANNEX I

LORD SUMNER'S FIRST DRAFT OF THE RESULTS OF THE MEETINGS
OF THE FIRST SUB-COMMITTEE UP TO 1 MARCH, 1919

(*Categories of Damage.*)

1. The first Sub-Committee has held (six) meetings and is now in a position to present a first interim report as directed by the Commission on Reparation.

It first took up the question of the categories of damage, under which the claims of the associated Powers might be classified. On the initiative of the Chairman of the Sub-Committee representatives of the different Delegations presented careful and detailed memoirs, in which they stated their respective views. These were then tabulated for the purpose of facilitating discussion, and after full examination the Sub-Committee has arrived with unanimity at certain conclusions in principle. In order that each Delegation may be enabled to rely on the expression of its views, which it has itself selected, the memoirs delivered to the Sub-Committee are annexed hereto for purposes of reference.

2. The subject of categories may be considered from the following points of view:

(I.) the persons whose conduct produces the loss for which reparation is claimed;

(II.) the persons who have suffered that loss and in whose right the reparation is claimed;

(III.) the nature and quality of the acts which produce the loss;

(IV.) the place where those acts are done, and the place where the subject matter on which loss is inflicted is situated;

(V.) the nature and quality of the things which are the subject matter of the loss inflicted;

(VI.) the extent to which the consequences of injurious acts form part of and are included in the loss to be repaired.

NOTE. Loss includes removal, destruction, deterioration or depreciation, and may also take the form of expenses incurred, beneficial enjoyment impaired, and sacrifices imposed.

3. As to (I.):

The enemy Powers and their forces, whether naval, military or aerial, and their subjects, whose acts or conduct have caused loss to the Associated Powers and their subjects, are all of them "persons" whose conduct may produce loss, for which reparation can be claimed.

As to (II.):

The State itself and all its subjects, and persons resident in its territory and under its protection, are "persons" in whose right reparation may be claimed, if they have suffered loss for which claims are otherwise admissible. "Persons" includes natural and artificial persons, incorporated societies, partnerships, companies, municipalities, communes and authorized associations. It is immaterial whether property damaged is public property or private property.

As to (III.):

It is immaterial whether the conduct causing loss is immediately the conduct of enemy persons or of persons belonging to the Associated Powers, or of the Associated Powers themselves, if such conduct occurred in the course of offensive, defensive or counter-offensive operations or was preparatory thereto, and whether in conformity to the laws of war or not, or occurred in the course of proceedings forming part of the conduct of the war by the Associated Powers, for in all such cases the conduct in question must be regarded as resulting from the aggressive war of the enemy Powers and as involving their responsibility. Decrees and orders by the representatives of the enemy Powers as administrators of regions invaded and occupied are included, as also illegal, unilateral or forced decisions of tribunals within the same.

As for (IV):

It is immaterial whether the conduct causing loss occurs on land or on the sea or in the air, and also whether the subject matter upon which loss was inflicted was situated on land or on the sea or in the air, loss inflicted within the territories of the Associated Powers or at sea and loss to the property of the Associated Powers or their subjects situated in enemy territory being also included, if it is otherwise the subject of an admissible claim.

As to (V.):

Among the subjects of loss for damage to which claims may be legitimately made are included property of all kinds, movable or immovable, corporeal or incorporeal, documents or title and instruments of credit, books of account and trade documents, patents and trade-marks; 'gisements' are also included with 'mines'.

As to (VI.):

Not only the immediate results of the conduct causing injury and loss but its natural and necessary consequences, in so far as they are certainly and exclusively caused thereby, may legitimately be claimed. This may include compensation for being deprived of the occupation or usufruct of immovables and movables.

Furthermore, persons as well as things are included among the subjects, loss or damage to which may be the ground of legitimate claims.

In this connection all natural persons are included, whether combatant or non-combatant, whether private or in public service, of whatever age, sex or occupation and whether held as prisoners of war or interned by the enemy Powers; such persons can claim for the material damage caused to them by all violence or compulsion applied to them, whether they are thereby affected in physical condition, in health, in modesty or liberty. Imprisonments, deportations, forced labor if insufficiently paid for, are included; widows, children and relations, ancestors or descendants, who may be entitled by law, can claim in the case of persons injured whose death has resulted from the injury:

For greater clearness and without restricting the generality of the above principles, the following cases may be mentioned as cases which are included:

Logement and cantonnement of troops; defensive inundations; floods caused by injury to canals, embankments or reservoirs;

Loss by torpedoes, submarine or floating mines and bombardment from the air;

Damage to and deterioration of railways, railway buildings and rolling-stock;

Requisitions of all kinds;

Forced loans and contributions, confiscations, sequestrations, forced sales and realizations by superior authority;

Ships and vessels of all kinds, whether used for inland navigation for the coasting trade and for fisheries or for use on the high seas, with their equipments, cargoes and freights;

Expenditure by the State or by persons under a legal obligation to incur it, for the purpose of assisting and supporting and transporting persons driven from their homes or reduced to want by enemy invasions and occupations, or for the purpose of assisting Allied prisoners of war and interned persons;

Allotments to the families of persons enlisted or called up for service, whether military or civil, including persons killed or injured in war factories;

Costs of maintaining and guarding enemy prisoners of war or interned persons;

All other expenses or charges resulting from the state of war imposed on the Allied nations;

The Commission then proceeded to investigate certain categories which presented greater difficulty.

ANNEX II [2]

NOTE on the different Memoranda which have been submitted by the United

[2] The Second Part of the first column of Annex II of Document 486 follows.

States of America, France, Greece, Poland, Roumania and the Czecho-Slovak Republic relating to the Methods of Evaluating Damage.*

[1. *General Observations:* Some Delegations have submitted no Memorandum. Their opinions on the various questions exposed below are therefore reserved.]

I

FRANCE

2. It will be the concern of the Allied and Associated [Powers] which have suffered damage to set forth and evaluate the damage which the enemy will be required to make good, each nation having regard to its own case.

3. The valuations thus established, in support of claims to be filed, shall conform to general and uniform rules as set forth in Chapter II below. [(Quoted in chapters II to VII.)]

4. The general rules set forth in Chapter II below apply exclusively to claims which are to be made on the enemy and do not necessarily govern the relations of the Allied and Associated States as between themselves, nor the relations of each State with its own nationals.

5. The registration and evaluation of claims referred to in the preceding paragraphs shall not be definitive until they have been [passed upon,] with a special view to uniformity, by Inter-Allied bodies composed of representatives of the Allied and Associated nations.

THE UNITED STATES

[6. General rules for measurement of damage should be adopted.]
[7. The other Memoranda do not deal with these points.]

II

FRANCE

8. Valuations of damage should be made with careful regard to placing every person having the right to reparation in a situation as nearly as possible identical with that in which he would have found himself if a state of war had not been imposed by the enemy Powers upon the Allied and Associated Powers.

THE UNITED STATES

[9. Reparation for damage within approved categories should be adequate to place the claimant in as nearly as may be the same position as he would have occupied had the damage not occurred.]

---

* See Ninth Meeting: Annexes I to VI. [Document 475.]

ROUMANIA

[10. "The enemy must restore the countries which have suffered the damage to the position in which they would have been if the act causing the damage had not been perpetrated."

[The other Memoranda do not deal with this.]

III

FRANCE

11. The valuations made should cover all the natural and necessary consequences of the acts giving rise to the claims for damages.

[12. This corresponds to the principle already adopted by the Sub-Committee.][3]

IV

FRANCE

13. Whatever the procedure adopted for the classification of categories of damage, or for the registration and valuation of claims, it shall never be possible to obtain payment twice for the same damage, either wholly or in part, whether to the same person or to different persons.

[14. This corresponds to the proposition already adopted by the Sub-Committee.]

V

FRANCE

15. Claims should be supported either by direct proof as to the reality and the amount of the damage suffered, or by any other acceptable evidence or credible testimony, the Allied and Associated Powers having the exclusive right to determine the form of evidence and the conditions under which it shall be admitted.

[16. This proposition corresponds to the proposition already adopted by the Sub-Committee, except that in the latter the words are: "It rests with the Powers concerned to determine in the first instance the particular form, etc."]

VI

FRANCE

17. Valuations shall be expressed in the currency of each nation concerned, without prejudice as to the currency in which the enemy will be obliged to make payment.

THE UNITED STATES

[18. Damage should be evaluated in terms of the same currency

---

[3] The French text omits this paragraph.

as that in which reparation by the enemy will be made payable (e.g., gold marks).]

POLAND

[19. Poland proposes a fixed rate of exchange, as set out, for evaluation of imposts, taxes, amendes, contributions de guerre de tous guises perçus par l'Ennemi.]

[20. The other Memoranda do not deal with this point.]

VII

FRANCE

21. The amount of a claim shall not be more than enough for the replacement of property or objects destroyed by other property of corresponding quality or importance, it being understood, however, that this provision does not refer to increases in value resulting from a rise in prices, or to the replacement of property or objects destroyed or damaged by similar property or objects in a new state.

[22. This proposition relates to the subject as to which the Sub-Committee has adopted the following: The cost of restoration of things injured, whether movables or immovables, does not extend to the cost of substituting for the things injured other things of a more expensive or valuable character or to rebuilding with better materials or on an enlarged scale.]

CZECHO-SLOVAK REPUBLIC

[23. The Memorandum of the Czecho-Slovak Delegation observes (Paragraph 30)[4] that in regard to certain kinds of damage: "No compensation can make good such damage, it can only atone for it; there must always be a certain element of arbitrariness."]

VIII

FRANCE

24. Destruction, deterioration and all damage caused to real or personal property, which property is of such a nature that it can be reconstructed, replaced or repaired, shall be valued at the amount of the estimated cost of such reconstruction, replacement or repair on the date of the conclusion of peace.

25. The cost of such reconstruction, replacement or repair is arrived at by applying to the corresponding pre-war cost an appropriate coefficient, calculated for each category of property in accordance with the market price, at the date of the conclusion of peace, in respect to materials, labor and all other factors to be considered.

---

[4] Error for "Paragraph 3."

26. In the case of labor hired or purchases made for reconstruction, replacement or repair, before the date of the conclusion of peace, the valuation may be based upon actual cost.

27. In case the same property or object has undergone repeated and successive damage, all labor and purchases that have actually gone to reconstruction, replacement or repair are to be taken into account in the valuation.

THE UNITED STATES

[28. "Damage by destruction or injury of property which is capable of restoration or replacement should be measured in terms of the cost of replacement or restoration as of the date of the conclusion of peace. The factors entering into replacement, such as materials, labor, etc., should be estimated as of this date."]

ROUMANIA

[29. Roumania considers that the date when reparation takes place is the time at which to make the valuation.]

POLAND

[30. The object must be valued on the basis of its market price on 20 June, 1914.]

[31. In the case of buildings the basis must be the net cost of construction at that date, with a suitable deduction for depreciation due to age.]

[32. A sum to cover the cost of restoration at the actual rates must be added to the above valuation. For this purpose each Government will classify the objects which have suffered through the war into categories, and will determine the percentage to be added to each category to cover the cost of reconstruction.]

[33. Other Memoranda do not define any rules on this subject.]

IX

FRANCE

34. Destruction, deterioration and all damage caused to real or personal property not susceptible of reconstruction, replacement or repair, are to be valued by reference to the amount the property would have been worth at the date of the conclusion of peace, deduction to be made proportionately for salvage, if any.

THE UNITED STATES

[35. Damage by destruction or injury of property not capable of replacement (e.g., forests, orchards, works of art, etc.) should be measured in terms of the value of the property, less salvage if any, as of the date of the conclusion of peace.]

X

FRANCE

36. Damage resulting from levies or seizures of sums of money, under whatever guise, or of assets of any kind expressed in cash, and damage resulting from expenses incurred, e.g., for the relief of the population of invaded territories or of interned civilians, are taken at the capital value of the sum involved, expressed in the currency of the State making the claim, with interest at 6 per cent from the day of the damage to the date of the conclusion of peace.

THE UNITED STATES

[37. Damage in the form of requisitions of currency should be estimated on the basis of its value, plus interest at an arbitrary rate for loss of use.]

POLAND

[38. Taxes, imposts, fines and war levies of every kind raised by the enemy will be estimated according to the total amount paid, a mark being held to equal Fr. 1.25, a krone Fr. 1.05 and a rouble Fr. 2.68.]

[39. See Section 65.]

[40. The other Memoranda do not make any special observations on this point.][5]

XI

FRANCE

41. Damage resulting from the seizure, loss or destruction of securities is valued on the basis of their average price on the Bourse during the first six months of 1914, or, in the case of securities issued after 1 July, 1914, on the basis of their issue price— provided that such price be not lower than the average for the fourth quarter of 1918; [to that should] be added the value of coupons, interest, or income in arrears which the owners would have been able to realize up to the date of the conclusion of peace if they had remained in possession of their securities.

[42. The other Powers do not make any specific proposals on this subject.]

XII

FRANCE

43. Damage resulting from the deprivation, wholly or in part, of the free exercise and enjoyment of every [property] right, is valued, for the period of such deprivation, on the basis of the average receipts or income of such property during the last three

---

[5] The French text omits this sentence. PV, CRD, p. 234.

calendar years, the [last] three fiscal years or the [last] three seasons [before] the war, including, in the case of agricultural property, the income of the landlord and that of the tenant; it being specified that the compensation shall not be less than the amount necessary to pay interest charges at 6 per cent and also to amortize the principal invested in the enterprise or representing the value of the property of which the nationals of the Allied and Associated States shall have been deprived.[6]

THE UNITED STATES

[44. Damage in the form of deprivation of use of income-producing property should be estimated for the period of dispossession on the basis of net income for normal (e.g., pre-war) years.]

[45. Other Memoranda do not specifically deal with this point.]

XIII

FRANCE

46. Damage resulting from the deprivation of opportunity to work or to obtain a fair remuneration for one's work or occupation is valued on the basis of the average wages or salary of the claimant during the three years preceding such deprivation.

THE UNITED STATES

[47. Damage in the form of forced labor or loss of opportunity to labor should be based on total-disability figures, reduced to terms of the time involved, from which should be deducted the value of such support, maintenance and wages, if any, as were supplied by the enemy.]

POLAND

[48. Losses caused through being deprived of the possibility of working or of earning a fair remuneration for work will be estimated according to the rates of pay in operation in Germany at the same period.]

XIV

FRANCE

49. Damage which consists in the disorganization of business houses, enterprises or professions is valued on the basis of the cost of reorganization.

THE UNITED STATES

[50. Damage in the form of a disorganization of business establishments should be estimated on an arbitrary basis, designed to meet the cost of reorganization.]

[6] There are differences in expression between this paragraph and the following text.

XV

FRANCE

51. Damage caused to industrial property through the enemy's knowledge of special processes of manufacture and the commercial damage resulting from the enemy's knowledge of books, correspondence and documents or information of a private nature, of all sorts, are to be valued in accordance with special rules agreed upon between the Allied and Associated Powers.

[52. No other Memoranda deals with this point.]

XVI

FRANCE

53. Damage relating to currency (marks, monetary instruments issued or falsified by the enemy, etc.) is valued on the basis of the face value of such currency, with interest at 6 per cent from 11 November, 1918, to the date of the conclusion of peace.

POLAND

[54. See Section 72 below.]

[55. The other Memoranda do not deal specifically with this.]

XVII

FRANCE

56. Damage resulting from every kind of personal injury, from every act, cruelty or violence leading to the death or total incapacity for labor of the injured person will be valued, for each person thus deceased or incapacitated, on the basis of a uniform scale of charges, applicable to all individuals and to all countries, which shall be agreed upon between the Allied and Associated Powers.

57. Damage resulting from every kind of personal injury, from every act, cruel treatment[7] or violence leading to wounds, illness or partial incapacity for labor, shall be valued for each person thus affected by applying to the scale of charges above mentioned a formula, which shall be uniform for all individuals and all countries and which shall be agreed upon between the Allied and Associated Powers.

58. Compensation which is due on account of all injuries to honor or health shall be determined in accordance with rules which shall be uniform for all individuals and for all countries and which shall be agreed upon between the Allied and Associated Powers.

THE UNITED STATES

[59. Damage to civilians in the form of personal injury or death

---

[7] The following text reads, "cruelty."

should be estimated on the basis of the Workmen's Compensation or similar national legislation, if any; otherwise in accordance with the similar law of some other country as may be agreed upon (e.g., Germany).]

POLAND

[60. Indemnities for physical injury, such as wounds, illness, total or partial disablement, shall include the cost of treatment, the wages lost through illness, and a life annuity fixed in proportion to the capacity for work and degree of disablement.]

XVIII

THE UNITED STATES

[61. Damage in the form of deprivation of use of non-income-producing private property should be estimated for the period of dispossession on the basis of an arbitrary percentage per annum on the pre-war value of the property.]

[62. Damage to civilians in the form of actual expenses in excess of normal, resulting directly from enemy military operations (e.g., expense of flight from invaded areas, etc.), should be measured in terms of such actual expense with interest to the date of the conclusion of peace.]

[63. Other Memoranda do not deal with these points specifically.]

XIX

POLAND

[64. Reparation for war losses must be whole and complete. The guiding principle must therefore be that the value of every object which has suffered destruction, deterioration, or seizure by the enemy owing to the war must be estimated as follows:]

[(The rules referred to are quoted in Sections 31, 32 and 33.)[8]]

[65. The losses suffered by the population by forced subscriptions to State loans will be estimated by calculating the difference between the sums invested by subscribers and the market price of the said securities six months after the signature of peace.]

[66. Expenses incurred by communes, towns and other public institutions for feeding, clothing and supporting the population thrown out of employment as a result of the war, will be settled according to the books kept by those institutions, such books having first been duly audited.]

[67. See section 38.]

68. Losses caused by compulsory administration are determined

[8] Error for "30, 31 and 32."

on the basis of the revenue of similar property for the same period. These losses will be refunded in francs at the rates of exchange mentioned in the preceding paragraph. [(Quoted in section 39.)][9] No debts contracted by such administration will be binding on the rightful owner unless admitted by the legal authorities to have been incurred for the benefit of the property.

69. The value of objects subjected to compulsory liquidation and which cannot by reason of their nature be restored, will be estimated according to the principle set forth in paragraph 1 [of this chapter XIX (i.e., sec. 64)]. [(Quoted in sections 30, 31 and 32.)] Objects which by reason of their nature can be restored must be returned to the owner free of charge.

70. The contract of sale drawn up between the liquidator and the purchaser will be considered *ipso facto* null and void, the purchaser merely being entitled to claim compensation from the enemy Government.

71. Deterioration caused by the liquidator or administrator will be estimated according to general rules.

[72. Bank-notes issued by the enemy in invaded countries and also all bank-notes left by the enemy in such countries, must be redeemed in gold at the rates above mentioned.]

[73. Besides reparation for actual damage, the enemy will be liable to pay compensation for the resulting stoppage of work and production, such compensation being estimated on the basis of the normal revenue.]

XX

CZECHO-SLOVAK REPUBLIC

[74. The Memorandum of the Czecho-Slovak Republic suggests a general scheme of evaluating damage, thus:]

[75. The following plan does not pretend to be, and is not, complete, yet it seems possible to classify damage under three heads, viz.:]

[Damage the existence and extent of which are obvious. Such damage would merely need to be recorded and described;]

[76. Damage which is not obvious, but which can be determined by statistics, such as a given number of acres devastated (or at least a number which can be calculated approximately), a given number of acres of forest land laid waste, a given number of houses demolished, etc. . . .[10]]

---

[9] Error for "38."
[10] The dots in this and the next paragraph are in the original.

[77. Finally, the amount of indemnity to be paid for certain damage, whether obvious or not, cannot be estimated by individual valuation, for the simple reason that the extent of the damage cannot be calculated. . . .]

[78. To prevent claims for compensation, treated as a whole in accordance with the present scheme, from differing too much in extent from the actual damage, or to prevent them from being groundless, it would be wise to add a round sum (not too small) to the total indemnity arrived at by the method explained in sections 1, 2 and 3 (see sections 75, 66 and 77 above).[11]]

XXI

THE UNITED STATES

[79. The United States Memorandum enunciates the following general principles:]

[80. Reparation for damage within approved categories should be adequate to place the claimant in as nearly as may be the same position as he would have occupied had the damage in question not occurred.]

[81. Items of alleged damage to be considered must be of a character susceptible of definite proof and of precise evaluation. Speculative damage is inadmissible.]

[82. In view of the magnitude of interests and multiplicity of cases involved, it will be impracticable to accord special consideration to each claimant. General rules for measurement of damage should be adopted.]

[83. In estimating damage we should, as far as possible, confine our attention to the specific individual who is the primary sufferer; otherwise it will be difficult to avoid duplications. When damage to an individual has in whole or in part been assumed by the State or some charitable organization, the relief thus accorded may be useful as a measure of the damage to the individual, but should not be treated as an additional item of damage. The State in its proprietary capacity should, of course, be treated as an individual proprietor.]

[84. It is believed that damage should be measured in terms of the actual damage to the person injured, and whether or not the State or any public or charitable organization has borne a part of such loss. In some cases the expenses of the benefactor may be useful as a measure of the damage.]

[11] Error for "75, 76 and 77."

DOCUMENT 477

First Subcommittee: Minutes of the Eleventh Meeting, March 11, 1919, 5:30 P. M.

[EOM, First Subcommittee, pp. 83-85. French stenographic minutes, PV, CRD, pp. 393-401; French condensed minutes, *ibid.*, pp. 402-5.]

The First Sub-Committee of the Commission on Reparation of Damage (Valuation of Damage) met on Tuesday, 11 March, 1919, at 5.30 P. M., at the Ministry of Finance, LORD SUMNER in the Chair.

Present: MR. DULLES (*U. S. A.*); LORD SUMNER (*British Empire*); MR. LEBRUN (*France*); MR. CHIESA (*Italy*); MR. MORI (*Japan*); MR. VAN DEN HEUVEL (*Belgium*); MR. MICHALACO-POULOS (*Greece*); MR. OLCHOWSKI (*Poland*); MR. DANIELOPOL (*Roumania*); MR. PROTITCH (*Serbia*); MR. OSUSKI (*Czecho-Slovak Republic*).[1]

Presentation of the minutes of the last meeting was postponed.

The CHAIRMAN said that the business before the meeting was to discuss the minimum figures of claims which had been submitted by various Delegations.

MR. LEBRUN (*France*) asked if discussion of the tabulation of methods of valuation was not to be continued.

The CHAIRMAN explained that it had been decided, in view of the urgency of the question of figures, to begin the discussion of such figures as were available. The Sub-Committee would return to the discussion of the tabulation when new drafts of certain disputed clauses had been prepared.

MR. LEBRUN stated his regret that he had been absent at the end of the last meeting, as he would have protested against this procedure. He pointed out that the Sub-Committee had begun a discussion of three questions, none of which it had brought to a solution.

MR. OLCHOWSKI (*Poland*) agreed with MR. LEBRUN'S view as to the proper procedure.

The CHAIRMAN said that the Commission had decided its procedure. Although, as MR. LEBRUN said, it was not perhaps a methodical or logical course, the Sub-Committee was now working under pressure. If the discussion of figures was postponed indefinitely, there would be no hope of making a useful report in time.

[1] According to the French stenographic minutes, McCormick (instead of Dulles) and Santos Viegas were also present.

Mr. Lebrun regretted that, as there was no fixed basis either for categories or for methods of valuation, he would be unable to discuss any figures which might be presented at the present time.

Explanation of American figures

Mr. Dulles (*U. S. A.*) then said that he would explain the methods adopted in estimating the American statement of minimum and maximum figures of claim which had been privately circulated to the Delegations.[2]

Taking the category "Immovables," Mr. Dulles explained that in the first item, "Damage done by enemy agents in the United States," the figure was based on explosions and similar acts as to enemy origin of which there could be little doubt. The maximum covered also doubtful cases as to many of which legal inquiry was still pending.

In answer to the Chairman, Mr. Dulles stated that damage done before the entry of the United States into the war had been included.

On the second item, "Property destroyed, etc., in enemy countries," Mr. Dulles said that the figures might be reduced by the return to its owners of part of this property, which was doubtless still in being, but that the question whether the owners must receive it back was not intended to be prejudged.

Mr. Mori (*Japan*) asked if loss of enjoyment and use was included.

Mr. Dulles said the figures were for the value only, loss of use not having yet been calculated.

Taking the category "Movables," Mr. Dulles said the figures were a rough calculation of the value of the tonnage sunk at an average of $300 per ton. A liberal margin was allowed between the minimum and maximum claims, because of the inadequacy of the available information as to the age and type of the ships.

In reply to the Chairman, Mr. Dulles said that the total tonnage had been taken, irrespective of the types of vessel involved, and that tonnage meant "dead weight" tonnage.

Mr. Dulles continued that the United States figures did not include vessels sailing under flags of foreign Powers represented at the Peace Conference, since these figures had been framed on the theory that the Government with which the ship was registered should, if possible, present the claim in the first instance. On the other hand, losses on ships flying the flags of Powers not represented were included.

[2] See section 19 of Document 368.

In reply to the CHAIRMAN, MR. DULLES said that this rule had been followed whether the United States or its subjects were interested in the vessels as charterers or as owners or as insurers.

Turning to cargoes, MR. DULLES said it might be inferred that the value was taken as at the date of loss, as the figures were based on the insurance value.

The CHAIRMAN asked if the figures were the sum of ascertained individual insurance values or were calculated from the total tonnage figure by use of average figures for insurance values.

MR. DULLES said the latter method had been followed. Personal effects lost at sea had been treated in the same manner as cargoes.

The claim for injury to merchant vessels, MR. DULLES continued, was based on the actual cost of repair, which was for the most part already completed.

MR. DULLES said that the item "Loss through Termination of Charters" represented actual losses, and in reply to the CHAIRMAN he added that a claim would probably also be made in respect of bill of lading freight which was being earned on cargoes which were sunk. Loss of use of ships had been calculated in a somewhat arbitrary manner, by taking the capital value as $100 per ton, and the annual earning capacity of 10 per cent, and reckoning the loss down to 1 July, 1919.

Turning to "Damage to Persons," MR. DULLES said that the minimum figure was based on $5,000 a life and the maximum on $25,000.

In the case of U. S. merchant seamen, MR. CHIESA (*Italy*) asked how many seamen and how much per head.

MR. DULLES replied that he did not have detailed figures. The figures were totals based on insurance borne and paid by the United States Government.

In regard to the claim for maintenance, etc., of alien enemies, Mr. DULLES said that the minimum figure was based on expenditure actually incurred, and the maximum based on budget estimates.

The cost of the army of occupation, MR. DULLES continued, was included because, although this claim had a special status under the Armistice Convention, it would involve a drain upon German resources. The minimum and maximum figures represented different interpretations of the Armistice Convention.

MR. VAN DEN HEUVEL (*Belgium*) said two points of principle were raised by the American statement: (1) the inclusion of damage by enemy agents before the entry of the United States into the war, and (2) the inclusion of claims against Turkey, although the United States had not been at war with Turkey.

Mr. DULLES said there could be no question as to the existence of these claims. The only possible questions were questions of priority and admissibility.

Mr. CHIESA agreed with Mr. DULLES that wrongs, such as the sinking of the Lusitania, which had led to the entry of the United States into the war, were certainly a proper matter for a claim for compensation. He asked if the United States would present a claim for war costs.

Mr. DULLES said the American Delegation had no present intention of submitting a claim for war costs. The American Delegation was opposed to claiming war costs from the enemy, not only on principle, but additionally because it as yet saw no way of determining actual "war costs" in an equitable sense, i.e., the real diminution in the national wealth as distinguished from mere transfer of wealth within the nation. This would at any rate require a much clearer definition of the term "war costs" than had hitherto been established.

Mr. CHIESA said that the Italian statement of war costs would represent actual Treasury expenditure alone.

After a discussion on procedure, in which the CHAIRMAN and Mr. LEBRUN (*France*) took part, it was decided to continue the discussion of the tabulation of methods of valuation at the next meeting.

The next meeting was fixed for Wednesday, 12 March, at 2.30 P. M.

The meeting was adjourned at 6.50 P. M.

SUMNER,
Chairman.

E. MINOST,
    Secretary.

DOCUMENT 478

First Subcommittee: Minutes of the Twelfth Meeting, March 12, 1919, 2:45 P. M.

[EOM, First Subcommittee, pp. 86-90. French stenographic minutes, PV, CRD, pp. 406-27; French condensed minutes, *ibid.*, pp. 428-32.]

The First Sub-Committee of the Commission on Reparation of Damage (Valuation of Damage) met on Wednesday, 12 March,

1919, at 2.45 P. M., at the Ministry of Finance, LORD SUMNER in the chair.

Present: MR. McCORMICK (*U. S. A.*); LORD SUMNER (*British Empire*); MR. LEBRUN (*France*); MR. CHIESA (*Italy*); MR. MORI (*Japan*); MR. VAN DEN HEUVEL (*Belgium*); MR. MICHALACO-POULOS (*Greece*); MR. OLCHOWSKI (*Poland*); MR. DOS SANTOS VIEGAS (*Portugal*); MR. ANTONESCO (*Roumania*); MR. PROTITCH (*Serbia*).[1]

Presentation of the minutes of the last meeting was postponed.

The CHAIRMAN proposed that the discussion of Methods of Valuation of Damage (Annex II, Tenth Meeting) should be continued.

Differences of opinion having appeared at a former meeting on the subject of section 34, the CHAIRMAN announced that a new draft was being prepared. The discussion of the section was accordingly postponed.

Sec. 36

The CHAIRMAN proposed to pass to the consideration of section 36.

MR. JOUASSET (*Expert for France*) asked whether it would not be well to reserve the words "expressed in the currency of the State making the claim," in order to avoid reopening a discussion which has already taken place upon a corresponding phrase in section 17.

MR. OLCHOWSKI (*Poland*) supported this view. He declared that Poland had no currency of her own, and suggested the adoption of the Polish proposal (section 67).

MR. MORI (*Japan*) asked the exact meaning of the word "avoirs." MR. JOUASSET (*Expert for France*) explained that the word comprised all assets expressed in terms of money; it therefore referred to credits of any kind existing in banking establishments, notaries' offices, etc.

MR. DANIELOPOL (*Roumania*) asked if the contemplated 6 per cent interest was to apply to a case in which a rate of interest had been fixed by agreement.

MR. JOUASSET (*Expert for France*), in view of this observation, proposed to add in the last line of the section the words: "interest which, in default of any agreement to the contrary, shall be fixed at 6 per cent." In further reply to an observation by MR. OLCHOW-SKI (*Poland*) he added that it would be desirable to bring the texts of sections 17 and 36 into agreement.

[1]According to the French stenographic minutes, Danielopol (instead of Antonescu) and Osuský were also present.

Mr. Danielopol (*Roumania*) proposed, with this object, to delete in section 36 the words "expressed in the currency of the State making the claim."

The Chairman supported this proposal and decided that the words in question should be struck out. The Powers interested would have liberty of choice as to currency, as had already been decided under section 17.

The Chairman then made three observations on the drafting of section 36:

(1) This section was drafted in very liberal terms. Was there not a danger that claims might be made without any real loss having been sustained? For example, credits might have been opened without there having been any actual deposit of funds.

(2) The section appeared not to provide for credits which might have been confiscated in Germany and which might have been set off against enemy credits with subjects of the Allied Powers.

(3) The 6 per cent rate of interest appeared to have been chosen arbitrarily.

Mr. Chiesa (*Italy*) remarked that the question of a set-off lay within the competence of the Second Sub-Committee.

Mr. Danielopol (*Roumania*) proposed that a distinction should be made between holdings of the Allied Powers in enemy countries and war damage properly so called. It might be decided in the Peace Treaty that the former should be simply restored, without its being necessary to show them in the list of war damages. Enemy claims, on the other hand, might serve as security for the settlement of claims for damage.

Mr. Jouasset (*Expert for France*) replied to the three criticisms made by the Chairman:

(1) Sections 15 and 17 removed all danger of duplication or of claims for fictitious losses.

(2) The question of a set-off was more delicate. It would be possible to add to section 36 the following words: "the right being fully reserved to regulate in any manner determined all questions as to reciprocal claims or debts arising from pre-war contracts between subjects of the enemy Powers and subjects of the Allied Powers."

(3) The 6 per cent rate of interest was quite normal. It was in close correspondence with the actual cost of the French Government borrowing.

Mr. Danielopol (*Roumania*) observed that if a special status was recognized for pre-war claims, there could no longer be any question in section 36 of "agreements to the contrary." He withdrew his amendment.

MR. JOUASSET (*France*) agreed with this observation. A new draft of the section would be prepared and presented to the Sub-Committee.

The CHAIRMAN said he accepted the explanations of MR. JOUASSET, and section 36 was adopted subject to the amendments suggested in the course of the debate. As the words "in default of any agreement to the contrary" were not to be inserted, the CHAIRMAN desired to reserve to each Power the right to regulate all questions affecting pre-war claims.

MR. MCCORMICK (*U. S. A.*) made the same reservation in the name of the American Delegation.

Sec. 41

The CHAIRMAN proposed that the Committee should pass to the consideration of section 41. He asked why two dates had been proposed.

MR. JOUASSET (*Expert for France*) replied that the intention was to secure that persons who had suffered from acts of war or invasion should not be placed in a worse position than that in which they would have found themselves if the war had not taken place, or if, despite the existence of a state of war, they had remained in possession of their securities. If this principle was accepted, it was immaterial whether the fourth quarter of 1918 was the period selected. If the Sub-Committee preferred to fix another period, the first quarter of 1919, for example, he was ready to support the wishes of the Delegates on this point.

The CHAIRMAN objected that the prices of 1918 and 1919 were abnormal, and that it would be dangerous to base the calculation upon the present value. He added that most of the thefts in question had taken place in 1914, the year of the great invasion.

MR. JOUASSET (*Expert for France*) recalled the facts that France had suffered a fresh invasion in 1918, during which many thefts had occurred; and that, as the Committee had accepted the principle that damage to movables should be assessed at the cost of replacement, it was natural to take the present value of securities, which would represent the cost of replacing what had been stolen. Furthermore, the enemy was at the moment restoring a large part of the securities which had been removed. It would be only fair that owners of securities which were definitely lost should be put in the same position as owners who had recovered their property.

The CHAIRMAN was afraid that if a date after the war was fixed there might be speculation upon the market for the purpose of artificially raising prices.

MR. VAN DEN HEUVEL (*Belgium*) and MR. MICHALACOPOULOS (*Greece*) cited actual examples in defense of the drafting of section 41.

MR. MCCORMICK (*U. S. A.*) proposed to substitute the first quarter of 1919 for the fourth quarter of 1918. He observed that the former period would probably be the last quarter before the signature of peace, and that there would be no possibility of speculation during that period.

This proposal was accepted and section 41 thus amended was adopted. The Delegations of the British Empire and Japan dissented.

Sec. 43

The CHAIRMAN proposed that the Committee should pass to the consideration of section 43, and asked whether the period of amortisement should not be stated. He suggested that MR. JOUASSET (*Expert for France*) should propose a new draft.

MR. JOUASSET (*Expert for France*) explained that the amortisement intended was such as was in operation in the concern in question before the war, and would be applicable to the whole period of deprivation of enjoyment. He offered to prepare a more explicit draft, if such was the CHAIRMAN'S desire.

In regard to agricultural property he proposed that net revenue, and not gross receipts, should be considered. Such net revenue comprised at once the rent of the land and the profits of its agricultural exploitation. It could be calculated by applying a percentage upon the pre-war selling value.

MR. DANIELOPOL (*Roumania*) considered that it was unfair to take the pre-war revenue, having regard to the increase in prices. If the enemy had cultivated the land and taken the crop, he had been able to sell at war prices. He would thus benefit by the difference between pre-war rates and the actual selling prices. On the other hand, where the soil had remained uncultivated the farmer would lose the present value of the crop which he would otherwise have produced.

MR. DULLES (*U. S. A.*) remarked that the difference between MR. JOUASSET and MR. DANIELOPOL was more apparent than real. The rise in the price of agricultural produce was due to the increase in the cost of production. If, therefore, the actual cost of production was deducted from the actual selling price, the result would be very nearly the net pre-war revenue.

MR. DANIELOPOL (*Roumania*) recognized that the rise in the cost of production had been an influence in raising prices; but he added that there were other reasons for this rise, in particular the depreciation in the value of money, due to the inflation of the paper currency. He admitted that a net revenue should be taken, but it should be calculated by reference to the present value of money.

MR. McCORMICK (*U. S. A.*) supported MR. DANIELOPOL'S opinion, and added that the rise in the price of agricultural produce was due to the general inadequacy of production.

The CHAIRMAN proposed to reserve the section and asked that it should be redrafted.

MR. VAN DEN HEUVEL (*Belgium*) laid stress upon the importance of the section, which applied to all invaded territory, and in particular to Belgian land which had been inundated and French land which had been broken up. In both cases, as the soil must remain for a long time unproductive, a serious depreciation had been inflicted.

MR. JOUASSET (*Expert for France*) asked what instructions should be followed in re-drafting the section. He added that it would be appropriate to discuss section 43 in connection with section 9, (g) of Annex XII, 4th Meeting.

The CHAIRMAN appreciated MR. JOUASSET'S desire for instructions, but was unable to give any, as the members of the Committee differed in opinion.

Section 43 was reserved.

[Sec. 46]

The CHAIRMAN passed to the consideration of section 46.

MR. JOUASSET (*Expert for France*) proposed that this section should be reserved in order that it might be redrafted in agreement with the draft accepted for section 43.

This proposal was adopted.

Sec. 49

The CHAIRMAN stated that no objection was taken to section 49.

Sec. 51

He passed to section 51, which he supported after an explanation by MR. JOUASSET to the effect that special agreements between the Allies would be necessary to regulate questions of patents and commercial documents, to which no general principle appeared to be applicable.

Section 51 was adopted.

The CHAIRMAN appointed the following business for the next meeting:

1. The continuation and conclusion of the examination of the Tabulation of Memoranda on Valuation of Damage.
2. The discussion of amendments in the Tabulation of Memoranda on Categories of Damage (Annex XII, 4th Meeting) and of any new text suggested for the reserved sections of the Tabulation of Memoranda on Valuation.
3. The discussion of Memoranda on actual figures of claim.

The next meeting was fixed for Thursday, 13 March, at 2.30 P. M. The meeting rose at 6.30 P. M.

SUMNER,
Chairman.

E. MINOST,
Secretary.

DOCUMENT 479

First Subcommittee: Minutes of the Thirteenth Meeting, March 13, 1919, 2:30 P. M.

[EOM, First Subcommittee, pp. 91-93. French stenographic minutes, PV, CRD, pp. 433-49; French condensed minutes, *ibid.*, pp. 450-52.]

The First Sub-Committee of the Commission on Reparation of Damage (Valuation of Damage) met on Thursday, 13 March, 1919, at 2.30 P. M., at the Ministry of Finance, LORD SUMNER in the Chair.

Present: MR. MCCORMICK (*U. S. A.*); LORD SUMNER (*British Empire*); MR. JOUASSET (*France*); MR. CHIESA (*Italy*); MR. MORI (*Japan*); MR. VAN DEN HEUVEL (*Belgium*); MR. OLCHOWSKI (*Poland*); MR. DOS SANTOS VIEGAS (*Portugal*); MR. DANIELOPOL (*Roumania*); MR. PROTITCH (*Serbia*).[1]

After the acceptance of amendments which were proposed the minutes of the 10th meeting were adopted.

The Committee then continued the discussion of methods of valuation.

Sec. 53

MR. JOUASSET (*France*) read the text of the new draft of

---

[1] According to the French stenographic minutes, Michalakopoulos and Osuský were also present.

Section 53 proposed by the French and American Delegations, as follows:

> "Damage relating to currency (marks, monetary instruments issued or falsified by the enemy, etc. . . .) is valued on the basis of the real net expenses resulting from operations for repurchase by the Allied and Associated Powers, when such operations have been made; and, in the contrary case, on the basis of the decline in value actually suffered by the holders; interest at 6 per cent to be added from 11 November, 1918, to the date of the conclusion of peace."

Messrs. JOUASSET (*France*) and DULLES (*U. S. A.*) drew attention to the advantage of this text as avoiding all ambiguity.

MR. OLCHOWSKI (*Poland*) called the attention of the Committee to the issue of bank-notes without cover, which had been made by the Germans in Poland. These bank-notes should be reimbursed in gold marks.

The CHAIRMAN pointed out the difficulties raised by the question of repurchase of currency. He also feared that the repurchase at par, and the stipulation of interest at 6 per cent proposed by the Franco-American text, might be favorable to speculation. Furthermore, he did not consider that interest should be paid, except on the assumption that the money had lost all value. Such claims could in no case be presented by individuals but only by their Governments.

MR. DANIELOPOL (*Roumania*) returned to an argument which he had already presented to the Committee. It was indispensable that all the Allied and Associated States adopt a common basis for the valuation of their damages; but the adoption of this common basis should in no way prejudge the question of what monetary unit the enemy should use in payment. There were two separate and distinct questions involved: 1. In what monetary unit should we calculate our claim? 2. In what monetary unit should the enemy pay?

MR. DANIELOPOL asked that this question be put on the agenda for a later meeting.

The CHAIRMAN thought there would be no objection to this, provided that such discussion did not delay the work of the Committee.

MR. JOUASSET (*France*) observed that the rule for valuation provided by the revised draft of Section 53 could be adopted, whatever was the solution of the question raised by MR. DANIELOPOL.

The CHAIRMAN proposed to reserve the second part of the text presented by the French and American Delegations, (that which dealt with the case where operations for repurchase had not been carried out), but to adopt immediately the first part (which dealt with the case where operations for repurchase had been made).

The Committee agreed with this proposal.

MR. VAN DEN HEUVEL (*Belgium*) observed that the last section of the Franco-American proposal, relative to fixing interest at 6 per cent, was applicable to the part adopted. The fixing of a rate of interest was completely justified if the operation of repurchase involved any charges, as the currency repurchased by the Allied States had been unproductive as far as they were concerned. After an exchange of opinion between the CHAIRMAN and MR. JOUASSET, the Committee seemed to be in favor of fixing a rate of interest at 6 per cent, from the date of damage until the conclusion of peace and adopted the following text:

Damage relating to currency (marks, monetary instruments, issued or falsified by the enemy, etc.) is valued on the basis of the real net expenses resulting from operations for repurchase by the Allied and Associated Powers, when such operations have been made, the right being reserved to the other Powers to present objections to any scheme which may have been put into operation. There shall be added interest at 6 per cent from the day of the damage to the date of the conclusion of Peace.

Secs. 56, 57 and 58

The Committee then took up sections 56, 57 and 58, relating to damage to persons. There was a discussion of the question whether the valuation of these damages should or should not be made on the basis of a fixed scale of charges adopted by all the creditor States, without regard to the earning capacity of the victims.

MR. JOUASSET (*France*) was in favor of the adoption of a fixed scale. It seemed to him that it would be difficult in dealing with the enemy States to maintain distinctions on the ground of the social status and of the nationality of the victims. An exception should be made, however, in the case of soldiers, for in their case all legislations varied the amount of pension according to rank.

The CHAIRMAN and Messrs. OLCHOWSKI (*Poland*) and VAN DEN HEUVEL (*Belgium*) were opposed to the adoption of a single fixed scale. The amount of our demands should correspond to the real amount of damage, and the real damage varied according to the position of the victim and the economic conditions of the country.

Sections 56, 57 and 58 were not adopted.

MR. JOUASSET (*France*), speaking for the French Delegation, reserved the right to present this question to the Plenary Commission.

The CHAIRMAN asked the Committee to accept the following resolution:

"It is understood that, in adopting the principles and resolutions which have already been adopted, the Sub-Committee does not exclude the adoption of additional resolutions subsequently, or regard those already adopted as exhaustive of all cases."

This resolution was accepted.

MR. CHIESA (*Italy*) asked that a table should be printed showing the various texts adopted by the Sub-Committee.

The CHAIRMAN said that this would be done.

MR. OLCHOWSKI (*Poland*) drew the attention of the Committee to the importance of section 68 and the following sections, presented by the Polish Delegation. These sections related to compulsory administration and to forced liquidations.

The CHAIRMAN feared that these sections might be, at least in part, a repetition of proposals already adopted. He asked MR. OLCHOWSKI to make a very complete verification, in this respect, and to go over the proposed texts before submitting them for discussion.

The next meeting was fixed for Saturday, 15 March, at 3 P. M.

The meeting adjourned at 6 P. M.

SUMNER,
Chairman.

E. MINOST,
Secretary.

DOCUMENT 480

First Subcommittee: Minutes of the Fourteenth Meeting (Including Annex), March 15, 1919, 3:30 P. M.

[EOM, First Subcommittee, pp. 94-100. French stenographic minutes, PV, CRD, pp. 463-75. There is no French text of the Annex.]

The First Sub-Committee of the Commission on Reparation of Damage (Valuation of Damage) met on Saturday, 15 March, 1919, at 3.30 P. M.,[1] at the Ministry of Finance, LORD SUMNER in the Chair.

---

[1] According to the French minutes, at 3 P. M.

Present: MR. MCCORMICK (*U. S. A.*); LORD SUMNER (*British Empire*); MR. LEBRUN (*France*); MR. CHIESA (*Italy*); MR. MORI (*Japan*); MR. VAN DEN HEUVEL (*Belgium*); MR. MICHALACOPOULOS (*Greece*); MR. OLCHOWSKI (*Poland*); MR. DOS SANTOS VIEGAS (*Portugal*); MR. DANIELOPOL (*Roumania*); MR. PROTITCH (*Serbia*); MR. BENES (*Czecho-Slovak Republic*).[2]

The minutes of the 9th and 11th meetings were approved.

The CHAIRMAN presented his first draft report on Methods of Valuation of Damage (see Annex).

It was decided to consider the amendments proposed by members of the Sub-Committee to the Tabulation of Memoranda on Categories of Damage (Annex XII (3,) Fourth Meeting.[3]

Sec. 9, g.

MR. JOUASSET (*Expert for France*) proposed the following new draft for this section, (Sec. 9, g.):

Loss caused to any person who has been deprived, wholly or partially, as a direct consequence of the fact of war or invasion, and without compensation from other sources of revenue, of the exercise of his proprietary rights or occupation, or generally of opportunity to work or to obtain fair remuneration for his work, during the whole period of such deprivation.

The CHAIRMAN announced that MR. VAN DEN HEUVEL (*Belgium*) had proposed upon the same section the following amendment:

Loss caused to persons who have refused to labor or to exercise their occupations in a manner contrary to the interests of their country and to the direct advantage of the enemy.

Loss caused to workers upon whom forced personal labor has been imposed by the enemy without remuneration.

Loss caused to workers by the necessity of consuming for their maintenance, during the period of occupation, the savings which they had deposited in public or private savings-bank.

Loss arising from unproductiveness of land or buildings directly caused by the operations of war or the measures taken by the enemy.

Recovery of the obligatory charges, which, as a direct consequence of the operations of war or of the measures taken by the enemy, have become a burden upon commercial or industrial undertakings.

MR. DANIELOPOL (*Roumania*) proposed the following new draft:

Loss arising in consequence of unproductiveness, inactivity,

[2] According to the French minutes, Dulles was present instead of McCormick.
[3] See Document 470.

immobilization or any other total or partial interference resulting from enemy occupation.

1. *To Agriculture:—*
    (a) By requisition of land and its cultivation by the enemy, and by all administrative measures of the enemy during the occupation affecting the exploitation of land;
    (b) By requisition, theft, destruction, depreciation, etc., of agricultural machines, instruments and tools of all kinds, and of every sort of large and small live stock, of seed, etc.;
    (c) By acts of interference with enjoyment, direct or indirect, emanating from the enemy.

2. *To Industry:—*
    (a) By the destruction, deterioriation or removal, in whole or part, of machines, fittings, tools;
    (b) By seizure of raw materials and their utilization for other concerns and in the exclusive interest of the enemy;
    (c) By the requisition of factories and their utilization by the enemy for his own account;
    (d) By the protection specially accorded to certain industries and their products, to the detriment of other industries, and by the exploitation of industries exclusively for the profit of the enemy;
    (e) By special utilization of the means of transport (alteration of railway lines, displacement of oil pipe lines, etc.) for the exclusive profit of the enemy.

3. *To Commerce:—*
    (a) By the requisitioning of commercial establishments;
    (b) By the closing of commercial establishments; by the restriction or prevention of commerce, and by its monopolization exclusively for the profit of the enemy and his subjects.

4. Loss caused to other professions in consequence of the enemy occupation.

MR. OLCHOWSKI (*Poland*) asked for an explanation of the words in the French proposal "and without compensation from other sources of revenue."

MR. JOUASSET (*Expert for France*) before replying to this question, desired to have the CHAIRMAN'S ruling as to the order in which proposed drafts would be examined.

The CHAIRMAN proposed that the three amendments should be considered together.

MR. LEBRUN (*France*) offered three criticisms upon MR. DANIELOPOL'S proposal:—

(1) Category "C" dealt with Miscellaneous Interests. The Roumanian draft spoke of losses resulting from requisition, theft, destruction and deterioration, which the Sub-Committee had already discussed;

(2) The Roumanian proposal did not deal with damage resulting from the loss of opportunity to work;

(3) The draft involved an enumeration which was restrictive in effect. Such an enumeration might be dangerous; a general formula was preferable.

Mr. Danielopol replied to these remarks:—

(1) As to the first point, he said that there could be no duplication of claims. The Sub-Committee had considered the reparation to be exacted in respect of thefts, requisitions, etc. The Roumanian proposal dealt with the losses resulting from the inactivity entailed by such thefts, requisitions, etc.

(2) He was under the impression that the Sub-Committee had decided to abandon the claim for losses caused to workers;

(3) He agreed with Mr. Lebrun that a general formula was always preferable to an enumeration; and for this reason he would be pleased to support the French proposal. He must, however, make the same reservation as Mr. Olchowski as to the words "without compensation from other sources of revenue."

Mr. Jouasset (*Expert for France*) explained the French text. Comparing it with the text previously submitted, he said that it was intended to make the following changes in that text:—

(1) The words referring to the normal development of resources had been suppressed, in order to exclude taking account of increase in value.

(2) It was intended to establish a direct relation of cause and effect between the interference with enjoyment of property and the fact of war or invasion.

(3) The word "libre" had been suppressed. The alteration did not change the meaning in the French text, but it had been felt that the word "libre" translated into a different language might affect the meaning of the clause.

(4) The words "without compensation from other sources of revenue" imported that damage had been suffered only to the extent to which the revenue which had been lost had not been replaced in whole or part by a new source of revenue.

Mr. Dulles (*U. S. A.*) declared himself satisfied by the explanation of Mr. Jouasset, and proposed that the text presented by him should be adopted.

MR. VAN DEN HEUVEL (*Belgium*) explained the Belgian proposal. As regarded wages, he considered that the relief which had been distributed to unemployed persons constituted a compensation whose amount should be deducted from the normal wage.

MR. OLCHOWSKI (*Poland*) asked if a more explicit draft could not be made.

The CHAIRMAN having approved the principle of the French proposal, the following amended draft of that proposal was accepted:—

"Loss caused to any person who has been deprived, wholly or partially, as a direct consequence of the operations of war or of the measures taken by the enemy, and without compensation from new sources of revenue, of the exercise of his proprietary rights, his occupation, or generally of opportunity to work or to obtain fair remuneration for his work, during the whole period of such deprivation."

MR. JOUASSET (*Expert for France*), replying to MR. VAN DEN HEUVEL (*Belgium*), explained that the words "without compensation from new sources of revenue" applied to labor as well as to property.

Sec. 27

MR. CHIESA (*Italy*) proposed the following amendment to Section 27:—

"Other costs of war: all expenses or charges resulting from the state of war imposed upon the Allied Nations, including exceptional and well-determined maritime and financial charges which any State, being in an exceptional position created by the fact of war, has been obliged to bear in consequence of the damage effected by submarines."

MR. CHIESA explained this proposal, giving as an example of exceptional charges the rise in freight costs, the losses due to unfavorable foreign exchange and losses caused by submarine war.

The CHAIRMAN remarked that all States had been placed more or less in an exceptional position by the war. While fully appreciating the serious losses suffered by Italy, he did not feel that the new Section now proposed removed the difficulties which the Sub-Committee had already encountered in reference to this category of damage. He added that the rules to be established by the Sub-Committee must be generally applicable to all countries.

MR. CHIESA (*Italy*) explained his proposal. He had hoped that the restriction of the claim by reference to circumstances which were exceptional and well-determined would have rendered his proposal acceptable.

The next meeting was fixed for Monday, 17 March, at 3 P. M. The meeting adjourned at 5.30 P. M.

SUMNER,
Chairman.

H. McKINNON WOOD,
Secretary.

ANNEX

FIRST DRAFT OF REPORT PRESENTED BY LORD SUMNER ON THE RESULTS OF THE WORK OF THE FIRST SUB-COMMITTEE

SECOND PART*

(Methods of Valuation of Damage.)

1. On 5 March the Sub-Committee proceeded to the consideration of the methods of evaluation of damage, and after discussion it adopted the following general propositions:—[4]

2. I. It is understood throughout that claims cannot be admitted under whatever categories so as to involve payment twice over for the same damages or payment to two persons of whatever sort for one injury.

3. II. Where injury is caused by acts for which the enemy Powers are responsible the damage to be claimed will include all the natural and necessary consequences of these acts.

4. III. Claims are not admissible which are incapable of being estimated with reasonable certainty by some means or other of proof whether direct and specific or statistical and general.

5. IV. Statistical methods of computation and evaluation may be resorted to in default of direct evidence of value or for other sufficient reasons subject to the application of proper methods for verification and corroboration.

6. V. The cost of restoration of things injured, whether movables or immovables, does not extend to the cost of substituting for the things injured other things of a more expensive or valuable character or to rebuilding with better materials or on an enlarged scale.

7. VI. Claims ought to be supported by credible testimony with reasonable certainty, but it rests with the Powers concerned to determine in the first instance the particular form in which such testimony is to be admitted.

---

* The First Part of this draft report is the document printed as Annex I, Tenth Meeting. [See Document No. 476.]

---

[4] These six general propositions are identical with Annex VII of Document 475.

8. In order to facilitate the discussion of particular rules, each Delegation was invited to present a Memorandum of its views on the appropriate principles and methods, and the following Delegations duly presented Memoranda, viz.: The American, French, Greek, Polish, Roumanian and Czecho-Slovak Delegations. To enable the views of each Delegation to be presented to the Plenary Commission in its own words, these Memoranda are annexed to this report. The proposition submitted were then co-ordinated in a tabular form, in which the Memorandum of the French Delegation, which was the most complete and detailed, occupied the leading place and formed the basis of discussion. This tabulation is annexed to the present report.

9. After full consideration the Committee adopted the following propositions:—

10. It will be the concern of the Allied and Associated Powers which have suffered damage, to set forth and evaluate the damage which the enemy will be required to make good, each nation having regard to its own case. (T.2.)†

11. The general rules set forth apply exclusively to claims which are to be made on the enemy, and do not necessarily govern the relations of the Allied and Associated States as between themselves, nor the relations of each State to its nationals. (T. 4.)

12. Valuations of damage shall be made with careful regard to placing every person having the right to reparation in a situation as nearly as possible identical with that in which he would have found himself if he had not sustained the loss resulting from the state of war imposed by the enemy Powers. (T. 8.)

13. Sections 11 and 12 were accepted in principle only. Sections 11, 13 and 15 of the Tabulation were:—

14. The valuations made should cover all the natural and necessary consequences of the acts giving rise to the claims for damages. (T. 11.)

15. Whatever the procedure adopted for the classification of categories of damage, or for the registration and valuation of claims, it shall never be possible to obtain payment twice for the same damage, either wholly or in part, whether to the same person or to different persons. (T. 13.)

16. Claims shall be supported, either by direct proof as to the reality and the amount of the damage suffered, or by any other acceptable evidence or credible testimony, the Allied and Associated

† The reference is to the numbered sections of the Tabulation of Memoranda on Valuation of Damage (Annex II, Tenth Meeting). [See Document 476.]

Powers having the exclusive right to determine the form of evidence and the conditions under which it shall be admitted. (T. 15.)

17. After considering these sections, the Sub-Committee reaffirmed the resolutions on the same subject set out in sections 2, 3, 4, 5 and 7 above.

The following propositions were then accepted:—

18. Valuations shall be expressed in the currency which each interested Power may consider it proper to adopt, without in any way prejudging the question of the currency in which payment shall be made by the enemy; and each Power shall state the rate of exchange upon which its calculation is based, so as to permit full verification. (T. 17.)

19. The amount of a claim shall not be more than enough for the replacement of property or objects destroyed, whether movables or immovables, by other property of corresponding quality or importance, it being understood, however, that this provision does not refer to increases in value resulting from a rise in prices, or to the replacement of property or objects destroyed or damaged by similar property or objects in a new state. (T. 21.)

Section 24 of the Tabulation was:—

20. Destruction, deterioration and all damage caused to real or personal property, which property is of such a nature that it can be reconstructed, replaced or repaired, shall be valued at the amount of the estimated cost of such reconstruction, replacement or repair as at the date of the conclusion of peace. (T. 24.)

MR. LEBRUN (*France*) explained that the word "reparation" used in the French text in this section had reference solely to the same objects as the words "reconstruction" and "remplacement."

The Committee passed to the consideration of the new section.

21. The cost of such reconstruction, replacement or repair is arrived at by applying to the corresponding pre-war cost an appropriate coefficient, calculated for each category of property in accordance with the market price at the date of the conclusion of peace, in respect to materials, labor and all other factors to be considered. (T. 25.)

22. The Committee reserved this section, together with section 34 of the Tabulation, which was:

23. Destruction, deterioration and all damage caused to real or personal property not susceptible of reconstruction, replacement or repair, are to be valued at the amount which the property would have been worth at the date of the conclusion of peace, deduction to be made proportionately for salvage, if any. (T. 34.)

The following propositions were accepted:

24. In the case of labor hired or purchases made for reconstruction, replacement or repair, before the date of the conclusion of peace, the valuation may be based upon actual cost. (T. 26.)

25. In case the same property or object has undergone repeated and successive damage, all labor and purchases which have actually gone to reconstruction, replacement or repair are to be taken into account in the valuation. (T. 27.)

26. Damage resulting from levies or seizures of sums of money, under whatever guise, or of assets of any kind expressed in cash, and damage resulting from expenses incurred, especially for the relief of the population of invaded territories or of interned civilians, are taken at the capital value of the sum involved, with interest at 6 per cent from the date of the damage to the date of the conclusion of peace, the right being fully reserved to regulate in any manner determined all questions as to reciprocal claims or debts arising from pre-war contracts between subjects of the enemy Powers and subjects of the Allied Powers. (T. 36.)

27. The following proposition was accepted, the Delegations of the British Empire and Japan dissenting:

28. Damage resulting from the seizure, loss or destruction of securities is valued on the basis of their average price on the Bourse during the first six months of 1914, or, in the case of securities issued after 1 July, 1914, on the basis of their issue price—provided that such price be not lower than the average for the first quarter of 1919; there shall be added the value of coupons, interest or income in arrears, which the owners would have been able to realize up to the date of the conclusion of peace if they had remained in possession of their securities. (T. 41.)

The following proposition was accepted in principle:

29. Damage which consists in the disorganization of business houses, enterprises or professions, is valued on the basis of the cost of reorganization.

The following propositions were accepted:

30. Damage caused to industrial property through the enemy's knowledge of special processes of manufacture, and the commercial damage resulting from the enemy's knowledge of books, correspondence and documents or information of a private nature, of all sorts, are to be valued in accordance with special rules agreed upon between the Allied and Associated Powers. (T. 51.)

31. Damage relating to currency (marks, monetary instruments issued or falsified by the enemy, etc.) is valued on the basis of the

actual net costs resulting from any operation of repurchase effected by the Allied and Associated Powers, when such operations have been made, the right being reserved to the other Powers to object to any scheme which may have been put into operation. There shall be added interest at 6 per cent from the date of the damage down to the date of the conclusion of peace. (T. 53.)

32. Sections 56, 57 and 58 of the Tabulation, in which was proposed a uniform tariff for the various kinds of injury to the person, were not accepted. The French Delegation reserved the right to put forward these sections for acceptance by the Plenary Commission.

33. The American Delegation withdrew those further sections of the Tabulation which were taken from its Memorandum.

34. The Polish Delegation called attention to sections 68-71 (inclusive) of the Tabulation; but no decision upon these sections was taken.

Having concluded the first consideration of the Tabulation of Memoranda, the Committee adopted the following resolution:

[35.] *"It is understood that in adopting the principles and resolutions which have already been adopted, the Sub-Committee does not exclude the adoption of additional resolutions subsequently, or regard those already adopted as being exhaustive of all cases."*

36. The Committee reserved the right to resume the review both of categories and of methods of valuation, with a view to supplementing its decisions upon the various points reserved.

DOCUMENT 481

First Subcommittee: Minutes of the Fifteenth Meeting, March 17, 1919, 3:20 P. M.

[EOM, First Subcommittee, pp. 101-3. French stenographic minutes PV, CRD, pp. 476-92; French condensed minutes, *ibid.*, pp. 493-95.]

The First Sub-Committee of the Commission on Reparation of Damage (Valuation of Damage) met on Monday, 17 March, 1919, at 3.20 P. M., at the Ministry of Finance, LORD SUMNER in the chair.

Present: MR. MCCORMICK (*U. S. A.*); LORD SUMNER (*British Empire*); MR. LEBRUN (*France*); MR. MORI (*Japan*); MR. VAN DEN HEUVEL (*Belgium*); MR. SPERANZA (*Greece*); MR. OLCHOWSKI (*Poland*); MR. DOS SANTOS VIEGAS (*Portugal*); MR. ANTONESCO (*Roumania*); MR. PROTITCH (*Serbia*); MR. KRECMAR (*Czecho-Slovak Republic*).[1]

[1] According to the French minutes, Michalakopoulos was present instead of Sperantzas, and Osuský instead of Krčmář. According to the French condensed minutes, Kramář was present instead of Krčmář.

The minutes of the 12th meeting were adopted.

Meaning of Reservations

In reply to a question by MR. JOUASSET (*Expert for France*) the CHAIRMAN explained that the reservation of any section or proposal did not imply its rejection or prevent its being brought forward again. Each Delegation remained free to bring forward its original proposal again and ask for a decision upon it, or to present it in a revised form, or to bring it forward in the Plenary Commission. The object was to preserve unanimity in face of the enemy as long as possible, and he asked if the Sub-Committee approved of the procedure thus outlined.

The Committee signified its approval.

Question about Interest on Claims

MR. JOUASSET (*Expert for France*) presented the following additional section to the Tabulation of Memorandum on Valuation (Annex II, Tenth Meeting).

"In all cases where the above sections do not provide for interest calculated in a special manner, the compensation for which the enemy is held responsible will bear interest at 6 per cent from 11 November, 1918 to the date of the conclusion of peace."

In reply to questions by Messrs. MORI (*Japan*) and VAN DEN HEUVEL (*Belgium*), MR. JOUASSET said that the new section provided for payment of interest upon all approved claims on which interest was not already payable under the sections already accepted by the Sub-Committee.

The Chairman considered that MR. JOUASSET'S proposal involved the danger of counting the same claim twice over, and might also be represented as an attempt to make Germany pay interest in respect of a delay in the settlement of peace terms for which she was not primarily responsible.

MR. VAN DEN HEUVEL (*Belgium*) agreed with the CHAIRMAN that the proposal involved duplication of claims for damage.

After explanations by MR. JOUASSET (*Expert for France*) the CHAIRMAN accepted the uniform rate of 6 per cent. interest as proper, where interest was charged in respect to seizure, etc., of money or securities by the enemy; but he was opposed to accepting the general imposition of interest provided by the suggested section.

The discussion of the proposal was then dropped.

[After adjournment, the CHAIRMAN stated that MR. JOUASSET had submitted an amended draft of his proposal to MR. VAN DEN

HEUVEL and himself, but they had not been able to accept it as excluding the danger of double counting of claims.][2]

The CHAIRMAN proposed the following new section for insertion after sections 24 and 25 of the Tabulation of Memoranda on Valuation (Annex II, Tenth Meeting.)

Date to be considered in valuing ships, etc.

"In the case of ships, cargoes and merchandise, the actual value at and after the time of the loss or damage may be taken whether there had been an actual replacement by purchase or not in order to avoid exposing the injured person to the risks of fluctuations of prices."

Supporting this proposal, the CHAIRMAN said that the British Delegation had accepted section 25 on the understanding that it did not apply to ships, cargoes and merchandise, but more careful study of its terms showed that it might be taken as applicable to such objects. The method of valuation which it provided was unsuitable for objects which were owned, employed and dealt in by reference to temporary conditions of markets, and its enforcement in the case of such objects would involve serious injustice. It would give the claimant not the value which he had lost, but something entirely different. Ships, cargoes and merchandise, regarded as the subjects of mercantile ventures, were not in reality objects capable of reconstruction, replacement or repair. The loss sustained was a loss of a particular venture; a new ship or supply of merchandise could be obtained, but it would probably be of a different character, and in any case its acquisition did not amount to restoration of the original mercantile opportunity, but to the commencing of another and quite different venture. The claim was different in kind from that of the man who lost a permanent property from which he obtained a regular income. The words "at or after the time of the loss or damage" were intended to take account of the fact that immediate replacement of losses had been very difficult during the war.

"Merchandise"

The CHAIRMAN added that he attached great importance to his proposal. He considered that sections 24 and 25 were applicable to a different class of property, and he had no objection to raise if their application was thus limited.

In reply to questions by MR. JOUASSET (*Expert for France*), the

---

[2] The brackets are in the original.

CHAIRMAN explained that the word "merchandise" covered all merchandise whether afloat or on land; merchandise meant any commodities anywhere which were dealt in for buying and selling in the ordinary course of business. He amended his proposal by substituting for the words "at or after the time of loss or damage" the words "at or within reasonable time after the time of loss or damage."

MR. VAN DEN HEUVEL (*Belgium*) called attention to the number of different persons interested in the fate of a ship or cargo. He was unable to see the soundness of the distinction drawn between merchandise and other movables, and thought that goods at sea and goods on land should be treated alike.

MR. JOUASSET agreed with MR. VAN DEN HEUVEL'S observations.

The CHAIRMAN said the question as to the person who should ultimately claim was a matter of detail. It was not intended to distinguish between goods at sea and goods on land; he would add the words "at sea or on land" after the word "merchandise" in the text of his proposal.

There was no question of preferential treatment for merchandise. Sections 24, 25, 26 and 34, as they stood, would inflict serious injustice in a class of cases with which he was very familiar; and it was to exclude such injustice that he had introduced and must insist upon his present proposal, which merely limited the application of these sections. The British Delegation could not accept the sections without this limiting amendment.

MR. DOS SANTOS VIEGAS (*Portugal*) supported the CHAIRMAN'S resolution, calling attention to the corresponding proposal in the Memorandum of the Portuguese Delegation (Annex XIII, Fourth Meeting).

MR. SPERANZA (*Greece*) also supported the proposal. He pointed out that ships were commonly bought and sold, whereas trains were not. MR. JOUASSET (*France*) observed that trucks and motor lorries were commonly sold and purchased.

On the proposal of MR. VAN DEN HEUVEL (*Belgium*) the discussion was adjourned.

The next meeting was fixed for Tuesday, 18 March, 1919, at 3 P. M.

The meeting adjourned at 6.45 P. M.

SUMNER,
Chairman.

BOURQUIN,
Secretary.

DOCUMENT 482

First Subcommittee: Minutes of the Sixteenth Meeting, March 18, 1919, 3:30 P. M.

[EOM, First Subcommittee, pp. 104-5. French stenographic minutes, PV, CRD, pp. 496-507; French condensed minutes, *ibid.*, pp. 508-9.]

The First Sub-Committee of the Commission on Reparation of Damage (Valuation of Damage) met on Tuesday, 18 March, 1919, at 3.30 P. M.,[1] at the Ministry of Finance, LORD SUMNER in the chair.

Present: MR. DULLES (*U. S. A.*); LORD SUMNER (*British Empire*); MR. LEBRUN (*France*); MR. CHIESA (*Italy*); MR. MORI (*Japan*); MR. VAN DEN HEUVEL (*Belgium*); MR. MICHALACO- POULOS (*Greece*); MR. OLCHOWSKI (*Poland*); MR. DOS SANTOS VIEGAS (*Portugal*); MR. DANIELOPOL (*Roumania*); MR. PROTITCH (*Serbia*).[2]

The minutes of the 13th meeting were adopted.

The first question on the Agenda was the discussion of sections 24, 25, 26 and 34 of the Tabulation of Methods of Valuation (Annex II, Tenth Meeting).

The CHAIRMAN proposed the following addition to section 24:

Dates to be considered in valuing ships, etc.

In case of ships, cargoes, or merchandise on land or at sea, the value at the moment of the loss or damage, or the value within a reasonable period after the moment of the loss or damage may be taken, whether there has been an actual re- placement by purchase or not, in order to avoid exposing the injured persons to the risks of fluctuations of prices.

MR. VAN DEN HEUVEL (*Belgium*) said that he could not support this proposal, as it made a distinction between merchandise and other movables. The same rule was necessary for all movables. But the same rule could be applied to movables as to securities (section 41), thus allowing movables and vessels to be valued "according to their value at the time of damage or their value at the date of peace.

MR. LEBRUN (*France*) agreed with MR. VAN DEN HEUVEL, but thought it would be sufficient to add to section 24: "provided that such value shall not be less than that of the damage."

MR. DANIELOPOL (*Roumania*) proposed the following wording:

---

[1] According to the French stenographic minutes, at 3:00 P. M. According to the French condensed minutes, "à 13 heures 30."

[2] According to the French stenographic minutes, Osuský was also present.

"estimated either at the date of the damage or at the date of the conclusion of peace."

The CHAIRMAN thought that a misunderstanding had arisen in the discussion from the fact that sections 24, 25 and 26 had been reserved, as the Sub-Committee had been in doubt as to the object of these sections. He had only accepted section 24 because he understood it was not applicable to vessels and merchandise. He must now make a reservation. The normal time for the valuation of damage was the time of loss; on account of the state of war it had been necessary to choose another date, that of the conclusion of peace. This procedure might be equitable in certain cases, but it departed from the general rule, and this general rule should be followed wherever possible. He was thus not asking for a special exception, but for conformity with a general rule which would avoid unjust treatment of injured persons. He could not support the amendments presented, as they would have the effect of allowing speculation in consequence of the choice permitted between two dates.

The CHAIRMAN, being obliged to attend a meeting of another Commission, requested MR. CHIESA (*Italy*) Vice-chairman of the Sub-Committee, to take the Chair.

MR. LEBRUN (*France*) observed that sections 24 and 26 had already been adopted without reserve, as was shown by the minutes of the 10th meeting.

MR. VAN DEN HEUVEL (*Belgium*) thought that LORD SUMNER could present an amendment on second reading.

MR. MICHALACOPOULOS (*Greece*) recalled the fact that it was at his suggestion that section 34 had been reserved, as it then seemed that this section was closely connected with sections 24 and 26. The three sections together should accordingly be reserved for discussion later.

MR. JOUASSET (*Expert for France*) remarked that LORD SUMNER'S amendment should be inserted after section 26, and did not affect section 34, which could, therefore, be discussed to-day.

MR. DULLES (*U. S. A.*) suggested waiting until LORD SUMNER was present before discussing these sections.

Sec. 34

Sec. 34. This section was reserved.

Secs. 43 and 46

Sec. 43 and 46. These sections were reserved for later discussion.

Sec. 39

Sec. 39. Section 39 was then considered.

MR. OLCHOWSKI (*Poland*) called the attention of the Sub-Committee to the importance of this section for Poland.

MR. JOUASSET (*Expert for France*) replied that in the opinion of the CHAIRMAN, who had prepared the Tabulation as well as in the opinion of the Sub-Committee, section 39 was covered by section 36. MR. OLCHOWSKI insisted that it would be preferable to add section 39 to 36, except in the case where it was clearly understood that the case in question under section 36 constituted a seizure.

MR. ANTONESCO (*Roumania*) asked that forced subscriptions be also included.

MR. JOUASSET (*Expert for France*) proposed adding to section 36, after the words "under whatever guise," the words "including forced subscriptions." This proposal was adopted.

The next meeting was fixed for Thursday, 19 March, at 2.30 P. M.

The meeting adjourned at 5 P. M.[3]

SUMNER,
Chairman.

E. MINOST,
Secretary.

DOCUMENT 483

First Subcommittee: Minutes of the Seventeenth Meeting,
March 19, 1919, 2:45 P. M.

[EOM, First Subcommittee, pp. 106-9. French stenographic minutes, PV, CRD, pp. 510-24; French condensed minutes, *ibid.*, 525-28.]

The First Sub-Committee of the Commission on Reparation of Damage (Valuation of Damage) met on 19 March, 1919, at 2.45 P. M., at the Ministry of Finance, LORD SUMNER in the chair.

Present: MR. DULLES (*U. S. A.*); LORD SUMNER (*British Empire*); MR. LEBRUN (*France*); MR. CHIESA (*Italy*); MR. MORI (*Japan*); MR. VAN DEN HEUVEL (*Belgium*); MR. MICHALACO-POULOS (*Greece*); MR. OLCHOWSKI (*Poland*); MR. DOS SANTOS VIEGAS (*Portugal*); MR. ANTONESCO (*Roumania*); MR. PROTITCH (*Serbia*) and MR. KRECMAR (*Czecho-Slovak Republic*).[1]

---

[3] According to the French condensed minutes, "à 15 heures 30."

[1] According to the French stenographic minutes, Osuský was present instead of Krčmář; and Van den Heuvel and Michalakopoulos were absent. According to the French condensed minutes, Kramář was present instead of Krčmář.

Presentation of the minutes of the last two meetings was postponed.

Methods of Valuation. Sec. 24

The CHAIRMAN, resuming the discussion of section 24 of the Tabulation of Methods of Valuation (Annex II, Tenth Meeting) proposed by way of compromise—

(1) to make his proposal applicable to all movables;

(2) to insert the provision "unless there has been an actual replacement by purchase," which would have the effect of leaving cases where there had been such replacements to be dealt with under section 24. By these changes the CHAIRMAN considered that he accepted the substance of MR. VAN DEN HEUVEL and MR. JOUASSET's proposals.

MR. VAN DEN HEUVEL (*Belgium*) pointed out that ships were immovables under some systems of law and would require to be specially mentioned. He suggested that the phrase "at the moment of the loss or damage, or within a reasonable period after the moment of loss or damage," in itself allowed an option as to date which was inconsistent with the CHAIRMAN's principles.

The CHAIRMAN accepted the suggestion that ships should be specially mentioned. He explained that the phrase quoted was not intended to give an option as to date, but to provide a practical definition of the term "time of loss or damage." The date of the loss of a ship was often not exactly known, but it could be ascertained within reasonable limits. In order to avoid even the appearance of an option, he was prepared to omit the words "at the moment of the loss or damage" and to read "within a reasonable period after the moment of the loss or damage." There would be no difficulty in practice in ascertaining what would be a "reasonable period."

MR. LEBRUN (*France*) asked whether the CHAIRMAN's proposal formed an addition to section 24, or was to be submitted for it. In the former case the injured party would still have an option as to date.

The CHAIRMAN replied that the proposal merely provided an exception to the general rule established by section 24.

MR. VAN DEN HEUVEL (*Belgium*) thought that the CHAIRMAN's intention was a modification of section 24 which would have the effect of establishing two general rules:—

(1) Immovables should be valued as at the date of the conclusion of peace;

(2) Movables should be valued as at the date of loss, unless there has been replacement by purchase.

He did not agree that the normal rule of law required the amount of an indemnification to be fixed at the value of the property at the actual moment of the damage. It would be necessary to take account of what the reparation would cost at the moment when it became possible.

A discussion followed upon this interpretation of the CHAIRMAN'S meaning.

MR. OLCHOWSKI (*Poland*) considered that to take the date of loss would inflict an almost universal injustice, in order to avoid unfairness in a particular class of claims. He proposed that a complete option be given.

MR. LEBRUN (*France*) vigorously protested against the danger of doing the greatest injustice to the population of devastated regio: is by requiring damage to be valued as at the date of loss. In this case there had been no possibility of replacement, and present prices were three times higher than at the time when the damage was suffered.

MR. CHIESA (*Italy*) quoted figures which he had just received from his government. In the case of 64,000 houses destroyed in Italy, an original estimate of the cost of reconstruction, based on pre-war prices, amounted to 584 million lire; the cost at present prices was now shown to be over 2,400 million lire. For this class of damage the date of the conclusion of peace must be taken. In other cases, however, such as crops cut by the enemy, the fairest date would be the date of loss.

MR. DULLES (*U. S. A.*), without expressing an opinion on the merits of the respective contentions, thought that there was less disagreement between the Delegations than appeared to be in the case, and that the CHAIRMAN'S intention had been misunderstood. MR. LEBRUN had urged that, in order not to do injustice in a vast number of cases, the ordinary rule of law that damage should be valued at the date of the damage should be disregarded in favor of valuation as at a date approximating that of actual replacement. MR. DULLES believed that the CHAIRMAN fully recognized this position and accepted section 24 as the general rule to be applied in estimating war losses. But there might be other cases, in particular the case of goods passing from hand to hand in the ordinary course of business, as objects of purchase and sale, where it would be fairer to revert to the ordinary rule and take the value at the time of loss. The CHAIRMAN's proposal merely provided an exception to section 24 in order to meet such cases.

The CHAIRMAN thanked MR. DULLES for explaining the misunderstanding which had arisen. MR. DULLES had correctly interpreted his intention. He moved his resolution in the following amended form as an addition to section 24:

"But in cases where the application of this rule would expose the persons injured to the risks of fluctuations of market prices, movables and ships shall be valued at their value within a reasonable time after the time of loss or damage, unless there has been an actual replacement by purchase."

MR. LEBRUN (*France*) accepted the proposal as now put, subject to its being made applicable to immovables as well as movables.

MR. JOUASSET (*Expert for France*) suggested the addition of the words "on land or at sea" after the words "damage caused to real or personal property" in section 24.

MR. MORI (*Japan*) congratulated the CHAIRMAN on the acceptance of his proposal, but said that the Japanese Delegation must, for the moment, reserve its attitude upon section 24 as amended.

Amendment Adopted

Subject to this reservation, the CHAIRMAN's and MR. JOUASSET's proposals were carried and section 24 was approved in the following form:—

Destruction, deterioration and all damage caused to real or personal property, on land or at sea, which property is of such a nature that it can be reconstructed, replaced or repaired, shall be valued at the amount of the estimated cost of such reconstruction, replacement or repair on the date of the conclusion of peace; but in cases where the application of this rule would expose the persons injured to the risks of fluctuation of market prices, damage caused to the property above mentioned shall be evaluated at its value within a reasonable time after the time of the loss or damage, except in the case, provided for in the section below, where there has been an actual replacement by purchase.

Sec. 34

Section 34, which had been reserved, was then accepted after an explanation by MR. JOUASSET that it referred solely to works of art and other unique objects.

Secs. 43 and 46

MR. JOUASSET (*Expert for France*) moved the following texts in substitution for sections 43 and 46.

(43) Damage resulting from the deprivation, wholly or in part, of the exercise of any proprietary right is valued, for the whole period of such deprivation, on the basis of the average receipts or net income of such property during the three

calendar years, the three fiscal years, or the three seasons last preceding the war, including, in the case of agricultural property, the net income of the landlord and that of the tenant; provided that the compensation shall not be less than the amount necessary to assure, after the payment of all charges and in particular the usual amortization, a net income of 6 per cent upon the capital invested in the enterprise, or representing the value of the property, of which the nationals of the Allied and Associated States shall have been deprived. In such valuation account shall be taken of all new resources whose addition to the existing income of the parties interested may have provided compensation, wholly or in part, for the loss suffered by them.

(46) Damage resulting from deprivation, wholly or in part, of the exercise of an occupation, or generally of opportunity to work or obtain a fair remuneration for work, is valued for the whole period of such deprivation on the basis of the average wages or salary of the claimant during the three years preceding the war.

After a discussion in which MR. JOUASSET (*Expert for France*) and the CHAIRMAN took part, consideration of these proposals was postponed.

The next meeting was fixed for Thursday, 20 March, at 2.30 P. M.

The meeting adjourned at 5 P. M.

SUMNER,
Chairman.

E. MINOST,
Secretary.

DOCUMENT 484

First Subcommittee: Minutes of the Eighteenth Meeting, March 20, 1919, 2:15 P. M.

[EOM, First Subcommittee, pp. 110-12. French stenographic minutes, PV, CRD, pp. 529-44; French condensed minutes, *ibid.*, 545-48.]

The First Sub-Committee of the Commission on Reparation of Damage (Valuation of Damage) met on Thursday, 20 March, 1919, at 2.15 P. M., at the Ministry of Finance, LORD SUMNER in the Chair.

Present: MR. DULLES (*U. S. A.*); LORD SUMNER (*British Empire*); MR. JOUASSET (*France*); MR. CHIESA (*Italy*); MR. MORI (*Japan*); MR. VAN DEN HEUVEL (*Belgium*); MR. MICHALACO-POULOS (*Greece*); MR. OLCHOWSKI (*Poland*); MR. DOS SANTOS VIEGAS (*Portugal*); MR. DANIELOPOL (*Roumania*); MR. PROTITCH (*Serbia*); MR. KRECMAR (*Czecho-Slovak Republic*).[1]

Sec. 43

The Sub-Committee continued the discussion of section 43 of

---

[1] According to the French stenographic minutes, Osuský was present instead of Krčmář. According to the French condensed minutes, Kramář was present instead of Krčmář.

the Tabulation of Methods of Valuation (Annex II, Tenth Meeting).[2]

MR. DANIELOPOL (*Roumania*) observed that the text proposed by the French Delegation would give the enemy an unjustifiable advantage in agricultural matters. This text took as a basis of valuation the mean revenue of the three years before the war. But the price of wheat during that time was appreciably lower than during the years 1915 to 1918. The loss suffered by cultivators of occupied regions, whom the enemy had deprived of their harvests, should be calculated on the basis of the value of those harvests at the time of loss.

MR. DANIELOPOL submitted an amendment to this effect.

After a suggestion by the CHAIRMAN, MR. DANIELOPOL changed the wording of his text so as to make clear that it applied only to loss of enjoyment.

His amendment was presented as follows:

"Damage through loss of enjoyment caused by the enemy in occupied territory to agriculture and agricultural produce by sequestration, consumption, destruction, or removal of produce, seed, live stock, agricultural machines, implements, etc., or in any other manner, shall be valued as at the time when the damage was caused."

MR. JOUASSET (*France*) explained the scope of section 43. The French Delegation persisted in believing that the basis of valuation proposed by them was more practical than that asked for by MR. DANIELOPOL. The mean revenue at the time of deprivation would be in a great number of cases very difficult to fix on account of the derangement of economic life and often through lack of terms of comparison. Nevertheless, the French Delegation would be ready to support the Roumanian proposal, on condition that the rules laid down in this proposal were applicable to all countries.

MR. DANIELOPOL (*Roumania*) said that he never had any idea of proposing a principle which was not applicable to all Allies indiscriminately.

MR. MORI (*Japan*) understood that the intention of MR. DANIELOPOL was not to establish different rules for different countries, but for different cases. If this was so, MR. MORI entirely agreed with this point of view and proposed the following amendment to the French text:

"In cases, however, where there is an actual means of estimating the net income which such property might have reasonably produced for the period of such deprivation, if the injury had not occurred, the damage may be valued on the basis of such net income thus estimated."

[2] See Document 476.

In certain cases the basis of valuation proposed by the French Delegation was the only one applicable. But in other cases it was possible to find a method of valuation more closely approaching reality and therefore preferable.

MR. VAN DEN HEUVEL (*Belgium*) cited the case of Belgium, where the situation of industry and that of agriculture were quite different. Industry had been entirely stopped throughout the whole territory except for coal mining. It was, therefore, impossible to find in the country itself points of comparison for establishing the mean net income during the period of occupation. On the other hand, agriculture had been paralyzed only in certain regions. In this latter case, therefore, terms of comparison existed, and the system proposed by the Roumanian Delegation was applicable. The system was more just than that of the French Delegation. The French system would in practice give an advantage to farmers whose land had not been ravaged over those whose land had been in the zone of fire. The former had been able to sell their products at the high war prices, while the latter would only be indemnified at a rate calculated on pre-war prices.

MR. VAN DEN HEUVEL therefore entirely supported the proposal of MR. DANIELOPOL.

MR. JOUASSET (*France*) was also inclined to support the spirit of the amendments presented by Messrs. DANIELOPOL and MORI; but he said that the rule should be so formulated as to be applicable in all cases and not act either directly or indirectly to the disadvantage of the countries which have suffered the first shock of the war.

He therefore proposed to value the mean revenue by applying a coefficient to the mean revenue of years preceding the war. His amendment was to add to the text of the French Delegation, after the words "at the time of damage," the following words: "the valuation to be made by applying an appropriate coefficient, according to the case and to the time, to the net receipts or the net mean revenue."

The CHAIRMAN observed that, if this amendment were accepted, the part of the French text allowing damaged persons a minimum of 6 per cent upon their invested capital was no longer necessary. This method was only justified by the arbitrary character of the proposed basis of valuation. With the amendment this arbitrary character would largely disappear.

MR. DANIELOPOL (*Roumania*) proposed, therefore, to suppress in the French text the part comprised between the words "or the three seasons last preceding the war" and the words "in the valuation, etc.——"

Mr. JOUASSET (*France*) accepted this proposal; but observed that he would have preferred extending to all categories of damaged persons the guaranty which Mr. DANIELOPOL had not thought necessary to mention. He realized, however, the difficulty of expressing this extension in a precise formula.

Mr. DULLES (*U. S. A.*) proposed to add after the words "during the whole period of such deprivation" the words "but not after the conclusion of peace." He justified his amendment by recalling that the Sub-Committee had already made a stipulation for an interest charge to the enemy on all sums which might not be paid immediately upon the conclusion of peace.

Messrs. VAN DEN HEUVEL (*Belgium*) and JOUASSET (*France*) called Mr. DULLES' attention to the fact that this interest charge was entirely foreign to the reparation of injury now being considered by the Sub-Committee. Mr. VAN DEN HEUVEL cited the case of Belgian factories situated along the line of the Escaut which had been destroyed just before the Armistice. Their restoration would require perhaps a year or two in certain cases. Could it be said that they should only be indemnified for loss of enjoyment until the conclusion of peace. This would be flagrant injustice.

The CHAIRMAN, having reviewed the two texts, asked that certain points be made clear:

(1) On the one hand, it should be made clear, beyond any possible ambiguity, that the measure proposed had reference only to deprivation of enjoyment and not to destruction.

(2) On the other hand, in order to avoid possible abuses, it should be clearly stated that the deprivation of enjoyment which gave rise to the claim for reparation could not exceed a reasonable period.

Mr. JOUASSET (*France*) replied to the first part of the CHAIRMAN's remarks that the scope of the text left no room for doubt. The text dealt only with deprivation of enjoyment, and not with material damage resulting from destruction.

As to the second point raised by the CHAIRMAN, Mr. JOUASSET agreed that there could be no question of counting the deprivation of enjoyment up to the actual time, whenever it might be, at which the enterprise should have actually recovered its full productivity. Deprivation of enjoyment could only reasonably give a right to reparation up to the time at which the exercise of the proprietary right should again have become possible. It would be necessary to make a draft which expressed this idea.

MR. CHIESA (*Italy*) was satisfied to note that for invaded regions there were being adopted methods of valuation whose application would have the effect of putting damaged persons back in the situation in which they would have stood if the war had not occurred, but he asked that these methods be generalized to include also uninvaded regions.

MR. MICHALACOPOULOS (*Greece*) thought that the wording of section 43 as proposed might give opportunity for controversy. The deprivation of the exercise of a proprietary right pre-supposed the existence of such a right. But when the object was destroyed, the right of proprietorship ceased through lack of object. It might thus be maintained that, according to the present text, section 43 was not applicable to cases where destruction has occurred. This was evidently not the idea of the Sub-Committee. He thought that the meaning should be more clearly presented.

The next meeting was fixed for Friday, 21 March at 2.30 P. M. The meeting adjourned at 5.30 P. M.

SUMNER,
Chairman.

E. MINOST,
Secretary.

DOCUMENT 485

First Subcommittee: Minutes of the Nineteenth Meeting, March 21, 1919, 2:30 P. M.

[EOM, First Subcommittee, pp. 113-15. French stenographic minutes, PV, CRD, pp. 549-62; French condensed minutes, *ibid.*, pp. 563-66.]

The First Sub-Committee of the Commission on Reparation of Damage (Valuation of Damage) met on Friday, 21 March, at 2.30 P. M.,[1] at the Ministry of Finance, LORD SUMNER in the Chair.

Present: MR. DULLES (*U. S. A.*); LORD SUMNER (*British Empire*); MR. LEBRUN (*France*); MR. CHIESA (*Italy*); MR. MORI (*Japan*); MR. VAN DEN HEUVEL (*Belgium*); MR. MICHALA-COPOULOS (*Greece*); MR. OLCHOWSKI (*Poland*); MR. DOS SANTOS VIEGAS (*Portugal*); MR. DANIELOPOL (*Roumania*); MR. PROTITCH (*Serbia*); MR. KRECMAR (*Czecho-Slovak Republic*).[2]

---

[1] According to the French stenographic minutes, at 11:30 A. M.

[2] According to the French stenographic minutes, Osuský was present instead of Krčmář. According to the French condensed minutes, Kramář was present instead of Krčmář.

Secs. 43 and 46

A new draft of sections 43 and 46 of the Tabulation of Methods of Valuation (Annex II, Tenth Meeting)[3] was presented by MR. JOUASSET (*Expert for France*).

After an explanation by MR. JOUASSET, MR. MORI (*Japan*) withdrew his proposal upon section 43 (see minutes of 18th meeting) and accepted the new draft.

MR. DULLES (*U. S. A.*) stated that he would withdraw the objection which he had previously made to section 43, as he understood that the principle already adopted, that there should be no double payment, would operate to prevent duplication, as through:—

1. Payment for a loss of use continuing after the lost property had been replaced in kind by an equivalent value;

2. Payment for a loss of use to the extent to which the value of such use was in whole or in part represented by the value attributed to the property in accordance with the principle indicated by section 24.

MR. VAN DEN HEUVEL (*Belgium*) asked that any relief received by claimants, such as subsidies to working men and their families, should be taken into account in the draft.

Approved text Secs. 43 and 46

The new sections 43 and 46 were then approved in the following form:—

Section 43: Damage resulting from the deprivation, wholly or in part, of the exercise of any proprietary right is valued on the basis of the average net receipts or income from such property at the time of damage for the whole period during which such deprivation shall have continued, both down to the date of the conclusion of peace and until such reasonable time after the said date as may be deemed necessary to secure the cessation of such deprivation. The valuation will be made by the application of a coefficient, appropriate to the cases and periods in question, to the average net receipts or income of the three calendar years, the three fiscal years or the three seasons last preceding the war. In such valuation account shall be taken of any new resources, or any subsidies, whose addition to the existing income of the parties interested may have furnished compensation, wholly or in part, for the loss suffered by them.

Section 46. Damage resulting from the deprivation, wholly or in part, of the exercise of an occupation, or generally of opportunity to work or to obtain a fair remuneration for work, is valued on the basis of the average wages or salaries of the parties interested at the time of the damage for the whole period during which such deprivation shall have continued, both down to the date of the conclusion of peace and until such reasonable time after the said date as may be deemed necessary to secure the cessation of such deprivation. The valuation will be made by the application of a coefficient, appropriate to the cases and periods in question, to

[3] See Document 476.

the average net wages or salaries for the three calendar years last preceding the war. In such valuation account shall be taken of any new resources, or any subsidies, whose addition to the existing income of the parties interested may have furnished compensation, wholly or in part, for the loss suffered by them.

Sec. 5

The CHAIRMAN proposed that section 5 should be finally approved in the following form:—

The registration and evaluation of claims referred to in the preceding section shall not be definitive until they have been verified by the Allied and Associated Powers.

MR. OLCHOWSKI (*Poland*) thought the section as it stood was satisfactory.

The CHAIRMAN thought it was not competent for the Commission to express an opinion on the procedure to be adopted by the Powers.

The CHAIRMAN'S proposal was then adopted.

Secs. 3 and 4

On the proposal of MR. JOUASSET (*Expert for France*), sections 3 and 4 were finally approved with the substitution of the words "in the following sections" for the words "in Chapter II below."

MR. DULLES (*U. S. A.*) proposed for acceptance by the Sub-Committee the following resolution, which sought to affirm in a more acceptable form the principle of the fifth general resolution proposed by the CHAIRMAN at the eighth meeting and withdrawn after discussion:—

"Claims should be net: i.e., credit should be given for all elements of value which survive the act of injury and its natural and necessary consequences, and the claim should be only for the residue."

MR. JOUASSET (*Expert for France*) considered that the principle in question was already sufficiently enforced by various sections which the Sub-Committee has accepted, for example, by sections 24 and 34. He understood that MR. DULLES was thinking, in particular, of forced loans. In the case of this class of damage he protested against the effect of the proposal, as it stood, which would be to compel the persons injured to retain the depreciated enemy securities and count them at their actual value as part of the reparation they received.

MR. CHIESA (*Italy*) pointed out that section 36 only allowed the claim to be made for the difference in value between the original property and the property now held.

The CHAIRMAN thought it might be advisable formally to affirm the principle of MR. DULLES' proposal, even if it was already enforced by other sections.

MR. JOUASSET (*Expert for France*) proposed the following revised draft of MR. DULLES' proposal:—

"Claims shall have regard only to net losses after deducting any values which may stand to the credit of the parties interested."

MR. DULLES (*U. S. A*) accepted MR. JOUASSET'S draft.

MR. MICHALACOPOULOS (*Greece*) asked that further time might be allowed for consideration of the draft. After MR. LEBRUN (*France*) had observed that the wording could be revised at a later stage, MR. JOUASSET'S draft was accepted.

Chairman's first draft report

The CHAIRMAN proposed that the Sub-Committee should now consider the first part of his Draft Report (Annex I, Tenth Meeting.) He explained that, before the Sub-Committee commenced its sittings, it had been directed by the Plenary Commission to be prepared to produce a Provisional Report at an early date. The draft had, therefore, been drawn up by him after the first consideration of categories had been concluded, with a view to stating the conclusions already accepted. Many Memoranda had been presented. It would have been invidious to select the text of a particular Memorandum. His intention had been to submit a short independent statement, to which the various Memoranda would be annexed in order that each Delegation might refer to the expression of its views in the terms which it had itself selected.

In reply to observations by MR. LEBRUN (*France*), the CHAIRMAN said he had not felt that in the case of categories of damage the Sub-Committee had accepted a series of precise texts, such as it had accepted when dealing with Methods of Valuation. The draft would, of course, require to be brought up to date by the addition of the resolutions as to categories which the Sub-Committee had accepted since its 6th meeting.

MR. LEBRUN (*France*) thought that the Tabulation of Categories of Damage (Annex XII, Fourth Meeting) as amended by the Sub-Committee, would constitute a series of precise texts, and should be submitted in its amended form to the Plenary Commission, together with the Draft Report, of which he fully approved, and the various Memoranda. The Sub-Committee's resolutions as to categories would probably be suitable for incorporation in some form in the Treaty of Peace.

The CHAIRMAN agreed that all resolutions formally accepted

should be submitted to the Plenary Commission and said that he had no desire to add comments of his own.

After a further discussion, in which MR. DANIELOPOL (*Roumania*), the CHAIRMAN, Messrs. LEBRUN (*France*), VAN DEN HEUVEL (*Belgium*) and CHIESA (*Italy*) took part, it was decided, with a view to a final report at an early date:—

(1) That Memoranda containing the amended texts of those paragraphs of the Tabulation of Categories of Damage and of Methods of Valuation (Annex XII, Fourth Meeting and Annex II, Tenth Meeting), which had been accepted, should be prepared by MR. JOUASSET and submitted for consideration at the next meeting;

(2) That an amendment to Annex 13 A already presented by MR. DANIELOPOL (*Roumania*), and any other amendments to this document, should be finally discussed at the next meeting.

The next meeting was fixed for Monday, 24 March, at 2.30 P. M.
The meeting adjourned at 5.15 P. M.

SUMNER,
Chairman.

E. MINOST,
Secretary.

DOCUMENT 486

First Subcommittee: Minutes of the Twentieth Meeting (Including Annexes I and II), March 24, 1919, 2:30 P.M.

[EOM, First Subcommittee, pp. 116-33. French stenographic minutes, PV, CRD, pp. 567-83; French condensed minutes, *ibid.*, pp. 584-86. French text of annexes, *ibid.*, pp. 587-607.]

The First Sub-Committee of the Commission on Reparation of Damage (Valuation of Damage) met on Monday, 24 March 1919, at 2.30 P. M., at the Ministry of Finance, LORD SUMNER in the Chair.

Present: MR. MCCORMICK (*U. S. A.*); LORD SUMNER (*British Empire*); MR. LEBRUN (*France*); MR. D'AMELIO (*Italy*); MR. FUKAI (*Japan*); MR. VAN DEN HEUVEL (*Belgium*); MR. SPERANZA (*Greece*); MR. OLCHOWSKI (*Poland*); MR. DOS SANTOS VIEGAS (*Portugal*); MR. DANIELOPOL (*Roumania*); MR. PROTITCH (*Serbia*); MR. KRECMAR (*Czecho-Slovak Republic*).[1]

The minutes of the 14th, 15th, 16th and 17th meetings were adopted.

---

[1] According to the French condensed minutes, Kramář was present instead of Krčmář.

The revised Tabulation of the Categories of Damage and of Methods of Valuation, which had been prepared by MR. JOUASSET (*Expert for France*), were presented to the meeting (see Annexes I and II).

Further discussion of Annex XII, 4th Meeting

Further discussion of Annex XII, 4th meeting.

The business upon the Agenda was the discussion of the amendments which had been presented upon the Tabulation of Categories of Damages, (Annex XII, Fourth Meeting).

MR. DANIELOPOL (*Roumania*) proposed the following addition to section II [*11*]:

"Injury resulting from the theft of stamps and articles which are the subject of State Monopolies, from their removal, or their sale at prices lower than those established by law, as well as from the failure to receive taxes, fines and other revenues due to the State, which can no longer be collected."

MR. DANIELOPOL explained that his amendment had reference to two distinct classes of acts:—

(1) Prevention by the enemy of the collection of certain taxes established by law;

(2) Theft of stamps and articles subject to State Monopolies. He cited several cases in point.

MR. LEBRUN (*France*) pointed out that the theft of stamps and monopolized articles was already covered by section 11 (b) of the revised Tabulation of Categories (Annex I).

The CHAIRMAN agreed with this point of view, but thought that as far as concerned the prevention of the collection of taxes, the Roumanian amendment would be difficult to justify.

MR. DANIELOPOL (*Roumania*) argued that the exportation of carloads of wheat without payment of the export duties fixed by Roumanian law constituted in reality a theft, for which the State had a right to claim compensation. As to monopolized articles, he explained that it was not the Roumanian population, but the troops of the enemy force of occupation, who profited by the sale at prices below those fixed by law.

MR. JOUASSET (*Expert for France*) considered that the prevention of collection of taxes was covered in the Second Part of the Tabulation of Categories of Damage, the first chapter of which gave the same right to reparation to the State as to individuals, as regarded deprivation of revenue. He noted moreover that the enemy had not always applied the taxes he had collected to the needs of the occupied regions, and that the countries which had suffered invasion had now to meet those expenses.

MR. DULLES (*Expert for U. S. A.*) thought that the State had still the possibility of recovering later the taxes which it had not been able to collect.

MR. JOUASSET (*Expert for France*) replied that such a view was illusory. He proposed, nevertheless, in order to take account of the objections which had been made, to add the words:—"In so far as the charges of the State in the occupied territories, or in the zone of operations, shall not have been reduced."

The CHAIRMAN considered that the amendment of the Roumanian Delegation was too wide, for in all countries the collection of taxes had been affected during the war. In his view MR. JOUASSET'S amendment was not a sufficient limitation of the original proposal.

MR. LEBRUN (*France*) cited a case in point to show that the invaded regions had today to meet expenses arising from the period of occupation; the departments, which had not been able to collect the "centimes additionnels," had been obliged, nevertheless, to pay their functionaries. He insisted on the point that no comparison was possible between damage resulting from the general risks of the war and that resulting directly from invasion, a hardship which only certain countries had suffered.

The CHAIRMAN asked MR. DANIELOPOL if he withdrew that part of his amendment which related to theft of stamps and monopolized articles.

MR. DANIELOPOL asked from the Sub-Committee the formal assurance that this category of damage was covered by the categories already adopted.

As the CHAIRMAN made certain reservations, MR. DANIELOPOL maintained this part of his amendment. Messrs. D'AMELIO (*Italy*), VAN DEN HEUVEL (*Belgium*), PROTITCH (*Serbia*) and KRECMAR (*Czecho-Slovak Republic*) supported MR. DANIELOPOL'S proposal, as amended by MR. JOUASSET.

MR. DOS SANTOS VIEGAS (*Portugal*) supported the opinion expressed by the American and British Delegations.

The CHAIRMAN declared the amendment to be adopted by a majority of votes.

Further discussion of Annex

The amendment, which was to be inserted between sections

20 and 21 of the revised Tabulation of Categories (Annex I), was carried in the following form:—

"Including loss resulting from the theft of stamps and articles which are the subject of State Monopolies, from their removal or their sale at prices lower than those established by law; and loss resulting from the failure to collect taxes, imposts and other revenues due to the State in occupied territory or in the zone of operations, in so far as such non-collection has not been balanced by a reduction in charges, and in so far as no material for taxation from which the State could recover such losses has been created anew by the admission of individual claims."

MR. DULLES (*Expert for U. S. A.*) could not accept the amendment as at present drafted. As to the question of principle, he observed that, taking into account Articles 48 and 49 of the annex regulation of The Hague Convention of 18 October, 1917, on the laws and customs of land warfare, he desired to reserve the opinion of the American Delegation.

Sec. 9c

The CHAIRMAN then submitted to the Sub-Committee the two following amendments proposed by the Serbian Delegation for insertion in section 9 (c).

(1) Claims with regard to debtors who have died during the war, which would remain unrealizable in spite of reparation of war damage.

(2) Life insurances contracted before the war by persons who have died during the war after having been prevented by the invasion from paying war-risk insurance premiums.

MR. BAYKITCH (*Expert for Serbia*) explained that his first amendment was intended to cover the case of debtors dying without family or estate.

MR. JOUASSET (*Expert for France*) called attention to the fact that there would always be a party claiming under the deceased, namely the State, against whom the interested party could establish his claim.

The CHAIRMAN thought that the adoption of this point of view would mean that a creditor whose claim would in normal times have remained unpaid, would derive a benefit from the war.

The Sub-Committee decided to adjourn until Tuesday, 25 March, at 11 A. M.

The meeting adjourned at 6 P. M.

SUMNER,
Chairman.

E. MINOST,
Secretary.

ANNEX I

CATEGORIES OF DAMAGE FOR WHICH REPARATION MAY BE DEMANDED

RESULTS OF THE DISCUSSION DOWN TO 21 MARCH, 1919
(NOTE FOR THE SUB-COMMITTEE)

TEXTS CONSIDERED BY THE SUB-COMMITTEE (ANNEX XII, FOURTH MEETING)[2]

FIRST PART

PRIVATE DAMAGE

DIVISION I.—CATEGORIES MENTIONED BY ALL OR THE MAJORITY OF THE DELEGATIONS.

CATEGORY A

Immovables

CHAPTER I.—DAMAGE CAUSED BY THE TWO GROUPS OF BELLIGERENTS IN EVERY THEATRE OF OPERATIONS.

Sec. 1

Destruction, deterioration or depreciation of immovable property on land or sea belonging to private persons (natural or artificial) and to public persons other than the State.

Sec. 2

1. Means employed:

The destruction, deterioration or depreciation may be the result either of an act of war or of the fact of invasion, as:—

(*a*) Bombardment by gun or aircraft on land or sea;

(*b*) Voluntary or involuntary action of troops (including lodging, billeting, etc.);

RESULTS OF THE DISCUSSION (*Texts Adopted*)[3]

FIRST PART

PRIVATE DAMAGE

[DIVISION I.—CATEGORIES MENTIONED BY ALL OR THE MAJORITY OF THE DELEGATIONS.]

CATEGORY A

Immovables

CHAPTER I.—DAMAGE CAUSED BY THE TWO GROUPS OF BELLIGERENTS IN EVERY THEATRE OF OPERATIONS.

Destruction, deterioration or depreciation of immovable property on land or sea belonging to private persons (natural or artificial) and to public persons other than the State;

1. Means employed:

The destruction, deterioration or depreciation may be the result either of an act of war or of the fact of invasion, as:—

(*a*) Bombardment by gun or aircraft on land or sea;

(*b*) Voluntary or involuntary action of troops (including lodging, billeting, etc.);

---

[2] Same as Annex XII of Document 470. The second column follows.

[3] The first column precedes. The Annex of Document 464 ("Categories of Damage for which Reparation May Be Demanded") follows.

(*c*) Defensive or offensive measures and measures pertaining thereto (including inundations, etc.);

(*d*) Torpedoes and submarine mines;

(*e*) Deterioration resulting from use by the enemy, felling and digging up;

(*f*) Requisition, expropriations, etc.

Sec. 3

2. Objects of destruction or deterioration:

(*a*) Land, forests, orchards and plantations, mines, quarries, roads, canals, railways in general, electric lines and conduits (telephone, telegraph or power), water supply, pipe lines, drains, works of all kinds, etc.;

(*b*) Private structures of all kinds and all public structures, other than those belonging to the State, buildings or monuments etc., artistic property included.

CHAPTER II.—DAMAGE OTHER THAN THAT PROVIDED FOR IN CHAPTER I ABOVE WHICH MAY HAVE BEEN CAUSED IN ALLIED OR ENEMY COUNTRIES.

Sec. 4

Damage caused [anywhere] to immovables [or to interests therein] either by the application of enemy war legislation or by any act ordered or committed by enemy authority or enemy population (Allied prop-

---

(*c*) Defensive or offensive measures and measures pertaining thereto (including inundations, etc.);

(*d*) Torpedoes and submarine mines;

(*e*) Deterioration resulting from use by the enemy, felling and digging up;

(*f*) Requisition, expropriations, etc.

2. Objects of destruction or deterioration.

(*a*) Land, forests, orchards and plantations, <u>deposits</u>, mines, quarries, roads, canals, railways in general, electric lines and conduits (telephone, telegraph or power), water supply pipe lines, drains, works of all kinds, etc.;

(*b*) Private structures of all kinds and all public structures, other than those belonging to the State, buildings or monuments, etc., artistic property included.

CHAPTER II.—DAMAGE OTHER THAN THAT PROVIDED FOR IN CHAPTER I ABOVE WHICH MAY HAVE BEEN CAUSED IN ALLIED OR ENEMY COUNTRIES.

Damage caused to immovable property:—

(*a*) <u>In enemy territory by any</u> act ordered or committed by enemy authority or population;

(*b*) <u>In enemy territory or in</u> invaded or occupied territory

erty sequestrated or liquidated by the enemy).

by the application of laws or by any act whatsoever under enemy authority relating to seizures, requisitions, sequestrations, and liquidations of sequestrated property.

CATEGORY B

Movables

CHAPTER I.—DAMAGE CAUSED BY THE TWO GROUPS OF BELLIGERENTS IN EVERY THEATRE OF OPERATIONS.

Sec. 5

1. Causes of Damage:—

All the causes referred to in clause 1 of Chapter I above, as well as all removals, with or without color of right, all thefts, forced sales, confiscations, or similar measures.

Sec. 6

2. Objects of Damage:—

(*a*) Equipment and furnishings of private structures and public structures, other than those belonging to the State, machinery and tools, articles of furniture, clothes, linen and personal effects of all sorts, art objects, raw and other materials, merchandise, live stock and animals of all kinds, crops, manufactured and non-manufactured products, provisions, drawings, models, patents, trade-marks, records, instruments, and documents of all kinds, etc.

(*b*) Merchant vessels, fishing-boats, etc., navigating upon the sea or inland waterways, as well as their equipment and cargo.

CATEGORY B

Movables

CHAPTER I.—DAMAGE CAUSED BY THE TWO GROUPS OF BELLIGERENTS IN EVERY THEATRE OF OPERATIONS.

1. Causes of damage:—

All the causes referred to in clause 1 of Chapter I above, as well as all removals, with or without color of right, all thefts, forced sales, confiscations or similar measures.

2. Objects of Damage:—

(*a*) Equipment and furnishings of private structures and public structures, other than those belonging to the State. machinery and tools, articles of furniture, clothes, linen and personal effects of all sorts, art objects, raw and other materials, merchandise, live stock and animals of all kinds, crops, manufactured and non-manufactured products, provisions, drawings, models, patents, trade-marks, records, instruments and documents of all kinds, etc.

(*b*) Merchant vessels, fishing-boats, etc., navigating upon the sea or inland waterways, as well as their equipment, freights and cargo.

CHAPTER II.—DAMAGE OTHER THAN THAT PROVIDED FOR IN CHAPTER I ABOVE WHICH MAY HAVE BEEN CAUSED IN ALLIED OR ENEMY COUNTRIES.

Sec. 7

Damage caused anywhere to movables, either by the application of enemy war legislation or by any act ordered or committed by enemy authority or enemy population (property sequestrated or disposed of by the enemy, etc.).

CHAPTER II.—DAMAGE OTHER THAN THAT PROVIDED FOR IN CHAPTER I ABOVE WHICH MAY HAVE BEEN CAUSED IN ALLIED OR ENEMY COUNTRIES.

Damage caused anywhere to movables:—

(*a*) In enemy territory by any act ordered or committed by enemy authority or population;

(*b*) In enemy territory or in invaded or occupied territory by the application of laws or by any act whatsoever under enemy authority relating to seizures, requisitions, sequestrations and liquidations of sequestrated property.

CATEGORY C

Miscellaneous Interests

CHAPTER I.—DAMAGE CAUSED BY THE TWO GROUPS OF BELLIGERENTS IN EVERY THEATRE OF OPERATIONS.

Sec. 8

1. Causes of damage:—

All causes referred to in clause 1 of Chapter I, Categories A and B, above, as well as illegal or *ex parte* sentences of all kinds, and every abolition or suspension by the enemy of laws or codes in force in invaded or occupied territories.

Sec. 9

2. Objects of Damage:—

(*a*) Shares and securities of all sorts, coupons;

(*b*) Requisition or hiring of labor or service;

CATEGORY C

Miscellaneous Interests

CHAPTER I.—DAMAGE CAUSED BY THE TWO GROUPS OF BELLIGERENTS IN EVERY THEATRE OF OPERATIONS.

1. Causes of damage:—

All causes referred to in clause 1, of Chapter I, Categories A and B, above, as well as illegal or *ex parte* sentences of all kinds, and every abolition or suspension by the enemy, of laws or codes in force in the invaded or occupied territories.

2. Objects of Damage:—

(*a*) Shares and securities of all sorts, coupons;

(*b*) Requisition or hiring of labor or service;

(*c*) [Claims of whatsoever description which can no longer be enforced (insurances included) and debts contracted;]

(*d*) Expenditures incurred [by any party (other than the State), and in any form whatsoever,] for the food supply, transport or relief of the population of invaded or occupied territories;

(*e*) Injury caused to industrial property by the discovery or use of special processes of manufacture, patents or special methods;

(*f*) Losses to trade caused by the disclosure of business books or ledgers and of public or private correspondence or records—and in general all documents or information not of a public nature—as well as by the use made of such documents and information. Losses caused by the new competition set up through the knowledge of such documents and information.

(*g*) [Partial or total deprivation of free exercise of proprietary rights of any kind, of the free exercise of any occupation or generally of opportunity to work or to obtain fair remuneration for work.]

[Loss caused by the total or partial unproductiveness, in-

(*c*) [Reserved;]

(*d*) Expenditure incurred under any form whatsoever by any public authority (other than the State) fulfilling an obligation, [or by private persons or societies upon whom has fallen the obligation of taking the place of the public authorities] for the food supply, transport or relief of the populations of invaded or occupied territories;

(*e*) Injury caused to industrial property by the discovery or use of special processes of manufacture, patents or special methods;

(*f*) Losses to trade caused by the disclosure of business books or ledgers, and of public or private correspondence or records —and in general all documents or information not of a public nature—as well as by the use made of such documents and information. Losses caused by the new competition set up through the knowledge of such documents and information.

(*g*) Loss caused to any person who has been deprived, wholly or partially, as a direct consequence of the operations of war or of the measures taken by the enemy, and without compensation from new sources of revenue, of the exercise of his proactivity or immobilization of property belonging to private or public persons, other than the State, the normal development of whose resources has been impeded by the fact of invasion:—

1. Up to the date of the Armistice.

2. From the date of the Armistice to the date at which normal exercise of the proprietary right or occupation shall again have become possible.]

Sec. 10

CHAPTER II. THE SAME CLASS OF DAMAGE AS UNDER CHAPTER II OF CATEGORY B ABOVE.

CATEGORY D
Exactions of a Financial Character

CHAPTER I. DAMAGE CAUSED BY THE TWO GROUPS OF BELLIGERENTS IN EVERY THEATRE OF OPERATIONS.

Sec. 11

(*a*) Taxes, imposts, contributions of war, fines, levies in cash of all kinds, thefts of currency—including balances of accounts transferred and assets converted into "bons," loan and other stock,—forced subscriptions and expenses imposed by the enemy upon individuals or corporations.

(*b*) Issues of bank-notes, "bons" [and] monetary instruments of any kind, [falsification, alteration or depreciation of the same.]

prietary rights, his occupation or, generally, of opportunity to work or to obtain fair remuneration for his work, during the whole period of such deprivation.

CHAPTER II. THE SAME CLASS OF DAMAGE AS UNDER CHAPTER II OF CATEGORY B ABOVE.

CATEGORY D
Exactions of a Financial Character

CHAPTER I.—DAMAGE CAUSED BY THE TWO GROUPS OF BELLIGERENTS IN EVERY THEATRE OF OPERATIONS.

Taxes, imposts, contributions of war, fines, levies in cash of all kinds, thefts of currency,—including balances of accounts transferred and assets converted into "bons," loan and other stock,—forced subscriptions and expenses imposed by the enemy upon individuals or corporations; issue, falsification, alteration or depreciation of bank-notes, "bons" or monetary instruments of any kind.

Sec. 12

CHAPTER II. THE SAME CLASS OF DAMAGE AS UNDER CHAPTER II CATEGORIES B AND C ABOVE.

CATEGORY E

Damage to Persons

CHAPTER I. DAMAGE CAUSED BY THE TWO GROUPS OF BELLIGERENTS IN EVERY THEATRE OF OPERATIONS.

Sec. 13

Pensions or allowances of every kind to civilian victims of acts of war (bombardment on land, on sea or from aircraft and all the consequences of operations of war), or to persons claiming under them.

(*a*) To the surviving wife or husband, orphans, descendants or parents;

(*b*) To mutilated, wounded or sick.

2. Pensions and allowances of every sort to civilian victims of acts, cruelties, violence or maltreatment committed or ordered by the enemy, or to persons claiming under them:—

(*a*) To persons shot, put to death or dead from the consequences of maltreatment;

(*b*) To persons exposed by the enemy to the fire of the Allied troops;

(*c*) To persons injured in life or health as a consequence of imprisonment, deportation, internment or evacuation;

(*d*) To persons who have suffered accidental death or injury,

CHAPTER II. THE SAME CLASS OF DAMAGE AS UNDER CHAPTER II CATEGORIES B AND C ABOVE.

CATEGORY E

Damage to Persons

CHAPTER I.—DAMAGE CAUSED BY THE TWO GROUPS OF BELLIGERENTS IN EVERY THEATRE OF OPERATIONS.

1. [Pensions or allowances of every kind] to civilian victims of acts of war (bombardment on land, on sea or from aircraft and all the consequences of operations of war), or to persons claiming under them:

(*a*) To the surviving wife or husband, orphans, descendants or parents, or persons claiming under them;

(*b*) To mutilated, wounded or sick.

2. [Pensions and allowances of every sort] to civilian victims of acts, cruelties, violence or maltreatment committed or ordered by the enemy, or to persons claiming under them:—

(*a*) To persons shot, put to death or dead from the consequences of maltreatment;

(*b*) To persons exposed by the enemy to the fire of the Allied troops;

(*c*) To persons injured in life or health as a consequence of imprisonment, deportation, internment or evacuation;

(*d*) To persons who have suffered accidental death or injury, or have become infirm or sick in consequence of forced labor [and especially of every kind of occupation contrary to the interests of their country.]

Sec. 15

Compensation for every kind of act injurious to health or capacity for work, or to honor.

CHAPTER II.—DAMAGE OTHER THAN THAT PROVIDED FOR IN CHAPTER I ABOVE WHICH MAY HAVE BEEN CAUSED IN ALLIED OR ENEMY COUNTRIES.

Sec. 16

Pensions, allowances and compensation for any injury to life, health or the capacity to work of interned civilians, including cost of relief of the said interned persons.

DIVISION II.—CATEGORIES NOT MENTIONED BY ALL OR THE MAJORITY OF THE DELEGATIONS.

CATEGORY C

Miscellaneous Interests

CHAPTER II.—DAMAGE WHICH MAY HAVE BEEN CAUSED IN ALLIED OR ENEMY COUNTRIES OUTSIDE OF EVERY THEATRE OF OPERATIONS OF THE TWO GROUPS OF BELLIGERENTS.

Sec. 17.

[(*a*) Claims no longer enforceable and debts contracted as a consequence of the war;

(*b*) Total or partial deprivation of free exercise of any

---

or have become infirm or sick in consequence of forced labor.

3. [Compensation for every kind of act] injurious to health or capacity for work, or to honor.

[CHAPTER II.—DAMAGE OTHER THAN THAT PROVIDED FOR IN CHAPTER I ABOVE WHICH MAY HAVE BEEN CAUSED IN ALLIED OR ENEMY COUNTRIES.

Sec. 16

Pensions, allowances and compensation for any injury to life, health or the capacity to work of interned civilians, including cost of relief of the said interned persons.]

DIVISION II.—CATEGORIES NOT MENTIONED BY ALL OR THE MAJORITY OF THE DELEGATIONS.

[CATEGORY C]

[Miscellaneous Interests]

[CHAPTER II.—DAMAGE WHICH MAY HAVE BEEN CAUSED IN ALLIED OR ENEMY COUNTRIES OUTSIDE OF EVERY THEATRE OF OPERATION OF THE TWO GROUPS OF BELLIGERENTS.]

Sec. 17.—[Reserved.]

proprietary right, occupation, or generally of opportunity to work or to obtain fair remuneration for work.

Loss caused by unproductiveness, inactivity or immobilization, total or partial, to any private person or public person, other than the State, the normal development of whose resources has been impeded by the fact of invasion, (*1*) up to the date of the Armistice; (*2*) from the date of the Armistice to the date at which normal exercise of the proprietary right or occupation shall again have become possible.

(*c*) All expenses imposed upon corporations, other than the State, and associations existing for the public benefit through the necessity of coming to the assistance of the population.

(*d*) All damage to individuals or corporations, other than the State, resulting from the annulment or suspension of contracts entered upon before the war with subjects of enemy Powers.

(*e*) All damage suffered by individuals or corporations, other than the State, in consequence of the increase in prices, freights, salaries and remunerations, etc.]

CATEGORY E

Damage to Persons

CHAPTER I.—DAMAGE CAUSED BY THE TWO GROUPS OF BELLIGERENTS IN EVERY THEATRE OF OPERATIONS.

Sec. 18

Damages for every person [employed] in any occupation contrary to the interests of his country, without injury to life, health or capacity for work.

CHAPTER II.—DAMAGE, OTHER THAN THAT PROVIDED FOR UNDER CHAPTER I ABOVE, WHICH MAY HAVE BEEN CAUSED IN ALLIED OR ENEMY COUNTRIES.

Sec. 19

Pensions and allowances of every kind:

(*a*) To victims of explosions in war factories;

(*b*) To victims of accidents while working in such factories.

SECOND PART

PUBLIC DAMAGE

DIVISION I.—CATEGORIES MENTIONED BY ALL OR THE MAJORITY OF THE DELEGATIONS.

CHAPTER I.—ALL DAMAGES ENUMERATED IN DIVISIONS I AND II OF PART I ABOVE WHICH HAVE BEEN SUFFERED BY THE STATE IN ITS NON-MILITARY PROPERTY AND IN ITS OWN RESOURCES.

Sec. 20

(Avoiding any duplication of claims for damage to individuals or corporations other than the State.)

[CATEGORY E]

[Damage to Persons]

[CHAPTER I.—DAMAGE CAUSED BY THE TWO GROUPS OF BELLIGERENTS IN EVERY THEATRE OF OPERATIONS.]

Damages [for] every person forced to engage in any occupation contrary to the interests of his country, without injury to life, health or capacity for work.[4]

CHAPTER II.—DAMAGE, [OTHER THAN THAT PROVIDED FOR UNDER CHAPTER I ABOVE,] WHICH MAY HAVE BEEN CAUSED IN ALLIED OR ENEMY COUNTRIES.

[Pensions and allowances of every kind:]

(*a*) To victims of explosions in war factories;

(*b*) To victims of accidents while working in such factories.[5]

SECOND PART

[PUBLIC] DAMAGE

[DIVISION I.—CATEGORIES MENTIONED BY ALL OR THE MAJORITY OF THE DELEGATIONS.]

CHAPTER I.—ALL DAMAGES ENUMERATED IN [DIVISIONS I AND II OF] PART I ABOVE WHICH HAVE BEEN SUFFERED BY THE STATE IN ITS NON-MILITARY PROPERTY AND [IN] ITS OWN RESOURCES.

(Avoiding any duplication of claims for damage to individuals or corporations other than the State.)

---

[4] Category E, Chapter 1, Section 4, of the following draft.
[5] Category E, Chapter 2, of the following draft.

Sec. 21

Including allowances to refugees, and to persons evacuated or out of work.

And furthermore:

Sec. 22

Injury resulting to Allied nations, from the necessity to which they have been put of redeeming monetary instruments and in general all obligations expressed in terms of enemy money held by the inhabitants (public or private persons) of territories which have been in the power *de jure* or *de facto* of the enemy Powers, or held by prisoners of war and interned civilians.

CHAPTER II.—MILITARY EXPENDITURE OF THE STATE OR OF ITS POSSESSIONS OR COLONIES.

Sec. 23

A. Pensions, allowances and bonuses of every kind to military victims of the war or persons claiming under them.

Sec. 24

To victims of acts of war, or persons claiming under them:

(*a*) To widows, orphans descendants or parents;

(*b*) To mutilated, wounded, sick and invalided.

Including allowances to refugees, [and] to persons evacuated [or out of work.

And furthermore:

Injury resulting to Allied nations from the necessity to which they have been put of redeeming monetary instruments and in general all obligations expressed in terms of enemy money held by the inhabitants (public or private persons) of territories which have been in the power *de jure* or *de facto* of the enemy Powers, or held by prisoners of war and interned civilians.

(This paragraph is reserved so far as regards such operations in territories which before the war were not included within the frontiers of the claimant State.)]

CHAPTER II.—[MILITARY] EXPENDITURE OF THE STATE OR OF ITS POSSESSIONS OR COLONIES.

A. Pensions, allowances and bonuses of every kind to military victims of the war or persons claiming under them.

To victims of acts of war, or persons claiming under them:

(*a*) [To] widows, orphans, descendants or parents or persons claiming under them;

(*b*) [To] mutilated, wounded, sick and invalided.

Sec. 25

To prisoners of war injured in life or health as a consequence of acts, cruelties, violence or maltreatment committed or ordered by the enemy.

Sec. 26

B. Expenditure for aid by the State or corporations rendered to prisoners of war. Allowances to families of mobilized persons.

C. Other war costs.

Sec. 27

All expenditures or charges resulting from the state of war imposed upon the Allied [nations.]

Sec. 28

Expenses of maintenance by the Allied States of enemy prisoners of war, officers and men and of interned persons.

DIVISION II.—CATEGORIES NOT MENTIONED BY ALL OR BY THE MAJORITY OF THE DELEGATIONS.

CHAPTER I.—DAMAGE OF EVERY KIND SUFFERED BY THE NATION IN ITS PRODUCTIVENESS.

Sec. 29

[Especially: damage resulting from deaths or any injury to the health or physical capacity of subjects; from the diminution of agricultural and industrial production—from excessive exploitation of forests—from loss on exchange caused by excess importation, etc.]

To prisoners of war injured in life or health as a consequence of acts, cruelties, violence or maltreatment committed or ordered by the enemy.

B. [Expenditure for aid] by the State [or corporations rendered] to prisoners of war. Allowances to families of mobilized persons.
C. Other war costs.

All expenditures or charges resulting from the state of war imposed upon the Allied Powers.

Expenses of maintenance by the Allied States of enemy prisoners of war, officers and men and of interned persons.

DIVISION II.—CATEGORIES NOT MENTIONED BY ALL OR BY THE MAJORITY OF THE DELEGATIONS.

CHAPTER I.—DAMAGE OF EVERY KIND SUFFERED BY THE NATION IN ITS PRODUCTIVENESS.

Sec. 29.—[Reserved.]

| CHAPTER II.—DAMAGE RESULTING FROM FORMER WARS. | CHAPTER II.—DAMAGE RESULTING FROM FORMER WARS. |

CHAPTER II.—DAMAGE RESULTING FROM FORMER WARS.

Sec. 30

A. [Greek Delegation: settlement of claims against Turkey and Bulgaria of earlier date than the European war.]

Sec. 31

B. [French Delegation: War of 1870-71 (war indemnity, war seizures, taxes, imposts, contributions, fines and payments imposed by the enemy).]

CHAPTER II.—DAMAGE RESULTING FROM FORMER WARS.

Sec. 30.—[Reserved.]

Sec. 31.—[Reserved.]

ANNEX II

METHODS OF VALUATION OF DAMAGE

RESULTS OF THE DISCUSSION DOWN TO 21st MARCH, 1919
(NOTE FOR THE SUB-COMMITTEE)

| TEXTS DISCUSSED BY THE SUB-COMMITTEE | RESULTS OF THE DISCUSSION (*Texts Adopted*) |

FIRST PART[6]

(*Propositions submitted by the Chairman Minutes of 8th Meetings, 5 March, 1919.*)

Sec. 1

1. It is understood throughout that claims cannot be admitted under whatever categories so as to involve payment twice over for the same damages, or payment to two persons of whatever sort for one injury.

FIRST PART[7]

I. It is understood throughout that claims cannot be admitted, under whatever categories, so as to involve payment twice over for the same damages, or payment to two persons of whatever sort for one injury.

---

[6] Same as text in Document 474. Annex VII of Document 475 follows. The section numbers in the margin are those referred to in Document 491.

[7] Annex VII of Document 475 precedes. The Annex of Document 464 ("Methods of Valuation of Damage") follows. The roman numerals at the beginning of the paragraphs (inserted by the editor after the seventh) correspond to the article numbers in the French minutes, PV, CRD, pp. 681-83, 687-88. The section numbers in the margins are those referred to in Document 491.

Sec. 2

2. Where injury is caused by acts for which the enemy Powers are responsible, the damage to be claimed will include all the natural and necessary consequences of those acts.

Sec. 3

3. [Claims are not admissible which are not substantially due to the acts of war, including the making of the war itself, for which the enemy Powers are reponsible, but which are only incidentally connected with them.]

Sec. 4

4. Claims are not admissible which are incapable of being estimated with reasonable certainty by some means or other of proof, whether direct and specific or statistical and general.

Sec. 5

5. [Claims should be net: that is to say, where the claimant has received already anything in reduction of or compensation for that which is the subject-matter of the claim, credit should be given for it and the claim should be made only for the residue.]

Sec. 6

6. Statistical methods of computation and evaluation may be resorted to in default of direct evidence of value, subject to the application of proper methods for verification and corrobation.

II. Where injury is caused by acts for which the enemy Powers are responsible, the damage to be claimed will include all the natural and necessary consequences of those acts.

III. Claims are not admissible which are incapable of being estimated with reasonable certainty by some means or other of proof, whether direct and specific or statistical and general.

IV. Claims shall have regard only to net losses, after deducting any values which may stand to the credit of the parties interested.

V. Statistical methods of computation and evaluation may be resorted to, in default of direct evidence of value or for other sufficient reasons, subject to the application of proper methods for verification and corroboration.

Sec. 7

7. The cost of restoration of things injured, whether movables or immovables, does not extend to the cost of substituting for the things injured other things of a more expensive or valuable character, or to rebuilding with better materials or on an enlarged scale.

Sec. 8

8. [Where the thing injured is not intended to be physically replaced or reconstructed, the amount of the claim is limited to its value without adding any expenses connected with replacement or reconstruction.]

Sec. 9

9. Claims ought to be supported by credible testimony with reasonable certainty, but it rests with the Powers concerned to determine in the first instance the particular form in which such testimony is to be admitted.

SECOND PART[8]

(*Annex II, Tenth Meeting.*)

Sec. 10

2. It will be the concern of the Allied and Associated [Nations] which have suffered damage, to set forth and evaluate the damage which the enemy will be required to make good, each nation having regard to its own case.

VI. The cost of restoration of things injured, whether movables or immovables, does not extend to the cost of substituting for the things injured other things of a more expensive or valuable character, or to rebuilding with better materials or on an enlarged scale.

VII. Claims ought to be supported by credible testimony with reasonable certainty, but it rests with the Powers concerned to determine in the first instance the particular form in which such testimony is to be admitted.

SECOND PART[9]

[VIII.] It will be the concern of the Allied and Associated Powers which have suffered damage, to set forth and evaluate the damage, which the enemy will be required to make good, each nation having regard to its own case.

[8] Annex II of Document 476 precedes. The second column follows.
[9] The first column precedes. The Annex of Document 464 ("Methods of Evaluation of Damage") follows.

Sec. 11

3. The valuations thus established, in support of claims to be filed, shall conform to general and uniform rules as set forth in [Chapter II below.]

[IX.] The valuations thus established, in support of claims to be filed, shall conform to general and uniform rules as set forth in the following paragraphs.

Sec. 12

4. The general rules set forth in [Chapter II below] apply exclusively to claims which are to be made on the enemy, and do not necessarily govern the relations of the Allied and Associated States as between themselves, nor the relations of each State with its own nationals.

[X.] The general rules set forth in the following paragraphs apply exclusively to claims which are to be made on the enemy, and do not necessarily govern relations of the Allied and Associated States as between themselves, nor the relations of each State [with its own nationals.]

Sec. 13

5.—The registration and evaluation of claims referred to in the preceding paragraphs shall not be definitive until they have been verified, [with a special view to uniformity, by Inter-Allied bodies composed of representatives of] the Allied and Associated Nations.

[XI.] The registration and evaluation of claims referred to in the preceding paragraph shall not be definitive until they have been verified by the Allied and Associated Powers.

Sec. 14

8. Valuations of damage should be made with careful regard to placing every person having the right to reparation in a situation as nearly as possible identical with that in which he would have found himself if [a state of war had not been] imposed by the enemy Powers upon the Allied and Associated Powers.

[XII.] Valuations of damage should be made with careful regard to placing every person having the right to reparation in a situation as nearly as possible identical with that in which he would have found himself if he had not sustained the damage resulting from the state of war imposed by the enemy Powers upon the Allied and Associated Powers.

Sec. 15

11. The valuations made should cover all the natural and necessary consequences of the acts giving rise to the claims for damages.

[XIII.] The valuations made [should] cover all the natural and necessary consequences of the acts giving rise to the claims for damages.

Sec. 16

13. Whatever the procedure adopted for the classification of categories of damage, or for the registration and valuation of claims, it shall never be possible to obtain payment twice for the same damage, either wholly or in part, whether to the same person or to different persons.

[XIV.] Whatever the procedure adopted for the classification of categories of damage, or for the registration and valuation of claims, it shall never be possible to obtain payment twice for the same damage, either wholly or in part, whether to the same person or to different persons.

Sec. 17

15. Claims should be supported, either by direct proof as to the reality and the amount of the damage suffered, or by any other acceptable evidence or credible testimony, the Allied and Associated Powers having the exclusive right to determine the form of evidence and the conditions under which it shall be admitted.

[XVI, *later* XV.] Claims should be supported, either by direct proof as to the reality and the amount of the damage suffered, or by any other acceptable evidence or credible testimony, the Allied and Associated Powers having the exclusive right to determine the form of evidence and the conditions under which it shall be admitted.

Sec. 18

17. Valuations shall be expressed in the currency [of each nation concerned, without prejudice as to the currency in which the enemy will be obliged to make payment.]

[XVII, *later* XVI.] Valuations shall be expressed in the currency each interested Power may consider it proper to adopt, without in any way prejudging the question of the currency in which payment shall be made by the enemy; and each Power shall state the rate of exchange upon which its calculation is based, so as to permit full verification.

Sec. 19

21. The amount of a claim shall not be more than enough for the replacement of property or objects destroyed by other property of corresponding quality or importance, it being understood, however, that this provision does not refer to increases in value resulting from a rise in prices, or to the replacement of property or objects destroyed or damaged by similar property or objects in a new state.

[XVIII, *later* XVII.] The amount of a claim shall not be more than enough for the replacement of property or objects destroyed whether movables or immovables, by other property of corresponding quality or importance, it being understood, however, that this provision does not refer to increases in value resulting from a rise in prices, or to the replacement of property or objects destroyed or damaged by similar property or objects in a new state.

Sec. 20

24. Destruction, deterioration and all damage caused to real or personal property, which property is of such a nature that it can be reconstructed, replaced or repaired, shall be valued at the amount of the estimated cost of such reconstruction, replacement or repair on the date of the conclusion of peace.

[XIX, *later* XVIII.] Destruction, deterioration and all damage caused to real or personal property, on land or at sea, which property is of such a nature that it can be reconstructed, replaced or repaired, shall be valued at the amount of the estimated cost of such reconstruction, replacement or repair on the date of the conclusion of peace; but in cases where the application of this rule would expose the persons injured to the risks of fluctuation of market prices, damage caused to the property above mentioned shall be evaluated at its value within a reasonable time after the time of the loss or damage, except in the case, provided for in the paragraph below, where there has been an actual replacement by purchase.

Sec. 21

25. The cost of such reconstruction, replacement or repair, is arrived at by applying to the corresponding pre-war cost an appropriate coefficient calculated for each category of property in accordance with the market price at the date [of the conclusion of peace] in respect to materials, labor and all other factors to be considered.[10]

[New article XIX.] Paragraph opposite reserved.

Sec. 22

26. In the case of labor hired or purchases made for reconstruction, replacement or repair, before the date of the conclusion of peace, the valuation may be based upon actual cost.

[XX.] In the case of labor hired or purchases made for reconstruction, replacement or repair, before the date of the conclusion of peace, the valuation may be based upon actual cost.

Sec. 23

27. In case the same property or object has undergone repeated and successive damage, all labor and purchases that have actually gone to reconstruction, replacement or repair are to be taken into account in the valuation.

[XXI.] In case the same property or object has undergone repeated and successive damage, all labor and purchases that have actually gone to reconstruction, replacement or repair are to be taken into account in the valuation.

Sec. 24

34. Destruction, deterioration and all damage caused to real or personal property not susceptible of reconstruction, replacement or repair, are to be valued by reference to the amount

[XXII.] Destruction, deterioration and all damage caused to real or personal property not susceptible of reconstruction, replacement or repair, are to be valued by reference to the

[10] The corresponding paragraph of the Annex of Document 464 follows this section.

which the property would have been worth at the date of the conclusion of peace, deduction to be made proportionately for salvage, if any.

Sec. 25

36. Damage resulting from levies or seizures of sums of money, under whatever guise, or of assets of any kind expressed in cash, and damage resulting from expenses incurred, for example, for the relief of the population of invaded territories or of interned civilians, are taken at the capital value of the sum involved, [expressed in the currency of the State making the claim,] with interest at 6 per cent from the day of the damage to the date of the conclusion of peace.

amount which the property would have been worth at the date of the conclusion of peace, deduction to be made proportionately for salvage, if any.

[XXIII.] Damage resulting from levies or seizures of sums of money, under whatever guise (including forced subscriptions) or of assets of any kind expressed in cash, and damage resulting from expenses incurred, for example for the relief of the population of invaded territories or of interned civilians, are taken at the capital value of the sum involved, with interest at 6 per cent from the date of the damage to the date of the conclusion of peace, the right being fully reserved to regulate in any manner determined all questions as to reciprocal claims or debts arising from pre-war contracts between subjects of the enemy Powers and subjects of the Allied and Associated Powers.

Sec. 26

41. Damage resulting from the seizure, loss or destruction of securities is valued on the basis of their average price on the Bourse during the first six months of 1914, or, in the case of securities issued after 1 July, 1914, on the basis of their issue price—provided that such price be not lower than the average

[XXIV.] Damage resulting from the seizure, loss or destruction of securities, is valued on the basis of their average price on the Bourse during the first six months of 1914, or, in the case of securities issued after 1 July, 1914, on the basis of their issue price, provided that such price be not lower than the average for the [fourth quarter of 1918;] there shall be added the value of coupons, interest, or income in arrears, which the owners would have been able to realize up to the date of the conclusion of peace, if they had remained in possession of their securities.

Sec. 27

43. Damage resulting from the deprivation, wholly or in part, of the free exercise or enjoyment of [every] proprietary right, is valued, [for the period of such deprivation,] on the basis of the average receipts or income [of] such property [during] the three calendar years, the three fiscal years or the three seasons last preceding the war [including in the case of agricultural property the income of the landlord and that of the tenant; provided always that the compensation shall not be less than the amount necessary to pay interest charges at 6 per cent and also to amortize the principal invested in the enterprise, or representing the value of the property, of which the nationals of the Allied and Associated States shall have been deprived.]

for the first quarter of 1919; there shall be added the value of coupons, interest or income in arrears, which the owners would have been able to realize up to the date of the conclusion of peace, if they had remained in possession of their securities.

[XXV.] Damage resulting from the deprivation, wholly, or in part, of the exercise of any proprietary right is valued on the basis of the average net receipts or income from such property at the time of damage for the whole period during which such deprivation shall have continued, both down to the date of the conclusion of peace and until such reasonable time after the said date as may be deemed necessary to secure the cessation of such deprivation. The valuation will be made by the application of a coefficient, appropriate to the cases and periods in question, to the average net receipts or income of the three calendar years, the three fiscal years or the three seasons last preceding the war. In such valuation account shall be taken of any new resources, or any subsidies, whose addition to the existing income of the parties interested may have furnished compensa-

46. Damage resulting from the deprivation of opportunity to work or to obtain [a] fair remuneration for [one's] work [or occupation] is valued on the basis of the average wages or [salary of the claimant during the three years preceding such deprivation.]

tion, wholly or in part, for the loss suffered by them.

[XXVI.] Damage resulting from the deprivation, wholly or in part, of the exercise of an occupation, or generally of opportunity to work, or to obtain fair remuneration for work, is valued on the basis of the average wages or salaries of the parties interested at the time of the damage for the whole period during which such deprivation shall have continued, both down to the date of the conclusion of peace and until such reasonable time after the said date as may be deemed necessary to secure the cessation of such deprivation. The valuation will be made by the application of a coefficient, appropriate to the cases and periods in question, to the average net wages or salaries for the three calendar years last preceding the war. In such valuation account shall be taken of any new resources, or any subsidies, whose addition to the existing income of the parties interested may have furnished compensation, wholly or in part, for the loss suffered by them.

49. Damage which consists in the disorganization of business

[XXVII.] Damage which consists in the disorganization of

houses, enterprises or professions is valued on the basis of the cost of reorganization.

business houses, enterprises or professions is valued on the basis of the cost of reorganization.

Sec. 30

51. Damage caused to industrial property through the enemy's knowledge of special processes of manufacture, and the commercial damage resulting from the enemy's knowledge of books, correspondence and documents or information of a private nature, of all sorts, is to be valued in accordance with special rules agreed upon between the Allied and Associated Powers.

[XXVIII.] Damage caused to industrial property through the enemy's knowledge of special processes of manufacture, and the commercial damage resulting from the enemy's knowledge of books, correspondence and documents or information of a private nature, of all sorts, is to be valued in accordance with special rules agreed upon between the Allied and Associated Powers.

Sec. 31

53. Damage relating to currency (marks, monetary instruments issued or falsified by the enemy, etc.) is valued on the basis of the [face value of such currency with interest at 6 per cent from 11 November, 1918, to the date of the conclusion of peace.]

[XXIX.] [Damage relating to currency (marks, monetary instruments issued or falsified by the enemy, etc.) is valued on the basis of the actual net costs resulting from any operation of repurchase effected by the Allied and Associated Powers, when such operations have been made, the right being reserved to the other Powers to present objections to any scheme which may have been put into operation. There shall be added interest at 6 per cent from the date of the damage down to the date of the conclusion of peace.]

Sec. 32

56. [Damage resulting from every kind of personal injury, from every act, cruelty or vio-

[Paragraph opposite reserved.]

lence leading to the death or total incapacity for labor of the injured person will be valued, for each person thus deceased or incapacitated, on the basis of a uniform scale of charges applicable to all individuals and to all countries, which shall be agreed upon between the Allied and Associated Powers.]

Sec. 33

57. [Damage resulting from every kind of personal injury, from every act, cruelty or violence leading to wounds, illness or partial incapacity for labor, shall be valued for each person thus affected by applying to the scale of charges above mentioned a formula which shall be uniform for all individuals and all countries and which shall be agreed upon between the Allied and Associated Powers.]

[Paragraph opposite reserved.]

Sec. 34

58. [Compensation which is due on account of all injuries to honor or health shall be determined in accordance with rules which shall be uniform for all individuals and for all countries and which shall be agreed upon between the Allied and Associated Powers.]

[Paragraph opposite reserved.]

Sec. 35

68. [Losses caused by compulsory administration are determined on the basis of the revenue of similar property for the same period. These losses

[Paragraph opposite reserved.]

will be refunded in francs at the rates of exchange mentioned in the preceding paragraph.* No debts contracted by such administration will be binding on the rightful owner unless admitted by the legal authorities to have been incurred for the benefit of the property.]

Sec. 36

69. [The value of objects subjected to compulsory liquidation and which cannot by reason of their nature be restored, will be estimated according to the principles set forth in paragraph (1).† Objects which by reason of their nature can be restored must be returned to the owner free of charge.]

[Paragraph opposite reserved.]

Sec. 37

70. [The contract of sale drawn up between the liquidator and the purchaser will be considered *ipso facto* null and void, the purchaser merely being entitled to claim compensation from the enemy Government.]

[Paragraph opposite reserved.]

Sec. 38

71. [Deterioration caused by the liquidator or administrator will be estimated according to general rules.]

[Paragraph opposite reserved.]

Sec. 39

Additional Paragraph. [In all cases where the above clauses do not provide for interest calculated in a special manner, the

[Additional paragraph reserved.]

*See section 67 of Annex II, Tenth Meeting.
†See paragraph I of Annex V, Ninth Meeting.

compensation for which the enemy is held responsible will bear interest at 6 per cent from 11 November, 1918, to the date of the conclusion of peace. This provision shall not apply to compensation in respect of deprivation of the exercise of proprietary rights of an occupation or of opportunity to work.]

DOCUMENT 487

First Subcommittee: Minutes of the Twenty-first Meeting, March 25, 1919, 11:20 A. M.

[EOM, First Subcommittee, pp. 134-36. French stenographic minutes, PV, CRD, pp. 608-21.]

The First Sub-Committee of the Commission on Reparation of Damage (Valuation of Damage) met on Tuesday, 25 March, 1919, at 11.20 A. M., at the Ministry of Finance, LORD SUMNER in the Chair.

Present: MR. DULLES (*U. S. A.*); LORD SUMNER (*British Empire*); MR. JOUASSET (*France*); MR. MORI (*Japan*); MR. VAN DEN HEUVEL (*Belgium*); MR. SPERANZA (*Greece*); MR. OLCHOWSKI (*Poland*); MR. DOS SANTOS VIEGAS (*Portugal*); MR. DANIELOPOL (*Roumania*); MR. PROTITCH (*Serbia*); MR. KRECMAR (*Czecho-Slovak Republic*).[1]

Sec. 9c

The Committee continued the discussion of the amendment to the Categories of Damage proposed by the Serbian Delegation at the last meeting.

MR. BAYKITCH (*Expert for Serbia*) gave a further explanation of the object of his amendment. MR. JOUASSET (*France*) stated that the French Delegation did not oppose the amendment. Upon the observation of the CHAIRMAN that at least three Delegations opposed the Serbian amendment, and as no Delegation seconded it, MR. BAYKITCH withdrew the amendment.

The Serbian Delegation then presented the following further amendment to section 9 (c).

[1] According to the French minutes, Kramář was present instead of Krčmář.

Contracts of life insurance made before the war by persons who have died during the war without having paid war-insurance premiums.

MR. BAYKITCH (*Expert for Serbia*) explained that the amendment was intended to meet the case of persons who had held ordinary life-insurance policies, but who had been prevented by the circumstances attending the sudden outbreak of the war from paying the special premiums to cover war risk.

MR. JOUASSET (*France*) said that the French Delegation did not oppose this amendment; but suggested the addition of words requiring that the persons in question should have been prevented from paying the necessary premiums by the fact of invasion.

The CHAIRMAN said that he must formally oppose the amendment, as it involved a great extension of the principles on which reparation was being claimed.

MR. DULLES (*U. S. A.*) sympathized with the Serbian case; but he observed that all the hardships arising from the war could not be put to the charge of the enemy. If the Sub-Committee admitted this particular case of failure to fulfill the conditions of a contract owing to the outbreak of the war, it would open the door to enormous claims in respect of losses on all classes of contracts. The case was, perhaps, rather one for domestic legislation.

MR. JOUASSET (*France*) replied to MR. DULLES that the claim in question arose solely from the fact of invasion. But he agreed that it was a case for domestic legislation, unless it were proved that there had been an actual diminution of the national wealth.

The CHAIRMAN thought that it was a clear case for domestic legislation. If the amendment were accepted, British Life Insurance Companies could sustain a claim for the heavy losses which they had suffered through bearing war risks without special premiums.

MR. BAYKITCH (*Expert for Serbia*) agreed that there had been no diminution of national wealth. The British Delegation being opposed to the acceptance of his amendment, he would withdraw it.

Secs. 20 and 21

MR. VAN DEN HEUVEL (*Belgium*) then moved the following paragraph for insertion between section 20 and section 21:—

Including the extraordinary expenses of administration which the State has had to incur in consequence of invasion and occupation.

In support of this proposal, MR. VAN DEN HEUVEL said that other countries besides Belgium were affected. The Belgian claim was for the extra expenditure involved in the removal of the civil administration to French soil, the ordinary revenues being collected in the meanwhile by the Germans.

The CHAIRMAN observed that, as section 21 was brought into discussion, he desired to say that the words "or out of work" were not accepted by the British Delegation.

Returning to MR. VAN DEN HEUVEL'S proposal, he thought the claim came under the Category "Exactions of a Financial Character." The taxes collected by the Germans in Belgium were forced taxes and were recoverable as such. Moreover, the matter involved the whole question of loans between the Allies. The extra expenditure referred to was to a large extent money borrowed from the Allies. If this claim were allowed and paid, would the money be allocated to the repayment of the loans?

MR. VAN DEN HEUVEL (*Belgium*) observed that in collecting taxes in Belgium, the Germans had merely applied existing laws. In view of the provisions of The Hague Convention, these taxes could not be called forced taxes. He recognized, too, that the proceeds were applied in large part to paying the costs of the public administration; the question of misappropriation by Germany was a separate one. To the CHAIRMAN'S question as to the disposal of the money, MR. VAN DEN HEUVEL replied that Belgium would loyally repay her loans in accordance with the terms on which the money was borrowed.

MR. JOUASSET (*France*) supported MR. VAN DEN HEUVEL'S position, and urged that the question as to the disposal of the money was irrelevant to the question as to whether the claim against Germany was just.

MR. DANIELOPOL (*Roumania*) proposed that, to avoid possible duplication of claims, the following words be added to the amendment:

In so far as these expenses have not been included in other claims.

The CHAIRMAN said that he had no intention of suggesting that obligations incurred by Allied States would not be loyally met. The question which he thought it necessary to raise, was whether loans spent on war purposes were to be claimed from Germany by the borrowing or the lending State. He contended that Great Britain was entitled to claim from Germany, under section 27, the loans made to her Allies. If this view were correct MR. VAN DEN HEUVEL'S proposal would involve a duplication of claims. If, on the other hand, the borrowing State made the claim, was it entitled to place the money received among its general assets, or must it treat it as allocated to repay the loans? Until this question was settled, the British Delegation could not accept MR. VAN DEN HEUVEL'S proposal. He suggested that its discussion be adjourned.

MR. DULLES (*U. S. A.*) said that the amendment brought up the even wider question as to which Power should present the claim against Germany in cases where two Powers were interested: for example in the case of American property destroyed in occupied territory. He suggested that this question be put on the Agenda for discussion at any early date.

MR. DANIELOPOL (*Roumania*) agreed that the question of loans was of great importance; he thought it could hardly be taken up at present.

MR. VAN DEN HEUVEL (*Belgium*) pointed out that section 27, as drafted, dealt with military expenses, whereas his claim was for costs of civil administration. There could, thus, be no danger of duplication. He could not accept the suggestion that the reparation in question should be allocated to the repayment of certain loans.

The CHAIRMAN was unable to agree that there was no danger of duplication, and urged that loans to an ally for carrying on military operations were to be considered military expenses no less than if the sums had been given outright.

The discussion of this section was then postponed, in order to be continued in connection with the whole question of loans.

The next meeting was fixed for Wednesday, 26 March, at 10.30 A. M.

The meeting adjourned at 1.25 P. M.

SUMNER,
Chairman.

E. MINOST,
Secretary.

DOCUMENT 488

First Subcommittee: Minutes of the Twenty-second Meeting,
March 26, 1919, 10:30 A. M.

[EOM, First Subcommittee, pp. 137-39. French stenographic minutes, PV, CRD, pp. 622-37; French condensed minutes, *ibid.*, pp. 638-41.]

The First Sub-Committee of the Commission on Reparation of Damage (Valuation of Damage) met on Wednesday, 26 March, 1919, at 10.30 A. M., at the Ministry of Finance, LORD SUMNER in the Chair.

Present: MR. DULLES (*U. S. A.*); LORD SUMNER (*British Empire*); MR. JOUASSET (*France*); MR. MORI (*Japan*); MR. VAN DEN HEUVEL (*Belgium*); MR. MICHALACOPOULOS (*Greece*); MR. OLCHOWSKI (*Poland*); MR. DOS SANTOS VIEGAS (*Portugal*); MR.

Danielopol (*Roumania*); Mr. Protitch (*Serbia*); Mr. Krecmar (*Czecho-Slovak Republic*).[1]

Annex I, 20th Meeting

The Sub-Committee proceeded to consider the Revised Tabulation of Categories of Damage prepared by Mr. Jouasset (Annex I, Twentieth Meeting).[2]

Submitting for discussion the heading of Chapter I of Division I, Category A, the Chairman referred to the discussion of the term "every theatre of operations" at the 4th meeting, as reported in the minutes,[3] and stated in correction of that report that the Sub-Committee had taken no decision as to the meaning of the term, which was to be regarded as a well-known phrase used in its ordinary sense.

Mr. Jouasset (*France*) thought it would be desirable to insert a precise definition of the term.

The Chairman felt that it would be unwise, as well as unnecessary to give a definition. The term was not used in a technical sense, and, as the clause would not be inserted in the Treaty of Peace, no difficulty as to its interpretation need be anticipated.

The Sub-Committee accepted the Chairman's view and adopted the heading and section without alteration.

Sec. 2

Section 2 was then submitted.

Mr. Protitch (*Serbia*) asked that the words "fait de guerre" in the French text be altered to "fait de la guerre," the phrase used in French legislation on the subject of reparation.

Mr. Jouasset (*France*) supported this proposal explaining that the term "fait de la guerre" had acquired almost a technical meaning in French.

Mr. Dulles (*U. S. A.*) pointed out that the Sub-Committee could not admit that words which it adopted were used in a technical meaning accorded to them by the legislation of any one country.

The Chairman associated himself with Mr. Dulles' observation.

After further discussion, the amendment was withdrawn on the suggestion of Mr. Jouasset (*France*) and section 2 was adopted without alteration.

---

[1] According to the French stenographic minutes, Sperantzas was present instead of Michalakopoulos and Kramář instead of Krčmář.

[2] Annex I of Document 486.

[3] See Document 470.

Sec. 3

Section 3 was then submitted.

MR. OLCHOWSKI (*Poland*) proposed that this section should be struck out as being an incomplete enumeration, which was unnecessary and possibly dangerous.

The CHAIRMAN thought the section innocuous, and the Sub-Committee adopted it without alteration.

Secs. 4, 5, 6, 7 and 8

Sections 4, 5, 6, 7 and 8 were adopted unaltered.

Sec. 9 (a), (b), (c)

In section 9, sub-sections (a) and (b) were adopted unaltered; sub-section (c) remained reserved.

On sub-section (d) MR. JOUASSET (*France*) pointed out that the text was that adopted at the 4th meeting, as reported in the minutes.[4]

The CHAIRMAN stated that the British Delegation understood this sub-section to apply only to expenditure incurred in consequence of a legal obligation. He felt that the draft did not make this clear, and he moved to insert the word "legal" before the words "obligation of taking the place of the public authorities."

MR. VAN DEN HEUVEL (*Belgium*) said that this insertion would defeat the purpose of his amendment, upon which the present draft had been based. He had moved it to meet the case of private persons, or of organizations, who came to the relief of dependents or communities because the public authority was unable to do so. In such a case there was no specific legal obligation, but a moral and social obligation. The case was, however, quite distinct from the work of voluntary charities, since the relief given was often out of proportion to the resources of those who had assumed the responsibility, and was not due to mere generosity, but to the absolute necessity of the circumstances. He agreed that voluntary charity should not be made the subject of a claim, but he refused to admit that persons who had drawn upon their capital in order to take the place of the public authorities should be refused reparation.

MR. JOUASSET (*France*) pointed out that the insertion of the word "legal" would have the effect of refusing compensation to manufacturers who had maintained their employees rather than allow them to be forced to work for the Germans; and to communes in occupied regions which, without legal obligation, had

[4] See Document 470.

maintained their destitute populations. Such an obligation could not have been imposed on them by the French Government, as they were outside its jurisdiction.

The CHAIRMAN considered that it was impossible to allow claims in respect of relief given under a merely moral and social obligation, without admitting claims for every kind of charitable relief. An employer was partly actuated by personal interest in assisting his employees. To recognize his demands and reject those of charity would be contrary to principle and dangerous.

MR. DULLES (*U. S. A.*) agreed that it was difficult to distinguish between the case of the employer, stated by MR. VAN DEN HEUVEL, and private charities. He suggested that the State would be entitled to claim the sums in question under section 9 (g) and could then reimburse the employer.

Sec. 9 (d)

After a further discussion between Messrs. JOUASSET, VAN DEN HEUVEL, the CHAIRMAN, Messrs. DANIELOPOL (*Roumania*), DULLES and OLCHOWSKI (*Poland*), who supported MR. VAN DEN HEUVEL's position, it was agreed that sub-section (d) should be considered again at a later stage, with a view to the proposal by MR. VAN DEN HEUVEL of a new draft. It was pointed out by MR. JOUASSET that MR. DULLES' suggestion would involve amendment of the method of valuation accepted for damage covered by sub-section (g) (section 25 of Annex II, Twentieth Meeting) [by] omission of the reference to compensation from "subsidies." The CHAIRMAN, therefore, proposed that MR. VAN DEN HEUVEL should move his new draft when the Sub-Committee came to consider the latter section.

Sec. 9 (e) and 9 (f)

Sub-Sections (e) and (f) of Section 9 were then considered.

The CHAIRMAN repeated on behalf of the British Delegation the reservation made on first reading (Minutes of Fourth Meeting) to the effect that these sub-sections were accepted on the understanding that their application should be governed by the practical possibilities of the case.

MR. JOUASSET (*France*) agreed that damage claimed under this sub-section must be clearly proved.

Sub-sections (e), (f) and (g) were then accepted unaltered.

Sec. 10

Section 10 was accepted unaltered.

Sec. 11

Section 11 was then considered.

GENERAL MCKINSTRY (*U. S. A.*), replacing MR. DULLES, proposed that this section should be limited to damage done by the enemy.

MR. JOUASSET (*France*) agreed that this limitation should be imposed, except as regarded thefts of currency and falsification, etc., . . . of bank-notes and other monetary instruments.[5] The Sub-Committee had from the first decided that damage arising as a consequence of defensive or offensive measures of the Allies was admissible. A parallel case was removal of woodwork from houses in order to obtain fuel.

The CHAIRMAN said that he had never understood the Categories of Damage approved by the Sub-Committee to include crimes committed by Allied subjects. There was a clear distinction in principle between looting by Allied soldiers, for example, or forging of notes by Allied subjects, and demolition of property in order to obtain the necessities of life in the trenches. To decide otherwise would be discreditable to the Sub-Committee.

MR. MORI (*Japan*) said that he entirely approved of the principle laid down by the CHAIRMAN.

MR. VAN DEN HEUVEL (*Belgium*) also agreed with the principle; but pointed out the difficulty of proving who had actually committed the thefts in question.

MR. DANIELOPOL (*Roumania*) agreed with the CHAIRMAN that a crime committed by an Allied subject could not be the basis of a claim against the enemy, but thought that to insist on proof of each case could make it easy for the enemy to throw the blame upon the Allies. The burden of proof should be upon the enemy. He suggested that the section might require to be redrafted, and that the discussion be adjourned.

The CHAIRMAN thought thefts of currency were already covered by the general provisions as to thefts in section 5 (Category B). He suggested that this section, also, might require to be redrafted and be limited to enemy acts.

It was agreed to postpone the discussion of section 11 and to consider at the same time the question of redrafting section 5.

Secs. 13, 14, 15 and 16

Sections 13, 14, 15 and 16 were accepted without alteration.

[5] Ellipsis in the original.

The next meeting was fixed for Thursday, 27 March, at 10.30 A. M.
The meeting adjourned at 1 P. M.

SUMNER,
Chairman.

E. MINOST,
Secretary.

DOCUMENT 489

*First Subcommittee: Minutes of the Twenty-third Meeting,
March 27, 1919, 10:30 A. M.*

[EOM, First Subcommittee, pp. 140-42. French stenographic minutes, PV, CRD, pp. 642-54; French condensed minutes, *ibid.*, pp. 655-57.]

The First Sub-Committee of the Commission on Reparation of Damage (Valuation of Damage) met on Thursday, 27 March, 1919, at 10.30 A. M., at the Ministry of Finance, LORD SUMNER in the Chair.

Present: MR. McCORMICK (*U.* S. A.); LORD SUMNER (*British Empire*); MR. JOUASSET (*France*); MR. CAMMEO (*Italy*); MR. MORI (*Japan*); MR. VAN DEN HEUVEL (*Belgium*); MR. SPERANZA (*Greece*); MR. OLCHOWSKI (*Poland*); MR. DOS SANTOS VIEGAS (*Portugal*); MR. DANIELOPOL (*Roumania*); MR. PROTITCH (*Serbia*); MR. KRECMAR (*Czecho-Slovak Republic*).[1]

The Sub-Committee resumed the discussion of the revised Tabulation of Categories of Damage (Annex I, Twentieth Meeting).[2]

Sec. 11

A new draft of section 11, proposed by the French Delegation, was accepted without discussion.

The new draft was in the following terms:

Destruction or disappearance of currency as a direct consequence of the causes referred to in section 2, above.

Taxes, imposts, contributions of war, fines, levies in cash of all kinds, imposed by the enemy, thefts of currency by the enemy including balances of accounts transferred and assets converted into 'bons,' loan or other stock—subscriptions and expenses imposed by the enemy upon individuals or corporations; issue, falsification, alteration or depreciation by the act of the enemy of bank-notes, 'bons' or monetary instruments of any kind.

The Sub-Committee proceeded to discuss Category E (Damage to Persons). After an exchange of views between Messrs. MORI (*Japan*), DULLES (*U. S. A.*) JOUASSET (*France*) and the CHAIR-

---

[1] According to both the French stenographic and the French condensed minutes, Santos Viegas was absent.

[2] See Document 486.

MAN, the words "pensions and allowances" and the word "damages" in sections 13, 14, 15, 16, 18 and 19, were replaced by the word "damage." These sections accordingly assumed the following form:—

Section 13—"Damage caused to civilian victims" etc.
Section 14—"Damage caused to civilian victims" etc.
Section 15—"Damage resulting from all acts" etc.
Section 16—"Damage resulting from any injury" etc.
Section 18—"Damage caused to every person" etc.
Section 19—"Damage caused:—

(a) to victims," etc.

On the proposal of the CHAIRMAN, and after observations by MR. JOUASSET (*France*), the words in section 16, "including cost of relief of the said interned persons," were struck out. It was agreed that these words should be added to section 9, and should be discussed at the same time as that section.

Sec. 20

Section 20 was adopted without discussion.

Sec. 21

The Sub-Committee then accepted the following new draft of section 21, which was proposed by the French Delegation:—

Including allowances to refugees, to persons evacuated, and to all persons who have been deprived, wholly or partially, as a direct consequence of the operations of war or of the measures taken by the enemy, of the exercise of their proprietary rights or occupation, or generally of opportunity to work or to obtain fair remuneration for their work.

MR. JOUASSET (*France*) reminded the Sub-Committee of the amendment proposed by MR. DANIELOPOL and himself and adopted at the meeting of 24 March (see Minutes of 20th Meeting).[3] After an exchange of views between MR. MORI (*Japan*), the CHAIRMAN, Messrs. JOUASSET (*France*) and DANIELOPOL (*Roumania*), it was agreed that this amendment should be inserted between sections 21 and 22.

Messrs. JOUASSET (*France*) and VAN DEN HEUVEL (*Belgium*) proposed to alter the title of the Second Part of the Tabulation (French version) by substituting the words "Dommages de l'État" for the words "Dommages Généraux." This proposal was accepted.

The Sub-Committee proceeded to discuss the reservation made upon section 22 (Purchase of enemy money in territories which

---

[3] See Document 486. Also PV, CRD, pp. 580, 585-86.

before the war were not included within the frontiers of the claimant State).

MR. JOUASSET (*France*) thought that a distinction might be
drawn between territories which at any date had formed part of
the claimant State and those which had never been so included.
In the former case he considered that the loss caused by operations
of redemption was as proper a subject for reparation as the corresponding claim which had been accepted for the case of occupied
territories.

MR. OLCHOWSKI (*Poland*) supported MR. JOUASSET'S views.

MR. DANIELOPOL (*Roumania*) also supported MR. JOUASSET.
He observed that in order to solve the question in a judicial spirit
all the consequences involved must be carefully weighed. It must
not be forgotten that those countries which were detaching themselves from Austria-Hungary held at present about 20 thousand
millions of kronen, the real value of which was almost nothing.

MR. CAMMEO (*Expert for Italy*) thought that all territories which
were reunited to Allied States should be treated upon the same
footing. In fact, in all cases such reunions would take place, not
arbitrarily, but as a matter of right. No distinction, therefore,
could be justifiable.

The CHAIRMAN asked MR. JOUASSET if France proposed to deduct from the indemnities claimed by her the value of public property in Alsace-Lorraine constructed at a date, later than 1870,
which would now become French State property.

MR. JOUASSET (*France*) stated that he could not reply to this
question at once, but, if the CHAIRMAN so wished, would give him
an answer in the near future.

MR. VAN DEN HEUVEL (*Belgium*) thought that, as regarded the
question raised by section 22,[4] a distinction must be made between
different states of fact. In the occupied territories, where the enemy
in virtue of the occupation had given forced currency to his money,
the question was simple. The case was one of unjustifiable injury,
which ought to be redressed. The position was different in the case
of territories which in 1914 formed part of enemy States. If such
territories were reunited to one of the Allied States, should not the
latter take them as they stood, both as regarded the credit and the
debit side of the account? If such territories were established as
independent States, should they not bear their proportionate part
of the debit not less than of the credit side? Such would appear to
be the principles hitherto accepted. Were there any legal or practi-

---

[4] The French condensed minutes read "section 12." That is obviously an error.

cal reasons for abandoning those principles? Possibly there were. He would wish to be fully informed on this point before expressing his opinion.

MR. DULLES (*U. S. A.*) declared that he could only admit the existence of a right to reparation in the case of repurchase of money in occupied territories, the claim being based upon the establishment of forced currency. He proposed that the Sub-Committee adopt Section 22, with the addition of the words:—

Excluding such operations in territories which before the war were not included within the boundaries of the claimant State.

The right would be reserved to the various Delegations to reopen the question, either before the Plenary Commission or before the Peace Conference.

The CHAIRMAN supported this proposal. He said that in his opinion section 22 was drafted in too comprehensive terms. It would be necessary to agree upon a new draft.

MR. DULLES (*U. S. A.*) proposed, as a matter of procedure, that the Sub-Committee should at an early date, and if possible on the following Monday, proceed to discuss the figures of the claims for damage. He considered it essential that some practical result should be attained at once.

The next meeting was fixed for Thursday,[5] 28 March, at 10.30 A. M. The meeting adjourned at 1.00 P. M.

SUMNER,
Chairman.

E. MINOST,[6]
Secretary.

DOCUMENT 490

First Subcommittee: Minutes of the Twenty-fourth Meeting, March 28, 1919, 10:15 A. M.

[EOM, First Subcommittee, pp. 143-46. French stenographic minutes, PV, CRD, pp. 658-71.]

The First Sub-Committee of the Commission on Reparation of Damage (Valuation of Damage) met on 28 March, 1919, at 10.15 A. M., at the Ministry of Finance, LORD SUMNER in the Chair.

Present: MR. DULLES (*U. S. A.*); LORD SUMNER (*British Empire*); MR. LEBRUN (*France*); MR. CHIESA (*Italy*); MR. MORI (*Japan*); MR. VAN DEN HEUVEL (*Belgium*); MR. SPERANZA (*Greece*); MR. OLCHOWSKI (*Poland*); MR. DOS SANTOS VIEGAS

[5] Error for "Friday."
[6] The French condensed minutes are signed by Maurice Bourquin.

(*Portugal*); MR. DANIELOPOL (*Roumania*); MR. PROTITCH (*Serbia*); MR. KRECMAR (*Czecho-Slovak Republic*).[1]

Draft minutes of the 18th, 19th and 20th meetings were presented, but their consideration was postponed.

Sec. 22

The Sub-Committee resumed the discussion of section 22 of the Revised Tabulation of Categories of Damage (Annex I, Twentieth Meeting).[2]

MR. DULLES (*U. S. A.*) thought that the terms of the draft under consideration were too wide; they might cover enemy securities, for example, Turkish bonds.

MR. VAN DEN HEUVEL (*Belgium*) produced photographs of German posters proving that forced currency at fixed rates had been given to marks in the occupied part of Belgium since 1914, first by local measures and afterward by general regulation.

MR. CAMMEO (*Expert for Italy*) said that in the occupied regions of Italy, not only had enemy money been given forced currency, but this money was a special issue made without any sort of cover by a bank established for the purpose by Germany and Austria-Hungary in co-operation.

Messrs. OLCHOWSKI (*Poland*), PROTITCH (*Serbia*) and JOUASSET (*Expert for France*) explained the manner in which enemy money had received forced currency in their respective countries.

The CHAIRMAN said that the British and American Delegations regarded the forced use and acceptance of the money in question as the test of admissibility of this class of claims. He suggested that the Delegations interested should prepare a new draft, defining more precisely the element of compulsion and also excluding application of the section to securities, such as the bonds mentioned by MR. DULLES. The section could in the meantime be reserved. He hoped the Sub-Committee would be able almost immediately to present a first Interim Report on the agreed Categories and Methods of Valuation. This would be followed by a report on the points which had given rise to controversy, in which the section when approved would find its place.

MR. JOUASSET (*Expert for France*) urged that this category of damage was too important to be omitted from any Interim Report.

MR. VAN DEN HEUVEL (*Belgium*) suggested that there be added in section 22, the words:

---

[1] According to the French stenographic minutes, Jouasset was present instead of Lebrun.

[2] See Document 486.

In consequence of the establishment, *de facto* or *de jure*, of forced currency therefor.

MR. CHIESA (*Italy*) supported this proposal.

The CHAIRMAN asked what was the precise meaning of the French phrase "tous avoirs exprimés en monnaie ennemie"?

MR. JOUASSET (*Expert for France*) replied that the term covered all paper money and also cases such as had occurred in France, where the enemy had cashed coupons payable in francs and had reimbursed the owners in marks at the rate arbitrarily fixed.

The CHAIRMAN said that in his opinion the section would be still too comprehensive even if MR. VAN DEN HEUVEL'S amendment were accepted. The Delegations interested would suffer no prejudice by postponing its discussion until after the Sub-Committee had presented its Interim Report.

MR. DULLES (*U. S. A.*) expressed sympathy with the general idea embodied in the section, but was afraid that adoption of the section, as at present drafted, might have consequences which no one intended.

MR. VAN DEN HEUVEL (*Belgium*) considered that the special case mentioned by MR. JOUASSET was not one to be dealt with under section 22.

The CHAIRMAN said that he could at once agree to the following text:—

> Injury resulting to Allied nations from the necessity to which they have been put of redeeming enemy money held by prisoners of war and interned civilians.

The phrase "les valeurs et tous avoirs, etc." of the French text was too vague.

MR. VAN DEN HEUVEL (*Belgium*) proposed to replace the phrase in question by the words: "les monnaies ennemies, espèce ou papier." To limit the application of the section to prisoners of war and interned civilians would be to deal with only a fraction of the question.

The CHAIRMAN then declared that for his part he could not at the moment accept a more comprehensive text than that which he had just suggested. MR. VAN DEN HEUVEL'S first amendment did not sufficiently define the element of compulsion.

MR. CHIESA (*Italy*), supporting MR. VAN DEN HEUVEL'S proposal, said that inhabitants of occupied regions were to be regarded as practically interned persons.

MR. MORI (*Japan*) said that, while he would be prepared to accept a rather more comprehensive draft than the CHAIRMAN, he felt the section must be made more precise, and he suggested the appointment of a sub-committee to discuss the whole question in collaboration with the sub-committee which had already been appointed by the Financial Commission to deal with the same subject-matter.

Messrs. DANIELOPOL (*Roumania*) and JOUASSET (*France*) supported MR. MORI'S proposal, which was accepted. It was agreed that section 22 be reserved *in toto* and the following sub-committee was appointed, viz.:—

Messrs. MORI, CAMMEO and VAN DEN HEUVEL.

Secs. 23, 24 and 25

Sections 23, 24 and 25 were adopted unaltered.

Sec. 26

Section 26 was adopted, subject to the deletion of the words "or corporations."

Sec. 27

Section 27 was then submitted.

The CHAIRMAN moved to add at the end of the section the words:—

Including loans by one of the combatant Powers to another made for the purpose of assisting or enabling it to prosecute or sustain the war.

The CHAIRMAN explained that the object of his amendment was to make it clear that loans to allies could be claimed under section 27. He reminded the Sub-Committee that section 21 had been reserved for discussion at the same time as section 27; and that the draft before it was MR. VAN DEN HEUVEL'S proposal, as amended by MR. DANIELOPOL, viz.:—

Including the extraordinary expenses of administration which the State has had to incur in consequence of invasion and occupation, in so far as these expenses have not been included in other claims.

Dealing with the question of loans, the CHAIRMAN argued that a loan of money for war purposes to an ally was as truly a war expenditure as the cost of furnishing direct military assistance. The question arose as to which party should make the claim upon the enemy, the Power which lent the money and bore the financial burden, or the borrowing and spending Power. An analogous problem was involved in cases where property of nationals of one Ally was destroyed in the territory of another. There the reparation was plainly due to the owner. The same principle should ultimately apply to loans. While the general question of the use of money recovered from Germany for the repayment of loans was clearly a matter for agreements among the Allies affected, he thought the Sub-Committee ought to lay the foundation for such agreements by recognizing such loans as a category of damage.

MR. DANIELOPOL (*Roumania*) said that there were two questions at issue: (1) What loans could be considered a subject of reparation; (2) the question of priority as between reparation for direct damage suffered and claims for money lent. He considered, for example, that reparation in respect of live stock and property, which were still actually in the hands of the enemy and whose recovery was the first requisite for the re-establishment of devastated areas, should be given priority over any other claim. The question of settlements between Allies was hardly within the competence of the Sub-Committee. He suggested that the CHAIRMAN'S amendment should be altered so as to state that loans to Allies were subjects for claims for reparation, without prejudging the question as to who should make the claim.

MR. CHIESA (*Italy*) considered that the CHAIRMAN'S amendment must involve duplication of claims, as borrowed money would be included in the expenditure for which reparation was demanded by the borrowing Powers.

The CHAIRMAN said that whatever categories might be voted would be subject to the rule against double counting. His acceptance of MR. VAN DEN HEUVEL'S proposal for section 21, and of many other categories, must be conditional upon the solution of the question he had raised. He welcomed MR. DANIELOPOL'S suggestion that the Sub-Committee should not prejudge the question as to which Power should make the claim against Germany. He did not ask that the money first received from Germany should be at once applied to repayment of loans, or that there should be any hypothecation or first charge in favor of loans; but for a mere expression of willingness to come to an amicable understanding. He requested the Delegations to express their readiness to recommend to their Governments to recognize the necessity for agreements between borrowing and lending Powers as to the repayment of the loans under reasonable and equitable conditions.

MR. VAN DEN HEUVEL (*Belgium*) said the CHAIRMAN had raised a very difficult question and he hoped his amendment would be withdrawn. It was not acceptable either as a legal or as a practical proposition. The Power which incurred an expenditure must ultimately bear the loss, if Germany failed to pay, whether the money was borrowed or taken from its own resources. The claim of a lending Power for repayment of its loans was different in kind from a claim for damage against the enemy. He thought that claims for damage must be presented separately by the Power immediately affected.

The discussion was adjourned.

The next meeting was fixed for Saturday, 29 March, at 10.30 A. M.

The meeting adjourned at 1 P. M.

SUMNER,
Chairman.

E. MINOST,
> *Secretary.*

DOCUMENT 491

First Subcommittee: Minutes of the Twenty-fifth Meeting, March 29, 1919, 10:45 A. M. and 2:40 P. M.

[EOM, First Subcommittee, pp. 147-50. French stenographic minutes (afternoon session only), PV, CRD, pp. 672-84; French condensed minutes (both sessions), *ibid.*, pp. 685-88.]

The First Sub-Committee of the Commission on Reparation of Damage (Valuation of Damage) met on Saturday, 29 March, 1919, at 10.45 A. M.[1] at the Ministry of Finance, LORD SUMNER in the Chair.

Present: MR. DULLES (*U. S. A.*); LORD SUMNER (*British Empire*); MR. JOUASSET (*France*); MR. CHIESA (*Italy*); MR. MORI (*Japan*); MR. VAN DEN HEUVEL (*Belgium*); MR. OLCHOWSKI (*Poland*); MR. DOS SANTOS VIEGAS (*Portugal*); MR. DANIELOPOL (*Roumania*); MR. PROTITCH (*Serbia*); MR. KRECMAR (*Czecho-Slovak Republic*).[2]

Sec. 27

Discussion was resumed upon the CHAIRMAN'S amendment to Section 27 of the Revised Tabulation of Categories of Damage (Annex I, Twentieth Meeting).[3]

The CHAIRMAN said that, having stated the position of the British Delegation, he was prepared to withdraw his amendment under all reservations, if the Sub-Committee would agree to the omission of the word "military" from the title of Chapter II of the Second Part of the Tabulation.

The Sub-Committee agreed to this omission.

Sec. 21

The amendment to section 21 proposed by Messrs. VAN DEN

---

[1] According to both the French stenographic and French condensed minutes, at 10 A. M.

[2] According to the French stenographic minutes, Sperantzas was also present.

[3] See Document 486.

HEUVEL (*Belgium*) and DANIELOPOL (*Roumania*) was then carried, the British Delegation dissenting (See Minutes of 21st Meeting).[4]

This amendment was in the following terms:—

Including the extraordinary expenditure which the State has been obliged to bear in consequence of invasion or occupation, in so far as such expenses have not been included in other claims.

Secs. 27 and 28

Sections 27 and 28 were then adopted without alteration.

MR. CHIESA (*Italy*) proposed the following three new categories of damage:

(1) Loss to the finances of the State in respect of the difference between the purchase price of raw materials, in warehouse or in transport at the date of the Armistice, and the sale price at that date.

(2) Cost of special measures of defense against asphyxiation and mustard gas.

(3) Loss to national agriculture arising from the fact of war for the duration of the war.

MR. CHIESA having explained his proposals, the CHAIRMAN said that he thought the first new category was either part of the war costs, in which case it was already covered, or was a claim for loss due to failure to sell war stocks, which was not in his opinion a category of damage. The second was covered by section 27. The third was either too indirect or was already included.

MR. CHIESA accepted the CHAIRMAN'S statement that his second category was already covered. He maintained the other two proposals, and explained the special circumstances which in the view of the Italian Delegation justified the presentation of the claims in question.

As MR. CHIESA'S proposals were not seconded by any Delegation, the CHAIRMAN declared them to be not adopted.

Secs. 29, 30 and 31

Sections 29, 30 and 31 remained reserved.[5]

Sec. 9 (d)

MR. JOUASSET (*France*) referred to section 9 (d) which had been reserved for redrafting (see Minutes 22d Meeting).[6] He stated that the French Delegation attached so much importance to this category that it was prepared to agree to the insertion of the word "legal," as proposed by the CHAIRMAN, in spite of the difficulties involved.

[4] See Document 487. Also PV, CRD, pp. 614-21.

[5] The French condensed minutes read, "29, 30 et 32." That is obviously an error.

[6] See Document 488. Also PV, CRD, pp. 626-31, 639-40.

The Sub-Committee adjourned at 11.15 A. M. and reassembled at 2.40 P. M.

MR. DANIELOPOL (*Roumania*) in the name of the Belgian and Roumanian Delegations, moved the following new draft of section 9 (d):—

Expenses incurred by any authority other than the State, or by any association or person for the relief, feeding and transport of the population in invaded or occupied territories: there shall be excluded from this category expenses incurred for this object from motives of charity.

Supporting this amendment, MR. DANIELOPOL pointed out that continental legislation did not in general impose on local authorities or individuals a legal duty of saving a destitute population from starvation. He agreed with the CHAIRMAN that charity or voluntary assistance were to be excluded. The relief in question was given under pressure of absolute necessity, and was neither a work of charity nor performance of a legal obligation.

MR. JOUASSET (*France*), supporting the amendment, agreed that there was no obligation imposed by law on a commune, or any other body of persons, to afford assistance to the distressed population. In France a thousand million francs had been spent in preventing actual famine, and this burden would have to be borne ultimately by the State.

The CHAIRMAN felt he must maintain his position as to the limitation of the claim to relief given under a legal obligation.

MR. JOUASSET said that, if it was clear that the expenditure of such bodies as the Commission de Ravitaillement Belge was covered, he might agree to the section with the insertion of the word "legal."

MR. VAN DEN HEUVEL (*Belgium*) described the various forms in which the population of Belgium had been relieved; and said that the persons who had spent their capital for this purpose under the pressure of necessity had always expected to be reimbursed by the enemy, who had failed in his duty under international law of using the food supplies of the country to feed the population.

MR. OLCHOWSKI (*Poland*), who supported MR. DANIELOPOL'S amendment, described the terrible conditions which had prevailed in Poland.

MR. DULLES (*U. S. A.*) said that he agreed with the CHAIRMAN that neither charitable relief, nor relief given from interested or mixed motives, could afford a basis for a claim; but there were cases where, under the pressure of an immediate necessity, persons had acted for the account of the State and in the expectation that the State would ratify the act and reimburse the expenditure. The State could retrospectively authorize such expenditure on its behalf, and the cost could then be claimed as "Damage to the State." He therefore proposed to strike out the words from "or by private persons" to the end of the section, and to incorporate the section in the Second Part of the Tabulation "Damage to the State."

After a further discussion in which the CHAIRMAN and Messrs. VAN DEN HEUVEL and JOUASSET took part, it was decided, on the proposal of MR. JOUASSET:—

(1) That section 9 (d) be adopted in the following form:
Expenditure incurred, under any form whatsoever, by any public authority fulfilling an obligation (other than the State) for the food supply, transport or relief of the population of invaded or occupied territories.

(2) That the following new clause be inserted in section 21:
Including expenses incurred under whatsoever form by the State, or by any corporation or individual intervening for the account and with the authorization of the State, for the food supply, transport or relief of the populations of invaded or occupied territories.

The Sub-Committee proceeded to consider the Revised Tabulation of Methods of Valuation of Damage (Annex II, Twentieth Meeting).[7]

Secs. 1, 2, 4, 5, 6, 7, 9, 10, 11, and 12 [Arts. 1-10]

Sections 1, 2, 4, 5, 6, 7, 9, 10, 11 and 12 were adopted without further discussion.[8]

Sec. 13 [Art. 11]

Section 13 was adopted with the substitution of the words "aux articles" for the words "au paragraphe" in the French version.

Sec. 14 [Art. 12]

Section 14 was adopted without discussion.

Secs. 15, 16, 17 and 19 [Arts. 13, 14, 16 and 18]

Sections 15, 16, 17 and 19 were adopted as reaffirming the principle, without in any way modifying the application of the corresponding sections of the First Part of the Tabulation.

Secs. 18 and 20 [Arts. 17 and 19]

Sections 18 and 20 were adopted without discussion.

On the proposal of MR. JOUASSET (*France*) and after a discussion in which MR. DANIELOPOL, the CHAIRMAN, Messrs. JOUASSET

[7] See Document 486.
[8] The English minutes refer to sections; the French, to articles. In the Revised Tabulation, English text, the roman numerals correspond to the French article numbers.

and DULLES took part, the following section based on section 25 of the original Tabulation of Methods of Valuation, was inserted after section 20:—

Sec. 21 [New article 19]

The cost of such reconstruction, replacement or repair is arrived at, wherever possible, by applying to the corresponding pre-war cost an appropriate coefficient, calculated for each category of property in accordance with the market price at the date prescribed by the preceding paragraph in respect to materials, labor and all other factors to be considered.

Secs. 22, 23, 24 and 25 [Arts. 20, 21, 22 and 23]

Sections 22, 23, 24 and 25 were adopted without discussion.

Sec. 26 [Art. 24]

Section 26 was adopted subject to the reservations made on first reading by the Delegations of the British Empire and Japan (see Minutes of the 12th Meeting).[9]

Secs. 27, 28, 29 and 30 [Arts. 25, 26, 27 and 28]

Sections 27, 28, 29 and 30 were adopted without discussion.

Sec. 31 [Art. 29]

Section 31 was reserved until a report should be received from the sub-committee appointed to discuss the corresponding Category of Damage (see Minutes of the 23rd Meeting).[10]

Secs. 32 to 39

Sections 32 to 39 (inclusive) remained reserved.

On the proposal of the CHAIRMAN, the Sub-Committee reaffirmed the resolution carried on 13 March (Minutes of the 13th Meeting).

"It is understood that in adopting the principles and resolutions which have already been adopted, the Sub-Committee does not exclude the adoption of additional resolutions subsequently, or regard those already adopted as being exhaustive of all cases."[11]

MR. JOUASSET (*France*) called attention to the failure of the Sub-Committee to adopt any method of valuing damage to persons, and expressed his surprise that no alternative to the proposal of the French Delegation had been presented.

The CHAIRMAN said that, in view of the importance of presenting an immediate report to the Plenary Commission, he thought it unwise to wait until agreement had been reached on this controversial subject. He urged that, despite their incompleteness, the

[9] See Document 478, debate on section 41. PV, CRD, pp. 414-18, 429-30.

[10] Error for "24th Meeting" (March 28). It was section 22 that was the "corresponding Category of Damage." See Document 490, and PV, CRD, p. 665.

[11] See Document 479. PV, CRD, pp. 446, 452.

resolutions already adopted should be at once embodied in a report, which would be purely provisional.

The Secretariat was instructed to print the resolutions adopted on the subjects of Categories of Damage and of Methods of Valuation so as to form a provisional report for presentation by the CHAIRMAN to the Chairman of the Plenary Commission.[12]

The next meeting was fixed for 31 March at 10.30 A. M.

The meeting adjourned at 5 P. M.

SUMNER,
Chairman.

E. MINOST,
Secretary.

DOCUMENT 492

First Subcommittee: Minutes of the Twenty-sixth Meeting, March 31, 1919, 10:30 A. M.

[EOM, First Subcommittee, pp. 151-54. French condensed minutes, PV, CRD, pp. 689-92.]

The First Sub-Committee of the Commission on Reparation of Damage (Valuation of Damage) met on Monday, 31 March, 1919, at 10.30 A. M., at the Ministry of Finance, LORD SUMNER in the Chair.

Present: MR. DULLES (*U. S. A.*); LORD SUMNER (*British Empire*); MR. JOUASSET (*France*); MR. D'AMELIO (*Italy*); MR. MORI (*Japan*); MR. VAN DEN HEUVEL (*Belgium*); MR. SPERANZA (*Greece*); MR. OLCHOWSKI (*Poland*); MR. DOS SANTOS VIEGAS (*Portugal*); MR. ANTONESCO (*Roumania*); MR. PROTITCH (*Serbia*); MR. BENES (*Czecho-Slovak Republic*).

The minutes of the 18th, 19th, 20th, 21st and 22nd meetings were adopted without observation.

MR. DULLES (*U. S. A.*) stated that, while he recognized that the titles were not a part of the text of the Categories of Damage which had been adopted, it might be wise to strike out in the title of the Revised Tabulation of Categories the words: "for which reparation may be demanded." The American Delegation had understood that this document represented a finding that damage and loss of certain kinds had occurred, without involving the question whether all such damage and loss was a proper subject of claims against all the enemy Powers.

The CHAIRMAN pointed out that MR. DULLES' proposal to alter the title of the report on categories was quite irregular. To convert the report into a mere statement that certain kinds of damage had

---

[12] See Annex of Document 464.

occurred, would reverse the whole proceedings of the past six weeks. It had always been understood that the Sub-Committee was to recommend Categories of Damage as bases of claims for reparation. The discussion would never have developed as it did, had not the categories been so intended. Moreover, merely to alter the title would not adequately express the reserves which MR. DULLES desired to make; the presentation of the report would imply that its contents had been approved. In the opinion of the CHAIRMAN, the proper course for the American Delegation would be to formulate its reserves in a separate statement.

MR. DULLES replied that, had the American Delegation understood that the categories discussed might be regarded as committing the respective Delegations, not only to a recognition of the fact of damage, but also to approval of presentation thereof in every case as a claim which the enemy was obliged to pay, it would have had to make reservations, which it now did, in the sense that the American Delegation accepted the Tabulation as adopted only as a finding that damage should be classified in categories, as therein named; and that the question of demands against the enemy should be resolved by the application to the categories of the principles which might be adopted by the Plenary Commission or by the Peace Conference.

MR. JOUASSET (*France*) associated himself with the CHAIRMAN'S declaration. He further observed that the reservations made by the various Delegations were mentioned in the minutes. He urged that the Tabulation should be retained without alteration, including its title, without which the document would lose all meaning.

The CHAIRMAN proposed that the Sub-Committee should now discuss the Memoranda as to figures of actual claims, in so far as such Memoranda had been presented by different Delegations.

MR. JOUASSET (*France*) stated that, despite its wish to meet the desire expressed by the Sub-Committee to receive figures of claims, and despite the efforts which it had made with this object, the French Delegation felt that, in consequence of the insuperable difficulties which it had encountered, obligations of loyalty towards the Allied and Associated Powers and the necessity of not compromising the interests of France made it impossible that it should present any figures.

Replying to suggestions made by the CHAIRMAN, MR. JOUASSET declared that the information furnished by the Press as to the amount of the losses suffered by France was not worthy of serious consideration. The figures which had been quoted in the Chamber were in no sense those of the French Government, and could not be regarded as official. MR. JOUASSET, furthermore, considered it inadmissible that any figures be taken as a basis for a valuation to be made by the Sub-Committee which had not been produced by the French Delegation itself. He stated that the French Delegation, being of the opinion that it was at the moment impossible to give an estimate of damage, would consider it proper to abstain from taking part in discussion of the figures presented by the other Delegations.

MR. PROTITCH (*Serbia*) declared that the Serbian Delegation had decided to supply figures in consequence of the position taken by MR. McCORMICK (*U. S. A.*) at the meeting of 4 March.[1] In view of the refusal of the French Delegation to take part in the discussion, he considered that such discussion would be useless.

MR. DULLES (*U. S. A.*) reminded the Sub-Committee that the Plenary Commission had received from the Peace Conference, and had accepted, the duty of determining the amount of the indemnity. France was represented at the meeting at which this decision was taken. The duty of the Sub-Committee was, therefore, to proceed at once to the examination of figures.

MR. OLCHOWSKI (*Poland*) felt that, though there was a theoretical possibility of presenting to Germany merely a list of Categories of Damage for which it must pay, and of indicating the methods of valuation which would be applied thereto, it would in practice be necessary to inform the enemy of the amount which he must pay.

MR. VAN DEN HEUVEL (*Belgium*) stated that serious difficulties had been encountered in the inquiries made by the Belgian Government for the purpose of valuing the damage suffered in accordance with the principles of the Sub-Committee. For this reason the Belgian Delegation could not present its figures for some little time, and they would in any case be only provisional.

MR. BENES (*Czecho-Slovak Republic*) thought that, despite the difficulty of establishing figures and the uncertainty resulting therefrom, those figures which had been presented could none the less usefully be examined at once.

MR. JOUASSET (*France*) said he must ask what could be the value of the estimates presented, having regard to the fact that the Sub-Committee had still not come to a decision on certain points of great importance, both in connection with Categories of Damage and with Methods of Valuation. As an example, he referred to losses suffered in consequence of the killing of civilians. These

[1] See Document 473. Also PV, CRD, pp. 341-47, 350-51.

lacunae might produce differences running into dozens of millions of francs.

MR. MORI (*Japan*) supported the proposal of the CHAIRMAN and MR. DULLES. There was in any case no question of binding the Delegations by the figures which they might present. It would be desirable for each to proceed as the American Delegation had done, and to state both a minimum and a maximum figure. The matter of importance, the purpose for which the Plenary Commission had been established, was to present a figure to the Peace Conference.

MR. PROTITCH (*Serbia*) pressed for an answer to the question whether the American Delegation maintained the point of view adopted by MR. MCCORMICK at the meeting of 4 March.

MR. DULLES (*U. S. A.*) replied in the affirmative; but pointed out at the same time that the object in view had been to lay down the following principle: "If a sum is to be demanded from Germany, there must be a minimum of established claims sufficient to absorb such sum."

Replying to MR. JOUASSET, MR. DULLES pointed out that the Delegations were allowed a very wide margin. It would be possible in any case for France to state at least the number of French civilians killed in the war, even if the method of valuing damage to persons had not yet been settled. He asked MR. JOUASSET if it was possible to be certain that the sum demanded from Germany would be covered by the claims which the Allies had against her.

MR. JOUASSET (*France*) replied that he did not think the summaries which would be presented to the Sub-Committee could be of such a nature as to allay anxiety on this point. Moreover, it was not certain that the sum to be paid by Germany would be fixed at present.

MR. ANTONESCO (*Roumania*) stated that the figures of the Roumanian Delegation were almost ready for presentation. He thought, however, that if France gave no estimate for herself, it would be impossible to establish even the minimum figure which was desired.

MR. BAYKITCH (*Expert for Serbia*) explained that the Serbian Delegation had made a great effort to present figures for its estimate in accordance with the principles established by the Sub-Committee and with statistical methods. He laid stress upon the vital interest which Serbia must take in the question of reparation, and upon the heavy responsibility resting upon the Serbian Delegation in view of the essentially provisional character of the figures which would serve as the basis for the indemnity.

In answer to a question by the CHAIRMAN, MR. BOURQUIN (speaking for MR. VAN DEN HEUVEL) said that the Belgian Delegation would be in a position to submit its Memorandum of figures in about a week.

The CHAIRMAN asked whether, in view of the absence of figures from the French and Belgian Delegations, the discussion could profitably be continued. He considered that it would be preferable first to inquire from members of the Peace Conference how far the work of the other Commissions had advanced.

The Sub-Committee approved of this procedure.

The next meeting was fixed for Tuesday, 1 April, at 3 P. M.

The meeting adjourned at 1 P. M.

SUMNER,
E. MINOST,   *Chairman.*
Secretary.

DOCUMENT 493

First Subcommittee: Minutes of the Twenty-seventh (and Final) Meeting, April 1, 1919, 3:15 P. M.

[EOM, First Subcommittee, p. 155. French condensed minutes, PV, CRD, p. 693.]

The First Sub-Committee of the Commission on Reparation of Damage (Valuation of Damage) met on Tuesday, 1 April, 1919, at 3.15 P. M., at the Ministry of Finance, LORD SUMNER in the Chair.

Present: GENERAL MCKINSTRY (*U. S. A.*); LORD SUMNER (*British Empire*); MR. LEBRUN (*France*); MR. CHIESA (*Italy*); MR. MORI (*Japan*); MR. VAN DEN HEUVEL (*Belgium*); MR. MICHALA-COPOULOS (*Greece*); MR. OLCHOWSKI (*Poland*); MR. DOS SANTOS VIEGAS (*Portugal*); MR. ANTONESCO (*Roumania*); MR. PROTITCH (*Serbia*); MR. BENES (*Czecho-Slovak Republic*).

The CHAIRMAN said that at the last meeting he had undertaken to ascertain what course it would be most useful for the Sub-Committee to follow with regard to the work of the Peace Conference as a whole. He had just received from his Government the suggestion that, in view of present circumstances, it would be most convenient for the Sub-Committee to defer any further discussion until the next meeting.[1]

The Sub-Committee agreed to this suggestion and adjourned.

SUMNER,
E. MINOST,   *Chairman.*
Secretary.

[1] The French reads "jusqu'au lendemain."

THE MINUTES OF THE SPECIAL COMMITTEE (POWERS NOT REPRESENTED ON THE COMMISSION)

DOCUMENT 494

First Subcommittee: Minutes of the First Meeting of the Special Committee (Powers Not Represented on the Commission), March 8, 1919, 3:15 P. M.

[TPG, II, 295-96. These minutes are part of Inclosure "O" to Document 497.]

The Special Committee appointed by the First Sub-Committee (Valuation of Damage) to get in statements of claims from powers not represented on the Commission on Reparation, held its first meeting on Saturday, March 8, 1919, at 3:15 P. M. at the Ministry of Finance.

Present: GENERAL MCKINSTRY (*U. S. A.*), COLONEL PEEL (*British Empire*), MR. JOUASSET (*France*).

The Committee elected GENERAL MCKINSTRY as CHAIRMAN and appointed MR. HENRY JAMES (*U. S. A.*) and MR. P. LAURE (*France*) as Secretaries.

The Committee has been charged to secure and report information relative to the amount and character of such reparation as may be claimed by or due to the Governments and people not represented on the Committee on Reparation of Damage.

It was decided to ask the Delegations of the Powers just referred to to forward all information needed for this purpose and also to give this Committee verbal explanations in case they deemed such explanations to be necessary.

The Secretaries were instructed to send a letter to this effect to the following Powers: BOLIVIA, BRAZIL, CUBA, ECUADOR, GUATEMALA, HAITI, HEDJAZ, LIBERIA, PANAMA, PERU, SIAM, URUGUAY, CHINA, NICARAGUA, HONDURAS.[1]

It was noted that CHINA had already supplied a memorandum.[2]

MR. JOUASSET (*France*) was charged to gather any information available in regard to Russian claims, so far as that could be done without official inquiry.

The next meeting was fixed for 11 March, at 11 A. M.

The meeting adjourned at 5 P. M.

[1] This letter was reproduced at the beginning of the Report of the Special Committee (see Document 497).

[2] See Document 498.

DOCUMENT 495

First Subcommittee: Minutes of the Second Meeting of the Special Committee (Powers Not Represented on the Commission), March 11, 1919, 11 A. M.

[TPG, II, 297-98. These minutes are part of Inclosure "O" to Document 497.]

The Special Committee appointed by the First Sub-Committee (Valuation of Damage) to get in statements of claims from Powers not represented on the Commission on Reparation, held its second meeting on Tuesday, March 11, 1919 at 11:00 A. M., at the Ministry of Finance.

Present: GENERAL McKINSTRY (*U. S. A.*), COLONEL PEEL (*British Empire*) and MR. JOUASSET (*France*).

The Committee decided to adopt the practice of translating all documents submitted to the Committee into English or French according to whether they were received in one or the other language and to present such documents for the Committee's consideration only after they had been examined by one of its members.

The CHAIRMAN was asked to consult LORD SUMNER about the course to be adopted with respect to a memorandum originating from the self-styled "Delegation of the American Republic to the Peace Conference."[1]

A memorandum had been received from the Siamese delegation setting forth damages sustained by Siam.[2] The Brazilian and Uruguayan Delegation had promised to send [?] memoranda shortly.

The Secretaries are to address a letter to the delegations of Honduras and Nicaragua, to [*two?*] powers which had not yet nominated delegates to the Peace Conference.

The meeting adjourned at noon.

DOCUMENT 496

First Subcommittee: Minutes of the Third (and Final) Meeting of the Special Committee (Powers Not Represented on the Commission), April 11, 1919, 3:30 P. M.

[TPG, II, 299-301. These minutes are part of Inclosure "O" to Document 497.]

The special committee met at 3:30 P. M. April 11, 1919, at the Ministry of Finance. MR. DUDLEY WARD (*British Empire*) and

---

[1] This should be "Armenian Republic." See Document 511.
[2] See Document 506.

M. LAURE (*France*) were present in the place of COL. PEEL and M. JOUASSET, respectively, who were unavoidably absent.

Present: GENERAL MCKINSTRY (*United States*), MR. DUDLEY WARD (*British Empire*) and M. P. LAURE (*France*).

MR. DUDLEY WARD stated that information regarding damages done in Lithuania would be received by him shortly from a British Agent.

M. OLCHOWSKI appeared before the committee and furnished the information given below in regard to damage in that part of Russia lying eastward of the territory covered by the Polish claims. He laid a map before the Committee, upon which the boundaries of Poland as advocated by his Government were outlined, and explained that the figures which he had already submitted to the Commission on Reparation covered the whole of this area.[1]

He then indicated a strip of territory to the east of the proposed boundary of Poland which included a considerable part of the Ukraine, and which had been invaded by the Germans. In this area the Poles constitute a very considerable element in the population and M. OLCHOWSKI could give figures relative to damage. He explained that in the Ukraine the Germans had been very solicitous of maintaining good relations with the people and had done little damage, but that to the north of the Ukraine the invaded area lying east of the proposed Polish boundary had been badly treated, and cattle, grain and farm equipment had been carried off on a large scale.

Area of invaded district east of the proposed Polish boundary, excluding the Ukraine, square kilometers 40,000. Arable land—hectares—1,300,000.

Reckoning 141 francs worth of cattle per hectare (pre-war value; coefficient 2½. Present value 354 francs [283.2 marks] per hectare), and estimating that 30% of the cattle in the whole region had disappeared, the losses in cattle equal	137,000,000 f.	[.1096 milliard marks]
Reckoning agricultural machinery at 50 francs per hectare and estimating the destruction at 10%, the losses equal	6,500,000 f.	[.0052 milliard marks]
Crops taken or destroyed	40,000,000 f.	[.0320 milliard marks]
Dispossession of farm rents	20,000,000 f.	[.0160 milliard marks]
Total	203,500,000 f.	[.1628 milliard marks]

The estimates of damage were made in roubles and converted to francs on the pre-war rate of exchange of 2.68 francs to a rouble.

[1] See Document 508.

The CHAIRMAN read a draft of the report to be submitted to the first Sub-Committee (Valuation of Damages).[2]

The Committee adjourned sine die.

DOCUMENT 497

First Subcommittee: Report of the Special Committee (Powers Not Represented on the Commission), April 14, 1919

[TPG, II, 104a-17. The title page of this document (p. 104) reads: "Report to Lord Sumner, President [of] First Sub-Committee (Valuation of Damage) of Special Committee Appointed to Report Information Relative to Amount and Character of Reparation Claimed by or Due to Governments and Peoples Not Represented on the Commission on Reparation of Damage."]

The First Sub-Committee of the Commission on Reparation of Damage (Valuation of Damage), at its Session of March 7th, 1919 (Procès-Verbal No. 9),[1] appointed a special Committee "to secure and report to the Sub-Committee information relative to the amount and character of such reparation as may be claimed by or due to the Governments and peoples not represented on the Commission on Reparation of Damage."

This special Committee was constituted as follows:

MEMBERS: GENERAL MCKINSTRY (*United States)*

COLONEL PEEL (*British Empire)*

M. JOUASSET (*France)*

SECRETARIES: MR. H. JAMES (*United States)*

M. P. LAURE (*France)*

The Committee met on the 8th. and 11th. of March 1919[2] and drew up the following circular letter:

"I have the honor to inform you that the Commission on Reparation of Damage, of the Preliminary Peace Conference, has charged a special Committee with the gathering together of claims which may be made against the enemy Powers.

"This Committee will be much indebted to you if you will address to it a written memorandum of the claims, classified by categories, which your Nation may make against the enemy. It will be glad, moreover, to receive information concerning the amount of these claims and the methods followed in evaluating the damages. In case it should not be possible to present at this time, exact or even approximate figures for all of the categories, it will be interesting to indicate at least a minimum figure which would certainly be reached by your evaluations.

"As the special Committee will have a meeting Tuesday morning March 11th, it would be opportune if the papers referred to above could be at its disposition at that time.

[2] The TPG contains only the Final Report (see Document 497). Probably what was read at this meeting was submitted without significant alteration.

[1] See Document 475.

[2] See Documents 494 and 495.

"I may add that in case your Delegation should consider it desirable to present verbal explanations on the subject of these documents, the Committee is disposed to hear a representative of your Nation at a date which will be fixed later."

This letter was sent to the delegations of the following Powers: BOLIVIA, BRAZIL, CUBA, ECUADOR, GUATEMALA, HAITI, HEDJAZ, HONDURAS, LIBERIA, NICARAGUA, PANAMA, PERU, SIAM, URUGUAY.

The Committee took note of the fact that CHINA had already presented a memorandum. (Inclosure "A")[3]

M. JOUASSET (*France*) was also requested to obtain the information relative to Russian damage in the possession of M. KLOTZ, Minister of Finance, and, unofficially, any information on the same subject obtainable from other sources.

In response to the above letter, data as to damage have been furnished by the delegations of BOLIVIA, BRAZIL, GUATEMALA, HAITI, HEDJAZ, LIBERIA, PERU, and SIAM (Inclosures "B", "C", "D", "E", "F", "G", "H", and "I")[4]

M. ARTHUR RAFFALOVITCH has presented, unofficially, memoranda relating to the damage suffered by Russia, but containing very little information as to the money value of the damage (Inclosure " J")[5]

M. OLCHOWSKI, Polish Delegate on the Commission on Reparation of Damage, came before the Committee and presented some information regarding the damage suffered in Russia Eastward of the territory covered by the Polish claims (Inclosure "K")[6]

The Republic of Panama has stated that she will refrain from presenting any claim. The Republic of Ecuador has likewise stated that she has no demand for reparation of damage to make against the enemy. (Inclosures "L" and "M")[7]

Prompt dispatch of memoranda has been promised by the delegations of Honduras, Nicaragua, and Uruguay.

No response has as yet been received from the Cuban delegation.

A memorandum was received from the "Delegation of the Armenian Republic to the Conference of Peace" (Inclosure "N.")[8]

All memoranda received are forwarded with this report.

Also the minutes of the Meetings of the Committee (Inclosure "O")[9]

[3] See Document 498.
[4] Bolivia, see Document 499; Brazil, 500; Guatemala, 501; Haiti, 502; Hejaz, 503; Liberia, 504; Peru, 505; Siam, 506.
[5] See Document 507.
[6] See Document 508.
[7] Panama, see Document 509; Ecuador, 510.
[8] See Document 511.
[9] See Documents 494, 495, and 496.

For the Special Committee:
    [HENRY JAMES][10]
      2nd. Lieutenant U. S. A.
    [P. LAURE][10]   SECRETARIES
      Adjoint à l'Inspection
      Générale des Finances

There follows a summary statement of the amounts for reparation claimed, with notes by the Committee:—

(The roman numerals on the right of the page refer to the attached general table of claims in which an attempt is made to divide the claims into categories)

ARMENIA

	Francs	
I. *Turkish Armenia*		
a) Losses suffered by the country population.............	4,601,610,000	I
b) Damage suffered by urban population and their needs for reconstruction (merchants, manufacturers and artisans)...........	3,235,550,000	I
c) General damage..................................	325,000,000	I
	840,000,000	II
	5,596,350,000	III
II. *Republic of Armenia and the provinces of Caucasus inhabited by Armenians*		
a) Localities absolutely devastated and destroyed, whose population has been driven out...................	1,831,872,000	I
b) Localities not abandoned by the population..........	1,293,600,000	I
c) General losses...................................	30,000,000	I
	240,000,000	II
	512,000,000	III
	625,000,000	IV
TOTAL.............	19,130,982,000 Fr	

NOTES

The claim includes reparation, at Frs 5,000 each, for 1,100,000 civilians massacred and 35,000 soldiers killed, in addition to claims for injuries, deportations, etc., regardless of whether there are heirs or dependents alive.

The claim also provides for re-establishing, with all their property, as many families as were comprised by the original people.

BOLIVIA

	Pounds Sterling	
a) Property lost as a consequence of the torpedoing of the steamer "Tubantia".............................	12,000	I
b) Death of Mr. Salinas Vega a few months after the torpedoing of S/S "Tubantia".......................	4,000	III
TOTAL..............	16,000	

NOTES

At the normal rate of exchange (1 pound Sterling = 25.22 francs) the claim is equivalent to Frs 403,520.

[10] The names are missing in the original, but the titles are included.

It is claimed that Mr. Vega's illness, which later resulted in his death, was aggravated by the shock experienced in the ship-wreck.

BRAZIL   Pounds Sterling

I. Anchorage rights and repairs	2,355,056-4-2	V
5% interest on anchorage rights (1,839,770-3-0)	245,102-4-0	
II. *War material	409,215-0-11	I
Interest compounded at 5% during 4 years and 11 months (August 1914-July 1919)	110,986-1-0	
III. *Naval material	17,733-6-8	I
Interest compounded at 5%	4,784-17-5	
IV. Coal of the "Strathroy"	3,838-4-0	I
Interest compounded at 5%	1,040-19-7	
V. Personal damages	27,000-0-0	III
VI. Losses of profits	271,230-0-0	II
VII. Personal property	10,000-0-0	I
VIII. Extraordinary expenditures	18,000-0-0	II
IX. Concentration, Food supply for enemy subjects	112,000-0-0	V
X. Clearance and dredging of the Pernambuco harbor	100,000-0-0	I
XI. Repairs of ships chartered to France (Frs 40,000,000)	1,600,000-0-0	V
TOTAL	5,285,986-17-9	

XII. In addition to the foregoing a *special claim* is made for restitution of 125,787,481 marks representing the sale value of coffee deposited to secure a loan (sold by the enemy), plus the loss resulting from the difference in rate of exchange and the difference in rate of interest.

NOTES

The claim contains an item of £1,839,770 for harbor dues on the German vessels interned in the harbor of Pernambuco, from August 1914 to April 1917, at the usual commercial rates; £245,102 for interest on this item, and £100,000 for extra expense of dredging the harbor, occasioned by the German boats. The claim also contains a total of £2,154,465 (part in item I and part in item XI) for repairs to German ships wilfully damaged by their crews before they were chartered to France.

The claim for personal damages is based on £1,000 each for common seamen, firemen, etc., £3,000 each for mechanics; £4,000 for a pilot and £5,000 for a master.

Losses of profits on Brazilian ships are estimated on the basis of 15 per cent per annum of the estimated value of the ships at the time they were lost, from that time until July 1.1919.

CHINA

A. CLAIMS AGAINST GERMANY   Taels

I. Victims of the submarine war (1968 persons)	1,416,960.00	III
II. Claims on account of the Lunghai Railroad	19,745,943.84	I
III. Damage suffered by other establishments of Chinese subjects	7,683,206.59	II

* Paid for before the war and not delivered.

IV. Reimbursement of sums paid for war material not delivered....................................	5,287,410.18	I
V. Cost of maintenance of war prisoners and civilians confined (Germany and Austria-Hungary)..........	1,489,680.00	V
VI. Damages caused in the province of Shantung........		
VII. War expenses....................................		
VIII. Interests..		
IX. Damage to Chinese State Railroads...............	4,406,620.25	I
X. Damage to privately owned Railroads..............	767,044.83	I
XI. Funds deposited in Germany by General Yung Tchang (Marks 446,593.11)......................	146,184.32	I
TOTAL................	40,943,050.01	

B. CLAIMS AGAINST AUSTRIA-HUNGARY   Taels

I. Reimbursement of sums paid for war ships etc., not delivered......................................	13,240,510.00	I
II. Damage suffered by Chinese subjects in Austria-Hungary..	281,505.73	II
III. Funds deposited in Austria by M. Hon Te Wang (16,765.78 Crowns).............................	4,663.65	I
TOTAL................	13,526,679.36	

NOTES

The total claim is 54,469,729 Taels or Frs 204,261,485.

The rates of exchange proposed by China and used in converting to a common standard of money, are the pre-war rates, i.e.

$$1 \text{ Tael} - 3.75 \text{ francs}$$
$$- 3 \text{ shillings}$$
$$- 1.796 \text{ florins (Holland)}$$
$$- 3.055 \text{ marks}$$
$$- 3.595 \text{ crowns}$$
$$1 \text{ Dollar} - 0.72 \text{ tael.}$$

The claim for submarine victims (Item I) is equivalent to Frs 2,700 per person.

ECUADOR

Will make no claim.

GUATEMALA   Dollars

I. Stopping of foreign commerce for the duration of the war......................................	40,000,000	II
II. Stopping of agricultural production.................	20,000,000	II
III. War expenditures (Mobilization of the Army).........	5,400,000	V
IV. Armaments and munitions.........................	4,500,000	V
V. Damages and interest of private property of Guatemalan citizens due to the cessation of business..............	9,000,000	II
TOTAL.................	78,900,000	

NOTE

At the normal rate of exchange (1 dollar = 5.18 francs) the claim is equivalent to Frs 408,702,000.

HAITI   Francs

    I. 6 Haitians disappeared on board of torpedoed steamers   180,000   III
   II. Vice-Consul of Haiti at Antwerp maltreated............   100,000   III
  III. M. Eugene de Pesaq maltreated.....................   100,000   III
  IV. N. A. Mackensie—140 bags of coffee taken............   152,593 ⎫
   V. Interest at 6% during 4 years on Frs 152,593..........   37,000 ⎬ I
                                           ⎭

                              Total.................   569,593

NOTE

    The lives of the Haitians lost are valued at Frs 30,000 each.

HEDJAZ   Francs

    I. Damage suffered by the railway and the telegraph in
       Hedjaz...   25,000.00   I
   II. Damaged Mosques and treasure of the Harem Babaoui
      (Tomb of the Prophet) stolen..................... 150,000.00   I
  III. Damage suffered by immovable objects (houses, roads,
      ports)...   5,000.00   I
  IV. Losses suffered by agriculture (Forests, harvests, etc.).. 200,000.00   I
   V. Destruction of houses belonging to private individuals,
      libraries and theft of rare books (18,000 volumes)......   I
  VI. Care of wounded and losses suffered by deported families 100,000.00   I
 VII. Miscellaneous expenses (relief, etc.)..................   2,000.00   II

                                Total..................

LIBERIA   Dollars

    I. For the loss of lives of seven Liberian citizens who were
      killed in the submarine bombardment of Monrovia,
      April 10th.1918 ....   70,000.00   III
   II. For the destruction of private property of Liberian
      citizens.......................................   14,000.00   I
  III. For the destruction of Public Property, that is, the Li-
      berian Revenue Schooner "President Howard" and its
      contents....................................... 116,000.00   I
  IV. For the loss of arms, ammunition and clothing for the
      Liberian Frontier Forces, which were on board a German
      ship, and not delivered to the Liberian Government...   45,000.00   I
   V. For the lives of about 300 Liberian citizens who were
      massacred in Duala, Cameroun..................... 2,400,000.00   III
  VI. On account of Liberian Minister in London for expense
      of Liberian subjects, maintenance and repatriation, bill
      for £147.5.11..................................   707.02   II
 VII. For one complete blacksmithing outfit with knock-down
      buildings, forge, tools, etc.......................   4,800.00   I
VIII. For loss of Custom Revenue to the Republic of Liberia 1,326,635.80   II
  IX. W. H. Blaine (goods lost in transit).................   735.10   I

                               Total................. 3,977,877.92

NOTES

    At the normal rate of exchange (1 dollar = 5.18 francs) the claim is equivalent
to Fr. 20,605,408. The lives of seven citizens killed by submarine bombardment

(Item I) are valued at Fr. 51,800 each ($10,000). The lives of 300 citizens massacred in Cameroun are valued at Fr. 41,440 each ($8,000).

PANAMA Claims waived

PERU	Pounds Sterling	
I. Steamship "Lorton" sunk...........................	55,236-8-0	I

NOTE

At the normal rate of exchange (1 pound sterling = 25.22 francs) the claim is equivalent to Frs 1,393,062.

SIAM	Francs	
I. Claims presented by the Royal Government on its own account.................................	10,396,015.82	I
	675,000.	V
II. Claims presented by the Royal Government on individual account.............................	1,272,952.50	I
	114,000.00	III
III. Military and administrative claims..............	14,000,000.00	V
	26,457,968.32	

NOTE

The lives of three civilians killed are valued at Frs 38,000 each. The remainder of the claims under items I and II are substantially all for securities, bank deposits and interest, and materials requisitioned.

CLAIMS PRESENTED BY NATIONS NOT REPRESENTED ON REPARATION COMMISSION

April 14, 1919

[Figures in brackets show milliards of marks, converted at ratio of 5:4.]

COUNTRY	I. Damage to physical property, requisitions, fines, taxes, etc.	II. Losses of Revenue, Support of civilians, repatriation of refugees etc.	III. Compensation for Civilian Injuries and Deaths.	IV. Compensation for Military Injuries and Deaths.	V. Other War Costs	VI. Total Claim
	Francs	*Francs*	*Francs*	*Francs*	*Francs*	*Francs*
Armenia	11,317,632,000	1,080,000,000	6,108,350,000	625,000,000	—	19,130,982,000 [15.304 786]
Bolivia	302,640	—	100,880	—	—	403,520 [.000 323]
Brazil*	16,584,633	7,294,381	680,940	—	108,752,635	133,312,589* [.106 650]
China†	163,493,913	29,867,672	5,313,600	—	5,586,300	204,261,485† [.163 417]
Cuba						
Ecuador						No claim
Guatemala§	—	357,420,000	—	—	51,282,000	408,702,000§ [.326 962]
Haiti	189,593	—	380,000	—	—	569,593 [.000 456]
Hedjaz‡	480,000‡	2,000	—	—	—	482,000‡ [.000 386]
Honduras						
Liberia§	935,172	6,875,636	12,794,600	—	—	20,605,408§ [.016 484]
Nicaragua						
Panama						Claims waived
Peru‖	1,393,062	—	—	—	—	1,393,062‖ [.001 114]
Russia						
Siam	11,668,968¶	—	114,000	—	14,675,000	26,457,968¶ [.021 166]
Uruguay						
TOTAL						[15.941 md. mks.]

* Claim made in Pounds Sterling; converted to Francs on basis of 1 Pound—25.22 francs. Brazil also claims the restitution of 125,787,481 marks representing the sale price of coffee deposited to secure a loan (sold by the enemy) plus the loss resulting from difference in rate of exchange and difference in rate of interest.

† Claim made in Taels; converted to Francs on basis of 1 Tael—3.75 Francs. No claims were made by China for damages in the Province of Shantung, for expenses of war or for interest.

‡ Claim noted as not yet complete.

§ Claim made in Dollars; converted to Francs on basis of 1 Dollar—5.18 francs.

‖ Claim made in Pounds Sterling; converted to Francs on basis of 1 Pound—25.22 francs.

¶ Includes 95,870 francs of taxes not yet due.

DOCUMENT 498

Chinese Memoranda on Claims for Reparation, about March 5, 1919, and Later]

[TPG, II, 118-38. Inclosure "A" to Document 497.]

*[The date of the first memorandum is derived from a reference to it in the second. The second (*TRANSLATION BUREAU—695*) is dated April 11. The claims of both are summarized in Document 497.]*

DOCUMENT 499

Bolivian Memorandum on Claims for Reparation, with Supplementary Letter, March 25 and March 30, 1919

[TPG, II, 139-41. Inclosure "B" to Document 497.]

[The memorandum is a translation. The supplementary letter, dated March 30, is headed. TRANSLATION BUREAU—*No. 639. The claims of both these documents are summarized in Document 497.]*

DOCUMENT 500

Brazilian Memoranda on Claims for Reparation, March 22 1919, and Later

[TPG, II, 142-76. Inclosure "C" to Document 497.]

*[The first memorandum (*TRANSLATION BUREAU—*497) is covered by a letter dated March 22. The second is dated March 31. The third (639) is undated. The fourth (*TRANSLATION BUREAU—*729) is also undated. The claims of all these are summarized in Document 497.]*

DOCUMENT 501

Guatemalan Memorandum on Claims for Reparation, March 27, 1919

[TPG, II, 177-78. Inclosure "D" to Document 497.]

[The memorandum is headed, TRANSLATION BUREAU—*639. Its claims are summarized in Document 497.]*

DOCUMENT 502

Haitian Memorandum on Claims for Reparation, with Covering Letter and with Annexes, March 19, 1919

[TPG, II, 179-208. Inclosure "E" to Document 497.]

[These documents are all headed, TRANSLATION BUREAU—*635. Their claims are summarized in Document 497.]*

DOCUMENT 503

Hejaz Memorandum on Claims for Reparation, with Covering Letter, March 11, 1919

[TPG, II, 209-10. Inclosure "F" to Document 497.]

[The memorandum is undated; the letter is dated March 11. The claims of the memorandum are summarized in Document 497.]

DOCUMENT 504

Liberian Memorandum on Claims for Reparation, with Covering Letter and with Annexes, March 10, 1919

[TPG, II, 211-35. Inclosure "G" to Document 497.]

[The memorandum is dated March 7; the letter, March 10. These claims are summarized in Document 497.]

DOCUMENT 505

Peruvian Letter on Claims for Reparation, March 22, 1919

[TPG, II, 236. Inclosure "H" to Document 497.]

[The letter is headed, TRANSLATION BUREAU—639. Its claims are summarized in Document 497.]

DOCUMENT 506

Siamese Memoranda on Claims for Reparation, Perhaps March 27, 1919

[TPG, II, 237-44. Inclosure "I" to Document 497.]

[One of the memoranda is dated March 27; the others are undated. Their claims are summarized in Document 497.]

DOCUMENT 507

Memoranda on Damages Suffered by Russia, Perhaps March 7, 1919, and Later

[TPG, II, 245-78. Inclosure "J" to Document 497.]

[Some of the sheets are headed, TRANSLATION BUREAU—634. An elaborate description of the damage suffered by Russia, without figures, however, except for war expenses. A map is annexed.

DOCUMENT 508

Statement by Olszowski in Regard to Damage in Russia East-ward of the Territory Covered by the Polish Claim, April 11, 1919

[TPG, II, 279-80. Inclosure "K" to Document 497.]

[Summarized in Document 497.]

DOCUMENT 509

Letter from Delegation of Panama Declining to Claim for Reparation, with Telegram from Polk, March 11, 1919

[TPG, II, 281-83. Inclosure "L" to Document 497.]

[Panama declines to claim on account of great losses suffered by France and by Belgium. Telegram to American Mission, March 11, reports same fact from Washington.]

DOCUMENT 510

Letter from Delegation of Ecuador Declining to Claim for Reparation, March 28, 1919

[TPG, II, 284. Inclosure "M" to Document 497.]

[Letter is headed, TRANSLATION BUREAU—633. Ecuador will not claim.]

DOCUMENT 511

Armenian Memorandum on Claims for Reparation, with Letter, before March 11, 1919

[TPG, II, 285-94. Inclosure "N" to Document 497.]

[Date derived from fact that this memorandum was mentioned in minutes of March 11 (see Document 495) as having been received. Claims summarized in Document 497. Accompanying letter from James to McKinstry, dated March 18, states that James' files have nothing on damages done in Armenia.]

THE MINUTES OF THE SECOND SUBCOMMITTEE (FINANCIAL CAPACITY OF THE ENEMY STATES —THEIR MEANS OF PAYMENT AND REPARATION)

DOCUMENT 512

Second Subcommittee: Minutes of the First Meeting, February 15, 1919, 3 P. M.

[EOM, Second Subcommittee, p. 5. French condensed minutes, PV, CRD, p. 707. The minutes of the thirty-two meetings of the Second Subcommittee are bound into one book. In addition to the minutes, this book also contains the following:

Cover. "PRELIMINARY PEACE CONFERENCE, COMMISSION ON THE REPARATION OF DAMAGE, SECOND SUB-COMMITTEE, FINANCIAL CAPACITY OF THE ENEMY STATES, THEIR MEANS OF PAYMENT AND REPARATION, MINUTES. MEETINGS: 1st—15 February . . . 32nd—19 [*18*] APRIL. PARIS, 1919."

Title Page. Same as Cover, except that "MINUTES" is omitted.

Page 3.   "SECOND SUB-COMMITTEE
"FINANCIAL CAPACITY OF THE ENEMY STATES—THEIR MEANS OF PAYMENT AND REPARATION.

"The Commission on Reparation of Damage voted on 4 February, 1919 (see minutes of its second meeting) to appoint Sub-Committees, including 'Sub-Committee No. 2—Study of financial capacity of the enemy States and of their means of payment and reparation.'

"It was decided (see Annex to the Minutes) that the Delegations of the United States of America, Great Britain, France, Italy and Japan should each have one representative on the Second Sub-Committee and that the Delegations of the other Powers should agree among themselves to nominate from among their members their representatives to the number of three.

"The following were appointed to the Committee thus created (meeting of 10 February, 1919: Annex):

"United States of America.................................Mr. Davis.
"British Empire.......................................Lord Cunliffe.
"France..Mr. Loucheur.
"Italy...Mr. Salandra.
"Japan...Mr. Tatsumi.
"Roumania...Mr. Danielopol.
"Serbia..Mr. Stoyanowitch.
"Poland..Mr. Chamiec."

Last Two Pages. "TABLE OF CONTENTS. . ."]

The Second Sub-Committee of the Commission on Reparation of Damage (Financial Capacity of the Enemy States—Their Means of Payment and Reparation) met on Saturday, 15 February, 1919, at 3 P. M., at the Ministry of Finance.

Present: MR. LAMONT (*U. S. A.*); LORD CUNLIFFE (*British Empire*); MR. LOUCHEUR (*France*); MR. D'AMELIO (*Italy*); MR. TATSUMI (*Japan*); MR. MARKOWSKI (*Poland*); MR. DANIELOPOL (*Roumania*); MR. STOYANOWITCH (*Serbia*).

Election of Officers

LORD CUNLIFFE (*British Empire*) was elected Chairman, on the proposal of MR. LOUCHEUR (*France*).

MR. LOUCHEUR (*France*) was elected Vice-Chairman on the proposal of MR. LAMONT (*U. S. A.*).

LORD CUNLIFFE took the Chair and thanked the Committee.

Tabulations to be Prepared

After an exchange of views to which the CHAIRMAN, and Messrs. LOUCHEUR (*France*), D'AMELIO (*Italy*) and DANIELOPOL(*Roumania*) contributed, it was decided that two tabulations should be prepared. The first was to show German money, and also claims, securities and receivables in foreign countries owned by Germany and other enemy States. The second was to give information about raw materials of which each of the Allied States had most need and which the enemy might be required to deliver in part payment.

After determining that even effects amenable to the jurisdiction of the enemy countries but situated in the territory of the Allied and Associated countries should contribute to the reparation of damage, it was decided that at the next meeting each Delegation should hand in a list of the different ways in which it considered that payment might be exacted.

Minutes to be Brief

It was agreed that the minutes should be brief summaries of the important features of the discussion. The Secretariat of the Commission appointed MR. FOBERTI as Secretary of the Second Sub-Committee.

The next meeting was fixed for Monday, 17 March,[1] 1919, at 5 P. M.

The meeting adjourned at 4 P. M.

CUNLIFFE,
Chairman.

F. FOBERTI,
   Secretary.

---

[1] Error for "February."

DOCUMENT 513

Second Subcommittee: Minutes of the Second Meeting, February 17, 1919, 5:15 P. M.

[EOM, Second Subcommittee, pp. 6-7. No French minutes in PV.]

The Second Sub-Committee of the Commission on Reparation of Damage (Financial Capacity of the Enemy States—Their Means of Payment and Reparation) met on Monday, 17 February, 1919, at 5.15 P. M., at the Ministry of Finance, LORD CUNLIFFE in the Chair.

Present: MR. LAMONT (*U. S. A.*); LORD CUNLIFFE (*British Empire*); MR. LOUCHEUR (*France*); MR. D'AMELIO (*Italy*); MR. TATSUMI (*Japan*); MR. CHAMIEC (*Poland*); MR. DANIELOPOL (*Roumania*); MR. STOYANOWITCH (*Serbia*).

Germany's Wealth

The CHAIRMAN circulated a pamphlet published in 1913 by the Dresdner Bank, on the Wealth of Germany. The figures should not be regarded as evidence of the present wealth, but only as proof of the increasing wealth of Germany in the years before the war.

MR. DANIELOPOL (*Roumania*) said that the Committee must consider, first, what wealth it must estimate, and, secondly, what methods of estimation should be adopted.

MR. LAMONT (*U. S. A.*) suggested that, as it would take time for the Delegations to procure from their countries the information necessary to answer the questions that had been raised, each Delegation should in the meanwhile supply the Commission with a statement of its own views of how much Germany could pay, with suggestions as to the method of payment.

Enemy Gold

The CHAIRMAN proposed to pass to the consideration of questions where the Committee was in possession of exact figures—gold and silver. He believed that Germany has:—

Gold, £120,000,000 [2.4 milliard marks].
Silver, £20,000,000 [0.4 milliard marks].
Gold in jewelry and objets d'art (negligible).

MR. LOUCHEUR (*France*) observed that, in addition to the gold officially acknowledged, there was certainly a large reserve of hoarded gold in the country; and after discussion, in which the CHAIRMAN and MR. CHAMIEC (*Poland*) took part, MR. LOUCHEUR suggested that the Allies should demand the total gold officially acknowledged and leave to Germany the hoarded gold as working capital. It was for Germany to take the measures necessary to force this hoarded gold into circulation.

The question: What is the gold reserve of each of the other enemy States? was then considered.

MR. DANIELOPOL (*Roumania*) claimed that a deduction should be made on the score of the gold standing to the credit of Roumania in Germany. Perhaps this gold appeared in the official figures of German gold.

MR. LOUCHEUR (*France*) said that he had the same reserves to make in respect to the gold stolen from Northern France, as also in Belgium. In the case of that gold the question was simply one of restitution.

Joint Liability

The CHAIRMAN suggested that the enemy States regarded as a whole should be asked to produce a sum, leaving it to them to apportion the burden among themselves.

MR. CHAMIEC (*Poland*) objected on the ground that Germany would attempt to lay the burden on the new States created out of the former Austrian Empire.

MR. DANIELOPOL (*Roumania*) agreed that there would be danger in leaving it open to Germany to determine the share that the other States must contribute.

The CHAIRMAN said that this question, being one for the Plenary Commission, was not within the competence of the Committee.

Gold to be Demanded

The CHAIRMAN put the following motion and it was resolved, that approximately £160,000,000 [3.2 milliard marks] in gold (apart from restitution) and £20,000,000 [0.4 milliard marks] worth of silver should be demanded from the enemy States.

MR. LAMONT (*U. S. A.*) proposed that the CHAIRMAN and MR. LOUCHEUR (*France*) be authorized to combine in a formula the questions contained in the different lists prepared by the Delegates. The CHAIRMAN and MR. LOUCHEUR agreed to do so.

Other Forms of Payment

The CHAIRMAN then turned to the question of means of payment other than gold and silver; for example, coal, potash, timber and dye-stuffs. He asked the members of the Committee to study these questions with a view to future discussion.

The next meeting was fixed for Tuesday, 18 February, at 4 P. M.
The meeting adjourned at 7 P. M.

CUNLIFFE,
Chairman.

F. FOBERTI,
Secretary.

DOCUMENT 514

Second Subcommittee: Minutes of the Third Meeting, February 18, 1919, 4 P. M.

[EOM, Second Subcommittee, pp. 8-10. French stenographic minutes, PV, CRD, pp. 708-23.]

The Second Sub-Committee of the Commission on Reparation of Damage (Financial Capacity of the Enemy States—Their Means of Payment and Reparation) met on Tuesday, 18 February, 1919, at 4 P. M., at the Ministry of Finance, LORD CUNLIFFE in the Chair.

Present: MR. LAMONT (*U. S. A.*); LORD CUNLIFFE (*British Empire*); MR. LOUCHEUR (*France*); MR. D'AMELIO (*Italy*); MR. TATSUMI (*Japan*); MR. CHAMIEC (*Poland*); MR. DANIELOPOL (*Roumania*); MR. STOYANOWITCH (*Serbia*).

COLONEL THÉRY and MR. CHEVALIER (*France*), and Messrs. DESPRET (*Belgium*), OSUSKI (*Czecho-Slovak Republic*) and MYLONAS (*Greece*) also attended.

The CHAIRMAN proposed the adoption of the minutes of the 1st meeting. The minutes were approved.

German Coal

The CHAIRMAN thereupon called upon MR. LOUCHEUR (*France*) to speak on the subject of the deliveries of coal to be demanded from Germany.

MR. LOUCHEUR considered such deliveries to be one of the principal means of payment.

On the one hand, Germany was in a position to meet the coal requirements of France and Italy to a large extent.

On the other hand, by exporting coal to neutral countries, Germany could obtain valuable supplies of foreign bills which she could hand over to the Allies.

The annual coal and lignite output of Germany before the war was about 280,000,000 tons, and her annual export 40,000,000 tons. Her home consumption being reduced by the falling off in her iron-ore output and metal industry, an export of 60,000,000 tons might be counted upon and, if necessary, demanded.

England would not have any reason to fear re-exportation of German coal from France or Italy; it was quite understood that former commercial relations were to be in no wise disturbed by the German deliveries.

Moreover, the extent to which France could absorb coal supplies was apparent from a study of her requirements.

France found herself deprived through the war of the output of the coal fields of the Nord and of part of that of the coal fields of the Pas-de-Calais. This had amounted to 20,000,000 tons before the war and, at the rate of progress attained during the last few years, should have reached 22,000,000 tons at the present time.

Amount Required by France

The demands made by France were as follows:—

(1) The annual delivery of a quantity equal to the lost output, by way of reparation—this quantity to be fixed at 22,000,000 tons at the beginning and to decrease year by year as and when the devastated mines resumed work. Germany to be credited with the value of such supplies calculated at cost price.

(2) In order to meet the prospective development of French industry, a supplementary annual delivery at market price, amounting in the first instance to 8,000,000 tons, to be increased in proportion to the decrease in the compensatory deliveries, so as to maintain the total quantity supplied at a constant figure of 30,000,000 tons annually.

Reverting to the idea of imposing an annual export of 60,-000,000 tons of coal on Germany, MR. LOUCHEUR pointed out that, at the probable price of 35 francs per ton, such export would represent an annual payment of 2,100,000,000 francs, and that the operation might easily be extended over a series of years, until the actual value of the capitalized annual payments would attain about forty milliards.

Silesian Coal Fields

MR. CHAMIEC (*Poland*) remarked that the figure mentioned by MR. LOUCHEUR for the German output (280,000,000 tons) would have to be reduced by 37,000,000 tons after the cession of Upper and Lower Silesia to Poland.

MR. DANIELOPOL (*Roumania*) quoted a German report to the International Congress at Stockholm (1913), according to which the total amount of Germany's coal deposits might be estimated at 437 milliard tons.

Reservations by Italy

MR. D'AMELIO (*Italy*) reserved the right to present Italy's coal requirements at a later date, and to make suggestions about means of transportation.

and Roumania

MR. DANIELOPOL (*Roumania*) also wished to defer the announcement of Roumania's requirements.

MR. LOUCHEUR (*France*) was anxious that the Delegates should give particulars of coal imported into their countries before the war, for it appeared to him important that the influx of German coal should not disturb existing commercial conditions.

None Required by Poland

MR. CHAMIEC (*Poland*) stated that, in view of the anticipated cession of Silesia to Poland, he did not think the question of the importation of coal would arise in the case of the latter.

Belgium

MR. DESPRET (*Belgium*) did not anticipate any necessity for the import of coal into Belgium, unless it be coal of certain special kinds, such, for example, as anthracite for gas.[1]

Limit of Requirement

The CHAIRMAN summed up the discussion and added that, in his opinion, MR. LOUCHEUR'S suggestion of exacting from Germany an export of coal exceeding the needs of the Allies would be beyond the powers of the Second Sub-Committee.

MR. LOUCHEUR (*France*) did not agree with this view; in his opinion Germany would only have to refuse to export in order to deprive herself systematically of the means of meeting her obligations; it was for the Allies to compel her to export such commodities as would ensure her these means.

As regards the coal requirements of the Allied countries, data were still lacking with respect to certain of those countries.

MR. LAMONT (*U. S. A.*) proposed deferring further discussion until a later meeting.

---

[1] In the French minutes, this paragraph reads:

"M. DESPRET, *Délégué de la Belgique*. Nous n'avons pas besoin d'importer du charbon, si ce n'est une certaine quantité de charbon à gaz." PV, CRD, p. 713.

At the tenth meeting of March 3, Despret had the following correction entered in the record:

"Il est dit au procès-verbal [de la troisième séance] que la Belgique échangerait de l'anthracite contre du charbon à gaz. Ce n'est pas exactement la pensée de M. Despret, qui a voulu dire que la Belgique pourrait prendre une certaine quantité de charbon à gaz." PV, CRD, p. 759.

The CHAIRMAN requested the Delegates to supply definite details as to the payments in cash or in kind which might be effected without delay. This would be only an insignificant proportion of the total amount acknowledged to be exactable. As to the balance, it would be necessary to draft a scheme of deferred payments.

Timber

He proposed for the present to turn to the question of the supply of timber by Germany. It was necessary to know the quantities of timber available in the enemy countries, the quantities that they could export and, finally, the needs of each of the Allied countries.

Requirements of France

MR. LOUCHEUR (*France*) estimated the value of the annual supply of timber which would be required by France at 100,000,000 francs.

and Greece

MR. MYLONAS (*Greece*) estimated the annual requirements of Greece at 20,000,000 francs.

Procedure

At the close of the meeting a discussion was opened on the question of the procedure to be adopted for the work of the Sub-Committee.

Messrs. LAMONT (*U. S. A.*) and STOYANOWITCH (*Serbia*) laid stress on the fact that it would be extremely useful for each Delegation to present a Memorandum on the capacity and means of payment of the enemy States.

The CHAIRMAN considered that this proposal supported his own repeated suggestions and wished to emphasize *the desire of the Sub-Committee to receive as much information as possible in writing from all the Delegates.*

Advance Payments

MR. STOYANOWITCH (*Serbia*) raised the question of advance payments for the benefit of devastated regions not in a position to await final settlements.

The CHAIRMAN thought that this question did not fall within the province of the Second Sub-Committee.

Procedure

COLONEL THÉRY and MR. CHEVALIER (*France*) reverting to the question of procedure, pointed out that the experts and technical advisers would be able to collect all the necessary documentation regarding each point if they were to receive due notice of the agenda.

The CHAIRMAN approved this suggestion and proposed that the question of the supply of potash by Germany should be dealt with at the next meeting.

The next meeting was fixed for Wednesday, 19 February, at 3.30 P. M.

The meeting adjourned at 6.30 P. M.[2]

CUNLIFFE,

F. FOBERTI, *Chairman.*
    Secretary.

DOCUMENT 515

Second Subcommittee: Minutes of the Fourth Meeting (Including Annexes I-IV), February 19, 1919, 3:30 P. M.

[EOM, Second Subcommittee, pp. 11-22. No French minutes in PV.]

The Second Sub-Committee of the Commission on Reparation of Damage (Financial Capacity of the Enemy States—Their Means of Payment and Reparation) met on Wednesday, 19 February, 1919, at 3.30 P. M., at the Ministry of Finance, LORD CUNLIFFE in the Chair.

Present: MR. LAMONT (*U. S. A.*); LORD CUNLIFFE (*British Empire*); MR. LOUCHEUR (*France*); MR. D'AMELIO (*Italy*); MR. TATSUMI (*Japan*); MR. MARKOWSKI (*Poland*); MR. DANIELOPOL (*Roumania*); MR. YANKOWITCH (*Serbia*).

MR. DESPRET (*Belgium*), COLONEL THÉRY (*France*) and MR. OSUSKI (*Czecho-Slovak Republic*) also attended.

The minutes of the 2d meeting were approved, subject to a modification suggested by MR. TATSUMI.

The CHAIRMAN stated that he had received Memoranda from Messrs. D'AMELIO (*Italy*), DANIELOPOL (*Roumania*) and STOYANOWITCH (*Serbia*).

Coal

The CHAIRMAN then returned to the question of coal, and asked MR. LOUCHEUR whether he was right in understanding that MR. LOUCHEUR suggested that Germany should be compelled to supply coal to France at the fixed price of 35 francs a ton over a period of 99 years.

---

[2] According to the French minutes, at 7 P. M.

He was of the opinion that it was impossible to fix the price for so many years.

Amount

MR. LOUCHEUR (*France*), without insisting on 99 years, maintained that Germany must be compelled to export coal for a great number of years in view of the great size of the debt to be extinguished and the impossibility of finding the means of extinguishing it except with the help of exports. Besides, an export of 60,000,-000 tons did not seem over-large in view of Germany's excessive export of coal before the war (40,000,000 tons per annum) and the coal consumption of Alsace-Lorraine (10,000,000 tons per annum).

The constant figure of 30,000,000 tons for annual delivery to France had been arrived at after a study of the curve of French consumption during the course of the years preceding the war. The increase in the production consequent upon the coal mines being restored to working condition would be exactly compensated by the increasing needs of French industry soon to develop.

Price

As to the figure of 35 francs a ton, that was given for purposes of discussion only. Evidently there could be no question of an unchanging price over a long series of years. Perhaps the best arrangement would be to make the price conform to the fluctuations on the English market.

The CHAIRMAN welcomed the explanation of MR. LOUCHEUR, and asked the Delegates to submit statements of their requirements of coal.

Requirement of Roumania

MR. DANIELOPOL (*Roumania*) stated that Roumania would require
1,500,000 tons per annum, mined coal.
400,000 tons per annum, coke.

Serbia

MR. YANKOWITCH (*Serbia*), speaking for Jugo-Slavia, said that their requirements would be
3,000,000 tons per annum, steinkohl.
150,000 tons per annum, coke.

Belgium

MR. DESPRET (*Belgium*) said he could give no exact figures without consulting expert opinion. It must not be understood that Belgium would not need any.

Czecho-Slovak Republic

MR. OSUSKI (*Czecho-Slovak Republic*) stated the requirements of his country at

5,000,000 tons per annum, coal.

1,000,000 tons per annum, coke.

The CHAIRMAN asked the Committee to take up the question of potash next.

Potash

COLONEL THÉRY (*France*) read a Memorandum attached to these minutes as Annex IV.

A discussion ensued in which COLONEL THÉRY and Messrs. LEFÈVRE (*France*), OSUSKI (*Czecho-Slovak Republic*) and DANIELOPOL (*Roumania*) took part, and the value of the potash as a means of payment was considered.

The CHAIRMAN, summing up, said he concluded from the discussion that we might perhaps expect potash to yield a revenue of about 100,000,000 francs. This conclusion was accepted by the Committee.

The next meeting was fixed for Thursday, 20 February, at 3.30 P. M. The subjects of discussion would be Timber and Dye-Stuffs.

The meeting adjourned at 6 P. M.

CUNLIFFE,
Chairman.

F. FOBERTI,
　Secretary.

ANNEX I[1]

METHODS BY WHICH THE ENEMY MAY BE REQUIRED TO MAKE PAYMENT

(*Presented by the Italian Delegation.*)

1. Cession of enemy State or Crown property or of property belonging to members of houses formerly reigning, whether these properties are in the territory of the Allied and Associated Powers or in the territories claimed from the enemy.

2. Annulment of claims of Enemy States or of their subjects (persons or juridical persons) against the Allied and Associated Powers.

3. Cession of raw material, plant, agricultural machinery, motors, manufactured goods, draft animals, and means of trans-

---

[1] French text, PV, CRD, p. 856.

port by land or air with their accessories, including hangars and hutments.

4. Liquidation of the property of subjects of enemy Powers in the Associated States.

5. Assignment to the Allied and Associated Powers of moneys owing to the enemy States or their subjects in neutral countries.

6. Enjoyment for a period of years of patents belonging to subjects of enemy States in countries of the Entente.

7. Restoration of works and objects of art or of historical interest and documents, removed from the Associated countries.

8. Cession of works and objects of art or of historical interest in compensation especially for those which have been destroyed by the enemy in the Associated countries.

9. Immunity of ceded territories from their share of enemy public debt.

10. Issue by the enemy states of a guaranteed loan (secured, for instance by customs duties, etc.)

[no date]

ANNEX II[2]

CAPACITY FOR REPARATION OF THE ENEMY COUNTRIES AND METHODS BY WHICH THEY MAY BE REQUIRED TO MAKE PAYMENT

(*Presented by the Roumanian Delegation.*)

The aim of our Sub-Committee is to investigate the financial capacity of the enemy countries and their means of payment.

In order to ascertain the wealth of the enemy countries, one must consider the question from a three-fold point of view:

1. Existing wealth of the countries themselves;
2. Existing wealth in the Allied and Associated countries;
3. Existing wealth in neutral countries.

I. Existing Wealth in the Countries Themselves

In the countries themselves one may consider as wealth:

(a) *Gold and Silver.* One must exclude from the quantity of gold possessed by Germany and her Allies the gold belonging to the Allied or Associated countries (States, private persons, etc.), which she must first return; thus, Germany must first return all the gold belonging to the Roumanian National Bank.

Germany and her allies must return the sums (with their interest) due to Allied or Associated countries (States, private persons,

---

[2] French text, PV, CRD, pp. 856-58.

etc.); thus, Germany and Austria-Hungary must return the sums due to the Roumanian National Bank and other institutions as well as to private persons.

(b) *Coal.* From the estimate made, Germany alone possesses 423,386,000,000 tons[3] of coal, of which 409,966,000,000 tons are coal and 13,390,000,000 tons are lignite. (See T. [*sic*] Ellis Barker, "Economic Statesmanship," quoting the report "Coal Resources of the World," which was presented to the International Congress of Geology at Ottawa in 1913.)[4]

(c) *Iron.* From the report "Iron Resources of the World," presented in the International Congress of Stockholm, 1910, quoted by the same author,[5] Germany possessed 1,270,000,000 tons of iron, as well as important reserves.

(d) *Mineral Salts and Particularly Potash Salts.* From various estimates, Germany possesses about 50,000,000,000 tons of Potash Salts. Germany, Austria-Hungary, Turkey and Bulgaria possess without doubt other elements of wealth, such as merchant marine, navy, products of industry, investments in various enterprises, public and private properties, all kinds of properties, cattle, securities, etc.

II. Wealth Existing in Allied or Associated Countries

Each Allied or Associated country has the right to retain as payment for her claims against the enemy countries all the public or private wealth that Germany and her allies, or their subjects, possess under any title, or in any manner in its own territory, such as all movable or immovable property, credits of all kinds, all State bonds, stocks, shares in companies and, in general, all rights of any kind.

III. Wealth Existing in Neutral Countries

What is the manner of ascertaining, appraising, and of levying on the wealth of Germany, her allies and their subjects in neutral countries?

METHOD OF PAYMENT

One may, for the present, consider as methods of payment:

(a) Restitution in kind of the goods carried away and replacing of the damaged goods by means of others in good condition.

(b) Payment with machines, merchandise and crops or any kind of products. The enemy's industries will have to sup-

---

[3] Error for "423,356,000,000 tons."

[4] J. Ellis Barker, *Economic Statesmanship: the Great Industrial and Financial Problems Arising from the War* (London, 1918), p. 335.

[5] *Ibid.*, p. 339.

ply, and manufacture if they have none in stock, all the machines and merchandise requested by each Allied or Associated State.

(c) Payment in cattle;
(d) Payment in raw materials;
(e) Payment in gold or silver coin and precious objects;
(f) Payment through credits possessed by Germany, Austria-Hungary, Turkey and Bulgaria in foreign countries;
(g) Payment in State bonds;
(h) Payment in war material of every kind which has been used or might have been used for war purposes.

For the countries having suffered from enemy occupation a preference must exist in their favor.

Through what process may one assure the immediate payment by Germany, Austria-Hungary, Turkey and Bulgaria of the debt for war damages?

Would it not be advisable to consider an inter-Allied organization, the aim of which would be to follow up the recovery of debts which could be settled at once?

Paris, 18 February, 1919.

ANNEX III[6]

ENEMY'S CAPACITY TO MAKE REPARATION: BULGARIAN RESOURCES

(*Presented by the Serbian Delegation.*)

If we wish to speak of Bulgaria's capacity to pay, with reference to reparation for damage caused in this war, which she, together with the Central Powers and Turkey, has waged against Serbia and her allies, it is first of all necessary to ascertain her economic strength—in other words, her resources. It is only after doing this that we shall be able to fix Bulgaria's capacity for participating in reparation for the damage that she and her allies have caused to their adversaries.

I

RESOURCES

The area of Bulgaria is to-day 111,000 square kilometers, with 5,000,050 inhabitants (46 per square kilometer). It is a country of small farmers; 80% of its inhabitants are farmers and there are 800,000 landowners who farm their land, whose property has increased from 3,970,000 hectares (1897) to 4,600,000 hectares (1908).

---

[6] No French text in PV.

The land may be classified thus:

A.—Private property: 48% of the total area.

B.—State property: 8% of the total area.

C.—Property of communes: 25% of the total area.

N. B. A.—The private property is divisible as follows:

(a) Property of peasants......................4,620,000 hectares
(b) Property of schools....................... 70,000 hectares
(c) Property of monasteries................... 56,000 hectares
(d) Property of churches...................... 28,000 hectares
(e) Property of farmers' banks................ 26,000 hectares

A. RURAL ECONOMY

I. *Agriculture.* The main part of Bulgaria's national wealth is agricultural. Of the entire area there are:

(a) Cultivated fields.........................3,500,000 hectares
(b) Forests.................................2,880,000 hectares

Farming is becoming more and more intensive, as can easily be proved by Bulgarian export statistics as well as by the more and more frequent use of modern implements for farm work. In 1893 there were only 18,710 iron plows in Bulgaria, and in 1910 about 114,245. There were formerly only 12,000 separators and in 1910 74,000. Recently there has been a rapid extension of the area under cultivation and the value of the ground cultivated has increased, in the last dozen years, by 300%.

1. The value of the cultivated land is estimated at 5,300,000,000 francs; the value of the forests at 700,000,000 francs.

2. The revenue from the harvests, that is, the yield of the cultivated land, usually exceeds a billion francs. The value of the products is as follows:

(a) Grains.................................500,000,000 francs
(b) Leguminous products.................... 43,000,000 francs
(c) Tobacco............................... 15,000,000 francs
(d) Forage................................100,000,000 francs
(e) Fruits................................. 3,000,000 francs
(f) Rose essence.......................... 14,000,000 francs
(g) Vineyards, etc......................... 60,000,000 francs

The same thing expressed in tons and kilograms:

(a) Wheat............................. 1,500,000,000 tons.
(b) Corn............................. 800,000,000 tons.
(c) Barley........................... 850,000,000 tons.
(d) Silk worms....................... 1,857,000,000 kilos.
(e) Tobacco.........................35,000,000,000 kilos.
(f) Rose essence..................... 4,500 kilos.

II. *Live stock.* Concerning the live stock, absolutely and relatively, it may be said to be satisfactory; to each square kilometer there were: 17.16 cattle, 4.94 buffaloes, 4.8 swine, 90 sheep and 15 goats.

1. Bulgaria possesses live stock to the following amount:

(a)	Horses	615,000
(b)	Mules and asses	155,000
(c)	Cattle	1,890,000
(d)	Sheep	9,900,000
(e)	Buffaloes	545,000
(f)	Goats	1,670,000
(g)	Swine	550,000

2. This live stock represents a value of 1,149,700,000 francs:

		Millions of Francs
(a)	Horses	184.5
(b)	Mules and asses	9.3
(c)	Cattle	567.0
(d)	Sheep	158.4
(e)	Buffaloes	163.5
(f)	Goats	26.0
(g)	Pigs	41.0
	Total	1,149.7

3. To this figure must be added the value of the poultry:

		Millions of Heads
(a)	Chickens	9,500
(b)	Geese	405
(c)	Turkeys	210
(d)	Ducks	162

Their value amounts to:

		Millions of Francs
(a)	Chickens	11,400
(b)	Geese	1,020
(c)	Turkeys	1,080
(d)	Ducks	260
	Total	13,760

Consequently the live stock and poultry of Bulgaria represent a value of 1,166 millions of francs.

B. INDUSTRY

The principal object of Bulgarian economic policy was to emancipate the country from foreign control. The following were the reasons:

The State has greatly assisted the development of her industry in general. In 1907 Bulgaria had 260 industrial factories and plants, the capital of which amounted to 65 millions of francs. Later conditions improved greatly; the State subsidized first of all the industries which manufactured the raw materials of the country—that is, flour mills, sugar refineries, breweries and the like; and, in the second place, textile industries. The following industrial enterprises were the most important: Sugar factories—one factory which refined one thousand carloads of sugar beets, and two which have been built during the recent war; the tobacco and alcohol industries; the textile industry; the clothing industry,—wearing apparel, hats; tanneries; iron industry,—foundries, spare parts of machinery, safety vaults; stoves; furniture; flour mills (steam); imitation articles.

The *value* of the industrial enterprises in Bulgaria exceeds 150 millions of francs. This capital is invested in the following enterprises:

(a) More than 43 millions of francs in industries connected with foodstuffs, namely:

Millions of Francs

    1. Sugar refineries.
    2. 16 Breweries.
    3. 1,100 Mills....................................57,000
(b) Textile Industry.......................................17,000
(c) 2 Electric Power Plants.............................. 7,500
(d) Ceramic Industries................................. 8,000
(e) 5 Soap Factories................................... 1,000
(f) 24 Leather Mills.................................... 2,700
(g) 23 Large Saw Mills................................. 6,500
(h) 4 Paper Mills (Pasteboard)......................... 1,570
(i) Rope Mills... 5,000
(j) Silk Factories...................................... 2,000
(k) Concrete.. 2,000
(l) Other Plants in the country........................16,000

To this value of the capital placed in the industries of the country must be added that of the capital invested in mining interests. Mining is still relatively undeveloped in Bulgaria, for the country is not very rich in mines. The appended table indicates the movement of the mining products obtained between 1902 and 1910. On the other hand, Bulgaria is very rich in coal. This coal is found partly in the mountainous regions of the Balkans and the Rhodopos, and partly in the plains of the Danube in the neighborhood of Sofia, of the Black Sea and of the Iskra. Nevertheless, the exploitation of coal is not developed. Some anthracite exists in the valley of the Iskra, north of Sofia and also in the neighborhood of Belogradjik. At the present day the following mines of black coal are of greater value; Pernik and Bodov Dol. The wealth of Pernik is estimated by experts at 1.5 billions of tons. Calculating the ton at 10 francs, this value amounts to 15 billions.

In the coal basins it is thought that there are 7 millions of tons of coal. During the war these basins have passed under the ownership of a Bulgaro-German stock company. The revenue from the State mines represents a value of 3.5 millions of francs.

It is estimated that a capital of 35 millions of francs has been invested in various mining enterprises.

C. CREDIT INSTITUTIONS

1. *Private Banks.* The economic progress of Bulgaria has occurred parallel to that of the banks. Before the war Bulgaria had more than 112 private banks; and many new establishments have been founded during the war. The capital of private credit institutions represented a total of 154.5 millions of francs.

2. *State Banks.* There are four large State establishments for credit.

	Francs
(a) The National Bulgarian Bank with a capital of	24,500,000
(b) The Farm Bank (Agricole)	70,000,000
(c) The Central Bulgarian Co-operative Banks	5,000,000
(d) Credit and Savings Institutions	178,000,000

In addition there are Postal Savings Banks which at the end of 1916 included 478 thousand depositors; in 1917, 55,000 new savings-bank books were issued. The total capital amounts to 117 millions of francs.

The total value of the wealth represented by State Credit Establishments, consequently amounts to 549 millions of francs.

N. B. Among the Credit Establishments mentioned in "1" above the following have a foreign capital:

(a) The Balkan Bank—Austrian Capital........6,000,000 Francs.
(b) The "Banque Générale"—Hungarian Capital.5,000,000 Francs.
(c) The Credit Bank—German Capital.........3,000,000 Francs.

D. COMMERCE

It is calculated that about 80,000 persons are engaged in trade in Bulgaria. Assuming that the capital invested in the enterprise of each person amounts on the average of 2,000 francs, we have the result that a capital of 160 millions of francs is invested in Bulgarian trade. The import and export trades of Bulgaria, that is, her annual commercial traffic, represent a value of 369 millions of francs. The annual income from commerce, therefore, exceeds 36 million.

E. TRADES

About 40 thousand persons are engaged in handicrafts; the annual income from these may be estimated at 40 millions of francs.

F. MOVABLE AND IMMOVABLE PROPERTY IN TOWNS AND VILLAGES

In default of exact data, we are compelled, in order to make an estimate of the value of the movable and immovable property, to make use of a comparison with the value of the same property in the towns and villages of Serbia, which amounts to about 2½ billions of francs.

In proportion to the population of Bulgaria and its density, it can be assumed that the value of its movable and immovable property in towns and villages represents a sum of 3½ billions of francs, that is, an average of 700 francs per capita.

G. RAILWAYS, ROADS, NAVIGATION, TELEGRAPHS, POSTS

Bulgaria had a railway system more than 6,500 kilometers in length. Before the war the rolling-stock was as follows:

(a) Locomotives... 212
(b) Coaches.. 335
(c) Cars..2626

Half of the public debt is invested in the railways; their value is estimated at 600 millions of francs. The value of the *Highways and Roads* can be estimated at 350 millions; the value of *Telephones and Telegraphs* is estimated at 30 millions. The capital invested in *Shipping* amounts to 40 millions. Consequently, the entire capital invested in communication facilities amounts to 1,020 millions of francs.

H. OTHER STATE ESTABLISHMENTS

According to the Budget, the revenue of these establishments is estimated at about 20 millions annually. Assuming that this income represents 20% of the capital, we should have a total value of 100 millions.

I. SUMMARY

In an estimate of the wealth of Bulgaria there must also be included 1.6 millions of hectares of uncultivated land. Attributing to it a value of 150 francs per hectare, we arrive at a total value of 240 millions of francs.

To sum up everything that has been set forth above, it is apparent that the total wealth of Bulgaria is valued at 12,935,000,000 francs.

To this sum must be added the value represented by the stretch of 1,500 square kilometers of territory annexed to Bulgaria, in so far as this has not been included in the calculation, that is, 1 billion francs. Its annual income amounts to 200 millions.

Consequently, the total fortune of Bulgaria represents a value of 14 billions of francs.

J. STATE FINANCE

The revenues of the Bulgarian State attained the sum of 251 millions; the expenditures were the same. The revenue was divided as follows:

Millions of Francs

(a) Direct Taxes	54.9
(b) Indirect Taxes	99.7
(c) Means of Communication	42.9
(d) Immovable Property and Capital	18.4
(e) Municipalities and Arrondissements	54.9
(f) Other sources of income	27.3
Total	251.0

Before the Balkan War, the Bulgarian public debt was 640 millions, that is, 140 francs per capita. The Balkan War has increased that debt to 1,113,000,000 francs, that is, 232 francs per capita.

If this sum be deducted from the total wealth of Bulgaria, it follows that *her net wealth before the last war represented a value of 13 billions of francs.*

II

ANNUAL REVENUE

In order to determine Bulgaria's capacity for payment, the annual income which she derives from her wealth must be determined with reference to that wealth.

1. The annual income from cultivated land totals a billion francs.

2. The revenue from uncultivated land, calculating it at 25% of the value (240 millions) of the land per hectare; 60 millions.

3. The annual revenue from live stock is 400 millions,

4. The revenue from the trades, calculating it at a thousand francs per person engaged therein, totals 40 millions.

5. The annual revenue from industry,—major and minor—the capital of which is 180 millions, on a basis of 30% of the capital, amounts to 55 millions. This revenue is really much greater on account of the mines.

6. The revenue from trade, in which a capital of 160 millions is invested, amounts to 40 millions, if estimated at 25% of the capital. This figure is obtained by reckoning the profit of the business men in the commerce of the country, which amounts to 38 millions yearly, as 11%.

7. The revenue of credit establishments, the capital of which amounts to 549 millions, and the annual transactions of which exceed 18 billions, amounts to 140 millions, at 8%.

8. The revenue from forests, which represents a value of 700 millions, and of which the State Forests alone appear in the State balance sheet, at a figure exceeding 660 millions, amounts to 180 millions, at 25% of the capital.

9. The revenue from Immovable and Movable Property in towns and villages, is 280 millions, taken at 8% of the value.

10. The revenue from State Economic Establishments, the value of which is 100 millions, represents 20 millions yearly, according to the Budget.

11. The revenue from new territories, fifteen thousand square kilometers, in so far as it is not already included in the above, is derived from a capital of 1 billion francs and amounts to 200 millions.

12. The revenue from railways, shipping, telephones, telegraphs and roads amounts to 120 millions yearly, at a rate of 12% of the value.

The total revenue from the entire national wealth of the Kingdom of Bulgaria totals 2.5 billions of francs, that is, nearly 20% of the value of that wealth.

Table B, appended hereto, gives a synopsis of the capital and gross revenues of the wealth of Bulgaria.

III

CAPACITY FOR PAYMENT

In view of the preceding, what is the capacity for payment of the Kingdom of Bulgaria? In 1918 her Budget was:

Revenue	480 millions of francs
Expenditures	479 millions of francs

This is the budget which the economic strength of Bulgaria had to support yearly. Among the expenditures were the following:

Expenditures for the Army................104 millions of francs
Expenditures for the Admin-
istration of the occupied
territories............................. 56 millions of francs

After the conclusion of Peace these two items will exist no longer. The expenditures for the Army will be reduced to a minimum. Consequently, the annual outlay will be the difference between 479 and 160 millions, or 319 millions. This outlay represents scarcely 15% of the total gross revenue of the country's national wealth.

If 20% of her gross revenue were imposed, that would mean a levy of 500 millions of francs. In view of the generally satisfactory conditions for the economic development of Bulgaria—her satisfactory situation with regard to international commerce, in view of the industriousness of her economical citizens and their thriftiness, and finally in view of the fact that the prices of products have doubled and that the annual revenue is not 2½ billions but almost twice that sum, Bulgaria will be able to bear a burden of 200 millions of francs in excess of this sum, which remains over and above her annual budget. Assuming that the gross revenue of Bulgaria will not exceed 4 billions yearly, even with the increase in prices, she will easily be able to support, besides the annual Budget, a burden of at least 300 millions of francs, if only 15% of her gross revenue is taken. Indeed, Bulgaria's annual payment might attain the *sum of 500 millions* if account is taken of the fact that Bulgaria, which was not invaded, greatly enriched itself during the war by the spoliation of the Serbian, Greek and Roumanian States.

This increase in the annual revenue of the Bulgarian national economy and the low rate of levy (15%) gives us the right to consider that Bulgaria could, in a large measure, recompense us at once in kind for the damage caused and the objects stolen, without danger that her capacity for future payment be too much weakened pending the time that she pay us during the coming years for the damages inflicted on Serbia, which she will be bound to pay.

Costa Stoyanowitch,
Delegate from Serbia.

Paris, 1 February, 1919.

TABLE A

Year	Copper Tons	Lead Tons	Zinc Tons	Zinc and Copper Tons	Lead and Copper Tons	Manganese Tons
1902	40		150			
1903		118	24	850		
1904	160	1170	848	2750		
1905	12011	379	746	1051	1034	
1906	2248	606	541	5434		
1907	6832	23	88	519		1900
1908	4180	28				30
1909	19040	3547		1495		
1910	18506	3419				
TOTALS	63017	9290	2397	12089	1034	1930

TABLE B

		Capital Millions of Francs	Revenue Millions of Francs
1.	Cultivated Lands	5300	1000
2.	Uncultivated Lands	240	60
3.	Live Stock	1166	400
4.	Trades	20	40
5.	Industries and Plants	180	55
6.	Commerce	160	40
7.	Credit Establishments	549	140
8.	Forests	700	180
9.	Movables and Immovables	3500	280
10.	State Economic Establishments	100	20
11.	New Territories	1000	200
12.	Railways, Roads, Shipping, Telephones and Telegraphs	1020	120
[no date]	TOTAL	13935	2535

ANNEX IV[7]

ENEMY'S CAPACITY TO MAKE REPARATION: GERMAN POTASH

(*Presented by the French Delegation.*)

The deposits of potash salts in Germany are very large. They extend over Saxony, Prussia, Brunswick and Hanover (representing an area of about 1,500 square kilometers, over which more than 200 mining undertakings are worked.

Before the war the whole world drew on Germany for potash, and more particularly on the Strassfurt mines, which were the centre of production; for at that time the yield of the Kaluce mines of Austrian Galicia was almost nil and the Alsatian deposits had not yet been worked.

[7] French text, PV, CRD, pp. 858-60.

This Memorandum will deal exclusively with the mines of Strassfurt, the production of which is officially known.

In 1900 these mines produced barely 3 millions of tons of unrefined salts, but as the demand increased this production increased to:

9,706,000 tons in 1911.
11,070,000 tons in 1912.
and 11,607,000 tons in 1913.

During 1913, which was the last year of normal working, the refineries produced 1,650,000 tons of concentrated salts for consumption, 485,000 tons of chloride of potassium and 111,000 tons of sulphate of potash.

Thanks to the immense deposits at Strassfurt, the output of which is practically only limited by the demand, Germany was able to increase the consumption of potash in industry and agriculture.

As regards industrial consumption, the Germans used potash chiefly to assist export. They had, for instance, a monopoly in the manufacture of cyanide of potassium used by Transvaal, Australian and American gold mines. They also used potash and its by-products in the most varied forms for the pharmaceutical products and dyes which they exported so largely.

Germany used a large part of the salts of potash prepared for agriculture herself, for the use of potash fertilizers had spread rapidly through all States of the Empire.

The rise in production was tremendous, advancing steadily from 273,000 tons in 1908 to 538,000 tons in 1913. All economists attribute the great prosperity attained by German agriculture before the war to this increase.

In 1913 the internal consumption of salts of potash in Austria-Hungary was only about 25,000 tons; it is therefore safe to conclude that of the production of 1,650,000 tons of concentrated salts of potash manufactured by Germany in 1913, hardly a third was used for the agricultural consumption of the two Central Empires and that the remaining two thirds was exported in the form of salts of potash prepared for agriculture or of numerous industrial by-products.

It is naturally impossible to ascertain the quantity of potash used and exported by German industry, but the statistics of the International Institute of Agriculture at Rome make it possible to specify the quantity of salts of potash imported from Germany in 1913 for agricultural use all over the world, excluding the two Central Empires.

The Allied Nations, for their part, took 309,000 tons, distributed as follows:

United States, 232,000 tons; France, 33,000 tons; United Kingdom, 23,000 tons; Belgium, 13,000 tons; Italy, 6,500 tons; Portugal, 1,200 tons.

German commercial statistics in my possession show a total export of chemical products and drugs to the value of 658 million marks in 1913, and of dyes valued at 298 millions, but they do not give details of the specific amount of salts of potash exported. According to figures compiled by the International Institute of Agriculture, this export is said to have been about 500,000 tons in 1913 (worth about 33 million marks, according to prices current that year in Germany).

Taking into account the fact that during that year prices at Strassfurt were Fr. 21.75 for chloride at 60% and Fr. 23.50 for sulphate, it is clear that the monetary value of the unrefined potash which Germany will be able to export in the future will have little effect on her capacity for business abroad, especially as German potash will have to compete in the world's markets with the Alsatian potash deposits, discovered in 1904 and not regularly worked until 1912 (that is, just before the war), and with deposits recently found in Spain (Catalonia) and the United States (California).

[no date]

DOCUMENT 516

Second Subcommittee: Minutes of the Fifth Meeting, February 20, 1919, 3:30 P. M.

[EOM, Second Subcommittee, pp. 23-24. French stenographic minutes, PV, CRD, pp. 724-34.]

The Second Sub-Committee of the Commission on Reparation of Damage (Financial Capacity of the Enemy States—Their Means of Payment and Reparation) met on Thursday, 20 February, 1919, at 3.30 P. M., at the Ministry of Finance, LORD CUNLIFFE in the Chair.

Present: MR. LAMONT (*U. S. A.*); LORD CUNLIFFE (*British Empire*); MR. LOUCHEUR (*France*); MR. D'AMELIO (*Italy*); MR. TATSUMI (*Japan*); MR. MARKOWSKI (*Poland*); MR. DANIELOPOL (*Roumania*); MR. STOYANOWITCH (*Serbia*).

Messrs. DESPRET (*Belgium*), MYLONAS (*Greece*) and LIST (*Czecho-Slovak Republic*) also attended.

Timber

The CHAIRMAN proposed to discuss the question of supplies of sawn and hewn timber, what quantities the enemy countries could export and what were the requirements of each of the Allies.

MR. LOUCHEUR (*France*) said that he had nothing to add to his [day before] yesterday's statement, according to which France required an annual supply of the approximate value of 100,000,000 francs, which he believed would correspond to a quantity of about 800,000 tons.

Requirements of Greece

MR. MYLONAS (*Greece*) estimated the approximate value of the annual requirements of Greece at 20,000,000 francs.

Italy

MR. D'AMELIO (*Italy*) valued the annual quantity required by Italy after the war at 1,500,000 tons.

Roumania

MR. DANIELOPOL (*Roumania*) gave the figure of 3,000,000 cubic metres as the requirements of his country.

Poland

MR. MARKOWSKI (*Poland*) reserved the right to state the requirements of Poland at a later date.

Timber Exports of Enemy Powers

The CHAIRMAN wished to know the approximate total of the export of timber by the enemy Powers.

MR. D'AMELIO (*Italy*) gave the figure of 400,000,000 francs as the value of the timber exports of Austria-Hungary.

The CHAIRMAN read out the following particulars: Annual export of soft timber by the Central Powers is 30,000,000 tons, representing a value of £150,000,000.

He added that the annual production of sawn and hewn timber in Germany was 15,000,000 tons, so that an annual export of about £75,000,000 might be counted on.

MR. LAMONT (*U. S. A.*) asked whether there would be sufficient market in Europe for such a large quantity.

The CHAIRMAN was of opinion that there would be no difficulty in that respect; it was only a question of transport, which, according to the experts, could easily be solved.

After an exchange of views between MR. LOUCHEUR (*France*) and the CHAIRMAN, it was decided to take provisionally as basis of calculation the figure of £75,000,000 as the value of annual export to be anticipated.

Payment in Raw Materials

The CHAIRMAN asked the Delegates to furnish a provisional list of all the raw materials which their countries could take in payment at a fair price.

At this point a discussion took place, in which Messrs. MYLONAS (*Greece*) and DANIELOPOL (*Roumania*) participated, on the question whether manufactured articles, particularly agricultural machinery, should be included in the lists.

It was decided that the lists in question should include only raw materials, but that Delegates might furnish separate lists of all categories of manufactured goods, and any other means of payment they might desire to specify.

Reparation in Kind

MR. DESPRET (*Belgium*) raised the question of the right of invaded countries to receive compensation in kind for stolen machinery.

The CHAIRMAN queried whether the Sub-Committee was competent to decide this point.

MR. LOUCHEUR (*France*) pointed out that the problem was a complicated one, because it concerned not only a means of payment but also the speed with which reconstruction might be effected.

Though he regarded the question as within the competence of the Sub-Committee, he considered this mode of payment might be dangerous to the interests of certain Allies, in so far as it might favor German commercial penetration. With regard to manufactured goods, reparation in kind should only be accepted where it offered exceptional material advantages.

MR. STOYANOWITCH (*Serbia*) again raised the question of advances to the invaded countries.

Dye-stuffs

The CHAIRMAN then proposed that the question of the supply of dye-stuffs should be dealt with.

MR. OSUSKI[1] (*Czecho-Slovak Republic*) stated that the annual value of the dye-stuffs exported by Germany before the war amounted to 170,000,000 marks.

---

[1] List, according to the French minutes.

After a short exchange of views between Messrs. LAMONT (*U. S. A.*) and LOUCHEUR (*France*) and the CHAIRMAN, the general opinion was expressed that dye-stuffs might furnish a means of payment of relatively small monetary value, but of considerable economic importance.

The CHAIRMAN proposed that the following question should be dealt with at the next meeting:

"How much can the enemy countries pay within the twelve months following the signature of peace?"

He further announced that he would lay before the Sub-Committee a general scheme relating to the means and forms of deferred payment extending over a long period of years.

MR. DANIELOPOL (*Roumania*) requested the CHAIRMAN to place upon the agenda the question as to what amount of machinery Germany could supply in payment.

The CHAIRMAN asked MR. DANIELOPOL to submit a Memorandum on the subject.

The next meeting was fixed for Friday, 21 February, at 10.30 A. M.

The meeting adjourned at 6 P. M.

CUNLIFFE,
Chairman.

F. FOBERTI,
Secretary.

DOCUMENT 517

Second Subcommittee: Minutes of the Sixth Meeting, February 21, 1919, 10:30 A. M.

[EOM, Second Subcommittee, pp. 25-27. French stenographic minutes, PV, CRD, pp. 735-42.]

The Second Sub-Committee of the Commission on Reparation of Damage (Financial Capacity of the Enemy States—Their Means of Payment and Reparation) met on Friday, 21 February, 1919, at 10.30 A. M., at the Ministry of Finance, LORD CUNLIFFE in the Chair.

Present: MR. LAMONT (*U. S. A.*); LORD CUNLIFFE (*British Empire*); MR. LOUCHEUR (*France*); MR. D'AMELIO (*Italy*); MR. TATSUMI (*Japan*); MR. MARKOWSKI (*Poland*); MR. DANIELOPOL (*Roumania*); MR. YANKOWITCH (*Serbia*).

Messrs. DESPRET (*Belgium*) and MYLONAS (*Greece*) also attended.[1]

---

[1] According to the French minutes, Stojanović was present instead of Janković; and Despret and Mylonas were not named as present.

The minutes of the 3d meeting were approved.

Enemy Capacity to Pay

The CHAIRMAN asked the Sub-Committee to consider the main question before them, namely, what recommendation they should make to the Commission as to the total amount that can be asked from the enemy Powers. The problem was difficult. It would be useless to submit figures unreasonably high, and on the other hand the Committee must not rest upon a needlessly low figure.

In making its calculations the Committee must reckon something more indeterminate than capital—viz.: The credit of a hard-working, well-trained industrial population.

In making these calculations, we should bear in mind that the enemy Powers, by reducing to a minimum their naval and military forces, would be able to pay over to us the economies so effected, and millions of men would be employed in useful work, and earning money, part of which could go to make good the damage done to the Allies.

It might be that the Committee would arrive at a figure that would appear too high to some persons. It would be well to recall that sums which the Allies had been able to raise by loans during the war, even at moments when things looked most critical, would have seemed absolutely fantastic five years before.

Any figures of the amount which the enemy Powers could pay over a series of years, which the CHAIRMAN suggested should be 50 years, must be merely approximate.

The Sub-Committee must decide, first, how much can the enemy pay in cash immediately, and, secondly, how much more can the enemy pay over a period of years.

As a sum total to be asked, MR. LLOYD GEORGE had suggested the figure £24,000,000,000—say 600 billions of francs.

The CHAIRMAN asked the Delegates to express their views as to the total to be exacted and the means for obtaining it.

Mr. Loucheur's Suggestion

MR. LOUCHEUR (*France*) expressed the view that, if costs of war were to be included, MR. LLOYD GEORGE'S figure must be increased to at least £40,000,000,000—say 1,000 billions of francs.

He distinguished between immediate and deferred payment and accepted 50 years as a term for the latter.

As to the first, he suggested that the enemy Powers should be required to pay 20 to 25 billions of francs immediately (say roughly £1,000,000,000), under the following heads:

Gold......................................	4,000,000,000 frs.
Merchant Ships...........................	2,000,000,000 frs.[2]
Submarine Cables.........................	1,000,000,000 frs.[3]
Foreign Assets of Enemy States and Individuals	6-10,000,000,000 frs.
Foreign Securities........................	5- 8,000,000,000 frs.[4]
Live Stock...............................	1,500,000,000 frs.

It might also be useful to demand say 10,000,000,000 marks, properly guaranteed, to meet the immediate payments the Allies might have to make in Germany.

After the deduction of these 20 to 25 billions, the Allies would remain creditors of the enemy Powers to the amount of 575 billions of francs,[5] the amortization of which would demand payments of 30 to 35 billions of francs annually for 50 years.

The means of payment hitherto considered by the Sub-Committee (coal, timber, potash, dye-stuffs, etc.) furnished a total of only 4 to 5 billions of francs per annum.

As for the balance of the 25 to 30 billions of francs, it would be necessary to leave the choice of methods of payment to the enemy, unless the Delegates had some further suggestions to offer on the point.

Mr. Lamont's Estimates

MR. LAMONT (*U. S. A.*) quoted American experts as making the following estimates:

Within 6 months of the signing of Peace...........	$1,800,000,000
At the end of the year...........................	1,200,000,000
At the end of the second year....................	2,400,000,000
Total......................................	$5,400,000,000

(These figures are exclusive of gold.)

The United States Delegation was not ready to offer an opinion as to whether the Allies should demand all the enemy gold. MR. LAMONT had not understood that the opinion had been formally called for at the second meeting or he would have explicitly reserved his own opinion.

Many people in America thought that to demand the gold reserve, already small, of the enemy States would have a bad effect, and might react unfavorably on the economic welfare of the Allies.

On the other hand, the above figures included, as did those

[2] According to the French minutes, 2½ milliard francs.
[3] According to the French minutes, 100 million francs.
[4] According to the French minutes, 5-10 milliard francs.
[5] According to the French minutes, 570.

supplied by MR. LOUCHEUR (*France*), the merchant marine and foreign securities.

The United States Delegation approached with great diffidence the question of deferred payments. The estimates of their experts, which are entirely approximative, point to the Allies being able to obtain annual payments of $1,500,000,000 over a series of 35 years, representing a capital of $57,900,000,000. They make every reservation as to the possibility of scientifically justifying these figures.[6]

MR. LAMONT hoped that the French and British estimates would be found to be much nearer the truth.

The difficulty was, in his opinion, not so much to raise the money as to get it into the hands of the Allies.

The next meeting was fixed for 3.30 P. M. on the same date.

The meeting adjourned at 1 o'clock.[7]

CUNLIFFE,
Chairman.

F. FOBERTI,
Secretary.

DOCUMENT 518

Second Subcommittee: Minutes of the Seventh Meeting, February 21, 1919, 3:30 P. M.

[EOM, Second Subcommittee, pp. 28-29. French stenographic minutes, PV, CRD, pp. 743-52; French condensed minutes, *ibid.*, 753-54.]

The Second Sub-Committee of the Commission on Reparation of Damage (Financial Capacity of the Enemy States—Their Means of Payment and Reparation) met on Friday, 21 February, 1919, at 3.30 P. M., at the Ministry of Finance, LORD CUNLIFFE in the Chair.

Present: MR. LAMONT (*U. S. A.*); LORD CUNLIFFE (*British Empire*); MR. D'AMELIO (*Italy*); MR. TATSUMI (*Japan*); MR. MARKOWSKI (*Poland*); MR. DANIELOPOL (*Roumania*); MR. STOYANOWITCH (*Serbia*).

---

[6] At the tenth meeting of March 3, Lamont offered the following correction, which was adopted at the eleventh meeting of March 4:

"M. LAMONT (*traduction*). Je désirerais voir insérer au procès-verbal de la sixième séance, à la dernière page, une rectification.

"Je veux parler du paragraphe qui commence: 'La Délégation des États-Unis a entamé avec beaucoup de difficultés la question du payement différé.' . . . 'A partir de cette phrase, je propose d'écrire: La Délégation des États-Unis espère que les Alliés pourraient obtenir des Puissances ennemies un payement annuel de 1.500 millions de dollars, qui devrait s'échelonner sur une période de trente-cinq ans, par exemple, ce qui représenterait une somme totale de 57.900 millions de dollars. Cette estimation est faite sous toute réserve car les experts des États-Unis n'ont pu arriver à justifier ces chiffres.' " PV, CRD, p. 759. Ellipsis in the original.

[7] According to the French minutes, at 12:25.

Messrs. DESPRET (*Belgium*), CHEVALIER (*France*), MYLONAS (*Greece*) and OLCHOWSKI (*Poland*) also attended.[1]

Machinery and Live Stock Urgently Needed

The CHAIRMAN asked the Delegates whose countries had the most pressing needs of certain products (machinery, live stock, etc.) to explain their requirements.[2]

MR. DESPRET (*Belgium*) asked the Committee to give a decision on the question of replacing machinery destroyed or stolen by the enemy, by taking other but similar machinery actually in use in Germany. Referring to MR. LOUCHEUR's point of view, he thought that the procedure was amply justified in this case by the necessity of putting an end to the disastrous unemployment and by the possibility of advancing by one or two years the process of reconstruction. Live stock must similarly be replaced by cattle handed over by the enemy.

MR. OLCHOWSKI[3] (*Poland*) made the same demand on behalf of his country. He proposed an international organization to manage the replacement.

Messrs. D'AMELIO (*Italy*) and DANIELOPOL (*Roumania*) made similar demands for Italy and Roumania.

The CHAIRMAN asked the Delegates to have lists of machinery and cattle destroyed or stolen by the enemy prepared for the consideration of the First Sub-Committee. Other lists of objects which the Allies concerned would wish to purchase from the enemy at a fair price must also be prepared. It was to be understood that by "purchase" he meant that credit, not money, should be given to the enemy.

In the case of Poland, a third list should be prepared of the machinery, etc., destroyed by the Russians.

Works of Art

The CHAIRMAN then passed to the consideration of works of art and of historic interest which figure in the Italian list. He regarded these as questions for the First Sub-Committee.

MR. D'AMELIO (*Italy*) submitted that in his opinion the proper method was first to establish categories of means of payment and then to apply them to the interests of the various Allies. He said that works of art of historic or archaeologic interest might form a

---

[1] According to the French stenographic minutes, Chevalier and Olszowski were absent; and Mylonas's name was reported as Myluks or Mylukas. The French condensed minutes do not list those present.

[2] The French condensed minutes omit this paragraph.

[3] According to the French stenographic minutes, Markowski.

means of payment, and therefore came within the competence of the Second Sub-Committee.

The CHAIRMAN was of the opinion that the question of principle should be referred to the Commission.

MR. D'AMELIO (*Italy*) asked about the replacement by equivalents of works of art taken from Lombardy by the Austrians in preceding wars.

The CHAIRMAN suggested that this was for the Council of Ten to decide.

Enemy Currency in Invaded Territory

Messrs. OLCHOWSKI[4] (*Poland*), STOYANOWITCH (*Serbia*) and DANIELOPOL (*Roumania*) raised the question of the repurchase of enemy currency and special money circulating in invaded territory.

Sugar

The CHAIRMAN was of the opinion that it was not within the competence of the Second Sub-Committee. So he proposed to pass on to the question of deliveries of sugar by Germany. He wished to know what Allied countries would be disposed to import German or Austrian sugar, and what the Austro-German exportation might amount to.

MR. MYLONAS (*Greece*) said that Greece imported sugar to the amount of six million francs per annum from Austria-Hungary.

MR. CHEVALIER (*French Expert*) thought that in view of the ruin of the sugar industry in the Nord, France ought to have recourse, as a temporary measure, to importation from Germany. He would prefer to reserve specifications until a later meeting.

The next meeting was fixed for Saturday, 22 February, at 10.30 A. M.

Business for the meeting: Further discussion of the total payable by the enemy Powers within 12 months from the signature of the Treaty of Peace.

The meeting adjourned at 6 P. M.[5]

CUNLIFFE,
Chairman.

F. FOBERTI,
Secretary.

[4] See note 2.
[5] According to the French stenographic minutes, at 5:30 P. M.

DOCUMENT 519

Second Subcommittee: Minutes of the Eighth Meeting, February 22, 1919, 10:30 A. M.

[EOM, Second Subcommittee, pp. 30-31. French condensed minutes, PV, CRD, pp. 755-56 (down to, but not including, the speech of M. de Lasteyrie).]

The Second Sub-Committee of the Commission on Reparation of Damage (Financial Capacity of the Enemy States—Their Means of Payment and Reparation) met on Saturday, 22 February, 1919, at 10.30 A. M., at the Ministry of Finance, LORD CUNLIFFE in the Chair.

Present: MR. LAMONT (*U. S. A.*); LORD CUNLIFFE (*British Empire*); MR. LOUCHEUR (*France*); MR. TATSUMI (*Japan*); MR. MARKOWSKI (*Poland*); MR. DANIELOPOL (*Roumania*); MR YANKOWITCH (*Serbia*).

Messrs. NEYMARK (*France*) and LIST (*Czecho-Slovak Republic*) also attended.[1]

Enemy Capacity to Pay

The CHAIRMAN invited the Committee to return to the discussion of the total sum which the enemy Powers can pay and how they can pay it.

MR. NEYMARK (*France*) said that on evidence in his possession, which he would lay before the Committee at a later meeting, he regarded the figures suggested by MR. LOUCHEUR (*France*) at the sixth meeting as very moderate.

He suggested that it would be advisable to take steps to obtain, in occupied territories, possession of official lists of income-tax papers.

Annual Payments

MR. LIST (*Czecho-Slovak Republic*), referring to MR. LOUCHEUR'S estimate that approximately 30,000,000,000 francs per annum should be paid by the enemy Powers, argued that Germany could furnish about 4,000,000,000 marks per annum, which would represent the approximate amount of the yearly increase in her movable wealth without dangerously affecting her economic life.

Being without similar data for the other enemy Powers, he called attention to their customs statistics. Austria-Hungary exported before the war upwards of 2,000,000,000 marks, Turkey 400,000,000 marks and Bulgaria 100,000,000 marks, making a

---

[1] The French minutes do not list those present.

total (inclusive of the amount suggested for Germany)[2] of about 7,000,000,000 marks available each year for the purpose of annual payments. To make up the difference between these figures and the 30,000,000,000 francs, sources must be found other than those already discussed.

He suggested the possibility of utilizing and developing the water power and mines of Austria, Turkey and Bulgaria. This course would, however, entail the investment of Allied capital.

MR. LIST made the further point that, if the enemy Powers were compelled to pay 30,000,000,000 francs per annum, there was a grave danger that they would turn themselves into the greatest "factory" in the world, and that after 50 years they would be in a very strong position to flood the world with their products.

Foreign Securities Held by Enemy

MR. LOUCHEUR (*France*) said that the Committee had gone as far as approximative statistics would lead them, and suggested that they should ask the Council of Ten to demand from the enemy States an exact statement of the foreign securities held by them and by their nationals, and of their gold and silver. He asked that the Delegates should produce statements of enemy assets in their countries.[3]

Another item, easy to ascertain, would be the amount of German-owned property in Allied countries. In France there was over one billion francs; in England doubtless at least as much; and, according to his information, about two and one half billions of francs in America. The Allies should supply each other with information on this point.

If we were to aim at the sum of 160 to 1,000 billions of francs, suggested by the American Delegate, MR. LOUCHEUR asked whether we must not demand enemy properties in enemy countries as a further means of payment. The taking by the Allies of 25 per cent of the shares of manufacturing or other stock companies might, for example, be considered.

Accordingly, and without undertaking to express any opinion of his own, MR. LOUCHEUR put the following question: "Can we regard as a means of payment enemy property in enemy countries?"

Resolutions Offered

Furthermore, he proposed the two following resolutions, of which the first one would necessarily go up to the Council of Ten:

---

[2] The phrase in parentheses is omitted from the French minutes.
[3] This sentence is omitted from the French minutes.

1st. To ask enemy Powers to make known immediately the amount: (1) of their cash holding in gold and silver; (2) of foreign securities held by enemy Powers and individuals, with complete details; (3) various assets held by the enemy Powers and individuals abroad.

2d. The Entente Powers are invited to make known, before 2 March, the approximate value of property held in their respective countries by enemy States and individuals, either already disposed of or capable of being disposed of.

MR. LAMONT (*U. S. A.*) said he was prepared, in general terms, to second the resolution. He suggested that no decision should be taken at the present meeting, but that the resolution should be circulated immediately and the decision deferred until a later meeting.

The CHAIRMAN agreed. He thought he could give figures of the exact amount of gold and securities held by the German and Austrian banks. He believed that *net* enemy assets would not amount to a large sum.

He thought that we might take enemy property in enemy countries. He would be in favor of taking it over a period of years and would suggest that a fixed sum, rather than a share of profits, should be asked.[4]

The Dilemma

The CHAIRMAN, referring to the question raised by MR. LIST (*Czecho-Slovak Republic*), said that he thought the Allies were in a dilemma. There were the dangers pointed out by MR. LIST on one side. On the other, if we did not keep the enemy at work to pay for the war, they would have time and opportunity to create another great army and to accumulate wealth for themselves with which they might wage another war within 40 years.

He asked that in future any calculations submitted by the Delegates should be expressed in gold marks.

The next meeting was fixed for Monday, 24 February, at 3.30 P. M.

The meeting adjourned at 12.30 P. M.[5]

CUNLIFFE,
Chairman.

F. FOBERTI,
Secretary.

[4] The last two paragraphs are omitted from the French minutes.
[5] See note 4.

DOCUMENT 520

Second Subcommittee: Minutes of the Ninth Meeting (Including Annexes I-IV), February 24, 1919, 3:30 P. M.

[EOM, Second Subcommittee, pp. 32-39. French condensed minutes, PV, CRD, p. 756 (beginning with speech of M. de Lasteyrie) to p. 758. French text of Annex I in PV, CRD, pp. 855-56; there are no French texts of Annexes II-IV.]

The Second Sub-Committee of the Commission on Reparation of Damage (Financial Capacity of the Enemy States—Their Means of Payment and Reparation) met on Monday, 24 February, 1919, at 3.30 P. M., at the Ministry of Finance, LORD CUNLIFFE in the Chair.

Present: MR. DAVIS (*U. S. A.*); LORD CUNLIFFE (*British Empire*); MR. LOUCHEUR (*France*); MR. D'AMELIO (*Italy*); MR. TATSUMI (*Japan*); MR. MARKOWSKI (*Poland*); MR. DANIELOPOL (*Roumania*); MR. STOYANOWITCH (*Serbia*).

Messrs. LAMONT (*U. S. A.*), DE LASTEYRIE (*France*) and MYLONAS (*Greece*) also attended.[1]

The minutes of the 4th meeting were approved.

Resolutions Adopted

The resolutions proposed by MR. LOUCHEUR (*France*) and seconded by MR. LAMONT (*U. S. A.*) at the previous meeting were adopted.

Bullion Reserves

MR. DE LASTEYRIE (*France*), referring to MR. LOUCHEUR'S resolutions, reported the facts disclosed by the German Delegates at Treves as to the gold and silver reserves of the Reichsbank and as to foreign securities held by Germany (see Annex I). He added similar information concerning Austria supplied by the Austrian Food Commission (Annex II).[2]

With reference to the second resolution, MR. LOUCHEUR (*France*) said he could supply figures on enemy property in France.

The CHAIRMAN and Messrs. MARKOWSKI (*Poland*), STOYANO-WITCH (*Serbia*) and D'AMELIO (*Italy*) said they would do their best to produce these figures by 2 March.[3]

A Tax on Capital Proposed

MR. LOUCHEUR (*France*) stated that we had decided on the

---

[1] The French minutes do not list those present.
[2] The French minutes omit this sentence.
[3] The French minutes replace Markowski and Stojanović by Lamont.

means of immediate payment and as to the remainder had found ways of getting 4 to 7 billions of marks, a small sum in comparison with the total that we must reach. Other methods must be sought and it was of use to consider what the Germans would have done if victorious.

They had intended to demand from France, in addition to costs of the war, an indemnity of 30 to 40 billions of francs in the form of a tax on capital.

Taking the wealth of Germany and Austria at roughly 800 billions of marks, a tax of 25 per cent would produce 200 billions of marks.

A discussion ensued in which MR. LAMONT (*U. S. A.*), the CHAIRMAN and MR. LOUCHEUR (*France*) took part, as to the practicability and desirability of imposing a capital tax.

MR. LOUCHEUR (*France*) explained that he had only suggested this as a means of payment. It was for the Committee to consider whether it would be practicable. The means of payment outstanding in foreign countries seemed to have been entirely exhausted.

Increase Public Debt

MR. D'AMELIO (*Italy*) suggested that another means of payment might be found in the increase of the German public debt, subject to proper guarantees.

Mr. Danielopol's Proposal

MR. DANIELOPOL (*Roumania*) submitted further* proposals for immediate payments:

(1) That the Allies should take over concessions to work part of the coal and potash mines of Germany and Austria.
(2) That the Allies should demand immediate delivery of a part of the stocks and shares of German financial and industrial companies.
(3) That the Allies should demand the immediate delivery of part of the 97 billions of German war bonds.

MR. STOYANOWITCH (*Serbia*) offered, as an estimate of the wealth of Germany, roughly, 650 billions of marks and a revenue of approximately 120 billions of marks. He argued that the Allies could demand annually 16 billions of marks: in view of the fact that the annual increase in the wealth of Germany, estimated at 3 per cent, would amount to 20 billions of marks, the Allies might take half of it, say 10 billions, and might impose a tax on the balance, which would produce 5 to 6 billions of marks.

MR. D'AMELIO (*Italy*) thought it unnecessary to determine with precision the means of payment. The Committee should only indicate on what data it relied in determining the total.

Mr. Loucheur's Conclusions

MR. LOUCHEUR (*France*) thought that in the end the Committee would always come back to the following conclusions:

(1) The enemy Powers could pay about 25 billions of francs within twelve months of the signing of peace.
(2) The Allies could count on an annual payment of 8 to 10 billions.
(3) To provide for the balance it would be necessary to consider taking part of enemy property in enemy countries.

He drew the attention of the Committee to the fact that they must shortly prepare a provisional report.

Bulgarian Wealth

MR. MYLONAS (*Greece*) stated that the wealth of Bulgaria appeared to have been:

In 1911.................................10,482,000,000 francs
Total revenue........................... 1,646,000,000 francs

A Memorandum to be offered in a few days would contain more detailed figures and the total of the annual payment which Bulgaria will be capable of making.

MR. STOYANOWITCH (*Serbia*) handed in a Memorandum on the capacity of Austria to pay (Annex III).[4]

The CHAIRMAN agreed that a preliminary report should be prepared, and suggested that two or three Delegates should assist the Secretariat in drawing up the report.

MR. TATSUMI (*Japan*) proposed that the CHAIRMAN, and Messrs. LOUCHEUR (*France*) and LAMONT (*U. S. A.*) should be charged with this task.

This proposal was adopted.[5]

The next meeting was fixed for Thursday, 27 February, at 3.30 P. M. The meeting adjourned at 6 P. M.[6]

CUNLIFFE,
Chairman.

F. FOBERTI,
Secretary.

---

[4] The French minutes insert after this sentence: "M. DANIELOPOL (Roumanie) dépose un projet sur les matières premières à exiger des pays ennemis (Annexe IV)."
[5] See Document 539, at note 3.
[6] The French minutes omit the last four paragraphs, beginning with "Mr. Tatsumi. . . ."

ANNEX I

FOREIGN SECURITIES OWNED BY GERMANS

(*Presented by the French Delegation.*)

Foreign securities owned by Germans, according to the statement made on September 30, 1916, corrected for changes reported up to November 30, 1918.

Securities	Marks
(A) Allied States (1916)............................	5,800,000,000
(B) Enemy States (1916)...........................	6,600,000,000
(C) Neutral States (1916).........................	1,700,000,000
(D) Other Foreign States.........................	900,000,000
	15,000,000,000

This figure includes................................	8,000,000,000
in round numbers of Austrian, Hungarian, Russian, Polish and Turkish securities which at the present time can hardly be utilized; out of the...................	7,000,000,000
that remain......................................	3,800,000,000
are in enemy countries, and have been apparently placed under sequestration, so that there are available at most.	3,200,000,000

But this figure also includes the securities owned by Alsace-Lorraine, the total of which, according to observations made on the financial market, must have increased considerably in recent times. Naturally, no claims to them can be made by Germany.

(The figures given refer to the par values.)

STATEMENT OF THE REICHSBANK, JANUARY 31, 1919

Assets	Marks	Liabilities	Marks
Gold Reserve	2,253,712,000	Capital	180,000,000
Silver Reserve	19,967,000	Reserve fund	94,828,000
		Bank bills	23,647,640,000
	2,273,679,000	Obligations falling due	
Imperial Treasury Notes	7,137,000	daily	12,522,737,000
Loan Treas. Notes	5,745,528,000	Miscellaneous	1,671,626,000
Notes of other Banks	2,945,000		
			38,116,831,000
	8,029,289,000		
"Portfeuilles," negotiable papers and Treasury			
Certificates	27,008,634,000[7]		
Loans on Securities	8,926,000		
Securities	148,150,000		
Miscellaneous	2,831,832,000		
	38,026,831,000		

Treves, February 14, 1919.

[7] According to the French text, 27,098,634,000. That makes the total assets equal to the total liabilities.

ANNEX II

FOREIGN SECURITIES HELD BY AUSTRIANS

(*Presented by the French Delegation.*)

Foreign securities (bonds, public funds, shares and other securities) owned by Austrians in enemy countries. All figures represent millions of the monetary unit.

Issuing Country	Francs	Pounds Sterling	Dollars	Dutch Florins
Belgium	11.5			
Great Britain		2.7	1.8	
France	48.0			
Italy	99.9			
Netherlands				1.6
United States			23.5	
Mexico			1.3	
South American States	0.7	0.4	0.1	
Egypt	0.5	0.2		
China		0.4		
	160.6	3.7	26.7	1.6

Total in francs: 395,500,000.

Foreign securities (bonds, shares, public funds and other securities) owned by Austrians in neutral countries.

Country of Issue	Value
Belgium	1,500,000 francs
England	400,000 pounds sterling
France	300,000 francs
Italy	24,100,000 lire
Holland	1,800,000 Dutch florins
Scandinavian Countries	5,600,000 Scand. crowns
Switzerland	30,800,000 francs
United States	12,800,000 dollars
Mexico	200,000 dollars Mexico
South America	1,400,000 francs
	200,000 pounds sterling
	100,000 dollars
Egypt	100,000 francs
	600,000 pounds sterling
China	1,500,000 pounds sterling
Japan	1,000,000 francs
	100,000 pounds sterling
Total	218,000,000 francs

Foreign securities (bonds, shares, public funds and other securities) owned by Austrians in Austria.

(a) Securities in denomination of francs issued in—

France	10,300,000
Italy	22,900,000
Belgium	2,200,000
Switzerland	2,100,000
South America	100,000
Egypt	100,000
Japan	1,100,000

Total in Francs.......38,800,000

(b) Securities in denomination of pounds sterling issued in—

England	1,500,000
Egypt	500,000
China	1,800,000

Total in pounds sterling...... 3,800,000

(c) United States Securities......1,400,000 dollars
(d) Swedish Securities......3,300,000 German marks
(e) Dutch Securities......1,700,000 florins

Total in francs......149,800,000

ANNEX III

ENEMY'S CAPACITY TO MAKE REPARATION: RESOURCES OF GERMANIC AUSTRIA

(*Presented by the Serbian Delegation.*)

Produce which Germanic Austria could deliver over, as payment and indemnity, to the United Kingdom of the Serbs, Croats and Slovenes:

A. AGRICULTURE

(a) *Grain.*—The annual production of grain (wheat, barley, rye, Turkish maize) of Germanic Austria is 946,000 tons.

The consumption (for seed and food) is 1,340,000 tons.

Germanic Austria therefore has a shortage of 400,000 tons which must be covered by importation.

(b) The potato crop furnishes 1,210,000 tons;
while the amount consumed is 1,700,000 tons.

Therefore there is a shortage of nearly 500,000 tons of potatoes which have to be imported.

(c) As for other agricultural products, Germanic Austria barely meets her own needs. Therefore agriculture does not contribute.

B. DOMESTIC ANIMALS

In the way of domestic animals, Germanic Austria possesses, at the present time:

230,000 horses;
22,200,000 head of cattle;
1,280,000 hogs;
350,000 sheep;
and the same number of goats.

Thus, in the matter of domestic animals, Germanic Austria is a producing country, and could furnish to the United Kingdom of Serbo-Croato-Slovenia 200,000 head of cattle and 100,000 head of calves.

C.   FORESTS

Germanic Austria owns 3,350,000 hectares of forest, the annual production of which is 10 million cubic metres of lumber. Her own consumption (for heat and construction) is 8 million cubic metres. Thus she could export 2 million cubic metres of lumber annually.

D.   INDUSTRIES

(a) *Coal* (anthracite or black coal).—The annual production is 90,000 tons.

This does not suffice to cover the country's own needs (not even those of the railroads).

(b) *Bituminous coal* (or lignite).—2,600,000 tons are produced, while 11 million tons of this coal are consumed.

Thus, Germanic Austria has a great shortage of anthracite and bituminous coal.

(c) *Crude iron.*—The production is 600,000 tons.

The consumption is 350,000 tons.

Thus, Germanic Austria could export at least 250,000 tons of crude iron.

However, it would be quite easy to increase the production and the capacity of production of crude iron to 900,000 tons a year.

Iron ores are found in great quantity in Germanic Austria. The output had reached more than 2 million tons. The production could be increased to 3 million tons.

The ore is exceedingly good. It can be obtained from the mountains without there being the need of making mine shafts.

E.   VARIOUS ORES

As for other ores, Germanic Austria produces:

Copper ore	16,000 tons
Lead ore	18,000 tons

Zinc... 2,000 tons
Graphite..16,000 tons

These products do not even meet the needs of the Austrians.

F. IRON INDUSTRY

This industry is highly developed in Germanic Austria. Especially during the war have foundries been built—for example:

1. In Northern Styria; Kapfenberg, Donavitz;
2. In Lower Austria; Vellersdorf, Blumau, Saint-Polton, etc.;
3. In Upper Austria; Steyer, Wells, etc.

At the present time the production from iron foundries greatly exceeds the needs of the country.

By reason of her remarkable production of iron Germanic Austria could deliver and export the following manufactures:

Dynamos;

Electric motors;

Transformers;

Sewing and knitting machines;

Looms;

Agricultural machinery;

Steam engines (locomotives, boilers, turbines);

Automobiles, bicycles, hydraulic engines, iron blooms, steel, iron and steel wire, blades and plates;

Forge lamps, arc lamps.

Cooking-utensils and all other kinds of iron-manufactory products.

The value of these articles which Germanic Austria could export represents between 150 and 200 millions a year, according to pre-war prices.

In this way Germanic Austria could cover the needs of the Serbo-Croato-Slovene Kingdom by furnishing these articles in reparation of damage done.

Aside from this, she could furnish also instruments of precision, such as optical instruments and measuring instruments.

G. MINERAL SALTS

The production of mineral salts in Germanic Austria is 165,000 tons, while the country consumes only 90,000 tons. She could thus export 75,000 tons annually.

H. PAPER

The annual production of paper is 200,000 tons (paper of various kinds).

The annual consumption is 40,000 tons.

Germanic Austria could thus export 160,000 tons of paper and paper articles.

I. BEER

In 1913 the production of beer was 6,900,000 hectolitres. This figure can be raised, and could reach 10 million hectolitres. Now the consumption comes to 4 million hectolitres; thus there remains a production of 2,900,000 hectolitres of beer for export.

J. SUGAR AND BEETS

The production of sugar-beets is 258,000 tons, which give 36,000 tons of sugar.

The consumption of sugar in Germanic Austria being 100,000 tons, the country thus has a deficit.

K. TEXTILE INDUSTRY

This industry is very highly developed.

The production greatly exceeds the needs of the country.

Naturally, the raw materials have to be imported; if the Austrian factories were supplied with the necessary raw materials, Austria could meet the needs of Jugo-Slavia in textiles (80,000 to 100,000 francs).

L. FURNITURE

The furniture industry is very highly developed.

It supplied almost all the Southern Slav countries before the war.

M. OTHER ARTICLES

The articles which Germanic Austria has exported are the following:

Medicines, perfumes, paints, varnish;

Essences, preserves and coffee.

N. FACTORIES

By reason of her centralized government Germanic Austria has concentrated a large number of factories in regions inhabited by Germans, to the detriment of the other nationalities.

These are the following factories:

Tobacco factories;

Petroleum refineries;

Textile mills;

Match factories;

Paper mills;

Wood mills;

Furniture factories;

Glass factories;

Machinery and implement factories.

This whole study has been calculated from official Austrian statistics of recent date.

From a statistical point of view, we take the following regions into account:

Statistics of Lower and Upper Austria;

Statistics of Northern Styria;

Statistics of Northern Corinth [*Carinthia*];

Statistics of Salzburg;

Statistics of the German Tyrol;

Statistics of Vorarlberg;

with a population of 6,400,000 inhabitants and an area of 83,000 square kilometers.

In the foregoing figures the German districts of Bohemia and Moravia are not included.

C. STOYANOWITCH, Delegate.

ANNEX IV

ENEMY PRODUCTS TO BE DEMANDED BY ALLIED STATES

(*Presented by the Roumanian Delegation.*)

Raw materials to be demanded from Germany and her allies:

Coal	1,500,000 tons annually.
Coke	400,000 tons annually.
Potassium Salts (40% KOH)	100,000 tons annually.
Building and other Wood	3,000,000 cubic meters annually.*
Dye-stuffs proper:	
Mineral Dyes	8,000 tons annually.
Graphite—183 tons	700 tons annually.
Lead (small shot, bars)	
Sheets, balls, etc. (3,000 tons)	10,000 tons annually.
Zinc (in fragments, melted, rolled, drawn, in sheets, plates) (150 tons)	4,500 tons annually.
Tobacco, in leaves (500 tons per year)	3,000 tons annually.
Avelendes [*valonia?*], myrobolamus [*myrobalans?*] and sumach	3,000 tons annually.
Marble, and other stone	10,000 tons annually.
Copper	500 tons annually.

* The quantities of building and other wood which the enemy removed from Roumania and which must be returned are not included in the figures above.

DOCUMENT 521

Second Subcommittee: Minutes of the Tenth Meeting, March 3, 1919, 5 P. M.

[EOM, Second Subcommittee, pp. 40-41. French stenographic minutes, PV, CRD, pp. 759-66.]

The Second Sub-Committee of the Commission on Reparation of Damage (Financial Capacity of the Enemy States—Their Means of Payment and Reparation) met on Monday, 3 March, 1919, at 5 P. M., at the Ministry of Finance, LORD CUNLIFFE in the Chair.

Present: MR. LAMONT (*U. S. A.*); LORD CUNLIFFE (*British Empire*); MR. LOUCHEUR (*France*); MR. D'AMELIO (*Italy*); MR. TATSUMI (*Japan*); MR. DANIELOPOL (*Roumania*); MR. STOYANO-WITCH (*Serbia*); MR. MARKOWSKI (*Poland*).

Messrs. DESPRET (*Belgium*), MICHALACOPOULOS (*Greece*), FREIRE D'ANDRADE (*Portugal*) also attended.[1]

The CHAIRMAN proposed that the minutes of the 5th, 6th, 7th and 8th meetings should be approved.

MR. LAMONT (*U. S. A.*) offered an amendment to the minutes of the 6th meeting.

The CHAIRMAN proposed the adoption of the minutes of the 5th, 7th and 8th meetings only, postponing the consideration of the minutes of the 6th meeting until a later occasion. This course was approved.

The CHAIRMAN regretted that the Sub-Committee of three was not ready to present definite proposals to this Committee and hoped that in a few days its members would have agreed upon proposals. The deliberations of this Committee need not be suspended, however.

Merchant Marine

Referring to the merchant marine, he expressed the opinion that a flat rate of so much per ton would not be adoptable. It would be better to get up a detailed exhibit of the ships that had been sunk, with particulars as to age, tonnage and state of repair, upon which a rational valuation might be based.

It was his view that the date of sinking should be looked at as the date for ascertaining value.

In respect to enemy vessels, it seemed to be a question whether

---

[1] The French minutes do not list those who "also attended."

they should be divided up into categories or whether they should all be taken over.

MR. LOUCHEUR (*France*), without intending to trespass on the province of the First Sub-Committee, to which the matter of lost tonnage appropriately belongs, wished to say that the French Government was of the view that the valuation should be based on replacement cost, due allowance being made for the depreciation of vessels according to their ages. Reciprocally the enemy fleet ought to be taken account of on the basis of actual values at the date of its being turned over to the Allies. Due regard should also be taken of the age of enemy vessels. As to a distribution of the enemy vessels, this was a question for the Peace Conference. Similarly the question of priority among the Allies was its question.

Finally he expressed the opinion that it would be necessary to leave in the hands of the enemy such coasting-vessels and fishing-boats as were necessary to their existence.

MR. D'AMELIO (*Italy*) urged that the merchant vessels of Austria-Hungary could not all be reckoned as available for distribution, as a number of them would have to be considered as attached to certain territory which is to be transferred. The Peace Conference would have to pass on a question here, and it should therefore be understood to be reserved. In other respects he wished to express his agreement with MR. LOUCHEUR'S position.

MR. MICHALACOPOULOS (*Greece*) found it impossible to agree that coasting-vessels and fishing-boats should be omitted from the list of those to be transferred. Greece would be particularly prejudiced by such a decision. His country had lost 50 per cent of her tonnage, and vessels for small traffic between the Greek ports were quite indispensable to the country.

MR. STOYANOWITCH (*Serbia*) also wished to have a reservation noted with respect to the division of the Austrian merchant fleet, of which more than one third is in the hands of Jugo-Slavs.

MR. DANIELOPOL (*Roumania*) joined in asking for this reservation with respect to the division of the Austro-Hungarian shipping.

MR. LAMONT (*U. S. A.*) suggested that the Allied Maritime Transport Council should be asked for a detailed schedule of the Allied ships which had been sunk and for a schedule of the enemy merchant shipping, with explanations that would help in arriving at valuations. The suggestion was approved.

Questions of Principle

MR. LOUCHEUR (*France*) reminding the Committee of the full

Commission's request, proposed to forward the following four questions of principle to the Commission for its decision:

(1) May the replacement of machinery that has been destroyed or stolen by means of machinery actually at work in enemy factories be reckoned as an available method of reparation?

(2) May a contribution of German labor be reckoned as one means of reparation?

(3) May a tax on capital or on consumption or on export be reckoned as one means of payment by the enemy and particularly by Germany?

(4) May the replacement of objects of art by others of similar sort or equivalent importance be reckoned as a method of reparation for the thefts of objects of art by the enemy?

The consideration of these questions was deferred until the next meeting.

The next meeting was called for Tuesday, March 4, at 4.30 P. M. The meeting adjourned at 6.30 P. M.

CUNLIFFE,
Chairman.

F. FOBERTI,
Secretary.

DOCUMENT 522

Second Subcommittee: Minutes of the Eleventh Meeting (Including Annexes I-IV), March 4, 1919, 4:30 P. M.

[EOM, Second Subcommittee, pp. 42-56. French condensed minutes, PV, CRD, p. 767. French text of Annex I, *ibid.*, pp. 768-69; of Annex IV, *ibid.*, pp. 867-69. There is no French text of Annexes II and III. Portuguese text of Annex III, in Moniz, pp. 301-8.]

The Second Sub-Committee of the Commission on Reparation of Damage (Financial Capacity of the Enemy States—Their Means of Payment and Reparation) met on Tuesday, 4 March, 1919, at 4.30 P. M., at the Ministry of Finance, LORD CUNLIFFE in the Chair.

Present: LORD CUNLIFFE (*British Empire*); MR. D'AMELIO (*Italy*); MR. TATSUMI (*Japan*); MR. STOYANOWITCH (*Serbia*); MR. DANIELOPOL (*Roumania*); MR. CHAMIEC (*Poland*).

COL. WEYL (*France*) and Messrs. WHITNEY (*U. S. A.*), DESPRET (*Belgium*), OSUSKI (*Czecho-Slovak Republic*), MYLONAS (*Greece*) and FREIRE D'ANDRADE (*Portugal*) were also present.[1]

---

[1] The French minutes do not list those who were "also present."

The CHAIRMAN proposed the adoption of the minutes of the 6th meeting, with the amendment offered by MR. LAMONT (*U. S. A.*) at the last meeting, and the minutes of the 6th meeting were adopted as thus amended.

The minutes of the 9th meeting were adopted after the incorporation of an amendment proposed by MR. MYLONAS (*Greece*).[2]

The CHAIRMAN asked the Sub-Committee to take up the questions submitted by MR. LOUCHEUR (*France*). (Cf. minutes of 10th meeting.)

Replacement of Machines, etc.

COLONEL WEYL (*France*), speaking for MR. LOUCHEUR, who was absent, explained the necessity of obtaining from the enemy, not only a restitution of machines which had been carried off, but also a replacement of machines that had been destroyed or could not be identified by machines of the same kind from among those working in enemy countries.

At the close of a discussion in which Messrs. DANIELOPOL (*Roumania*), DESPRET (*Belgium*), STOYANOWITCH (*Serbia*) and CHAMIEC (*Poland*) participated, it was agreed that MR. LOUCHEUR'S question should be submitted to the Commission in a broader form, which should cover not only machinery, but also tools, rolling-stock, animals, timber and other objects.

Contribution of Enemy Labor

COLONEL WEYL (*France*) presented MR. LOUCHEUR'S second question: Shall the enemy make a contribution of labor?

The CHAIRMAN, expressing his own strong doubt of the practicability of such a method of reparation, asked the Committee to postpone its decision respecting MR. LOUCHEUR'S question until the next meeting.[3]

It was decided to hold the next meeting on Wednesday, 5 March, at 4.30 P. M.

The meeting adjourned at 6.30 P. M.

CUNLIFFE,
Chairman.

F. FOBERTI,
Secretary.

---

[2] The French minutes omit the last two paragraphs.

[3] The French minutes insert here the names of those who presented the Annexes: D'Amelio (Annex I), Mylonas (Annex II), Freire d'Andrade (Annex III), Osuský (Annex IV).

ANNEX I

ENEMY'S CAPACITY TO MAKE REPARATION: AUSTRO-HUN-GARIAN REVENUES—COMMUNICATION FROM THE ITALIAN DELEGATION

AUSTRIA

	Average per Year Budget 1906-1910	Budget 1911-1912	Budget 1912-1913
Taxes, land*	53,521	51,985	51,971
Taxes, immovables	104,500	118,020	118,040
Taxes, industrial	98,000	100,000	102,000
Taxes on interest, on capital and public securities	9,700	12,200	13,100
Taxes, supplemental on personal income and salaries	65,100	95,300	101,700
TOTAL DIRECT TAXES	330,821	377,505	386,811 [4]
Taxes, on food, etc.	377,020	423,960	410,070
Monopolies	346,913	399,930	430,993
Taxes, on business (stamps, registrations, etc.)	219,873	257,623	289,118
Customs charges	165,622	205,733	210,152
TOTAL INDIRECT TAXES	1,109,428	1,287,246	1,340,333 [5]

HUNGARY

	Average per Year Budget 1906-1910	Budget 1911-1912	Budget 1912-1913
Taxes, Land*	74,630	72,846	66,970
Taxes, immovables	38,540	44,780	45,520
Taxes, industrial	73,730	75,140	75,030
Taxes on interest, on capital and public securities	16,800	21,100	23,500
Taxes, supplementary, on personal income and salaries	42,100	44,600	44,160
TOTAL DIRECT TAXES	245,800	258,466	255,180
Taxes, on food, etc.	228,280	265,110	297,080
Monopolies	187,637	216,311	231,513
Taxes, on business (stamps, registrations, etc.)	164,604	209,002	208,025
Customs charges	40,980	34,745	42,199
	621,501	725,168	778,817

* The figures on revenue from taxes are published in the ÖSTERREICHISCHES STATISTICHES-HANDBUCH, Vienna, 1913; and in the STATISTICAL ABSTRACT FOR FOREIGN COUNTRIES, 1901-1912. London, 1914.

[4] The French text reads, 386,817. The English is correct.
[5] The French text reads, 1,304,223. The English is correct.

SYNOPSIS

AUSTRIA

Direct taxes	330,821	377,505	386,811
Indirect taxes	1,109,428	1,278,246[6]	1,340,333[7]
Total	1,440,249	1,664,751	1,727,144[8]

HUNGARY

Direct taxes	245,800	258,466	255,180
Indirect taxes	621,501	725,168[9]	778,817
Total	867,301	983,634	1,033,997

P.S.—In addition to the totals given above, various other revenues (Railway, Postal, Public Land Administration) appear in the budgets of the late Monarchy.

ANNEX II

ENEMY'S CAPACITY TO MAKE REPARATION: BULGARIAN

RESOURCES

(*Presented by the Greek Delegation.*)

METHOD: SOURCES OF INFORMATION

1. To arrive at an approximate estimate of the economic capacity of Bulgaria to make reparation for war damage, it is necessary to examine her national wealth: on the one hand revenues, and on the other finances.

2. We have when possible drawn our economic information from sources furnished by the enemy. Thus we have used the German work, "BULGARIA, LAND AND PEOPLE," by the professor of Geography at the University of Sofia, A. Ischirkoff (published, Leipzig, 1917),[10] who states that he has taken advantage of the *excellent* book of the Director of the Bulgarian Statistical Service, Kyrill Popoff, "LA BULGARIE ÉCONOMIQUE."[11] Another German book has also stood us in good stead: "GRÜNDUNGS-WESEN UND FINANZIERUNG in UNGARN, BULGARIEN UND DER TÜRKEI." by the Budapest lawyer, Öd. Makai

---

[6] The French text reads, 1,287,246. That is correct and makes the total so.

[7] The French text reads, 1,304,223. The English is correct. See note 5.

[8] The French text reads, 1,727,034. The English is correct.

[9] The French text reads, 729,168. The English is correct.

[10] Anastas Ishirkov (*French*, Ichirkov; *German*, Ischirkoff), *Bulgarien, Land und Leute* ("Bulgarische Bibliothek," No. 2), II, "Bevölkerung, Volkswirtschaft, Siedelungsverhältnisse" (Leipzig, 1917), 128 pp.

[11] Kiril G. Popov (*French*, Popoff), *La Bulgarie économique, 1879-1911*, translated by V. Robeff (Sofia, 1920), 520 pp. Obviously a later edition or translation than that available at the Peace Conference in 1919.

(Berlin, 1916).[12] We find less recent information in the official publication in English of the Bulgarian Ministry of Commerce and Industry, "BULGARIA OF TO-DAY" (London, 1907).[13] Upon certain details we lack particulars. We have not yet procured a much more recent German work by Weiss Baltenstein [*sic*] (Berlin, 1918), "BULGARIENS VOLKSWIRTSCHAFT UND IHRE ENTWICKLUNGSMÖGLICHKEITEN," although we do not believe that this book would have led us to different calculations and conclusions.[14] The data following do not include the new provinces annexed to Bulgaria after the Balkan wars. We have been able to obtain no information about these regions.

AGRICULTURE—ANIMAL INDUSTRY

3. The principal source of wealth for Bulgaria is agriculture. In 1911, before the Balkan wars, 83% of the population (4,337,516) was agricultural. Of her exports, 85% consists of agricultural products, notably grain, live stock and animal products.

4. The territory of Bulgaria (1911) covers 96,345 square kilometers, or 9,634,500 hectares. Of this region 83% is susceptible of cultivation.

5. After the Balkan wars (1913) the net additions to Bulgarian territory by annexation were 17,660 square kilometers, after deduction of that part of the Dobruja ceded to Roumania (8,340 square kilometers). The population of these new regions was estimated at 1,180,184.

6. The country is fertile and its inhabitants are industrious. Nevertheless, the agricultural yield is far from giving a large return. About 20% of the land suitable for cultivation had not yet been cultivated in 1911. Farming methods are not yet up to date and modernized. Artificial fertilizer is little used, and lands are allowed to lie fallow two or three years.

In 1911 there were 420,084 wooden plows as against 114,245 of iron. But the introduction of modern implements and machinery is increasing from year to year. Thus between 1909 and 1912 the importation more than doubled (from 2,764,000 francs to 6,880,000 francs, worth).

[12] Ödön Makai, *Gründungswesen und Finanzierung in Ungarn, Bulgarien und der Türkei* (Berlin, 1916), 377 pp.

[13] Bulgaria, Ministerstvo na t''rgovilata i zemledielieto, *Bulgaria of To-Day*, official edition of the Bulgarian Ministry of Commerce and Agriculture (London, 1907), 299 pp.

[14] Walter K. Weiss-Bartenstein, *Bulgariens Volkswirtschaft und ihre Entwicklungsmöglichkeiten, seine Wirtschaftspolitik und Wirtschaftslage im Hinblick auf den Abschluss neuer Handelsverträge und deutsche Kapitalbetätigung auf dem Balkan* (Berlin, 1918), 495 p.

7. Following is a list of the agricultural products of 1912 (average year):

Value in francs

1.	Grain	62.89% of the arable land.	436,487,337
2.	Plants for Industry	0.91% of the arable land.	14,666,984
3.	Spices	2.19% of the arable land.	23,127,317
4.	Truck and Vegetable	0.72% of the arable land.	8,630,220
5.	Dried Vegetables	0.27% of the arable land.	10,160,748
6.	Forage	14.05% of the arable land.	95,990,624
7.	Fruits	0.29% of the arable land.	3,208,830
8.	Vineyards	1.51% of the arable land.	56,122,988
9.	Roses	0.19% of the arable land.	6,505,535
10.	Produce of fallow land	16.98% of the arable land.	576,439

TOTAL..665,477,076[15]

8. Grains, therefore, are the principal product of the country. The weight of this staple was (1912) 2,672,038 tons, of which 1,218,075 tons were wheat, and 723,301 tons maize.

9. Green vegetables give an important revenue, although they are cultivated in a primitive fashion. This produce serves not only for internal consumption, but is exported abroad in considerable quantities. Moreover, thousands of gardeners emigrate into the neighboring countries, and after a few years return with considerable earnings. In Budapest, for example, these Bulgarian gardeners earn more than six million francs per year.

10. Rose-growing is the famous specialty of Eastern Roumelia. For one kilogram of rose extract, the price of which varies, according to the quality and harvest, from 8 francs to 1,400 francs, about 3,000 rose petals are used. The average value of this production is estimated at more than 5,000,000 francs. In 1911 the exports amounted to 7,500,000 francs.

11. In many parts of Bulgaria, stock breeding is an important industry; but Bulgaria's arid climate and the backward civilization especially favor small stock, notably sheep. According to the stock census of 1910, there were:

		Increase from 1892 to 1910
Horses	478,222	39.04%
Mules	12,238	48.09%
Asses	118,488	45.19%
Cattle	1,606,363	12.67%
Sheep	8,669,260	26.22%
Buffaloes	412,978	20.70%
Goats	1,464,719	15.90%
Pigs	527,311	14.20%
Poultry	8,688,853	153.57%

[15] The items listed total 655,477,022.

The total value of the live stock was set at 512 millions of francs, while the average increase was 54.5% for the period 1892–1910, and the increase in prices amounted to 104%. In 1911 the exportation of live stock and their food products formed 14.3% of the total exports.

FORESTS

12. In spite of the great extent of the forests of Bulgaria, (29.4% of the territory in 1908), their economic value is not considerable. The greater part belongs to the Communes (58.8%). The State owns the most valuable (22.7%), and private persons and corporations 15.5%.

13. In 1911 the forest products consisted of 526,227 cubic meters of building wood, 2,054,738 cubic meters of firewood, and 6,343,660 kilograms of coal.

Bulgaria has not sufficient forest products for its own consumption. It is true that she exports more firewood and coal than she imports; but the importation of building wood is much greater than the export. A wiser exploitation in the future could increase the value of the Bulgarian forests, which in 1911 were valued at approximately 600,000,000 francs.

INDUSTRY—MINES

14. Bulgarian industry owes its development to a protective legislation (since 1894) which has not imposed tariffs on imports from abroad, but granted exemption from taxes and other encouragements to home industries.

Undertakings by the State, and the enterprises of private citizens, must be distinguished. In 1912 the number of the various private enterprises (mining, metallurgical, ceramic, chemical industries; manufacture of articles of food and drink; textile, wood, furniture, leather and paper industries; and electric power) amounted to 381, with a total capital of 87,590,565 francs, and a motor power of 31,747 h.p. The value (in 1912) of the products was 108,142,677 francs; the export of those products amounted to 17,539,519 francs. State enterprises (mining and metallurgical industries) were only 8 in number, with a total capital of 14,725,623 francs, and a motor power of 1,348 h.p. The value of the output (1912) totals 6,964,987 francs.

15. Minor industries, engaging a large part of the urban population, were also encouraged by the State.

16. The production of copper, which is exported, is also of some importance. Mineral wealth, however, is not yet skillfully exploited.

The production of copper in 1912 was 20,180 tons, as against 3,225 tons in 1905; and that of lead 5,083 tons, as against 379. Coal (2 mines belonging to the State) is used for internal consumption.

COMMERCE—BANKS

17. Inasmuch as the export commerce, as we have seen, consists of agricultural products, 85%, notably grain, it depends largely upon the quality of the harvest. Following is a table of the five years preceding the Balkan wars:

	Imports	Exports	Total
1908	130,150,642 francs	112,356,997 francs	242,507,639 francs
1909	160,429,624	111,433,683	271,863,307
1910	177,359,723	129,052,205	306,408,928[16]
1911	199,344,808	184,633,945	383,978,753
1912	213,110,269	156,406,624	369,516,893

18. Imports into Bulgaria from Greece are insignificant, while exports represent quite considerable sums:

	Value in 1,000 Francs	
	Imports	Exports
1909	811	4,601
1910	421	6,340
1911	488	12,650
1912	833	8,383

Exports into Greece consist mainly of grain; live-stock and animal-stock products form only a small part thereof. As regards the quantity of Bulgarian grain imported into Greece, there have been years when it amounted to as much as one third of the total grain import.

19. The National Bank of Bulgaria, a State bank, had on 31 December, 1915, a capital of 20,000,000 francs, and various reserves totaling 14,547,026 francs. The gold and silver reserve was 83,-000,000 francs against a note circulation of 370,000,000 francs. At the same date (i.e., after the entry of Bulgaria into the war) the National Bank had a foreign credit of 204,000,000. We are not informed of the distribution of these credits among the Allied countries, but it is probable that Bulgaria would have liquidated before entering the war at least a part of the credits in Entente countries. Moreover, the reserve of the Bank has no doubt increased since then, as has happened in other countries. We do not think that the Bulgarians would have allowed the Germans to carry their reserve away to Berlin. According to information which remains to be verified, it seems that they have even required the

[16] The total of the exports and imports as given is 306,411,928.

Central Empires to assume two thirds of the Bulgarian war loans, so that Bulgaria is carrying only one-third.

20. Still other State Banks exist in Bulgaria: the "Banque Agricole," ("Farmers' Bank"), with a capital (1912) of 45,000,000 francs, and the "Banque Centrale Co-opérative" (Central Co-operative Bank), with a capital of 5,000,000 francs.

21. The Postal Savings Banks had 46,000,000 francs, deposits in 1912.

22. The number of credit institutions not under the State amounts to 60. Of these, however, only 12 are important, with a capital of more than 1,000,000 francs (total 56,000,000 francs). The most important banks have been founded with foreign capital; we are not aware of the exact sum that the capitalists of each of the Allied countries have contributed. The "Banque Générale" owes its creation to Hungarian, Dutch and French capital (Banque de Paris); the "Banque de Crédit" to German capital; the "Banque Balkanique" to Austrian capital; and so on in the cases of the "Banque Commerciale de Bulgarie" the "Crédit Foncier de Bulgarie," the "Banque Franco-Bulgare d'Hypothèques," etc.

RAILWAYS AND MERCHANT MARINE

23. The railway system, which belongs in its entirety to the State, was 1948 kilometers long in 1912. The capital invested amounted to 305,000,000 francs, and the net profits to 5,479,371 francs.

Number of locomotives	212
Number of passenger coaches	335
Number of mail cars	34
Number of freight cars (box and flat)	4,729

24. Sea transportation is effected entirely by foreign shipping. In 1912 there was only one Bulgarian shipping concern, which owned 6 vessels, of 4,027 tons register.

TOTAL NATIONAL WEALTH AND REVENUE

25. Any estimate of this nature can be only approximate. We will limit ourselves to quoting the following figures given by the Director of the Bulgarian statistical service for the year 1911 (see above, Paragraph 2).

A. PRIVATE WEALTH

		Millions of Francs
1.	Unimproved realty	3,765
2.	Buildings	2,360
3.	Live stock	511
4.	Other farm property (not including land)	46

5.	Commercial capital	250
6.	Industrial capital (not including stock shares)	110
7.	Foreign securities	10
	Bulgarian State Securities	80
	Shares in Bulgarian corporations	100
8.	Gold	50
	Silver	57
9.	Household furniture	330
10.	Foodstuffs in possession of the population	350
	TOTAL	8,019

B. PUBLIC WEALTH

(Of the State, Departments, Communes, and State Banks)

Millions of Francs

1.	Unimproved realty		2,166
2.	Buildings		240
3.	Railways and Harbors	317,100	
	Roads and Highways	139,300	
	Telegraphs and telephones	5,100	461
4.	Capital of the "Banque Nationale" and of the "Banque Agricole"		67
5.	Military property (not including fortifications and other immovable structures)		250
	TOTAL		3,184
	From this sum must be deducted debts to foreign countries (of the State, the Communes, and the two banks)		753
	BALANCE		2,431

According to this estimate, the total wealth, public and private, would therefore amount to 10,482,000,000 francs.

26. It should be noted that during the last few years (1916-19), the national wealth of Bulgaria has trebled. The increase in land values is largely responsible for this rise. On a per capita basis the wealth would come to 2,400 francs, (still referring to the year 1911).

27. As to NATIONAL REVENUE (not including that from the national domains), the Director of Bulgarian statistics affords us the following statistics for the year 1911:

Millions of Francs

1.	Agriculture	723
2.	Stock-raising	213
3.	Industry	200
4.	Commerce	80
5.	Miscellaneous	15
6.	Buildings	115
7.	Wages	300
	TOTAL	1,646

The revenue per capita would thus be 378 francs.

FINANCE

28. Before the entry of Bulgaria into the world war (1915), the public debt totaled 616,459,242 francs. At the end of 1917 the consolidated debt was 108,000,000; the floating debt, 2,324,000,000, including a debt of 413,000,000 to the National Bank. The debt of the departments and towns, at the end of 1912, amounted to 94,000,000, of which 55,000,000 were owed by Sofia.

29. Before the Balkan wars, in 1911, the total receipts were 265,000,000; and the expenditures, 229,000,000, of which 38,000,000 went for the army and 66,000,000 to meet the public debt.

30. Let us now examine the figures for the 1918 budget (in "THE STATESMAN'S YEARBOOK"):

Receipts.......................................481,100,000 francs
Expenditures..................................479,414,019 francs

of which 56,000,000 went to new Bulgaria—which, from our point of view, can mean only the Serbian, Greek, and Roumanian territories which were under the Bulgarian invasion of 1913. The ministry of war appears therein at the figure 104,000,000, and the public debt at the figure 128,000,000 francs (that is, about 62,-000,000 more than in 1911 (29)).

CONCLUSIONS

31. What sum would Bulgaria be capable of paying annually? Let us base our calculations upon the national revenues for the year 1911, for which we shall have to estimate and deduct the various taxes.

In the first place, we must contemplate a diminution of the military expenses: thus, of the 104,000,000 of the 1918 military budget, we could leave a maximum of 34,000,000, taking into account principally military pensions, inasmuch as in 1911 the war budget did not exceed 38,000,000. And let us not forget the fact that the army, which was striving to imitate Prussian traditions in the Balkans, must be limited at most to half its strength of 1911, which was a year of military preparations for the Balkan War. We therefore have 60,000,000 less by reason of the reduction of military expenses. From the budget of expenditures must also be deducted the following:

(a) The costs of administration of the regions annexed in 1913, which constitute more than one fourth of the total territory and one sixth of the total population of Bulgaria for 1913 (5) and

(b) The costs of the administration of the regions invaded by the Bulgars during the war (56,000,000 francs) (30), for we have not counted in the national revenues (of 1911), the revenue of these rich occupied provinces, which, moreover, will not all be a part of post-bellum Bulgaria. The expenses for these regions would not be less than 100,000,000 francs. Therefore this makes 60 plus 100, or 160 millions of francs to be deducted from the 1918 budget of expenditures—

> plus 479 millions of francs,
> minus 160 millions of francs,
> equals 319 millions of francs.

32. Furthermore it must not be forgotten that a part of the budget receipts do not appear in the accounts of the annual revenue from the people, but that they accrue from the State domain, the State railways, and other enterprises carried on by the State. These receipts would seem to be not less than 85,000,000 francs. Not to enter into detailed calculations as long as we can speak only approximately and in round numbers, it seems that after the war Bulgaria will have to meet annually by taxation (exclusive of the interest on the indemnity) a sum of 250,000,000 (taking Bulgaria with her 1911 frontiers). If we add to this sum departmental and communal taxes, which we can take roundly as 100,000,000 (in France they form about 50% of the total burdens), we obtain the total of 350,000,000, which will be deducted from the national revenue (1,646,000,000) not including the war indemnity to be paid.

33. But it must be recalled that these estimates of national wealth and revenue are calculated for 1911, while the ordinary burdens of taxation are estimated according to the 1918 budget; consequently the pre-war revenues, by reason of the general rise in prices, should increase to a much greater value, at least to twice as much, after the war, according to the opinion expressed by Mr. Loucheur in one of the sessions of the Sub-Committee.

This increase in value would be further justified by the fact that, Bulgaria being an agricultural country, her farmers have earned great profits during the war, and that these profits will continue for a long time. Moreover, it is to be noted that:

(a) The means of production have been subjected to no damage in Bulgaria, and that agriculture especially may be increased upon a much greater scale, as has been said before.

(b) In our calculations the revenues of the annexed territories do not figure. Thus the national revenues, doubled, would be 3,300,000,000.

34. Consequently, taking into account only the evident rise in prices, the following calculations of an *annual levy* may be made:

(a) 200,000,000 francs, which, plus the ordinary expenditures of 350,000,000, would total 550,000,000, or only 16% of the national revenue.

(b) 300,000,000 francs,—650,000,000, or 20% of the revenue;

(c) 400,000,000 francs,—750,000,000, or 25% of the revenue;

(d) 500,000,000 francs,—850,000,000, or 30% of the revenue; and so on.

It is to be noted that before the war the burden of taxation in France had already reached 17%, and in Italy 18.3% of the total national revenue; and it is to be anticipated that these quotas will be considerably increased after the war.

35. The result at which we have thus arrived is not at all exaggerated: on the contrary, it is the minimum; and there would also be a large margin for the subtraction from the national revenues of the non-recoverable minimum. Indeed, on the German national income, estimated by the German banker Helffrich at 50 billions of marks for 1913, a levy of 9 billions minimum to 20 billions maximum has been considered practicable; that is, from 18% to 40% of the revenue.

Of the national revenue of Bulgaria (1,646,000,000 in 1911), the levy of 200,000,000 annually contemplated above would be 12%; a levy of 300,000,000, 20%; 400,000,000, 25%; and 500,-000,000, 30%. This quota would be only half, if the value of the revenue of 1911 is doubled.

We learn that the British "Industrial Federation," in a study which it has made upon the enemy's capacity of payment, estimates that Bulgaria would be able to pay 775,000,000 francs annually. If that is true, it is evident that our evaluation is only too moderate.

36. We have attempted here to arrive at figures most nearly exact as the basis for a levy either upon income or upon capital. The method and the quota of the levy will depend upon the decision of the Peace Conference, which will be uniform for all enemy countries.

PAYMENT IN KIND

37. Of the produce of Bulgaria which we have reviewed, certain Allied countries might accept an annual quantity of products in payment for the annuities of the indemnity. Thus Greece, which imports cereals, live stock and animal products, would be willing to receive in payment a quantity worth approximately 30,000,000

francs yearly, without disturbing her pre-war commercial relations with the other friendly countries. It is of course understood that this statement holds true only until we obtain a sufficiency by more intensive exploitation of our own soil.

38. Greece would also have to deduct from the indemnity the value of the Bulgarian property sequestrated in Greece.

Paris, 27 February, 1919.

Technical Advisor,

ALEXANDER C. MYLONAS,
General Secretary of the Greek
Department of Agriculture.

SUPPLEMENT TO ANNEX II
ECONOMIC STATISTICS ON BULGARIA IN 1917

The German Review *Südost* (Berlin, August, 1918) reproduces verbatim a report of the "Banque de Crédit" of Sofia on Bulgaria's economic situation during the year 1917. We believe that this text, which sets forth the country's economic capacity in a very satisfactory fashion, should be reproduced here:

"From an economic point of view the year 1917 was an exceptional year. Prices were paid for all agricultural products such as had not been known hitherto, especially for products sold out of the country. Among these tobacco was pre-eminent. Its production in 1917 rose to the amount of 700 millions of lewa as against 100 millions of lewa during the pre-war period. The large sums which thus flowed into the country produced an exceptional surplus of money. Consequently bank deposits reached very high figures. Money did not depreciate, however, because the immediate result was a lively activity in new enterprises and speculation in various securities and investments which produced not only a general high level in prices but also an increased demand for money. In 1917, fifty-seven stock companies, with a capital of 345 millions of lewa, were incorporated. Other still more remarkable increases in capital were brought about. Already the question is being asked, with reference to these figures, whether the new enterprises correspond to the needs of the country. The majority of the stock companies newly organized have not yet begun to do business regularly. Nevertheless, some of their shares are sold above par in the open market. In January, 1918, the official stock and security exchange was opened. This will, it is hoped, contribute to a saner development of business and will result in Bulgarian capital's being directed to good domestic investments, especially to State issues and municipal obligations. The 1917 harvest did not come up to the average. The crops of summer wheat, maize, beans and potatoes in particular were poor by reason of the dry summer. Nevertheless, thanks to the measures adopted by the government, there were no great difficulties with respect to food requirements."

It is clear that this document corroborates the forecasts and conclusions of the Memorandum which we have already submitted regarding Bulgaria's economic capacity (Annex II).

SECOND SUPPLEMENT TO ANNEX II
PROSPERITY OF BULGARIAN BANKS DURING THE WAR

Additional information confirms the conclusions of our Memorandum. Bulgaria, far from being impoverished by the war, has been able to extract important profits from it, and her economic prospects need not excite sympathy. We read the following in the German review *Südost* of September, 1918, respecting Bulgarian banks during the war:

"To-day Sofia has thirty-four banks, eighteen of which were established during the war, particularly in 1916 and 1917.

"Among the other banks five are foreign banks or supported by foreign banks. The war found Bulgaria with ten banks, each having a million capital; in all, 33 millions of lewa. Their reserves of all sorts amounted to more than 6 millions of lewa. During the war, and until 1917, eight of these banks put out new issues (the remaining two are now doing the same thing), so as to increase their capital to 67 millions of lewa, which amounts to their doubling their capital in three years. During the same period these banks increased their reserves to 19 millions of lewa; that is to say, they tripled them. In 1914 the reserves were 19% of the capital, whereas in 1917 they had risen to 28%, a very significant sign. Whereas the banks paid a dividend below normal in 1914 and in 1915, they raised an interest rate in 1916 of 8.05% and in 1917 went as high as 9.60%."

ANNEX III
THE PROBLEM OF REPARATION OF WAR DAMAGE BY MEANS OF MERCHANDISE, TOOLS AND MONEY
(*Memorandum Submitted by the Portuguese Delegation.*)

I. MERCHANDISE

Importations on a large scale

Upon consultation of the statistics of pre-war importations, it is evident that the commodities which the State could easily import and distribute are few.

It is necessary that the merchandise should be more or less homogeneous, that its quality should easily be controlled; that the prices could be established in accordance with quotations on the great world markets; that the amount to be imported should be considerable; and that the yearly imported tonnage should be somewhat stable.

Importations on a large scale fulfilling more or less the above-mentioned conditions are those shown in Table A, appended to this document.

In this table appear nine kinds of goods which seem to be satisfactory; but, upon closer examination of the question, they are reduced to those under Nos. 1, 2 and 4, which lowers the quantities to be imported by the State to

Cotton...	2,600 contos
Pit coal...	4,500 contos
Fertilizer..	600 contos
	7,700 contos
	£1,700,000

This sum, placed as an annuity for 20 years at the rate of 5%, corresponds to a capital of £21,250,000.

The organization of the iron industry necessary to national economic life as regulating the balance of trade and compensating the instability of maritime tonnage, would be detrimentally affected by the obligatory importation of those grades of iron that are most common on the market. This explains the exclusion of No. 3.

The forced importation of foreign cereals is detrimental to the agricultural development of Portugal and its colonies, which should, on the contrary, be encouraged. The high total of importations of cereals, the heavy taxes imposed on them and the lack of stability in the relation between trade and the rate of exchange show clearly the necessity of following the foregoing procedure and therefore the exclusion of Nos. 5, 6, 7 and 8, which however, if necessary, might be maintained for some time.

As to salted codfish, No. 9, it stands to reason that, only in case of absolute necessity, should it be considered admissible for State importation.

The relative importance of our imports from the countries which export most to Portugal is shown in the following table of percentages:

April	Total	Germany	Belgium	U.S.A.	France	England	Argentine
1913	100	17.80	4.55	11.12	8.53	26.40	5.62

To form an idea of the proportion in which goods to be imported could be utilized as compensation of the war burden, statistics on exportations must also be consulted, and it will certainly be useful to consult the statistics concerning the origin of the produce and its destination. This holds equally for importations and exportations. We will limit ourselves, for the present, to the numbers corresponding to those indicated for importations in Table B (below).

In general, one may estimate the importance of our exports to enemy countries from the relation of their value to total exports and by comparing them to exports to countries to which the exports are of greater value.

Values of certain exports in percentages of total exports.

	Total	Germany	Spain	Brazil	England
1913	100	9.66	15.53[17]	17.55	21.54

The re-exportation of colonial products, not included in this table, materially increases the proportion of our export commerce with enemy countries. This can easily be verified by the figures given in the table appended to this document.

II.   WORKING IMPLEMENTS

Maritime Transportation

Our trade is for the most part carried on under foreign flags.

The following list shows the part taken by each of the great Powers in 1913.

Movements of Cargoes Loaded and Unloaded in Portugal according to Flags

	Coasting Trade at large	Coasting Trade in shore	Total
Portugal	264,115	409,025	....
Germany	580,209	....	....
Denmark	94,638	....	....
Spain	342,567	....	....
France	201,041	....	....
Holland	61,792	....	....
England	1,260,684	....	....
Italy	102,725	....	....
Norway	725,248	....	....
Sweden	150,260	....	....
			R. 4,357,674[18]

[17] According to Moniz, 15.63.
[18] The items listed total 4,192,304. The figure in the minutes is the same as in Moniz.

It suffices to compare the relative totals of Germany, Spain and the small nations mentioned, with ours, to make evident the place we ought to occupy in the maritime transportation of our own trade. We must lay hold of these resources if we wish to avoid the ruin of our economic life. This has already been shown in a preceding Memorandum.

We estimate at 150,000 tons net the shipping which we could easily handle aside from that now in our possession and in that of our Allies.[19]

Railway Transportation

The equipment and the development of our railroads make it possible to receive in material:

For Portugal itself:

100 locomotives with 100-ton tenders.

For Portugal and her colonies;

250,000 tons of rails, to be received in ten years.

The rolling-stock of new railroads is not taken into account, because it is difficult at the present moment to foresee what will be the requirements of these lines.

III.   MONEY

Portuguese Internal Debt

The war has impoverished the economic situation of the country and has ruined her financial condition. We turned everything we could into gold in order to import, on our account and without borrowing abroad, whatever we needed for the war and for our foods. We have lost important enemy markets for farm products, the only ones at our disposal; and devastated our forests because of the impossibility of exporting any more gold to import fuel. Finally, we were obliged to resort to foreign credit, accepting financial assistance from Great Britain. This credit has not yet affected our unstable financial condition.

In spite of this, our rate of exchange has lowered considerably as compared with that of the Allies, though we were all equally at war.

It is therefore peremptory to obtain money compensation for this damage at least in so far as concerns the foreign debt.

This debt was on July 1, 1918, $187,173,330,[20] and the respective interest was $8,619,965.40, which at par amounts to £1,900,000.

We estimate the increase of this debt, up to the end of the war,

[19] The text in Moniz has additional details.

[20] According to Moniz, 137.173.330$. These figures, here and following, represent *escudos*, not dollars.

when our debt to the English treasury will be added, at £16,-000,000 more—a sum to which corresponds approximately an interest charge of £880,000. We will therefore have an annual burden of £2,780,000.[21]

In 20 years this interest, if taken at 5%, will equal the sum of £34,800,000. The foreign debt would during these 20 years remain intrusted to the financial organization which might be created to liquidate the war debts, and would free the income from our customs, which constitute at present its special guarantee.

Gold Reserve

The circulation of paper money for commercial transactions of the Bank of Portugal necessitates a gold reserve of $17,000,000—£3,800,000.

It would therefore be very useful to incorporate the Bank in the legal system, viz., a gold reserve of 25% for the circulation in commercial transactions, not including the State debt. The metallic quota involved being very small, the enemy would encounter no difficulty.

IV.   SUMMARY

To sum up, the proportions in which Portugal can receive reparation for her war burdens, in merchandise, working implements and money are the following:

	Duration of the Annuities. Years	Annuity	Present value of the capital at 5%.
Merchandise	20	£1,700,000	£21,250,000 (approximately)
Ships			[£ 7,050,000]
Rolling Stock (railroad)			[£ 800,000]
Railroad Property (permanent)	10	[£ 200,000]	[£ 1,550,000 (approximately)]
Interest on Foreign Debt	20	£2,780,000	£34,800,000 (approximately)
Gold			£ 3,800,000
			[£69,250,000]
Money or Material for Industrial Development, etc. (cement, iron, etc.)	20	[£2,405,000]	[£ 30,750,000]
			[£100,000,000]

It is probable that the collection and the distribution of the volume of the reparation, as well as the fixing of the prices, the control and specifications for the receipt of merchandise and

---

[21] According to Moniz, £2,730,000.

working implements, will be intrusted to an Inter-Allied Economic and Financial Commission.

Paris [14 February, 1919].[22]

TABLE A

Import for consumption in 1913

Customs Rates		Commodities	Total		From Enemy Country		Part that the State can Import		
			Amount Tons	Value Contos	Amount Tons	Value Contos	Per Cent	Amount Tons	Value Contos
1. II	43	Cotton	17,639	5,676	424	146	50	8,000	2,500[23]
2.	87	Pit Coal	1,351,820[24]	5,602	8,957	42	75	1,000,000	4,500
3.	114	Wrought Iron or Rolled Iron	68,052	2,426	27,806	1,000	50	30,000	1,000
4.	150	Fertilizer (Farm)	144,493[25]	1,313[26]	12,980	207	50	50,000	600
5. IV	326	Corn (Indian)*	104,490	3,319	20				
6.	327	Wheat*	174,159[27]	7,581	7,970	357			
7.	331	Rice	30,968	2,019	10,025	689	30	10,000	700
8.	339[28]	Sugar	38,842	3,045	20,876	1,427	25	10,000	700
9.	348	Salt Codfish	33,259	4,385	2,210	337	25	7,500	11,000[29]

* The importation varies considerably.

TABLE B

Principal Commodities of Large-Scale Exportation

(Year 1913)

	Customs Rates	Commodities	Total		Enemy Countries	
			Tons	Contos	Tons	Contos
1.	II	Rough and manufactured cork	93,210	5,100	14,502	1,308
2.		Rough and sawed wood	349,000	1,132		
3.		Ore: Copper, tungsten, iron, etc.	486,552	1,714	61,524	216
4.	IV	Ordinary wines and vinegars*	72,978	4,960	1,004	45
5.		Liqueurs*	33,431	7,235	4,158	737
6.		Canned fish (Tunny fish, sardines)	26,793[30]	2,485	3,994	364
7.		Dried and fresh fruit (pineapples, almonds, figs, grapes, apples, etc.)		1,306		400
		Colonial Re-exportation				
8.	II[31]	Rubber	921	1,150	133	163
9.		Wax	420	705	271	167
10.		Cocoa	33,360	8,540	10,357	2,645
11.		Coffee	2,205	524	226	55
12.		Oil seeds	431	32	394	28

* The unit is 1,000 liters.

[22] The date, and the figures in brackets above, are supplied from Moniz.
[23] According to Moniz, 2,600.
[24] According to Moniz, 1,351,320.
[25] According to Moniz, 144,496.
[26] According to Moniz, 1,315.
[27] According to Moniz, 174,150.
[28] According to Moniz, 338.
[29] According to Moniz, 1,000.
[30] According to Moniz, 86,793.
[31] There is no "II" in Moniz.

WAYS IN WHICH THE ENEMY STATES SHOULD MAKE
REPARATION

(Presented by the Czecho-Slovak Delegation.)

The indemnity due from Germany to Allied States, even the part estimated in kind, will be estimated in gold.

It will therefore be necessary to come to an understanding about the principles by which the amount of indemnity to be paid and the amount forfeit in case of a delay in delivery, are to be valued. As far as fixing the amount is concerned, the fact must not be lost sight of that Germany and her allies must as a matter of principle furnish indemnity "in natura" at the very place of the damage. It will therefore be necessary to establish stations situated so far as possible at the frontier where merchandise would be received and where prices established by free competition would serve as a basis for valuation.

The enemy States could make up the difference resulting from expense of transport from the frontier to the interior of the country by being obliged to allow the receiving State free and gratuitous use of means of transport during the time necessary for travel and unloading.

Interest resulting from delay and delivery of merchandise would also be payable in kind.

As the compensation imposed on enemy States is payable annually and will be distributed among the different Allied States, according to the nature of their claims, the establishment of a special International Commission for the recovery and distribution of the indemnities imposed on the enemy is recommended.

This Commission, within the limits set forth in the Treaty of Peace, would have as object:

(a) To prescribe the quality and quantity of indemnities to be furnished during each new period of five years from the total compensation imposed. The enemy States will be notified of these provisions two years in advance and the desire of the Allied States will be taken into account as much as possible.

(b) To settle differences between the Allies or between the latter and the enemy States as far as delivery price of merchandise is concerned.

(c) The mode of procedure will be according to principles laid down in the clause of the League of Nations concerning investigations by the Executive Committee.

(d) By means of special machinery of control, especially created with a view to making sure that the enemy States fulfill their obligations in commercial good faith, and examining complaints on this subject.

(e) To keep account of indemnities actually furnished up to the end of each year and to fix the interest charges for delay.

(f) To resort if necessary to methods of compulsion in case of failure to execute clauses of the Treaty of Peace.

(g) To prescribe and if necessary to enforce measures to insure the proper system of bookkeeping for indemnities furnished and to maintain indispensable organizations for control in the receiving stations of creditor States.

(h) In order to prevent the enemy from discriminating in favor of one of the Allied States the following principles must be adopted:

1. Agreements of whatever nature and until the final settlement of war damages shall be valid only upon the approval of the International Commission.

2. The reparation of damage in the interior of each Allied State will be brought about by regulations special to each one of them, but the creation or tolerance of organizations which permit citizens of different Allied States to communicate directly with enemy States or their citizens concerning the payment of indemnities will be absolutely prohibited, as, for example, communication with a representative of an enemy commercial house.

All dealings of this nature will be carried on through the creditor State and under the control of the International Commission which will fix the method of procedure.

DOCUMENT 523

Second Subcommittee: Minutes of the Twelfth Meeting, March 5, 1919, 4:30 P. M.

[EOM, Second Subcommittee, pp. 57-58. French stenographic minutes, PV, CRD, pp. 770-79; French condensed minutes, *ibid.*, pp. 780-81.]

The Second Sub-Committee of the Commission on Reparation of Damage (Financial Capacity of the Enemy States—Their Means of Payment and Reparation) met on Wednesday, 5 March, 1919, at 4.30 P. M., at the Ministry of Finance, LORD CUNLIFFE in the Chair.

Present: LORD CUNLIFFE (*British Empire*); MR. D'AMELIO (*Italy*); MR. TATSUMI (*Japan*); MR. DANIELOPOL (*Roumania*); MR. CHAMIEC (*Poland*).

COLONEL WEYL (*France*) and Messrs. DESPRET (*Belgium*), FREIRE D'ANDRADE (*Portugal*), OSUSKI (*Czecho-Slovak Republic*), R.-G. LÉVY and THÉRY (*French Technical Advisers*), WHITNEY (*U. S. A.*) and STANAREWITCH (*Serbia*) were also present.[1]

The CHAIRMAN proposed the adoption of the minutes of the 10th meeting. The minutes were approved.

[1] The French stenograpnic minutes omit the names of those who were "also present."

Contribution of Enemy Labor

The CHAIRMAN recurred to the question of payment by means of a contribution of labor, that had been under consideration at the last meeting.

After a discussion to which the CHAIRMAN, MR. DESPRET (*Belgium*), COLONEL WEYL (*France*), and MR. CHAMIEC (*Poland*) contributed, it was decided that a question of principle should be laid before the Commission in the following form:

"May the supply of a certain amount of labor be considered as one method of reparation to the Allies by the enemy States?"

Taxation of Enemy Countries

The CHAIRMAN asked the Committee to take up the question of principle respecting reparation by means of a tax on enemy countries, which had been proposed for submission to the Commission.

COLONEL WEYL (*France*) *read a Memorandum* by MR. LOUCHEUR on this point.

A discussion ensued between the CHAIRMAN, COLONEL WEYL (*France*), and Messrs. R.-G. LÉVY (*French Technical Adviser*) and THÉRY (*French Technical Adviser*) as to the character and methods of collection of such a tax on enemy countries.

The CHAIRMAN thought it best to present the question of principle to the Commission in broad terms. The following wording of the question was adopted:

"Should the Sub-Committee now consider the imposition of taxes on the enemy Powers for the payment of reparation?"

Restoration of Works of Art

COLONEL WEYL (*France*) read a Memorandum by MR. LOUCHEUR on the question of replacing works of art stolen or destroyed by the enemy by similar works of art.

MR. D'AMELIO (*Italy*) favored this kind of reparation, which appeared to him particularly appropriate to the damage.

A brief discussion ended in the adoption of the following wording of the question:

"Should the replacement of destroyed or stolen works of art by other works of art equivalent and of the same kind taken from the enemy be considered as one means of reparation?"

MR. D'AMELIO (*Italy*) asked if the question of requiring the enemy countries to raise the means of payment by contracting a foreign loan should not be presented to the Commission.

The CHAIRMAN stated that this question was clearly within the province of the Committee and was already being considered by the Committee's Special Committee of Three and that such method of providing for payment seemed inevitable.

MR. D'AMELIO (*Italy*) expressed satisfaction with this answer.

The Committee agreed to meet again on 6 March, at 6.30 P. M.[2]

The Committee adjourned at 7 P. M.[3]

CUNLIFFE,
Chairman.

F. FOBERTI,
Secretary.

DOCUMENT 524

Second Subcommittee: Minutes of the Thirteenth Meeting, March 6, 1919, 3:30 P. M.

[EOM, Second Subcommittee, pp. 59-60. French condensed minutes, PV, CRD, pp. 782-83.]

The Second Sub-Committee of the Commission on Reparation of Damage (Financial Capacity of the Enemy States—Their Means of Payment and Reparation) met on Thursday, 6 March, 1919, at 3.30 P. M., at the Ministry of Finance, LORD CUNLIFFE in the Chair.

Present: LORD CUNLIFFE (*British Empire*); MR. D'AMELIO (*Italy*); MR. TATSUMI (*Japan*); MR. CHAMIEC (*Poland*); MR. DANIELOPOL (*Roumania*); MR. STOYANOWITCH (*Serbia*).

There were also present Messrs. DESPRET (*Belgium*), MYLONAS (*Greece*), FREIRE D'ANDRADE (*Portugal*) and LIST (*Czecho-Slovak Republic*).

The CHAIRMAN suggested that the Delegates take up the discussion of the questions submitted to the Commission. In view of the absence of the American and French Delegates, full reserve must be made as to any decisions which might be taken.

Restitution of Stolen Articles

MR. CHAMIEC (*Poland*), referring to the first question,—that concerning the recovery of identified property,—suggested that the Committee proceed to the discussion of the details of application. He suggested that representatives of other countries which had suffered from enemy occupation could be added to the Commission for the recovery of property stolen in France or Belgium, which Commission is now operating in Germany in virtue of the Armistice Convention. Similar Commissions should be formed in Turkey, Bulgaria and Austria. MR. CHAMIEC proposed, accord-

---

[2] According to the French stenographic minutes, at 3:30 P. M.
[3] According to the French stenographic minutes, at 6:40 P. M.

ingly, that there be drawn up a common Memorandum in which would be set forth the various measures to be taken to this end.

MR. DANIELOPOL (*Roumania*) considered that it would be preferable (in order to simplify things and to avoid any addition to the machinery of the Armistice) to proceed to the nomination of a Commission for each country—it being understood that the necessary powers for operating in enemy territory would be obtained from the competent authority.

The CHAIRMAN accepted the principle of an International Commission. While awaiting the decision of the Conference on this point, it would be useful for every Delegation to prepare a list of suitable nominees (experts, etc.), as well as a list of objects which had been stolen.

Reparation by Deliveries in Kind

In regard to the second question—that relative to levies in kind to be carried out in enemy territory—MR. DESPRET (*Belgium*) insisted on the absolute urgency of the economic re-establishment of his country. This urgency justified resorting to this method of reparation. An International Commission, with a sub-committee (also international) for every country presenting claims, could be charged with the duty of determining the extent of the immediate needs and of carrying out the levies deemed justified.[1]

The CHAIRMAN, in view of the absence of the American and French Delegates, suggested postponing the discussion of the third question (supply of labor) until the next meeting.

Works of Art

As regards the replacement of stolen or destroyed works of art by similar or equivalent objects to be taken in enemy countries, after observations by Messrs. D'AMELIO (*Italy*), CHAMIEC (*Poland*), DANIELOPOL (*Roumania*) and MYLONAS (*Greece*), the CHAIRMAN proposed that the Delegations should present detailed lists of works of art, antiquities or objects of historical value which had been destroyed or stolen. An International Commission would be given the duty of carrying out the replacement.

The next meeting was fixed for Saturday, 8 March, 1919, at 10.30 A. M.

The meeting adjourned at 5 P. M.

CUNLIFFE,
Chairman.

F. FOBERTI,
Secretary.

[1] The French minutes omit this sentence.

DOCUMENT 525

Second Subcommittee: Minutes of the Fourteenth Meeting, March 8, 1919, 10:30 A. M.

[EOM, Second Subcommittee, pp. 61-62. French condensed minutes, PV, CRD, pp. 784-85.]

The Second Sub-Committee of the Commission on Reparation of Damage (Financial Capacity of the Enemy States—Their Means of Payment and Reparation) met on Saturday, 8 March, 1919, at 10.30 A. M., at the Ministry of Finance, LORD CUNLIFFE in the Chair.

Present: MR. LAMONT (*U. S. A*); LORD CUNLIFFE (*British Empire*); MR. LOUCHEUR (*France*); MR. TATSUMI (*Japan*); MR. CHAMIEC (*Poland*); MR. DANIELOPOL (*Roumania*); MR. STANARE-WITCH (*Serbia*).

There were also present Messrs. DESPRET (*Belgium*), FREIRE D'ANDRADE (*Portugal*), NEYMARK (*France*) and LIST (*Czecho-Slovak Republic*).

The CHAIRMAN invited the Committee to resume its discussion of the five questions referred back by the Commission.

Recovery of Stolen Property

MR. LOUCHEUR (*France*) reminded the Committee that the Commission had adopted the principle of recovering stolen property from the enemy as applicable against all the enemy countries in favor of all the Allied Powers, and that the terms of the Armistice already settle this point with respect to the rights of France and Belgium as against Germany. He proposed to present a formula to the next meeting of the Committee which would extend the application of the principle thus recognized in the Armistice and would be in form appropriate for embodiment in a preliminary Treaty of Peace.

Replacement of Machines and Animals by Equivalents

He then took up the second question and observed again that the removal of machines and other objects from the enemy countries in order to replace what had been stolen or destroyed would raise difficult questions with respect to amounts to be taken in any one place and to methods of taking. It was his view that an Inter-Allied Commission would have to be set up to supervise the takings and to assure reasonable methods in obtaining replacements. The Committee might well direct one of its members to draw up an article for incorporation in the Preliminary Treaty of Peace, in which should be set out the principles governing the replacements and the measures to be taken to provide for their proper application.

The CHAIRMAN emphasized the need of getting agricultural machinery and animals immediately if the spring work were to be done on the farms. He asked MR. LOUCHEUR (*France*) to lay the urgency of this before higher authority.

MR. LOUCHEUR (*France*) replied that he had already raised the point in appropriate quarters and that he would do so again without delay.

MR. DESPRET (*Belgium*) acceded to the CHAIRMAN'S request to him to draw up such a text as MR. LOUCHEUR (*France*) had proposed, but asked that two other members of the Committee might be appointed to help him.

MR. CHAMIEC (*Poland*) and MR. DANIELOPOL (*Roumania*) were accordingly appointed.

MR. DANIELOPOL (*Roumania*) agreed that it was impossible at present to settle what amount of material Germany could safely be made to part with; but he considered that it was quite possible to require the immediate delivery of a safe minimum. He urged the importance of doing this in respect to agricultural materials[1] for Roumania. The CHAIRMAN expressed his agreement with MR. DANIELOPOL.

Some further discussion took place as to the constitution of the Commissions which would have to visit the enemy countries to investigate their available material.

Undeveloped Resources of the Enemy

At the invitation of the CHAIRMAN, several members, particularly MR. DANIELOPOL (*Roumania*) and MR. NEYMARK (*France*), then expressed their views on the increased economic capacity of the enemy Powers which would result from the restriction of military service and from the development, more especially, e.g., in Hungary and German Austria, of mineral and hydraulic resources.[2]

MR. LIST (*Czecho-Slovak Republic*) recalled in this connection the suggestions which he had made at a previous meeting regarding the exploitation for the benefit of the Allies of the water power of German Austria and the mineral wealth of Hungary, Turkey and Bulgaria.

[1] The French text omits "in respect to agricultural materials."

[2] The French text reads: ". . . exposent leurs vues quant aux perspectives de l'expansion allemande et au développement économique devant résulter de la réduction des charges militaires en Allemagne."

The next meetings were fixed for 10.30 A. M. and 4.30 P. M. on Monday, 10 March, 1919.

The meeting adjourned at 12.30 P. M.

CUNLIFFE,
Chairman.

F. FOBERTI,
Secretary.

DOCUMENT 526

Second Subcommittee: Minutes of the Fifteenth Meeting (Including Annexes I and II), March 10, 1919, 10:30 A. M.

[EOM, Second Subcommittee, pp. 63-66. French condensed minutes and Annexes, PV, CRD, pp. 786-91.]

The Second Sub-Committee of the Commission on Reparation of Damage (Financial Capacity of the Enemy States—Their Means of Payment and Reparation) met on 10 March, 1919, at 10.30 A. M., at the Ministry of Finance, LORD CUNLIFFE in the Chair.

Present: LORD CUNLIFFE *(British Empire)*; MR. LOUCHEUR *(France)*; MR. D'AMELIO *(Italy)*; MR. TATSUMI *(Japan)*; MR. CHAMIEC *(Poland)*; MR. DANIELOPOL *(Roumania)*; MR. MARKOVITCH *(Serbia)*.

There were also present Messrs. DESPRET *(Belgium)*; FREIRE D'ANDRADE *(Portugal)*; THION DE LA CHAUME *(France)*.

The minutes of the 11th, 12th and 13th meetings were approved.[1]

Restoration of Stolen Objects

MR. LOUCHEUR *(France)* read a text which he had phrased so that it might be inserted in the Preliminary Treaty of Peace and which covered the restoration of objects taken from territories occupied by the enemy. (See Annex I.)

The CHAIRMAN proposed that discussion of this text should be postponed until the next meeting in order that the Delegates might have received copies of it in English and in French.

Reparation by Equivalents

MR. LOUCHEUR *(France)*, passing to the second question recommitted to the Committee (viz., the taking of "equivalent" objects from the enemy countries), read the text drawn by Messrs. CHAMIEC *(Poland)*, DANIELOPOL *(Roumania)* and DESPRET *(Belgium)*. (See Annex II.)

This text was approved subject to the omission of the last clause ("The vote of the majority shall be final"), which the Committee decided to strike out.

---

[1] The French minutes omit this paragraph.

At the close of a discussion in which the CHAIRMAN and Messrs. LOUCHEUR (*France*), DESPRET (*Belgium*), and DANIELOPOL (*Roumania*) exchanged views about the composition of the Inter-Allied Commission to be charged with effectuating the restitution, the Committee agreed that it should be prepared to be called upon by the Peace Conference to nominate such an Inter-Allied Commission.

MR. LOUCHEUR (*France*) remarked that there was no present question of enforcing any restitution, but only of preparing a clause for insertion in the Preliminary Treaty of Peace. He knew that the Supreme War Council was not disposed to adopt new demands until the time for executing the Preliminary Treaty.

This statement disclosed ground for the fear that there would be long delays in obtaining what ought to be secured immediately. The CHAIRMAN accordingly asked the Delegations to whom the matter was of immediate consequence to furnish him with memoranda showing briefly and exactly:

(a) The importance to their countries of obtaining agricultural machinery, draught animals and cattle for the farm work that must be done immediately.

(b) The consequence of delaying.

He undertook to transmit these Memoranda to the Chairman of the Council of Ten directly.

MR. LOUCHEUR (*France*) promised his own hearty support to such an appeal to the Chairman of the Council of Ten.

MR. D'AMELIO (*Italy*) thought the recovery of identified objects and the taking of objects by way of equivalents should proceed simultaneously, in order that stolen and identifiable objects might not get sent (as equivalents) to other countries than those from which they had been taken.

The CHAIRMAN asked Messrs. DESPRET (*Belgium*), CHAMIEC (*Poland*) and DANIELOPOL (*Roumania*) to amend the text (Annex II) which they had reported in order that it should cover the point raised by MR. D'AMELIO.

Enemy Sub-Marine Cables

The CHAIRMAN called the attention of the Delegates to the desirability of considering the revenue that Germany had been drawing from her submarine cables.

MR. THION DE LA CHAUME (*France*) presented figures on the point.

The net income from the German submarine cables in the year 1913 was about 5,500,000 marks.

The meeting adjourned at 12.30 P. M.

CUNLIFFE,
Chairman.

F. FOBERTI,
Secretary.

ANNEX I

DRAFT OF ARTICLE TO BE INSERTED IN THE TREATY OF PEACE GOVERNING RESTORATION OF ALLY PROPERTY

(Proposal by Mr. Loucheur (France).)[2]

The enemy States must make immediate restitution of all property, generally, and of whatsoever kind, belonging to the Allied Powers and their citizens of which they have possessed themselves for any purpose and which is now [to be] found on their territory.

Annex No.   of the Treaty provides conditions according to which restitution shall be made.

ANNEX

In accordance with Article No.   of the Treaty, the enemy States shall return to the Allied Powers all effects, whether movables or fixtures, public property or that of artificial or natural persons, which enemy nationals have carried off and which are now in enemy territory. This clause applies to each and every object thus carried off which may now be situated in the enemy States.

Accordingly, these States shall execute a solemn undertaking immediately to collect from their nationals returns setting forth the whereabouts of effects now in the possession of the said nationals drawn from territories of the Allied and Associated Powers.

Laws shall immediately be enacted which shall provide that every person who fails to make return will be regarded as a receiver of stolen goods, and will be liable to severe penalties, to be determined by agreement with the Allied and Associated Powers.

An interval of one month from the signing of the Preliminary Treaty of Peace will be allowed for the making of these returns.

A comprehensive return, setting forth the sources from which objects have been drawn, if they have been identified, the nature of the objects and their present location, shall be made to the representatives of the Allied and Associated Powers within a period of two months after the signature of the Preliminary Treaty of Peace.

[2] Clause A of Annex II of Document 543 follows.

The provisions hereinafter recited show broadly what measures are to be adopted to the end that complete restitution shall be made with the least possible delay. It is the purpose of the High Contracting Parties, however, that all necessary measures shall be taken to assure, in the fullest degree, complete restitution of objects carried off, (subject to reservations hereinafter stated in the interest of the Allied and Associated Powers.) The enemy Governments formally undertake to do all in their power to facilitate search and return shipments.

The Plan of Procedure that follows is applicable to objects of all sorts: furniture, securities, objects of art, etc.

PLAN OF PROCEDURE

I

Machines, machine parts, machine tools, agricultural implements and accessories of every sort and industrial or agricultural equipment of every kind, including cattle, beasts of burden, etc., which were taken from the territory occupied by the enemy armies under any pretence whatsoever, by military or civil authority of the enemy, or by private citizens of enemy countries, shall be at the disposal of the Allied and Associated Powers for return to the places from which they were taken, if the interested Government so determines.

II

In order to prepare for this restitution, the enemy Government shall, with the utmost expedition, supply the duly appointed representatives of the Allied and Associated Powers with all records, official or private, relating to the objects in question; also with all contracts for sale, lease or other purposes, all correspondence thereto pertaining, all declarations and all useful indications as to their existence, source, change of form, present state and place of deposit.

III

Delegates of the Allied and Associated Governments shall, in their discretion, take steps to make in the enemy countries surveys and examinations on the spot of the objects indicated.

IV

Re-shipments shall be made according to special instructions given under the authority of the nation to which the particular objects belong.

V

Particularly, declarations shall be made with a view to an immediate restitution of all accumulations in yards, on the rails, in boats or in factories, of belting, electric motors, motor parts, accessories, etc., that have been taken from the invaded territories.

VI

The retaking of an object of any kind that may be found or identified shall in no case be obligatory upon the Allied and Associated Powers, which shall be in no wise bound to take back objects. They shall have the right to declare without assigning cause that they waive claim to the restitution of particular objects and require reparation in lieu thereof by any other method contemplated by the Treaty.

VII

All expenses incurred in searching for, reshipping and completely reinstalling objects that are restored shall be borne by the enemy Power concerned. The restoration of objects as herein required shall in no case affect the right to recover compensation for what has not been so restored.

VIII

It is formally stipulated that no argument drawn whether from the law or from the interpretation of any text whatsoever shall be invoked by the enemy Powers in order to suspend or delay the execution of any measure of restitution prescribed by the representatives of the Allied or Associated States. The execution of such a measure shall always be immediate, a right to claim damages accruing only in case it is subsequently adjudged that the measure in question was contrary to the provisions of the Treaty.

ANNEX II

DRAFT OF ARTICLE TO BE INSERTED IN THE TREATY OF PEACE
GOVERNING REPARATION BY DELIVERY OF EQUIVALENTS[3]

(Drawn by Messrs. Danielopol, Chamiec and Despret.)

Where it is necessary to meet an urgent need, the Allied States may take objects whether at present in use or not, from the enemy countries, especially rolling stock, equipment and tools, timber, live stock, etc. these to be the equivalent of similar objects removed, worn-out, consumed or destroyed by the enemy or by military operations.

[3] The Annex of Document 527 follows; and this latter is almost identical, in the French texts, with Clause B of Annex II of Document 543. It seems likely, therefore, that the French texts were what was

To this end an Inter-Allied Commission of members shall be constituted with the duty of passing upon the claims of each one of the Allied States in regard to its urgent need of objects of the various categories and to determine the quantities of these objects which the enemy countries are to deliver, the same to be apportioned to the recognized needs of each one of the interested parties.

Each Allied country shall appoint national Commissions, to be presided over by Delegates of the Inter-Allied Commission, who shall proceed to the enemy countries in order to select and take the objects of the various categories, within the authorized limitations.

The Chairman of the different National Commissions operating in the same enemy countries shall confer together with a view to coordinating the work of the Commission. Their decisions shall be taken by majority vote.

10 March, 1919.

DOCUMENT 527

Second Subcommittee: Minutes of the Sixteenth Meeting (Including Annex), March 10, 1919, 4:30 P. M.

[EOM, Second Subcommittee, pp. 67-68. French condensed minutes, PV, CRD, p. 792. French text of the Annex, *ibid.*, pp. 870-71.]

The Second Sub-Committee of the Commission on Reparation of Damage (Financial Capacity of the Enemy States—Their Means of Payment and Reparation) met on 10 March, 1919, at 4.30 P. M., at the Ministry of Finance, LORD CUNLIFFE in the Chair.

Present: MR. LAMONT (*U. S. A.*); LORD CUNLIFFE (*British Empire*); MR. LOUCHEUR (*France*); MR. D'AMELIO (*Italy*); MR. TATSUMI (*Japan*); MR. CHAMIEC (*Poland*); MR. DANIELOPOL (*Roumania*); MR. STANAREVITCH (*Serbia*).

---

considered by the Subcommittee; and so the changes have been shown in them rather than in the English. The French text is as follows (PV, CRD, p. 791):

"Dans tous les cas où il s'agit d'assurer des besoins immédiats, les États alliés peuvent prélever des objets, actuellement utilisés ou non, dans les pays ennemis, notamment des machines, du matériel roulant, des équipements et de l'outillage, du bois, du bétail, etc., équivalents à des objets de même nature, enlevés ou usés, ou consommés, ou détruits par l'ennemi, ou par des faits de guerre.

"[A cette fin,] une Commission interalliée de membres sera constituée avec mission de se prononcer sur les demandes de chacun des États alliés, en ce qui concerne ses besoins immédiats d'objets des différentes catégories et de fixer les quantités de ces objets à livrer par les pays ennemis, lesquelles seront réparties proportionnellement aux besoins admis pour chacun des intéressés.

"Chaque Pays allié nommera des Commissions nationales, qui seront présidées par [des] Délégués de la Commission [nationale,] qui se rendront dans les pays ennemis, pour choisir et prélever les objets des différentes catégories, dans les limites autorisées.

"Les Présidents des différentes Commissions nationales, opérant dans le même pays ennemi, auront à délibérer pour harmoniser les travaux de celles-ci; [leurs décisions seront prises à la majorité.]"

Messrs. DESPRET (*Belgium*) and FREIRE D'ANDRADE (*Portugal*) were also present.

MR. LAMONT withdrew before the end of the meeting.

Text Governing Reparation by Equivalents Adopted

MR. DESPRET (*Belgium*) offered the text drawn by his Special Committee in an amended form such that it covered the point raised in the morning session. (See Annex.) The amended text was adopted.

Contribution of Enemy Labor

The CHAIRMAN asked the Delegates to express their views about the question of demanding a supply of Enemy labor. He believed that it would be better to call, not for a certain amount of German labor, but for labor necessary to the completion of such and such named jobs (like railways, canals, etc.), the work to be done under the supervision of the authorities of the creditor countries.

MR. LOUCHEUR (*France*) assented to this view. He thought it would be better to apply the enemy labor to work of reparation, particularly to restoring land to a cultivatable condition, and feared that it would be difficult to particularize undertakings on which enemy labor might best be employed until a later date.

The Committee decided, without going into details, to ask Messrs. DESPRET (*Belgium*), CHAMIEC (*Poland*) and DANIELOPOL (*Roumania*) to draw a text for consideration at the next meeting of the Committee.

The next meeting was fixed for Wednesday, at 3.30 P. M., for the discussion of the following:

(a) The use of enemy labor.

(b) The levying of taxes in the enemy countries.

The Committee adjourned.[1]

CUNLIFFE,

F. FOBERTI,   *Chairman.*

Secretary.

ANNEX

AMENDED DRAFT OF ARTICLE TO BE INSERTED IN THE TREATY OF PEACE GOVERNING REPARATION BY DELIVERY OF EQUIVALENTS

(Drawn by Messrs. Danielopol, Chamiec and Despret.)[2]

Where it is necessary to meet an urgent need the Allied States may take objects whether at present in use or not, from the enemy

[1] According to the French minutes, at 5:30 P. M.

[2] Annex II of Document 526 precedes. Clause B of Annex II of Document 543 follows; and the

countries, especially rolling stock, equipment and tools, timber, live stock, etc. these to be the equivalent of similar objects removed, worn out, consumed or destroyed by the enemy or by military operations.

Objects found in enemy countries which have been previously taken from the territories of the Allied States cannot be availed of as equivalent objects except upon condition that their owners do not claim them in accordance with the procedure laid down in Article No.   of the Treaty of Peace.

In order that the takings herein provided for may be effected, an Inter-Allied Commission of   members shall be constituted with the duty of passing upon the claims of each one of the Allied States in regard to its immediate needs of the objects of the various categories and to determine the quantities of those objects which the enemy countries are to deliver, the same to be apportioned to the recognized needs of each one of the interested parties.

Each Allied country shall appoint commissions, to be presided over by Delegates of the Inter-Allied Commission, who shall proceed to the enemy countries, in order to select and take the objects of the various categories, within the authorized limitations.

The Chairman of the different National Commissions operating in the same enemy country shall confer together with a view to co-ordinating the work of the Commissions.

French text of the present document is almost identical with the French text of the following document. It therefore seems reasonable to assume that the original was in French; and that the differences in the English are due only to differences in translation. The French text of the present draft is as follows (PV, CRD, pp. 870-71):

"Dans tous les cas où il s'agit d'assurer des besoins immédiats, les États alliés peuvent prélever des objets, actuellement utilisés ou non, dans les pays ennemis, notamment des machines, du matériel roulant, des équipements et de l'outillage, du bois, du bétail, etc., équivalents à des objets de même nature, enlevés ou usés ou consommés ou détruits par l'ennemi ou par des faits de guerre.

"Les objets se trouvant en pays ennemis et qui auraient été enlevés dans les territoires des États alliés ne pourront être prélevés à titre d'équivalents qu'à la condition qu'ils ne seraient pas réclamés par leurs propriétaires suivant la procédure indiquée à l'article   du Traité de paix.

"A l'effet de réaliser les prélèvements prévus ci-dessus, une Commission interalliée de   membres sera constituée avec mission de se prononcer sur les demandes de chacun des États alliés en ce qui concerne ses besoins immédiats d'objets des différentes catégories et de fixer les quantités de ces objets à livrer par les pays ennemis, lesquelles seront réparties proportionnellement aux besoins admis pour chacun des intéressés.

"Chaque Pays allié nommera des Commissions nationales qui seront présidées par les Délégués de ¡a Commission interalliée et qui se rendront dans les pays ennemis pour choisir et prélever les objets des différentes catégories, dans les limites autorisées.

"Les Présidents des différentes Commissions nationales, opérant dans le même pays ennemi, auront à délibérer pour harmoniser les travaux de celles-ci."

DOCUMENT 528

Second Subcommittee: Minutes of the Seventeenth Meeting (Including Annexes I and II), March 12, 1919, 3:30 P. M.

[EOM, Second Subcommittee, pp. 69-75. French condensed minutes and Annexes, PV, CRD, pp. 793-802.]

The Second Sub-Committee of the Commission on Reparation of Damage (Financial Capacity of the Enemy States—Their Means of Payment and Reparation) met on Wednesday, 12 March, 1919, at 3.30 P. M., at the Ministry of Finance, LORD CUNLIFFE in the Chair.

Present: LORD CUNLIFFE (*British Empire*); MR. D'AMELIO (*Italy*); MR. TATSUMI (*Japan*); MR. CHAMIEC (*Poland*); MR. FREIRE D'ANDRADE (*Portugal*); MR. STOYANOWITCH (*Serbia*).

There were also present MR. DESPRET (*Belgium*) and MAJOR ARON, representing MR. LOUCHEUR (*France*).

The CHAIRMAN proposed the adoption of the minutes of the 14th meeting. The minutes were adopted.[1]

Text Governing Supply of Labor

MR. DESPRET (*Belgium*) read a text which he had drafted with MR. CHAMIEC (*Poland*) and MR. DANIELOPOL (*Roumania*) and which covered the matter of a supply of labor in accordance with the discussion at the previous meetings.

At the close of a discussion to which the CHAIRMAN and Messrs. DESPRET (*Belgium*) and D'AMELIO (*Italy*) contributed, several amendments were proposed and an amended text was adopted. (See Annex I.)

MAJOR ARON, speaking in the name of MR. LOUCHEUR (*France*), asked that the conditions governing labor and wages should be regulated in accordance with conditions governing labor and wages of workmen of similar occupations in the country of sojourn instead of in the country of origin.

MR. D'AMELIO (*Italy*) spoke in support of MR. LOUCHEUR'S proposal.

MR. DESPRET (*Belgium*), although maintaining that the regulation should be according to conditions prevailing in the country of origin, was disposed to add to the fourth paragraph, which provides for the regulation of the conditions of work, a final phrase reading "under the control of the Inter-Allied Commission."

---

[1] The French minutes omit this paragraph.

The CHAIRMAN requested the Delegates to postpone a decision until the next meeting, and to consider further those fundamental difficulties which appeared more and more clearly as one proceeded in the consideration of practical details with respect to the use of enemy labor.

MR. STOYANOWITCH (*Serbia*) presented a Memorandum on the capacity of the new republic of Hungary to make reparation. (See Annex II.)

The next meeting was fixed for 13 March at 4.30 P. M.

The meeting adjourned.[2]

CUNLIFFE,
Chairman.

F. FOBERTI,
Secretary.

ANNEX I

ARTICLES PROVIDING FOR A SUPPLY OF ENEMY LABOR DRAFTED FOR INSERTION IN THE TREATY OF PEACE—AMENDED[3]

In the devastated region the enemy states shall with the least possible delay restore cities, villages, farms and factories, roads, communications and works of construction and shall restore land to cultivable condition and plant woods, etc., in accordance with a project of work to be defined by an Inter-Allied Commission upon the basis of proposals submitted by each country interested.

The Commission shall specify the quantity and kind of labor needed each year for the accomplishment of the project thus determined.

The enemy laborers and supervising personnel engaged upon this work shall be governed by conditions set forth in the Annex.

ANNEX

Article   of the Treaty refers to the performance of clearly specified and limited undertakings of which a project will be provided by the Inter-Allied Commission and for which the country bound to make restoration (acting through such agents as it may designate), shall assume the role of contractor but for which it shall in no case supply anything whatsoever except labor.

The country of origin (supplying the labor) shall define the rights and obligations of the workmen whom it enrolls for the purposes herein specified. Such definition shall be subject to the approval of

---

[2] According to the French minutes, at 5:30 P. M.
[3] See Article 2 of Document 250.

the Inter-Allied Commission. Liberal provisions may thus be made in so far as compatible with a faithful and complete discharge of the duty assumed and with the internal police regulations of the country of sojourn. Working gangs shall be organized on the model of military labor battalions.

The workmen shall be under the control of their overseers in whatever concerns discipline within the gangs; with respect to breaches of discipline by combined numbers calculated to disturb the public peace,[4] and offenses against common law, they shall be subject to the police power of the country of sojourn and to its laws.

Working conditions shall be such as prevail for workmen of similar kinds in the country of origin, subject to regulation by the Inter-Allied Commission.

The country of origin shall be bound to lodge, feed and insure the workmen and their supervisors at its own expense. The country of sojourn shall decide whether to permit the sale to the country of the workmen's origin of objects necessary to the foregoing purposes. The country of origin shall pay wages, of which the sum total including issues of goods shall be equivalent to that of laborers of the same kind. It shall provide and deposit with the country of sojourn an amount of its national currency, equal to three months' wages. This fund shall be maintained and replenished, if there be occasion, throughout the duration of the undertaking.

The value of the labor supplied upon each piece of work shall be determined by the Inter-Allied Commission and the amount estimated shall be credited to the country of the workmen's origin.

The laborers enrolled shall be of good average character and skill. Each workman shall carry an identification card with his photograph on it and his police record shall be in the hands of the supervisor of the detachment to which he belongs. Any enemy laborer or enemy member of the working force may be rejected as undesirable by the country of sojourn without the latter having to show cause for its decision, and such person shall immediately be sent away and replaced.

Jobs shall be performed under the direction of engineers and architects of the country of sojourn, who shall transmit their orders to the supervisors of the gangs of workmen in whatever manner is usual for jobs of the kind in hand.

The shifts shall relieve each other as detachments and when work stops laborers shall go off by detachments.

[no date]

---

[4] The French text omits the phrase, "with respect . . . public peace."

ANNEX II

ENEMY'S CAPACITY TO MAKE REPARATION—CAPACITY OF THE NEW REPUBLIC OF HUNGARY

(Presented by the Serbian Delegation.)

The frontiers of the new Hungarian Republic not being as yet determined, it is very difficult to make definite statements in regard to the paying capacity of the new Hungarian State.

We shall, therefore, limit ourselves to giving as precise figures as possible, taking as a basis the ethnographic division and the territorial configuration of the former country of Hungary.

The new Hungarian State will have an area of about 130,000 square kilometers and will comprise about 10,000,000 inhabitants. It will embrace almost the whole of the two Hungarian plains (the great and the small Hungarian plains)—that is to say, those vast lands which lie between the middle portion of the course of the Danube and its two great tributaries, the Drave and the Fisza;[5] while the entire massif of the Carpathians will at last, after long centuries, become again the property of the Czecho-Slovak, Ukrainian, and Roumanian nations. When this change is effected, the Hungarian State will become still more an agricultural country, having lost the great mineral wealth of the Carpathian Mountains and the vast virgin forests which covered those mountains almost to the tops of their highest peaks.

It is true that the greater part of the industries of old Hungary will remain on the territory of the new Hungarian State; but more than ever these industries will feel the need of coal and iron, which will have to be imported in much larger quantities than heretofore.

With these remarks as a preface, we shall attempt to draw a rapid sketch of the economic resources of the new Hungarian Republic and of its means of paying the greatest possible sum for war indemnities.

This task is evidently very difficult at this time, particularly for the two following reasons; in the first place, no one can figure out definitely the economic development that will take place in the new State after it has lost the boundaries that have existed throughout long centuries; in the second place, the existing official statistics are not made in such a way that one can, taking into consideration the general state of affairs resulting from the war, immediately utilize them for the purpose in view.

To accomplish our task, we must consider:

[5] Error for "Tisza." The Theiss River.

1. The entire wealth, private and public, of the new Hungarian State;

2. The income from this national wealth;

3. Foreign commerce;

4. The financial condition of the new republic.

The private and public wealth of the new State may be divided as follows:

A.—Lands.

	Hectares	Value in Francs
Arable land	6,750,000	13,500,000,000
Gardens	150,000	450,000,000
Meadows	1,100,000	1,980,000,000
Vineyards	190,000	570,000,000
Pasturage	1,400,000	700,000,000
Forests (counting the land and timber)	2,050,000[6]	6,325,000,000
Uncultivated land	700,000	

B.—Agricultural Inventory.
   (a) Live stock:

	Head	
Cattle	3,000,000	1,770,000,000
Horses	1,040,000	680,000,000
Pigs	3,700,000	615,000,000[7]
Sheep	3,000,000	120,000,000
Goats	50,000	2,000,000
Fowl	50,000,000	75,000,000
(b) Inanimate real property		300,000,000
C. Buildings and building sites		8,000,000,000
D. Iron and coal mines		500,000,000
E. Railroads		2,000,000,000
F. Telegraph and telephone lines		50,000,000
G. Boats		230,000,000
H. National capital invested:		
(a) In industries		800,000,000
(b) In banks and savings-banks		1,850,000,000
(c) In trust companies		175,000,000
I. Savings accounts		2,150,000,000
J. Gold and silver coin		300,000,000
K. Other gold and silver objects		200,000,000
L. Foreign securities		200,000,000
M. Furniture, works of art, etc.		1,000,000,000
N. Foreign bonds		2,000,000,000
O. Bonds of the former Hungarian debt		1,000,000,000
Total		47,542,000,000

We must note here that we have not indicated above various categories representing immense amounts of capital, but which

---

[6] The French text reads, 1,400,000. This is evidently a mistake.

[7] The French text reads, 614,000,000. The English figure makes the total correct.

give no direct return,—as, for example, roads, certain public buildings, churches, etc.,—and which, therefore, cannot be reckoned with the figures which it is our purpose to set forth.

The returns from Hungary's national resources which we have just enumerated may be estimated as follows:

	Quintals	Value in Francs
Wheat	24,000,000	600,000,000
Rye	8,200,000	157,500,000
Barley	7,600,000	128,000,000
Oats	6,750,000	126,000,000
Indian corn	22,000,000	340,000,000
Other cereals	850,000	10,000,000
Beans	1,020,000	24,500,000
Peas and lentils	66,000	2,600,000
Tobacco	425,000	18,200,000
Other indigenous plants	525,000	36,500,000
Moha (German millet)	100,000	1,500,000
Melons	1,600,000	9,600,000
Pumpkins	18,000,000	26,000,000
Cabbages	9,000,000	54,000,000
Fruit	1,500,000	41,250,000
Forage seed	300,000	13,000,000
Forage	70,000,000	400,000,000
Straw	180,000,000	360,000,000
Wine (unfermented)	2,165,000	78,660,000
Beets	21,120,000	48,500,000
Potatoes	25,850,000	187,000,000[8]
Wood		100,000,000
Coal	25,000,000	26,000,000
Iron	1,000,000	8,000,000
Stock-farm animals		500,000,000
Products of the industry of the country, exclusive of tobacco and of material consumed already deducted		600,000,000[9]
Products of foreign commerce, plus freight costs paid out to local transport organizations		400,000,000
Interest on foreign securities		80,000,000
Money receipts (from savings of emigrants)		100,000,000
Products of the tobacco industry		90,000,000
Various other returns		100,000,000
Total		4,667,310,000

We do not mention under special headings certain returns (such as interests on savings, stock dividends, etc.), since they are as a matter of fact included in other returns appearing in the above list under agriculture, industry or foreign or local commerce, and

[8] The French text reads, 187,500,000. That makes the total correct.
[9] The French text omits this item, which is needed to make the total correct.

since, if we cited them separately, it would then be necessary to deduct them from these latter categories.

Thus, it would be necessary to deduct from the returns mentioned:

1. The value of imports, with the exception of raw materials, the value of which is already deducted from the value of the products of local industries;

2. The interest on foreign debts. The latter, however, will be investigated when we come to deal with the finances of the new Hungarian State, while the imports not as yet deducted, consisting either of raw materials destined for direct consumption or of manufactured articles, reach a figure of about 600 million francs, which brings the net sum of returns to about 4,000,000,000 francs.

However, as all these figures are calculated from pre-war prices, and as these prices must be increased by at least 50%, it may be estimated that the returns from the national Hungarian wealth amount to about 6,000,000,000 francs.

After investigating the wealth comprised in the returns of the new republic, let us pass to the third heading—foreign commerce. Here we shall limit ourselves to giving a brief summary of the most important articles of export, and if we take as a basis the statement of the foreign commerce of the former kingdom of the crown of Saint-Étienne, we shall see that the new Republic of Hungary will be able to export the following quantities:

		Francs
Wheat (in grain and flour)	5,260,000 quintals	171,500,000
Rye	1,620,000 quintals	31,110,000
Barley	1,230,000 quintals	23,610,000
Oats	850,000 quintals	15,850,000
Beets (in form of raw and of refined sugar)	1,160,000 quintals	37,100,000
Potatoes	400,000 quintals	2,900,000
Beans	270,000 quintals	6,500,000
Wine	615,000 hectolitres	26,250,000
Cattle	125,500 head	70,000,000
Horses	23,500 head	15,250,000
Pigs	270,000 head	45,000,000
Fowl, dead	85,000 quintals	13,200,000
Fowl, live	2,800,000	7,000,000
Eggs	200,000 quintals	26,000,000
Wood (European lumber)	1,500,000 quintals	15,500,000
Wood (unmilled logs)	650,000 quintals	3,200,000

The produce listed above, if we take as a basis of our proportion, for example, the statement of the year 1913, would form about 50% of the entire exportation of the new republic. The remaining 50%

would consist of products of minor importance and of manufactures. Imports would be chiefly minerals and manufactured
products, and would also amount to about one billion francs.

It must be emphasized that these prices which we have taken as
the basis of our calculations are those of pre-war days, and that at
least during the years directly following the war these prices will
be much higher.

Having thus set forth a study of the first three headings which
covered the resources and the income of the new Hungarian State,
we shall pass to the study of the fourth and last heading, State
finances. This is the more necessary, in that these determine in
great measure the possibility of the new State's carrying out its
obligations toward the victorious nations.

Before commencing the study of the financial situation of the
Hungarian Republic, we must take note of the fact that the Kingdom of Hungary suffered for many years from the malady common
to newly formed States; indeed, constituted as it was in 1867 on
an entirely new basis, the basis of dualism, it was able with the aid
of the powerful resources of the entire monarchy to make rapid
economic progress. But in its desire thus to pass directly from the
condition of an agricultural and patriarchal society to that of a
highly developed industrial organization, it suffered grave financial
crises, which caused it to float large foreign loans and thereby
forced the whole monarchy to maintain a large amount of paper
currency, while actually it had a gold standard. A few months
before the beginning of the war preparations were being made to
return, in part at least, to payments in gold coin; but since gold
disappeared from circulation during the war, and since the old
monarchy has crumbled under the weight of events, the effort
once begun will never be resumed.

The new Hungarian Republic thus finds itself confronted by
tremendous difficulties, obliged as it is to bear the load of a heavy
and troublesome heritage, as well as all the debts that now en-
cumber it as a result of the war.

The Hungarian State was in former times unable to regulate its
budget without resorting to exceptional measures, and it had contracted new debts, almost every year up to the end of 1913—debts
which, at that time, amounted to 6,195,975,000 kronen net. Since
by the rules of international law the portions of the former Hungarian State detached from it must assume a portion of these debts,
the new republic will be alloted a total of pre-war debts amounting
to about 4 billions. Taking this as a basis, let us pass to the forma-
tion of the budget of the new State.

Income

	Francs
Direct taxes	180,000,000
Tolls	150,000,000
Stamp taxes	25,000,000
Transit rights	60,000,000
Monopolies	80,000,000
Revenues from railroads, mail service, etc. (State industries)	550,000,000
Customs	50,000,000
Other revenues	50,000,000
Total income	1,145,000,000

Expenses

President of the Republic	1,250,000
Parliament	4,700,000
Pensions of State employees	50,000,000
Invalid pensions	100,000,000
Pre-war debts	200,000,000
Cour des comptes (a tribunal of finance)	500,000
Administrative tribunal (Council of State)	850,000
Presidency of the ministry	2,500,000
Ministry of home affairs	60,000,000
Ministry of finance	180,000,000
Ministry of commerce	220,000,000
Ministry of agriculture	35,000,000
Ministry of public worship and instruction	60,000,000
Ministry of justice	30,000,000
Ministry of war	50,000,000
Ministry of foreign affairs	20,000,000
Quarterly investments	120,000,000
Total	1,134,800,000

Thus, the receipts exceed the expenditure by about 10 millions. It must be added that all these figures are based on the Hungarian budgets before the war, and that the fact that they are not reduced in proportion to the diminution of the area of the new State and of its population is explained by special factors which we shall now indicate. For example, the figure cited for pensions of State employees even exceeds the pre-war figure; this results by reason of the fact that the new State will be obliged to assume the responsibility for the maintenance of many employees whom the detached districts will not wish to accept. It must be borne in mind that nearly 90% of the State employees and officers of former Hungary were Magyars and served as pioneers in the movement of Magyarization in the Slovak, Roumanian, Serbo-Croat, etc., countries as well as in the army; and since the new State cannot take them all into its service and must therefore indemnify them, at least in part, by pensions, the item for pensions had to be increased.

Moreover, the figures cited for the maintenance of the army and the figures for the expenses of the ministry of commerce are estimated below pre-war prices; in the case of the former, this is done because of the inevitable reduction of the peace-time army; and in the case of the latter, by reason of the fact that the greatest expenditures of the ministry of commerce were devoted partly to the support of railroads, roads, mail service, telegraph and telephone services in the mountainous districts of the former State, and partly to the support of the port of Fiume and of the merchant marine. Nevertheless, the figure of investments is left in proportion to its amount in previous budgets, since, now that the rolling-stock of the railroads has in large part been worn out or destroyed during the war, it will be necessary to go to great expense in order to renew it, so that the entire item will have to be expended to this end; and this expenditure will be all the more possible since the other institutions depending on the Ministries of Finance, Public Worship, etc., and located in the territory of the new State, are already so abundantly endowed that they can dispense for a long time with relief loans.

On examination of the budget of the new State appearing above, it is apparent that it balances automatically, without recourse being necessary to exceptional measures such as loans; and this result may be realized if the Hungarian administrators will have due regard for the new state of affairs in their country.

It remains to find means of paying the war indemnities of the victorious States. It is only natural that these indemnities should be in proportion to the national revenues. Now, these revenues amount to about 6 billion francs, as we have just calculated; it follows that on a national revenue of 6 billion francs the State will levy taxes amounting to about 1,100,000,000 francs (that is, about 19%) to defray its regular expenses; 19%, or at most 25%, could, in our estimation, serve for the payment of war indemnities; in that this sum could constitute a special item in the budget of the new State, an item which could be raised from the returns on a special tax. The obligation to pay, which would thereby be imposed, would perhaps not quite correspond, we must admit, to the proportion to which Germany will probably be held; but if one bears in mind the capacity of each State for development, and above all the fact that Germany, by uniting with Germanic Austria, will be larger even than she was heretofore, while Hungary will lose more than half of her territory, falling thus from her position of a great Power before the war to the position of a middle Power, and in addition will lose direct access to the sea as well as almost all her mineral deposits, one must concede that it would be difficult to obtain from Hungary more than is calculated above.

In conclusion, we must repeat that, in our estimation, the Hungarian Republic should be required to pay, in the twelve months following the conclusion of the Peace, a capital sum of about 2 billion francs.

Paris, 11 March, 1919.　　Dr. Svetimir Korporitch,
　　　　　　　　　　　　Lawyer, Secretary of National Food
　　　　　　　　　　　　Supply (joint stock company of
　　　　　　　　　　　　Zagreb) Technical Expert.

DOCUMENT 529

Second Subcommittee: Minutes of the Eighteenth Meeting, March 13, 1919, 4:30 P. M.

[EOM, Second Subcommittee, pp. 76-77. French condensed minutes, PV, CRD, pp. 803-4.]

The Second Sub-Committee of the Commission on Reparation of Damage (Financial Capacity of the Enemy States—Their Means of Payment and Reparation) met on Thursday, 13 March, 1919, at 4.30 P. M., at the Ministry of Finance, Lord Cunliffe in the Chair.

Present: Lord Cunliffe (*British Empire*); Mr. d'Amelio (*Italy*); Mr. Tatsumi (*Japan*); Mr. Chamiec (*Poland*); Mr. Danielopol (*Roumania*); Mr. Stoyanowitch (*Serbia*).

There were also present: Messrs. Despret (*Belgium*), Freire d'Andrade (*Portugal*), List (*Czecho-Slovak Republic*) and Mylonas (*Greece*).[1]

The Chairman proposed the adoption of the minutes of the 15th meeting. The minutes were adopted.[2]

Supply of Enemy Labor

He then submitted the following fresh draft of the article to be inserted in the Peace Preliminaries, dealing with the supply of enemy labor:—

"As a further means of covering the enemy's debt, it may be permissible, in suitable cases and at stated times, for enemy workers to take part in the work of reconstruction in devastated regions, it being understood that they shall be subject to the conditions specified below and formulated for the purpose of assuring their good behavior and guaranteeing the fact that their pay shall not be higher than the rate of pay existing in the district in question."

[1] According to the French minutes, List was not present.
[2] The French minutes omit this paragraph.

MR. DESPRET (*Belgium*) remarked that there was a fundamental difference between the present text and the one discussed at the preceding meeting (17th Meeting, Annex I). The furnishing of labor by the enemy was left to his option according to one text—made obligatory according to the other.

After an exchange of views in which the CHAIRMAN, and Messrs. DESPRET, MYLONAS, D'AMELIO, CHAMIEC and DANIELOPOL took part, it became evident that it was impossible to arrive at a satisfactory mean between compulsory and optional supply of labor by the enemy countries.

The CHAIRMAN therefore proposed that the question be referred to the Plenary Commission, with the explanation that the Committee had been unable to arrive at an agreement on the subject.

The Committee accepted this proposal.

Taxation of Enemy Countries

The CHAIRMAN suggested to the Delegates that they should discuss the question of taxes to be raised in enemy countries, and reminded them that, in his opinion, a bill should be presented to the enemy States and they should be left to find the means of paying it, subject to coercion later on in the event default of payment occurred.

MR. DESPRET (*Belgium*) considered that nothing would be obtained in this way and that enemy States should, on the contrary, be informed of the stated sources of revenue which they would have to tap.

MR. CHAMIEC (*Poland*) was also of this opinion.

MR. D'AMELIO (*Italy*) pointed out that, after the question of principle had been referred to the Plenary Commission, the Committee would be able to consider the question of the levying of taxes in enemy States as an acceptable mode of payment and to discuss the means of applying the same.

Tax on Capital Discussed

The Committee therefore proceeded to discuss the question of a tax on capital.

The CHAIRMAN pointed out that a tax on capital would, in effect, be a tax on the bankers who would have to advance it. This they could only do by inflating the paper currency, and then the advantage to foreign creditors would be illusory.

After a discussion between the CHAIRMAN, and Messrs. CHAMIEC (*Poland*) and LIST (*Czecho-Slovak Republic*), the general opinion was arrived at that some other forms of tax should be considered.

Other Taxes

The CHAIRMAN suggested more particularly taxes on towns, railways, canals, etc., adding that it would be best not to settle the amount to be yielded by each tax, but to allow this to be done by the enemy countries, merely giving the latter the figure of the total to be received.

MR. D'AMELIO (*Italy*) asked that the provisional report which the American, British and French Delegates had to present might be submitted to the Committee as soon as possible, in order that it might serve as a basis for a discussion which, without it, threatened to end in nothing.[3]

The CHAIRMAN stated that his draft was ready, but that he could not submit it without the consent of the two other *rapporteurs*.

The next meeting was fixed for Friday, 14 March, at 2.30 P. M., to consider the following questions: (1) Indemnity payable in enemy merchant ships; (2) Continuation of discussion on taxes to be levied in enemy countries.

The meeting adjourned at 6.30 P. M.

CUNLIFFE,
Chairman.

F. FOBERTI,
Secretary.

DOCUMENT 530

Second Subcommittee: Minutes of the Nineteenth Meeting, March 14, 1919, 2:30 P. M.

[EOM, Second Subcommittee, pp. 78-79. French condensed minutes, PV, CRD, pp. 805-7.]

The Second Sub-Committee of the Commission on Reparation [of Damage] (Financial Capacity of the Enemy States—Their Means of Payment and Reparation) met on 14 March, 1919, at 2.30 P. M. at the Ministry of Finance, LORD CUNLIFFE in the Chair.

Present: MR. STRAUSS (*U. S. A.*); LORD CUNLIFFE (*British Empire*); MR. D'AMELIO (*Italy*); MR. TATSUMI (*Japan*); MR. DANIELOPOL (*Roumania*) and MR. STOYANOWITCH (*Serbia*).

There were also present Messrs. DESPRET (*Belgium*), MYLONAS (*Greece*) and FREIRE D'ANDRADE (*Portugal*).[1]

Taxation of Enemy Countries

The CHAIRMAN asked the Committee to resume consideration of the question of levying taxes in enemy countries.

---

[3] See at the end of Document 520.

[1] According to the French minutes, Mylonas was not present.

MR. DESPRET (*Belgium*) stated the matter as follows:[2] He assumed a total enemy debt of 200 billions; and that the Allies might collect about 25 billions in gold or its equivalent immediately. There would remain 175 billions. He assumed that this sum should be amortized by an annual payment of 10 billions, including interest, and that 3½ billions of this, or more, would be covered by deliveries of goods. Then the Committee might content itself with reporting as to the balance "that it would consider it advisable to impose taxes in the enemy countries up to an amount sufficient to complete the payment in gold or its equivalent."

The CHAIRMAN was of the opinion that if the Delegates were in favor of accepting paper money in payment from the enemy it would be necessary to fix the rate of exchange in advance.

MR. STOYANOWITCH (*Serbia*) wished to see a careful study of Germany's resources and wished that such study might not only include German figures of 1914 but reductions due to war losses and corrections on account of the development of war industries and the plundering of occupied territory, etc.

MR. DANIELOPOL (*Roumania*) thought that the question of payment by the enemy should be regarded as two-fold.

(a) Immediate payment from existing wealth.

(b) Payment from production and from future wealth, extending over a time to be determined.

In comparison with the total sum to be paid by the enemy, the amount which they could pay either immediately or within twelve months after the conclusion of peace would be very small. As a matter of fact this amount had been placed at about 25 or 30 billion francs by some and at about 40 billion francs by other members of this Committee.

The question of payment in paper marks did not appear to have any great importance because if a large amount of paper marks (about 30 or 40 billions) were to be exported it was certain that this paper would have no great value; but he thought that there was a possibility of obtaining effective results from the taking over by the Allies of a part of the existing wealth of the enemy, such as stocks, bonds and shares of all kinds which would be turned over to a financial organization to be constituted, either as a part of the League of Nations or in some other manner and which would administer these shares for the benefit of the Allies.

The most serious question would be the manner of assuring the payment by the enemy of the annuity within the time necessary for

---

[2] The French text inserts here, "en ne citant des chiffres que pour la mieux faire saisir."

the liquidation of their debt. He thought that this could be done only by the Allies controlling German production. The Allies might control the enemy production by means of an organization to be constituted, perhaps as a part of the League of Nations, and might direct it in the different parts of the world according to their needs and would thus be able to assure the payment of the annuity owed by the enemy.

MR. D'AMELIO (*Italy*) put the question—"Do we want marks or do we not?" which he considered might be put in another form— "Are we going to buy from Germany?" It would only be in case this question were answered in the affirmative that the question of levying taxes in Germany would become practically interesting.

Proposed Report on the Question

The CHAIRMAN proposed to report to the Commission as follows: The Second Sub-Committee believes that taxes should be imposed at once in Germany, but what taxes should be imposed and by whom they should be imposed the Second Sub-Committee has not been able to agree.

MR. DESPRET (*Belgium*) thought it would be better to report the opinion of the majority of the Sub-Committee to the full Committee and to add a minority report if need be.

The CHAIRMAN preferred to make a report confined to the statement that the Sub-Committee had not been able to reach an agreement.

MR. STRAUSS (*U. S. A.*) agreed with the CHAIRMAN'S view.

MR. D'AMELIO (*Italy*) proposed a report in the following form as preferable to the CHAIRMAN'S last suggestion:—The Sub-Committee recommends to the Commission that special taxes leviable in Germany and other enemy countries ought to be considered as a means of payment and reparation.

The CHAIRMAN reserved his own opinion in respect to this proposal and thought it better, in view of the absence of certain Delegates, to postpone further discussion until the next meeting.

Enemy Merchant Marine

He then proposed to go back to the consideration of the enemies' Merchant Marine as a means of payment. He had obtained full details about the enemy Merchant Marine from British experts, except that he had not been able to obtain figures on the Turkish and Bulgarian shipping.

MR. MYLONAS (*Greece*) called attention to the figures on the Bulgarian shipping contained in Annex II, 11th Meeting.

The CHAIRMAN took up the problem of appraisal and thought there were three points to be considered:

(1) The date as of which ships should be appraised.

(2) The method of appraisal.

(3) The degree of moderation to be adopted in demanding deliveries, especially with respect to fishing-boats and coasting-vessels of less than 1600 tons.

The next meeting was fixed for Monday at 3.30 P. M., for the consideration of the following: (1) Final action on the first two questions referred back by the Commission. (2) Further consideration of: (a) the enemy merchant marine; (b) the levying of taxes in enemy countries.

The meeting adjourned at 6.30 P. M.

CUNLIFFE,

F. FOBERTI,   *Chairman.*

Secretary.

DOCUMENT 531

Second Subcommittee: Minutes of the Twentieth Meeting, March 17, 1919, 3:30 P. M.

[EOM, Second Subcommittee, pp. 80-81. French condensed minutes, PV, CRD, pp. 808-9.]

The Second Sub-Committee of the Commission on Reparation of Damage (Financial Capacity of the Enemy States—Their Means of Payment and Reparation) met on Monday, 17 March, at 3.30 P. M., at the Ministry of Finance, LORD CUNLIFFE in the Chair.

Present: MR. LAMONT (*U. S. A.*); LORD CUNLIFFE (*British Empire*); MR. D'AMELIO (*Italy*); MR. TATSUMI (*Japan*); MR. RYBARSKI (*Poland*); MR. GHEORGHIU (*Roumania*); MR. STOYANO-WITCH (*Serbia*).

There were also present Messrs. DESPRET (*Belgium*), MYLONAS (*Greece*) and FREIRE D'ANDRADE (*Portugal*).

The CHAIRMAN proposed the adoption of the minutes of the 16th meeting and the Annex thereto. These were adopted.[1]

MR. DESPRET (*Belgium*), referring to the Annex, wished to observe that the list of categories contained in the first paragraph, "machinery, rolling-stock . . . live-stock, etc.," was purely illustrative and not limitative. The Belgian Delegation especially reserved the right to demand:

(a) boats for inland waterways, and

(b) semi-manufactured articles (iron profiles and sheet iron) to replace similar objects destroyed or stolen.

---

[1] The French minutes omit this paragraph.

The CHAIRMAN agreed with this interpretation.

In the Annex, paragraph 1, after the words "Allied Powers" the words "and to their citizens" should be added.[2]

Taxation of Enemy Countries

The CHAIRMAN, returning to the question of taxes to be levied in enemy countries, asked the Delegates to submit any new proposals they might have.

Arguments presented by Messrs. LÉVY, NEYMARK and CHEVALIER (*French Experts*) tended to show that, by merely increasing actually existing taxes in Germany, an annual income of 2½ or 3 milliards of marks could be produced.

The CHAIRMAN, while drawing the attention of the Committee to the difficulties of the application of such proposals, thanked the Delegates for the exact figures which they had presented and expressed a wish to continue the discussion along the same lines.

MR. DESPRET (*Belgium*) thought that the Allies should neither assume the task of collecting taxes in enemy countries nor content themselves with presenting a bill to enemy countries, but should determine, in the Treaty of Peace, not only the sum total of their claims but also certain obligatory methods of payment.

The CHAIRMAN insisted on the importance of selecting taxes of a sort easy to collect, i.e., customs duties preferably to income taxes, etc.

A discussion followed in which Messrs. GHEORGHIU (*Roumania*), STOYANOWITCH (*Serbia*) and MYLONAS (*Greece*) took part which indicated that there might be an advantage in obliging the enemy countries to establish monopolies, especially of tobacco, coffee and petrol, the revenues from which would be under control of Allied Commissions.

MR. STOYANOWITCH (*Serbia*) estimated that by some such means a revenue of 4,200,000,000 francs could be obtained.

The CHAIRMAN expressed his satisfaction with the line the discussion was following and hoped that further definite proposals would be forthcoming.

The next meeting was fixed for Tuesday, 18 March, 1919, at 3.30 P. M., discussion of taxes upon enemy countries to be resumed.

The meeting adjourned at 6.30 P. M.[3]

CUNLIFFE,
Chairman.

F. FOBERTI,
Secretary.

[2] The French minutes omit the last two sentences.
[3] According to the French minutes, at 5:30 P. M.

DOCUMENT 532

Second Subcommittee: Minutes of the Twenty-first Meeting (Including Annex), March 18, 1919, 3:30 P. M.

[EOM, Second Subcommittee, pp. 82-84. French condensed minutes, PV, CRD, pp. 810-13.]

The Second Sub-Committee of the Commission on Reparation of Damage (Financial Capacity of the Enemy States—Their Means of Payment and Reparation) met on 18 March, 1919, at 3.30 P. M., at the French Ministry of Finance, LORD CUNLIFFE in the Chair.

Present: LORD CUNLIFFE (*British Empire*); MR. TATSUMI (*Japan*); MR. STOYANOWITCH (*Serbia*); MR. GHEORGHIU (*Roumania*).

There were also present Messrs. R. B. [*G.*] LÉVY, and CHEVALIER (*Experts for France*), DESPRET (*Belgium*) and LIST (*Czecho-Slovak Republic*).[1]

Taxation of Enemy Countries

The CHAIRMAN, returning to the question of taxes which might be raised in enemy countries, asked the Delegates to submit further proposals.

MR. LIST (*Czecho-Slovak Republic*) submitted comparative statistics of the public revenues and of the total per capita taxation in France, England, Austria-Hungary and Germany[2] tending to show that the latter was much the least heavily taxed. If the military budget of Germany were taken into account, a considerable margin of taxation was left, which could be turned to the profit of the Allies.

MR. R. G. LÉVY (*Expert for France*), referring to his remarks at the previous meeting, thought it would be simpler to confine taxation to additions to already existing taxes, with, perhaps, the addition of a new tax on coal. By this means an annual revenue of several billion marks could be obtained, according to detailed figures he submitted for reference.

MR. STOYANOWITCH (*Serbia*) thought that by obliging Germany to establish monopolies of tobacco and coffee, together with taxes on importations of foodstuffs and raw materials, an annual revenue of about 3 billion marks could be obtained, but that, as a

---

[1] According to the French minutes, Freire d'Andrade was also present.
[2] According to the French minutes, in Serbia also.

result of the economic development to be counted on after the war, this figure might easily reach 10 billion marks in a few years.

After an exchange of opinions between Messrs. R. G. LÉVY and CHEVALIER (*Experts for France*), STOYANOWITCH (*Serbia*), D'ANDRADE (*Portugal*) and LIST (*Poland*)[3] as to the respective advantages of taxes and monopolies, the CHAIRMAN requested the Delegates to submit their expert opinion in the form of a list of taxes proposed.

MR. DESPRET (*Belgium*) observed that the Sub-Committee, as far as the first part of its work was concerned (Capacity of Enemy Countries to Pay), had contented itself with giving only general indications. He thought it would be well, in order to avoid unnecessary delay in the work of the Sub-Committee, to treat in the same way the second part (Method of Payment) which had now been reached. That it would merely be necessary to submit a general scheme of taxation, without entering into details of application.

The CHAIRMAN agreed, and asked MR. LÉVY, MR. CHEVALIER and MR. STOYANOWITCH to submit proposals of the nature indicated.

MR. GHEORGHIU (*Roumania*) presented a Memorandum on the subject of the Constanza-Constantinople Cable (see Annex).

The next meeting was fixed for Thursday, 20 March, 1919, at 3.30 P. M.

The meeting adjourned at 6 P. M.

CUNLIFFE,
Chairman.

F. FOBERTI,
    Secretary.

ANNEX

NOTE ON THE CONSTANZA-CONSTANTINOPLE CABLE

(*Presented by [the] Roumanian Delegation.*)

The Roumanian Delegation presents a note concerning the telegraphic cable between Constanza and Constantinople which reverts, by right, to Roumania according to the clauses of the contract of concession.

The cable was laid down by the Osteuropaeische Kabelgesellschaft of Cologne, and was put into operation in June, 1905, with a single conductor and a total length of 343 kilometers 212 meters (185 sea miles).

---

[3] Error for *Czecho-Slovak Republic.*

According to the clauses of the contract of concession, the Roumanian Government was to pay to the Company an annual subsidy of 50,000 francs; but in case the gross revenue of the company from cable charges between Constanza and Constantinople exceeded 50,000 francs per year, the above subsidy was to be reduced by 5,000 francs for each 10,000 francs of excess.

The gross revenue between July, 1905, and April, 1906, was 111,806 francs and the only subsidy paid by the Roumanian Government during this time was 17,694 francs.

After 1906 Roumania ceased to pay any subsidy, as the revenue from the cable for the succeeding years was as follows:

1906	Frs.	143,438.36
1907	Frs.	173,823.07
1908	Frs.	207,878.00[4]
1911	Frs.	300,948.11
1912	Frs.	458,680.96[5]

This revenue has continued to increase from year to year, reaching, during the latter years, a sum equal to the amount of capital invested in the construction, exploitation and maintenance of the cable.

In 1912 the Company requested authority to lay down a new cable, the existing one being no longer adequate to the needs of the traffic. This plan could not be carried out on account of events in the Balkans and in order to increase the capacity of the existing cable rapid instruments such as "Siemens" instruments had to be employed.

The concession was to expire in 1935. The cable has been in effective use for 11 years without any interruption.

At the beginning the charges paid in to the Roumanian Government for transit through its territory of all correspondence utilizing the Constanza-Constantinople cable were the regular international telegraphic charges. Later, in order to attract more correspondence over this cable, the charges were materially reduced and Roumania shared in these reductions by diminishing its participation in terminal and transit charges.

The ownership of this cable therefore reverts by right to Roumania, in view not only of the sacrifices consented to by the State in the reduction of charges in order to assure an appreciable revenue to the Company, but also by the clauses of the contract of concession which reserved the exploitation of the cable to the Roumanian administration.

[4] According to the French text, 208,078.00.
[5] According to the French text, 158,680.96.

DOCUMENT 533

Second Subcommittee: Minutes of the Twenty-second Meeting (Including Annexes I-III), March 20, 1919, 3:30 P. M.

[EOM, Second Subcommittee, pp. 85-94. No French minutes. French text of Annexes I and III, PV, CRD, pp. 860-67. No French text of Annex II.]

The Second Sub-Committee of the Commission on Reparation of Damage (Financial Capacity of the Enemy States—Their Means of Payment and Reparation) met on Thursday, 20 March, at 3.30 P. M., at the Ministry of Finance, LORD CUNLIFFE in the Chair.

Present: LORD CUNLIFFE (*British Empire*); MR. D'AMELIO (*Italy*); MR. TATSUMI (*Japan*); MR. ANTONESCO (*Roumania*); MR. STOYANOWITCH (*Serbia*).

There were also present Messrs. DESPRET (*Belgium*), MYLONAS (*Greece*) and FREIRE D'ANDRADE (*Portugal*).

The CHAIRMAN proposed the adoption of the minutes of the 17th and 18th meetings. These were adopted without remark. MR. D'ANDRADE (*Portugal*) asked for an alteration in the 14th minutes already adopted, and the CHAIRMAN requested him to present his statement, which would be made a part of the present record.

MR. D'ANDRADE recalled that during the 14th meeting he had asked the question whether the text to be prepared on the subject of replacement in kind of objects destroyed or stolen by act of war was applicable also to the colonies, and that the CHAIRMAN had said that the question of this special application would be taken up later.

The CHAIRMAN proposed the examination of the minutes of the 19th and 20th meetings and after the discussion of several alterations the adoption of these minutes was reserved for the next meeting.

MR. STOYANOWITCH (*Serbia*) presented a note on methods of payment to be imposed upon Germany (Annex I).

MR. ANTONESCO (*Roumania*) presented a note on the financial situation of European countries before the war (Annex II).

The CHAIRMAN, in the absence of MR. LOUCHEUR (*France*), postponed further discussion of additional taxation in enemy countries as a means of payment until a later meeting.

State Property as a Means of Payment

MR. D'AMELIO (*Italy*) observed that the Italian Delegation had proposed to consider, as a means of payment, the surrender of property of enemy States situated in Allied countries. He recalled that the Sub-Committee had already admitted, as a means of payment, the property of enemy private citizens, and that this decision could be extended to include State property. For this purpose each Delegation could present a list of such property situated within the boundaries of its country.

After a discussion in which Messrs. DESPRET (*Belgium*), MYLONAS (*Greece*) and D'AMELIO (*Italy*) took part it was admitted, as a principle, that State property might form a means of payment.

The CHAIRMAN observed there might be difficulty in identifying such property in Allied countries, as it was often disguised in trust or in the name of nominees, especially in the case of bank deposits.

MR. MYLONAS (*Greece*) pointed out that a large part of such property could be identified through the records of sequestration in the various Allied countries. He also presented a study of Germany's capacity to make reparation (Annex III).

The question of State property of enemy countries situated in countries to be ceded to other Powers by the Peace Treaties was raised, and the CHAIRMAN thought that this question was outside the province of this Sub-Committee.

The next meeting was fixed for Saturday, 22 March, at 3.30 P. M. The meeting adjourned at 5.30 P. M.

CUNLIFFE,
Chairman.

F. FOBERTI,
  Secretary.

ANNEX I

ENEMY'S CAPACITY TO MAKE REPARATION: TAXATION IN GERMANY

(*Presented by the Serbian Delegation.*)

I

From 1873 there were two powerful and large groups in Germany: the agrarian conservatives and the representatives of the iron industry who spread the idea of creating economic autocracy. In 1875 the "Association of German Industrials" was founded with the aim of combating the principle of free exchange. In 1879 the agrarians succeeded in protecting the production of wheat by customs duties. By successive increases these duties reached almost prohibitive rates extending not only to all other agricultural products but also to live stock. At the end the protection of agricultural products was completed by the protection of the great industries. "The production of iron was protected by duties on iron, that of hard coal by a railway rate, which extravagantly increased the cost of coal transported from the frontier to the interior."

The policy was to make Germany self-sufficient. This policy partially succeeded. From 1901 to 1913 the population increased by almost 10 millions—the total amount of wheat imported remained almost constant, 1.9 millions of tons in 1901 against 2 million tons in 1913. The same situation is revealed for the other agricultural products. But Germany paid more for her bread, and also for her meat and other provisions than if she had given up the protection of her agriculture. The policy of economic self-government considers only the interests of the producer; it has been possible to develop production in considerable proportions, but the interests of the consumers have been neglected or even sacrificed. Between 1900 and 1912 the general increase of prices raised the cost of living of a German working family from 45 to 50%, and wages by no means followed the same proportion. The improvement in the existence of workmen brought by the increased wages has been more than offset by the increase in the price of the principal staples (bread, butter, meat). *The policy followed by Germany enriches a few privileged ones, does not help the peasants and the rural workmen at all, and has only little effect on the industrial workman.*

Germany, at the time of its unification, was still a country mainly agricultural. After 44 years it has become an industrial State. In 1882 the agricultural class comprised 19.2 millions, 43% of the number of inhabitants; in 1907 only 17.7 millions, or 29%; numerically, the agricultural class had diminished by more than 1 million and its proportion to the whole by one quarter.

During the same period the effectiveness of the classes given to industry and commerce was raised from 20.6 to 34.7 millions, 56.3% of the total population instead of 45%. Another social transformation had begun in the industrial class as a necessary consequence of the movement of concentration which characterized the economic development of all Germany. During this time, from 1910 to 1913, Germany's share in world commerce had increased from 4.6 billions of francs to 10.1 billions of francs. This increase in export trade is due especially to the development of German industry, proportionally to the action of the number of inhabitants employed in industry.

II

Let us sum up all that we have said above:

German industry is the basis of its whole economic structure; it represents the principal part of its economic force. Agriculture, considering the situation and the conditions which govern agricultural development, is developing to the detriment of the mass of workmen and consumers. During the last 30 years the area of territory cultivated has hardly increased, while the agricultural production has increased by 80%. Germany's harvests yield the greatest crops by hectare.

In its economic power agricultural production plays an inferior part. In 1913 Germany spent more than 10 billions of francs for purchases abroad; more than 12 millions (one fifth of the population) lived by foreign trade.

The few ideas stated below best characterize the economic structure of Germany as well as its economic development:

The importation of raw materials for industry, which amounted to 1.5 billions in 1879 was raised to more than 5 billions in 1913. The importation of manufactured objects increased from 600 millions of francs in 1879 to only 1,478 billions of francs, while the export of manufactured objects which amounted in 1879 to only 1 billion, increased to 7.535 billions of francs. The production of iron ore increased from 6 to 27 billion tons. From 1888 to 1908 the production of hard coal increased by 127%; the pig-iron production from 4,024,000 tons increased to 17,853,000 tons in 1912. The same is true in the production of steel. The net tonnage of the merchant fleet increases for the same period from 1,240,182 to 3,153,724.

Parallel with this development of German economic life, the principal basis of which is the development of its industrial work, the revenues as well as the capitalization of the national revenues have developed. The revenue of the national economic life amounted before the war to 43 billions, against 23 in 1895; of these 43 billions about 7 billions of marks (1/6) are used for public purposes; 27 to 28 billions are used for private purposes; and about 10 billions represent the increase of national property, which 15 years ago was only 4.5 billions. The national property of Germany is valued at about 300 billions (Dr. Helfferich, 1913, estimates it at 310 billions; S[t]einma[n]n-Bucher, 1909, at 350 billions; Prof. Ballod at 270 billions, 1912; and Dr. R[i]esser at 230 billions, 1909). This figure, if one considers the property and the gross annual income, appears inferior to reality. In Germany each year 30 billions,

part of her live stock, of her 20,182 million head of horned stock, 21,920 million head of swine and 82,700 [million] head of poultry, that she had before the war.

In consequence of the preceding and in order to arrive at a certain method of enabling Germany to pay, during the years to come, the debt that she owes to the Allies, her national economy must be be taxed in two directions: her industrial production must first be taxed and afterward her consumption.

Consequently, after a cursory examination of Germany's import commerce, we will arrive at the conclusion that we should impose import duties on the following articles:

(a) raw materials (46.5% of the importation);

(b) foodstuffs, except cereals and meat (25% of the importation).

In this way we should succeed in diminishing, by means of taxation, the 10 billion representing the annual increase in national property before the war, an increase which will be much greater, doubtless, in the future. In the second place, we might also partially tax the consumption of the country.

The following is a table showing the consumption of some important articles in Germany:

(1) sugar................1,179,200 tons.............17.6 per head
(2) salt..................1,507,000 tons.............23.4 per head
(3) petroleum............ 978,200 tons.............14.6 per head

If we add to these articles: alcohol; matches; tobacco (importation of 136 million marks; consumption of tobacco, 17,382 billion cigars and cigarettes); beer (65,089 hectolitres); and if we oblige Germany to introduce a State monopoly for these articles, there is no doubt that they will be the source of enormous annual revenue. In this way we will succeed in taxing the great mass of consumers of Germany and we will be able to distribute among this mass the sums necessary to meet the debt. Supposing that these monopolies take from each inhabitant only 60 francs a year, their annual revenue would amount to 4.2 billion francs.

Signed: Technical Councillor,
DR. BOGDAN MARKOVITCH,

Presented by
COSTA STOYANOWITCH, Delegate.

COUNTRY	AREA SQUARE KILO	POPULATION	POPULATION PER SQUARE KILO	RAILROADS KILO	KILO OF RAILROAD PER SQUARE KILO OF AREA	EXPENDITURES	EXPENDITURES FOR ARMY AND NAVY	PERCENT OF TOTAL EXPENSE	PUBLIC DEBT	PUBLIC DEBT PER CAPITA	PUBLIC DEBT AS PERCENTAGE OF
						lei.	lei.		lei.	lei.	lei
(a) German Empire...						4,620,041,000			6,532,800,000		
(b) Prussia..........	348,780	41,165,219				6,061,100,000			12,944,420,000		
(c) Bavaria..........	75,870	6,877,291				920,760,000			3,111,138,000		
(d) Saxony..........	14,993	4,806,661				615,606,000			1,091,466,000		
(e) Wurtemberg	19,507	2,437,574				161,250,000			799,265,000		
(f) Other States.....	81,693	10,629,248				455,300,000			1,742,023,000		
TOTAL Germany.....	540,833	64,925,993	120	62,207	8.7	12,834,057,000	2,118,125,000	16.50	26,041,112,000	401.00	203
(a) Austro-Hungarian Empire........						830,106,000			5,398,365,000		
Hungary.........									7,840,713,000		
(b) Austria..........	351,205	30,503,736		22,888		3,633,760,000					
(c) Hungary.........	325,411	20,886,487		23,200		2,377,300,000			6,922,488,000		
TOTAL Austria-Hungary........	676,616	51,390,223	76	46,088	14.7	6,841,166,000	1,012,250,000	14.08	20,161,566,000	392.59	293
Turkey..............	1,096,100	23,028,900	12	6,660	293.3	1,317,630,000	637,263,000	48.39	3,437,677,000	149.30	261
Bulgaria.............	96,345	4,337,513	54	1,928	50.7	256,000,000	53,000,000	20.70	914,785,000	211.10	357
Luxembourg.........	2,586	259,891	100	525	4.9	24,400,000	669,000	2.75	52,000,000	123.15	131
TOTAL 1–5.........	3,251,924	143,942,520		117,408	27.7	21,273,253,000	3,821,307,000	17.95	50,587,140,000	351.45	237
Russia..............	22,556,520	166,107,700	7	74,061	304.8	9,395,280,000	2,256,280,000	24.01	22,988,480,000	138.55	4
European Russia......	5,066,279	133,879,000									
Belgium.............	29,456	1,490,411	254	4,720	6.3	770,347,000	100,000,000	13.21	3,759,000,000	499.10	485
Serbia.............	48,303	2,957,207	61	949	53.6	131,000,000	29,527,000	22.53	654,000,900	221.15	491
Montenegro.........	9,080	285,000	31	18	504.4	10,096,000	273,000	2.70	9,500,000	33.33	(
Spain..............	504,517	19,611,334	40	14,805	36.0	1,139,593,000	258,544,000	22.69	9,941,920,000	506.80	872
Roumania..........	131,353	7,250,000	4	3,690	36.4	600,000,000	98,100,000	16.33	1,769,000,000	244.00	283
Holland............	33,079	6,022,452	182	3,234	10.2	548,465,000	111,233,000	20.49	2,451,584,000	407.05	447
Portugal............	91,993	5,423,132	61	2,894	32.8	382,410,000	56,651,000	14.82	4,267,612,000	786.90	1119
Sweden............	447,864	5,561,799	12	13,972	34.4	534,908,000	112,590,000	21.09	865,358,000	155.60	162
Norway............	322,909	2,391,782	7	3,085	10.6	212,670,000	29,589,000	13.95	695,000,000	347.50	357
Switzerland.........	41,324	3,753,293	91	5,112	8.1	98,296,000	44,799,000	45.68	255,130,000	290.95	260
Italy..............	280,682	35,950,077	125	17,420	16.0	2,863,200,000	784,700,090	27.40	14,783,148,000	411.20	517
Greece.............	64,657	2,631,952	41	1,609	40.3	254,000,000	30,330,000	11.94	1,073,000,000	407.90	422
Denmark...........	40,368	2,775,076	69	3,445	11.8	164,313,000	42,990,000	26.21	545,764,000	196.70	332
England............	314,435	45,362,281	144	41,868	7.6	6,304,700,000	1,944,900,000	30.85	16,380,000,000	361.10	260
France.............	536,464	39,601,599	74	50,249	10.7	5,091,643,000	1,814,570,000	34.95	32,500,000,000	820.70	626
TOTAL 1–21........	28,710,878	497,117,615		358,539	80.2	49,874,174,000	11,537,473,000	23.17	163,505,636,000	328.85	1418
CENTRAL POWERS										REC	AP
Germany............	540,833	64,925,993	120	62,207	8.7	12,834,057,000	2,118,125,000	16.50	26,041,112,000	401.00	203
Austria-Hungary.....	676,060	51,390,223	76	46,088	14.7	6,841,166,000	1,012,566,000	14.08	20,161,566,000	392.50	293
Other States.........	2,035,031	27,626,304	166	9,113	226.1	1,598,030,000	690,932,000	43.45	4,384,462,000	157.25	274
TOTAL............	3,251,924	143,942,520		117,408	27.7	21,273,253,000	3,821,307,000	17.95	50,587,140,000	351.45	237
Allied Powers........	23,780,940	207,754,275		189,285	126	24,666,266,000	6,930,260,000	28.17	91,054,128,000	305.80	367
Neutral Powers.......	1,678,014	55,420,820		51,846	32.9	3,934,656,000	785,906,000	20.00	21,864,968,000	394.50	582
GRAND TOTAL	28,710,878	497,117,615		358,539	80.2	49,874,174,000	11,537,473,000	23.13	163,505,636,000	328.85	1418

[2] See Annex III of Document 536.

INTEREST ON DEBT	INTEREST ON DEBT AS PER CENT OF TOTAL EXPENDITURE	INTEREST ON DEBT AS PERCENT OF TOTAL DEBT	TAXES	PERCENT OF EXPENDITURES PROVIDED BY TAXATION	PER CAPITA TAX	EXPENSE OF COLLECTING REVENUE	TOTAL EXPENSES AS PER CENT OF TOTAL EXPENDITURES	IMPORTS	EXPORTS	TOTAL	TOTAL TRADE AS PERCENT OF EXPENDITURES	SERIAL NUMBER
						FOREIGN TRADE						
lei.			lei.		lei.	lei.		lei.	lei.	lei.		
304,437,000	......	..	3,111,338,000	..	...	3,484,000,000	58	....	....	....	......	1
567,835,000	......	..	857,500,000	..	...	....	..	....	....	....	..	
25,603,000	......	..	232,500,000	..	...	....	..	....	....	....	......	
48,750,000	......	..	131,400,000	..	...	....	..	....	....	....	......	
36,450,000	......	..	69,375,000	..	...	....	..	....	....	....	......	
70,000,000	......	..	160,000,000	..	...	....	..	....	....	....	......	
,053,075,000	8	4	4,562,113,000	36	70	....	..	13,462,992,000	12,622,430,000	26,085,422,000	203	
												2
378,000,000	......	..	227,276,000		...	....	..					
556,697,000	......	..	1,965,180,000		...	....	..					
294,000,000	......	..	1,138,515,000		...	....	..					
,228,697,000	1.80	6	3,330,971,000	55	64	....	..	3,351,297,000	2,524,519,000	5,875,816,000	85	
												3
345,750,000	26.00	10	587,000,000	44	25	....	..	980,915,000	508,937,000	1,489,852,000	113	4
73,000,000	29.00	8	176,000,000	68	41	....	..	199,345,000	184,634,000	383,979,000	150	5
3,166,000	13.00	9	14,000,000	58	54	....	..	....	....	....		
703,688,000	12.00	6	8,670,084,000	41	60	....	..	17,994,549,000	15,840,520,000	33,835,069,000	161	
,000,478,000	12.00	5	5,499,000,000	58	33	....	..	2,819,559,000	3,767,711,000	6,587,270,000	70	6
209,000,000	26.00	5	317,000,000	41	42	....	..	4,508,500,000	3,580,300,000	8,088,800,000	10	7
32,400,000	249.00	5	94,000,000	72	31	....	..	115,425,000	116,916,000	232,341,000	177	8
								6,490,000	2,557,000	9,047,000	90	9
409,250,000	36.00	4	1,060,000,000	97	54	....	..	1,415,000,000	1,195,000,000	2,610,000,000	229	10
112,593,000	18.00	6	286,000,000	47	39	....	..	637,905,000	642,103,000	1,280,008,000	213	11
9,740,000	15.00	3	322,500,000	58	54	....	..	8,387,150,000	6,587,600,000	14,974,750,000	2,730	12
320,000	35.00	3	237,120,000	62	43	....	..	314,172,000	160,771,000	474,943,000	124	13
39,770,000	7.00	4	382,493,000	71	68	....	..	933,569,000	824,080,000	1,757,649,000	328	14
23,908,000	11.00	3	113,980,000	53	47	....	..	689,090,000	452,315,000	1,141,415,000	536	15
7,108,000	7.00	3	80,947,000	81	21	....	..	1,802,359,000	1,257,309,000	3,059,668,000	3,121	16
604,000,000	21.00	3	2,074,000,000	72	57	....	..	3,358,094,000	2,169,312,000	5,527,406,000	193	17
37,650,000	15.00	3	101,000,000	39	38	....	..	172,002,000	140,903,000	312,905,000	123	18
24,936,000	15.00	4	156,979,000	95	56	....	..	866,406,000	745,939,000	1,612,345,000	982	19
617,400,000	9.00	3	4,107,600,000	65	90	733,000,000	11	19,372,115,000	15,997,464,000	35,369,579,000	561	20
306,585,000	25.00	4	4,602,000,000	88	116	676,000,000	13	10,724,000,000	9,260,000,000	19,984,000,000	385	21
392,820,000	15.00	4	28,104,703,000	57	56	....	..	74,116,385,000	62,740,800,000	136,857,185,000	274	
ATION												
,453,075,000	8.00	4	4,562,113,000	36	70	....	..	13,462,992,000	11,622,430,000	26,085,422,000	203	
,228,697,000	1.80	6	3,330,971,000	53	64	....	..	3,351,297,000	2,224,519,000	5,875,816,000	85	
,421,916,000	26.00		777,000,000	47	28	....	..	1,180,260,000	693,571,000	1,873,831,000	119	
703,688,000	12.00	6	8,670,084,000	41	60	....	..	17,994,549,000	15,840,520,000	33,825,069,000	161	
,314,863,000	15.00	4	10,693,600,000	67	56	....	..	40,904,183,000	34,894,260,000	75,798,443,000	307	
,874,269,000	22.00	4	2,741,019,000	69	49	....	..	15,217,653,000	12,006,020,000	27,223,673,000	692	
392,820,000	15.00	4	28,104,703,000	57	56	....	..	74,116,385,000	62,740,800,000	136,857,185,000	274	

II. REVENUES OF THE GERMAN EMPIRE

(1911.)	Marks
Posts and Telegraphs	791,381,000
Printing	11,788,000
State Railways	141,780,000
Imperial Banks	25,635,000
Miscellaneous	99,991,000
From Pension Funds	61,240,000
Other Revenues	46,229,000
Matricular Contributions	228,512,000
Customs Fees	131,000
Duties	699,308,000
Tobacco	12,290,000
Tax on Cigarettes	29,983,000
Tax on Sugar	143,500,000
Tax on Salt	59,167,000
Tax on Alcohol	195,046,000
Other Imposts	150,757,000
Tax on Champagne	11,329,000
Tax on Petroleum	11,653,000
Tax on Matches	18,210,000
Tax on Beer	122,100,000
Stamp Tax	17,954,000
Stamps	62,940,000
Taxes on Increments	18,000,000
Succession Duties	43,500,000
Receipt Stamps	141,000,000
Revenues of the Imperial Territories	5,777,338,000
Total	8,843,762,000

ANNEX III

GERMANY'S CAPACITY TO MAKE REPARATION

(*Presented by the Greek Delegation.*)

1. To estimate the capacity of a State to pay, that is, its economic strength, it is not sufficient to know what articles it exports annually, either in raw material (coal, potash, etc.) or in manufactured goods.

In fact, very often the export of these products serves either to balance the importation of other products absolutely necessary to the State or to pay the arrears of debts previously contracted abroad. Moreover, to employ this method would be to neglect all research and all estimation of the most important source of wealth, that is, the labor of the nationals of the State under consideration. In fact, it is by the national labor that the exploitation of the natural resources of a State is continually developed, that its industrial progress is assured and its export commerce increased. And if we consider the gold reserve and credits on foreign countries as capital available to-day to serve for a first payment, and that, on the other hand, capital is only accumulated labor, it would not be logical not to take into consideration the revenue which is to accrue from the future national labor.

We must therefore adopt a different procedure to determine the hostile countries' capacity to pay.

2. In the first place, it must be observed that, if a State is not able to pay its debts, it would be necessary and even simply just to leave it such a part of its revenues as is absolutely necessary to meet its expenses of administration. Without administration, a State can neither preserve itself nor work nor produce. It goes without saying that among these expenses we do not count those for an army and navy, except such as are necessary to maintain order.

3. On the other hand, it must not be forgotten that the public debts contracted before the war must be respected. But in proportion as the holders of these securities are nationals of a hostile State, it would be just to recognize the priority of debts resulting from war indemnities. It would not be difficult to find out how many securities are in the possession of holders of this category.

4. As to the loans concluded during the war, we should distinguish; (a) The loans which the German State has extended to Austria, Bulgaria and Turkey cannot be recognized by the Allies. In fact neither the common nor the moral law would authorize the reimbursement of the chief of a band of criminals for what he gave his accomplices for the perpetration of the crime.

(b) The loans floated by the State in the interior and whose holders are individuals or corporations. It would not be well to cancel these loans; if such a principle were to prevail it might be feared that in case of a future war (although this is highly improbable after the founding of the League of Nations), it might be very difficult to persuade the nationals of a State to subscribe to loans in the interior. Nevertheless the claims of the conquerors should take priority over those of the holders in question.

5. The State revenues are only a part of the national revenue. The State levies on the revenue of each citizen as much as it needs for the accomplishment of its duties and the interest on its debts, leaving, of course, to the taxpayer enough for him to work and so as not to reduce him to famine or force him to emigrate. At the same time we must not lose sight of the fact that if a State pre-

cipitates a universal war, as did Germany and her accomplices, the citizens must suffer the consequences. The principle is all the more applicable to Germany and her accomplices, since they wished the war and marched to it with enthusiasm. They must consequently suffer the levying of a much greater part of their resources than before the war. There might even have been included in the estimation of capital destined to the immediate payment of the claims of the Allies, besides the gold and foreign securities, the product of a tax on capital which would be levied only once, but which might be payable in annual payments. On the eve of the war Germany had already had recourse to this sort of taxation, so that we might use as a basis the method already employed by her. It must be noted, however, that this tax did not give altogether satisfactory results. Still, if it is admitted that the Allies may count on a tax of this nature, they might, by broadening the bases, use these annuities for a financial combination, all the more so as some international banking organization might discount these annuities.

6. To establish the annual budget of the economic revenue and the capacity for payment of each one of the hostile States, it would be necessary to inscribe in the assets all their revenues (domains, industrial and commercial enterprises of the State, taxes, monopolies, existing at present or to be created, etc.).

The taxes must naturally be increased more than they will be increased in England, for example, or in France. And, moreover we must estimate not only the revenues of the State but those of the Departments and the Communes, and, for Germany, those of the confederated States. As for the liabilities, there should be inscribed the expenses indispensable for the administration and for the interest on the loans floated before the war, all the more so as these securities would belong to Allied nationals. The balance would be applied to the interest on the sums due for the reparation of damage caused by the war.

7. This method presupposes a permanent economic and financial control exercised by the League of Nations by means of Commissions appointed to each one of the hostile States and sitting in the country itself. But this question would fall under the jurisdiction of the third Sub-Commission, which would at the same time indicate the measures to be imposed on the enemy, in order to prevent and to punish frauds in the matter of the taxes and levies which might possibly be assigned especially to the interest on the war credits.

It would be especially necessary to forbid our enemies to change their financial laws and to give the taxes a basis which might be harmful to the interests of the Allies. We might, on the other hand, allow them to make changes which promised a greater revenue.

8. If the revenues assigned to the interest on the war debts should surpass the estimations made, the surplus would return, half to the enemy State, and half would be assigned to the improvement of the payment of the conquerors' credits. In this way, on one hand we would leave to the State the liberty of improving its financial situation and of paying its domestic credits, which would have lost their priority, as we have already said; the State and the citizens would not lose all hope of improving their situation, and we would not run the risk of suppressing all effort on the part of the Government and of individuals to increase their revenue. On the other hand, it being understood that the yield from each tax increases automatically every year, the creditors, that is the Allied and Associated States, will have a large share of this surplus.

9. The payment of each annuity shall be made in gold, if necessary, or in well-secured drafts on foreign countries, or even in kind, according to the current price.

Special arrangements would have to be made for cases analogous to that of France, for whom, seeing that her coal mines have been destroyed, it would be fair to assign every year the payment in kind of a part of the annuity due her; the same for Roumania and Serbia for the devastation suffered, and for Greece for the destruction of her important industry of merchant marine.

10. In the preceding we have not spoken of the restitution in kind of material, farming, industrial and other, taken by the Germans and their Allies. In fact, that is not a case of reparation, but of the restitution of material stolen or otherwise removed.

11. Finally, the question might be asked: Is it certain that the annuities will be paid? The answer is clear: The future of any method of payment whatever will always depend on the international situation. And, if ever Germany feels herself strong enough to repudiate her obligations, she will refuse to pay. The League of Nations would be an effective guarantee to prevent such an event.

DOCUMENT 534
Second Subcommittee: Minutes of the Twenty-third Meeting, March 22, 1919, 3:30 P. M.

[EOM, Second Subcommittee, p. 95. French condensed minutes, PV, CRD, p. 814.]

The Second Sub-Committee of the Commission on Reparation of Damage (Financial Capacity of the Enemy States—Their Means of Payment and Reparation) met on Saturday, 22 March, 1919, at 3.30 P. M., at the Ministry of Finance, LORD CUNLIFFE in the Chair.

Present: LORD CUNLIFFE (*British Empire*); MR. D'AMELIO (*Italy*); MR. FUKAI (*Japan*); MR. DANIELOPOL (*Roumania*); MR. STOYANOWITCH (*Serbia*).

There were also present Messrs. DESPRET (*Belgium*) and CHEVALIER (*France*).[1]

The CHAIRMAN proposed the adoption of the amended minutes of the 19th and 20th meetings and the minutes of the 21st meeting. These were adopted.[2]

Discussion of Procedure

MR. DANIELOPOL (*Roumania*) raised the question of possible improvement in the co-ordination of the work of the various Sub-Committees, with the idea of avoiding duplication of work and divergence of decisions.

MR. DESPRET (*Belgium*) thought that up to the present time no overlapping had taken place in the work of the various committees and that the questions of common interest had been treated in the various Commissions according to their competence.

MR. D'AMELIO (*Italy*) defined the object of the work of the Second Sub-Committee of the Economic Commission and thought that the members of the various Commissions could mutually keep one another informed of the progress of their own particular part of the work, thus securing proper co-ordination.

The CHAIRMAN thought that, where there were so many Commissions, a certain amount of overlapping was unavoidable and that it would indeed be well if the Delegates kept themselves informed of the progress of the work in other Commissions.

MR. CHEVALIER (*France*) observed that it might be necessary to take into account the results of the deliberations of the other commissions, especially with regard to territorial changes, before

---

[1] According to the French minutes, Freire d'Andrade was also present.
[2] The French minutes omit this paragraph.

coming to a final decision upon the capacity for payment of enemy countries.

As to methods of payment, he suggested (without making a definite proposal) a progressive annuity in order to take advantage of future economic development in enemy countries after the war. This progression would be automatically realized by a super-tax on already existing methods of taxation in enemy countries and by a tax on exports.

The CHAIRMAN observed that the work of this Committee had not lost sight of the points raised by MR. CHEVALIER and proposed that the next meeting be devoted to the discussion of shipping.

The next meeting was fixed for Monday, 24 March, at 3.30 P. M. The meeting adjourned at 5.15 P. M.

CUNLIFFE,
Chairman.

F. FOBERTI,
   Secretary.

DOCUMENT 535

Second Subcommittee: Minutes of the Twenty-fourth Meeting, March 24, 1919, 10 A. M.

[EOM, Second Subcommittee, p. 96. French condensed minutes, PV, CRD, pp. 815-16.]

The Second Sub-Committee of the Commission on Reparation of Damage (Financial Capacity of the Enemy States—Their Means of Payment and Reparation) met on Monday, 24 March, 1919, at 10 A. M., at the Ministry of Finance, LORD CUNLIFFE in the Chair.

Present: LORD CUNLIFFE (*British Empire*); MR. LOUCHEUR (*France*); MR. TATSUMI (*Japan*); MR. STOYANOWITCH (*Serbia*).[1]

Taxation of Enemy Countries

The CHAIRMAN proposed that with the assistance of MR. LOUCHEUR the Sub-Committee continue the discussion of taxes to be raised in enemy countries.

MR. LOUCHEUR (*France*) said that, after reflection on the subject, he was of the opinion that it would be better merely to fix the amount of the annual sums to be paid by enemy countries and to demand of them their foreign securities and credits, and that, for the surplus, payable in enemy currency, the enemy countries be allowed to establish the methods of taxation for themselves.

---

[1] According to the French minutes, Freire d'Andrade was also present.

These taxes, which should be easily controllable, should be submitted for the approval of the creditor Powers. He thought that in order to complete this proposal it would be necessary to know as exactly as possible the sum-total of the war costs in Germany (debt, loans, bank note issues and other necessary details) so as to compare the per capita tax-burden of Germany with that in Allied countries, taking into account changes of territory which might result from the Peace Treaties.

Enemy Merchant Fleet

The CHAIRMAN recalled that he had been opposed to fixing the details of methods of taxation in enemy countries,[2] and thought that the Committee should state in its report that this subject had been thoroughly examined without being able to arrive at a more detailed solution. While awaiting the details asked for by MR. LOUCHEUR, the CHAIRMAN proposed the discussion of the enemy merchant fleet as a means of payment. He was of the opinion that the Allied Powers could take (a) all enemy vessels over 1600 tons, (b) some enemy vessels between 1600 and 1000 tons, (c) a larger number of vessels between 1000 and 500 tons and (d) very few vessels lower than 500 tons, and no fishing-vessels, on account of the question of food supply in Germany.

MR. LOUCHEUR (*France*) observed that the Commission on Inland Waterways had established a figure of about 500 million francs as the value of the Rhine merchant fleet and the German port equipment at Rotterdam, which would be an immediately realizable sum for the Allies.

The CHAIRMAN asked the Delegates to present a list of enemy merchant vessels smaller than 1600 tons which they would propose to demand from the enemy.

In reply to a question by MR. STOYANOWITCH, the CHAIRMAN said that this list should be compiled on the basis of registered tonnage as of 1914, taking into account construction and destruction during the war but no transactions since the Armistice.

The next meeting was fixed for Thursday, 27 March, at 3 P. M.[3]

The meeting adjourned at 11.30 A. M.

F. FOBERTI,   CUNLIFFE,
    Secretary.   *Chairman.*

---

[2] The French minutes insert here: "il se rallie donc entièrement à la thèse qui vient d'être exposée."
[3] According to the French minutes, the next meeting was fixed for Friday, March 28, at 10 A. M.

DOCUMENT 536

Second Subcommittee: Minutes of the Twenty-fifth Meeting (Including Annexes I-IV), March 28, 1919, 10 A. M.

[EOM, Second Subcommittee, pp. 97-104. French condensed minutes, PV, CRD, pp. 817-18. French text of Annex I, *ibid.*, p. 870; of Annexes II-IV, *ibid.*, pp, 819-26.]

The Second Sub-Committee of the Commission on Reparation of Damage (Financial Capacity of the Enemy States—Their Means of Payment and Reparation) met on Friday, 28 March, 1919, at 10 A. M., at the Ministry of Finance, LORD CUNLIFFE in the Chair.

Present: MR. LAMONT (*U. S. A.*); LORD CUNLIFFE (*British Empire*); MR. D'AMELIO (*Italy*); MR. TATSUMI (*Japan*); MR. STOYANOWITCH (*Serbia*); MR. RYBARSKY (*Poland*); MR. NECULCEA (*Roumania*).

There were also present Messrs. MYLONAS (*Greece*), LAURENT-VIBERT (*Expert for France*), BANAZ (*Expert for Serbia*), and CAPTAIN HARDY, COMMANDER GOODHART and MR. HIPWOOD (*Experts for British Empire*).[1]

Available Enemy Shipping

The CHAIRMAN, continuing the discussion of the question of the enemy merchant fleet, asked the Committee to consider the two following problems: (1) What boats should be taken; and (2) How should these be valued?

He proposed to consider, first, the category of boats of more than 1600 tons. The sense of the meeting appeared to favor taking all these without exception.

The second category to be considered was that of boats between 1000 and 1600 tons. In reply to an observation by CAPTAIN HARDY, the CHAIRMAN said that fishing-boats would not be included in this category.

In reply to remarks by Messrs. STOYANOWITCH (*Serbia*), BANAZ (*Serbia*) and D'AMELIO (*Italy*), tending to exclude from the enemy commercial fleet boats belonging to former Jugo-Slav or Italian citizens of the ex-Austro-Hungarian Empire, the CHAIRMAN again affirmed the principle already adopted in a former meeting that the Sub-Committee should take as a basis for its discussions the state of enemy fleets as they existed on the eve of the war.

[1] According to the French minutes, Freire d'Andrade was also present; and McCormick-Goodhart and Hipwood were not.

MR. STOYANOWITCH (*Serbia*) presented a note on the Adriatic commercial fleet and on the Danube and Save river fleets. (Annex II).

The CHAIRMAN thought that, for the category of boats from 1000 to 1600 tons, it would be well not to take too large a proportion, and proposed 35 or 40 per cent.

MR. LAURENT-VIBERT (*Expert for France*) thought that this was too small a percentage and that the restoration of the French Mediterranean Fleet would require the percentage to be raised to 50 per cent, but that as an offset all boats of less than 1000 tons could be left to the enemy.

The CHAIRMAN agreed to the proposal of the Expert for France.

MR. MYLONAS (*Greece*) accepted the proposal of 50 per cent for boats from 1000 to 1600 tons, but awaited authorization from his Government before accepting the total exclusion of boats below 1000 tons.

MR. BANAZ (*Expert for Serbia*) insisted that the Austro-Hungarian fleet should not be considered, and the CHAIRMAN reaffirmed the principle he had stated above with regard to the basis for the discussions of the Committee.

River Fleet

He then proposed consideration of the question of the river fleet and asked the Delegates to present the desiderata of their respective countries.

CAPTAIN HARDY (*Expert for British Empire*) said that Great Britain only asked for the restitution of English river boats stolen during the war.

The CHAIRMAN observed that this restitution would result from the principles stated by the Sub-Committee in a preceding meeting.

MR. RYBARSKY (*Poland*) stated that his country desired to receive a proportion of the German river fleet corresponding to the relative importance of the river traffic of the territory ceded to Poland with regard to the total traffic of Germany. (See Annex I.)

The CHAIRMAN presented a draft of articles to be inserted in the Preliminaries of Peace, the discussion of which was put off until the next meeting.

Valuation

He said that, with regard to the valuation of surrendered boats, this valuation should be made by an Inter-Allied commission of experts which would operate in each port, taking as a basis for estimates the value on the day of the surrender.

In reply to a question by Mr. d'Andrade (*Portugal*), he stated that replacement in kind or by an equivalent was not to be allowed for boats that had been sunk.

Mr. d'Andrade (*Portugal*) submitted a text of corrections to Annex II of the 22d meeting (Annex III).

Mr. List (*Czecho-Slovak Republic*) submitted a note on methods of payment (Annex IV).

The next meeting was fixed for Monday, 31 March, 1919, at 3.30 p. m.

The meeting adjourned at 12.15 p. m.

Cunliffe,
Chairman.

F. Foberti,
    Secretary.

ANNEX I

DISPOSAL OF THE GERMAN MERCHANT VESSELS, BOTH SEAGOING AND RIVERINE

(*Presented by the Polish Delegation.*)

The Peace Treaty will grant Poland her national coast line and her internal waterways, such as the lower part of the Vistula, the canal of Bydgoscz and the upper part of the Oder. It is plain that the ships attached to the territories to be restored to Poland can be taken into account in the partition, since such are the property of Polish citizens. But this argument should not affect the just claims of Poland regarding the surrender of ships by the Germans. The fact must not be overlooked that many of the ships that ply in the sea and river ports which should belong of right to Poland, may be considered as attached to territory outside of the future frontiers of Poland. The material left in these ports will not be enough to satisfy the elemental needs of our territories, which naturally demand considerable traffic in transportation. It suffices to say that on 1 January, 1913, only 101 steam or sail ships, representing 24,666 tons gross, were registered in all the ports of western Prussia. This is a very small number, explained by the fact that Danzig was supplied by ships attached to important western ports. The figure given is but 0.4 per cent of the total German tonnage; at the same time it is worth noting that in 1911, for example, ships carrying 1,491,580 tons sailed in or out of Danzig itself, which amounts to about 3 per cent of the total traffic of the German Empire. The same proportions can be found in river navigation.

By reason of the facts that we have just set forth, the following proposals are made:

1. Ships attached to the territories ceded by Germany are not available for the partition.

2. If the commercial wants of these territories were once supplied by ships attached to ports located outside of these frontiers, Germany should deliver up a number of ships corresponding to the proportion between the total import and export of ports situated in these territories, and the total figure of commerce of German ports.

3. Moreover, Germany shall deliver to the Polish State 20,000 tons gross of ships able to navigate the Vistula to replace those destroyed by them in the Kingdom of Poland.

ANNEX II

THE FORMER AUSTRO-HUNGARIAN MERCHANT MARINE

(Presented by the Serbian Delegation.)

I

When the Armistice was concluded between the Allies and Austria-Hungary, Italy took the whole of the merchant marine, ceding a part thereof to France. By reason of this, the Serbs, Croats and Slovenes, who owned a large part of this marine, were deprived of their ships, not only to their own damage but to the damage of the nation which hoped to use this marine for the importation and exportation of goods, and for commerce in general.

In submitting this report on the situation of the Austro-Hungarian merchant marine to the Commission, we wish particularly to emphasize the need of lifting the blockade as soon as possible, which is so harmful to us. We also emphasize that the ships belonging to subjects of the Kingdom of the Serbs, Croats, and Slovenes should not be considered an object of the indemnity to be paid by the former Austro-Hungarian merchant marine, since Paragraph 5 of the Naval Clauses of the Armistice with Austria-Hungary is to the effect that these ships should be freed from the blockade, and should be returned to their Jugo-Slav ship-owners.

II

As shown in this Memorandum, the whole of the river fleet of the Serbs on the Danube and the Save was destroyed during the war. As compensation for all this damage, we ask the transfer to the State of the Serbs, Croats and Slovenes, of the boats, canal-boats, tugs, ship-yards, implements of navigation, etc., which were possessed by the former Austro-Hungarian Monarchy on the Save, the Danube, the Tisza, the Maros, the Drave, etc., and which our State has been temporarily using since the conclusion of the Armistice.

III

In addition, we claim a part of the merchant marine of former Austria-Hungary belonging to Austro-German or Magyar ship-owners, by way of an installment of the restitutions and reparation that we are entitled to exact from Austria-Hungary.

COSTA STOYANOVITCH, Delegate

MEMORANDUM ON MERCHANT MARINE

In 1914 the steam merchant marine of the former Austro-Hungarian Monarchy consisted in a total tonnage of 1,100,000 gross tons.

TABLE I (a and b) shows what enterprises are to be considered strictly as Jugo-Slav, in terms of tonnage as well as according to ownership.

TABLE II shows the enterprises of mixed capital where, side by side with important Jugo-Slav capital, there is a great amount of capital of Austro-Germans, Hungarians and Italians who are represented in important posts of the management.

TABLE III shows enterprises where German, Hungarian and Italian capital predominates, and where Jugo-Slav capital is in a much weaker proportion.

TABLE I

Jugo-Slav Enterprises

(a) Coastal Trade, 1914

Name of the Company	Number of ships	Tonnage gross	Capital Jugo-Slav %	Sunk during War Ships	Sunk during War Tonnage
1. Ungaro-Croata, Fiume	46	17,450	90	5	2,273
2. Dalmatia, Triest	33	9,570[2]	70	1	405
3. Dubrovačkg, Dubrovnik	6	3,520	90	2	1,320
4. Hrvatsko Parobr. D. Senj	3	470	100	..	.....
5. Austro-Croata, Punat	4	555	100	..	.....
6. Bokeska Plovidba, Kotor	3	175	100	..	.....
7. Jadran, Spalato	2	708	100	1	362
8. Dubrovacka, Ob. Plovidba Dubrovnik	4	444	100	..	.....
9. Miscellaneous	8	659	100	..	.....
TOTAL	109	33,551	100	9	4,360

[2] The French text reads, 6,570. The English reading makes the total correct.

(b) Free Navigation (Transatlantic)

Name of the Company	Number of ships	Tonnage gross	Capital Jugo-Slav %	Sunk during War Ships	Tonnage
1. Ungaro-Croata for Free Navigation, Fiume..................	6	22,696	90	2	6,708
2. Dubrovacka, Plovidba...........10		31,147	90	2	5,513
3. Racich & Co., Dubrovnik........10		29,112	90	3	12,517
4. T. Cossovich & Co. Triest........	4	13,287	60	..	.....
5. Oceania, Triest..................	4	11,696	90	..	.....
TOTAL 34		112,910[3]	...	7	24,938[4]

N. B. The "Oceania" was formed in 1918 for the acquisition of 4 steamships belonging to Jugo-Slav owners.

TABLE II

Mixed Enterprises

Ships in Free Navigation

Name of the Company	Number of ships	Tonnage gross	Capital Jugo-Slav %	Sunk during War Ships	Tonnage
1. D. Tripkovich, Triest............17		63,337	50	..	.....
2. Libera Triestina, Triest..........	9	36,786	40	..	.....
3. Orient[e], Fiume.................	6	26,405	40	..	.....
TOTAL......................32		126,528	...	..	.....

TABLE III

In the other enterprises and companies for steam navigation belonging to the former Austro-Hungarian Monarchy, such as the "Austrian Lloyd," the "Adria," the "Levant," etc., Jugo-Slav capital is represented to a small amount, varying from 5 to 20%, but reaching certainly at least 100,000 tons. The total Jugo-Slav capital invested in steam merchant marine of the former Austro-Hungarian Monarchy is valued at about 250 million francs. This figure is arrived at by averaging the value before the war and to-day.

Sailboats of the local coasting-trade registered in the different Dalmatian ports belong almost exclusively to Jugo-Slav capital.

The tonnage shown above as being part of Jugo-Slav capital, cannot be taken into consideration in connection with the indemnities to be exacted from Austria-Hungary for tonnage sunk by the enemy during this war, since, under Paragraph 5 of the Naval Clauses of the Armistice with Austria-Hungary, said tonnage should be free from the blockade and returned to the Jugo-Slav ship-owners. Our Delegation has already applied to the

[3] The total of the items listed is 107,938.
[4] The total of the items listed is 24,738.

Inter-Allied Supreme Economic Council to have the paragraph in question put into execution.

SHIPS OF THE KINGDOM OF SERBIA SUNK DURING THE WAR PASSENGER SHIPS OF RIVER NAVIGATION ON THE DANUBE AND THE SAVE:

	HP	R.T.
1. One ship	650	300.0
2. One ship	550	309.0
3. One ship	420	209.0
4. One ship	400	275.0
5. One ship	360	182.0
6. One ship	320	120.0
7. One ship	180	98.5
8. One ship	830	285.0
9. One ship	340	176.0
10. One ship	320	120.0
11. One ship	320	109.0
12. 3 tugs	300	150.0
TOTAL		2,333.5

CANAL-BOATS SUNK OR SEIZED DURING THE WAR

Numbers	Numbers of ships	Tonnage
1. 70	1	70
2. 100—103	3	120
3. 201—203	2	200
4. 251—252	2	280
5. 351—352	2	360
6. 353—354	2	320
7. 400—409	10	480
8. 600—609	10	680
9. 501—512	12	620
10. 650—658	9	700
11. In shipyards	6	700
12. For raw materials	6	700
13. Private property	10	600
TOTAL		5,830

As a means of paying for the losses inflicted on the Serb River-Navigation Company, we propose that the ships and canal-boats seized by the Serb and Allied military authorities be transferred to the State of the Serbs, Croats and Slovenes, with a view to restoring its means of transportation, which were totally destroyed during the war by the Austro-Germans.

Austria-Hungary should also transfer to them the equipment of its river-navigation companies, with a view to restoring the Serbian ship-yards destroyed during the war.

The State of the Serbs, Croats and Slovenes claims in addition a part of the former Austro-Hungarian merchant marine belonging to Austro-German or Magyar ship-owners, as an installment on the restitutions and reparation that this State is entitled to claim from Austria-Hungary; otherwise, in the present economic situation of the Austro-German and Magyar populations, upon whom the entire responsibility for the war rests, it would be very hard to realize said credits.[5]

ANNEX III

ADDENDA TO ANNEX 21-B[6]

Having taken note of Annex 21-B of the minutes of the Second Sub-Committee of the Commission on the Reparation of Damage, in which the economic and financial situation of Portugal prior to the year of 1914 is represented in the table designated as "Situation économique et financière des pays européens avant les guerres des années 1912—1913 et 1913—1914" (Economic and Financial situation of European countries prior to the wars of 1912—13 and 1913—14), the Portuguese Delegation presents the following corrections and addenda:

FINANCIAL AND ECONOMIC SITUATION OF PORTUGAL PRIOR TO WARS OF 1912–13 AND 1913–14

Area in sq. kilometers (1918)		91,943
Area not under cultivation		28,428
Population—1911		5,957,985
Population per square kilometer		64.7
Railways in operation, kilometers (1918)		3,198
Area in square kilometers, per kilometer of track		28.8
State expenditures (1913–14)	386,000,000 francs	69,514,643 écus
Expenditures for army and navy	76,000,000 francs	13,681,843 écus
Per cent of total expenditure	19.7	
Public debt in circulation (1914)		
Internal	2,600,000,000 francs	468,973,245 écus
Abroad	1,020,000,000 francs	181,919,190 écus
TOTAL	3,620,000,000 francs	650,892,435 écus
Public debt per capita	607 francs	109.23 écus
Per cent budgetary outlay	937.82	
Annual interest on debt (1914)	125,000,000 francs	22,511,286 écus
Per cent of total expenditure	32.40	
Per cent of public debt	3.46	
Per cent of taxes proceeds	41	

[5] These last three paragraphs are omitted from the French text.
[6] Annex II of Document 533.

Proceeds from taxes (1914)

Indirect (duties, tobacco and matches)....	180,000,000 francs	32,356,400 écus
Direct (stamps, etc.)....................	125,000,000 francs	22,522,367 écus
TOTAL...........................	305,000,000 francs	54,878,767 écus
Per cent of total expenditures (covered by taxes).......................	79	
Per capita tax—		
Indirect (duties, tobacco and matches)	30.20 francs	
Direct (stamps, etc.)................	20.95 francs	
TOTAL...........................	51.15 francs[7]	9.21 écus
Special commercial (1913)		
Imports...........................	500,000,000 francs	89,941,000 écus
Exports...........................	203,000,000 francs	36,684,700 écus
TOTAL...........................	703,000,000 francs	126,625,700 écus
Per cent of total State expenditures......	182[8]	

PRINCIPAL TYPES OF EXPORTS, 1913

	Annual Production Tons	Tons	Exports Value in Francs
Cork (Raw and manufactured).............	75,000*	92,210	28,300,000
Wood (Rough and sawed, timber for mines)		349,000	6,200,000
Ores (copper, iron, tungsten)...............		486,552	9,520,000
Dressed stone (marble and granite).........		26,731	278,000
Artificial fertilizer........................120,000		25,856	695,000
Jute and cotton clothes...................		1,847	5,825,000
Common wines and vinegars—.............		[72,978]	[27,600,000][9]
Port and Madeira wines† and liqueurs‡....645,000		33,431	13,750;000
Fish, canned in oil (sardines and tunny).....		26,793	13,800,000
Olive oil..............................	50,000†	2,133	2,885,000
Dried and green fruits (pineapples, grapes, apples, almonds, figs and carobs)§........		22,000	7,200,000
TOTAL...116,053,000			

NOTES:

  * About half of the world production.

  † 1000 litres.

  ‡ Vineyards in the region Porto (Portuguese town at the mouth of the Douro). Vineyards of Madeira (island in the Atlantic).

  § Pineapples grown in the hothouses of the Azores.

The principal seaports are Lisbon, at the mouth of the Tagus, and Porto, at the mouth of the Douro. The port of Lisbon was in direct communication with Paris, 1894 kilometers away, by three express trains de luxe, which made the trip in 31 hours, 54 minutes, and was in communication with Madrid and Barcelona, by expresses.

---

[7] The French text reads, 51.16 francs.

[8] The French text reads, 102 percent. That is incorrect.

[9] The figures in brackets are supplied from the French text.

EMIGRATION TO BRAZIL, THE UNITED STATES (MASSACHUSETTS, CALIFORNIA), COLONIES, ETC.

	1903—1913	
Permanent.................................424,734	or	42,473 per year
Temporary................................. 12,579	or	1,256 per year
Total.................................437,313	or	43,729 per year

	1909	1910	1911	1912
Per 1000 inhabitants...................6.32[10]	6.68	10.01	14.81

NOURISHMENT OF THE WORKINGMAN

	Portuguese Laborer	(Average) Laborer
Albuminous substances..................... 86.47 grammes	150 grammes
Fats...................................... 45.46 grammes	60 grammes
Hydrocarbonates..........................414.18 grammes	563 grammes

PUBLIC WEALTH

	Portuguese	Average France and England
Per capita.............................2,000—2,500 francs	8,575 francs
Gross proceeds of private wealth (salaries and incomes)		
Per capita.............................. 525 francs	1,250 francs

ANNEX IV

METHODS BY WHICH THE ENEMY MAY BE REQUIRED TO MAKE REPARATION

REPARATION OF WAR DAMAGE

(Presented by the Czecho-Slovak Delegation.)

According to the declarations of the Italian Delegation, Annex IV,[11] the Czecho-Slovak Delegation proposes sources of reparation as follows:

I. Imposition of customs taxes of 10% on exportation, except on raw materials intended for the reparation of war damage; we would thus gain foreign securities. Taking the prices and the amount of business of 1913 as a basis and considering the territory which would remain to the States in which we are interested, taxes may thus be figured out:

German Republic: Exportation, raw material intended for the reparation of war damage excepted:............................10,000,000,000 francs
Germanic Austria: id.............................. 500,000,000 francs
Magyar Republic: id.............................. 500,000,000 francs
Bulgaria and Turkey: id.......................... 300,000,000 francs

Total.....................................11,300,000,000 francs

[10] The French text reads, 6.52.

[11] The French text reads, "Annexe I du procès-verbal n° 4." The reference is to Annex I of Document 515.

so that the taxes of 10% on exportation would give about 1,100,-000,000 francs on pre-war rate of exchange.

II. Operating of monopolies in the countries with small capital. According to pre-war prices, the income from monopolies in Germanic Austria and the Magyar State can be estimated as follows:

Monopoly on salt.....................................	13,000,000 francs
Monopoly on tobacco.............................	71,000,000 francs
Monopoly on matches.............................	10,000,000 francs

III. In the non-industrial countries and countries with small capital, we might obtain the concession of operating the natural riches:

Turkey possesses salt, coal, lead, emery, borax, copper, chromium ores. These substances brought, in 1908-1909, 25 million francs.

Bulgaria owns antimony, chromium, arsenic, copper, gold, silver.

Germanic Austria has unexploited hydraulic power which can yield about 1,200,000 H.P. and which, transformed into electricity, represents the equivalent of about 1,000,000 tons of coal annually.

IV. The reduction of transport rates on goods coming from Allied and friendly countries on the railroads of enemy States, to be deducted from annuities to be paid for the reparation of damage.

DOCUMENT 537

Second Subcommittee: Minutes of the Twenty-sixth Meeting (Including Annex), March 31, 1919, 3:30 P. M.

[EOM, Second Subcommittee, pp. 105-8. French condensed minutes, PV, CRD, pp. 827-29.][1]

The Second Sub-Committee of the Commission on Reparation of Damage (Financial Capacity of the Enemy States—Their Means of Payment and Reparation) met on Monday, 31 March, 1919, at 3.30 P. M., at the Ministry of Finance, LORD CUNLIFFE in the Chair.

Present: LORD CUNLIFFE (*British Empire*); MR. CLÉMENTEL (*France*); MR. D'AMELIO (*Italy*); MR. FUKAI (*Japan*); MR. RYBARSKI (*Poland*); MR. NECULCEA (*Roumania*); MR. STOYANOWITCH (*Serbia*).

There were also present: Messrs. ROBINSON (*U. S. A.*); HARDY and HIPWOOD (*Experts for British Empire*); DESPRET (*Belgium*); MYLONAS (*Greece*); and FREIRE D'ANDRADE (*Portugal*).

---

[1] The French minutes have no Annex.

The CHAIRMAN proposed the adoption of the minutes of the 22nd, 23rd and 24th meetings. These minutes were adopted.[2]

British Draft Merchant Ship Clauses

The CHAIRMAN asked the Committee to discuss the British Draft of Clauses Governing Taking of Enemy Merchant Ships (Annex).

MR. CLÉMENTEL (*France*) proposed to place at the beginning of these clauses the following additional text:

"The enemy Powers recognize the right of the Allied and Associated Powers to the replacement ton for ton (gross) and class for class of all the merchant and fishing vessels lost or damaged by act of war.

"Nevertheless and although the total tonnage of the ships of the enemy Powers now in existence is much below that of the tonnage lost by the Allied and Associated Powers, the right recognized above shall be exercised in the case of the enemy ships under the following conditions."

In reply to a question by MR. ROBINSON (*U. S. A.*), MR. CLÉMENTEL (*France*) explained that his intention was to establish the principles of reparation, ton for ton in each category and that the "pool" system was not in question.

The CHAIRMAN proposed to add the text presented by MR. CLÉMENTEL to the beginning of the English Draft and to proceed to the discussion of the Draft itself.

MR. DESPRET (*Belgium*) referring to the exclusion of boats of less than 1,000 tons stated that Belgium had great need for trawlers and fishing boats owing to the fact that a great number of such boats belonging to Belgium had been taken or destroyed and that no construction had been possible during the war.

After a discussion in which MR. CLÉMENTEL (*France*); MR. MYLONAS (*Greece*); MR. DESPRET (*Belgium*); and CAPTAIN HARDY (*Expert for British Empire*) took part, on the subject of the wording an additional text which would cover this observation it was decided to add at the end of Article I of the British Draft:

". . . and 25 per cent. of steam trawlers as well as 25 per cent. of other fishing boats.

MR. D'AMELIO (*Italy*) again made the reservations which he had presented at a preceding meeting on the subject of the merchant fleet of the ex-Austro-Hungarian Empire.

MR. STOYANOWITCH (*Serbia*) asked that the following amendment be inserted:

"The vessels of subjects of liberated territory which belonged before the war to the Central Powers shall not be delivered under the provisions of Article I."

[2] The French minutes omit this paragraph.

The CHAIRMAN recalled that the Committee had taken as a basis for its discussion the state of the enemy fleets as they existed on the eve of the war and that it would be outside the competence of the Committee to depart from this rule.

Upon a remark from MR. D'AMELIO (*Italy*) it was decided to substitute "the enemy" for "Germany" and "enemy Powers" for "Central Powers" throughout the text.[3]

The CHAIRMAN asked the Delegates to take up paragraph 2 substituting "All the Ships" for "all the merchant ships." Paragraph 2 was so adopted.

In reply to a question by MR. CLÉMENTEL (*France*) on the subject of paragraph 3, MR. HIPWOOD (*Expert for British Empire*) said that the intention of the writer of the text had been to exclude from the delivery to be demanded only boats captured and definitely condemned by Prize Courts.

MR. ROBINSON (*U. S. A.*) proposed to put at the beginning of paragraph 3, the following additional text:[4]

1. The seizures during the war of merchant ships by the Allied and Associated Powers respectively

2. The legality and sufficiency of the title to such ships acquired through such seizures irrespective of the process or means used to effect such seizures

3. The full divesting of the [Central] Powers and each and every [subject] thereof interested in such ships, of any right, title or interest in such seized property.

The [Central] Powers on behalf of themselves; so as to bind all other persons interested in such ships, hereby [cede to the Allied and Associated Governments respectively; all property and interests in merchant ships belonging to the Central Powers or to subjects thereof] so seized and taken possession of by the [said] Allied and Associated Governments respectively during the war.

He also desired the adoption of the following principle:

The reasonable value of such ships shall be determined and such value shall be charged against the government holding such ships and credited to the enemy [country] formerly owning the same on all such claims as are finally allowed respectively to [the] Allied and Associated Powers as a result of the Treaty of Peace. [In the event the credit to the enemy power] exceeds the aggregate of [such] claims in the case of [the] Allied and Associated Powers, the excess shall be used and applied in accordance with the [general] provisions of the Treaty of Peace in [relation to] excess credits.

MR. CLÉMENTEL (*France*) wished the principle of the pool to be safeguarded. The principle proposed by MR. ROBINSON seemed to him to be inequitable in the results it might bring about. The

[3] According to the French minutes, the term "Puissances ennemies" was substituted for the terms "Allemagne" and "Puissances centrales."

[4] The French text inserts here, "Les Puissances ennemies reconnaissent: . . ." The Amendments to Clause C of Annex II of Document 543 follow.

United States, which had only lost 389 thousand tons and had been able to build during the war would receive 660 thousand tons while France which had lost 906 thousand tons and had not been able to build would only receive 40 thousand. He asked therefore that the following text be substituted for paragraph (a) of Article 3:

". . . which since 2 August, 1914, have flown and had the right to fly the flag of one of the enemy powers and which have neither been the object of a sale to a neutral or allied power recognized as valid and regular by the Allied and Associated Powers nor the object of a regular and definite condemnation by a tribunal or Prize Court of one of the Allied and Associated Powers in conformity with the rules of international law."

The CHAIRMAN proposed to defer the rest of this discussion to the next meeting.

The next meeting was fixed for Thursday, 3 April, 1919, at 10 A. M.

The meeting adjourned at 6 P. M.

CUNLIFFE,
Chairman.

F. FOBERTI,
  Secretary.

ANNEX

DRAFT OF CLAUSES GOVERNING TAKING OF GERMAN MERCHANT
SHIPS IN PART REPARATION

(*Proposed by British Delegation.*)[5]

1. The [Central] Powers hereby, on behalf of themselves and so as to bind all other persons interested therein, cede to the Allied and Associated Governments the property in all Merchant Ships belonging to the subjects of the [Central] Powers which are of 1600 tons gross and upwards and also one half of the ships which are between 1600 tons gross and 1000 tons gross.

2. The [Central] Powers will, within two months of the signature of the Preliminaries of Peace, hand over to a Representative of the Allied and Associated Governments, duly authorized by them for this purpose, all the [merchant] ships mentioned in Article I.

3. The [merchant] ships mentioned in Article I include all [merchant] ships which (a) fly, or may be entitled to fly the merchant flags of any of the Central Powers, (b) are owned by any enemy subject, company or corporations or by any neutral company or corporations which is under the control or direction of

---

[5] The Annex of Document 539 follows.

enemy subjects, (c) which are now under construction in enemy or neutral countries [and have already been launched.]

4. For the purpose of providing documents of title for each of the ships to be handed over as above mentioned, the Central Powers will,

(a) Deliver to the representative of the Allied and Associated Governments in respect of each vessel a bill of sale or other document of title evidencing the transfer of the entire property in the vessel free from all encumbrances, charges and liens of all kinds to that officer;

(b) Take all measures that may be indicated by the said Representative of the Allied and Associated Governments for ensuring that the ships themselves shall be placed at his disposal.

DOCUMENT 538

Second Subcommittee: Minutes of the Twenty-seventh Meeting, April 3, 1919, 10 A. M.

[EOM, Second Subcommittee, pp. 109-10. No French minutes.]

The Second Sub-Committee of the Commission on Reparation of Damage (Financial Capacity of the Enemy States—Their Means of Payment and Reparation) met on Thursday, 3 April, 1919, at 10 A. M., at the Ministry of Finance, LORD CUNLIFFE in the Chair.

Present: LORD CUNLIFFE (*British Empire*); MR. CLÉMENTEL (*France*); MR. D'AMELIO (*Italy*); MR. FUKAI (*Japan*); MR. RYBARSKI (*Poland*); MR. NECULCEA (*Roumania*); MR. STOYANOWITCH (*Serbia*).

There were also present: Messrs. DESPRET (*Belgium*); HOSTIE (*Expert for Belgium*); ROBINSON (*U. S. A.*); HIPWOOD and CAPTAIN HARDY (*Experts for British Empire*); LIST (*Czecho-Slovak Republic*).

The CHAIRMAN proposed the adoption of the minutes of the 25th meeting. These minutes were adopted.

The discussion of the amendments to the British Draft (Annex to the 26th Meeting) proposed by MR. ROBINSON (*U. S. A.*) was deferred until the next meeting.

Par. 3 of British Draft

The CHAIRMAN asked the Committee to continue the examination of paragraph 3 of the British Draft.

As a result of an observation by CAPTAIN HARDY (*Expert for*

British Empire) it was decided to delete the words "and have already been launched" at the end of Article (c).

MR. CLÉMENTEL (*France*) in anticipation of the insufficiency of the tonnage which the enemy countries would be able to deliver for the replacement of vessels destroyed by act of war thought that it would be necessary to oblige the enemy countries to construct vessels for the Allied and Associated countries up to the amount of this deficit.

MR. HOSTIE (*Expert for Belgium*) agreed with this suggestion.

The CHAIRMAN asked the French Delegation to prepare a draft on this point which after having been translated and distributed could be discussed at the next meeting. He proposed to proceed to the examination of paragraph 4.

MR. HOSTIE (*Expert for Belgium*) proposed to substitute in the French text of Article (a) the words "privilèges, hypothèques et charges quelconques" for the words "servitudes, charges et hypothèques."

Par. 4

Paragraph 4 was so adopted.

River Fleet

MR. DESPRET (*Belgium*) proposed to take up the question of the river fleet. It was an important one for his country, which had suffered heavy losses of this kind. The Belgians would demand (a) boats which had been requisitioned and were now in Germany and (b) the replacement of such boats as had been destroyed or sold to neutral countries.

MR. HOSTIE (*Expert for Belgium*) thought that for the sake of clearness in the discussions it would be well to treat the different categories of naval fleets separately, i.e., the Rhine, the Elbe, the Danube, etc. . . .[1] He submitted a text with regard to Belgian claims.

MR. STOYANOWITCH (*Serbia*) was prepared to frame a clause giving to his country as replacement in kind the Austro-Hungarian boats and yards which the Allied military authorities had taken possession of in liberated territories.

MR. CLÉMENTEL (*France*) insisted that as far as the enemy was concerned the principle of the pool should be maintained.

MR. NECULCEA (*Roumania*) agreed with MR. CLÉMENTEL. He wished to record a reservation on account of Rumanian boats

---

[1] Ellipsis in original.

that, having been captured by the enemy and made to appear as Austrian boats would suffer the fate of Austrian boats.

MR. LIST (*Czecho-Slovak Republic*) asked (1) that the treaty by which the Austrian Navigation Company had delivered to a German company boats which had been before the war in Czecho-Slovak territory be annulled and (2) that Danube boats registered before the war in Czecho-Slovak territory be allotted to the Czecho-Slovak Republic.

MR. RYBARSKI (*Poland*) asked that a portion of the German river fleet corresponding to the relative importance between the traffic in ceded territory and the total traffic of Germany be allotted to his country.

The CHAIRMAN thought that the delegates of the countries interested in the question of the river fleet should meet together to frame clauses similar to those which had been presented by the British Delegation with regard to the merchant marine. He drew the attention of these delegates to the difficulty of exactly defining the elements which should be comprised in the term river fleet.

Referring to a question raised in previous meetings on the subject of transactions made since 1914 with regard to merchant vessels, he thought it safe to say that a special committee would be constituted to treat these questions.

The next meeting was fixed for Saturday, 5 April, 1919, at 5 P. M.

The meeting adjourned at 12 Noon.

CUNLIFFE,
Chairman.

F. FOBERTI,
Secretary.

DOCUMENT 539

Second Subcommittee: Minutes of the Twenty-eighth Meeting (Including Annex), April 5, 1919, 5 P. M.

[EOM, Second Subcommittee, pp. 111-14. French condensed minutes, PV, CRD, pp. 830-32. French text of the Annex, *ibid.*, p. 869.]

The Second Sub-Committee of the Commission on Reparation of Damage (Financial Capacity of the Enemy States—Their Means of Payment and Reparation) met on Saturday, 5 April, 1919, at 5 P. M., at the Ministry of Finance, LORD CUNLIFFE in the Chair.

Present: MR. ROBINSON (*U. S. A.*); LORD CUNLIFFE (*British Empire*); MR. CLÉMENTEL (*France*); MR. D'AMELIO (*Italy*); MR.

Fukai (*Japan*); Mr. Rybarski (*Poland*); Mr. Neculcea (*Roumania*); Mr. Stoyanowitch (*Serbia*).

There were also present Messrs. Despret (*Belgium*); Hostie (*Expert for Belgium*); Captain Hardy and Mr. Hipwood (*Experts for British Empire*).[1]

The Chairman proposed the adoption of the minutes of the 26th and 27th meetings.

The minutes of the 27th meeting were approved after the acceptance of corrections.[2]

Mr. Robinson (*U. S. A.*) referring to the minutes of the 26th meeting, desired to be recorded as having offered the following addition to the Annex:

"The enemy powers represent that they have requisitioned the property and interest of their nationals and other persons interested in all merchant ships belonging to or under the control of the nationals of the enemy powers at the outbreak of the war."

The Chairman proposed that the minutes of the 26th meeting be approved as they stood and that this amendment of Mr. Robinson's should appear in the minutes of the current meeting. This was approved.

Interim Report

The Chairman recalled that at a previous meeting a committee of three consisting of the Chairman, Mr. Loucheur and Mr. Lamont had been appointed to draw up an interim report. He said that this committee had held a number of meetings and had reached a substantial agreement except as regards the sum-total which the enemy countries could be called upon to pay. This small committee, however, had drawn up a provisional report embodying the results of their discussions with a suggestion for arriving at the sum which the enemy could pay and this report would be submitted to the delegates for perusal before the next meeting.[3]

Clause 3. British Draft and American Amendments

He then invited the Committee to proceed with the discussion of Clause 3 of the British Draft (Annex-26th Meeting) and the amendments proposed by the American Delegation.

Mr. Hipwood (*Expert for British Empire*) pointed out that although the American amendment agreed with the British proposal in providing for a complete surrender by the enemy of all

---

[1] According to the French minutes, Freire d'Andrade was also present; and Despret and Hardy were absent.

[2] The French minutes omit the last two paragraphs.

[3] See Document 520, at note 5.

title in their merchant vessels, the use of the word "respectively" in paragraph 1 of the amendment implied the substitution of individual for collective action in the matter. This method would be open to grave objection. Such a method of distribution would appear to be inequitable in that (1) it would act in favor of particular states as against the claims of the Allied Powers as a whole and that certain States which had suffered least might gain most and that (2) it was based on the physical possession of the vessels and the accident of their having taken refuge in certain ports. Furthermore, neutrals might consider themselves justified in claiming the enemy ships which had taken refuge in their harbors.

Whatever view might be taken of this question, he suggested that the final distribution of the enemy merchant marine among the Allies was not a matter which need be introduced into the Treaty of Peace. The question before the Committee was to provide for the complete surrender by the enemy of the property in their merchant shipping.

MR. CLÉMENTEL (*France*), MR. HOSTIE (*Expert for Belgium*) and MR. FUKAI (*Japan*) expressed themselves as in entire agreement with the remarks of MR. HIPWOOD.

MR. ROBINSON (*U. S. A.*) said that the American Delegation did not desire to provide for the final allocation of the enemy shipping, but that they did desire to maintain the validity of the American title to ships seized in American harbors under the Act of Congress (May, 1917.)[4]

He did not think that the adoption of the American Amendment would lead to the seizure by neutrals of the enemy ships detained in their harbors. It was not obvious in what way ships differed from any other form of property and he considered that the question resolved itself thus: Was the American title to these ships to be questioned? On what grounds was redistribution claimed? A claim to redistribution would involve an attempt to estimate the respective contributions to the war of the various

[4] United States, Laws, statutes, etc., *The Statutes at Large of the United States of America*, XL (Washington: Government Printing Office, 1919), 75. Joint Resolution of May 12, 1917 (65th Cong., 1st sess.: S. J. Res. 42—Pub. Res. No. 2). The text follows:

"CHAP. 13.—Joint Resolution Authorizing the President to take over for the United States the possession and title of any vessel within its jurisdiction, which at the time of coming therein was owned in whole or in part by any corporation, citizen, or subject of any nation with which the United States may be at war, or was under register of any such nation, and for other purposes.

"*Resolved by the Senate and House of Representatives of the United States of America in Congress assembled,* That the President be, and he is hereby, authorized to take over to the United States the immediate possession and title of any vessel within the jurisdiction thereof, including the Canal Zone and all territories and insular possessions of the United States except the American Virgin Islands, which at the time of coming into such jurisdiction was owned in whole or in part by any corporation, citizen, or subject of any nation with which the United States may be at war when such vessel shall be taken, or

Allied and Associated Powers, which was, in his opinion, impossible.[5]

MR. CLÉMENTEL (*France*) argued that the seizure of enemy shipping could only be legally justified in one of the two following ways:

1. In accordance with the principle of reparation which had been specifically laid down in President Wilson's Fourteen Points and consequently accepted by the enemy. This principle did not justify the delivery to the United States of all the enemy tonnage seized in United States ports which greatly exceeded American losses.

2. By right of capture. According to the Hague Convention this right did not exist for merchant ships in hostile ports at the outbreak of hostilities. Although the United States had not ratified this clause they had observed it during the Spanish-American War and the clause might be considered as forming part of the Law of Nations.

As for considering vessels like other property, the mere existence of a separate maritime law containing stipulations about the right of refuge would tend to show that this consideration could not be admitted. Furthermore, it would be contrary to the natural state of affairs.

He would like to ask MR. ROBINSON two questions:

(1) Did he consider that Brazil, which had lost 25,000 tons of shipping, should keep the 218,000 tons of enemy shipping now in her harbors?

(2) Did he think that a neutral state had the right to pass a law over-riding the claims of the Allies as affecting the enemy shipping in its harbors?

MR. ROBINSON (*U. S. A.*) replied that as regards Brazil, he was not prepared to give an opinion and to the second question he replied in the negative.

On the suggestion of the CHAIRMAN, MR. ROBINSON agreed to

---

was flying the flag of or was under register of any such nation or any political subdivision or municipality thereof; and, through the United States Shipping Board, or any department or agency of the Government, to operate, lease, charter, and equip such vessel in any service of the United States, or in any commerce, foreign or coastwise.

"SEC. 2. That the Secretary of the Navy be, and he is hereby, authorized and directed to appoint, subject to the approval of the President, a board of survey, whose duty it shall be to ascertain the actual value of the vessel, its equipment, appurtenances, and all property contained therein, at the time of its taking, and to make a written report of their findings to the Secretary of the Navy, who shall preserve such report with the records of his department. These findings shall be considered as competent evidence in all proceedings on any claim for compensation.

"Approved, May 12, 1917."

[5] The French minutes omit this sentence. But it may be found as the last sentence on p. 869 of PV. See note 7 below.

the approval of the British Draft as revised,[6] reserving the right to offer an addition in the sense of his amendments which he would present with the report of the Committee. It was approved with this understanding. (See Annex.)

The next meeting was fixed for Monday, 7 April, at 4 P. M.

The meeting adjourned at 7.15 P. M.

CUNLIFFE,
Chairman.

F. FOBERTI,
Secretary.

ANNEX
ARTICLE GOVERNING TAKING OF ENEMY MERCHANT SHIPS AS PART REPARATION (*As Revised*)[7]

1. The enemy Powers recognize the right of the Allied and Associated Powers to the replacement ton for ton (gross) and class for class of all [the] merchant and fishing [vessels] lost or damaged [by acts of war.]

[Nevertheless and although the total tonnage of the ships of the enemy Powers now in existence is much below that of the tonnage] lost by the Allied and Associated Powers, the right recognized [above shall be exercised in the case of the enemy ships] under the following conditions.

2. The Enemy Powers [hereby,] on behalf of themselves and so as to bind all other persons interested [therein,] cede to the Allied and Associated Governments the property in all merchant ships [belonging to the subjects of the Enemy Powers] which are of 1,600 tons gross and upwards [and also] one half of the ships which are between 1,600 tons gross and 1,000 tons gross, [and 25 per cent. of steam trawlers as well as 25 per cent. of other fishing boats.]

3. The Enemy Powers will, within two months of the signature of the Preliminaries of Peace, [hand over] to a Representative of the Allied and Associated Governments, duly authorized by them for this purpose, all the ships mentioned in Article 1.

4. The ships mentioned in Article 1 include all ships which (a) fly, or may be entitled to fly, the merchant flags [of any of the Central Powers] (b) are owned by any enemy subjects, company

---

[6] The French minutes read, ". . . amendé ainsi qu'il est dit aux procès-verbaux nos 26 et 27. . . ."

[7] The Annex of Document 537 precedes. Part I of Clause C of Annex II of Document 543 follows. At the end of the French text of the present document there is an extra sentence: "Une discussion sur la contribution relative apportée à l'oeuvre commune par chacun des Alliés lui paraît sans issue." This appears to be the missing sentence mentioned in note 5 above.

or corporations or by any neutral company or corporations which is under the control or direction of enemy subjects: (c) which are now under construction in enemy or neutral countries.

5. For the purpose of providing documents of title for each of the ships to be handed over as above mentioned, the [Central] Powers will

(a) Deliver to the representative of the Allied and Associated Governments in respect of each vessel a bill of sale or other document of title evidencing the transfer of the entire property in the vessel free from all encumbrances, charges and liens of all kinds to that officer;

(b) Take all measures that may be indicated by the said Representative of the Allied and Associated Governments for ensuring that the ships themselves shall be placed at his disposal.

DOCUMENT 540

Second Subcommittee: Minutes of the Twenty-ninth Meeting, April 7, 1919, 4 P. M.

[EOM, Second Subcommittee, pp. 115-16. French condensed minutes, PV, CRD, pp. 833-34.]

The Second Sub-Committee of the Commission on Reparation of Damage (Financial Capacity of the Enemy States—Their Means of Payment and Reparation) met on Monday, 7 April, 1919, at 4 P. M., at the Ministry of Finance, LORD CUNLIFFE in the chair.

Present: MR. ROBINSON (*U. S. A.*); LORD CUNLIFFE (*British Empire*); MR. D'AMELIO (*Italy*); MR. FUKAI (*Japan*); MR. RYBARSKI (*Poland*); MR. DANIELOPOL (*Roumania*); MR. STOYANOWITCH (*Serbia*).

There were also present Messrs. DESPRET (*Belgium*); FREIRE D'ANDRADE (*Portugal*); MYLONAS (*Greece*); CHAMIEC (*Poland*); LIST (*Czecho-Slovak Republic*) and POISSON (*Expert for France*).[1]

Interim Report

The CHAIRMAN invited the Committee to discuss the provisional report.

MR. CHAMIEC (*Poland*) presented an additional text to be placed at the beginning of the report recalling the principle of restitution for all stolen objects which could be found in enemy countries before all disposition with regard to methods of payment. This text was adopted.

MR. DESPRET (*Belgium*) presented an additional text to be in-

---

[1] According to the French minutes, Michalakopoulos was also present; and Rybarski was absent.

serted immediately after the foregoing with the idea of affirming the principle of reparation in kind and equivalent independently of methods of payments indicated in the rest of the report. This text was adopted.

MR. DANIELOPOL (*Roumania*) asked that specific mention be made of payments in kind.

MR. DESPRET (*Belgium*) agreed with this proposal, but insisted that the mention asked by MR. DANIELOPOL be inserted among the methods of deferred payment and not following his own amendments, which had in view immediate reparation.

It was decided that the amendment of MR. DANIELOPOL should form a special paragraph, "Payments in Kind" which would be inserted immediately after the paragraph "Specific Objects of Export."

In reply to observations by MR. MYLONAS and MR. MICHALA-COPOULOS on the subject of enemy properties sequestrated in Allied countries, the CHAIRMAN replied that this part of enemy assets was already included in the sum total of 20 billion marks.

MR. LIST (*Czecho-Slovak Republic*) thought that if the figure fixed as the value of enemy liquid assets included the value of the merchant shipping and also the value of enemy properties in foreign countries, the total of 20 billion marks was too low.

The CHAIRMAN thought that this figure, which was the result of previous deliberations, should not be changed.

MR. POISSON (*Expert for France*) reverting to the paragraph "Anticipation of Payments" asked if the last sentence with regard to export taxes implied on the part of the Committee an opinion unfavorable to this method of payment. If so, he desired to make every reservation on the subject.

The CHAIRMAN suggested that a paragraph be added at the end of the report so worded as to allow later admission of subsequent resolutions.[2]

The report so amended was adopted in its entirety. (See Annex to the 15th Meeting of the Plenary Commission.)[3]

The next meeting was fixed for Wednesday, 9 April, at 2.30 P. M.[4]

The meeting adjourned at 7 P. M.

CUNLIFFE,
Chairman.

F. FOBERTI,
Secretary.

[2] The French minutes insert here: "La Sous-Commission se rallie à cette suggestion."
[3] See Annex I of Document 543.
[4] The French minutes omit this paragraph.

DOCUMENT 541

Second Subcommittee: Minutes of the Thirtieth Meeting (Including Annexes I and II), April 9, 1919, 2:30 P. M.

[EOM, Second Subcommittee, pp. 117-19. No French minutes or texts of Annexes.]

The Second Sub-Committee of the Commission on Reparation of Damage (Financial Capacity of the Enemy States—Their Means of Payment and Reparation) met on Wednesday, 9 April, 1919, at 2.30 P. M., at the Ministry of Finance, LORD CUNLIFFE in the chair.

Present: MR. ROBINSON (*U. S. A.*); LORD CUNLIFFE (*British Empire*); MR. DESPRET (*Belgium*); MR. TATSUMI (*Japan*); MR. RYBARSKI (*Poland*); MR. DANIELOPOL (*Roumania*); MR. STANARE-VITCH (*Serbia*).

There were also present Messrs. HOSTIE (*Expert for Belgium*), HIPWOOD (*Expert for the British Empire*), GRUNEBAUM-BALLIN and LAURENT-VIBERT (*Experts for France*), MYLONAS (*Greece*), and FREIRE D'ANDRADE (*Portugal*).

River Shipping

The CHAIRMAN proposed the consideration of the text presented by the Powers interested with regard to river shipping. (See Annex I.)

MR. ROBINSON (*U. S. A.*) said that as far as the last paragraph ("one or more umpires appointed by the Government of the United States") was concerned he could not approve without asking for authority from his Government.

MR. HOSTIE (*Expert for Belgium*) recalled the arbitration commissions constituted by the Harbor Commission for each river system to decide the questions of transfer of flag due to changes of territory affecting the inhabitants of the borders of inter-national rivers; he thought that with the consent of the United States Government there would be an advantage in turning over to these Commissions the settlement of methods of transfer provided for in the text under discussion.

MR. ROBINSON (*U. S. A.*) approved the general idea of this solution, while reserving the opinion of his Government. The Committee, upon the proposal of the CHAIRMAN and with the assent of MR. ROBINSON, decided to consider the solution proposed by MR. HOSTIE as adopted if the United States Delegation did not formally object within a short delay.

The CHAIRMAN opened the discussion of the first paragraph.

MR. HIPWOOD (*Expert for British Empire*) observed that the wording "for any reason whatsoever" would imply the obligation on the part of the enemy to restore river vessels which they might have bought: in this special case the purchase price should be refunded.

MR. DESPRET (*Belgium*) affirmed that this was the intention of the Drafting Committee and thought that it would suffice to record it in the minutes.

MR. HIPWOOD (*Expert for British Empire*) declared himself satisfied and the first paragraph was approved.

The Committee then took up the second paragraph.

As a result of observations by MR. DANIELOPOL (*Roumania*), who thought the wording of the clause not exact enough, it was decided to insert after the words "by the Allied and Associated Powers and which" the words "cannot be eventually made good by means of restoration" instead of "might eventually not be made good by means of restoration provided in the above section."

The second paragraph was so approved.

The CHAIRMAN proposed the examination of the text (See Annex II) which the French Delegation offered with the idea of imposing on Germany during ten years the construction of merchant shipping for the benefit of the Allies in order to make up as far as possible the deficiency of the enemy merchant fleet with regard to the admitted principle of replacement ton for ton.

MR. LAURENT-VIBERT (*France*) laid great stress on the vital importance to France of reparation in kind for her losses which had not been offset by any new construction during the war due to the fact that all yards and factories had been exclusively devoted to war work for the Allies.

MR. HIPWOOD (*Expert for British Empire*), while he admitted the value of the arguments presented, thought that it would be difficult to force this work on Germany and, furthermore, feared unfavorable reaction on the industry of shipbuilding nations.

MR. ROBINSON (*U. S. A.*) thought there would be ample tonnage in the world before very long and that the French proposal might cause over-production.

MR. LAURENT-VIBERT (*France*), in reply to MR. HIPWOOD, observed that any form of payment of indemnity would force the enemy to work for the benefit of the Allies. He did not think that the question of competition with Allied shipbuilding nations was well taken because the German yards had a fixed capacity for construction and it was only a question whether a part of their product should fly the enemy or the Allied flag.

With regard to refrigerating machinery the text was intended to mean such as was under construction.

With regard to raw materials, MR. LAURENT-VIBERT agreed with MR. HIPWOOD and accepted the suppression of any reference thereto in the text. He replied to MR. ROBINSON that the abundance of tonnage in the world foreseen by the latter, would not suffice for countries like France which had suffered very great losses and for which it was of the utmost importance to resume the place to which they considered themselves justified among maritime nations.

MR. MYLONAS (*Greece*) supported the French proposal and merely suggested that the percentage of enemy construction to be demanded by the Allies be fixed.

MR. HOSTIE (*Expert for Belgium*) supported the suggestion.

MR. LAURENT-VIBERT (*France*) proposed to amend the French text by adding at the end of the first clause "up to 25 per cent. of the annual new construction."

Following a discussion between the CHAIRMAN and MR. ROBINSON (*U. S. A.*) it was decided to reserve the amended text until the next meeting.

The next meeting was fixed for Thursday, 10 April, at 10.30 A. M. The meeting adjourned at 7 P. M.

CUNLIFFE,
Chairman.

F. FOBERTI,
　Secretary.

ANNEX I

ARTICLE GOVERNING DELIVERY OF RIVER SHIPPING

(*Proposed for insertion in the Treaty of Peace by the Delegations of France, Italy, Belgium, Roumania, Yugo-Slavia, Czecho-Slovakia and Poland.*)[1]

The enemy Powers bind themselves to restore in kind and in normal conditions of keeping, to the Allied and Associated Powers, within two months from the signature of those preliminaries, any boats and other movable appliances belonging to inland navigation, which, since the 2 August, 1914, have come anyhow into the

---

[1] Part III of Clause C of Annex II of Document 543 follows, with differences of translation not shown.

possession of any one of the enemy Powers or any dependents of the same and which can be identified.

With a view to compensate the inland navigation tonnage decrease, suffered during the war by the Allied and Associated Powers and which cannot be eventually made good by means of restoration, the enemy Powers bind themselves to hand over to the Allied and Associated Powers a part of their river vessels up to the value of the said decrease, provided that such delivery shall not exceed 20 per cent of the same fleet as it was at the date of the 11 November, 1918.

The conditions of this [delivery shall be settled by one or several umpires appointed by the United States of America Government.]

ANNEX II

ARTICLE GOVERNING CONSTRUCTION OF MERCHANT SHIPS BY THE ENEMY AS PARTIAL REPARATION

(*Offered by the French Delegation.*)[2]

As an additional part of reparation, the German Government agrees to cause merchant ships to be built in German yards for Allied account, as follows:

1. Within three months of the signature of the preliminaries of peace, the Allied and Associated Powers will notify the German Government of the amount of tonnage to be laid down in German ship-yards in each of the two years next succeeding the three months mentioned above;

2. Within twenty-four months of the signature of the preliminaries of peace, the Allied and Associated Governments will notify to the German Government the amount of the tonnage to be laid down in each of the three years following the two years mentioned above;

3. The amount of tonnage to be laid down in each year will not exceed 200,000 tons, gross tonnage.

4. The specifications of the ships to be built, the conditions under which they are to be built and delivered, the price per ton at which they are to be accounted for in the reparation account, and all other questions relating to the accounting, ordering, building and delivery of the ships, shall be determined by a Commission nominated by the Allied and Associated Powers.

---

[2] Part II of Clause C of Annex II of Document 543 follows. The two are identical.

DOCUMENT 542

Second Subcommittee: Minutes of the Thirty-first Meeting (Including Annex), April 10, 1919, 10:30 A. M.

[EOM, Second Subcommittee, pp. 120-22. No French minutes or text of Annex.]

The Second Sub-Committee of the Commission on Reparation of Damage (Financial Capacity of the Enemy States—Their Means of Payment and Reparation) met on Thursday, 10 April, 1919, at 10.30 A. M., at the Ministry of Finance, LORD CUNLIFFE in the chair.

Present: MR. ROBINSON (*U. S. A.*); LORD CUNLIFFE (*British Empire*); MR. TATSUMI (*Japan*); MR. RYBARSKI (*Poland*); MR. STOYANOWITCH (*Serbia*).

There were also present Messrs. MYLONAS (*Greece*), FREIRE D'ANDRADE (*Portugal*), LIST (*Czecho-Slovak Republic*), HIPWOOD (*Expert for British Empire*), HOSTIE (*Expert for Belgium*), LAURENT-VIBERT (*Expert for France*), CAPTAIN JUNG (*Expert for Italy*).

Ship Construction as Reparation

The CHAIRMAN proposed the adoption of the minutes of the 28th meeting. These minutes were adopted. He then invited the Delegates to continue the discussion of the amendments presented by the French Delegation in regard to imposing on the enemy the obligation of constructing shipping for the Allies as a means of reparation. (See Annex II, Thirtieth Meeting.)

MR. LAURENT-VIBERT (*Expert for France*) said that as the objection to the amendment on the part of the British and United States Delegations seemed to rest on the actual demand by the Allies of construction on the part of the enemy, the French Delegation was prepared to propose a wording which would "allow the Allied Powers the right to demand" etc. "up to the mentioned percentage (25 per cent.)."

MR. ROBINSON (*U. S. A.*) observed that while he still felt that there would be great practical difficulties in carrying out this clause, he was ready to assent to the proposal in general, but he considered that the total amount of tonnage to be demanded for construction by the enemy should be fixed with as little delay as possible to avoid the menace to the shipping market which would be raised by a continued option.

He pointed out that as he understood that the Reparation Commission proposed to constitute a High Commission for the treatment of questions of reparations in kind it would seem unnecessary to make other arrangements for regulating the delivery of shipping.

After a discussion in which MR. LAURENT-VIBERT *(France)*, MR. ROBINSON *(U. S. A.)*, MR. HOSTIE *(Belgium)* and MR. MY-LONAS *(Greece)* took part with regard to the difficulties involved in the application of the proposed amendment, it was decided to appoint four Delegates (British Empire, France, U. S. A. and Belgium) to draw up a text embodying the following points:

(1) The Allied Powers to have the right to demand construction by the enemy up to a certain limit as reparation.

(2) The total amount of the tonnage to be demanded to be fixed with as little delay as possible.

(3) The definite specifications for construction to be fixed at least a year in advance.

(4) The regulating of deliveries to be in the hands of a special commission as proposed by the French Delegation or of such other authority as might be constituted by the High Commission.

No Transfer of Marine Property

The CHAIRMAN invited the Committee to discuss a text offered by the French Delegation with a view to (1) forbidding until the conclusion of peace any transfer of marine property belonging to enemy Powers; any acquisition of participation or shares in marine enterprises belonging to said Powers, and, in general, any agreements with a view to causing or preparing for a transfer of flag which might alter the status of the various merchant fleets; (2) declaring null and void all transactions of such character which had happened either during hostilities or since the Armistice.

MR. LAURENT-VIBERT *(Expert for France)* stated that the basic idea of the amendment, from the point of view of the French Delegation, was that for the purposes of reparation Germany's assets as they existed on 2 August, 1914, should be regarded as now available.

CAPTAIN JUNG *(Expert for Italy)* observed that in his opinion this Sub-Committee was not competent to deal with this question, which involved the neutral as well as the Allied Powers.

Furthermore, he opposed the proposal on two grounds, a technical and a general one. Technically, the question has been settled by a ruling of the Allied Maritime Transport Council and in general the principle that no retroactive nullification was valid in law.

After further discussion between MR. LAURENT-VIBERT *(Expert for France)*, MR. ROBINSON *(U. S. A.)* and CAPTAIN JUNG *(Expert for Italy)* the CHAIRMAN pointed out that the matter did not really fall within the competence of this Committee and at any rate was not a question to be inserted in the Treaty of Peace.

MR. LAURENT-VIBERT (*Expert for France*) on the part of the French Delegation reserved the right to present the question at a later time.

Financial Clauses

The CHAIRMAN then invited the attention of the Delegates to two articles referred to the Reparation Commission by the Finance Commission. (See Annex.)

At the suggestion of MR. STOYANOWITCH (*Serbia*) it was agreed to insert a clause at the beginning of these articles providing for their application to all enemy Powers.

With this addition the articles were adopted.

The CHAIRMAN directed the Secretariat to draw up a second Interim Report for examination at the next meeting.

The next meeting was fixed for Wednesday, 16 April, at 3 P. M.[1]

The meeting adjourned at 1 P. M.

CUNLIFFE,
Chairman.

F. FOBERTI,
Secretary.

ANNEX

ARTICLE REFERRED TO THE REPARATION COMMISSION BY THE FINANCIAL COMMISSION[2]

(ART. 10 REVISED)

The German Government shall convey to the Allied and Associated Governments, within three months and along with such details as may be called for, the following information which shall be supplied as of date of the signature of this convention.

A. The total gold reserve in the Reichsbank: in other banks of issue: and in public treasuries.

B. Whether situated in Germany* or outside of Germany.

1. All foreign securities and obligations of foreign states held by Germany or its nationals.

2. All foreign bank notes or other foreign paper currency held by Germany or its nationals.

*Approved by the Second Committee of the Reparation Commission subject to the modification that provisions applying to Germany shall be made applicable to the other enemy Powers also.

†NOTE.—As her boundaries shall have been established by this Treaty. [This is a note without a reference in the text.]

---

[1] The Subcommittee did not meet again until April 18.

[2] See Clause D of Annex II of Document 543.

3. All foreign "devises" held by Germany and its nationals.

C. All property and interest of whatsoever nature belonging to Germany and its nationals and situated in foreign territory such as:

1. Immovable property.
2. Movable property of every kind.
3. Merchandise.
4. Cash not included in B. 2 above.
5. Participations and credits of every kind not included in paragraph 2, a. b. and c. above.
6. Options and contracts for work or materials, orders unexecuted or incompletely executed that involve products, merchandise, tools and materials of every kind, and concessions of whatever sort.

ARTICLE II. (Revised)

The German Government undertakes to adopt all measures necessary to acquire, if it does not own them already, and to transfer to the Allied and Associated Governments all property and effects above mentioned for which [it] may be called upon by the aforesaid Governments. Notice stating the effects to be transferred shall be given within six months from the date of the report which the German Government is to furnish under the terms of Article 2. The transfer is to be effected by the German Government with the least delay possible and at the most within six months of the date of the notice.

Property and effects shall be valued by an Inter-Allied Financial Commission and the total shall be credited on account of reparation due from Germany to the Allied and Associated Powers.

The provisions of this article shall not apply to property and effects of the German Government or its nationals that, at the date of this convention have already been sequestered by the Allied and Associated Powers, nor to what is situated on territory ceded by Germany.

DOCUMENT 543

Second Subcommittee: Minutes of the Thirty-second (and Final) Meeting (Including Annexes I and II), April 18, 1919, 3 P. M.

[EOM, Second Subcommittee, pp. 123-39. French stenographic minutes, PV, CRD, pp. 872-89. French text of Annex (printed as Annex to the twenty-ninth meeting of the Second Subcommittee, April 7, 1919), PV, CRD, pp. 835-54.]

The Second Sub-Committee of the Commission on Reparation

of Damage (Financial Capacity of the Enemy States—Their Means of Payment and Reparation) met on Friday, 18 April, 1919, at 3 P. M., at the Ministry of Finance, LORD CUNLIFFE in the chair.

Present: MR. ROBINSON (*U. S. A.*); LORD CUNLIFFE (*British Empire*); MR. TATSUMI (*Japan*); MR. RYBARSKI (*Poland*); MR. DANIELOPOL (*Roumania*); MR. STOYANOWITCH (*Serbia*).

There were also present Messrs. MYLONAS (*Greece*), FREIRE D'ANDRADE (*Portugal*), HIPWOOD (*Expert for British Empire*) and LAURENT-VIBERT and DAYRAS (*Experts for France*).[1]

The CHAIRMAN proposed the adoption of the minutes of the 29th, 30th and 31st meetings.

Second Interim Report

The CHAIRMAN then passed to the discussion of the Second Interim Report. The report was examined paragraph by paragraph.

The CHAIRMAN proposed the addition of a clause about chemical and electrical products with a view to giving the Allied and Associated Powers the right to demand a certain percentage of her output of these products from Germany at fair prices.

With regard to the existing stocks, on the proposal of MR. ROBINSON (*U. S. A.*), it was decided that the percentage to be demanded should be fixed by the Inter-Allied Commission.

With regard to future production of these German industries, the clause proposed the following percentages:

1920 and 1921	25 per cent.
1922 and 1923	20 per cent.
1924 and 1925	15 per cent.

for all the Allies.

MR. DAYRAS (*Expert for France*) observed that in view of the difficulty of making a present estimate of future production as a basis for these percentages it was impossible to forecast the effect of such a limiting clause. He thought it would be better to leave the fixing of these percentages to the Inter-Allied Commission as had been decided with respect to stocks on hand.

The CHAIRMAN and MR. ROBINSON (*U. S. A.*) were not inclined to agree with this, and desired to keep to the proposed percentages.

MR. DAYRAS (*Expert for France*), therefore, in the absence of

---

[1] According to the French minutes, Théry, Lévy, Neymarck, and Neculcea were also present; and Dayras was absent (although mentioned later in the course of the meeting).

any French Delegate, reserved the right to add to the report, if it were deemed necessary, a note with regard to deliveries in question with a view to guarding against of the taking as establishing maximum [*sic*].

The Second Interim Report, with the addition[al] insertion of the proposed clause on electrical and chemical products, was then adopted.

The Committee then passed to the discussion of the Annexes to the report.

On the proposal it was decided to accept certain minor changes in the phraseology of the English version of the Shipping Clauses which had been suggested by MR. HIPWOOD (*Expert for British Empire*) to include in the Annexes to the report a clause relating to the delivery or release of clear titles to ships, (see Annex to Supplementary Report, Clause C, Article IV), which had been drawn up by the experts of Great Britain, France, the United States and Belgium.

The Annexes were so adopted.

MR. ROBINSON (*U. S. A.*), on behalf of the shipping experts, presented a note intended for the assistance of the two Drafting Committees and after discussion it was left to the Plenary Commission to decide whether to add their note to the report.

The meeting adjourned at 5.30 P. M.

CUNLIFFE,
Chairman.

F. FOBERTI,
Secretary.

ANNEX [*I*]

FIRST INTERIM REPORT[2]

(*Presented by the Second Sub-Committee.* (*Financial Capacity of the Enemy States: Their Means of Payment and Reparation*).)

On 4 February, 1919, the following representatives were appointed to study the financial capacity and the means of payment of the enemy States:—

[2] Except as otherwise stated in the notes, the various sections of this First Interim Report (beginning with that on Restitution) are preceded by the corresponding sections of Document 143, which is Lamont's Preliminary Draft of this Report, submitted to the Special Committee of Three as a basis of discussion. The present document is the Report as finally adopted by the Second Subcommittee. The Report as submitted to the Subcommittee by the Special Committee is not in the minutes, but presumably would consist of the present text minus the following: (1) Chamiec's text on Restitution; (2) Despret's text, with the Text of Resolution, on Reparation in Kind and Equivalent; (3) Danielopol's text on Payment in Kind; and (4) Cunliffe's final paragraph on the later admission of subsequent resolutions.

Mr. Norman H. Davis.....................United States of America.
Lord Cunliffe (*Chairman*)...................Great Britain.
Mr. Loucheur.............................France.
Mr. Salandra.............................Italy.
Mr. K. Tatsumi...........................Japan.
Mr. Chamiec.............................Poland.
Mr. Danielopol...........................Roumania.
Mr. Stoyanowitch........................Serbia.

The following were also present at the meetings:—

Mr. Despret.............................Belgium.
Mr. Mylonas.............................Greece.
Mr. List................................Czecho-Slovakia.
Mr. Freire d'Andrade.....................Portugal.

The Sub-Committee have held twenty-eight meetings and have very carefully considered and reviewed all the evidence, information and figures at their command; they have also been greatly assisted in their deliberations by certain expert witnesses and hope to obtain further details for their final report, which, for various reasons, are to-day unprocurable.

For the purposes of this Report, the "mark" is taken as equivalent to 0.358,423 grammes of fine gold.

Restitution[3]

In the first place the Sub-Committee recommend that the enemy States should immediately restore all property belonging to the Allied Powers or their subjects which they have taken for any purpose and which are and can be identified in the enemy territory.

Reparation in Kind and Equivalent[4]

The Sub-Committee were of opinion that one method of immediate payment to be considered as essential in the reparation of damage caused by the Enemy in the territories of the Associated nations should consist in the right of removing, for the benefit of such nations, from the enemy countries material equivalent in kind to that which has been taken, worn out, consumed or destroyed by the enemy or as the result of acts of war. This right of removal to be exercised apart from any claim to the liquid assets available and to further payments which are dealt with below. The Sub-Committee attach a special importance to this kind of reparation, having regard to the moral considerations which favor its adoption and to the fact that it would thus be possible for the

[3] This section was added at the request of Chamiec (Poland) (see Document 540).
[4] This section was added at the request of Despret (Belgium) (see Document 540).

areas which have been intentionally and systematically devastated by the enemy to be more rapidly reconstituted.

The Sub-Committee have formulated their views on this question in the following resolution. It should be understood that the enumeration of material therein contained is no way exhaustive, and that consequently the text is intended to apply to all forms of damage without exception.

Text of Resolution[5]

"In cases where immediate needs must be provided for, the Allied States may take objects, whether at present in use or not, from the enemy countries: viz., machinery, rolling-stock, equipment, tools, timber, cattle, etc., equivalent in kind to the objects which have been taken, worn out, consumed or destroyed by the enemy, or as a result of acts of war.

"Objects found in enemy countries which have been taken from the territories of the Allied States can only be removed for the purpose of reparation in this manner on condition that they are not claimed by their owners in accordance with the procedure indicated in article   of the Treaty of Peace.

"For the purpose of undertaking the removals described above an Inter-Allied Commission of   members shall be constituted which will be entrusted with the task of considering the demands of each of the Allied States in regard to their immediate need of the objects falling under the various categories, and of fixing the quantities of such objects to be surrendered by the enemy countries, these objects to be distributed in proportion to the recognized needs of the interested parties.

"Each Allied country shall appoint National Commissions which will be presided over by Delegates of the Inter-Allied Commission and which will visit the enemy countries to select and remove objects falling under the various categories within the authorized limits. The heads of the different National Commissions operating in the same enemy country shall consult together in order to co-ordinate the work of their Commissions."

Available Liquid Assets[6]

The first endeavor of the Sub-Committee has been to determine the amount of the so-called "liquid assets" in the possession of the

---

[5] The Annex of Document 527 precedes this section, which is the same as Clause B of Annex II of the present document. It was added at the request of Despret (Belgium) (see Document 540).

[6] This section is preceded by the corresponding section of Document 143. The two are so different, however, that the changes cannot be indicated by brackets and by underlining.

enemy countries which can be made available within a period of about 18 months or two years from the signing of the Preliminary Peace. This amount of liquid assets obtainable within the period named the Sub-Committee have estimated at M. 20,000 million. Included in these assets there is an amount of gold and silver reported as being approximately M. 3,200 million, but it has come to the knowledge of the Sub-Committee that considerable sums have been deposited for safekeeping in the German banks by nationals and others—notably about £6,000,000 by the Ottoman Public Debt. It is not within the province of this Sub-Committee to determine what precise amount of this gold and silver shall be taken from the enemy countries; but it is apparent that the total amount (whatever it may finally prove to be) is all available as one of the liquid assets.

Ships, like gold, are one of the actually known assets which can be liquidated easily; the method of such liquidation is at the present moment under discussion and must be reported on later.

Prompt Liquidation Necessary

It should be noted that the realization of the great bulk of the total amount within the period named is dependent upon the possibility of liquidating these assets within that period. For instance, one of the chief items is that of investments by the enemy countries in the securities of foreign Governments and of enterprises located outside the enemy countries. In order to realize this item it will be necessary to find purchasers of or persons prepared to lend on these securities. There is no assurance that this can be accomplished; but the judgment of the Sub-Committee is, as above expressed, that the amount of M. 20,000 million can, under reasonably favorable conditions, be made available within the period named.

The Sub-Committee have not attempted to indicate in what installments and at what intervals (within the period mentioned) the total sum should be paid, but measures must obviously be taken to control and to expedite the payment of the sum indicated.

The Sub-Committee have not considered the sums which the enemy Powers may be called upon to pay in cash or securities for the armies of occupation or for foodstuffs.

Possible Exports[7]

In addition to gold, silver and securities, whether in enemy,

[7] This section is new, from Document 143.

Allied or neutral countries, the Sub-Committee have carefully examined and explored the following industries, to ascertain the possible amount of exports from the enemy countries of coal, iron, timber, sugar, potash, dyes, machinery, woolen and cotton and leather goods, etc., etc., being careful that such exports should as far as possible be readily and willingly consumed by the Allies and should in no case interfere with or militate against their trade.

Subsequent Payment[8]

The second endeavor of the Sub-Committee has been to determine what amount of reparation the enemy countries can pay subsequent to the above-named period following the conclusion of peace. Upon this point the Sub-Committee assumes as the beginning of the period in question 1 January, 1921. If, as the Sub-Committee believe, the enemy Powers, after the exhaustion of a long war, can still pay by means of exports or credit the sum of M. 20,000 million in about two years, it may be reasonably held that when their industries and credit are better established, they can well pay a very considerable amount annually, increasing as time goes on. What that sum is the Sub-Committee have, so far, been unable unanimously to determine, but the following scheme is submitted:

1919-20:—M. 20,000 million as set forth in this report, and thereafter a sum (to be fixed as hereinafter provided) to be paid each year until the total amount of the proved claims shall have been discharged, which total amount is hereinafter referred to as the debt.

Inter-Allied Commission[9]

In order to fix the amount of the claims by suitable proof and the amount of the said annual payments, the Allied Powers should create an Inter-Allied Commission, which will hear such evidence as to the capacity of the enemy Powers to pay as it may think just and proper (including evidence brought forward by the enemy Powers), and then fix the above amounts with due regard to the said capacity.

The said Commission shall be instructed and bound not to decide that the capacity of the enemy Powers to pay will fall short of the full amount of the proved claims, unless and until the enemy Powers shall have imposed on their subjects taxation per head for

---

[8] This section replaces the two sections of Document 143 entitled *Additional Principal Sum to be Paid, Marks 100,000,000,000* and *Total Payments Throughout Period.*

[9] This section is new, from Document 143.

the service of this debt at least as heavy as the highest taxation imposed on its subjects for the service of its debt by any Allied Power.

Debt to be Funded[10]

The Sub-Committee suggest that the debt should be funded by the enemy Powers in the form of 5 per cent gold-mark bearer bonds free from all enemy Power taxes, etc., etc., which would create a negotiable instrument—a matter of considerable importance.

Anticipation of Payments to be Encouraged[11]

The Sub-Committee express the judgment that the enemy countries should be permitted and encouraged upon proper notice to anticipate in whole or in part payment of the total principal sum remaining unpaid at the end of any given year.

Your Committee have very carefully considered the vast commercial importance to the enemy of the loss of the very rich provinces of Alsace-Lorraine and of their mercantile navy, and have also been duly mindful of their territorial and colonial losses. No discussion has taken place on the subject of the Saar valley or other territory bordering on the Rhine, while any export taxes imposed on enemy manufactures or duties on raw materials imported must considerably reduce their capacity to pay the cost of reparation.

Estimates largely a matter of conjecture

In respect of any forecast of the capacity of the enemy countries for payment extending over a series of years, the Sub-Committee desire to make particular note of the fact that no forecast can be accepted as attaining complete exactitude and certainty. The factors which may influence the ability of the enemy countries to pay are so many and of so fluctuating a nature that it is impossible, as regards even a few years—still more as to a period of fifty years—to forecast conditions, and to say positively what can or cannot be done.

Specific Objects of Export

In arriving at a forecast of what the enemy countries can pay the Sub-Committee have taken tesimony covering a large number of articles which the enemy countries can, in all probability, export

[10] This section is new, from Document 143.
[11] This section is new, from Document 143.

in future upon a scale far heavier than that prevailing before the war, and testimony has been presented to show that the peoples of the Associated Governments can also absorb such exports upon a similar scale. The list of such articles as enumerated to the Sub-Committee is extensive, the chief items being coal and timber and iron.

As to the item of coal, it is recommended that such Commission (whose appointment is hereinafter suggested) as may be empowered to carry out the general provisions for reparation should give its special attention to the opportunity afforded to create heavy payments through the export of coal from Germany. France is represented as requiring 30,000,000 tons of coal per annum throughout the period required for the payment of reparation, particularly in order to replace the output of the mines dismantled by the Germans in Northern France. The experts of the French Delegation calculate that Germany may be able to export 60,000,000 tons of coal per annum to the value of approximately M. 1,600 million, which, by arrangement, can be utilized, at any rate to a certain extent, for reparation payments.

In considering such testimony, the Sub-Committee have thought it proper largely to disregard the figures of the pre-war export trade of the enemy countries (especially that of Germany) and to assume that in such industries (such as coal and timber just mentioned), the exports of the enemy countries can be vastly stimulated over those of the pre-war period, and that to this particular end practically the whole of the interior industrial life of the enemy countries will be able to conform.

Payment in kind[12]

The Sub-Committee also consider that another very efficacious and useful method of payments would consist in obliging the enemy Powers to hand over to such Allied countries as may desire it, supplies of all kinds, manufactured goods, live stock, etc., the value of which would be deducted for each Allied country from the claim for damages preferred by that country against the enemy Powers.

Germany must continue on war basis of economy and imports

For instance, in the case of Germany prior to the war, its annual merchandise exports were less rather than more than its imports.

---

[12] This section was added at the request of Danielopol (Rumania) (see Document 540).

It is plain, therefore, that in order to reverse this trade balance so that Germany's annual exports may largely exceed its imports, the industrial and the domestic life of Germany must adapt itself and cut down imports to the least figure commensurate with the amount of raw materials which she actually requires from abroad for the conduct of her domestic and industrial life; and must turn herself into a nation of exporters, organized for the purpose of paying the reparation claims of the Associated Governments.

Economic dangers involved for Associated Governments

The Sub-Committee appreciate that the development by the enemy countries of such a policy as just described may lead to the creation, especially in Germany, of an organization so highly developed and so skilled as to be calculated in the future to have considerable and perhaps unfavorable influence upon the markets of the world.

It must not be overlooked that such internal organization is based on a minimum of consumption by the German population and that such diminished consumption by 70,000,000 people may seriously affect the ability of the Associated Governments to dispose of their surplus products. On the other hand, it must be remembered that if but a comparatively small sum be demanded of the Germans, which, with their great assiduity, perseverance and thrift, they are able to repay within a short term of years, they will the sooner be in a position to resume their former commercial tactics and will no doubt work even harder to build up their own wealth than to restore what they have so wantonly destroyed.

Method of Reasoning Employed

The Sub-Committee have been unable, as they have already stated, to demonstrate scientifically upon the basis of pre-war figures of industry and trade, the ability of the enemy countries to pay the amount of the proved claims as they are set forth. The Sub-Committee feel that in any event it is wiser to fix an amount, even though that should prove to be in excess of the resources of the enemy countries, rather than to run the risk of naming a sum well within their ability to pay without any extraordinary effort— especially as the Sub-Committee further realize that in any event the proved claims fall well below the actual amount of the injury and destruction inflicted upon the peoples of the Associated Governments.

Possibility of Increasing Capacity to Pay

It must be remembered that the productive capacity of a nation may, owing to improvement in the arts and sciences, increase at a rate far more rapid than would now be considered possible. In the estimate considered by the Sub-Committee, allowance has been made for a certain increase of productive capacity on the part of the enemy countries. But it is only necessary to look back a few years to show how much values can vary. Figures which to-day appear out of all proportion to the productive capacity of Germany may be considered as quite moderate in twenty or thirty years. A glance at the development of Germany during the last fifty years gives food for thought about the possible increase in Germany's capacity to pay. For example, according to the best figures obtainable, the production of coal in Germany increased five times during these fifty years; the production of steel twelve times; the number of laborers employed in mechanical industries five times, while the number of kilometers of railroads has tripled and exports have increased five times.

Recommendation as to Commission of Control[13]

In view of the above, and, in some contingencies, of the possible dangers in the situation as already described, the Sub-Committee regard it as important that some permanent international body be established, to be vested with the power to supervise the payment of reparation. The Sub-Committee have excluded from their consideration any plan which would involve the assumption by the Associated Powers of the internal management of German industries, and also the use of power as a method of compulsion; and no system of reparation must be entertained, or, if established, allowed to continue by which the regular trade of the Associated Powers would be prejudiced or disturbed. In the opinion of the Sub-Committee, the best guarantee for the payment of her debt by Germany will be her consciousness of the necessity for maintaining her financial and commercial credit, a consciousness which will steadily become stronger if the securities are issued as above proposed, and become spread in all countries of the world, and as

[13] This section is preceded by the section of Document 143 entitled *Recommendation as to Committee of Control.*

the approach of the time for the final discharge of the debt increases the financial stability of Germany beyond the risk of any temptation to repudiate.

Having concluded the first consideration of the financial capacity of the enemy States, and their means of payment and reparation the Sub-Committee adopted the following resolution:—[14]

> "It is understood that in adopting the principles and resolutions which have already been adopted the Sub-Committee does not exclude the adoption of additional resolutions subsequently, or regard those already adopted as exhaustive in all cases."

CUNLIFFE,
Chairman of the Second Sub-Committee.
8 April, 1919[15]

ANNEX [II]
SUPPLEMENTARY INTERIM REPORT OF THE SECOND SUB-COMMITTEE ON REPARATION

SINCE presenting its first interim report, the Second Sub-Committee has held three meetings in order to conclude its discussions of the enemy merchant fleet considered as a means of reparation, and on other matters. In these meetings the Committee has had the advantage of the advice of experts.

Merchant Shipping

The Committee started from the principle that the enemy should be required to recognize the right of the Allied and Associated Powers to the replacement, ton for ton and class for class, of all the merchant ships and fishing-boats which they have destroyed or damaged during the war. The Allied merchant tonnage destroyed by the enemy is, in round figures, 10,750,000 tons, and the total enemy merchant shipping tonnage available about 5,500,000 tons. There is, therefore, only enough enemy merchant tonnage to meet about half the Allied claim, and yet it has been deemed necessary to leave the enemy the major portion of his coasting and fishing fleets as being essential to his economic needs.

The Committee agree that the enemy Powers should be required to cede the whole of their merchant tonnage over 1,600 tons gross, half of the vessels between 1,600 and 1,000 tons, and one-quarter

---

[14] This last paragraph and the resolution were added at Cunliffe's request (see Document 540).
[15] The French text is dated April 7, which is the date the Report was actually adopted in its entirety by the Subcommittee.

of the steam trawlers and of the other fishing craft. This leaves to Germany the greater portion of her coasting and fishing vessels.

An additional means of securing reparation in kind for the merchant ships destroyed during the war is to require Germany to undertake to build merchant ships for the Allies over a period of five years. The maximum amount to be built in any one year is fixed at 200,000 tons, this being about one-third of the total output of all German shipyards before the war.

In addition, the Committee consider it essential that the enemy Powers should be bound to cede to the Allies a certain proportion of the river craft now in their possession. The craft taken by force or otherwise acquired from the Allies during the war, which can be identified, should be restored, and in addition a further amount of river tonnage should be ceded by way of reparation. The total amount to be surrendered is so calculated as not to impair seriously the economic life of the enemy Powers.

Draft clauses for giving effect to these proposals are appended (see Clause C in the Annex), and it is recommended that these clauses should be referred to the Inter-Allied Drafting Committee in order that any necessary amendments of form may be made, so as to enable the clauses to be embodied in the Peace Treaty.

On the main principle, viz., that the enemy should be required to relinquish all title in the merchant shipping and fishing tonnage, the Committee were unanimous. The Committee generally were of opinion that the enemy should be required to cede the tonnage to the Allies as a whole. The American Delegation proposed that the enemy should be required to acknowledge the validity of the seizures made by each individual Allied or Associated Power, and to recognize the title of that Power to the ships which it had seized.

This question is so important and so far-reaching that the Committee consider it desirable to set out the arguments on each side at some length.

American Contention and Amendment

The amendment which is offered by the American Delegation for the purpose of validating the title to the seized ships is offered for the reasons following:

(a) That no question of title may be raised by any of the enemy Powers or by any of their nationals, or by any one interested in any manner in such seized ships.

(b) That no Allied or Associated Power should question the validity of the title to the ships seized by any other Associated or Allied Power.

The amendment relating to the payment of compensation for such seized ships is for the purpose of determining the value and the application of the payment for such ships at the value so determined.

In making these reservations and presenting the amendments, the United States Delegation submits the following:

(*a*) That it does not admit the right of any enemy Power or Allied or Associated Power to question the title to the enemy ships seized during the war under the authority of the Congress of the United States approved 12 May, 1917, and the proclamation of the President of the United States based thereon.

(*b*) That the amendments are submitted in view of the interpretation made by the British Delegation as set out in the *procès-verbal* for the twenty-sixth meeting to the effect that paragraph 3 of Clause C (see Annex) is intended to exclude from delivery under the general provisions of Clause C only such enemy ships as have been "captured and definitely condemned by prize courts," and that prize-court condemnations were made only in the cases of ships taken by Great Britain and Portugal.

The United States Delegation further submits that as the title to the seized enemy ships should be accepted as valid by the enemy Powers and by the Allied and Associated Powers, the suggestion to transfer such ships to a "pool" for redistribution on the basis of losses, ton for ton and category for category, is tantamount to asking for a contribution on the part of certain of the Allied and Associated Powers.

The principle involved in such a request would compel a complete analysis and consideration of the causes and progress of the war and the relations of various Allied and Associated Powers to the war and, in addition, a complete survey and determination of the relations of the Allied and Associated Powers to each other.

British and French Contention

The British and French Delegations pointed out that the American proposal was open to the following objections:

1. It substituted individual for collective action, Germany being bound to recognize as valid the seizures made by each State, instead of ceding the ships to the Allies collectively.

2. It is based frankly and implicitly on physical possession, not on justice, and establishes the doctrine that the disposal of enemy ships after a war is decided not by international law or agreement, but by the accident of ships having taken refuge in certain ports to

escape capture. In the present war the very large numbers of German and Austrian ships which took refuge in North and South American ports on the outbreak of war fled to these ports and remained there in order to escape capture by the British and French naval forces.

3. If this principle is admitted in the case of an Ally, it will be difficult in practice to prevent the neutrals from adopting it and keeping for their own use, in satisfaction of their claims against Germany, the enemy tonnage in their ports. As this amounts to 794,000 tons, the loss to the Reparation Fund will be considerable.

4. It would cause great injustice, for some of the States which have suffered least from the war, such as the United States and Brazil, will gain most under this proposal, while the States which have suffered most from the war would be seriously injured.

The United States and Brazil would have an absolute priority in the payment of their claims over any one else, including Belgium, for they would be able to pay themselves.

Under the most favorable circumstances there are not enough enemy ships to replace half the Allied losses, there being only 5,500,000 tons of enemy shipping to meet claims in respect of Allied losses amounting to 10,750,000, but under this arrangement the United States would get nearly twice as much tonnage as they have lost, for they have lost 389,000 tons and would get 628,000. Brazil would get nearly ten times as much as she lost, for she has lost 25,000 tons and would get 216,000. Great Britain, on the other hand, which has lost 7,746,000 tons, would only be able to keep 480,000, and France, who has lost 950,000 tons, would only be able to keep 45,000.

5. The proposal cannot be made a general rule, because it is obviously impossible to grant to, say, Brazil and Spain, the special right which is now claimed by the United States.

6. The American proposal, if agreed to, would insert in the Treaty of Peace with Germany a clause prescribing the method by which some of the enemy ships are to be allocated amongst the Allied and Associated Powers. The enemy have nothing to do with this allocation, which is a matter for the Allies to settle amongst themselves, and the Treaty should be confined to compelling the enemy to cede the ships to the Allies as a whole.

The Committee approved reporting the clause drafted by the British Delegation (Annex, Clause C) subject to the reservation of the United States Delegation, whose amendment was also to be reported.

Reservations were also made by some of the Delegations, including some representing new countries, who claimed that their nationals were entitled to the property in some of the enemy ships. The Committee felt that they were not competent to consider or decide the claims of this kind, and that they could only deal with the facts as they existed in August, 1914. It was understood that a Special Committee had been appointed to investigate claims of this kind.

Methods of Valuing Ships

With respect to the enemy merchant fleet, the Committee agreed that the actual value should be estimated at the date of surrender to the Allies.

The Committee is of the opinion that the work connected with such valuation should be entrusted to an Inter-Allied Commission of Experts.

Supply of Labor

In considering means of payment which might be imposed on the enemy, the Committee discussed the desirability of requiring the enemy to supply labor for the construction of the devastated regions. The imposition of such a requirement was found likely to give rise to numerous difficulties and complications which were accordingly exhaustively examined by the Committee. On the one hand, representatives of those countries which had suffered greatly at the hands of the enemy during the war felt strongly that the restoration of destroyed towns and ravaged land should be a burden upon the enemy States. They were not, in view of the many attendant difficulties, anxious to avail themselves of enemy labor, but, in view of the shortage of labor in their own countries, felt that they had no alternative but to call for it. On the other hand, it was pointed out that the difficulties involved in the utilization of such labor would be such as really outweigh any advantage that could be derived from it. The employment of large bodies of enemy workmen in an Allied country might give rise to endless industrial complications in that country in regard to conditions of work, pay, employment, etc. There was considerable ground for thinking that, notwithstanding the most careful safeguards, the quality of the labor might be very unsatisfactory. Further, though under the circumstances the employment of enemy labor in this manner might be completely justified, yet there was a great danger that public opinion might at no very distant date come to regard it as indistinguishable from forced labor and refuse to tolerate its continuance. After prolonged discussion of the subject and consideration of various detailed proposals for the organization of such labor, the Committee regrets that it was not possible to arrive at any agreement, and consequently is unable to make any recommendations on the matter.

Imposition of Taxes

Other means of payment which were discussed included calling upon the enemy to levy certain taxes, the total sum derived therefrom to be applied in reduction of the debt to the Allied and Associated Powers. The Committee considered various forms of new tax that might be imposed, including monopolies and capital taxes, and also whether it might not be preferable to force the enemy to increase taxes already in existence without creating new ones. But the Committee came to the conclusion that it was wiser to leave it to the enemy Powers to devise the means of meeting the liabilities they would assume by the signature of the Peace Treaty.

Liquid Assets

A Sub-Committee of the Financial Commission submitted to the Second Sub-Committee for Reparation two proposals for the control and assurance of the payment of a great part of the liquid assets. The Sub-Committee approved these proposals, which it submits in the form of clauses to be inserted in the Preliminary Peace Treaty (see Annex, Clause D), with the intention that they shall also be applied with regard to the other enemy countries.

Chemical and Electrical Products

The Sub-Committee recommend that the Allied and Associated States should claim an option to require delivery at fair prices to be fixed by the Inter-Allied Commission and credited against reparation a proportion of all and any chemical and electrical products of Germany as follows:—

Present Stocks.............Any or all—subject to the approval of the Inter-Allied Commission.
Stocks of 1920 and 1921....25 per cent. of output.
Stocks of 1922 and 1923....20 per cent. of output.
Stocks of 1924 and 1925....15 per cent. of output.
for the benefit of the Allies jointly.*

* The French Delegation considers that, as it is difficult to determine at present the production of the electrical and chemical industries in Germany, the percentages given should not be regarded as a maximum.

Works of Art

As to the works of art carried off or destroyed, the Committee is unanimously of the opinion that the Clauses A and B, to be inserted in the Preliminary Treaty of Peace, are applicable to the reparation of this class of damage.

Having concluded the first consideration of the financial capacity of the enemy States and their means of payment and reparation, the Sub-Committee adopted the following resolution:—

"It is understood that in adopting the principles and resolutions which have already been adopted, the Sub-Committee does not exclude the adoption of additional resolutions subsequently, or regard those already adopted as exhaustive of all cases."

CUNLIFFE,
Chairman of the Second Sub-Committee.
April 18, 1919

ANNEX—(OF THE SUPPLEMENTARY INTERIM REPORT)

CLAUSES PROPOSED FOR INSERTION IN THE TREATY OF PEACE

Clause A[16]

Article Governing Restitution

(See the First Interim Report under "Restitution.")

The enemy States must make immediate restitution of all property, generally, and of whatsoever kind, belonging to the Allied Powers of which they have possessed themselves for any purpose, and which is now found on their territory.

Annex No.   of the Treaty provides conditions according to which restitution shall be made.

ANNEX

In accordance with Article No.   of the Treaty, the enemy States shall return to the Allied Powers all effects, whether movables or fixtures, public property or that of artificial or natural persons, which enemy nationals have carried off and which are now in enemy territory. This clause applies to each and every object thus carried off which may now be situated in enemy States.

Accordingly those States shall execute a solemn undertaking immediately to collect from their nationals returns setting forth the whereabouts of effects now in the possession of the said nationals drawn from territories of the Allied and Associated Powers.

---

[16] Clause A is preceded, practically without change, by Annex I of Document 526.

Laws shall immediately be enacted which shall provide that every person who fails to make a return will be regarded as a receiver of stolen goods and will be liable to severe penalties to be determined by agreement with the Allied and Associated Powers.

An interval of one month from the signing of the Preliminary Treaty of Peace will be allowed for the making of these returns.

A comprehensive return, setting forth the sources from which objects have been drawn, if they have been identified, the nature of the objects and their present location, shall be made to the Representatives of the Allied and Associated Powers within a period of two months after the signature of the Preliminary Treaty of Peace.

The provisions hereinafter recited show broadly what measures are to be adopted to the end that complete restitution shall be made with the least possible delay. It is the purpose of the High Contracting Parties, however, that all necessary measures shall be taken to assure, in the fullest degree, complete restitution of objects carried off (subject to reservations hereinafter stated in the interest of the Allied and Associated Powers). The enemy Governments formally undertake to do all in their power to facilitate search and return [shipments].

The Plan of Procedure that follows is applicable to objects of all sorts; furniture, securities, objects of art, &c.

Plan of Procedure

I

Machines, machine parts, machine tools, agricultural implements and necessaries[17] of every sort and industrial or agricultural equipment of every kind, including cattle, beasts of burden, etc., which were taken from the territory occupied by the enemy armies under any pretense whatsoever, by military or civil authority of the enemy, or by private citizen of enemy's countries, shall be at the disposal of the Allied and Associated Powers for return to the places from which they were taken, if the interested Government so determines.

II

In order to prepare for this restitution, the enemy Government shall, with the utmost expedition, supply the duly appointed representatives of the Allied and Associated Powers with all records, official or private, relating to the objects in question; also with all

---

[17] Error for "accessories."

contracts for sale, lease or other purposes, all correspondence thereto pertaining, all declarations and all useful indications as to their existence, source, change of form, present state and place of deposit,

III

Delegates of the Allied and Associated Governments shall, in their discretion, take steps to make in the enemy countries surveys and examinations on the spot of the objects indicated.

IV

Reshipments shall be made according to special instructions given under the authority of the nation to which the particular objects belong.

V

Particularly, declarations shall be made with a view to an immediate restitution of all accumulations in yards, on the rails, in boats, or in factories, of belting, electric motors, motor parts, accessories, &c., that have been taken from the invaded territories.

VI

The retaking of an object of any kind that may be found or identified shall in no case be obligatory upon the Allied and Associated Powers, which shall be in no wise bound to take back objects. They shall have the right to declare, without assigning cause, that they waive claim to the restitution of particular objects and require reparation in lieu thereof by any other method contemplated by the Treaty.

VII

All expenses incurred in searching for, returning and completely reinstalling objects that are restored shall be borne by the enemy Power concerned. The restoration of objects as herein required shall in no case affect the right to recover compensation for what has not been so restored.

VIII

It is formally stipulated that no argument drawn whether from the law or from the interpretation of any text whatsoever shall be invoked by the enemy Powers in order to suspend or delay the execution of any measure of restitution prescribed by the Representatives of the Allied or Associated States. The execution of such a measure shall always be immediate, a right to claim damages accruing only in case it is subsequently adjudged that the measure in question was contrary to the provisions of the Treaty.

Clause B[18]

Article providing for Reparation by Equivalents

(See the First Interim Report.)

In every case where it is a matter of satisfying immediate needs, the Allied States may take away objects in the enemy countries, whether in actual use or not, especially rolling-stock, equipment and tools, timber, livestock, etc.: these to be the equivalent of similar objects removed, consumed, or destroyed by the enemy or worn out as the result of acts of war.

Objects found in enemy countries which have been previously taken from the territory of the Allied States cannot be taken as equivalents, except upon condition that their owners do not claim them in accordance with the procedure laid down in Article of the Treaty of Peace.

In order that the renewals herein provided for may be effected, an Inter-Allied Commission of members shall be constituted with the duty of deciding the claims of each one of the Allied States in regard to its immediate needs of the objects falling under various categories, and to determine the quantities of those objects which the enemy countries are to deliver, the same to be apportioned in accordance with the recognized needs of each one of the interested parties.

Each Allied country shall name Commissions, to be presided over by Delegates of the Inter-Allied Commission, who shall proceed to the enemy countries in order to select and take the objects falling under various categories, within the authorized limitations.

The Chairman of the different National Commissions operating in the same enemy country shall be expected to confer together with a view to co-ordinating the work of the Commissions.

Clause C

Articles relating to Merchant Shipping

I[19]

1. The enemy Powers recognize the right of the Allied and As-

---

[18] Clause B is preceded by the Annex of Document 527; and the French text of the preceding document is almost identical with the French text of the present document. It therefore seems reasonable to assume that the original was in French; and that the differences in the English are due only to differences in translation.

[19] This section is preceded by the Annex of Document 539.

sociated Powers to the replacement, ton for ton (gross tonnage) and class for class, of all merchant ships and fishingboats lost or damaged owing to the war.

Nevertheless, and in spite of the fact that the tonnage of enemy shipping at present in existence is much less than that lost by the Allied and Associated Powers, the right thus recognized will be enforced on enemy ships and boats under the following conditions:—

> The enemy Powers, on behalf of themselves and so as to bind all other persons interested, cede to the Allied and Associated Governments the property in all the enemy merchant ships which are of 1,600 tons gross and upward; in one-half, reckoned in tonnage, of the ships which are between 1,600 tons and 1,000 tons gross; in one-quarter, reckoned in tonnage, of the steam trawlers; and in one-quarter, reckoned in tonnage, of the other fishingboats.

2. The enemy Powers will, within two months of the signature of the Preliminaries of Peace, deliver to a representative of the Allied and Associated Governments, duly authorized by them for this purpose, all the ships and boats mentioned in Article I.

3. The ships and boats mentioned in Article I include all ships and boats which (*a*) fly, or may be entitled to fly, the enemy merchant flag; (*b*) are owned by any enemy subject, company or corporation or by any neutral company or corporation which is under the control or direction of enemy subjects; (*c*) which are now under construction in enemy or in neutral countries.*

4. For the purpose of providing documents of title for the ships and boats to be handed over as above mentioned, the enemy Powers will:

(*a*) Deliver to the representative of the Allied and Associated Governments in respect of each vessel a bill of sale or other document of title evidencing the transfer of the entire property in the vessel, free from all encumbrances, charges and liens of all kinds, to that officer;

(*b*) Take all measures that may be indicated by the said representative of the Allied and Associated Governments for ensuring that the ships themselves shall be placed at his disposal.

* See below for amendment proposed by United States Delegation.

II[20]

As an additional part of reparation, the German Government agrees to cause merchant ships to be built in German yards for Allied account as follows:—

(1) Within three months of the signature of the Preliminaries of Peace, the Allied and Associated Powers will notify the German Government of the amount of tonnage to be laid down in German ship-yards in each of the two years next succeeding the three months mentioned above;

(2) Within twenty-four months of the signature of the Preliminaries of Peace, the Allied and Associated Governments will notify to the German Government the amount of tonnage to be laid down in each of the three years following the two years mentioned above;

(3) The amount of tonnage to be laid down in each year will not exceed 200,000 tons, gross tonnage.

(4) The specifications of the ships to be built, the conditions under which they are to be built and delivered, the price per ton at which they are to be accounted for in the reparation account, and all other questions relating to the accounting, ordering, building and delivery of the ships, shall be determined by a Commission nominated by the Allied and Associated Powers.

III[21]

The enemy Powers undertake to restore in kind and in normal condition of upkeep to the Allied and Associated Powers, within two months of the signature of these preliminaries, any boats and other movable appliances belonging to inland navigation which since 2 August, 1914, have by any means whatever come into their possession or into the possession of their nationals, and which can be identified.

With a view to make good the loss in inland navigation tonnage, from whatever cause arising, which has been incurred during the war by the Allied and Associated Powers, and which cannot be made good by means of the reparation in kind prescribed in the above paragraph, the enemy Powers agree to cede to the Allied and Associated Powers a portion of the enemy river fleet up to the amount of the reparation in kind mentioned above, provided

[20] This section is preceded by Annex II of Document 541.

[21] This section is preceded by Annex I of Document 541, with some differences of translation not shown.

that such cession shall not exceed 20 per cent of the river fleet as it existed on 11 November, 1918.

The conditions of this <u>cession shall be settled by the same arbitrators as are charged with the settlement of difficulties relating to the apportionment of river tonnage resulting from the new international regime applicable to certain river systems or from the territorial changes affecting those systems.</u>

IV[22]

1. The enemy Powers undertake to take any measures that may be indicated to them by the Allied and Associated Governments for obtaining the full title to the property in all ships which have during the war been transferred, or are in process of transfer, to neutral flags, without the consent of the Allied and Associated Governments.

2. The enemy Powers abandon, in favor of the Allied and Associated Governments, all claims of all descriptions against the Allied and Associated Governments and against subjects or citizens of Allied and Associated countries in respect of the detention, employment, loss or damage of any enemy ships or boats.

3. The enemy Powers abandon, in favor of the Allied and Associated Powers, any claim to vessels or cargoes sunk by or in consequence of enemy naval action and subsequently salved, in which any of the Allied or Associated Governments or their citizens or subjects may have any interest either as owners, charterers, insurers or otherwise, notwithstanding any decree of condemnation which may have been made by an enemy Prize Court.

4. The enemy Powers will, within three months of the signature of the Preliminaries of Peace, take all necessary legislative and administrative measures to enable them to carry out the provisions of this chapter.

Amendments to Clause C proposed by the United States Delegation (but not accepted by all Delegations)

(For explanation, see text of the Second Interim Report above,

---

[22] This section was first submitted to the delegates at the thirty-second meeting of the Second Sub committee, April 18, 1919 (PV, CRD, p. 882; *English minutes have nothing on this point*) (see Document 543). This was the meeting at which the whole present document was being finally passed upon. Hipwood (British expert) made the following statement (*ibid.*, p. 883): "The fourth section consists of four clauses which have not yet been submitted to the deliberations of the Subcommittee. They have been drafted and they are proposed by the Drafting Committee which should concern itself (*qui devait s'occuper*) with questions relating to the river fleet and to the construction of ships by the German Government." The section was adopted later without objection (*ibid.*, p. 885).

p. 2 [at "Merchant Shipping" at the beginning of the present Annex II].)[23]

The Enemy Powers recognize as valid:

1. The seizure during the war of enemy merchant ships by the Allied and Associated Powers respectively.
2. The legality and sufficiency of the title to such ships acquired through such seizures irrespective of the process or means used to effect such seizures.
3. The full divesting of the enemy Powers and of each and every national thereof, and of each and every other party interested in such ships, of any right, title or interest in such seized property.

The enemy Powers, on behalf of themselves and so as to bind all other persons interested in such ships, hereby acknowledge the divesting of all and every right, title, property and interest of such enemy Power, and/or of their nationals or others interested in the ships so seized and taken possession of during the war by the Allied and Associated Governments respectively, and further confirm the vesting of such right, title, interest and property in such ships in the Allied and Associated Governments respectively.

The reasonable value of such ships shall be determined and such value shall be charged against the Government holding such ships and at the option of such Government shall be credited to the respective enemy Power which either itself or through its nationals or others formerly owned the same, on all such claims as are finally allowed respectively to such Allied or Associated Power as a result of the Treaty of Peace, and/or shall be credited and paid to any subject, citizen or other national of any enemy Power and/or others having or claiming to have any interest in any such ships as their respective interests may appear.

In the latter event, the balance, if any, shall be credited to such enemy Power which, through itself or its subjects, citizens, nationals or others, formerly owned such ships.

If such final credit so established in favor of any particular enemy Power, when taken together with other credits that may be allowed such Power under the terms of the Treaty of Peace, exceeds

[23] The text in Document 537 precedes.

the aggregate of claims allowed in the case of any Allied or Associated Power establishing such credit, the excess shall be used and applied in accordance with the provisions of the Treaty of Peace in respect to such excess credits.

Clause D[24]

Articles providing for control and assurance of the payment of part of their liquid assets by enemy Powers

(Approved by the Second Sub-Committee, subject to the modification that provisions applying to Germany shall be made applicable to the other enemy Powers also.)

ARTICLE 1

The German Government shall convey to the Allied and Associated Governments, within three months, and along with such details as may be called for, the following information, which shall be supplied as of the date of the signature of this Convention:

(*a*) The total gold reserve in the Reichsbank; in the other banks of issue; and in public treasuries.

(*b*) Whether situated in Germany* or outside of Germany.

1. All foreign securities and obligations of foreign States held by Germany or its nationals.
2. All foreign bank-notes or other foreign paper currency held by Germany or its nationals.
3. All foreign bills of exchange held by Germany and its nationals.

(*c*) All property and interest of whatsoever nature belonging to Germany and its nationals and situated in foreign territory, such as:

1. Immovable property.
2. Movable property of every kind.
3. Merchandise.
4. Cash not included in (*b*) 2 above.
5. Participations and credits of every kind not included in paragraph (*b*), 1, 2 or 3 above.
6. Options and contracts for work or materials, orders unexecuted or incompletely executed, that involve products, merchandise, tools and materials of every kind, and concessions of whatever sort.

---

* As her boundaries shall have been established by this Treaty.

[24] Clause D is derived from the Annex of Document 542.

ARTICLE 2

The German Government undertakes to adopt all measures necessary to acquire, if it does not own them already, and to transfer to the Allied and Associated Governments, all property and effects above mentioned, for which it may be called upon by the aforesaid Governments. Notice stating the effects to be transferred shall be given within six months from the date of the report which the German Government is to furnish under the terms of Article 1. The transfer is to be effected by the German Government with the least delay possible, and at most within six months of the date of the notice.

Property and effects shall be valued by an Inter-Allied Financial Commission, and the total shall be credited on account of reparation due from Germany to the Allied and Associated Powers.

The provisions of this article shall not apply to property and effects of the German Government or its nationals that, at the date of this Convention, have already been sequestrated by the Allied and Associated Powers, nor to what is situated on territory ceded by Germany.

Clause E[25]

From the date of bringing into force the present Treaty all the concessions, privileges and favors enjoyed on German territory by the subjects of Austria, Bulgaria, Hungary and Turkey, as the result of any act of a German Public Authority after 1 August, 1914, are assigned and transferred by Germany to the Allied and Associated Powers, under conditions which shall be determined by the said Powers.

The same shall apply in respect of the concessions, privileges and favors granted since 1 August, 1914, and enjoyed on German territory by German subjects as the result of an act of an Austrian, Bulgarian, Hungarian or Turkish Public Authority.

Germany undertakes to cancel any sale, cession, or other measure of disposal of the said concessions, privileges or favors which might interfere with the assignment and transfer of these rights.

For this purpose Germany shall, as from the coming into force of the present Treaty, take all necessary preservative measures, such as requisition, sequestration, seizure, etc.

The Allied and Associated Powers shall not be liable on their part for any claim for compensation or indemnities arising out of the present stipulation.

April 18, 1919.

[25] According to the French text of Clause E (PV, CRD, p. 854), this was an article referred to the Commission on the Reparation of Damage by the Commission on Economic Questions.

ADDITIONAL NOTE (*For the Drafting Committee.*)[26]

In the case of ships, as in the case of other property in kind ceded by the Germans to the Allies, there may be cases in which there are claims on the part of the Governments, or citizens, or subjects of Allied and Associated States against the ships or property. These claims should be considered on their merits before the ships or property are distributed or otherwise dealt with by the Allies, in the event of the Germans not having satisfied the claims themselves and before credit is given to Germany on account of these ships or other property.

The Committee recommended that the Allied Drafting Committee should have their attention called to these cases and should be asked to formulate a clause for inclusion in the Peace Treaty providing that cases of this kind shall be considered and that provisions be inserted to safeguard the legal and equitable interests of the Allied and Associated Governments and their nationals.

[26] There is no evidence as to the origin of this Additional Note.

THE MINUTES OF THE THIRD SUBCOMMITTEE (MEASURES OF CONTROL AND GUARANTEES)

DOCUMENT 544

Third Subcommittee: Minutes of the First Meeting, February 24, 1919, 11:40 A. M.

[EOM, Third Subcommittee, p. 5. French stenographic minutes, PV, CRD, pp. 895-97. The minutes of the Third Subcommittee have been available to the editors in a photostat copy, which is bound into one book. In addition to the minutes, this book also contains the following:

Cover. Not in the photostat copy.

Title Page. "PRELIMINARY PEACE CONFERENCE, COMMISSION ON THE REPARATION OF DAMAGE, THIRD SUB-COMMITTEE, MEASURES OF CONTROL AND GUARANTEES. MEETINGS: 1st—24 FEBRUARY . . . 4th—2 MAY. PARIS, 1919."
Unnumbered Page. "TABLE OF CONTENTS . . ." This page is probably out of place in the binding of the photostats.

Page 3. "COMMISSION ON REPARATION AND [*sic*] DAMAGE
"TERMS OF REFERENCE
"At its meeting on 4 February, 1919, the Commission on Reparation of Damage decided to appoint for the study of measures of control and guarantees a Sub-Committee of eight members, one to represent each of the Great Powers (United States of America, British Empire, France, Italy and Japan), and the remaining three members chosen among the representatives of the Powers with Special Interests."

Page 4.   "MEMBERS
"By the appointments made by the various Delegations, the Sub-Committee was constituted as follows:—

"United States of America.....................Mr. Bernard M. Baruch.
"British Empire..........................The Rt. Hon. W. M. Hughes.
"France...Mr. L. L. Klotz.
"Italy...Mr. d'Amelio.
" Japan...Mr. H. Nagaoka.
"Belgium...Mr. Despret.
"Greece...Mr. A. Romanos.
"Poland.......................................Mr. Casimir Olchowski."]

The Third Sub-Committee of the Commission on Reparation of Damage (Measures of Control and Guarantees) met on Monday, 24 February, 1919, at 11.40 A. M., at the Ministry of Finance, MR. KLOTZ in the chair.[1]

Present: MR. BARUCH (*U. S. A.*); MR. HUGHES (*British Empire*); MR. KLOTZ (*France*); MR. D'AMELIO (*Italy*); MR. NAGAOKA

---

[1] According to the French minutes, Hughes was in the chair at the beginning.

(*Japan*); MR. MICHALACOPOULOS (*Greece*); MR. BENES (*Czecho-Slovak Republic*).[2]

Election of Officers

MR. KLOTZ (*France*) nominated MR. HUGHES (*British Empire*) as Chairman. This proposal was accepted unanimously. MR. HUGHES then took the chair.

The CHAIRMAN nominated as Vice-Chairman MR. BARUCH (*U. S. A.*) who was also elected unanimously.

After a discussion in which Messrs. BENES (*Czecho-Slovak Republic*), BARUCH (*U. S. A.*), D'AMELIO (*Italy*), and KLOTZ (*France*) took part, it was decided that the Committee should adjourn until the Supreme War Council had given the Commission on Reparation a reply to the question which had been referred to it,—or until the First and Second Sub-Committee[s] had been able to provide the Third Sub-Committee with the necessary materials for its work.

It was understood that the CHAIRMAN would keep in touch with the Chairman of the Reparation Commission and the Chairman of the First and Second Sub-Committees.

The meeting adjourned at 11.50 A. M.

W. M. HUGHES,
Chairman.

HENRY JAMES,
Secretary.

DOCUMENT 545

Third Subcommittee: Minutes of the Second Meeting, March 11, 1919, 2:45 P. M.

[EOM, Third Subcommittee, pp. 6-7. French stenographic minutes, PV, CRD, pp. 898-902.]

The Third Sub-Committee of the Commission on Reparation of Damage (Measures of Control and Guarantees) met on Tuesday, 11 March, 1919, at 2.45 P. M., at the Ministry of Finance, MR. HUGHES in the chair.

Present: MR. BARUCH (*U. S. A.*); MR. HUGHES (*British Empire*); MR. DE VERNEUIL (*France*); MR. D'AMELIO (*Italy*); MR. TATSUMI (*Japan*); MR. DESPRET (*Belgium*); MR. MICHALACO-POULOS (*Greece*); MR. OSUSKI (*Czecho-Slovak Republic*).[1]

---

[2] According to the French minutes, Moniz was also present; D'Amelio and Beneš were replacing Romanos and Osuský, respectively.

---

[1] According to the French minutes, Nagaoka (instead of Tatsumi) and Danielopol (error for Osuský?) were also present.

The minutes of the 1st meeting were approved.

The CHAIRMAN stated that he had called the Committee together because the Supreme War Council had requested the Reparation Commission to present its report by the end of the week. Even though the other Sub-Committees had not yet reported, it was apparent that, whatever they might determine the enemy should pay, the Committee must be prepared to suggest the method of guaranteeing the payment. He invited suggestions.

MR. BARUCH (*U. S. A.*) expressed the opinion that an army of occupation might be the best means of securing the payment of the first instalments by the enemy, but that it would be undesirable to prolong such occupation after perhaps two years, some sort of Commission of control might have to be substituted.

Methods of Securing Payment

After a discussion in which Messrs. D'AMELIO (*Italy*) and BARUCH (*U. S. A.*) took part, the CHAIRMAN said that the methods of securing payment which had been suggested or which had occurred to him might be classified as follows:

1. An army of occupation, either permanent or for a limited time.
2. Economic control.
3. The military occupation of strategic points.
4. An International Commission to act as receivers and Controllers of revenues, customs, railway receipts and perhaps taxes.
5. An issue by the enemy Government of a loan to cover the indemnity; the bonds of this loan to be issued to enemy nationals and subscription to be obligatory upon persons possessing a prescribed property.
6. A limitation of expenditure on luxuries in the enemy countries.
7. Import duties on raw materials required by the enemy countries, coupled with the right of stoppage of such imports.

MR. D'AMELIO (*Italy*) raised the question whether the 5th proposal did not fall within the province of the Financial Commission of the League of Nations.

The CHAIRMAN expressed the opinion that even, if this was the case, the Sub-Committee was in no way relieved of its responsibility for recommending methods of securing payment of the indemnity.

After a brief further discussion the CHAIRMAN requested the Delegations represented on the Committee to present their views upon the seven heads enumerated, and upon any others which might occur to them, in the form of brief written memoranda, such memoranda to be in the hands of the Secretariat by 6 P. M. on 12 March.

The next meeting was fixed for 13 March, at 2.30 P. M.

The meeting adjourned at 3.30 P. M.

W. M. HUGHES,

HENRY JAMES, *Chairman.*

Secretary.

DOCUMENT 546

Third Subcommittee: Minutes of the Third Meeting (Including Annexes I-VI), March 13, 1919, 2:30 P. M.

[EOM, Third Subcommittee, pp. 8-15. The French minutes for this meeting are partly condensed and partly stenographic. PV, CRD, pp. 903-11.]

The Third Sub-Committee of the Commission on Reparation of Damage (Measures of Control and Guarantees) met on Thursday, 13 March, 1919, at 2.30 P. M., at the Ministry of Finance, MR. HUGHES in the chair.

Present: MR. BARUCH (*U. S. A.*); MR. HUGHES (*British Empire*); MR. CIIIESA (*Italy*); MR. DESPRET (*Belgium*); MR. MICHALACOPOULOS (*Greece*); MR. TATSUMI (*Japan*); and MR. OSUSKI (*Czecho-Slovak Republic*).

There were also present, MR. DE LA CHAUME and MR. DE VERNEUIL (*Experts for France*).[1]

The minutes of the second meeting were adopted.

French Proposal

The CHAIRMAN stated that a number of proposals had been submitted to him by the Delegations and invited the Committee to take the French proposal (Annex I) as a basis of discussion.

MR. DE LA CHAUME (*Expert for France*) explained the principles on which the French proposals were based. He thought that the first step would be to determine the sum to be paid by the enemy Powers and the second to decide whether it should be paid entirely in money or partly in materials. In the former case the articles of the French proposal relating to delivery of merchandise would disappear. The French Delegation had next considered the question whether the Commission to enforce payments should be an Inter-Allied Commission representing creditor countries or an International Commission representing the League of Nations. The French Delegation would itself prefer an Inter-Allied Commission and the French proposal had been so drawn.

[1] According to the French minutes, De la Chaume was not present.

Messrs. CHIESA (*Italy*) and BARUCH (*U. S. A.*) remarked on the similarity of the proposal submitted by Italy (Annex III) and that of the American Delegation (Annex VI) to the French proposal as explained by MR. DE LA CHAUME.

A discussion arising out of a suggestion of MR. CHIESA (*Italy*) that the French proposal should be amended to cover all the enemy Powers, instead of Germany alone, ended in an understanding that the details of the proposal should first be discussed with reference to one country only, but that they might be extended to cover all enemy Powers after the question of joint liability as between those Powers had been decided by the Commission.

MR. BARUCH (*U. S. A.*) urged that paragraph 3 should be adopted only upon condition that the Second Sub-Committee decided upon reparation in kind.

MR. DE LA CHAUME (*Expert for France*) pointed out that paragraph 4 implied the abandonment of the idea of controlling German foreign trade and substituted instead a right to receive part of the profits of such trade.

A discussion of paragraph 5 followed, in which the CHAIRMAN and MR. BARUCH (*U. S. A.*) objected to the idea of a tax on German exports, and MR. OSUSKI (*Czecho-Slovak Republic*) urged that no such tax should in any case be placed on raw materials.

MR. DE LA CHAUME (*Expert for France*) pointed out that paragraph 9 gave the proposed Inter-Allied Commission discretionary powers with respect to postponements of payment, the object being to avoid the necessity of referring such questions to all the creditor nations.

Subject to these observations and to the consideration of amendments offered by MR. CHIESA (*Italy*) (Annex II) the Committee provisionally approved the French memorandum.

It was decided that the French proposal and those of the other Delegations should be further discussed at a meeting to be called when the Second Sub-Committee should have reported.

The meeting adjourned at 4.40 P. M.

W. M. HUGHES,
Chairman.

HENRY JAMES,
Secretary.

ANNEX I[2]

CONTROL AND GUARANTEES

Memorandum presented by the French Delegation

1. For the purpose of carrying into effect the financial stipula-

[2] French text in PV, CRD, pp. 915-16. The latter part of Annex I of Document 547 follows.

tions of the Treaty of Peace with Germany, the Allied and Associated Governments shall be represented by an "Interallied Financial Commission of the German Debt," the constitution of which shall be determined by the Treaty of Peace.

2. It shall be the duty of the Commission to collect all payments to be made by Germany, and to divide the amount thereof among the Allied and Associated States in accordance with principles established by a special agreement to be concluded between the said States.

3. The Commission will determine and notify to Germany the nature, amount and destination of payments to be effected in kind. After having assured itself that its instructions have been carried out, the Commission will determine the amount in cash with which Germany shall be credited.

4. The Commission will accept foreign bills tendered in payment by Germany, and fix the rate of exchange [therefor.]

5. [The Commission will supervise and collect the amounts accruing from certain taxes, dues or charges, either already in existence or to be created with its consent, which are to be specially appropriated, as for instance:

[Taxes on alcohol, beer, sugar, salt, tobacco, luxuries (amusements, the purchase of works of art, jewelry, precious stones and metals, etc.), petroleum, coal, phosphates, etc.[3]

[Customs, posts and telegraphs, ports, canals (Kiel Canal), mines, forests etc.

[Direct taxes.

[Germany shall in particular establish an export duty (of so much per cent) on products of German manufacture or origin; such duty to be payable in the currency of the country of destination.]

6. [The Commission will administer a portfolio of German stocks and securities ceded or assigned to it by the German Government by way of security and pledges,][4] and will collect the revenue arising therefrom.

7. The Commission will administer all real estate of any description temporarily or permanently ceded to it by the German Government and will collect the revenue arising therefrom.

8. The Commission will convert into bills of Allied and Associated States all amounts in Marks accruing from the sources enumerated in articles 5 to 7 hereof.

---

[3] The French text adds, "sous forme de monopoles ou autrement."
[4] The French text omits "by way of security and pledges."

9. Should the proceeds of the different sources of payment specified in articles 3 to 7 hereof fail to produce an amount sufficient to cover the fixed yearly payments at the proper dates, the Commission shall be entitled either to grant an extension or delay (with or without continuation interest thereon) or to demand from the German Government payment of a sum in Marks corresponding to the ascertained deficit.

[The approval of the Commission must be obtained for the ways and means employed by the German Government to raise such sum in Marks.

[Should the said deficiency of proceeds continue during two consecutive years, the Commission shall be entitled, in accordance with the stipulations of article 5 hereof, to demand the appropriation of the proceeds of further taxes, either already existing or to be created, the anticipated revenue from which shall at least equal the minimum deficiency which has occurred during one of the two years in question.]

The payments in Marks effected under the present article shall be used, either to meet bills on the German State sold by the Commission, or for the purchase in Germany of goods chosen by the Commission and for payment of the transport charges thereon as far as the German frontier.

10. Should the proceeds of the different sources of payment specified in articles 5 to 7 exceed the amount necessary to cover the fixed yearly payments at the proper dates, the balance of the sums received by the Commission shall, after setting aside an amount corresponding to the service of the yearly payments for the following year, be paid to the German Government.

11. Should Germany not conform to the obligations specified above, the Commission may propose to the League of Nations, through the Financial Section thereof, the following coercive measures:—

(a) Occupation of strategic points or of property capable of yielding a fiscal or industrial revenue;

(b) Complete or partial blockade of a financial or economic nature.

12. The following temporary measures shall remain in force until Germany shall have: (1) effected the payments required by the Treaty of Peace for the first two years after signature thereof; (2) assigned to the Commission, by way of guarantee or pledge, the taxes, securities or real estate specified in articles 5 to 7 hereof:—

(a) Military occupation of strategic points;

(b) Economic and financial blockade according to the conditions laid down in article 1 of the Financial Protocol signed at Treves on 13 December 1918.

Subject to alteration or additions.

Paris 12 March, 1919.

ANNEX II[5]

PROPOSALS OF THE ITALIAN DELEGATION FOR ADDITIONS AND AMENDMENTS TO ANNEX I

The Italian Delegation proposes the following additions:—

Add at the end of paragraph 5 the following sentences:—

"The Financial Commission will superintend the payment thereof."

Add the following additional paragraph 13:—[6]

"The Provisions laid down in the present text concerning Germany shall be equally applicable to the other enemy Powers."

Add the following additional paragraph 14:—

"In the event of an obligation being imposed on the enemy Powers to contract an exterior debt in favor of the Allies, the Financial Commission shall assure the proper administration thereof and superintend the guarantees provided. It shall also [be charged with the allotment of] the bonds to the Allied and Associated Powers in accordance with their respective rights."

ANNEX III[7]

REPLY OF THE ITALIAN DELEGATION TO THE QUESTIONS SUBMITTED BY THE CHAIRMAN

I

Proposal No. 1. Military occupation of a zone of the enemy territories by way of guarantee can be suggested only in reference to payments in cash, in credits, in bonds, or in any other form of property, which the enemy States would be able to make within a maximum period of one year from the date of the conclusion of peace. Occupation extending further than the provision of such a guarantee may be considered as a means of preventing delay in payment by the enemy.

If, as is suggested in Proposal No. 5, the enemy countries are obliged either to create an exterior debt or to levy, once and for all, a tax on capital, it might be stipulated that the military occupation should extend until the final completion of this financial operation.

[5] French text in PV, CRD, pp. 916-17.

[6] The two following additional paragraphs, suggested by the Italians, were incorporated into Annex I of Document 547. The words in brackets were changed.

[7] French text in PV, CRD, pp. 917-18.

II

Proposal No. 2. It should be observed that continuance of the blockade would make the life of our debtors very difficult, as they would be unable to do their work for want of proper nourishment. The present system of provisioning should, perhaps, be continued. In any case, the tendency now seems to be to eliminate rather than to continue the existing blockade.

III

Proposal No. 3. Occupation of strategic points entails greater difficulties than the proposal outlined in paragraph I. It may, moreover, become superfluous in the event of Proposal No. 1 being accepted.

IV

Proposal No. 4. The constitution of an International Commission to control loans, customs, railways, taxes, etc. is undoubtedly the best method of guaranteeing the payment of debts claimed from the enemy countries.

Such control might be extended also to some of the ports, such as Hamburg, etc., or to the Kiel Canal.

This system of control would become all the more necessary if the following proposal were accepted.

V

Proposal No. 5. An obligation to be imposed on the enemy countries to contract abroad a loan which would be guaranteed in a special manner, has already been suggested by the Italian Delegation to the Second Sub-Committee, which is studying the means of payment. In order to avoid overlapping, it would be advisable to act in agreement with the Second Sub-Committee in this matter.

VI

Proposal No. 6. Sumptuary laws have always been difficult to apply and have invariably had a disappointing result. This would be still more the case were they imposed by victors on the vanquished.

VII

Proposal No. 7. Deficiency in imports of raw material into the enemy countries would result in the impoverishment of their industries, and create conditions such as might prevent them from meeting their obligations as to payments for war damage. At the same time, those States which export raw materials might themselves be injured by this circumstance.

ANNEX IV[8]

REPLY OF THE CZECHO-SLOVAK DELEGATION TO THE QUESTIONS SUBMITTED BY THE CHAIRMAN

I. Occupation.

The Delegation accepts the proposal, but points out that in order to render such occupation effective, at least the following towns should be occupied:—Bremen, Hamburg, Kiel, Lübeck, Stettin, Berlin, Leipsig, Essen, Magdeburg, Vienna, Munich and Budapest.

Moreover, the Delegation asks whether a nominal occupation would not be advisable to compel Germany by moral pressure to hasten the payment of the war indemnities. Such occupation should consist only of small Allied garrisons in fairly large towns, so that the mere sight of the uniforms of the Allied soldiers might compel the population to pay quickly. To guarantee the safety of such troops, severe penal measures might be introduced into the Peace terms against towns in which offences were committed against soldiers, and, in case of need, distinguished German citizens might be taken as hostages, such hostages being changed in the event of an extended occupation. Measures of this kind could not be considered a breach of International Law, since, unlike the brutal and illegal measures of Germany and her Allies, they would be taken with the formal consent of the nations concerned.

II. Economic Control.

The Delegation signifies its approval.

III. Occupation of Strategic Points.

The Czecho-Slovak Delegation approves of the suggestion, on condition that the towns mentioned in Paragraph 1 be considered as such strategic points in the event of their not being occupied under I.

IV. Interallied Commission.

The Delegation signifies its approval.

V. Forced Internal Loan.

The Delegation asks for an explanation of the refusal of the Second Sub-Committee to acquiesce in the proposal as to payment in securities belonging to Germany or her Allies and as regards a probable heavy depreciation of such securities.

VI. Prohibition of Luxuries in Germany and countries allied to her until full payment has been made.

[8] French text, *ibid.*, pp. 918-19.

The Delegation signifies its approval.

VII. Retention of Raw Materials indispensable to the Enemy States.

The Delegation approves of this suggestion, and gives a list of raw materials indispensable to the Enemy States, viz.:—

Germany. Animal and vegetable fats; petroleum and naphtha; colonial products; wheat and flour; timber; cotton; wool; copper; tin; sulphur; pyrites.

German-Austria. The same products, except timber, but with the addition of coal.

Magyar Republic. Petroleum; cotton; wool; copper; tin; coal.

ADDITIONAL SUGGESTIONS

VIII. Control of important industrial concerns, such as Krupps at Essen, the Potash Syndicate (Kali-Syndicat), the General Electrical Company, the Coal Syndicate, chemical works, and in particular those manufacturing artificial saltpetre, and naval ship yards.

IX. Germans to be forbidden to set up in business in foreign countries or to acquire real estate, by direct or indirect means, or to participate in industrial, commercial or other undertakings, until the war indemnity has been paid.

EXPLANATION OF REASONS

These measures are required to prevent emigration of Germans in large numbers from Germany, particularly to countries of lesser importance such as Russia, which in its present unsettled state the Germans might very easily Germanize, exploit economically, and subsequently consolidate from the military point of view against the Allies.

X. The right to sequestrate commercial, industrial and other undertakings in enemy countries.

XI. Enemy States shall be bound to frame laws on this subject within two months from the date of signature of the Peace Preliminaries.

ANNEX V[9]

REPLY OF THE JAPANESE DELEGATION TO THE QUESTIONS SUBMITTED BY THE CHAIRMAN

I. Army of Occupation

The first payments to be made by Germany may be comparatively easy, but only experience will show how the later payments

[9] French text, *ibid.*, p. 920.

will be made. It would seem reasonable, therefore, to maintain an Army of Occupation during some years of this later period.

II. Economic Control

The question of the blockade is extremely delicate as it appears to involve the rights of neutrals.

III. Occupation of Strategic Points

This question would seem to be included in paragraph I.

IV. International Commission

It will be necessary to define exactly the composition of the International Commission. It will probably be composed of representatives of the Allied and Associated Powers and of the former enemy Powers.

The paragraph should be completed by adding the words: "payable by the enemy Powers under the terms of the Treaty of Peace."

As regards the supervision of revenues, or of customs and railway receipts, it would perhaps not be desirable to include these questions within the jurisdiction of an International Commission, for, to be effective, all supervision must be accompanied by a certain amount of executive authority, and any such executive authority would tend to diminish the sense of responsibility of enemy officials and would, consequently, have an adverse influence on the receipts.

The following additional clauses might prove useful:—
(a) Determination of the sequence in which debts shall be paid;
(b) Control of future emigration from enemy countries, whether of persons or of capital, and also of any emigration which has taken place during the war.

V. Issues by the Enemy Government

It would appear that bonds representing the total value of reparation claimed should be held by the Allied Governments, until such time as (enemy) nationals may be willing to take them.

VI. Limitation of Expenditure on Luxuries in Enemy Countries

This would appear to be a question of taxation.

VII. Restriction of Import of Raw Materials necessary to Enemy Countries

This point might be included in paragraph IV as being a matter which should be controlled by the International Commission.

ANNEX VI[10]

REPLY OF THE AMERICAN DELEGATION TO THE QUESTIONS SUBMITTED BY THE CHAIRMAN

1 and 3. An army of occupation, either permanent or for a limited time.

We believe it would be unwise to maintain an army of occupation; except possibly that a limited number of troops of the Powers primarily interested in Reparation might be maintained at strategic points until the good faith of Germany in assuming reparation obligations had been demonstrated. It is suggested that the points, if any, occupied be such as would assist the Commission established to administer the collection of indemnity.

2. Economic Control.

This is probably the most effective measure, but no economic action should be taken unless there is default or evidence of bad faith. Otherwise the making of reparation should be handled by Germany pursuant to the agreement between the enemy governments and the Associated Powers. It must be borne in mind that economic control exercised by the Associated Powers while the indemnity is being paid will almost inevitably lessen the amount which the enemy can pay.

4. An International Commission to act as receivers and controllers of revenues, customs, railway receipts and perhaps taxes.

We agree this should be put into execution in the event of default; and in the meantime this Commission should sit to visé all receipts and expenditures.

5. An issue by the enemy Governments of a loan to cover the indemnity; the bonds of this loan to be issued to enemy nationals and their purchase by citizens of certain wealth to be obligatory.

We believe this measure to be impracticable, and that it lies within the province of the Second Sub-Committee.

6. A limitation of expenditure on luxuries in enemy countries.

This subject is one of the measures that should be recommended by the Second Sub-Committee as a means of raising revenue, and as a means of regulating an adverse balance of trade.

7. Import duties on raw materials required by the enemy countries coupled with the right of stoppage of such imports.

If this is one of the methods recommended by the Second Sub-Committee for raising the agreed indemnity, it should be put into effect; but it has the objection of decreasing the industrial activity, and limiting Germany's ability to pay.

[10] French text, *ibid.*, p. 921.

DOCUMENT 547

Third Subcommittee: Minutes of the Fourth (and Final) Meeting (Including Annexes I-II, May 2, 1919, 3 P. M.

[EOM, Third Subcommittee, pp. 16-19. French condensed minutes, PV, CRD, p. 912.]

The Third Sub-Committee of the Commission on Reparation of Damage (Measures of Control and Guarantees) met on Friday, 2 May, 1919, at 3 P. M., at the Ministry of Finance, MR. HUGHES (*British Empire*) in the Chair.

Present: MR. BARUCH (*U. S. A.*); MR. HUGHES (*British Empire*); MR. DE VERNEUIL (*France*); MR. D'AMELIO (*Italy*); MR. FUKAI (*Japan*); and MR. OSUSKI (*Czecho-Slovak Republic*).

There were also present: Messrs. THION DE LA CHAUME (*Expert for France*), MARKOWITCH (*Serbia*) and SLAVIK (*Czecho-Slovak Republic*).[1]

The minutes of the third meeting were adopted.

Draft Report

The CHAIRMAN explained that he had called the meeting of the Committee to consider its position and to decide whether it should make a report. A report had been drafted by the British Delegation which included certain definite proposals drafted by the French Delegation. The CHAIRMAN had copies of this draft distributed to the Committee and also copies of a letter which he had addressed to the General Secretary of the British Delegation to the Peace Conference but which had not been replied to (See Annexes I and II). The CHAIRMAN pointed out that the draft report would now be rendered after decisions of a final sort had been reached by the Council of Four, and that under such circumstances the definite proposals which it contained might be superfluous suggestions.

MR. DE VERNEUIL (*Expert for France*) thought that it would still be interesting to render a report containing suggestions that might be helpful at some later stage.

After a discussion in which Messrs. BARUCH (*U. S. A.*) DE VERNEUIL (*Expert for France*), and FUKAI (*Japan*) took part it was decided that the draft report should be adopted to the extent of its general statements, but that the particular proposals contained in the numbered paragraphs should be omitted, and that a

[1] According to the French minutes, Tatsumi (instead of Fukai), Chiesa (instead of D'Amelio), Despret and Michalakopoulos were also present; and De la Chaume, Marković and Slavík were absent.

closing paragraph offered by the CHAIRMAN should be adopted in the following form:

"Under all the circumstances, the Sub-Committee thinks that no useful purpose can be served by proceeding to make recommendations, unless the Supreme War Council expresses a wish that it should do so."

The Committee decided to forward the report thus modified to the Council of Ten.

The CHAIRMAN stated that he would call another meeting of the Committee only in case the Council asked to have detailed proposals addressed to it.

The Committee adjourned *sine die* at 4.15 P. M.

W. H. [*M.*] HUGHES,
Chairman.

HENRY JAMES,
Secretary.

ANNEX I[2]

DRAFT REPORT OF THE THIRD SUB-COMMITTEE

The Third Sub-Committee was appointed by the Commission on Reparation to consider and report on "Measures of Control and Guarantees."

The Sub-Committee held three meetings in February and March, and, having considered the question as it then stood, adjourned pending the reports of the First and Second Sub-Committees.

The First and Second Sub-Committees having now reported,[3] and the Council of the Great Powers being understood to have arrived at certain decisions on the subject, which have not been communicated to the Commission, the Third Sub-Committee still finds itself in a position of considerable difficulty.

The first Sub-Committee has not been able to indicate any figures of the amount of damages claimable; but has established a list of Categories of Damage, which include the general costs of the war. The Sub-Committee has no information as to whether the Council accepts this basis.

The Second Sub-Committee, in its report, has not indicated, either specifically or by implication, the total amount which the enemy States are able to pay, or the period which should be allowed them for payment.

On the 10th April, the Chairman of this Sub-Committee wrote

---

[2] French text in PV, CRD, pp. 912-15. Annex I to Document 546 precedes.
[3] The French text reads, "n'ayant pas déposé de rapports."

to the Secretariat of the Peace Congress setting out the position and asking for instructions from the Council of Four as to whether, under the circumstances, a report from this Sub-Committee was desired. To this no reply, has, as yet, been received.

Under these circumstances, and in the absence of definite data on the above essential elements of the problem, it is clear that any conclusion of the Third Sub-Committee as to the measures of control and the guarantees which are appropriate to enforce payment can only be provisional in their nature and general in their terms; and must be subject to comprehensive reservations.

It is obvious that the measures of control and the guarantees applicable to the enforcement of the obligations of the enemy States must depend to a very large extent on the amount which they are called upon to pay, their capacity and means of payment, and the mode and period of payment stipulated for.

But, subject to the above and other obvious qualifications and reservations, the Sub-Committee ventures to submit the following suggestions:—[4]

1. For the purpose of carrying into effect the financial stipulations of the Treaty of Peace with Germany, the Allied and Associated Governments shall be represented by an "Interallied Financial Commission of the German Debt" the constitution of which shall be determined by the Treaty of Peace.

2. It shall be the duty of the Commission to collect all payments to be made by Germany, and to divide the amount thereof among the Allied and Associated States in accordance with the principles established by a special agreement to be concluded between the said States.

3. The Commission will determine and notify to Germany the nature, amount and destination of payments to be effected in kind. After having assured itself that its instructions have been carried out, the Commission will determine the amount in cash with which Germany shall be credited.

4. The Commission will accept foreign bills tendered in payment by Germany, and fix the rate of exchange thereof.

5. If it is decided that any German taxes, dues, charges or revenues, either already in existence or to be created, are to be specially appropriated to purposes of reparation, the Commission will supervise and collect the amounts accruing from these sources.

---

[4] The French text has a note here: "Toutes les dispositions numérotées ont disparu du texte du rapport adressé au Conseil suprême."

6. Similarly, if it is decided that any German stocks and securities shall be ceded or assigned by way of security[5] by the German Government, the Commission will administer the same and will collect the revenue arising therefrom.

7. The Commission will administer all real estate of any description temporarily or permanently ceded to it by the German government and will collect the revenue arising therefrom.

8. The Commission will convert into bills of Allied and Associated States all amounts in Marks accruing from the sources enumerated in articles 5 to 7 hereof.

9. Should the proceeds of the different sources of payment specified in articles 3 to 7 hereof fail to produce an amount sufficient to cover the fixed yearly payments at the proper dates, the Commission shall be entitled either to grant an extension or delay (with or without continuation interest thereon) or to demand from the German Government payment of a sum in Marks corresponding to the ascertained deficit.

The payments in Marks effected under the present article shall be used, either to meet bills on the German State sold by the Commission, or for the purchase in Germany of goods chosen by the Commission and for payment of the transport charges thereon as far as the German frontier.

10. Should the proceeds of the different sources of payment specified in articles 3 to 7 exceed the amount necessary to cover the fixed yearly payments at the proper dates, the balance of the sums received by the Commission shall, after setting aside an amount corresponding to the service of the yearly payments for the following year, be paid to the German Government.

11. Should Germany not conform to the obligations specified above the Commission may propose to the League of Nations, through the Financial Section thereof, the following coercive measures:—

(a) Occupation of strategic points or of property capable of yielding a fiscal or industrial revenue.

(b) Complete or partial blockade of a financial or economic nature.

12. The following temporary measures shall remain in force until Germany shall have; (1) effected the payments required by the Treaty of Peace for the first two years after signature thereof:

---

[5] The French text omits "by way of security."

(2) assigned to the Commission, by way of guarantee or pledge, the taxes, securities or real estate specified in articles 5 to 7 hereof:—

(a) Military occupation of strategic points.

(b) Economic and financial blockade according to the conditions laid down in article 1 of the Financial Protocol signed at Treves on 13 December, 1918.

13. The provisions laid down in the present text concerning Germany shall be equally applicable to the other enemy Powers.

14. In the event of an obligation being imposed on the enemy Powers to contract an Exterior Debt in favor of the Allies, the Financial Commission shall assure the proper administration thereof and superintend the guarantees provided. It shall also *undertake to allot* the bonds thereof to the Allied and Associated Powers in accordance to their respective rights.[6]

ANNEX II[7]

CHAIRMAN'S LETTER TO THE GENERAL SECRETARIAT OF THE BRITISH DELEGATION

Dear Sir:

As Chairman of the 3rd Sub-Commission of the Reparations Commission, I am authorized by the Commission to ask you to obtain instructions from the Council of Four as to whether—under the circumstances set out below—a report from that Sub-Commission is desired.

The position is this. The Third Sub-Commission has been unable to proceed far with its work before receipt of the reports of the 1st and 2nd Sub-Commission had been received—as the nature of guarantees obviously depended on the question of the amount of which the enemy powers were able to pay and the amount demanded of them.

On Friday last, the Council of Four called for reports of all Commissions to be sent in by Monday last. On Monday, a Provisional Report of the First Sub-Commission was adopted by the Commission, and on Tuesday the First Provisional Report of the Second Sub-Commission was adopted; and these have both been forwarded to you.

---

[6] Paragraphs 13 and 14 were Italian additions. See Annex II to Document 546. The italics indicate a change from the original wording (in English texts only); they are inserted by the editor.

[7] This letter is not printed in PV. It was written April 10, 1919. See PV, CRD, p. 913; also Draft Report of the Third Subcommittee.

The Third Sub-Commission found itself in some difficulty as to furnishing a report. The report of the Second Sub-Commission does not state a figure of the total amount which the enemy powers should be called upon to pay, nor of the period over which payment is to be spread. (It states a figure for the first payments to be made within 18 months, but specifies no total). Both reports are provisional and it is not certain that the categories set out in them will not be varied or added to.

It obviously makes a great difference to the deliberations of the 3rd Sub-Commission whether the amount claimed is £50,000,000 a year or £500,000,000 a year.

I therefore have to ask whether under these circumstances it is desired that the 3rd Sub-Commission should furnish a report, and if so, upon what basis or within what limits, as regards the amount to be claimed, the 3rd Sub-Commission should proceed.

Yours faithfully,
(Signed) W. M. HUGHES,
Chairman of 3rd Sub-Commission.

INDEX

worth of new securities are issued (stocks, bonds, etc.) If one considers as exact the figure given for the national property, we should have, for 1912, a national property amounting per capita to:

In France..5,100 marks
In England..7,700 marks
In Germany..4,100 marks

Nevertheless, the figures of the yearly increase of national property (10 billions), as well as the figures of the movement of German trade (more than 21 billions), show that the national property and the annual revenue in Germany are much greater.

The diminution of the number of unemployed laborers is also a sign of the favorable economic situation of Germany: in 1913 the number of unemployed laborers was 2.9% (in England 2.1%): in 1908 only 20,000 inhabitants emigrated from Germany, while 336,000 people had emigrated from England during the same year.

The increase of salaries is also a sign of the general progress in Germany. On the average, salaries increased by 80% from the last decade of the past century to 1910. The savings of the great masses of the people (in Germany 16,780 billions; in France 4,514 billions; in England 4,422 billions) is also a sign of the enormous progress realized.

In 1913 its export and import trade was as follows:

	Import Millions of Marks	%	Export Millions of Marks	%
Raw materials...............	5,003.5	46.5	1,518.0	15.0
Partly finished products......	1,238.8	11.5	1,139.4	11.3
Manufactured goods.........	1,478.8	13.7	6,395.8	63.3
Food products..............	2,759.5	25.6	1,035.9	10.3
Live stock.................	289.7	2.7	7.4	0.1
Total..................	10,770.3	100.	10,096.5	100.

Per capita, 160 marks worth of import and 150 of export.

If we consider in detail these statistics, we arrive at the following results: Germany pays abroad for foodstuffs not more than 2 billion marks yearly, and for raw materials about 3.5 billions of marks, a total for the two of 5.5 billion marks.

If Germany's import trade is examined still more in detail, it will be seen that it is composed of the following articles:

I—FOODSTUFFS

(a) cereals................................1000 million marks
(b) eggs.................................. 188 million marks
(c) fruit.................................. 223 million marks
(d) rice.................................. 103 million marks

(e) wines.................................. 62 million marks
(f) coffee................................. 253 million marks
(g) Indian corn........................... 143 million marks
(h) cacao................................. 67 million marks

II—FOREIGN SPECIALTIES

(a) drugs................................. 421 million marks
(b) silk.................................. 193 million marks[1]
(c) rubber................................ 146 million marks
(d) petroleum............................. 69 million marks
(e) heavy benzine......................... 54 million marks
(f) copper................................ 313 million marks

III—RAW MATERIALS

(a) cotton................................ 644 million marks
(b) wool.................................. 511 million marks
(c) hides................................. 672 million marks
(d) wood.................................. 438 million marks
(e) iron ore.............................. 238 million marks
(f) coal.................................. 193 million marks

Admitting, as a principle, that taxation is to be a method of payment enforced against Germany to indemnify ourselves for the damage that she has inflicted on the Allies during the war, the following ideas especially must be brought out:

Germany will be obliged to abandon the policy of agrarian protection, for this policy weighed, to the profit of the large landholders, on the ultimate consumers of the working class, which is the principal factor in its economic development. Import duties on flour and wheat must in the future take on a fiscal character. In this way it will come about that these articles will be imported from agricultural countries which produce these foodstuffs at a much lower cost of production. The ultimate consumer, who has, up to the present, been exploited by the large landholders, will be rid of this burden and his power will be increased, which will allow him to bear the other burdens which will be laid on him for the liquidation of the damage inflicted by Germany on the Allies. The progress of agriculture, which, for the last 45 years has been artificially directed toward an economic autarchy, which has motives only too imperialistic, should also be checked, for the reasons above mentioned. Without suffering a great upheaval in its general economic situation, when she will have to give up what will be asked of her in kind, Germany can easily dispense with a great

[1] According to the French text, 493 million marks.